JOHN WILLIS

SCREEN WORLD

1998

VOLUME 49

ASSOCIATE EDITOR
BARRY MONUSH

NEW YORK • LONDON

COPYRIGHT © 1998 BY JOHN WILLIS. ALL RIGHTS RESERVED.
LIBRARY OF CONGRESS CARD NO. 50-3023
ISBN: 1-55783-341-9 (CLOTH)
ISBN: 1-55783-342-7 (PAPER)

1957   1957   1964

1966   1972   1973

1978   1984   1990

To
JOANNE WOODWARD

one of the most gifted actresses of her generation, who has found truth in a rich collection of characters of edgy intelligence and indomitable spirit.

FILMS:*Count Three and Pray* (1955), *A Kiss Before Dying* (1956), *The Three Faces of Eve* (1957; Academy Award for Best Actress), *No Down Payment* (1957), *The Long Hot Summer* (1958), *Rally 'Round the Flag, Boys!* (1958), *The Sound and the Fury* (1959), *The Fugitive Kind* (1959), *From the Terrace* (1960), *Paris Blues* (1961), *The Stripper* (1963), *A New Kind of Love* (1963), *Signpost to Murder* (1964), *A Fine Madness* (1966), *A Big Hand for the Little Lady* (1966), *Rachel, Rachel* (1968; Academy Award nomination), *Winning* (1969), *King: A Filmed Record...Montgomery to Memphis* (1970), *WUSA* (1970), *They Might Be Giants* (1971), *The Effect of Gamma Rays on Man-in-the-Moon-Marigolds* (1972), *Summer Wishes, Winter Dreams* (1973; Academy Award nomination), *The Drowning Pool* (1975), *The End* (1978) *Harry and Son* (1984), *The Glass Menagerie* (1987), *Mr. and Mrs. Bridge* (1990; Academy Award nomination), *The Age of Innocence* (narrator), *Philadelphia* (1993)

Leonardo DiCaprio, Kate Winslet in *Titanic*
Academy Award Winner for Best Picture of 1997
© Paramount Pictures/Twentieth Century Fox

CONTENTS

Dedication: Joanne Woodward...3

Top Box Office Stars of 1997 6

Domestic Films released in the United States
from January 1 through December 31, 1997...............................8

Academy Award "Oscars" for 1997
presented Monday, March 23, 1998 in the
Shrine Auditorium 185

Promising New Actors of 1997..197

Academy Award Acting Nominees for 1997 192

Top 100 Box Office Films of 1997 200

Foreign Films released in the United States
from January 1 through December 31, 1997.............................202

Biographical Data on Film Actors 267

Obituaries for 1997 297

EDITOR: JOHN WILLIS

ASSOCIATE EDITOR: BARRY MONUSH

Staff: Marco Starr Boyajian, William Camp, Jimmie Hollifield, II,

Tom Lynch, John Sala

Acknowledgements: John Alston, Ed Arentz, Arrow Releasing, Artistic License, Castle Hill, Castle Rock Entertainment, Cinepix Films Properties, City Cinemas, Cline & White, Richard D'Attile, Dennis Davidson Associates, Alex Dawson, Samantha Dean, Dream Works, Brian Durnin, The Film Forum, First Look, First Run Features, Fox Serchlight, Adrian Goycoolea, Gramercy Pictures, Khan & Jacobs, Craig Keleman, Kino International, Legacy Releasing, Leisure Time Features, LIVE Entertainment, Mike Maggiore, David Mazor, Robert Milite, Jr., Miramax Films, Jennifer Morgerman, David Munro, New Line Cinema/Fine Line Features, New Yorker Films, Northern Arts Entertainment, October Films, PMK Publicity, Paramount Pictures, Phaedra Films, PolyGram, Quad Cinema, George Scherling, Kimberly Scherling, 7th Art Releasing, Sony Pictures Entertainment, Sheldon Stone, Strand Releasing, Paul Sugarman, Twentieth Century Fox, Universal Pictures, Jen Wallace, Walt Disney Pictures, Glenn Young, Zeitgeist Films.

1. Harrison Ford

2. Julia Roberts

3. Leonardo DiCaprio

4. Will Smith

5. Tom Cruise

6. Jack Nicholson

7. Jim Carrey

8. John Travolta

9. Robin Williams

10. Tommy Lee Jones

11. Brad Pitt

12. Neve Campbell

13. Pierce Brosnan

14. Jodie Foster

15. Nicolas Cage

16. Tim Allen

TOP BOX OFFICE STARS OF 1997

17. Michael Douglas   18. Demi Moore   19. Michelle Pfeiffer   20. Sandra Bullock

1997 RELEASES

January 1 Through December 31, 1997

21. Cameron Diaz   22. Brendan Fraser   23. Denzel Washington   24. Robert De Niro

25. Meg Ryan   Dustin Hoffman   Jamie Lee Curtis   Ethan Hawke

TURBULENCE

(MGM) Producer, Martin Ransohoff, David Valdes; Executive Producer, Keith Samples; Director, Robert Butler; Screenplay, Jonathan Brett; Photography, Lloyd Ahern II; Designer, Mayling Cheng; Editor, John Duffy; Music, Shirley Walker; Costumes, Robert Turturice; Visual Effects Supervisor, Mark Vargo; Casting, Phyllis Huffman; a Rysher Entertainment presentation of a Martin Ransohoff production; Distributed by MGM/UA; Dolby Digital SDDS Stereo; Super 35 Widescreen; Color; Rated R; 103 minutes; January release

CAST

Ryan Weaver	Ray Liotta
Teri Halloran	Lauren Holly
Stubbs	Brendan Gleeson
Detective Aldo Hines	Hector Elizondo
Rachel Taper	Rachel Ticotin
Brooks	Jeffrey DeMunn
Sinclair	John Finn
Captain Sam Bowen	Ben Cross
Maggie	Catherine Hicks
Betty	Heidi Kling
Carl	Gordy Owens
Captain Matt Powell	J. Kenneth Campbell
First Officer Ted Kary	James MacDonald
Marshal Douglas	Michael Harney
Marshal Arquette	Grand L. Bush
Marshal Riordan	Richard Hoyt Miller
Marshal Green	Michael F. Kelly
Mr. Kramer	Alan Bergmann
Mrs. Kramer	Danna Hansen
Kip	R.J. Knoll
Career Woman	Sondra Spriggs
LAX Manager	Garrett Brown
Limato	Darryl Theirse
Asian Businessman	Fritz Mashimo
Mr. Hollywood	Tom Todoroff

and Jeffrey Joseph (Detective), Dennis Redfield (Desk Sergeant), Malachy McCourt (Ray the Doorman), Gary Rodriguez (Rodriguez), Billy Burton (Port Authority Cop), Callie Thorne (Laura), John Elsen (Stone), Bill Cross (William Harris), Tannis Benedict, Don Dowe, Scott Gurney (Controllers), Cooper Huckabee (Wing Commander), Ken Thatcher II (SWAT Member), Kevin O'Rourke (Mark Pavone), Scott Lawrence (Felix), Ken Mosley (Tower Air Co-Pilot)

During a stormy Christmas Eve flight from New York to Los Angeles, a gun battle errupts killing the pilots and leaving a murderer free of his police escorts, as stewardess Teri Halloran tries to bring the plane safely to the ground.

©Rysher Entertainment

Lauren Holly, Ray Liotta

Tom Sizemore, Penelope Ann Miller

THE RELIC

(PARAMOUNT) Producers, Sam Mercer, Gale Anne Hurd; Executive Producers, Gary Levinsohn, Mark Gordon; Director/Photography, Peter Hyams; Screenplay, Amy Jones, John Raffo, Rick Jaffa, Amanda Silver; Based upon the novel by Douglas Preston and Lincoln Child; Designer, Philip Harrison; Editor, Steven Kemper; Visual Effects Supervisor, Gregory L. McMurry; Creature Effects, Stan Winston; Costumes, Dan Lester; Music, John Debney; Casting, Penny Perry; a Pacific Western production, presented in association with Cloud Nine Entertainment; Dolby DTS Stereo; Panavision; Deluxe color; Rated R; 110 minutes; January release

CAST

Dr. Margo Green	Penelope Ann Miller
Lt. Vincent D'Agosta	Tom Sizemore
Dr. Ann Cuthbert	Linda Hunt
Dr. Albert Frock	James Whitmore
Detective Hollingsworth	Clayton Rohner
Greg Lee	Chi Muoi Lo
Parkinson	Thomas Ryan
Mayor Owen	Robert Lesser
Mayor's Wife	Diane Robin
John Whitney	Lewis Van Bergen
Mrs. Blaisedale	Constance Towers
Mr. Blaisedale	Francis X. McCarthy
Dr. Zwiezic	Audra Lindley
McNally	John Kapelos
Bailey	Tico Wells
Bradley	Mike Bacarella

and Gene Davis (Martini), John DiSanti (Wootton), David Proval (Johnson), David Graubart (Eugene), Ronald Joshua Scott (Josh), Jophery C. Brown (Frederick Ford), Thomas Joseph Carroll (Evans), Montrose Hagins (Chanting Woman), Santos Morales (Captain Borne), Ralph Seymour (Sergeant), La Donna Tittle (Teacher), Edward Jemison (Museum Worker), David Hollander (Charlie), Amanda Ingber (Donna), Katharine Mitchell, Candy Coburn, Kurt Naebig, Don MacLellan, Marc P. Shelton (Police Officers), Don Harvey (Spota), Ken Magee (Coroner's Assistant), Aaron Lustig (Dr. Brown), Kent George (Student), Lynn A. Henderson (Perri Masai), Ron Cummins (Dr. Gross), Matthew Daniel Moses Furlin (Crazy Man), Elwood Forbes (Graduate Student), Dina Bair (Reporter), Mark Lake (Swat Team Guy), Ned Schmidtke (Captain Martin), Vincent Hammond, Brian Steele (Kothoga)

A deadly creature, unwittingly brought back from the jungles of South America, breaks loose and creates havoc at the Chicago Natural History Museum.

© Paramount Pictures

ALBINO ALIGATOR

(MIRAMAX) Producers, Brad Krevoy, Steve Stabler, Brad Jenkel; Director, Kevin Spacey; Screenplay, Christian Forte; Photography, Mark Plummer; Designer, Nelson Coates; Editor, Jay Cassidy; Music, Michael Brook; Costumes, Isis Mussenden; Casting, David Rubin; a Brad Krevoy & Steve Stabler production presented in association with Motion Picture Corporation of America; Dolby Stereo; Color; Rated R; 105 minutes; January release

Matt Dillon, Gary Sinise

CAST

Dova	Matt Dillon
Janet	Faye Dunaway
Milo	Gary Sinise
Law	William Fichtner
Guy	Viggo Mortensen
Jack	John Spencer
Danny	Skeet Ulrich
Marv	Frankie Faison
Jenny	Melinda McGraw
Dino	M. Emmet Walsh
G.D. Browning	Joe Mantegna

and Doug Spinuzza, Spencer Garrett, Enrico Colantoni (Agents), Tulsy Ball (ATF Agent), Travis Appel (Another Agent), Brad Koepenick (Browning's Assistant), Jock Worthen (Medic), Willie C. Carpenter, Alexander Smith, Michael Unger (Reporters), Toni Montgomery (Officer), Jeff Hoffman (Jenny's Cameraman)

After their heist goes awry, three criminals take refuge in Dino's Last Chance Bar and find themselves surrounded by the police. This film marked the directorial debut of actor Kevin Spacey.

©Miramax Films

Joe Mantegna

Faye Dunaway, Skeet Ulrich, Viggo Mortensen, John Spencer

METRO

Eddie Murphy, Michael Rapaport

(TOUCHSTONE) Producer, Roger Birnbaum; Executive Producers, Mark Lipsky, Riley Kathryn Ellis; Director, Thomas Carter; Screenplay, Randy Feldman; Co-Producers, George W. Perkins, Ray Murphy, Jr., Randy Feldman; Photography, Fred Murphy; Designer, William Elliott; Costumes, Ha Nguyen; Editor, Peter E. Berger; Music, Steve Porcaro; Casting, Ellen Chenoweth; a Roger Birnbaum production, presented in association with Caravan Pictures; Distributed by Buena Vista Pictures; Dolby Digital Stereo; Panavision; Technicolor; Rated R; 117 minutes; January release

CAST

Scott Roper	Eddie Murphy
Kevin McCall	Michael Rapaport
Michael Korda	Michael Wincott
Ronnie Tate	Carmen Ejogo
Captain Frank Solis	Denis Arndt
Lieutenant Sam Baffert	Art Evans
Earl	Donal Logue
Clarence Teal	Paul Ben-Victor
Detective Kimura	Kim Miyori
Officer Forbes	James Carpenter
Debbie	Jeni Chua
Bank Manager	Dick Bright
SWAT Officer Jennings	David Michael Silverman
Reporters	Frank Somerville, Malou Nubla
Repoman	Nino Degennaro
Screaming Lady	Val Diamond
Ronnie's Boyfriend Greg	Charleston Pierce
Detective Glass	Will Marchetti
Racetrack Announcer	Trevor Denman
SWAT Captain	Joe Vincent
Jewelry Salesgirls	Corie Henninger, Karen Kahn
Jewelry Customer Dotson	Nellie Cravens
Jewelry Manager	Danny Teal

and Jeff Mosley (Cable Car Brakeman), Ralph Peduto (Bail Bondsman Hawkins), James Cunningham (Postrio Waiter), C.W. Morgan (Jail Laundry Room Guard), Nick Scoggin (Property Room Sergeant Frank), Marie Villatuya (Tahitian Waitress)

Hostage negotiator Scott Roper teams with SWAT team sharp-shooter Kevin McCall to trap a deadly jewel thief.

©Touchstone Pictures

Eddie Murphy

Carmen Ejogo, Eddie Murphy

Michael Wincott

BEVERLY HILLS NINJA

(TRISTAR) Producers, Brad Krevoy, Steve Stabler, Brad Jenkel; Executive Producers, Jeffrey D. Ivers, John Bertolli, Michael Rotenberg; Director, Dennis Dugan; Screenplay, Mark Feldberg, Mitch Klebanoff; Photography, Arthur Albert; Designer, Ninkey Dalton; Editor, Jeff Gourson; Costumes, Mary Claire Hannan; Music, George S. Clinton; Co-Producers, Marc S. Fischer, Mitch Klebanoff; Casting, Gary M. Zuckerbrod; Stunts, Rick Barker; a Motion Picture Corporation of America production in association with Brad Krevoy & Steve Stabler; Dolby SDDS Stereo; Technicolor; Rated PG-13; 90 minutes; January release

CAST

Haru	Chris Farley
Alison	Nicollette Sheridan
Gobei	Robin Shou
Tanley	Nathaniel Parker
Sensei	Soon-Tek Oh
Nobu	Keith Cooke Hirabayashi
Joey	Chris Rock
Izumo	Francois Chau
Old Japanese Man	Dale Ishimoto
Head Kobudosai	Da Ming Chan
Mr. Ozaru	Burt Bulos
Billy	Curtis Blanck
Billy's Dad	Tom Bailey
Busboy	Jason J. Tobin
Driver	Richard Kline
Traveler	Anna Mathias
Fisherman	Nathan Jung
Policemen	John Farley, Kevin Farley
Porter	Gerry Del Sol
Reporters	Cynthia Allison, Francesca Cappucci
Security Person	Hideo Kimura
Woman	Saachiko
Guard	James Laing

and Robbie Thibaut, Jr. (Grandson at Hotel) Michael Cardenas (Patron at Hop Louie's), Brett Golov, Joe Decker (Club Patrons), Charles Dugan (Man with Shoes), Jason Davis (Young Haru), Alexandra Stabler (Girl on Rodeo Drive), Nicolas Stabler (Boy on Rodeo Drive), Tania L. Pearson, Lisa C. Boltanzer, Nancy Howard (Dancers), Conrad Goode, Bryan Hays Currie, Caesar Luisi (Bouncers), Rick Miller (Motorcycle Rider), Eric C. Charmelo (Guy at Plant), Sarah Pierce (Poodle Lady)

Haru, believing himself to be the Great White Ninja, travels to Beverly Hills to save a mysterious and beautiful woman.

©TriStar Pictures

Chris Farley, Robin Shou

Roxanne, Kathleen Quinlan

Zeus, Jessica Howell, Majandra Delfino, Miko Hughes

ZEUS AND ROXANNE

(MGM) Producers, Frank Price, Gene Rosow, Ludi Boeken; Executive Producers, Laura Friedman, Hilton Green; Director, George Miller; Screenplay, Tom Benedek; Photography, David Connell; Designer, Bernt Capra; Editor, Harry Hitner; Co-Producer, Frederic W. Brost; Music, Bruce Rowland; Casting, Karen Rea; a Rysher Entertainment presentation of a Frank Price production; Dolby DTS Stereo; Color; Rated PG; 97 minutes; January release

CAST

Terry Barnett	Steve Guttenberg
Mary Beth Dunhill	Kathleen Quinlan
Dr. Claude Carver	Arnold Vosloo
Becky	Dawn McMillan
Jordan Barnett	Miko Hughes
Judith Dunhill	Majandra Delfino
Nora Dunhill	Jessica Howell
Mrs. Rice	Duchess Tomasello
Linda	Shannon K. Foley
Phil	Jim R. Coleman
Floyd	Alvin Farmer

and Harri James (Airline Attendant), Justin Humphrey (Craig), James Stone (Security Guard), Maury Covington (Reverend), Michael A. Xynidis (Messenger), Nikki, Tito, Rosa (Zeus), Cayla, Bimini, Stripe (Roxanne), Benjamin Pettijohn (Additional Zeus Vocals), David Nathaniel Hoyte (Lead Steel Pan Performer)

Marine biologist Mary Beth Dunhill is surprised to discover that her neighbor's dog, Zeus, has its own form of communication with a captive dolphin named Roxanne.

©Rysher Entertainment

FIERCE CREATURES

(UNIVERSAL) Producers, Michael Shamberg, John Cleese; Executive Producer, Steve Abbott; Directors, Robert Young, Fred Schepisi; Screenplay, John Cleese, Iain Johnstone; Co-Producer, Patricia Carr; Photography, Adrian Biddle, Ian Baker; Music, Jerry Goldsmith; Editor, Robert Gibson; Designer, Roger Murray-Leach; Costumes, Hazel Pethig; Chief Animal Trainer, Jim Clubb; Casting, Priscilla John; a Fish Productions/Jersey Films production; Digital DTS Stereo; Panavision; Eastmancolor; Rated PG-13; 93 minutes; January release

Michael Palin, John Cleese, Jamie Lee Curtis, Kevin Kline

CAST

Rollo Lee	John Cleese
Willa Weston	Jamie Lee Curtis
Vince McCain/Rod McCain	Kevin Kline
Bugsy Malone	Michael Palin
Reggie Sealions	Ronnie Corbett
Cub Felines	Carey Lowell
Sydney Small Mammals	Robert Lindsay
Neville Coltrane	Bille Brown
Gerry Ungulates	Derek Griffiths
Pip Small Mammals	Cynthia Cleese
Hugh Primates	Richard Ridings
Di Admin	Maria Aitken
Ant Keeper	Michael Percival
Flamingo Keeper	Fred Evans
Sealion Keeper	Lisa Hogan
Parrot Keeper	Choy-Ling Man
Vulture Keeper	Tim Potter
Aquarium Keeper	Jenny Galloway
Tiger Keeper	Kim Vithana
Buffalo Keeper	Sean Francis
Rodent Keeper	Julie Saunders

and Susie Blake (Woman in Red Dress), Pat Keen (Her Mother), Denis Lill (Her Husband), Gareth Hunt (Inspector Masefield), Ron Donachie (Sergeant Scott), Paul Haigh (Sergeant Irving), Leon Herbert, Stewart Wright (Octopus Security Guards), Kerry Shale (Frightened Executive), Mac McDonald (TV Producer), Amanda Walker (Zoo Secretary), Terence Conoley (Man in Straw Hat), Tom Georgeson, John Bardon, Anthony Pedley (Sealion Spectators), Jennie Goossens, Georgia Reece, Hilary Gish, Kenneth Price, Brian King, Peter Silverleaf (Sponsors), Kevin Moore (Hotel Manager), Leslie Lowe, Iain Mitchell (Assistant Hotel Managers), Valerie Edmond (Hotel Maid), Nick Bartlett (Policeman), Ricco Ross, Kate Harper (TV Journalists), Nicholas Hutchison (TV Reporter), Kate Alderton, Jack Davenport, Jo Ann Geary, William Grove, Francis Pope, Jaqui Thomas, David Wood (Student Zoo Keepers), John Alexander (Gorilla Performer—Jambo), Peter Elliott (Gorilla Performer), Tessa Crockett, Phillip Hill, Holly Hoffman, Mario Kalli, Tina Maskell, Elizabeth O'Brien (Background Gorillas), Ailsa Berk (Panda Performer)

Hoping to keep media mogul Rod McCain from closing the floundering Marwood Zoo, Rollo Lee comes up with the marketing idea of stocking the place exclusively with violent, man-eating creatures.

Kevin Kline, Jamie Lee Curtis

John Cleese

Michael Percival, Carey Lowell, Robert Lindsay, Fred Evans, John Cleese, Richard Ridings

PREFONTAINE

(HOLLYWOOD PICTURES) Producers, Irby Smith, Jon Lutz, Mark Doonan, Peter Gilbert; Director, Steve James; Screenplay, Steve James, Eugene Corr; Co-Producer, Shelly Glasser; Photography, Peter Gilbert; Designer, Carol Winstead Wood; Editor, Peter Frank; Music, Mason Daring; Costumes, Tom Bronson; Casting, Pam Dixon Mickelson; an Irby Smith/Jon Lutz/Mark Doonan production; Distributed by Buena Vista Pictures; Dolby Digital Stereo; Technicolor; Rated PG-13; 106 minutes; January release

CAST

Steve Prefontaine	Jared Leto
Bill Bowerman	R. Lee Ermey
Bill Dellinger	Ed O'Neill
Pat Tyson	Breckin Meyer
Elfriede Prefontaine	Lindsay Crouse
Nancy Alleman	Amy Locane
Elaine Finley	Laurel Holloman
Mac Wilkins	Brian McGovern
Curtis Cunningham	Kurtwood Smith

and Adrian Amadeus (Finnish Teammate), Laurence Ballard (O'Hara), Ryan Brewer (12 Year Old Black), Robert Karl Burke (Young Pre), Gaard Swanson, Kevin Calabro (Airport Reporters), George Catalano, Jim Freeman (Patrons), Wade Clegg (German Security), Wally Dalton (Dick Burke), Adam Fitzhugh (Thomas Becker), Tom Glasgow, David Grosby (NCAA Press), Geoff Haley (German Soldier), Dag Hinrichs (Jeff Galloway), Tracy Hollister (Lasse Viren), Peter Anthony Jacobs (Ray Prefontaine), Eric Johnson (Olympic Trials Reporter), Eric Keenleyside (James Buck), Steve Kelley (U of O Reporter), Stephen J. Lang (Bar Back), Shannon Leto (Bar Patron), Eric Liddell (Gary Powers), Jochen Liesche (German Newscaster), Henry Lubatti (Frank Shorter), Jeff McAtee (Reporter at Village Gate), Michael Patten (Munich Stadium Official), John Charles Pavlich (Husband), Wendy Ray (Himself), Brad Tuinstra (Finnish Runner), Brad Upton (Neighborhood Man), Bruce Walker (Olympic Village Reporter), Hugh P. Wallace (Man on Winding Road), Mac Wilkins (Track Official), Phaedra Wilson (German Security Girl), Pauly Yarnold (Reporter at Trailer Park)

The true story of long distance runner Steve Prefontaine and his partici-pation in the 1972 Munich Olympics. Prefontaine's life was also the basis for the 1998 film Without Limits starring Billy Crudup and Donald Sutherland.

©Hollywood Pictures Company

Jared Leto, Ed O'Neill, R. Lee Ermey

Tim Roth, Tupac Shakur

GRIDLOCK'D

(GRAMERCY) Producers, Damian Jones, Paul Webster, Erica Huggins; Executive Producers, Ted Field, Russell Simmons, Scott Kroopf; Co-Executive Producers, Preston Holmes, Stan Lathan; Co-Producers, Michael Bennett, Steven Siebert; Director/Screenplay, Vondie Curtis Hall; Photography, Bill Pope; Designer, Dan Bishop; Editor, Christopher Koefoed; Costumes, Marie France; Music, Stewart Copeland; Casting, Robi Reed-Humes; a PolyGram Filmed Entertainment presentation of an Interscope Communicatios production in association with Def Pictures/Webster/Dragon Pictures; Dolby Digital Stereo; Deluxe Color; Rated R; 90 minutes; January release

CAST

Stretch	Tim Roth
Spoon	Tupac Shakur
Cookie	Thandie Newton
Mr. Woodson	Charles Fleischer
Blind Man	Howard Hesseman
Supervisor	James Pickens, Jr.
Cops	John Sayles, Eric Payne
D-Reper's Henchman	Tom Towles
Koolaid	Tom Wright
Patrolmen	James Shanta, Jim O'Malley
Chuck	George Poulos
Clerk	Debbie Zaricor
Officer #1	Mik Scriba
Cee-Cee	Lucy Alexis Liu
Resident Doctor	Richmond Arquette
Medicaid Women	Billie Neal, Debra Wilson
Nurse	Rusty Schwimmer
Admissions Person	Elizabeth Anne Dickinson
Vendor	Joey Dente
Panhandler	Darryl Jones

and Jasen Govine (Medicaid Security Guard), Tim Truby (Man with Directions), Venssia Valentino (Woman in ER), Ron Cummins (Man in ER), Bradley Jordan Spencer, Rory J. Shoaf (Paramedics), Tracy Vilar (Screaming Woman), Roslyn McKinney (Clerk), Roderick Garr (Welfare Security Guard), William Long, Jr. (Right Wing TV Show Host), Mark Ericson (Bill the Anchor Man), Tonia Rowe (Woman on TV), Lynn Blades (Alexia Cruz), Kasi Lemmons, Henry Hunter Hall (Madonna and Child), Vondie Curtis Hall (D-Reper)

When the singer in their band overdoses and ends up in a coma, Stretch and Spoon decide it is time that they clean up their drug habits.

© Gramercy Pictures

JOHNS

(FIRST LOOK PICTURES) Producers, Beau Flynn, Stefan Simchowitz; Executive Producer, P. Holt Gardiner; Director/Screenplay, Scott Silver; Photography, Tom Richmond; Editor, Dorian Harris; Co-Executive Producer, Dolly Hall; Line Producer, Elyse Katz; Designer, Amy Beth Silver; Costumes, Sara Jane Slotnick; Music, Charles Brown, Danny Caron; Casting, Mary Vernieu; a Flynn/Simchowitz production, presented in association with Bandeira Entertainment; Dolby Stereo; CFI color; Rated R; 96 minutes; January release

CAST

Donner	Lukas Haas
John	David Arquette
John Cardoza	Arliss Howard
Homeless John	Keith David
Eli	Christopher Gartin
David	Josh Schaefer
Mikey	Wilson Cruz
Jimmy the Warlock	Terrence Dashon Howard
Mix	Nicky Katt
Nikki	Alanna Ubach
Manny Gould	Elliott Gould
Paul Truman	Richard Kind
Old Man	Harper Roisman
Danny Cohen	John C. McGinley
Mr. Popper	Richard Timothy Jones
John Wayne	Louis Mustillo
Santa Claus	Tony Epper
Tourist Mom	Ruth Silver
Young Hustler	Kurtis Kunzler
Tiffany the Prostitute	Nina Siemaszko
Christmas Preacher on Radio	Craig Bierko

As Christmas approaches John, a Hollywood prostitute, hopes to come up with the $300 he needs to spend a night in a luxury hotel.

Lukas Haas

David Arquette

David Arquette, Lukas Haas

14

MEET WALLY SPARKS

(TRIMARK) Producer, Leslie Greif; Director, Peter Baldwin; Screenplay, Rodney Dangerfield, Harry Basil; Story, Harry Basil; Co-Producers, Harry Basil, Elliot Rosenblatt; Photography, Richard Kline; Designer, Bryan Jones; Costumes, Alexandra Walker; Editor, Raul Davalos; Music, Michel Colombier; Casting, Fern Champion, Mark Paladini; a Leslie Greif production; Dolby DTS Stereo; Color; Rated R; 104 minutes; January release

Rodney Dangerfield

CAST

Wally Sparks .... Rodney Dangerfield
Governor Floyd Preston .... David Ogden Stiers
Sandy Gallo .... Debi Mazar
Harvey Bishop .... Mark L. Taylor
Emily Preston .... Cindy Williams
Priscilla Preston .... Lisa Thornhill
Dean Sparks .... Michael Weatherly
Lola Larue .... Cindy Ambuehl
Joey .... Lenny Clarke
Judge Randal Williams .... Alan Rachins
Helen Williams .... Rita McKenzie
Canadian Ambassador .... Edmund L. Shaff
Canadian Ambassador's Wife .... Kay Gerhard
Alan Miller .... Eamonn Roche
Mr. Spencer .... Burt Reynolds
Robby Preston .... Glenn Walker Harris, Jr.
Butler .... Albert Able Eisenmann
Bartender .... George Wallace
Mr. Harry Karp .... Gilbert Gottfried
Mrs. Martha Karp .... Julia Sweeney
Actor .... Ron Jeremy
Robby's Friend #1 .... Ryan Tomlinson
Commercial Director .... Sandy Helberg
Bum .... Carmen Filpi
Nurse .... Lesley-Anne Down

and George Greif, Dee Booher (Guests), Barry Nolan, "Stuttering" John Melendez, Karen Duffy, Bob Saget (Reporters), Connie Danese, Jennifer Koppelman, Michael Stadvec (Fans), Big Nate Kanae, Randy Kiyabo (Sumo Wrestlers), Nils Allen Stewart, Scott L. Schwartz (American Wrestlers), Laura Basil, Patricia Forte (Constituents), Janice Hart (Agnes Farber), Andre Rosey Brown (Teamster), Lewis Arquette (Cardinal), Rochelle Swanson (Dixie), Tim Allen, Morton Downey Jr., Michael Bolton, Jay Leno, John Hensen, Richard Bey, George Hamilton, Sally Jessy Raphael, Geraldo Rivera, Roseanne, Jerry Springer, Alana Stewart, Rolanda Watts (Themselves), Tony Danza (Taxi Driver), Sir Mix-a-Lot (Rapper Announcer), Michael Rooker (Bar Patron), Harry Basil (Stable Boy), Marzia Greif (Miss Bussone), Ron Jeremy (Porn Actor), Thomas Weber (Agent Cameron)

Glenn Walker Harris Jr., David Ogden Stiers, Cindy Williams

Uncouth talk show host Wally Sparks, told to clean up his program or else, pursues a seemingly safe story on Georgia governor Floyd Preston, only to uncover a scandal.

Rodney Dangerfield, Cindy Williams

Burt Reynolds

Debi Mazar

Fred Willard, Catherine O'Hara, Christopher Guest, Parker Posey, Eugene Levy

Bob Balaban

Matt Keeslar

WAITING FOR GUFFMAN

(SONY CLASSICS) Producer, Karen Murphy; Director, Christopher Guest; Screenplay, Christopher Guest, Eugene Levy; Photography, Roberto Schaefer; Designer, Joseph T. Garrity; Editor, Andy Blumenthal; Costumes, Julie Carnahan; Music/Lyrics, Michael McKean, Harry Shearer, Christopher Guest; a Castle Rock Entertainment presentation of a Pale Morning Dun production; Dolby Stereo; Color; Rated R; 84 minutes; January release

CAST

Corky St. Clair	Christopher Guest
Dr. Allan Pearl	Eugene Levy
Sheila Albertson	Catherine O'Hara
Ron Albertson	Fred Willard
Libby Mae Brown	Parker Posey
Lloyd Miller	Bob Balaban
Clifford Wooley	Lewis Arquette
Johnny Savage	Matt Keeslar
Gwen Fabin-Blunt, Councilwoman	Deborah Theaker
Steve Stark, Councilman	Michael Hitchcock
Tucker Livingston, Councilman	Scott Williamson
Glenn Welsch, Mayor	Larry Miller
Phil Burgess, Blaine Historian	Don Lake
UFO Expert	David Cross
Singing Auditoner	Jim McQueen
Ping Pong Ball Juggler	Turk Pipkin
Raging Bull Auditioner	Jerry Turman
UFO Abductee	Paul Dooley
Mrs. Allan Pearl	Linda Kash
Red Savage	Brian Doyle-Murray
Costume Designer	Miriam Flynn
Stage Manager	Jill Parker-Jones
Costume Dresser	Margaret Bowman
Not Guffman	Paul Benedict

Mock-documentary spotlights director Corky St. Clair as he stages a lavish musical revue to commemorate the 150th anniversary of the town of Blaine, Missouri, the Stool Capital of the World.

DANTE'S PEAK

(UNIVERSAL) Producers, Gale Anne Hurd, Joseph M. Singer; Executive Producer, Ilona Herzberg; Director, Roger Donaldson; Screenplay, Leslie Bohem; Photography, Andrzej Bartkowiak; Designer, Dennis Washington; Editors, Howard Smith, Conrad Buff, Tina Hirsch; Visual Effects Supervisor, Patrick McClung; Associate Producer, Geoff Murphy; Co-Producer, Marliese Schneider; Costumes, Isis Mussenden; Music, John Frizzell, James Newton Howard; Casting, Mike Fenton, Allison Cowitt; a Pacific Western production; DTS Digital Stereo; Super 35 Widescreen; Deluxe color; Rated PG-13; 112 minutes; February release

CAST

Harry Dalton	Pierce Brosnan
Rachel Wando	Linda Hamilton
Lauren Wando	Jamie Renée Smith
Graham Wando	Jeremy Foley
Ruth	Elizabeth Hoffman
Paul Dreyfus	Charles Hallahan
Greg	Grant Heslov
Terry Furlong	Kirk Trutner
Nancy	Arabella Field
Stan	Tzi Ma
Les Worrell	Brian Reddy
Dr. Jane Fox	Lee Garlington
Sheriff Turner	Bill Bolender
Mary Kelly	Carol Androsky
Norman Gates	Peter Jason
Jack Collins	Jeffrey L. Ward
Elliot Blair	Tim Haldeman
Marianne	Walker Brandt
Warren Cluster	Hansford Rowe
Karen Narlington	Susie Spear
Hot Spring Man	David Lipper
Hot Springs Woman	Heather Stephens

and Ingo Neuhaus (National Guardsman), Patty Raya MacMillan (News Stringer), R.J. Burns (Man at Helicopter), Tammy L. Smith (Town Meeting Woman), Christopher Murray (Pilot), Justin Williams (Paramedic), Donna Deshon, Tom Magnuson (Road Block Newspersons), Marilyn Leubner (Babysitter)

Volcanologist Harry Dalton arrives in the mountain town of Dante's Peak predicting that a sleeping volcano will soon errupt.

Jeremy Foley, Jamie Renée Smith, Pierce Brosnan, Linda Hamilton

Pierce Brosnan, Linda Hamilton

Pierce Brosnan, Linda Hamilton

THE BEAUTICIAN AND THE BEAST

(PARAMOUNT) Producers, Howard W. "Hawk" Koch, Jr., Todd Graff; Executive Producers, Roger Birnbaum, Fran Drescher, Peter Marc Jacobson; Director, Ken Kwapis; Screenplay, Todd Graff; Photography, Peter Lyons Collister; Designer, Rusty Smith; Editor, Jon Poll; Music, Cliff Eidelman; a Koch Company production in association with High School Sweethearts; Dolby Stereo; Color; Rated PG; 105 minutes; February release

Timothy Dalton, Fran Drescher

CAST

Joy Miller	Fran Drescher
Boris Pochenko	Timothy Dalton
Grushinsky	Ian McNeice
Kleist	Patrick Malahide
Katrina	Lisa Jakub
Jerry Miller	Michael Lerner
Judy Miller	Phyllis Newman
Karl	Adam LaVorgna
Masha	Heather DeLoach
Yuri	Kyle & Tyler Wilkerson
Alek	Timothy Dowling
Stage Manager	Michael Immel
Model	Tonya Watts
Consuela	Tamara Mello
Lupe	Celeste Russi
Hector	Daniel R. Escobar
Fireman	Bill Brown
Photographer	Jorge Noa
Students	Carmela Rappazzo, Clyde Wrenn
Factory Worker	Earl Carroll
Jailer	Vincent Schiavelli
Chef	Marianne Muellerleile
Cousin Doris	R. Sparkle Stillman
Elderly Man	Ed Cambridge
Denny	Todd Graff
Servant	Gene Chronopoulos
Agent	Paul Beringer
Kitchen Worker	David Shackelford
Neighbor at Party	J.J. Chaback

Queens Beautician Joy Miller is mistaken for a school instructor and asked to come to the nation of Slovetzia to teach the children of barbaric dictator Boris Pochenko.

Fran Drescher, Timothy Dalton

Fran Drescher, Timothy Dalton

Timothy Dalton, Lisa Jakob, Fran Drescher, Heather DeLoach, Adam LaVorgna

Giovanni Ribisi, Nicky Katt

Jayce Bartok, Parker Posey

Steve Zahn, Dina Spybey

SUBURBIA

(SONY CLASSICS) Producer, Anne Walker-McBay; Executive Producer, John Sloss; Director, Richard Linklater; Screenplay, Eric Bogosian, based on his play; Photography, Lee Daniel; Designer, Catherine Hardwicke; Editor, Sandra Adair; Music, Sonic Youth; Casting, Judy Henderson, Alycia Aumuller; a Castle Rock Entertainment presentation of a Detour Film production; Dolby Stereo; Color; Rated R; 118 minutes; February release

Steve Zahn

CAST

Pony	Jayce Bartok
Sooze	Amie Carey
Tim	Nicky Katt
Nazeer	Ajay Naidu
Erica	Parker Posey
Jeff	Giovanni Ribisi
Pakeesa	Samia Shoaib
Bee-Bee	Dina Spybey
Buff	Steve Zahn

A group of aimless twenty-year-olds hang out at a strip-mall parking lot awaiting the arrival of an old friend who has made it big as a rock singer. Steve Zahn and Samia Shoaib repeat their roles from the 1994 Off-Broadway production.

Samia Shoaib

THE PEST

(TRISTAR) Producers, Sid Sheinberg, Jon Sheinberg, Bill Sheinberg; Executive Producer, Robert A. Papazian; Director, Paul Miller; Screenplay, David Bar Katz; Story, David Bar Katz, John Leguizamo; Photography, Roy H. Wagner; Designer, Rodger E. Maus; Editors, Ross Albert, David Rawlins; Costumes, Tom McKinley; Co-Producers, John Leguizamo, David Bar Katz; Music, Kevin Kiner; Casting, Wendy Kurtzman; a presentation of The Bubble Factory of a Sheinberg production; Dolby SDDS Stereo; Technicolor; Rated PG-13; 82 minutes; February release

John Leguizamo, Tammy Townsend

CAST

Pestario "Pest" Vargas	John Leguizamo
Gustav Shank	Jeffrey Jones
Himmel Shank	Edoardo Ballerini
Ninja	Freddy Rodriguez
Xantha Kent	Tammy Townsend
Chubby	Aries Spears
Mr. Kent	Joe Morton
Angus	Charles Hallahan
Leo	Tom McCleister
Gladyz	Ivonne Coll
Glen Livitt	Pat Skipper

and Jorge Luis Abrell (Piercer), Jennifer Broughton (Bank Employee), Yau Gene Chan (Cook), Judyann Elder (Mrs. Kent), Paul Harris (Karaoke Singer), Joe Jokubeit (Laphroig), David Bar Katz, Will Potter (White Guys), Les Lannom (Bagpipe Player), Jim Lau (Mr. Cheung), Barrie Mizerski (Host), Hugh Murphy (Emcee), Kristin Norton (Trixy), Yelba Osorio (Malaria), Tony Perez (Felix), Cantor Aviva Rosenbloom (Cantor), Julian Scott Urena (Sergio)

Con-man Pestario "Pest" Vargas agrees to become the target for crazed hunter Gustav Shank, assuming that if he survives for a 24-hour period he will receive $50,000.

© Tristar Pictures, Inc.

Freddy Rodriguez, John Leguizamo, Aries Spears

Tom McCleister, John Leguizamo, Jeffrey Jones

Edoardo Ballerini, John Leguizamo

FOOLS RUSH IN

(COLUMBIA) Producer, Doug Draizin; Executive Producer, Michael McDonnell; Director, Andy Tennant; Screenplay, Katherine Reback; Story, Joan Taylor, Katherine Redback; Photography, Robbie Greenberg; Designer, Edward Pisoni; Editor, Roger Bondelli; Costumes, Kimberly A. Tillman; Co-Producer, Anna Maria Davis; Music, Alan Silvestri; Casting, Juel Bestrop; a Doug Draizin production; Dolby SDDS Stereo; Technicolor; Rated PG-13; 106 minutes; February release

CAST

Alex Whitman	Matthew Perry
Isabel Fuentes	Salma Hayek
Jeff	Jon Tenney
Chuy	Carlos Gomez
Tomas Fuentes	Tomas Milian
Lanie	Siobhan Fallon
Richard Whitman	John Bennett Perry
Judd Marshall	Stanley DeSantis
Cathy Stewart	Suzanne Snyder
Amalia	Anne Betancourt
Nan	Jill Clayburgh
Great Grandma	Angelina Calderon Torres
Donna	Debby Shively
Juan Fuentes	Mark Adair Rios
Dr. Lisa Barnes	Annie Combs
Aunt Carmen	Shelley Morrison
Aunt Yolanda	Maria Cellario
Aunt Rosa	Irene Hernandez
Antonio Fuentes	Josh Cruze
Petra	Angela Lanza
Dam Policemen	Randy Sutton, Christopher Michael
Carlos	Angel Valdez
Enrique	Cesar Santana
Osha Rep	Garret Davis
Priest	Chris O'Neill
Man in Lobby	John Tripp
Assorted Cheeses	Andrew Hill Newman
Phil	Chris Bauer
Hank	Douglas Weston

and Rupert Baca (Porter), Jan Austell (Bruce Stewart), Cydney Arther (Diane Stewart), Leslie Silva (Process Server), Maryann Plunkett (Heliport Mother), Juel Mendel (Receptionist), Eddie Powers (Elvis), Salvador Saldaña (Mariachi Singer)

Three months after a one night stand, businessman Alex Whitman decides to marry Isabel Fuentes after discovering that she is pregnant.

© Columbia Pictures Industries, Inc.

Jon Tenney, Mathew Perry, Salma Hayek

Bill Pullman, Patricia Arquette

Natasha Gregson Wagner

LOST HIGHWAY

(OCTOBER) Producers, Deepak Nayar, Tom Sternberg, Mary Sweeney; Director, David Lynch; Screenplay, David Lynch, Barry Gifford; Photography, Peter Deming; Designer/Costumes, Patricia Norris; Editor, Mary Sweeney; Music, Angelo Badalamenti, Barry Adamson; Casting, Johanna Ray, Elaine J. Huzzar; a Ciby 2000/Asymmetrical production; Dolby Digital Stereo; Panavision; Color; Rated R; 135 minutes; February release

CAST

Fred Madison	Bill Pullman
Renee Madison/Alice Wakefield	Patricia Arquette
Pete Dayton	Balthazar Getty
Mystery Man	Robert Blake
Mr. Eddy/Dick Laurent	Robert Loggia
Arnie	Richard Pryor
Bill Dayton	Gary Busey
Candace Dayton	Lucy Butler
Sheila	Natasha Gregson Wagner

and John Roselius (Al), Lou Eppolito (Ed), Jenna Maetlind (Party Girl), Michael Massee (Andy), Henry Rollins (Guard Henry), Michael Shamus Wiles (Guard Mike), Mink Stole (Forewoman), Leonard Termo (Judge), Ivory Ocean (Guard Ivor), Jack Kehler (Guard Johnny Mack), David Byrd (Dr. Smordin), Gene Ross (Warden Clements), F. William Parker (Capt. Luneau), Guy Siner, Alexander Folk (Prison Officials), Carl Sundstrom (Hank), John Solari (Lou), Jack (The Dog), Al Garrett (Carl), Heather Stephens (Lanie), Giovanni Ribisi (Steve "V"), Scott Coffey (Teddy), Amanda Anka (Girl #1), Jennifer Syme (Junkie Girl), Matt Sigloch (Assistants), Greg Travis (Tail Gate Driver), Jack Nance (Phil), Lisa Boyle (Marian), Leslie Bega (Raquel), Marilyn Manson, Twiggy Ramirez (Porno Stars)

A jazz musician, certain his wife is having an affair, is accused of her murder; a garage mechanic becomes involved with a dangerous woman who is cheating on her gangster lover.

© October Films

Clint Eastwood, Laura Linney

ABSOLUTE POWER

(COLUMBIA) Producers, Clint Eastwood, Karen Spiegel; Director, Clint Eastwood; Executive Producer, Tom Rooker; Screenplay, William Goldman; Based on the novel by David Baldacci; Photography, Jack N. Green; Designer, Henry Bumstead; Editor, Joel Cox; Music, Lennie Niehaus; Casting, Phyllis Huffman; a Castle Rock Entertainment presentation of a Malpaso production; SDDS Stereo; Panavision; Technicolor; Rated R; 121 minutes; February release

CAST

Luther Whitney	Clint Eastwood
President Alan Richmond	Gene Hackman
Seth Frank	Ed Harris
Kate Whitney	Laura Linney
Bill Burton	Scott Glenn
Tim Collin	Dennis Haysbert
Gloria Russell	Judy Davis
Walter Sullivan	E.G. Marshall
Christy Sullivan	Melora Hardin
Sandy Lord	Ken Welsh
Laura Simon	Penny Johnson
Michael McCarty	Richard Jenkins
Red	Mark Margolis
Valerie	Elaine Kagan
Art Student	Alison Eastwood
Waiter	Yau-Gene Chan
Airport Bartender	George Orrison
Medical Examiner	Charles McDaniel
Repairman	John Lyle Campbell
White House Tour Guide	Kimber Eastwood
Oval Office Agent	Eric Dahlquist, Jr.
Watergate Doorman	Jack Stewart Taylor
Reporter	Joy Ehrlich
Cop	Robert Harvey

While pulling off a heist, master thief Luther Whitney accidentally witnesses the President of the United States involved in the death of his mistress.

Gene Hackman, Judy Davis

© Castle Rock Entertainment

Clint Eastwood, Ed Harris

Scott Glenn, Judy Davis

THAT DARN CAT

(WALT DISNEY PICTURES) Producer, Robert Simonds; Executive Producer, Andrew Gottlieb; Director, Bob Spiers; Screenplay, S.M. Alexander, L.A. Karaszweski; Based on the novel *Undercover Cat* by The Gordons, and the screenplay by The Gordons and Bill Walsh; Photography, Jerzy Zielinski; Designer, Jonathan Carlson; Editor, Roger Barton; Costumes, Marie France; Music, Richard Kendall Gibbs; Head Animal Trainer, Larry M. Madrid; Casting, Gary Zuckerbrod; Distributed by Buena Vista Pictures; Dolby Digital Stereo; Technicolor; Rated PG; 89 minutes; February release

CAST

Patti Randall	Christina Ricci
Zeke Kelso	Doug E. Doug
Mr. Flint	Dean Jones
Boetticher	George Dzundza
Pa	Peter Boyle
Peter Randall	Michael McKean
Judy Randall	Bess Armstrong
Mrs. Flint	Dyan Cannon
Dusty	John Ratzenberger
Lu	Megan Cavanagh
Old Lady McCracken	Estelle Parsons
Ma	Rebecca Schull
Melvin	Tom Wilson
Marvin	Brian Haley
Rollo	Mark Christopher Lawrence
D.C. ("That Darn Cat")	Elvis
Lizzy	Rebecca Koon

and Ned Bellamy, Brad Sherwood, Rob Cleveland, Jeffrey King (Agents), Tom Turbiville (Field Agent #1), Libby Whittemore (Another Agent), Cassandra Lawton (Newscaster), Margo Moorer (Teacher), Hillary Tolle, Paula Jones, Kinsey McLean (Kids), Jon Kohler (Hollywood Cat Choreographer), Wilbur T. Fitzgerald, Terrence Gibney (Scientists), Harvey Reaves, Michael Genevie (Cops), Bill Coates (Old Ticket Man), Alex Van (Trash Man), Michelle B. Cooper (Nurse), Stephen Michael Ayers (Disbelieving Cop #1), Douglas Myers (Judge), Frank Smith (Announcer), Larue Stanley (Widow), David Wayne Evans, Margaret Ellis (Agents)

Patti Randall's tomcat, D.C., returns home with a watch that turns out to be an important clue in a mysterious kidnapping. Remake of the 1965 Disney film which starred Hayley Mills, Dean Jones, Dorothy Provine, and Roddy McDowall. Jones, who played Kelso in the original film, also appears in this version.

Doug E. Doug, Christina Ricci

Dyan Cannon, Dean Jones

BOOTY CALL

(COLUMBIA) Producer, John Morrissey; Director, Jeff Pollack; Screenplay, Takashi Bufford, Bootsie; Photography, Ron Orieux; Designer, Sandra Kybartas; Editor, Christopher Greenbury; Costumes, Vicki Graef; Music, Robert Folk; Co-Producer, John M. Eckert; Casting, Mary Vernieu, Ronnie Yeskel; a Turman/Morrissey Company production; Dolby SDDS Stereo; Technicolor; Rated R; 77 minutes; February release

CAST

Bunz	Jamie Foxx
Rushon	Tommy Davidson
Lysterine	Vivica A. Fox
Nikki	Tamala Jones
Singh	Scott LaRose
Mr. Chiu	Ric Young
Chan	Gedde Watanabe
Akmed	Art Malik
Judge Peabody	Bernie Mac
Arguing Woman	Amy Monique Waddell
Arguing Man	Wiley Moore
Ug Lee	Kam Ray Chan
Yoyo	Ammie Sin
Judge's Woman	Olivia Yap

and Bill MacDonald (Hold Up Man), John Moraitis (Greek Cabbie), Karen Robinson (Admitting Nurse), Donna Preising (Triage Nurse), Johnie Chase (Guard), Amanda Tapping (Dr. Moore), Beatriz Pizano (Pregnant Woman), Bootsie (Older Man), James Mainprize (Another Patient), Pedro Salvin (Male Nurse), Robert Bidaman (Dr. Zevroloski), Julia Paton (Nurse), Valerie Boyle (O.R. Nurse), David Hemblen (Dr. Blade), James Kidnie (Mummified Man), Michael Anthony Joseph, Dominic Marcus, George Ramsey, Derrick Simmons (Dice Players)

Bunz and Rushon find that their dates, Nikki and Lysterine, are so adamant about safe sex, that the two men end up on a frantic pursuit to find condoms.

© Columbia Pictures Industries, Inc.

Vivica A. Fox, Jamie Foxx, Tamala Jones, Tommy Davidson

Paul Mazursky, Lolita Davidovich

Christopher Walken, Bridget Fonda

TOUCH

(UNITED ARTISTS) Producers, Lila Cazès, Fida Attieh; Director/Screenplay, Paul Schrader; Based upon the novel by Elmore Leonard; Co-Producer, Llewellyn Wells; Photography, Ed Lachman; Designer, David Wasco; Editor, Cara Silverman; Costumes, Julie Weiss; Music, David Grohl; Casting, Ronnie Yeskel, Mary Vernieu; a Lumiere International presentation of a Lila Cazès production; Distributed by MGM/UA; Dolby Stereo; CFI color; Rated R; 97 minutes; February release

CAST

Lynn Faulkner	Bridget Fonda
Bill Hill	Christopher Walken
Juvenal	Skeet Ulrich
August Murray	Tom Arnold
Debra Lusanne	Gina Gershon
Antoinette Baker	Lolita Davidovich
Artie	Paul Mazursky
Kathy Worthington	Janeane Garofalo
Elwin Worrel	John Doe
Virginia Worrel	Conchata Ferrell
Father Nestor	Mason Adams
Greg Czarnicki	Breckin Meyer
Father Donahue	Anthony Zerbe
Himself	LL Cool J
Alisha	Maria Celedonio
Scruffy Staff Worker	Chris Hogan
Court Clerk	William Newman
Bailiff	Matt O'Toole
Judge	Richard Fancy
Prosecutor	Tamlyn Tomita
Father Navaroli	Don Novello
Jerry	Richard Schiff
Bib Overalls	O-Lan Jones
Arnold	Brent Hinkley
Song Leader	Diana Georger
Richie Baker	Theo Greenly
Roman Governor	Richard Coe
Shelly	Julie Condra
Palsied Man	John Gay
Waitress	Missy Hargraves
Stripper	Casey Gray
Edith	Kate Williamson
Hillbilly	Dennis Burkley

A young man whose touch can heal, arrives in Los Angeles to work at a rehab center and finds himself being exploited by a pair of con-men.

Gina Gershon   Janeane Garofalo

Bridget Fonda, Skeet Ulrich

BLOOD AND WINE

(FOX SEARCHLIGHT) Producer, Jeremy Thomas; Executive Producers, Chris Auty, Bernie Williams; Director, Bob Rafelson; Screenplay, Nick Villiers, Alison Cross; Story, Nick Villiers, Bob Rafelson; Photography, Newton Thomas Sigel; Designer, Richard Sylbert; Editor, Steven Cohen; Costumes, Lindy Hemming; Co-Producers, Hercules Bellville, Noah Golden; Music, Michal Lorenc; a Recorded Picture Company presentation of a Jeremy Thomas production; Dolby Stereo; Deluxe color; Rated R; 98 minutes; February release

CAST

Alex Gates	Jack Nicholson
Jason	Stephen Dorff
Gabriela	Jennifer Lopez
Suzanne Gates	Judy Davis
Victor Spansky	Michael Caine
Henry	Harold Perrineau, Jr.
Dina	Robyn Peterson
Mike	Mike Starr
Frank	John Seitz
Guard	Marc Macaulay
Todd	Dan Daily
Gabriela's Cousin	Marta Velasco
Jeweler #2	Thom Christopher

and Mario Ernesto Sanchez (Artie—Fishing Ace), John Hackett (Gas Station Attendant), Hector Montano (Gabriela's Grandfather), Vanessa L. Hernandez (Cuban Little Girl), Carmen Lopez (Head Nurse), Antoni Corone (Caribbean Club Bartender), Jim Torres Towers (Father of Gabriela's Cousin), Glice Montano (Gabriela's Grandmother)

Wine merchant Alex Gates creates further friction between himself, his wife Suzanne and his stepson Jason when he helps his safe-cracker buddy Victor steal a valuable diamond necklace.

Jennifer Lopez, Jack Nicholson

Stephen Dorff, Jack Nicholson

Jack Nicholson, Michael Caine

Jack Nicholson, Michael Caine

Al Pacino, James Russo, Bruno Kirby, Michael Madsen, Johnny Depp

Johnny Depp

Al Pacino, Johnny Depp

Johnny Depp, Anne Heche

DONNIE BRASCO

(TRISTAR) Producers, Mark Johnson, Barry Levinson, Louis DiGiaimo, Gail Mutrux; Executive Producers, Patrick McCormick, Alan Greenspan; Director, Mike Newell; Screenplay, Paul Attanasio; Based on the book *Donnie Brasco: My Undercover Life in the Mafia* by Joseph D. Pistone, with Richard Woodley; Photography, Peter Sova; Designer, Donald Graham Burt; Editor, Jon Gregory; Costumes, Aude Bronson-Howard, David Robinson; Music, Patrick Doyle; Casting, Louis DiGiaimo, Brett Goldstein; a Mandalay Entertainment presentation of a Baltimore Pictures/Mark Johnson production; Dolby SDDS Stereo; Super 35 Widescreen; Technicolor; Rated R; 121 minutes; February release

Johnny Depp, Al Pacino

CAST

Lefty Ruggiero	Al Pacino
Joe Pistone (Donnie Brasco)	Johnny Depp
Sonny Black	Michael Madsen
Nicky	Bruno Kirby
Paulie	James Russo
Maggie Pistone	Anne Heche
Tim Curley	Zeljko Ivanek
Dean Blandford	Gerry Becker
Sonny Red	Robert Miano
Bruno	Brian Tarantina
Richie Gazzo	Rocco Sisto
Dr. Berger	Zach Grenier
Sheriff	Walt MacPherson
Annette	Ronnie Farer
Strip Club Owner	Terry Serpico
Sonny's Girlfriend	Gretchen Mol
Philly Lucky	Tony Lip
Big Trin	George Angelica
Trafficante	Val Avery
Jilly	Madison Arnold
Daughters	Delanie Fitzpatrick, Katie Sagona, Sara Gold
Tommy	Larry Romano
FBI Technicians	Tim Blake Nelson, Paul Giamatti
FBI Agent	James Michael McCauley
U.S. Attorney	Jim Bulleit
Hollman	Andrew Parks
Japanese Maitre D'	Keenan Shimizu
Trafficante's Men	Rocco Musacchia, Joe Francis
Mare Chiaro Bartender	Sal Jenco

and Billy Capucilli, Laura Cahill (Communion Party Couple), Doreen Murphy, Elle Alexander, Denise Faye, Elaine Del Valle (Mob Girlfriends), John Horton (FBI Director), Dan Brennan (FBI Photographer), LaJuan Carter, Sandy Barber, Joyce Stovall (Singers), Frank Pesce, Randy Jurgensen, John DiBenedetto, Richard Zavaglia, Tony Ray Rossi, Edward Black, Gaetano LoGiudice, Carmelo Musacchia, Pat Vecchio (Wiseguys)

True story of how FBI agent Joe Pistone, under the identity of Donnie Brasco, gained the confidence of hit-man Lefty Ruggerio and infiltrated the Mafia. This film received an Oscar nomination for screenplay adaptation.

Al Pacino

Terry Serpico, Johnny Depp

HARD EIGHT

(GOLDWYN) Producers, Robert Jones, John Lyons; Executive Producers, Keith Samples, Hans Brockmann, Francois Duplat; Director/Screenplay, Paul Thomas Anderson; Photography, Robert Elswitt; Designer, Nancy Deren; Editor, Barbara Tulliver; Co-Producer, Daniel Lupi; Music, Michael Penn, Jon Brion; Costumes, Mark Bridges; Casting, Christine Sheaks; a Rysher Entertainment presentation of a Green Parrot production in association with Trinity of a P.T. Anderson Picture; Dolby Stereo; Super 35 Widescreen; Color; Rated R; 101 minutes; February release

CAST

Sydney	Philip Baker Hall
John	John C. Reilly
Clementine	Gwyneth Paltrow
Jimmy	Samuel L. Jackson
Hostage	F. William Parker
Young Craps Player	Philip Seymour Hoffman
Restroom Attendant	Nathanael Cooper
Waitress	Wynn White
Keno Bar Manager	Robert Ridgely
Keno Girl	Kathleen Campbell
Pitt Boss	Michael J. Rowe
Bartender	Peter D'Allessandro
Stickman	Steve Blane

and Xaleese (Cocktail Waitress), Melora Walters (Jimmy's Girl), Jean Langer (Cashier), Andy Breen (Groom), Renee Breen (Bride), Jane W. Brimmer (Aladdin Cashier), Mark Finizza (Desk Clerk), Richard Gross (Floorman), Cliff Keeley (Aladdin Change Booth Attendant), Carrie McVey (El Dorado Cashier), Pastor Truman Robbins (Pastor), Ernie Anderson, Wendy Weidman, Jason "Jake" Cross (Pants on Fire People)

Sydney, a professional gambler, takes young John under his wing and teaches him the art of gambling. Two years later their bond is challenged by a small-time crook, Jimmy, and a cocktail waitress named Clementine.

Samuel L. Jackson

Gwyneth Paltrow

John C. Riley, Philip Baker Hall

JUNGLE 2 JUNGLE

(WALT DISNEY PICTURES) Producer, Brian Reilly; Executive Producers, Richard Baker, Rick Messina, Brad Krevoy; Director, John Pasquin; Screenplay, Bruce A. Evans, Raynold Gideon; Based on the film *Un Indien Dans La Ville (Little Indian, Big City)* written by Herve Palud, Thierry Lhermitte, Igor Aptekman, Philippe Bruneau de la Salle; Co-Producer, William W. Wilson III; Associate Producers, Thierry Lhermitte, Louis Becker, Kimberly Brent, Bruce Economou; Photography, Tony Pierce-Roberts; Designer, Stuart Wurtzel; Editor, Michael A. Stevenson; Costumes, Carol Ramsey; Music, Michael Convertino; Casting, Renee Rousselot; Stunts, Danny Aiello III; Dolby Digital Stereo; Technicolor; Rated PG; 105 minutes; March release

Tim Allen, Martin Short

CAST

Michael Cromwell	Tim Allen
Mimi-Siku	Sam Huntington
Dr. Patricia Cromwell	JoBeth Williams
Charlotte	Lolita Davidovich
Richard	Martin Short
Jan	Valerie Mahaffey
Karen	LeeLee Sobieski
Andrew	Frankie Galasso
Abe	Luis Avalos
Langston	Bob Dishy
Sarah	Rondi Reed
Madeleine	Oni Faida Lampley
Ian	Dominic Keating
Fiona	Carole Shelley
Gino	Michael Mastro
Mrs. Prelot	Joan Copeland
Mr. Uhley	Jack McGee
Jovanovic	David Ogden Stiers
Jovanovic Thugs	Nicholas J. Giangiulio, Don Picard
Stewardess	Christine Toy
Homeless Person	Jack O'Connell
Benjamin	Jake Cooper
Ride Operator	Ken Larsen
Broker	Lowell Sanders
Morrison	Adam LeFevre
Deli Clerk	John Tormey

and Diana Roberts ("Hello You" Girl), Derek Smith (Louis), Tanya Memme (Trader's Assistant), R.M. Haley (Hot Dog Vendor), Glen Trotiner (Dart Booth Attendant), Eva Veronika (Jovanovic's Mother), Georgina Kess (Fish Market Employee), Maureen Beitler (Nurse), Shthd Right-Turn Clyde (Matitika), Brian M. Reilly (Fingerless Hand), John Pasquin (Bearded Man in Times Square)

Tim Allen, Sam Huntington

New York commodities trader Michael Cromwell travels to the Amazon jungle to finalize a divorce with his wife only to find that he has a 13 year old son, raised in the ways of the jungle tribesmen. Remake of the film Little Indian, Big City which was released in the U.S. in 1996 by the Walt Disney Company.

Lolita Davidovich, Tim Allen

29

Howard Stern, Fred Norris

Mary McCormack, Howard Stern

Robin Quivers

PRIVATE PARTS

(PARAMOUNT) Producer, Ivan Reitman; Executive Producers, Daniel Goldberg, Joe Medjuck, Keith Samples; Director, Betty Thomas; Screenplay, Len Blum, Michael Kalesniko; Based on the book by Howard Stern; Photography, Walt Lloyd; Designer, Charles Rosen; Editor, Peter Teschner; Co-Producer, Celia Costas; Music Supervisor, Peter Afterman; Costumes, Joseph G. Aulisi; Casting, Phyllis Huffman, Olivia Harris; a Rysher Entertainment presentation of an Ivan Reitman production; Dolby Stereo; DuArt color; Rated R; 109 minutes; March release

CAST

Himself	Howard Stern
Herself	Robin Quivers
Alison Stern	Mary McCormack
Himself	Fred Norris
Kenny	Paul Giamatti
Himself	Gary Dell'Abate
Himself	Jackie Martling
Gloria	Carol Alt
Ben Stern	Richard Portnow
Ray Stern	Kelly Bishop
Moti	Henry Goodman
Griff	Jonathan Hadary
Ross Buckingham	Paul Hecht
Dee Dee	Allison Janney
Roger Erlick	Michael Murphy
Payton	James Murtaugh
Vallesecca	Reni Santoni
Marvin Mamoulian	Lee Wilkof
Brittany	Melanie Good
Orgasm Woman	Theresa Lynn
Julie	Amber Smith
The Kielbasa Queen	Althea Cassidy
Mandy	Jenna Jameson
Seven-year-old Howard	Bobby Borriello
12-year-old Howard	Michael Maccarone
16-year-old Howard	Matthew Friedman
Music Awards Technician	John Michael Bolger
Howard's Agent	Steven Gilborn
Airline Representative	Curtis McClarin
Symphony Sid	Richard B. Shull
Elliot	Evan Roberts
Herbie	Gabriel De Silva
Coeds	Jennifer Gareis, Mandy Steckelberg
Blind Coed	Ali Marsh
Friends	Scott Cohen, James Villemaire
Elyse	Wendy Hoopes
Film Professor	Richard Russell Ramos
Unshaven Deejay	Gordon Joseph Weiss
Barb	Allison Furman
Patricia Fonfara	Julie Gawkowksi
Nurse	Davenia McFadden
Duke of Rock	Michael Gwynne
The Leather Weather Lady	Irene DeCook
Rubberbound Man	Jordan Derwin
Trembling Patient	Stuart Rudin

and John Stamos, Chris Barron, Flava Flav, Hammer, Ted Nugent, Ozzy Osbourne, John Popper, Slash, Dee Snider, Renee Suran, Tiny Tim, David Letterman, "Stuttering" John Melendez, George "Crackhead Bob" Harvey, Nicole Bass (Themselves), Richard Ziman (Salesman), Adam LeFevre (Sales Manager), Janine Lindemulder (Camp Director's Wife), Scott Lawrence (News Guy), Christine Tucci (Doctor), Kim Chan (Waiter), Nick Wyman (Douglas Kiker), Stephen Pearlman (Husband), Catherine Wolf (Wife), Luke Reilly (Imus), Rick Levi, Peter Jacobson (Lawyers), Leslie Bibb (NBC Tour Guide), Joanne Camp (Reenie), Peter Maloney (Researcher), Sarah Zinsser (Kenny's Secretary), Barry Papick (Engineer), Christine Toy, Alison Stern (NBC Switchboard Operators), Brian Johnson, Angus Young, Malcolm Young, Phil Rudd, Cliff Williams (AC/DC), Susan Pratt (Stewardess), Sasha Martin, Sarah Jane Hyland (Howard's Daughters), Larry Grey (Dr. Larry), Camille Donatacci (Bikini Girl in Westchester), Danna Bradley, Seth Silver (Transvestites), Carrie Flaska (Wife in Car), Steve Ballot (Husband), Brian Constantini, Barnett Milton Lloyd (DC Cops), Aimee Luzier (Betty Jean Rushton).

The true story of how Howard Stern rose from obscurity to become the number one rated nationally syndicated radio disc jockey.

Liev Schreiber, Parker Posey, Anne Meara, Hope Davis, Pat McNamara

Hope Davis, Liev Schreiber, Parker Posey

Hope Davis, Stanley Tucci

THE DAYTRIPPERS

(CFP) Producers, Nancy Tenenbaum, Steven Soderbergh; Executive Producers, Lawrence S. Kamerman, David Heyman, Campbell Scott; Director/Screenplay, Greg Mottola; Photography, John Inwood; Designer, Bonnie J. Brinkley; Editor, Anne McCabe; Costumes, Barbara Presar; Music, Richard Martinez; Casting, Sheila Jaffe, Georgianne Walken; a Nancy Tenenbaum Films presentation; Dolby DTS Stereo; Color; Not rated; 87 minutes; March release

CAST

Eliza D'Amico	Hope Davis
Louis D'Amico	Stanley Tucci
Jo Malone	Parker Posey
Carl	Liev Schreiber
Rita Malone	Anne Meara
Jim Malone	Pat McNamara
Eddie, The Author	Campbell Scott
Ronnie	Andy Brown
Leon, Ronnie's Father	Paul Herman
Aaron, Book Publicist	Marc Grapey
Libby	Marcia Gay Harden
Molly	Marcia Haufrecht
Doris	Carol Locatell
Chap, Louis' Boss	Douglas McGrath
Amy Corinne Fairbright-Lebow	Amy Stiller
Cassandra, the Receptionist	Stephanie Venditto
Nick Woodman	Peter Askin
Libby's Ex-Boyfriend	Adam Davidson
Monica	Jill Rowe
Monica's Friend	Tracey Barry
Sandy	F. Evanson

After Eliza finds a love letter written to her husband, she collects together her family to venture into New York City for a confrontation.

© CFP Distribution

CITY OF INDUSTRY

(ORION) Producers, Evzen Kolar, Ken Solarz; Executive Producer, Barr Potter; Director, John Irvin; Screenplay, Ken Solarz; Co-Producers, Matthew Gayne, Frank K. Isaac; Photography, Thomas Burstyn; Designer, Michael Novotny; Music, Stephen Endelman; Editor, Mark Conte; Costumes, Eduardo Castro; Casting, Henderson/Zuckerman; from Largo Entertainment; Dolby Stereo; Deluxe Color; Rated R; 97 minutes; March release

Timothy Hutton, Harvey Keitel

CAST

Roy Egan	Harvey Keitel
Skip Kovich	Stephen Dorff
Lee Egan	Timothy Hutton
Rachel Montana	Famke Janssen
Jorge Montana	Wade Dominguez
Odell Williams	Michael Jai White
Cathi Rose	Lucy Alexis Liu
Keshaun Brown	Reno Wilson
Gena	Dana Barron
Sunny	Tamara Clatterbuck
Backus	Brian Brophy
Uncle Like	Francois Chau
A Roc	Flex
Pai-Gow Dealer	Brian Shen
Gwen	Ai Wan
Steady	Cyrus Farmer
Henry Montana	Eli Ruiz
Gingerhead	Vien Hong
Shrimp Boy	Michael Trac
Droutzkoy	Evzen Kolar
Jewelry Manager	Jonathan Schmock

and Raymond Ma (Paradise Hotel Clerk), Georg D. Rice (Royal Sentry Security Guard), Brian Habicht (Phone Company Employee), Arthus Louis Fuller (Bouncer), Sarah Sullivan (Nurse), Jane Crawley (Waitress), Antonio Molina (Mailman), Philip Tan (Jimmie), Stuart Quan (Onion Head), Anthony James DeJesus (Jorge, Jr.), John Koyama (Two Gun), Steven Ho (Gang Member), Brian Imada (Sweet Plum), Leo Lee (Redman), William Leong (Jesse), Andrew Markell (Kangol), Eddie Yansick, Eddie Mathews, Tim Rigby (Bodyguards), Fred Lerner (Security Guard), Elliott Gould

Famke Janssen

Lee Egan talks his brother Roy into joining him in a heist which goes terribly wrong when one of the other participants decides to take the haul for himself.

Stephen Dorff

MANDELA

(ISLAND) Producers, Jonathan Demme, Edward Saxon, Jo Menell; Executive Producers, Chris Blackwell, Dan Genetti; Co-Producer, Peter Saraf; Photography, Dewald Aukema, Peter Tischhauser; Music, Cedric Gradus Samson, Hugh Masekela; Editor, Andy Keir; a Clinica Estetico production; Dolby Stereo; Color; Not rated; 120 minutes; March release. Documentary on Nelson Mandela and his journey from childhood to presidency of a reborn South Africa.

This film received a 1996 Oscar nomination for feature documentary.

BOYS LIFE 2

(STRAND) Color; Not rated; 74 minutes.

MUST BE THE MUSIC

Producer, Rafi Stephan; Director/Screenplay, Nickolas Perry; Photography, Steve Adcock; Editor, Craig A. Colton; Casting, Aaron Griffith.

CAST

Eric	Michael Saucedo
Kevin	Justin Urich
Dave	Travis Sher
Jason	Milo Ventimiglia

and Germane Montel (Eric's Friend/Lead Dancer), Gabriel Fuller, Ryan Vernotico (Kissing Boys), Grant Swanson (Matt), Eddie Mui (Gregg), Jason Adelman (Michael), David Ko (Michael's Friend), Chris Fuentes (D.J.)

Travis Sher, Gabriel Fuller, Ryan Vernotico in *Must Be the Music*

NUNZIO'S SECOND COUSIN

Executive Producer, Camille Taylor; Director/Screenplay, Tom DeCerchio; Photography, Steve Poster; Editor, Mike Murphy; Line Producer, Gayle S. Newborn; Music, Robert Folk; Casting, Ferne Cassel.

CAST

Sgt. Tony Randozza	Vincent D'Onofrio
Jimmy	Miles Perlich
Mrs. Randozza	Eileen Brennan

and David Fresco (Mr. Perlin), Harry Walters, Jr. (Tony's Date), Christian Meoli, Seth Green, Jarred Blancard, Josh Scheafer (Homophobes)

ALKALI, IOWA

Producer, Ann Ruark; Director/Screenplay, Mark Christopher; Photography, Jamie Silverstein; Editor, Gloria Whittemore; Music, Julian Harris.

CAST

June Gudmanson	Mary Beth Hurt
Jack Gudmanson	J.D. Cerna
Blondie	Kent Broadhurst

and Ellen Hamilton-Latzen (Carol), Ed Seamon (Bill Gudmanson), Greg Villepique (Jacko)

Jonah Rooney, Brett Barsky in *Trevor*

TREVOR

Producers, Peggy Rajski, Randy Stone; Director, Peggy Rajski; Screenplay, James Lecesne; Photography, Marc Reshovsky; Editor, John Tintori; Music, Danny Troob; Casting, Avy Kaufman.

CAST

Trevor	Brett Barsky
Father Joe	Stephen Tobolowsky
Trevor's Mom	Judy Kain
Trevor's Dad	John Lizzi
Pinky	Jonah Rooney
Walter	Allen Doraine

Four short films dealing with gay young men and their different journeys from adolesence to manhood. Trevor was the recipient of the 1994 Academy Award for Best Live Action Short Subject.

Miles Perlich, Vincent D'Onofrio in *Nunzio's Second Cousin*

Larenz Tate, Nia Long

LOVE JONES

(NEW LINE CINEMA) Producers, Nick Wechsler, Jeremiah Samuels; Executive Producers, Julia Chasman, Jay Stern, Amy Henkels, Helena Echegoyen; Director/Screenplay, Theodore Witcher; Photography, Ernest Holzman; Editor, Maysie Hoy; Designer, Roger Fortune; Music, Darryl Jones; Costumes, Shawn Barton; Casting, Jane Alderman, Robi Reed-Humes; an Addis-Wechsler production; Dolby Stereo; Deluxe color; Rated R; 110 minutes; March release

CAST

Darius Lovehall	Larenz Tate
Nina Mosley	Nia Long
Savon Garrison	Isaiah Washington
Josie Nichols	Lisa Nicole Carson
Hollywood	Bill Bellamy
Eddie Coles	Leonard Roberts
Sheila Downes	Bernadette L. Clarke
Marvin Cox	Khalil Kain
Troy Garrison	Cerall Duncan
Publisher	David Nisbet
Roger Lievsey	Simon James
Model (Lievsey Studio)	Oona Hart
Lisa Martin	Jacqueline Fleming
Nina's Assistant	Manao DeMuth
Tracey Powell	Marie-Francoise Theodore
Themselves	Reginald Gibson, Malik Yosef

and Kahil El Zabar (Percussionist), Darryl "Munch" Jones (Bassist), Teodross Avery (Saxophonist), Everette Dean (Porter), Benjamin LeVert (Savon's Son), John M. Watson, Sr. (Tiki Room Bartender), William Yancey (Sanctuary Bartender), Ernest Perry (Model), Helena Echegoyen (Woman on Train), Troy Borisy (Taxi Driver), Michelle Poole, Kevin Bell (Kissing Couple)

Darius, a struggling writer, and Nina, a disillusioned photographer's assistant, begin a relationship which is tested when Nina's former fiancee shows up wanting her back.

Lisa Nicole Carson, Nia Long

Nia Long, Larenz Tate

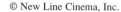

THE DEVIL'S OWN

(COLUMBIA) Producers, Lawrence Gordon, Robert F. Colesberry; Executive Producers, Lloyd Levin, Donald Laventhall; Director, Alan J. Pakula; Screenplay, David Aaron Cohen, Vincent Patrick, Kevin Jarre; Story, Kevin Jarre; Photography, Gordon Willis; Designer, Jane Musky; Editors, Tom Rolf, Dennis Virkler; Costumes, Bernie Pollack; Music, James Horner; Casting, Alixe Gordin; a Lawrence Gordon presentation; Dolby SDDS Stereo; Panavision; Technicolor; Rated R; 110 minutes; March release

CAST

Tom O'Meara...Harrison Ford
Rory Devaney (Frankie McGuire)................................Brad Pitt
Sheila O'Meara...Margaret Colin
Edwin Diaz ....Ruben Blades
Billy Burke ....Treat Williams
Peter Fitzsimmons ....George Hearn
Chief Jim Kelly ....Mitchell Ryan
Megan Doherty ....Natascha McElhone
Sean Phelan...Paul Ronan
Harry Sloan..Simon Jones
Bridget O'Meara...Julia Stiles
Morgan O'Meara...Ashley Carin
Annie O'Meara ....Kelly Singer
Martin MacDuff..David O'Hara
Dessie ....David Wilmot
Gerard...Athony Brophy
Young Frankie..Shane Dunne
Frankie's Father ....Martin Dunne
Frankie's Mother..Gabrielle Reidy
Frankie's Sister ....Samantha Conroy
Customs Agent...Baxter Harris
Teenager..Hassan Johnson
Rookie Cop...Scott Nicholson
Jerry ....Jonathan Earl Peck
Hispanic Man..Sixto Ramos
Hispanic Woman ....Mya Michaels
Hispanic Girl ....Jessica Marie Kavanagh
Teddy...Brendan Kelly
Thug ....Kevin Nagle
Tony ....Greg Salata
Joey the Bartender...Joseph Dandry
Jack Fitzsimmons ....Jack McKillop
and Mac Orange (The Maid), Malachy McCourt (Bishop), Marian Tomas Griffin (Cousin Eileen), Peggy Shay (Aunt Birdie), Danielle McGovern (Brooke), Ciaran O'Reilly (Father Canlon), Rob McElhenny (Kevin), Donald J. Meade, Patrick Reynolds, Peter Rufli (Irish Musicians), Debbon Ayer (Tour Guide), Mario Polit (Young Domincian), Chance Kelly (Masked Burglar), Greg Stebner (Uniformed Cop), William Paulson (Detective), Bill Hoag (Trucker), Victor Slezak (Evan Stanley, FBI), Damien Leake (Art Fisher, FBI)

New York cop Tom O'Meara allows a young Irishman, Rory Devaney, to take room and board in his home, unaware that he is in actuality a terrorist sent to the United States to buy weapons.

© Columbia Pictures Industries, Inc.

Harrison Ford, Brad Pitt

Brad Pitt, Natascha McElhone

Harrison Ford, Margaret Colin, Julia Stiles, Brad Pitt, Kelly Singer

Jim Carrey, Jennifer Tilly

Swoosie Kurtz, Eric Pierpont, Jennifer Tilly, Jim Carrey

LIAR LIAR

(UNIVERSAL) Producer, Brian Grazer; Executive Producers, James D. Brubaker, Michael Bostick; Director, Tom Shadyac; Screenplay, Paul Guay, Stephen Mazur; Photography, Russell Boyd; Designer, Linda DeScenna; Editor, Don Zimmerman; Costumes, Judy L. Ruskin; Music, John Debney; Casting, Junie Lowry Johnson, Ron Surma; an Imagine Entertainment presentation of a Brian Grazer production; DTS Stereo; Deluxe color; Rated PG-13; 86 minutes; March release

Jim Carrey, Justin Cooper

CAST

Fletcher Reede	Jim Carrey
Audrey Reede	Maura Tierney
Max Reede	Justin Cooper
Jerry	Cary Elwes
Greta	Anne Haney
Samantha Cole	Jennifer Tilly
Miranda	Amanda Donohoe
Judge Marshall Stevens	Jason Bernard
Dana Appleton	Swoosie Kurtz
Mr. Allan	Mitchell Ryan
Kenneth Falk	Chip Mayer
Richard Cole	Eric Pierpoint
Skull	Randall "Tex" Cobb
Jane	Cheri Oteri
Pete	SW Fisher
Randy	Ben Lemon
Zit Boy	Jarrad Paul
Ms. Berry	Marianne Muellerleile
Lady in Elevator	Krista Allen
Police Officer	Stephen James Carver
Beggar at Courthouse	Don Keefer
Beggar at Office	Paul Roache
Detective Bryson	Randy Oglesby
Restroom Man	Charlie Dell
Pilot	Jim Hansen
Co-Pilot	Terry Rhoads
Tow Yard Employee	Michael Leopard
Skycap	Charles Walker
Mechanic	Ed Trotta
Bailiff	Ernest Perry, Jr.
Court Guard	Skip O'Brien
Cop	Tony Carreiro
Publicist	Amanda Carlin
Cole Children	Matthew Michael Goodall, Samantha Heyman
Fred	Anthony Lee
Sharpo the Clown	Eric Sharp
Lupe	Christine Avila
Playground Teacher	Hope Allen
Stenographer	Carrie Armstrong
Deputy	Craig Barnett
Flight Attendant	Brandi Burkett
Macho Attorney	Charles Emmett
Driver	Mike Grief
Colleague	Matthew Arkin

and Steven M. Gagnon, Moon Jones, Rick Hill (Jail Guards), Kelly Anne Conroy, Richard Jones (Passengers on Plane), Dennis Napolitano (Piano Player), Michael Adler, Joe Barnaba, Ben Brown, Mark Chaet, Catherine Evans, Colleen Fitzpatrick, David Fresco, Sue Goodman, Michael Kostroff, Howard S. Miller (Conference Room Attorneys), Edward Amuwa, Ashley Monique Clark, Derrick Friedman, David Kikuta, Oliver Kindred, Patrick Lawrence McTavish, Sara Paxton, Ashley Rumph, Jacob Stein, Mercedes Villamil (Children at Party and School)

Cary Elwes   Maura Tierney

Max Reede, tired of the undependability of his slick lawyer dad, makes a birthday wish that his father not be able to lie, a wish that comes true for a twenty-four hour period.

Jim Carrey, Maura Tierney

© Universal Studios Inc.

THE SIXTH MAN

(TOUCHSTONE) Producer, David Hoberman; Executive Producer, Jody Savin; Director, Randall Miller; Screenplay, Christopher Reed, Cynthia Carle; Photography, Michael Ozier; Designer, Michael Bolton; Editor, Eric Sears; Music, Marcus Miller; Co-Producer, Justis Greene; Costumes, Grania Preston; Special Effects Coordinator, Stewart Bradley; Casting, Dan Parada; a Mandeville Films production; Distributed by Buena Vista Pictures; Dolby Digital Stereo; Technicolor; Rated PG-13; 107 minutes; March release

CAST

Kenny Tyler	Marlon Wayans
Antoine Tyler	Kadeem Hardison
Coach Pederson	David Paymer
R.C. St. John	Michael Michele
Mikulski	Kevin Dunn
Gertz	Gary Jones
Malik Major	Lorenzo Orr
Zigi Hrbacek	Vladimir Cuk
Danny O'Grady	Travis Ford
Luther LaSalle	Jack Karuletwa
Jimmy Stubbs	Chris Spencer
Coach Nichols	Kirk Baily
Camille Tyler	Saundra McClain
James Tyler	Harold Sylvester
Nativity Watson	Octavia L. Spencer
Cheryl	Danielle Saklofsky
Jordy	Christopher Turner
Ernie	Scott LaRose
Bernie	Paul Ben-Victor

and Emil Pinnock (Young Antoine), Allan Lindo (Young Kenny), Tyronne L'Hirondelle (Doctor), Tony Marr (Paramedic), Rod Crawford (Man in Bathroom), Jody Savin, Dave Young (Reporters), Randall Miller (Booster), Lauro Chartrand (Husky Mascot), William Sasso (Guy in Bar), Flex (Jerrod Smith), Brent Kerray (Wilson), Greg Collins, Kevin Benton, Howard Storey (Refs), Keith Gibbs (O'Neil), Brad Nessler, James "Bruiser" Flint, Jerry Tarkanian, Billy Packer, John Thompson, Nolan Richardson, George Raveling, Todd Bozeman (Themselves), Chris Reimer, Mark Poyser, Brady Ibbetson, Dave Nelson, Craig Wayans, Shaun Hawke, Mark Lewis (Husky Players)

The ghost of former college basketball star Antoine Tyler materializes to help his younger brother Kenny and his last place team to victory.

© Touchstone Pictures

Paulina Porizkova, Tilda Swinton

Kadeem Hardison, Marlon Wayans

FEMALE PERVERSIONS

(OCTOBER) Producer, Mindy Affrime; Executive Producers, Zalman King, Gina Resnick, Rena Ronson; Director, Susan Streitfeld; Screenplay, Julie Hebert, Susan Streitfeld; Based upon the book Female Perversions: The Temptation of Emma Bovary by Dr. Louise J. Kaplan; Photography, Teresa Medina; Designer, Missy Stewart; Costumes, Angela Billows; Editors, Curtiss Clayton, Leo Trombetta; Music, Debbie Wiseman; Associate Producer, Janine Gold; Line Producer, Rana Joy Glickman; Casting, Christine Sheaks; a Trans Atlantic Entertainment and Mindy Affrime Productions presentation; Dolby Stereo; Color; Rated R; 119 minutes; March release

CAST

Eve Stephens	Tilda Swinton
Madelyn Stephens	Amy Madigan
Renee	Karen Sillas
Langley Flynn	Paulina Porizkova
John	Clancy Brown
Annunciata	Frances Fisher
Margot Fuchs	Lisa Jane Persky
Edwina	Dale Shuger
Emma	Laila Robins
Jake Rock	John Diehl
Make-up Salesgirl	Shawnee Smith
Lingerie Saleswoman	Nina Wise
Boutique Saleswoman	Judy Jean Berns
Wallace Leishman	J. Patrick McCormack
Homeless Man	Abdul Salaam el Razzac
Trudy (License to Flirt)	Sandy Martin

and Elizabeth Cava (Jail Guard), Scotch Ellis Loring (Joey—Cab Driver), John Cassini (Gas Station Attendant), Rick Zieff (Office Boy), Marcia Cross (Eve's Mother), Don Gettinger (Eve's Father), Marra Racz (Earthwoman), Ruben Knight (Judge), Russ Gething (Courthouse Guard), Bailee Bileschi (Young Eve), Kim Blank (Mother in Boutique), Robert Rider (Old Man in Boutique), Bea Marcus (Old Lady on Bus Bench), Jim James (Detective), Evangelina Rodriguez (Latina Corn Seller), Kirstie Tyrone (Young Madelyn), Tere Wierson, Rana Joy Glickman, Viktor Manoel, Torry Pendergrass (Caryatids in Fantasy), Wade Durbin (King), Azalea Davila (Queen)

A drama exploring the erotic fantasies, nightmares and memories of various women.

©October Films

38

THAT OLD FEELING

(UNIVERSAL) Producers, Leslie Dixon, Bonnie Bruckheimer; Executive Producer, Tom Joyner; Director, Carl Reiner; Screenplay, Leslie Dixon; Photography, Steve Mason; Designer, Sandy Veneziano; Editor, Richard Halsey; Music, Patrick Williams; Song: "Somewhere Along the Way" by Sammy Gallop and Ada Kurtz/performed by Bette Midler; Costumes, Robert De Mora; Casting, Nancy Nayor; The Bubble Factory presentation of a Sheinberg production in association with Boy of the Year and All Girl Productions; DTS Digital Stereo; Deluxe color; Rated PG-13; 105 minutes; April release

Bette Midler, David Rasche

CAST

Lilly	Bette Midler
Dan	Dennis Farina
Molly	Paula Marshall
Rowena	Gail O'Grady
Alan	David Rasche
Keith	Jamie Denton
Joey	Danny Nucci
Bar Pianist	Blu Mankuma
Aunt Iris	Jayne Eastwood
Senator Marks	Michael J. Reynolds
Senator Marks' Wife	Joan Luchak
Man at Wedding	Mike Wilmot
Granny Tapper	Lula Franklin
Bandleader	George Hevenor
Inn Proprietress	Arlene Meadows
Desk Clerk	Don Allison
Rufus	Ian Clark
Cops	David Huband, Tony Craig
Waitresses	Kim Bourne, Cara Chisholm
Waiter	Pedro Salvin
Best Man	Doug Murray
Sanford (Usher)	John Nightingale
Gordon (Usher)	Scott Gibson
Girl at Tabloid	Mary Jo Eustace
Busboy	Simon Barry
Minister	Ian Downie

and Marjorie Lowe, Michelle Carberry, Justina Taglialatela (Bridesmaids), Tabitha Lupien, Brittney Kuczynski, Alexandra Longo (Flower Girls), Gerry Mendicino (Maitre d'), Jerry Schaeffer (Fan), Madeline Lee (Woman at Sidewalk Cafe)

At their daughter's wedding Lily and Dan, happily divorced for 12 years, find their passions for one another being unexpectedly reignited.

Dennis Farina, Bette Midler

Dennis Farina, Gail O'Grady

Danny Nucci, Paula Marshall

Dwight Ewell, Ben Affleck, Jason Lee

Jason Mewes, Kevin Smith

CHASING AMY

(MIRAMAX) Producer, Scott Mosier; Executive Producer, John Pierson; Director/Screenplay, Kevin Smith; Photography, David Klein; Associate Producer, Robert Hawk; Designer, Robert "Ratface" Holtzman; Editors, Kevin Smith, Scott Mosier; Line Producer, Derrick Tseng; Costumes, Christopher Del Coro; "Bluntman & Chronic/Chasing Amy" Artwork, Mike Allred; Music, David Pirner; Casting, Shan Lory; a View Askew production; Dolby Stereo; Color; Rated R; 111 minutes; April release

Ben Affleck, Joey Lauren Adams

CAST

Holden McNeil	Ben Affleck
Alyssa Jones	Joey Lauren Adams
Banky Edwards	Jason Lee
Hooper	Dwight Ewell
Jay	Jason Mewes
Silent Bob	Kevin Smith
Fan	Ethan Suplee
Collector	Scott Mosier
Little Kid	Casey Affleck
Singer	Guinevere Turner
Kim	Carmen Lee
Executives	Brian O'Halloran, Matt Damon
Train Attendant	Dan Lunney
Cashier	Tony Torin
Dalia	Rebecca Waxman
Tory	Paris Petrick
Jane	Welker White
Nica	Kelli Simpkins
Cohee Lundin	John Willyung
Young Black Kid	Tsemach Washington
Bystander	Ernie O'Donnell
Waitress	Kristin Mosier
Con Woman	Virginia Smith

Comic book creator Holden McNeil finds himself falling in love with fellow artist Alyssa Jones though her preference for women dictates the two function strictly as friends.

© Miramax Films

Joey Lauren Adams, Ben Affleck

Ben Affleck, Joey Lauren Adams, Jason Lee

Joey Lauren Adams, Dwight Ewell

Elisabeth Shue, Val Kilmer

Elisabeth Shue, Val Kilmer

Elisabeth Shue

THE SAINT

(PARAMOUNT) Producers, David Brown, Robert Evans, William J. MacDonald, Mace Neufeld; Executive Producers, Paul Hitchcock, Robert S. Baker; Director, Phillip Noyce; Screenplay, Jonathan Hensleigh, Wesley Strick; Story, Jonathan Hensleigh; Based on the character created by Leslie Charteris; Photography, Phil Meheux; Designer, Joseph Nemec III; Editor, Terry Rawlings; Associate Producer, Lis Kern; Music, Graeme Revell; Costumes, Marlene Stewart; Casting, Patsy Pollock, Elisabeth Leustig; a David Brown and Robert Evans production, presented in association with Rysher Entertainment; Dolby Stereo; Panavision; Rated PG-13; 116 minutes; April release

CAST

Simon Templar	Val Kilmer
Dr. Emma Russell	Elisabeth Shue
Ivan Tretiak	Rade Serbedzija
Ilya Tretiak	Valery Nikolaev
Dr. Lev Botvin	Henry Goodman
Chief Inspector Teal	Alun Armstrong
Tretiak's Aide—Vereshagin	Michael Byrne
President Karpov	Evgeny Lazarev
Frankie	Irina Apeximova
General Sklarov	Lev Prigunov
Inspector Rabineau	Charlotte Cornwell
Woman on Plane	Emily Mortimer
Russian Prostitute	Lucija Serbedzija
Skinhead	Velibor Topic
Scarface	Tommy Flanagan
Scratchface	Yegor Pozenko
Young Simon Templar	Adam Smith
Catholic Priest	Pat Laffan
Agnes	Verity Dearsley

and Michael Marquez (Boy in Orphanage), Lorelei King (TV Reporter), Alla A. Kazanskaya (Old Russian Lady), Ronnie Letham (Old Russian Man), Tusse Silberg (Prostitute's Mother), Peter Guinness (Frankie's Curator), Stefan Gryff (President's Aide), Malcolm Tierney (Russian Doctor), Stephen Tiller (Russian Policeman), Christopher Rozycki (Russian Chief of Police), Etela Pardo (President Karpov's Wife), Nikolai Veselov (Red Square Tramp), David Schneider (Rat Club Comedian), Oxana Popkova (Ilya's Girlfriend), Agnieszka Liggett (Rat Club Party Girl), Lydia Zovkic (Rat Club Beauty), Alexander Tutin (Russian Colonel), Vadim Stepashkin (Russian Soldier), Ravil Isyanov (Tretiak Guard), Alexander Kadanyov (Tretiak Security Guard), Petar Vidovic (Tretiak's Builder), Susan Porrett (Orphanage Nun), Cliff Parisi (Pub Waiter), Richard Cubison, Tony Armatrading (Customs Officers), Benjamin Whitrow (Chairman at Oxford), Julian Rhind-Tutt (Young Student), Kate Isitt (Second Student), Barbara Jefford (Academic Woman), Sean O'Kane (Running Student), Lucy Akhurst (Policewoman), Nigel Clauzel (Marine Guard), Eric Loren (Embassy Official), William Hope (State Department Official), Michael Cochrane (Cold Fusion Broker), Ginny Holder (Jamaican Video Girlfriend), Akiko (Japanese Video Girlfriend), Melissa Knatchbull (English Video Girlfriend), Caroline Lee Johnson (Private Hotel Receptionist), Roger Moore (Voice on Radio)

Spy Simon Templar is hired to steal a valuable formula for cold fusion and winds up in love with the scientist responsible for its development. The character of "The Saint" first appeared on screen in the 1938 RKO film The Saint in New York, starring Louis Hayward; he was subsequently played by George Sanders(The Saint Strikes Back, The Saint in London, The Saint's Double Trouble, The Saint Takes Over, and The Saint in Palm Springs), Hugh Sinclair (The Saint's Vacation and The Saint Meets the Tiger), again by Louis Hayward (The Saint's Girl Friday)and on tv by Roger Moore in the series "The Saint" (syndication: 1963-66; NBC: 1967-68), and Ian Ogilvy in the CBS series "Return of the Saint" (1979-80).

© Paramount Pictures

INVENTING THE ABBOTTS

(20TH CENTURY FOX) Producers, Ron Howard, Brian Grazer, Janet Meyers; Executive Producers, Karen Kehela, Jack Cummins; Director, Pat O'Connor; Screenplay, Ken Hixon; Based on the story by Sue Miller; Photography, Kenneth MacMillan; Designer, Gary Frutkoff; Editor, Ray Lovejoy; Music, Michael Kamen; Costumes, Aggie Guerard Rodgers; an Imagine Entertainment production; Dolby Stereo; Deluxe color; Rated R; 110 minutes; April release

Billy Crudup, Liv Tyler, Joaquin Phoenix

CAST

Doug Holt	Joaquin Phoenix
Jacey Holt	Billy Crudup
Lloyd Abbott	Will Patton
Helen Holt	Kathy Baker
Eleanor Abbott	Jennifer Connelly
Steve	Michael Sutton
Pamela Abbott	Liv Tyler
Alice Abbott	Joanna Going
Joan Abbott	Barbara Williams
Peter Vanlaningham	Alessandro Nivola
Giggling Girls	Nicole M. Vassallo, Amanda Sherman
Victor	Shawn Hatosy
Webb Crosby	Garrett M. Brown
Co-ed	Julie Benz
Sandy	Zoe McLellan
Ted	David Frazier
Store Clerk	Margaret Ash
Principal	Clive Rosengren
Mrs. Porter	Susan Barnes
Waitress	Andrea Post
Funeral Director	Jack Cummins
Pre-Record Singer	David Heckendorn
Narrator	Michael Keaton

In a Midwestern town during the 1950s, the working class Holt Brothers find themselves becoming involved with the three Abbott sisters from the wealthy side of town.

Liv Tyler, Joaquin Phoenix

Joaquin Phoenix, Billy Crudup

Kathy Baker, Joaquin Phoenix, Billy Crudup

8 HEADS IN A DUFFEL BAG

(ORION) Producers, Brad Krevoy, Steve Stabler, John Bertolli; Director/Screenplay, Tom Schulman; Co-Producer, Tim Foster; Photography, Adam Holender; Designer, Paul Peters; Editor, David Holden; Costumes, Sanja Milkovic Hays; Music, Andrew Gross; Executive Producer, Jeffrey D. Ivers; Line Producer, Andrew G. Lamarca; Special Makeup Effects Creator, Greg Cannom; Casting, Janet Hirshenson, Jane Jenkins, Amy IcIntyre Britt; a Brad Krevoy & Steve Stabler production, presented in association with Rank Film Distributors; Dolby Digital Stereo; Deluxe color; Rated R; 93 minutes; April release

CAST

Tommy Spinelli	Joe Pesci
Charlie	Andy Comeau
Laurie Bennett	Kristy Swanson
Steve	Todd Louiso
Dick Bennett	George Hamilton
Annette Bennett	Dyan Cannon
Ernie	David Spade
Rico	Anthony Mangano
Benny	Joe Basile
Paco	Frank Roman
Big Sep	Howard George
Hugo	Tom Platz
Marty	Endre Hules
Jamal	Calvin Levels

and John Zurlo (Little Joey), Roger Cobra (Frank), Jeff Sanders (Isaiah), Ric Sarabia (Benito), Tony Montero (So-So Stu), Michael Groh (Bad Frank), Wendy Clifford (Woman with Baby), Matthew Fonda (Organ Carrier), Michael Nickles (Juan the Bandito), Suzanne Krull (Woman at Phone), Miguel Perez (Customs Inspector), John Webber (Airline Ticket Agent), Eduardo Ricard (Hotel Doctor), Sally Colon, Irene Olga Lopez (Maids), Charles Martiniz (Airport Security Guard), Glenn Taranto (Mr. Escobedo), Bart Braverman (Rental Dealer), Phillip Suriano (Gangster), Ellis E. Williams (Newark Porter), Horacio LeDon (Airport Customs Inspector), Joe Xavier Rodriguez (La Purisima Police Officer), Darius Anderson (Mexican Man)

Mob courier Tommy Spinelli, transporting the heads of eight slain gangsters, finds that he has accidentally swapped his bag at the airport with that of an innocent graduate student.

© Orion Pictures Corp

David Spade, Todd Louiso, Joe Pesci

Jean-Claude Van Damme, Dennis Rodman

DOUBLE TEAM

(COLUMBIA) Producer, Moshe Diamant; Executive Producers, Don Jakoby, David Rodgers; Director, Tsui Hark; Screenplay, Don Jakoby, Paul Mones; Story, Don Jakoby; Photography, Peter Pau; Editor, Bill Pankow; Designer, Marek Dobrowolski; Music, Gary Chang; Costumes, Magali Guidasci; Co-Producers, Rick Nathanson, Nansun Shi; Casting, Penny Perry, Illana Diamant; Stunts, Charles Picerni; a Mandalay Entertainment presentation of a Moshe Diamant production/a One Story Pictures production; Dolby SDDS Stereo; Super 35 Widescreen; Technicolor; Rated R; 91 minutes; April release

CAST

Jack Quinn	Jean-Claude Van Damme
Yaz	Dennis Rodman
Stavros	Mickey Rourke
Goldsmythe	Paul Freeman
Kath	Natacha Lindinger
Dr. Maria Trifioli	Valeria Cavalli
Brandon	Jay Benedict
Stavros' Girlfriend	Joelle Devaux-Vullion
Kofi	Bruno Bilotta
James	Mario Opinato
Carney	Grant Russell
Roger	William Dunn
Moishe	Asher Tzarfati
Dieter Staal	Rob Diem
Stevenson	Ken Samuels
Delta Two	Sandy Welch
Delta Three	Jessica Forde
Delta Four	Malick Bowens
Delta Five	Dominic Gould
Delta Six	Frederick Renard
Bravo One	Dufaut Cyrille
Bravo Two	Eric Gauchy
Bravo Three	Patrick Gauderlier

and Orso Maria Guerrini (Colony Resident), Alexander Koumpaan (Russian Man), Hans Meyer (British Man), Jesse Joe Walsh (Jacseck), Peter Nelson (American CIA Agent), Paolo Calissano (Rome CIA Agent), Pascal Lopez, Dominique Fouassier (Stavros' Men), Paolo Paoloni (Old Monk), Jean-Pierre Stewart (Yamir), Ted Russof (Brother Ramulu), Umberto Raho (Brother Regulo), Adam Kaci (Cyrus), Xin Xin Xiong (Stavros' Man—Hotel), Pascaline Girardot (Domestic), Nathalie Grac (Mermaid), M. Benabiles (Pilot), M. Szkolnic (Co-Pilot), Sigal Diamant (Giada), Angelo Ragusa (Stavros Goon), Gabriella D'Olive (Nurse), Nick Brett (Hospital Guard)

On his final mission counter-terrorist Jack Quinn fails to dispose of Stavros and winds up the target of his evil vengeance.

© Columbia Pictures Indusrtries, Inc.

GROSSE POINTE BLANK

(HOLLYWOOD PICTURES) Producers, Susan Arnold, Donna Arkoff Roth, Roger Birnbaum; Executive Producers, Jonathan Glickman, Lata Ryan; Director, George Armitage; Screenplay, Tom Jankiewicz, D.V. DeVincentis, Steve Pink, John Cusack; Story, Tom Jankiewicz; Co-Producers, John Cusack, Steve Pink; Photography, Jamie Anderson; Designer, Stephen Altman; Editor, Brian Berdan; Costumes, Eugenie Bafaloukos; Music, Joe Strummer; Casting, Junie Lowry Johnson, Ron Surma; a Roger Birnbaum & Roth/Arnold production in association with New Crime Production, presented in association with Caravan Pictures; Dolby Digital Stereo; Technicolor; Rated R; 107 minutes; April release

Dan Aykroyd, John Cusack

CAST

Martin Q. Blank	John Cusack
Debi Newberry	Minnie Driver
Dr. Oatman	Alan Arkin
Grocer	Dan Aykroyd
Marcella	Joan Cusack
Lardner	Hank Azaria
McCullers	K. Todd Freeman
Mr. Newberry	Mitchell Ryan
Paul Spericki	Jeremy Piven
Bob Destepello	Michael Cudlitz
Felix	Benny Urquidez
Ultimart Carl	Duffy Taylor
Arlene	Audrey Kissel
Ken	Caros Jacott
Husky Man	Brian Powell
Amy	Ann Cusack
Dan Koretzky	D.V. DeVincentis
Mary Blank	Barbara Harris
Melanie the Waitress	Wendy Thorlakson
Mrs. Kinetta	Belita Moreno
Nathaniel	Pat O'Neill
Tanya	Jenna Elfman
Terry Rostand	Steve Pink
Tracy	K.K. Dodds
Waiter	Bill Cusack

and Traci Dority (Jenny Slater), Doug Dearth (Eckhart), Colby French (Bartender), Brent Armitage (Cosmo), Jackie Rubin (Marie), Sarah DeVincentis (Dr. Oatman's Patient), Eva Rodriguez (Nurse), David Barrett (Bicycle Messenger), Bobby Bass, Lance Gilbert, Pete Antico, Laurence Bilzerian (Assassins)

Jeremy Piven

Alan Arkin

Hoping to find some meaning to his empty life as a professional hit man, Martin Blank returns to his home town for his high school reunion, unaware that his rival, Grocer, is on his trail intending to exterminate him.

Minnie Driver, John Cusack

John Cusack, Joan Cusack

ANACONDA

(COLUMBIA) Producers, Verna Harrah, Leonard Rabinowitz, Carole Little; Executive Producer, Susan Ruskin; Director, Luis Llosa; Screenplay, Hans Bauer, Jim Cash, Jack Epps Jr.; Photography, Bill Butler; Designer, Kirk M. Petruccelli; Editor, Michael R. Miller; Music, Randy Edelman; Co-Producer, Beau Marks; Visual Effects, John Nelson; Animatronic Effects, Walt Conti; Casting, Mindy Marin; a CL Cinema Line Films Corporation Production; Dolby SDDS Stereo; Super 35 Widescreen; Color; Rated PG-13; 90 minutes; April release

Vincent Castellanos, Jon Voight

CAST

Terri Flores	Jennifer Lopez
Danny Rich	Ice Cube
Paul Sarone	Jon Voight
Dr. Steven Cale	Eric Stoltz
Warren Westridge	Jonathan Hyde
Gary Dixon	Owen Wilson
Denise Kalberg	Kari Wuhrer
Mateo	Vincent Castellanos
Poacher	Danny Trejo

A film crew's expedition down the Amazon is sidetracked by a mysterious loner who leads them into dangerous waters in his attempt to track a deadly 40-foot Anaconda.

Kari Wuhrer, Owen Wilson, Jennifer Lopez

Jennifer Lopez, Eric Stoltz

Jennifer Lopez, Ice Cube

Mark Wahlberg, Bill Paxton

TRAVELLER

(OCTOBER) Producers, Bill Paxton, Brian Swardstrom, Mickey Liddell, David Blocker; Executive Producers, Robert Mickelson, Rick King; Director, Jack Green; Screenplay, Jim McGlynn; Designer, Michael Helmy; Music, Andy Paley; Editor, Michael Ruscio; Casting, Joseph Middleton; a Banner Entertainment production; Dolby Stereo; Color; Rated R; 100 minutes; April release

CAST

Bokky	Bill Paxton
Pat O'Hara	Mark Wahlberg
Jean	Julianna Margulies
Double D	James Gammon
Boss Jack	Luke Askew
Kate	Nikki Deloach
Shane	Danielle Wiener
Lip	Michael Shaner
Bimbo	Vincent Chase
Pincher	Andrew Porter
Bokky's Grandmother	Jean Howard
Farmer	Rance Howard
Farmer's Son	Robert Peters
Boss Jack's Wife	Jo Ann Pflug
Snipe	Scott Schultz

and John Bennes (Hearse Driver), Barbara Rowan (Pregnant Wife), Trenton McDevitt (Pregnant Wife's Husband), Moses Gibson (Porter), Bonnie Cook (Cashier), John Paxton (Financial Planner), Jim Flowers, Frederick E. Dann (Bar Regulars), Walter Cobb (Priest), Joanne Pankow (Elderly Woman), Chuck Kinlaw (Elderly Woman's Son), Blaque Fowler (Gas Station Owner), Ted Manson (First Trailer Buyer), Kerry Maher (Bartender), John Easterbrook (Trailer Salesman), Paddy Keenan, John Williams, Nigel Stevens, Jackie Moran (Traveller Musicians), Mary K. Heneghan (Traveller Camp Dancer)

A young man, cast out of a band of Irish grifters for marrying an outsider, returns to the group and is taken under the wing of Bokky who intends to teach him the way of their forefathers.

Julianna Margulies

Scott Schultz, Mark Wahlberg

Don Cheadle

Tommy Lee Jones, Gaby Hoffman

VOLCANO

(20TH CENTURY FOX) Producers, Neal H. Moritz, Andrew Z. Davis; Executive Producer, Lauren Shuler Donner; Director, Mick Jackson; Screenplay, Jerome Armstrong, Billy Ray; Story, Jerome Armstrong; Photography, Theo van de Sande; Designer, Jackson DeGovia; Editors, Michael Tronick, Don Brochu; Costumes, Kirsten Everberg; Music, Alan Silvestri; Stunts, Mic Rodgers; Special Effects Supervisor, Dale Ettema; Special/Mechanical Effects Coordinators, Clay Pinney, Marty Bresin; a Shuler Donner/Donner and Moritz Original production; Dolby Stereo; Deluxe color; Rated PG-13; 102 minutes; April release

CAST

Mike Roark	Tommy Lee Jones
Dr. Amy Barnes	Anne Heche
Kelly Roark	Gaby Hoffmann
Emmit Reese	Don Cheadle
Dr. Jaye Calder	Jacqueline Kim
Lt. Ed Fox	Keith David
Norman Calder	John Corbett
Gator Harris	Michael Rispoli
Stan Olber	John Carroll Lynch
Kevin	Marcello Thedford
Rachel	Laurie Lathem

and Bert Kramer (Fire Chief), Bo Eason (Bud McVie), James G. MacDonald (Terry Jasper), Dayton Callie (Roger Lapher), Michael Cutt (Armstrong), Kevin Bourland (Bob Davis), Valente Rodriguez (Train Driver), Sheila Howard (Panicked Woman/Nanny), Gerry Black (Train Passenger), Susie Essman (Anita), Lou Myers (Pastor Lake), Gareth Williams (Pete), Juan Gabriel Reynoso (Carlos), Angela Albarez (Lydia Perez), Richard Penn (Middle Aged Man), Jennifer Bill (Nurse Fran), Mickey Cottrell (Councilman Gates), M. Darnell Suttles (Chief Sindelar), Ken Kerman (Museum Guard), Sal Rendino (Chuck), Michael Manuel (Del), Jared Thorne, Taylor Thorne (Tommy), Richard Schiff (Haskins), Brad Parker (Ken Woods), Pete Kasper (Kenny Lopez), Brian Markinson, Robert Wisdom, Katie Rich, Ceal Coleman, Phil Nee, Carlos Cervantes, George Zaver, Marty Levy, Wayne Grace (OEM Staffers), Mother Love (Traffic Cop), Kayli DeGregorio, Kelsi DeGregorio (5 Year Old Chuckie), Steven Mainz (K-Rail Driver), Josie Dapar, Joy Baggish (Survivors), Ron Perkins (Fire Chief), Todd Sible (Scott), Joshua Fardon (Medic), Catherine Schreiber (Displeased Protestor), David Pressman (Second Protestor), Danny Comden (Ascending Cop), Michael McGrady (Policeman), Michole Briana White (ER Nurse #1), Steve MacLaughlin (Construction Supervisor), Howard DuVall, Sam Alejan, Gary Kent James, Robert Tittot, John Perry Edson, Jr., David T. Mabowe, Ken Thomas, Eddie J. Low (Engineers), Georganna Barry (Java Lady), Tom Crabson (Passenger on Train), Rick Rogers (Sgt. Riley), Terry Anzur, Kerry Kilbride, Jennifer Bjorklund, Lonnie Lardner, Frank Buckley, Harvey Levin, Larry Carroll, Chris Myers, Angie Crouch, Shepard Smith, Steve Edwards, Christopher Spinder, Sasha Foo, Jeremy Thompson, Rick Garcia, Peter Trunk, Penny Griego, Michael Louis Villani, Pat Lalama, Bruce Orchid, Paula Bond, Charles Perez, Sandra Clark, Teresa Quevedo-Stoll, Rich Goldner, Leo Quinones, Juan Carlos Gonzalez, Alina Recasens, James Scott Hodson, Walter Richards, Jere Laird, Richard L.D. Saxton, Luann Lee, Sergio Urquidi, D. Lucey, Jane Velez-Mitchell, Jean Martirez, Jillian Warry, Chris McWatt, Jane Wells, Al Naipo, Karl T. Wright, Warren Olney, Andrea Wynn, Takayuki Yamauchi (The Media—Themselves)

A volcano errupts in the La Brea Tar Pits in the middle of downtown Los Angeles causing a lava flow that threatens to destroy the city.

Tommy Lee Jones, Anne Heche

Tommy Lee Jones, Anne Heche

49

A BROTHER'S KISS

(FIRST LOOK PICTURES) Producers, Bob Potter, E. Bennett Walsh; Executive Producer, Jim Walton; Director/Screenplay, Seth Zvi Rosenfeld; Based on his play; Co-Producers, Al Corley, Bart Rosenblatt; Photography, Fortunato Procopio; Designer, Roger Fortune; Music, Frank London; Editor, Donna Stern; Casting, Francine Maisler, Tracey Marable Moore; a Rosefunk Pictures Ltd. production; Ultra-Stereo; Color; Rated R; 92 minutes; April release

CAST

Lex	Nick Chinlund
Mick	Michael Raynor
Young Lex	Justin Pierce
Doreen	Cathy Moriarty
Young Mick	Joshua Danowsky
Debbie	Rosie Perez
Missy	Marisa Tomei
Jimmy	Richard Palmer
Lefty	John Leguizamo
Nancy	Erica Nicole Grier
Referee	Andre Blake
Dope Fiend	Adrian Pasdar
Junita	Anjeanette Dejesus
Reefer Kid	Rafael Nunez
Lucy	Jennifer Esposito

and Scott Cohen (Rapist), Arthur Nascarella (Lex's Father), Michael Rapaport (Stingy), Jason Andrews, Kevin Thigpen (Cops), Talent Harris (Vic), Frank Minucci (Uncle Mac), Maurice Ballard (Ball Player), Aesha (Young Lex's Girlfriend), Ulysses Torrero, Ian Kelly (Variety Boys), Cameron Lucente (Baby), Blaze (Gunman), Pitzly You (Dealer), Seth Zvi Rosenfeld (Spam Man)

Two brothers, raised in a tough East Harlem neighborhood, vow to live a clean life and realize their dreams. Years later Mick becomes a cop while his younger, sensitive brother Lex gets lost in the world of drug dealing and addiction.

© First Look Pictures

Michael Raynor, Nick Chinlund

Joshua Danowsky, Cathy Moriarty, Justin Pierce

Shiloh, Blake Heron

SHILOH

(LEGACY) Producers, Zane W. Levitt, Dale Rosenbloom; Executive Producers, Carl Borack, Mark Yellen; Director/Screenplay, Dale Rosenbloom; Based on the novel by Phyllis Reynolds Naylor; Photography, Frank Byers; Editor, Mark Westmore; Music, Joel Goldsmith; Designer, Amy Ancona; Costumes, Charmain Schreiner; Casting, Laura Schiff; a Utopia Pictures/Carl Borack production in association with Zeta Entertainment; Dolby Digital Stereo; Color; Rated PG; 93 minutes; April release

CAST

Ray Preston	Michael Moriarty
Doc Wallace	Rod Steiger
Marty Preston	Blake Heron
Judd Travers	Scott Wilson
Mrs. Wallace	Bonnie Bartlett
Louise Preston	Ann Dowd
Becky Preston	Tori Wright
Dara Lynn Preston	Shira Roth
Samantha	J. Madison Wright
Sue	Rachel Winfree
Mrs. McCallister	Montrose Hagins
Mrs. Young	Amzie Strickland

A beagle, abused by its cantankerous owner, runs away and finds a friend in young Marty Preston who hopes to keep the dog for his own.

© Overseas Filmgroup

ROMY AND MICHELE'S HIGH SCHOOL REUNION

(TOUCHSTONE) Producer, Laurence Mark; Executive Producers, Barry Kemp, Robin Schiff; Director, David Mirkin; Screenplay, Robin Schiff, based on characters from her play *Ladies' Room*; Co-Producer, Richard Luke Rothschild; Photography, Reynaldo Villalobos; Designer, Mayne Berke; Editor, David Finfer; Costumes, Mona May; Music, Steve Bartek; Character Makeup Designer/Supervisor, Kevin Haney; Choreographer, Smith Wordes; Casting, Marcia Ross; a Laurence Mark production in association with Bungalow 78 productions; Distributed by Buena Vista Pictures; Dolby Digital Stereo; Technicolor; Rated R; 91 minutes; April release

Lisa Kudrow, Mira Sorvino

CAST

Romy	Mira Sorvino
Michele	Lisa Kudrow
Heather Mooney	Janeane Garofalo
Sandy Frink	Alan Cumming
Christie	Julia Campbell
Cheryl	Mia Cottet
Kelly	Kristin Bauer
Lisa	Elaine Hendrix
Billy	Vincent Ventresca
Toby	Camryn Manheim
Cowboy	Justin Theroux
Ramon	Jacob Vargas
Receptionist at "Singled Out"	Tami-Adrian George
Boutique Manager	Neil Dickson
Mr. Lish	E.J. Callahan
Kick Boxing Instructor	Kathy Long
Spinning Instructor	Betsy Folsom
Head of Personnel	Zack Phifer
Guy at Rehab Meeting	Ricky Paull Goldin
Creepy Manager	Robb Skyler
Service Guys	Deezer D, Kivi Rogers
Brat	Brian McGregor
Truck Stop Waitress	Pat Crawford Brown
Bartender Vic	Victor Wilson
Suit Salesman	Paul Keeley

and Amelinda Smith, Keana Hall, Alison Gale, Anne Jensen (Reunion Guests), Elizabeth Norment (Irate Customer), Rick Pasqualone (Mark), Tate Taylor (Casey), Linda Clements (Beverly Hills Lady), Alan Purwin (Helicopter Pilot)

Best friends Romy and Michele decide they must revamp themselves and their lives in order to make an impression at their ten-year high school reunion. Lisa Kudrow repeats her role from the original L.A. stage production.

Alan Cumming, Julia Campbell

© Tuchstone Pictures

Lisa Kudrow, Janeane Garofalo, Mira Sorvino

Vincent Ventresca, Mira Sorvino

ALL OVER ME

(FINE LINE FEATURES) Producer, Dolly Hall; Executive Producers, Andreas Buhler, Stephen X. Graham, Nina M. Benton; Director, Alex Sichel; Screenplay, Sylvia Sichel; Photography, Joe DeSalvo; Designer, Amy Beth Silver; Editor, Sabine Hoffmann; Music, Miki Navazio; Costumes, Victoria Farrell; Casting, Lina Todd; a Medusa Pictures presentation in association with Baldini Pictures and Slam Pictures; Ultra-Stereo; Color; Rated R; 90 minutes; April release

CAST

Claude	Alison Folland
Ellen	Tara Subkoff
Mark	Cole Hauser
Jesse	Wilson Cruz
Claude's Mom	Ann Dowd
Lucy	Leisha Hailey
Luke	Pat Briggs
Gus	Shawn Hatosy
Don	Vincent Pastore

Claude, a fifteen year-old girl living in New York's Hell's Kitchen, becomes jealous when her best friend Ellen begins showing interest in a guy, bringing her to the realization that she herself is in love with Ellen.

Tara Subkoff, Alison Folland

Tara Subkoff, Pat Briggs

Anthony LaPaglia, Courteney Cox, Aidan Quinn

Courteney Cox, Aidan Quinn

COMMANDMENTS

(GRAMERCY) Producers, Michael Chinich, Joe Medjuck, Daniel Goldberg; Executive Producer, Ivan Reitman; Director/Screenplay, Daniel Taplitz; Photography, Slawomir Idziak; Designer, Robin Standefer; Editor, Michael Jablow; Music, Joseph Vitarelli; Costumes, John Dunn; Co-Producer, Nellie Nugiel; Casting, Lynn Kressel; a Northern Lights Entertainment production; DTS Stereo; Deluxe color; Rated R; 87 minutes; May release

CAST

Seth Warner	Aidan Quinn
Rachel Luce	Courteney Cox
Harry Luce	Anthony LaPaglia
Sylvia	Shirl Bernheim
Melissa Murphy	Pamela Gray
Rudy Warner	Louis Zorich
Detective Mahoney	Scott Sowers
Police Chief Warren	Pat McNamara
Gordon Bloom	Jack Gilpin
Mr. Mann	Tom Aldredge
Mrs. Mann	Alice Drummond
Mr. Neer	Stephen Singer

and Peter Jacobson, Patrick Garner (Bankers), Marcia Debonis (Receptionist), Lisa Louise Langford (Paramedic), Chris McGinn (Nurse), Amy Sedaris (Scholar), Stephen Pearlman (Rabbi), Frank Girardeau (Bartender), John Tormey (Desk Sergeant), Michael Badalucco (Detective), Stu "Large" Riley (Inmate), Tom Riis Farrell (Marine Biologist)

When one unspeakable tragedy after another strikes Seth Warner he decides to challenge God by breaking all of the Ten Commandments.

NIGHT FALLS ON MANHATTAN

(PARAMOUNT) Producers, Thom Mount, Josh Kramer; Director/Screenplay, Sidney Lumet; Based upon the book *Tainted Evidence* by Robert Daley; Co-Producer, John H. Starke; Photography, David Watkin; Designer, Philip Rosenberg; Editor, Sam O'Steen; Costumes, Joseph G. Aulisi; Music, Mark Isham; Casting, Billy Hopkins, Suzanne Smith, Kerry Barden; a Spelling Films presentation of a Mount/Kramer production; Dolby Stereo; Deluxe color; Rated R; 113 minutes; May release

Andy Garcia, Richard Dreyfuss, Dominic Chianese

CAST

Sean Casey	Andy Garcia
Liam Casey	Ian Holm
Joey Allegretto	James Gandolfini
Peggy Lindstrom	Lena Olin
Jordan Washington	Shiek Mahmud-Bey
Elihu Harrison	Colm Feore
District Attorney Morgenstern	Ron Leibman
Sam Vigoda	Richard Dreyfuss
Judge Impelliteri	Dominic Chianese
McGovern	Paul Guilfoyle
Instructor	Bonnie Rose
Detective	Norman Matlock
Judge	Sidney Armus
Man in Asylum	Jim Murtaugh
Legal Aid Attorney	Melba Martinez
Eduardo	Santo Fazio
Shmuel	Anthony Alessandro
Half-Naked Girl	Nafisah Sayyed
Eileen	Marcia J. Kurtz
Lieutenant Wilson	Jude Ciccolella

and David Wolos-Fonteno, John Seitz, Robert Sean Miller (Captains), John Randolph Jones (Captain Lawrence), Chuck Pfeiffer (Captain Gentile), Stephen Beach, Vincent Pastore, Allen Collodow, Dennis Paladino, Salvatore Paul Piro (Cops), Clark D. Williams, Tamara Phillips, Bill Boggs (News), Louis Guss (Court Clerk), Richard Bright (64 Precinct Lieutenant), Ronald von Klaussen (65 Precinct Sergeant), John DiBenedetto (Patrolman #2), Kevin Ramsey (Sean's Assistant), Kermit Frazier (Jury Foreman), Vernica Hall (Pier Cop), Vic Noto (Diver), Jim Moody (Mayor Williams), Socorro Santiago (Lab Assistant), Fran Anthony (Moderator), Donna Hanover, Jack Cafferty, Kaity Tong (TV Newsperson), Mike Cammallere, Mike Sheehan (Sergeants), Jim Mauro, Joe Mosso (Lieutenants), Frank Vincent (Captain), Teddy Coluca, Roslyn Coh, Elliot Cuker (Reporters), Yvette Mercedes (Meter Maid), Kristina Lear (Girl in Restaurant), Joe Drago (D.A. Driver), Catherine Schreiber (Sean's Assistant #2), Bobby Cannavale (Vigoda Assistant #1)

A young Manhattan District Attorney, Sean Casey, is assigned to a high profile case in which his father, a cop, has been wounded in a shoot out with a drug dealer.

Lena Olin, Andy Garcia

© Spelling Films

Ian Holm, Andy Garcia

Ron Liebman, Colm Feore, Andy Garcia

Kathleen Quinlan, Kurt Russell

Kurt Russell

J.T. Walsh, Kurt Russell, Kathleen Quinlan

Kurt Russell, J.T. Walsh

BREAKDOWN

(PARAMOUNT) Producers, Martha De Laurentiis, Dino De Laurentiis; Executive Producers, Jonathan Fernandez, Harry Colomby; Director/Story, Jonathan Mostow; Screenplay, Jonathan Mostow, Sam Montgomery; Line Producer, Jeffrey Sudzin; Photography, Doug Milsome; Designer, Victoria Paul; Editors, Derek Brechin, Kevin Stitt; Costumes, Terry Dresbach; Music, Basil Poledouris; Casting, Carol Lewis; Presented in association with Dino De Laurentiis and Spelling Films; Dolby Digital Stereo; Super 35 Widescreen; Deluxe color; Rated R; 95 minutes; May release

Kurt Russell

CAST

Jeff Taylor	Kurt Russell
Red Barr	J.T. Walsh
Amy Taylor	Kathleen Quinlan
Earl	M.C. Gainey
Billy	Jack Noseworthy
Sheriff Boyd	Rex Linn
Al	Ritch Brinkley
Arleen	Moira Harris
Deputy Len Carver	Kim Robillard
Calhoun	Thomas Kopache
Bartender	Jack McGee
Deke	Vincent Berry
Flo	Helen Duffy
Barfly	Ancel Cook
Tow Truck Driver	Gene Hartline
Cowboy in Bank	Steve Waddington
Truck Stop Trucker	Rick Sanders

After their jeep breaks down in the desert, Jeff Taylor stays with the vehicle while his wife accepts a lift from a trucker. Hours later Jack discovers that she has disappeared without a trace.

Kathleen Quinlan, Kurt Russell

© Paramount Pictures

Kurt Russell, J.T. Walsh, Rex Linn

Mike Myers, Elizabeth Hurley

Mike Myers

Robert Wagner

AUSTIN POWERS:
INTERNATIONAL MAN OF MYSTERY

(NEW LINE CINEMA) Producers, Suzanne Todd, Demi Moore, Jennifer Todd, Mike Myers; Executive Producers, Eric McLeod, Claire Rudnick Polstein; Director, Jay Roach; Screenplay, Mike Myers; Photography, Peter Deming; Designer, Cynthia Charette; Editor, Debra Neil-Fisher; Costumes, Deena Appel; Music, George S. Clinton; Casting, John Papsidera; a Moving Pictures/Eric's Boy production, presented in association with Capella International/KC Medien; Dolby Digital Stereo; Super 35 Widescreen; CFI color; Rated PG-13; 89 minutes; May release

CAST

Austin Powers/Dr. Evil..Mike Myers
Vanessa Kensington ....Elizabeth Hurley
Basil Exposition ....Michael York
Mrs. Kensington..Mimi Rogers
Number Two..Robert Wagner
Scott Evil ....Seth Green
Alotta Fagina ....Fabiana Udenio
Frau Farbissina..Mindy Sterling
Patty O'Brien ....Paul Dillon
Commander Gilmour ....Charles Napier
Mustafa ....Will Ferrell
'60s Models.......Joann Richter, Anastasia Nicole Sakelaris, Afifi Alaouie
Mod Girl..Monet Mazur
Andy Warhol ....Mark Bringelson
Radar Operator ....Clint Howard
Borschevsky..Elya Baskin
Gary Coleman ....Carlton Lee Russell
Vanilla Ice ....Daniel Weaver
Quartermaster Clerk ....Neil Mullarkey
Random Task ....Joe Son
Las Vegas Tourist ....Tyde Kierny
Casino Dealer ....Larry Thomas
Himself ....Burt Bacharach
UN Secretary ....Brian George
Mrs. Exposition ....Kay Wade
and Lea Sullivan, Chekesha Van Putten, Heather Marie, Sara Smith, Laura Payne-Gabriel (Go-Go Dancers), Cheryl Bartel, Cindy Margolis, Donna W. Scott, Barbara Ann Moore, Cynthia Lamontagne (Fembots), Steve Monroe (Son), Vince Melocchi (Dad), Patrick Bristow (Virtucon Tour Guide), Jim McMullan (American UN Representative), Robin Gammell (British UN Representative), Ted Kairys (Eastern European Technician), Carrie Fisher (Session Leader), Tom Arnold (Man in Toilet)

Swingin' sixties secret agent Austin Powers is put into deep freeze in order to trap his nemesis Dr. Evil, both men finding themselves hopelessly out-of-date when they are defrosted in the 1990s.

© New Line Cinema

Mike Myers

Robert Wagner

Mike Myers

Elizabeth Hurley

Mike Myers

Mike Myers, Elizabeth Hurley

John Glover, Stephen Bogardus, Jason Alexander, Justin Kirk, Randy Becker, Stephen Spinella, John Benjamin Hickey

Stephen Bogardus, Jason Alexander

Stephen Bogardus, Randy Becker

John Benjamin Hickey, Stephen Spinella

Jason Alexander

LOVE! VALOUR! COMPASSION!

(FINE LINE FEATURES) Producers, Doug Chapin, Barry Krost; Executive Producers, Ruth Vitale, Jonathan Weisgal, Amy Labowitz; Director, Joe Mantello; Screenplay, Terrence McNally, based on his play; Line Producer, Diane Conn; Photography, Alik Sakharov; Editor, Colleen Sharp; Designer, François Seguin; Music, Harold Wheeler; Costumes, Jess Goldstein; Choreographer, John Carrafa; a Krost/Chapin production; Dolby Stereo; Color; Rated R; 110 minutes; May release

CAST

John Jekyll/James Jekyll	John Glover
Perry Sellars	Stephen Spinella
Gregory Mitchell	Stephen Bogardus
Arthur Pape	John Benjamin Hickey
Bobby Brahms	Justin Kirk
Ramon Fornos	Randy Becker
Buzz Hauser	Jason Alexander

A look at the lives, loves and relationships of eight gay friends as they spend three separate weekends together during the course of a summer. All of the principles (except Jason Alexander) repeat their roles from the original 1994 Off-Broadway production. The 1995 Tony Award-winning Broadway production featured Anthony Heald in the role of Perry. Nathan Lane played the role of Buzz in both productions.

© Fine Line Features

Stephen Spinella, John Benjamin Hickey

Randy Becker

Stephen Bogardus, Justin Kirk, John Glover, John Benjamin Hickey, Jason Alexander, Randy Becker

NOWHERE

(FINE LINE FEATURES) Producers, Gregg Araki, Andrea Sperling, Why Not Productions; Director/Screenplay/Editor, Gregg Araki; Photography, Arturo Smith; Designer, Patti Podesta; Costumes, Sara Jane Slotnick; Casting, Rick Montgomery, Dan Parada, Mary Margiotta, Karen Margiotta; from Desperate Pictures/Blurco/Why Not Productions (France); U.S.-French; Color; Rated R; 85 minutes; May release

CAST

Dark	James Duval
Mel	Rachel True
Montgomery	Nathan Bexton
Kriss	Chiara Mastroianni
Kozy	Debi Mazar
Lucifer	Kathleen Robertson
Zero	Joshua Gibran Mayweather
Alyssa	Jordan Ladd
Dingbat	Christina Applegate
Egg	Sarah Lassez
Cowboy	Guillermo Diaz
Bart	Jeremy Jordan
Handjob	Alan Boyce
The Teen Idol	Jaason Simmons
Shad	Ryan Phillippe
Lilith	Heather Graham

and Scott Caan (Ducky), Thyme Lewis (Elvis), Mena Suvari (Zoe), Beverly D'Angelo (Dark's Mom), Charlotte Rae (Fortune Teller), Denise Richards (Jana), Teresa Hill (Shannon), Kevin Light (Noah), Traci Lords, Shannen Doherty, Rose McGowan (Val Chicks), John Ritter (Moses Helper), Christopher Knight (Mr. Sigvatssohn), Eve Plumb (Mrs. Sigvatssohn), Lauren Tewes (Julie, the Newscaster), David Leisure (Egg & Ducky's Dad), John Enos III, Nicolette Gato, Brian Buzzini (The Scary Drag Queens), Aaron Smith, Tres Trash Temperilli, Sara Jane (The Atari Gang), Devon Odessa (What), Stacy Keanan (Ever), Gibby Haynes (Jujyfruit), Keith Brewer (Surf), Derek Brewer (Ski), Roscoe (The Alien)

A look at the lives of various aimless L.A. teenagers and their experiences with love, sex, crime, and drugs.

© Fine Line Features

James Duvall

Joe Torry, Rusty Cundieff, Tisha Campbell, Paula Jai Parker

SPRUNG

(TRIMARK) Producer, Darin Scott; Executive Producer, Mark Amin; Director, Rusty Cundieff; Screenplay, Rusty Cundieff, Darin Scott; Co-Producer, Jonathan Komack Martin; Photography, Joao Fernandes; Designer, Terrence Foster; Editor, Lisa Bromwell; Associate Producer, Andrew Hersh; Line Producer, Elaine Dysinger; Music, Stanley Clarke; Costumes, Tracey White; Casting, Tony Lee; a Darin Scott production; Dolby Stereo; Color; Rated R; 105 minutes; May release

CAST

Brandy	Tisha Campbell
Montel	Rusty Cundieff
Adina	Paula Jai Parker
Clyde	Joe Torry
Detective	John Witherspoon
Veronica	Jennifer Lee
Grand Daddy	Clarence Williams III
Bride's Mother	Loretta Jean
Party Guard	Ronny Willis
Watch Commander	Ron Brooks

and John Ganun, David McKnight (Patrol Officers), Bobby McGee (First Suspect), Moon Jones (Godzilla Nuts Suspect), Bobby Mardis (Foreign Suspect), J.P. Stevenson (Flaming Suspect), Maryn Tasco (Cute Older Lady), Rai Tasco (Cute Older Man), Jeri Gray (Dancing Older Lady), Nick LaTour (Dancing Older Man), Angela Dickerson (Consuela), Darin Scott (Inconsiderate "Husband"), Isabel Sanford, Angela Means, Yolanda Whitaker, Homselle Joy (Sistas), Sherman Hemsley, Reynaldo Rey, Mark Christopher Lawrence, Tim Hutchinson (Brothas), Freda Payne (Vocalist), Shari Randolph, Karlotta Nelson, Trina Davis, Robyn Lattaker (Restaurants)

Montel, looking for a serious relationship, and his sex-hungry friend Clyde go to a sorority alumni jam where they meet and pair up with the jaded Brandy and her money-obsessed friend Adina.

© Trimark Pictures

THE LOST WORLD: JURASSIC PARK

(UNIVERSAL) Producers, Gerald R. Molen, Colin Wilson; Executive Producer, Kathleen Kennedy; Director, Steven Spielberg; Screenplay, David Koepp; Based on the novel The Lost World by Michael Crichton; Photography, Janusz Kaminski; Designer, Rick Carter; Editor, Michael Kahn; Music, John Williams; Associate Producers, Bonnie Curtis; Full Motion Dinosaurs, Dennis Muren; Live Action Dinosaurs, Stan Winston; Special Dinosaur Effects, Michael Lantieri; Visual Effects Producer, Ned Gorman; Casting, Janet Hirshenson, Jane Jenkins; an Amblin Entertainment production; Dolby DTS Stereo; Deluxe color; Rated PG-13; 134 minutes; May release

Jeff Goldblum, Vanessa Lee Chester, Vince Vaughn, Julianne Moore, Richard Schiff

CAST

Ian Malcolm	Jeff Goldblum
Sarah Harding	Julianne Moore
Roland Tembo	Pete Postlethwaite
Peter Ludlow	Arliss Howard
John Hammond	Richard Attenborough
Nick Van Owen	Vince Vaughn
Kelly Curtis	Vanessa Lee Chester
Dieter Stark	Peter Stormare
Ajay Sidhu	Harvey Jason
Eddie Carr	Richard Schiff
Dr. Robert Burke	Thomas F. Duffy
Tim	Joseph Mazzello
Lex	Ariana Richards
Carter	Thomsa Rosales
Cathy Bowman	Camilla Belle
Mrs. Bowman	Cyd Strittmatter
Mr. Bowman	Robin Sachs
Senior Board Member	Elliott Goldwag
Board Member	J. Patrick McCormack
Curious Man	Ross Partridge
Butler	Ian Abercrombie
Workman	David Sawyer
Barge Captain	Geno Silva

and Alex Miranda (Barge Captain's Son), Robert "Bobby Z" Zajonc (Ingen Helicopter Pilot), Bob Boehm, Bradley Jensen, Alan Purwin, Ben Skorstad, Rick Wheeler, Kenyon Williams (Cargo Helicopter Pilots), Gordon Michaels, J. Scott Shonka, Harry Hutchinson, Bill Brown, Brian Turk (Ingen Workers), Jim Harley (Harbor Master), Colton James (Benjamin), Carey Eidel (Benjamin's Dad), Katy Boyer (Benjamin's Mom), David Koepp (Unlucky Bastard), Eugene Bass, Jr. (Attorney), Bari Buckner (Screaming Woman), P.B. Hutton, David St. James, Mark Brady, Marjean Holden, Jacqueline Schultz, Domini Hofmann De Salgado, Thomas Stuart (Screamers), Ransom Walrod (Ship Driver), David Gene Gibbs (Police Helicopter Pilot), Michael N. Fujimoto, Paul Fujimoto, Darryl A. Imai, Darryl Oumi (Asian Tourists), Vincent Dee Miles (Screaming Hunter), Bernard Shaw (CNN Reporter/Himself)

Richard Schiff, Julianne Moore, Jeff Goldblum, Vince Vaughn

Chaos theorist Ian Malcolm arrives on the dinosaur manufacturing facility for Jurassic Park where his girlfriend Dr. Sarah Harding has gone to study the surviving dinosaurs. Meanwhile Peter Ludlow dispatches a team of hunters to capture the creatures and bring them back to the mainland. Sequel to the 1993 Universal release Jurassic Park with Jeff Goldblum, Richard Attenborough, Joseph Mazzello, and Ariana Richards repeating their roles from that film. This film received an Oscar nomination for visual effects.

© Universal Studios

Jeff Goldblum, Richard Schiff, Vince Vaughn

Dylan McDermott, Sarah Jessica Parker, Jeanne Tripplehorn

'TIL THERE WAS YOU

(PARAMOUNT) Producers, Penney Finkelman Cox, Tom Rosenberg, Alan Poul; Executive Producers, Sigurjon Sighvatsson, Ted Tannebaum; Director, Scott Winant; Screenplay, Winnie Holzman; Photography, Bobby Bukowski; Designer, Craig Stearns; Editors, Richard Marks, Joanna Cappuccilli; Music, Miles Goodman, Terence Blanchard; Costumes, Enid Harris, Rita Salazar; Co-Producers, Richard S. Wright, Julie Golden; Associate Producers, Karen Montgomery, James McQuaide; Casting, Amanda Mackey Johnson, Cathy Sandrich; a Lakeshore Entertainment presentation of a Penney Finkelman Cox production; Dolby Stereo; Deluxe color; Rated PG-13; 113 minutes; May release

CAST

Gwen Moss	Jeanne Tripplehorn
Nick Dawkan	Dylan McDermott
Francesca Lansfield	Sarah Jessica Parker
Debbie	Jennifer Aniston
Jon Haas	Craig Bierko
Sophia Monroe	Nina Foch
Harriet	Alice Drummond
Beebee Moss	Christine Ebersole
Saul Moss	Michael Tucker
Bob	Reg Rogers
Angenelle	Kasi Lemmons
Timo	Patrick Malahide
Kevin	Steven Antin
Robin	Susan Walters
Vince	Kale Browne
Saul (age 25)	John Plumpis
Beebee (age 25)	Janel Moloney
Gwen (age 7)	Yvonne Zima
Nick (age 7)	Kellen Fink
Betty	Karen Allen
Taffy (age 7)	Alexandra Theriault
Taffy (age 12)	Kimberly Paige
TV Dad	Jim Jansen
Gregory	Ken Olin
Jonny (age 8)	Andrew Armbruster
Debbie (age 13)	Amanda Fuller
Gwen (age 12)	Madeline Zima
Nick (age 12)	Joshua Rubin
Gwen's Prom Date	Matt Alexander

and John Mascaro (Gwen's College Date), Michael Moertl (Dean), Richard Fancy (Murdstone), Earl Carroll (Heep), Ian Gomez (Scott), Matt Roth (Todd), Karen Mayo Chandler (Awful Truth Woman), Anthony Guidera (Maitre' D), Alexa Jago (Suzanne), John Hawkes (Gawayne), Jack Kruschen (Mr. Katz), Danielle Wiener (Chelsea), Julio Oscar Mechoso, Bruce Winant (Movers), Cinders (Himself), David C. Miller (Man with Flyer), Tiffany Paulsen (Tiffany), William Utay (Paul Pullman), William Forward (Chairman), David Elliot (Waiter with Tray), Kelly McCarthy (Waitress), Annabelle Gurwitch (Woman in Bathroom), Marina Malota (Gwen's Daughter)

Gwen Moss and Nick Dawkan literally bump into one another as children then spend their lives going their separate ways, searching for perfect relationships, always just missing one another despite the fact that they share common friends and acquaintances.

© Paramount Pictures

Jeanne Tripplehorn, Dylan McDermott

Jennifer Aniston, Jeanne Tripplehorn

TRIAL AND ERROR

(NEW LINE CINEMA) Producers, Gary Ross, Jonathan Lynn; Executive Producers, Mary Parent, Allen Alsobrook; Director, Jonathan Lynn; Screenplay, Sara Bernstein, Gregory Bernstein; Story, Sara Bernstein, Gregory Bernstein, Cliff Gardner; Photography, Gabriel Beristain; Designer, Victoria Paul; Editor, Tony Lombardo; Music, Phil Marshall; Costumes, Shay Cunliffe; Associate Producers, Jane DeVries Cooper, Edward Lynn; Casting, Terry Liebling; a Larger Than Life production; Dolby Digital; Super 35 Widescreen; CFI Color; Rated PG-13; 98 minutes; May release

CAST

Richard Rietti	Michael Richards
Charles Tuttle	Jeff Daniels
Billie Tyler	Charlize Theron
Elizabeth Gardner	Jessica Steen
Judge Paul Z. Graff	Austin Pendleton
Benny Gibbs	Rip Torn
Tiffany	Alexandra Wentworth
Jacqueline	Jennifer Coolidge
Whitfield	Lawrence Pressman
Dr. Stone	Dale Dye
Dr. Brown	Max Casella
Charles' Assistant	McNally Sagal
Hank Crabbit	Kenneth White
Buck Norman	Keith Mills
Bailiff	Zaid Farid
Mrs. Sussex	Rachel Winfree
Clerk	Ken Magee
Court Reporter	Michelle Bonilla
Eric	Mark Davenport
Kurt	Kelly Perine
Phil	Rick La Fond

and Paul Joseph Dworkin, John Bigham (Bartenders), Nancy Linehan Charles (Witness), Jim Cody Williams (Tattooed Lowlife), Jodi Faith Cahn (Elizabeth's Secretary), Brian Mahoney (Man in Bar), Gerry Spence (Himself), Norman Brennar (Courtroom Janitor)

When lawyer Charles Tuttle is unable to make a court appearance his best friend, Richard, an actor, fills in for him, little realizing that he will have to go on posing as Charles for the remainder of the trial.

© New Line Cinema

Danny Glover, Joe Pesci

Michael Richards, Jeff Daniels

GONE FISHIN'

(HOLLYWOOD PICTURES) Producers, Roger Birnbaum, Julie Bergman Sender; Executive Producer, Jill Mazursky Cody; Director, Christopher Cain; Screenplay, Jill Mazursky Cody, Jeffrey Abrams; Photography, Dean Semler; Designer, Lawrence Miller; Editor, Jack Hofstra; Co-Producers, Richard H. Prince, Lou Arkoff; Music, Randy Edelman; Costumes, Lizzy Gardiner; Casting, Rick Montgomery, Dan Parada; Stunts, Shane Dixon; a Roger Birnbaum production, presented in association with Caravan Pictures; Dolby Digital Stereo; Technicolor; Rated PG; 94 minutes; May release

CAST

Joe Waters	Joe Pesci
Gus Green	Danny Glover
Rita	Rosanna Arquette
Angie	Lynn Whitfield
Billy "Catch" Pooler	Willie Nelson
Dekker Massey	Nick Brimble
Phil Beasly	Gary Grubbs
Donna Waters	Carol Kane
Cookie Green	Edythe Davis
Gina Waters	Jenna Bari
Tracy Green	Samantha Brown
Mack Waters	Jeff DiLucca
Gregory Green	Jamil Akim O'Quinn
Young Joe	Frank Nasso

and Raynor Scheine (Glenn), Robyn Hackett (Nicky), James R. Greene (Bubba), Steve Wise (JP), Claudia Haro (Julie), Jonathan Avildsen (Parking Valet), Bob Noble (Manager), Jeff Prettyman (Maitre D'), Judy Clayton (Deana Bernini), Antoni Corone (Front Desk Clerk), Dana Adamstein, Valerie J. Boey (Reporters), Joseph Scalora (Officer), Tommy DeVito (Construction Foreman), Leonard Termo, Alfred Nittoli (Vending Workers), Gary Morgan (Bergman), Lisa Hewlett Keen (Dining Room Guest), Dave Corey (Actor), Baynor Foy Crane (Actress), Mark Futch (Seaplane Pilot), John Griffen (Blind Driver), Louise Fletcher, Maury Chaykin

Gus and Joe, on their way to the Florida Everglades for a fishing vacation, have their car stolen by a mysterious man on his way to recover some stolen cash.

© Hollywood Pictures Company

Nicolas Cage

Rachel Ticotin

Steve Buscemi

Ving Rhames

Danny Trejo

Nicolas Cage, Mykelti Williamson

CON AIR

(TOUCHSTONE) Producer, Jerry Bruckheimer; Executive Producers, Chad Oman, Jonathan Hengsleigh, Peter Bogart, Jim Kouf, Lynn Bigelow; Director, Simon West; Screenplay, Scott Rosenberg; Photography, David Tattersall; Art Director, Edward T. McAvoy; Editors, Chris Lebenzon, Steve Mirkovich, Glen Scantlebury; Music, Mark Mancina, Trevor Rabin; Costumes, Bobbie Read; Visual Effects Supervisor, David Goldberg; Visual Effects, Dream Quest Images; Stunts, Kenny Bates; Casting, Victoria Thomas; a Jerry Bruckheimer production; Distributed by Buena Vista Pictures; Dolby Digital Stereo; Panavision; Technicolor; Rated R; 115 minutes; June release

John Cusack, Colm Meaney, John Roselius

CAST

Cameron Poe	Nicolas Cage
U.S. Marshal Vince Larkin	John Cusack
Cyrus "The Virus" Grissom	John Malkovich
Garland Greene	Steve Buscemi
Billy Bedlam	Nick Chinlund
U.S. Marshal Guard Sally Bishop	Rachel Ticotin
Duncan Malloy	Colm Meaney
Swamp Thing	M.C. Gainey
Diamond Dog (Nathan Jones)	Ving Rhames
Conrad	Brendan Kelly
Baby-O	Mykelti Williamson
Johnny 23	Danny Trejo
Sally Can't Dance	Renoly
Francisco Cindino	Jesse Borrego
"Pinball" Parker	Dave Chappelle
Con #1	Carl N. Ciarfalio
Ajax	Jerry Mongo Brownlee
Falzon	Steve Eastin
Sims	Jose Zuniga
Chopper Pilot	Ned Bellamy
Gator	John Marshall Jones
Devers	John Roselius
Pilot	Fredric Lane
Co-Pilot	Martin McSorley
Starkey	Dylan Haggerty
Chambers	Matt Barry
Tricia Poe	Monica Potte
Casey Poe	Landry Allbright
Fuel Jockey	Dan Bell
Ted, the Pilot	Robert Stephenson
Bus Guard	Scott Ditty
Sheriff	Tommy Bush

and Lauren Pratt (Debbie 6yrs. old), Steve Hulin (Ronnie), Don Charles McGovern (Smoke), Angela Featherstone (Ginny), Doug Hutchinson (Donald), Jeris Poindexter (Watts), David Ramsey (Londell), Conrad Goode (Viking), Emillio Rivera (Carlos), Tyrone Granderson Jones (Blade), Mario Roberts (Mongoose—Stunt), Earl Billings, Greg Collins, Billy Devlin, Mark Ginther, Joseph Patrick Kelly (Guards), Jeff Olson (Uncle Bob), Dawn Bluford (Baggage Handler), Charlie Paddock (Transportation Officer #1), Randee Barnes (Stickman), Don Davis (Man in Car), Barbara Sharma (Woman in Car), Tommy Rosales, Eddie Perez, Scott McCoy (Cindino Gunmen—Stunts), Brian Hayes Currie (Cop in Vegas), Ashley Smock (Huey Pilot), Charles Lynn Frost (DEA Agent), Joey Miyashima (Tech Guy), Scott Burkholder (Air Traffic Controller), Kevin Cooney (Judge), Gerard L'Heureux (Guard Renfro), Peter Antico (Guard Garner), John Robotham (Guard Ryan), Gilbert Rosales (Ramirez—Stunt), Richard Duran (Warlock—Stunt), George Randall (Old Con on Plane), James Bozian, Harley Zumbrum, Doug Dearth (Cons), David Roberson (Supervisor), Alexandra Balahoutis (Waitress), Dick "Skip" Evans (Airplane Pilot), Sheldon Worthington (Co-Pilot), Robert Taft, Robert White (Soldiers), Chris Ellis (BOP Official Grant), John Campbell (BOP Bus Driver), Brian Willems, Bill Cusack (Paramedics), Dabbs Greer (Old Man under Truck), Marco Kyris (Cindino's Pilot)

John Malkovich

Eager to get home to his wife and child, recently paroled Cameron Poe takes passage on a plane transporting a group of dangerous criminals only to find that it is up to him to save the day when the convicts take over the vehicle. This film received Oscar nominations for song ("How Do I Live") and sound.

Mykelti Williamson, Nicolas Cage, Rachel Ticotin

BUDDY

(COLUMBIA) Producers, Steve Nicolaides, Fred Fuchs; Executive Producers, Francis Ford Coppola, Stephanie Allain, Brian Henson; Director/Screenplay, Caroline Thompson; Based upon the book Animals Are My Hobby by Gertrude Davies Lintz; Screen Story, William Joyce, Caroline Thompson; Photography, Steve Mason; Designers, David Nichols, Daniel Lomino; Editor, Jonathan Shaw; Music, Elmer Bernstein; Costumes, Colleen Atwood; Creature Effects, Jim Henson's Creature Shop; Casting, Carrie Frazier; a Jim Henson Pictures presentation of an American Zoetrope production; Dolby SDDS Stereo; Panavision; Technicolor; Rated PG; 84 minutes; June release

Buddy, Rene Russo

CAST

Trudy Lintz	Rene Russo
Dr. Bill Lintz	Robbie Coltrane
Dick Kroener	Alan Cumming
Emma	Irma P. Hall
Buddy	Peter Elliott, Mak Wilson
	(and Lynn Robertson Bruce, Mark Sealey, Rob Tygner, Michelan Sisti, Peter Hurst, Leif Tilden, Star Townshend)
Professor Spatz	Paul Reubens
Mr. Bowman	John Aylward
Mrs. Bowman	Mimi Kennedy
Theater-goer	Jon Simmons
Movie Woman	Kathleen Klein
Usher	Russell Young
Zoo Keeper	Frank Collison
Barker	Al Weber
Minister	Philip Baker Hall
Bellowing Man	Kyle Galyean
Fair Cop	Dane Cook
Skinny Man	Michael Reid Mackay
Policemen	John Ennis, Jeff Hatz
Ali Baba	Bradley J. Lesley
Cornered Woman	Julianna Wheeler
Buddy Vocals	Frank Welker, Gary Hecker, Hector C. Gika

The true story of eccentric socialite Gertrude "Trudy" Lintz who kept a menagerie of wild animals on her New York estate, most notably a gorilla named "Buddy" that she raised since he was a baby.

Alan Cumming

Rene Russo

Mimi Kennedy, John Aylward, Buddy

Vanessa Zima, Peter Fonda

Patricia Richardson

Jessica Biel, Peter Fonda, Vanessa Zima

ULEE'S GOLD

(ORION) Co-Producers, Sam Gowan, Peter Saraf; Executive Producers, Edward Saxon, John Sloss, Valerie Thomas; Director/Screenplay, Victor Nunez; Photography, Virgil Mirano; Designer, Pat Garner; Music, Charles Engstrom; Costumes, Marilyn Wall-Asse; Casting, Judy Courtney; a Jonathan Demme presentation of a Nunez-Gowan/Clinica Estetico production; Dolby Stereo; Deluxe color; Rated R; 111 minutes; June release

CAST

Ulee Jackson	Peter Fonda
Connie Hope	Patricia Richardson
Helen Jackson	Christine Dunford
Jimmy Jackson	Tom Wood
Casey Jackson	Jessica Biel
Penny Jackson	Vanessa Zima
Eddie Flowers	Steven Flynn
Ferris Dooley	Dewey Weber
Sheriff Bill Floyd	J. Kenneth Campbell
Chance Barrow	Traber Burns
Charley Myers	Ryan Marshall
Markie	Chad Fish
Child at Rest Stop	Will Sexton
Beekeeper Assistants	Dale C. Marshall, James Whitehurst, Charles Branner

Florida beekeeper Ulee Jackson, raising his two granddaughters, must cope again with the girls' irresponsible, drug-addicted mother when he is asked by his son to retrieve the woman from a pair of dangerous criminals. This film received an Oscar nomination for actor (Peter Fonda).

Christine Dunford   Tom Wood

J. Kenneth Campbell

SPEED 2: CRUISE CONTROL

(20TH CENTURY FOX) Producers, Jan De Bont, Steve Perry, Michael Peyser; Director, Jan De Bont; Screenplay, Randall McCormick, Jeff Nathanson; Story, Jan De Bont, Randall McCormick; Based on characters created by Graham Yost; Executive Producer, Mark Gordon; Photography, Jack N. Green; Designers, Joseph Nemec III, Bill Kenney; Editor, Alan Cody; Music, Mark Mancina; Special Effects Supervisors, Stefen Fangmeier (ILM), Bert Terreri (Rhythm & Hues, Inc.); Costumes, Louise Frogley; Stunts, Dick Ziker; Casting, Risa Bramon Garcia, Randi Hiller; a Blue Tulip production; Dolby Digital Stereo; Panavision; Deluxe color; Rated PG-13; 121 minutes

CAST

Annie Porter	Sandra Bullock
Alex Shaw	Jason Patric
John Geiger	Willem Dafoe
Juliano	Temuera Morrison
Merced	Brian McCardie
Drew	Christine Firkins
Harvey	Michael G. Hagerty
Debbie	Colleen Camp
Celeste	Lois Chiles
Rupert	Francis Guinan
Sheri	Tamia
Ashton	Jeremy Hotz
Alejandro	Enrique Murciano, Jr.
Isabel	Jessica Diz
Fran	Connie Ray
Ruby	Patrika Darbo

and Kimmy Robertson (Liza the Cruise Director), Charles Parks (Frank), Susan Barnes (Constance), Bo Svenson (Captain Pollard), Royale Watkins (Dante), Alex Montesino (Control Room Chief Engineer), Glenn Plummer (Maurice), Allison Dean (Marifa), Joe Foster (Pool Officer), Richard Speight, Jr. ("C" Deck Officer), Tim Conway (Mr. Kenter), Mark Adair-Rios, Xavier Coronel, Tyler Patton, Craig A. Pinckes (Engine Room Crew Members), Michael Robinson, Joe d'Angerio (Muster Deck Officers), Michael O'Hagan (Supertanker Captain), Christopher Wynne, Robert Herrick (Supertanker Officers), Ivory Broome (Supertanker Crew Member #1), Thomas J. Huff (Diaper Van Driver), Jay Lacopo (Real Estate Salesman), Alexander De Bont (Little Boy—Condo), Kathryn Rossetter (Mother at Condo), Mark Beltzman (Convertible Owner), Mark Kriski (News Reporter), Ben Meyerson, Gustavo Laborie (Bridge Officers), Ben Siegler (Policeman), Jennifer S. Badger, Cheryl Bermeo, Jeff Brockton, Don Pulford, Cliff McLaughlin, Matthew Taylor, PJ Wagner, May R. Boss, Nancy Collet (Passengers), Wilma Edward (Woman on phone)

Annie and Alex take a Caribbean cruise only to discover that the ship they are sailing on has been hijacked by a crazed terrorist. Sequel to the 1994 20th Century Fox release Speed with Sandra Bullock and Glenn Plummer repeating their roles from that film.

© Twentieth Century Fox

Illeana Douglas, Paulina Porizkova, Julie Warner

Jason Patric, Sandra Bullock

Sandra Bullock, Willem Dafoe

WEDDING BELL BLUES

(LEGACY/BMG) Producers, Ram Bergman, Dana Lustig, Mike Curb, Carole Curb Nemoy; Director, Dana Lustig; Screenplay, Annette Goliti Gutierrez; Story, Dana Lustig, Annette Goliti Gutierrez; Photography, Kent Wakeford; Editor, Caroline Ross; Designer, Shay Austin; Costumes, Dana Allyson; Music, Paul Christian Gordon, Tal Bergman; Casting, Margiotta Casting; from Bergman Lustig productions/Curb Entertainment International Corp.; Color; Rated R; 100 minutes; June release

CAST

Jasmine	Illeana Douglas
Tanya	Paulina Porizkova
Micki	Julie Warner
Cary	John Corbett
Matt	Jonathan Penner
Oliver	Charles Martin Smith
Tom	Richard Edson
Jeff	Joseph Urla
Tanya's Mother	Stephanie Beacham
Violet	Carla Gugino
Robert	Leo Rossi
Herself	Debbie Reynolds

and John Capodice (Jasmine's Father), Liz Sheridan (Micki's Mother), Stephen Gilborn (Micki's Father), Jeff Seymour (Jan), Victoria Jackson (Boutique Customer), Kamala Dawson (Pregnant Woman), Carol Ann Susi (Aunt Anash), Andrew Heckler (Zane), Marcy Lafferty Shatner (Sonya), Bill Elliot (Anxious Husband), Carlos Montilla (Gustavo), David Wilbur (Priest), Kate Asner (Alice), Danny Koker (Beautiful Groom), Kevin Hunt (All-American Man), Brendan "Reno" Duffy (Elvis Impersonator)

Three women drive to Las Vegas where they hope to find husbands, marry them and divorce them within 24 hours, in order to say they were wed before they reached the age of thirty.

© BMG Independents

DREAM WITH THE FISHES

(SONY CLASSICS) Producers, Johnny Wow, Mitchell Stein; Co-Producers, David Arquette, Laurie A. Miller, Jeffrey Brown; Executive Producers, John Sideropoulos, Charles Hsiao; Director/Screenplay, Finn Taylor; Story, Finn Taylor, Jeffrey Brown; Photography, Barry Stone; Editor, Rick Le Compte; Designer, Justin McCartney; Costumes, Amy Brownson; Casting, Joseph Middleton; a 3 Ring Circus Films presentation; Dolby Stereo; Color; Rated R; 96 minutes; June release

Brad Hunt, David Arquette

CAST

Terry	David Arquette
Nick	Brad Hunt
Aunt Elise	Cathy Moriarty
Liz	Kathryn Erbe
Don	Patrick McGaw
Joe, Nick's Father	J.E. Freeman
Michelle	Timi Prulhiere
Mary	Anita Barone
Sophia	Allyce Beasley
Pharmacist	Peter Gregory
Sheriff	Richmond Arquette
Funeral Director	George Maguire
Terry's Bowling "Date"	Kristina Robbins
Nick's Bowling "Date"	Katherine Copenhaver
Drug Dealer	Gary Brickman
Psychic	Nina Peschcke-Koedt
Priest	Orril Fluharty

and Michael Halton (Liquor Store Clerk), Mike Por (Donut Shop Clerk), Chris Pay (Emergency Room Doctor), Felix Justice, James Carraway (Nick's Doctors), Michael Vaughn (Bank Security Guard), Beth Daly (Librarian), Banda El Rincon (Band in Bar), Michael Hsiao (Restaurant Pianist), Alec Ingalls (Bartender), Jack A. Roe (Angry Taxi Passenger), Xris (Convenience Store Clerk), Capt. Greg Love, Officer Ken Cunningham, Officer Mike Price (Cops at Funeral/Pharmacy), Roland Absolo (Aquarium Security Guard), Sophia Stefanek (Mary's Daughter), Mark Hager (Garbage Man), Peaches (Nick's Ashes)

Terry, determined to commit suicide, hooks up with terminally ill Nick and the two decide to drop out of society to live life on the edge.

Phuong Duong, Eddie Cutanda, Tyrone Burton

SQUEEZE

(MIRAMAX) Producers, Ari Newman, Garen Topalian, Stephanie Danan, Patricia Moreno; Executive Producer, Mitchell B. Robbins; Director/Screenplay, Robert Patton-Spruill; Photography/Editor, Richard Moos; Associate Producers, Emmett Folgert, Laura Bernieri, H. Forrest Logan; Designer, Maximilian Cutler; Line Producer, Lee Beckett; a Robbins Entertainment presentation of a ca*thar*tic film Works and Danan/Moreno Films production in association with the Dorcester Youth Collaborative Extreme Close-Up; Dolby Stereo; Color; Rated R; 89 minutes; June release

CAST

Tyson	Tyrone Burton
Hector	Eddie Cutanda
Bao	Phuong Duong
JJ	Geoffrey Rhue
Tommy	Russell G. Jones
Marcus	Leigh Williams
Uzi	Robert Agredo
Derick	Beresford Bennett
Lisa	Jennifer Maxcy
Fiend	Harlem Logan
Aunt C.	Diane Beckett
Pearl	Ingrid Askew
Psychiatrist/Homelessman	James Spruill
Jason	William Butler
Mason	Daryl Bugg
Tisha	Maleah Liggins
Pinky	Pinky Lugo
Angela	Milagros Jones

and Catherine Oberg, Patrick Ruth (Cat Fighters), Sean Henderson, Johnny Henderson (Bad Kids), Lynda Patton, Georgette Leslie (Women in Car), Bruce Serefin (Police Officer), Gerry Nuzollo (Gas Station Attendant), Jessica Edwards (Marrisa), Victor Nunez (Julio), Alfredo Rivera (Doorman), John Bonaparte (Man with Burning Book), Juanita Rodriguez (Youth Center Receptionist), Monique Douglas (Youth Worker), Sparkle Henderson, Nicole Kelly, Melissa Khomblassen (Girls with Rakes), Aaron Stewart, Roy J. Lynch (Barbers), Max Cutler (Hospital Patient)

Three Boston teens are faced with the decision of helping out at a local youth center or taking the dangerous road of gangs and drug dealing.

Pegasus, Phil, Hercules

Hades, Meg

Hercules, Hydra

Hercules, Nessus

Panic, Pain

HERCULES

(WALT DISNEY PICTURES) Producers, Alice Dewey, John Musker, Ron Clements; Directors, John Musker, Ron Clements; Animation Screenplay, Ron Clements, John Musker, Donald McEnery, Bob Shaw, Irene Mecchi; Art Director, Andy Gaskill; Designer, Gerald Scarfe; Editor, Tom Finan; Associate Producer, Kendra Haaland; Music, Alan Menken; Lyrics, David Zippel; Artistic Supervisors: Story, Barry Johnson; Production Stylist, Sue C. Nichols; Layout, Rasoul Azadani; Background, Thomas Cardone; Visual Effects, Mauro Maressa; Computer Graphics Imagery, Roger L. Gould; Clean-Up, Nancy Kniep; Artistic Coordinator, Dan Hansen; Distributed by Buena Vista Pictures; Dolby Digital Stereo; Technicolor; Rated G; 92 minutes; June release

Hades, Hercules

VOICE CAST

Alemene	Barbara Barrie
Young Hercules (singing)	Roger Bart
Earthquake Lady	Mary Kay Bergman
Burnt Man	Corey Burton
Nessus	Jim Cummings
Apollo	Keith David
Phil	Danny DeVito
Hercules	Tate Donovan
Fate	Paddi Edwards
Meg	Susan Egan
Hera	Samantha Eggar
Heavyset Woman	Kathleen Freeman
Muse (Melpomene)	Cheryl Freeman
Panic	Matt Frewer
Pain	Bobcat Goldthwait
Little Boys	Bug Hall, Kellen Hathaway
Narrator	Charlton Heston
Amphitryon	Hal Holbrook
Young Hercules (speaking)	Joshua Keaton
Demetrius	Wayne Knight
Muse (Terpsichore)	LaChanze
Ithicles	Aaron Michael Metchik
Cyclops	Patrick Pinney
Fate	Amanda Plummer
Muse (Thalia)	Roz Ryan
Hermes	Paul Shaffer
Fate	Carole Shelley
Muse (Clio)	Vaneese Thomas
Zeus	Rip Torn
Lead Muse (Calliope)	Lillias White
Hades	James Woods

and Tawatha Agee, Jack Angel, Shelton Becton, Bob Bergen, Rodger Bumpass, Jennifer Darling, Debi Derryberry, Bill Farmer, Milt Grayson, Sherry Lynn, Mickie McGowan, Denise Pickering, Phil Proctor, Jan Rabson, Riley Steiner, Fonzi Thorton, Erik Von Detten, Ken Williams (Additional Voices)

Phil, Hercules

Hoping to rule the Universe the evil god of the Underworld, Hades, has Zeus's son Hercules abducted from Mount Olympus and taken to earth. There the boy is raised as mortal despite having retained his super-human strength. Previous film versions of Hercules include the 1957 release starring Steve Reeves and the 1983 MGM production with Lou Ferrigno. This film received an Oscar nomination for song ("Go the Distance").

Meg, Hercules, Pegasus

Julia Roberts, Cameron Diaz

Julia Roberts, Rupert Everett

Cameron Diaz, Dermot Mulroney, Julia Roberts

MY BEST FRIEND'S WEDDING

(TRISTAR) Producers, Jerry Zucker, Ronald Bass; Executive Producers, Gil Netter, Patricia Whitcher; Director, P.J. Hogan; Screenplay, Ronald Bass; Photography, Laszlo Kovacs; Designer, Richard Sylbert; Editors, Garth Craven, Lisa Fruchtman; Costumes, Jeffrey Kurland; Music, James Newton Howard; Casting, David Rubin; a Jerry Zucker/Predawn production; Dolby SDDS Stereo; Panavision; Technicolor; Rated PG-13; 105 minutes; June release

CAST

Julianne Potter	Julia Roberts
Michael O'Neal	Dermot Mulroney
Kimmy Wallace	Cameron Diaz
George Downes	Rupert Everett
Walter Wallace	Philip Bosco
Joe O'Neal	M. Emmet Walsh
Samantha Newhouse	Rachel Griffiths
Amanda Newhouse	Carrie Preston
Isabelle Wallace	Susan Sullivan
Scott O'Neal	Chris Masterson
Title Sequence Performers	Raci Alexander, Jennifer Garrett, Kelly Sheerin, Bree Turner
Flower Girl	Cassie Creasy
Kimmy's Grandma	Lucina Paquet
Old Woman #2	Aida Baggio
Oldest Lady	Shirley Kelly
Party Guests	George Bozonelos, Loretta Paoletti
Stoner Guys	Joseph Sikora, Shale Marks
Wedding Singer	Phillip Ingram
Seamstress	Rose Abdoo
Tailor	JoBe Cerny
Bellman	Paul Giamatti
Himself	Chef Charlie Trotter
Chef	Guillermo Tellez
Captain	Ned Schmidtke
Karaoke Singer	Mark Swenson

and Mara Casey (Karaoke Girl), Tonray Ho (Karaoke Waitress), Michelle Hutchison (Drunken Trashy Girl), Robert Sutter (Crabhouse Pianist), Charlotte Zucker, Susan Breslau, Burton Zucker, Sharon Haight (Customers), Nydia Rodriguez Terracina (Walter's Secretary), Mike Bacarella (Office Janitor), Larry Santori (Conductor), Gene Janson, Kevin Michael Doyle (Sport Magazine Guys), Scott Kuhagen (Werner), Sid Hillman, Norman Merrill, Renata Scott, Anh Duong (Dining Guests), Harry Shearer (Jonathan P.E. Rice), Jennifer McComb (Excited Woman), Mary-Pat Green (Angry Woman), Davenia McFadden (Angrier Woman), Jo Farkas (Loony Woman), The Morning Choir of the 4th Presbyterian Church of Chicago (Wedding Choir)

Julianne, realizing she still has very strong feelings for her best friend Michael, tries to break up his relationship with his fiancee in the four days leading up to their wedding. This film received an Oscar nomination for original music or comedy score.

© Tristar Pictures

Philip Bosco, Susan Sullivan

Chris Masterson, Dermot Mulroney

Julia Roberts, Cameron Diaz

Julia Roberts, Dermot Mulroney, Rupert Everett

Nicolas Cage, John Travolta

Joan Allen, John Travolta

Dominique Swain

Nicolas Cage, Alessandro Nivola

FACE/OFF

(PARAMOUNT) Producers, David Permut, Barrie M. Osborne, Terence Chang, Christopher Godsick; Executive Producers, Jonathan D. Krane, Michael Douglas, Steven Reuther; Director, John Woo; Screenplay/Co-Producers, Mike Werb, Michael Colleary; Photography, Oliver Wood; Designer, Neil Spisak; Editors, Christian Wagner, Steven Kemper; Costumes, Ellen Mirojnick; Music, John Powell; Associate Producer, Jeff Levine; Visual Effects Supervisors, Richard Hollander, Boyd Shermis; Special Makeup Effects Creator, Kevin Yagher; Stunts, Brian Smrz; Casting, Mindy Marin; a Douglas/Reuther—WCG Entertainment — David Permut production; Dolby Stereo; Panavision; Deluxe color; Rated R; 138 minutes; June release

John Travolta, Nicolas Cage

CAST

Sean Archer	John Travolta
Castor Troy	Nicolas Cage
Eve Archer	Joan Allen
Pollux Troy	Alessandro Nivola
Sasha Hassler	Gina Gershon
Jamie Archer	Dominique Swain
Dietrich Hassler	Nick Cassavetes
Lazzaro	Harve Presnell
Dr. Malcolm Walsh	Colm Feore
Prison Guard Walton	John Carroll Lynch
Hollis Miller	CCH Pounder
Tito	Robert Wisdom
Wanda	Margaret Cho
Buzz	Jamie Denton
Loomis	Matt Ross
Leo Fry	Tommy J. Flanagan
Lars	Dana Smith
Kimberly	Romy Walthall
Fitch	Paul Hipp
Aldo Adino	Kirk Baltz
Dubov	Chris Bauer
Burke Hicks	Thomas Jane
Agent Winters	Lauren Sinclair
Pilot	Ben Reed
Janitor	Del Zamora
Cindee	Lisa Boyle
Livia	Linda Hoffman
Karl	Danny Masterson
Priest	Father Michael Rocha
Adolescent Girl	Megan Paul
Iris' Dad	Mike Werb
LAPD Cop	Tom Reynolds
Interrogating Agent	Steve Hytner

and Myles Jeffrey (Michael Archer), Carmen Thomas (Reporter Valerie), John Bloom (Prison Medical Technician), Walter Scott (Port Police Commander), Brooke Leslie (ER Nurse), David McCurley (Adam Hassler), Cam Brainard (Dispatcher), David Warshofsky (Bomb Leader), John Neidlinger (Bomb Technician), Norm Compton (Cigarette Guard), Gregg Shawzin (Lock Down Guard), Clifford Einstein (Restorative Surgeon), Marco Kyris (Recreation Guard), Tom Fridley (Prison Guard), Andrew Wallace (Altar Boy), Jacinto Rodriguez (Prisoner), Chic Daniel (FBI Squad Leader), Laurence Walsh (Walsh Clinic Nurse)

Gina Gershon, Nicolas Cage

Having captured Castor Troy, the crazed terrorist who killed his son, FBI agent Sean Archer agrees to a bizarre experiment wherein he will swap faces with Troy in order information from Troy's brother, a plan which goes terribly awry. This film received an Oscar nomination for sound effects editing.

Nicolas Cage, John Travolta

Will Smith, Tommy Lee Jones

Will Smith, Tony Shalhoub

Mikey

Rip Torn

Tommy Lee Jones, Will Smith, Linda Fiorentino

MEN IN BLACK

(COLUMBIA) Producers, Walter F. Parkes, Laurie MacDonald; Executive Producer, Steven Spielberg; Director, Barry Sonnenfeld; Screenplay/Story, Ed Solomon; Based on the Malibu Comic by Lowell Cunningham; Co-Producer, Graham Place; Photography, Don Peterman; Designer, Bo Welch; Editor, Jim Miller; Costumes, Mary E. Vogt; Music, Danny Elfman; Visual Effects Supervisor, Eric Brevig; Visual Effects, Industrial Light & Magic; Alien Make-up Effects, Rick Baker; Casting, David Rubin, Debra Zane; an Amblin Entertainment production in association with MacDonald/Parkes productions; Dolby DTS Stereo; Technicolor; Rated PG-13; 98 minutes; July release

CAST

K	Tommy Lee Jones
J	Will Smith
Dr. Laurel Weaver	Linda Fiorentino
Edgar	Vincent D'Onofrio
Zed	Rip Torn
Jeebs	Tony Shalhoub
Beatrice	Siobhan Fallon
Gentle Rosenberg	Mike Nussbaum
Van Driver	Jon Gries
Jose	Sergio Calderon
Arquillian	Carel Struycken
INS Agent Janus	Fredric Lane
D	Richard Hamilton
1st Lt. Jake Jensen	Kent Faulcon
Mikey	John Alexander
Perp	Keith Campbell
Orkin Man	Ken Thorley
Mr. Redgick	Patrick Breen
Mrs. Redgick	Becky Ann Baker
Passport Officer	Sean Whalen
News Vendor	Harsh Nayyar
Cop in Morgue	Michael Willis
Police Inspector	Willie C. Carpenter
Tow Truck Driver	Peter Linari
Morgue Attendant	David Cross
MIB Agent Bee	Charles C. Stevenson, Jr.
Cook	Boris Leskin

and Steve Rankin, Andy Prosky (INS Agents), Michael Goldfinger (NYPD Sergeant), Alpheus Merchant (Security Guard), Norma Jean Groh (Mrs. Edelson), Bernard Gilkey (Baseball Player), Sean Plummer, Michael Kaliski (First Contact Aliens), Richard Arthur (2nd First Contact Alien), Debbie Lee Carrington (Alien Father), Verne Troyer (Alien Son), Mykal Wayne Williams (Scared Guy), Tim Blaney (Frank the Pug), Mark Setrakian (Rosenberg Alien), Brad Abrell, Thom Fountain, Carl J. Johnson, Drew Massey (Worm Guys)

J joins the goverment agency known as Men in Black whose mission it is to regulate all alien immigration from other planets. 1997 Academy Award-winner for Best Makeup. This film received additional Oscar nominations for art direction and original musical or comedy score.

Baby Redgick, Will Smith

Vincent D'Onofrio

Tommy Lee Jones, Will Smith

OUT TO SEA

(20TH CENTURY FOX) Producers, John Davis, David T. Friendly; Executive Producers, Dylan Sellers, Barry Berg; Director, Martha Coolidge; Screenplay, Robert Nelson Jacobs; Photography, Lajos Koltai; Designer, James Spencer; Editor, Anne V. Coates; Music, David Newman; Choreography, Kim Blank; Costumes, Jane Robinson; Casting, Jackie Burch; a Davis Entertainment Company production; Dolby Stereo; Deluxe color; Rated PG-13; 109 minutes; July release

CAST

Herb Sullivan	Jack Lemmon
Charlie Gordon	Walter Matthau
Liz LaBreche	Dyan Cannon
Vivian	Gloria DeHaven
Gil Godwyn	Brent Spiner
Mavis	Elaine Stritch
Mac	Hal Linden
Jonathan	Donald O'Connor
Mrs. Carruthers	Rue McClanahan
Cullen Carswell	Edward Mulhare
Shelly	Alexandra Powers
Alan	Sean O'Bryan
Maria	Esther Scott
Sebastian	Allan Rich
Bridget	Estelle Harris
Willie	Leon Singer
Madge	Concetta Tomei
Tanaka	Goh Misawa
Dance Instructor	Kim Blank
Edie	Louisa Abernathy
Purser	Michael Laskin
Parrot	Hector Mercado
Flight Attendant	Carol Barbee
Sylvia	Dale Raoul
Shapiro	Lomax Study
Pearl	Beverly Polcyn
Bettor in Front	Shaun Troub

and Bert Rosario (Cab Driver), Paul Kievit (Ship Captain), Henk Ijdens (Ship Officer), Frank Patton (Dealer), Natalia Momtchilova (Shopgirl), Rod Phillips (Julian), P.D. Mani (Floor Person), Trevor Denman (Track Announcer), Bubba Dean Rambo, Allen Walls (Dance Hosts), Laura Canellias, Cindera Che, Leslie Cook, Andre Fortin, Dotti Karlstein, Albert Torres (Ballroom Dancers), Michelle Elkin, Sharon Ferguson, Diane Mizota, Andrea Paige Wilson (Showgirls), Bubba Carr, Ronnie Willis (Showguys), Ungela Brockman, John R. Corella, Joaquin Escamilla, Eddie Garcia, Sal Lorez, U. Lucero, Rosero, Darrell W. Wright (Mexican Dancers), Thomas DeLuca (Piano Player)

Charlie cons his brother-in-law Herb into joining him on a luxury cruise where the two will get free passage under the guise of dance instructors. This was the last film of actor Edward Mulhare who died on May 24, 1997.

Walter Matthau, Dyan Cannon, Edward Mulhare

Gloria DeHaven, Jack Lemmon

Jack Lemmon, Brent Spiner, Walter Matthau

Donald O'Connor, Rue McClanahan, Hal Linden

THIS WORLD, THEN THE FIREWORKS

(ORION CLASSICS) Producers, Chris Hanley, Brad Wyman, Larry Gross; Executive Producer, Barr Potter; Co-Executive Producer, Billy Zane; Director, Michael Oblowitz; Screenplay, Larry Gross; Based on the story by Jim Thompson; Photography, Tom Priestley, Jr.; Designer, Maia Javan; Music, Pete Rugolo; Costumes, Dan Moore; Special Effects, Michael Schorr; Casting, Mary Vernieu; a Largo Entertainment presentation of a Muse, Balzac's Shirt, Wyman Production; Dolby Stereo; Color; Rated R; 100 minutes; July release

Gina Gershon, Billy Zane

CAST

Marty Lakewood	Billy Zane
Carol Lakewood	Gina Gershon
Lois Archer	Sheryl Lee
Mrs. Lakewood	Rue McClanahan
Police Lt. Morgan	Will Patton
Joe	Richard Edson
Police Detective Harris	Seymour Cassel
Marty's Father	Philip Loch
Little Marty	Christian Durango
Little Carol	Sloan Cobb
Young Carol	Megan Leigh Brown
Young Marty	Christopher Jones

and Elizabeth Imboden (Neighbor's Wife), Roberta Hanley (Younger Mom Lakewood), Robert Pentz (Lou), Marianna Alacchi (Glenda), Orson Oblowitz (Eugene), Willy Cobbs (Blues Musician), Max Maxwell, Max O'Toole (Thugs in Bar), Mert Hatfield (Bus Driver), Tom Keeley (Cousin Lyle), Thad Mace (Tim), Jonathan Taylor Luthren (Ben), Stephanie Fisher (Claire), Mark Jeffrey Miller (Lloyd), Vincent Schilling (Patron), Lou Criscuolo (McCloud), Jeffrey Pillars (Galloway), Paul Allan Sincoff (Assistant), William Hootkins (Jake Krutz), Barry Bell (Barnett Gibons), David Lenthall (Doctor), Brian Gamble (Undertaker), Terry Nienhuis (Minister), Val DeVargas (Mexican Doctor), Dean Mumford (Capt. Miles Archer), Rick Warner (Real Estate Guy)

The incestuous Marty and Carol Lakewood, a con man and a hooker, team up to fleece a repressed police woman who has been seduced by Marty.

Billy Zane, Rue McClanahan

Billy Zane, Sheryl Lee

A SIMPLE WISH

(UNIVERSAL) Producers, Sid, Bill and Jon Sheinberg; Director, Michael Ritchie; Screenplay, Jeff Rothberg; Photography, Ralf Bode; Designer, Stephen Hendrickson; Editor, William Scharf; Co-Producers, Michael S. Glick, Jeff Rothberg; Costumes, Luke Reichle; Music, Bruce Broughton; Computer Generated Visual Effects, Blue Sky Studios Inc; Special Visual Effects, Matte World Digital, Pacific Data Images; Casting, Rick Pagano; DTS Stereo; Deluxe color; Rated PG; 89 minutes; July release

CAST

Murray	Martin Short
Claudia	Kathleen Turner
Anabel Greening	Mara Wilson
Oliver Greening	Robert Pastorelli
Boots	Amanda Plummer
Charlie Greening	Francis Capra
Hortense	Ruby Dee
Rena	Teri Garr
Tony Sable	Alan Campbell
Lord Richard	Jonathan Hadary
Jeri	Deborah Odell
Duane	Lanny Flaherty
Ms. Bramble	Clare Coulter
Manny	Neil Foster
Joe	Jaime Tirelli
Officer O'York	Jack McGee
Schoolgirls	Lillian Ritchie, Miriam Ritchie
Tony's Agent	David Crean
Grocer	Kwok-Wing Leung

and H.D. Trayer, Sabine Thomson, Peter Linari, Maja Niles (German Tourists), Bunty Webb, Valerie Boyle, Barbara Stewart, Kathryn Kirkpatrick (Fairy Godmothers), Adam David (Sable's Chauffeur), Rick Fox (Pianist), Derek Carkner (Shaw's Assistant), Henry Gomez (Investor), Frank Cee (Vendor), John Douglas Williams (Paperboy)

Anabel Greening, desperate to help her father land a part in a Broadway musical, calls on her fairy godmother for help and ends up with a bumbler named Murray.

© Universal City Studios/ The Bubble Factory

Kathleen Turner, Mara Wilson, Martin Short

4 LITTLE GIRLS

(HBO/40 ACRES AND A MULE) Producers, Spike Lee, Sam Pollard; Director, Spike Lee; Photography, Ellen Kuras; Music, Terence Blanchard; Editor, Sam Pollard; Associate Producer, Michele Forman; Color; Not rated; 102 minutes; July release.

A documentary on four Birmingham, Alabama school girls who, in September of 1963, were killed when a terrorist bomb exploded in the basement of a Baptist church. This film received an Oscar nomination for feature documentary.

WITNESSES

Chris McNair, Maxine McNair, Helen Pegues, Queen Nunn, Arthur Hanes Jr., Bill Baxley, Howell Raines, Alpha Robertson, Wamo Reed Robertson, Harold McNair, Carole C. Smitherman Esq., Diane Braddock, Carolyn Lee Brown, Reverend Fred Shuttlesworth, Wyatt Tee Walker, Florence Terrell, Gwendolyn White, Doris Lockhart, Gerald Colbert, Dr. Freeman Hrabowski III, Nadean S. Williams, Shirley Wesley King, Carolyn M. McKinstry, David J. Vann, Reverend Andrew Young, Taylor Branch, Janie Gaines, Rhonda Nunn Thomas, Barbara Nunn, Reverend James Bevel, Tommy Wrenn, George Wallace, Nicholas Katzenbach, Lillie Brown, Billie Harris, Rickey Powell, Ossie Davis, Reverend John Cross, Barbara Cross, Morris Marshall, Junie Collins, Diane Nash, Faye Davis, Coretta Scott King, Walter Cronkite, Bill Cosby, Reverend Jesse L. Jackson Sr., Reverend Reggie White

Shirley Wesley King

GEORGE OF THE JUNGLE

(WALT DISNEY PICTURES) Producers, David Hoberman, Jordan Kerner, Jon Avnet; Executive Producer, C. Tad Devlin; Director, Sam Weisman; Screenplay, Dana Olsen, Audrey Wells; Story, Dana Olsen; Based upon Characters Developed by Jay Ward; Photography, Tom Ackerman; Designer, Stephen Marsh; Editors, Stuart Pappé Roger Bondelli; Visual Effects, Dream Quest Images; Special Creature Effects, Jim Henson's Creature Shop; Co-Producer, Lou Arkoff; Music, Marc Shaiman; Title song by Stan Worth and Sheldon Allman/Performed by the Presidents of the United States of America; Costumes, Lisa Jensen; Casting, Amanda Mackey Johnson, Cathy Sandrich; a Mandeville Films, Avnet/Kerner production; Distributed by Buena Vista Pictures; Dolby Digital Stereo; Color; Rated PG; 89 minutes; July release

CAST

George	Brendan Fraser
Ursula Stanhope	Leslie Mann
Lyle Van de Groot	Thomas Haden Church
Kwame	Richard Roundtree
Max	Greg Cruttwell
Thor	Abraham Benrubi
Beatrice Stanhope	Holland Taylor
Betsy	Kelly Miller
Arthur Stanhope	John Bennett Perry
Voice of an Ape Named "Ape"	John Cleese
N'Dugu	Michael Chinyamurindi
Kip	Abdoulaye N'Gom
Bateke	Lydell Cheshier
The Narrator	Keith Scott
Guests at Party	Spencer Garrett, Jon Pennell
Ursula's Friends	Lauren Bowles, Afton Smith, Samantha Harris
Lion	Joseph, Kaleb, Bongo
Shep	Tai
Tookie	Tookie, Scooper, Hopper
Little Monkey	Binx, Zachery, Emely
Ape Body Actor	Nameer El-Kadi
Jailer	Rodney Johnson

and Hans Schoeber, Alexander Denk, Sven-Ole-Thorsen (Mercenaries); Peter F. Giddings, C.C.M. (TV Weatherman), Terilyn Joe (TV Anchor), Michel Camus (Cameraman), Valerie Perri (TV Reporter), Mayor Willie L. Brown, Jr. (Himself), Carrie Zanoline (Perfume Lady), Garrett Griffin (Fireboat Captain), Harve Cook, Aristide Sumatra (Bongo Drummers at Dance Studio), Noah John Cardoza, Benjamin John Cardoza (George, Jr.), Tom Fisher, Philip Tan, Jody St. Michael, Leif Tilden (Gorilla Body Actors)

George, a young man raised in the jungle by animals, falls in love with career woman Ursula on an expedition with her fiancee to capture the "great white ape." Based on the animated series on ABC from 1967 to 1970.

Brendan Fraser, Leslie Mann

Brendan Fraser

Thomas Haden Church, Greg Cruttwell, Abraham Benrubi

Brendan Fraser, Ape

Tim Robbins, Martin Lawrence

NOTHING TO LOSE

(TOUCHSTONE) Producers, Martin Bregman, Dan Jinks, Michael Bregman; Executive Producer, Louis A. Stroller; Director/Screenplay, Steve Oedekerk; Photography, Donald E. Thorin; Designer, Maria Caso; Editor, Malcolm Campbell; Music, Robert Folk; Casting, Gretchen Rennell Court; a Bergman production; Distributed by Buena Vista Pictures; Dolby Digital Stereo; Panavision; Technicolor; Rated R; 97 minutes; July release

CAST

Kelly Preston, Tim Robbins

T. Paul ....Martin Lawrence
Nick Beam ....Tim Robbins
Davis "Rig" Lanlow ....John C. McGinley
Charlie Dunt ....Giancarlo Esposito
Ann ....Kelly Preston
Phillip Barrow ....Michael McKean
Danielle ....Rebecca Gayheart
Delores..Susan Barnes
Bertha ....Irma P. Hall
Lisa ....Samaria Graham
Joey ....Marcus Paulk
Tonya ....Penny Bae Bridges
Security Guard Baxter ....Steve Oedekerk
Grace...Mary Jo Keenen
Emma ....Lisa Mende
Alan...Clark Reiner
Zach ....Ned Gill
Henry...Patrick Cranshaw
Sheriff ....Randy Oglesby
Sheriff Officer #1 ....Steven M. Porter
Hillbilly Attendant ....Robert Louis Kempf
English Driver...Dave Lea
LAPD Sergeant...Dan Martin
LAPD Officer...Lance August
Security Guard..Joe Minjares
Overweight Security Guard ....Carl Sundstrom
Manny..Hank Garrett
and Selma Stern (Old Woman in Elevator), Caroline Keenan (Ann's Sister), Jim Meskimen (Business Suit Man), J.J. Boone (Ginger), Kim Kim (Mary Ann), Jodi Jinks (Girl at Checkout), Willy Parsons (Truck Driver), Victoria Redstall (Woman in Bar)

Giancarlo Esposito, Martin Lawrence, John C. McGinley

Nick Beam, at the end of his rope after finding his wife carrying on with his boss, meets up with a would-be carjacker, T. Paul, and promptly takes his attacker hostage.

© Touchstone Pictures

STAR MAPS

(FOX SEARCHLIGHT) Producer, Matthew Greenfield; Executive Producers, Esther Shapiro, Chris Iovenko, Scott King, Mitchell Kelly, Beth Colt; Co-Producers, Eden J. Shapiro, Ron Nyswaner, Kathleen Brown Corbin; Director/Screenplay, Miguel Arteta; Story, Miguel Arteta, Matthew Greenfield; Photography, Chuy Chavez; Editors, Jeff Betancourt, Tom McArdle, Tony Selzer; Designer, Carol Strober; Casting, Belinda Gardea; a Flan de Coco Films production in association with King Pictures; Dolby Stereo; Color; Rated R; 95 minutes; July release

CAST

Carlos	Douglas Spain
Pepe	Efrain Figueroa
Jennifer	Kandeyce Jorden
Teresa	Martha Velez
Maria	Lysa Flores
Letti	Annette Murphy
Martin	Robin Thomas
Juancito	Vincent Chandler
Fred	Al Vicente
Cantinflas' Ghost	Herbert Siguenza
Frank Rivers	Jeff Sanna
Bartender	Jeff Michalski
Carmel County Stage Manager	Beth Colt
Carmel County Writers	Zak Penn, Michael White
Star Map Boys	Luis Fernando Guizar, Alejandro Parra, Caesar Garcia, Elvis Saint Hilaire, Michael Peña
Carmel County Casting Director	Alisa Steen
Nanny	Anna Padgett
Hotel Guard	Danny De La Paz
Angry Customer	Mark Beltzman
Bel Air Woman	Hana Delaney
Bel Air Man	Bill Gordon
Young Carlos	Andrew Garcia
Jennifer's Son	T.J. Forster

and Kate Movius (Carmel County Actress), Joshua Fardon (Carmel County Actor), Adam Parker (Man Mistaken for Customer), Joe Mayesh (Guard at Gate), Michael Caldwell, Rachel Winfree (Tourists), Doug Kieffer (Waiter)

Young Carlos joins his family in Los Angeles where he is immediately forced by his father to work on the streets, using the cover of selling maps to the stars' homes while actually working as a prostitute.

© Twentieth Century Fox

Kenan Thompson, Shaquille O'Neal, Kel Mitchell

Douglas Spain

GOOD BURGER

(PARAMOUNT) Producers, Mike Tollin, Brian Robbins; Executive Producer, Julia Pistor; Director, Brian Robbins; Screenplay, Dan Schneider, Kevin Kopelow, Heath Seifert, based on their characters created for Nickelodeon's tv series "All That;" Photography, Mac Ahlberg; Designer, Steven Jordan; Editor, Anita Brandt-Burgoyne; Co-Producers, Diane Batson-Smith, Dan Schneider; Music, Stewart Copeland; Casting, Jaki Brown-Karman, Robyn M. Mitchell; a Tollin/Robbins production; Presented in association with Nickelodeon Movies; Dolby Stereo; Deluxe color; Rated PG; 97 minutes; July release

CAST

Ed	Kel Mitchell
Dexter Reed	Kenan Thompson
Mr. Wheat	Sinbad
Otis	Abe Vigoda
Monique	Shar Jackson
Mr. Bailey	Dan Schneider
Kurt Bozwell	Jan Schwieterman
Spatch	Ron Lester
Fizz	Josh Server
Deedee	Ginny Schreiber
Heather	Linda Cardellini
Himself	Shaquille O'Neal
Dancing Crazy	George Clinton
Huge Scary Man	Richard Haje
Angry Customer	Robert Wuhl
Corey	Corrie Harris
Connie Muldoon	Lori Beth Denberg
Jake	Marques Houston
News Reporter	Matthew Gallant
Customer	Teresa Ganzel
Upset Customer	Brian Peck
Troy	Hamilton Von Watts
Griffen	J. August Richards

and Kevin Kopelow (Sad Clown), Floyd Levine (Ice Cream Man), Brett Jones (Driving Attendant), Brad Wilson (Scared Customer), Melissa Spell (Frightened Customer), Andrew Aybar (Mondo Worker), Eve Sigall, Jo Farkas (Elderly Ladies), Paul Parducci, Kim Delgado (Police Officers), Wendy Worthington (Demented Hills Nurse), Chet Nichols, Carl A. McGee (Guards), David Shackelford, Rob Elk (Attendants), Carmit Bachar, Stella Choe, John Corella, Kelly Devine, Cindy Leos, Courtney Miller, Nezester Ponder, Chonique Sneed, Miranda Stamatelatos (Demented Hills Dancers)

Two high schoolers get jobs at a failing burger joint, Good Burger, causing a competitor at Mondo Burger to hound them for the recipe for their secret sauce.

©Paramount Pictures

AIR FORCE ONE

Gary Oldman, Harrison Ford

Harrison Ford

(COLUMBIA) Producers, Armyan Bernstein, Jon Shestack, Wolfgang Petersen, Gail Katz; Executive Producers, Thomas A. Bliss, Marc Abraham, David Lester; Director, Wolfgang Petersen; Screenplay, Andrew W. Marlowe; Photography, Michael Ballhaus; Designer, William Sandell; Editor, Richard Francis-Bruce; Visual Effects Supervisor, Richard Edlund; Costumes, Erica Edell Phillips; Music, Jerry Goldsmith; Casting, Janet Hirshenson, Jane Jenkins; a Beacon Pictures presentation of a Radiant Production; Dolby SDDS Stereo; Super 35 Widescreen; Technicolor; Rated R; 118 minutes; July release

CAST

President James Marshall ....Harrison Ford
Ivan Korshunov...Gary Oldman
Vice President Kathryn Bennett ....Glenn Close
Grace Marshall...Wendy Crewson
Alice Marshall ....Liesel Matthews
Chief of Staff Lloyd Shepherd ....Paul Guilfoyle
Agent Gibbs ....Xander Berkeley
Major Caldwell..William H. Macy
Defense Secretary Walter Dean ....Dean Stockwell
NSA Advisor Jack Doherty ....Tom Everett
General Alexander Radek...Jurgen Prochnow
Press Secretary Melanie Mitchell ....Donna Bullock
AFO Pilot Colonel Axelrod..Michael Ray Miller
AFO Co-Pilot Lt. Col. Ingrahams ....Carl Weintraub
AFO Navigator ....Elester Latham
Andrei Kolchak...Elaya Baskin
Sergei Lenski...Levani
Igor Nevsky...David Vadim
Boris Bazylev..Andrew Divoff
Vladimir Krasin ....Ilia Volokh
Major Perkins..Chris Howell
White House Aide Thomas Lee ....Spencer Garrett
General Northwood ....Bill Smitrovich
U.S. Attorney General Ward ....Philip Baker Hall
"Football" Colonel ....Albert Owens
White House Comm. Officer ....Willard Pugh
Assistant Press Secretary ....Michael Monks
Russian President Petrov ....Alan Woolf
Future Postmaster General ....Messiri Freeman
Steward Mike ....Thomas Crawford
Steward Joey ....Fenton Lawless
Notre Dame Aide ....Dan Shor
Agent Johnson...David Gianopolous
Agent Walters..Glenn Morshower
AFO Back-up Pilot ....Richard Doyle
F-15 Leader Colonel Carlton ....Don R. McManus
F-15 "Halo 2" Fighter Pilot...Duk Miglin
and Pavel D. Lychnikoff, Oleg Taktarov (Prison Guards), Mario Roberts, Keith Woulard, J. Mark Donaldson, Bruce Holman (Special Service Agents), Brian Libby (Chief Mechanic), Diana Bellamy (Switchboard Operator), Thom Barry (Ramstein S.O.F. Watch Officer), Harry Hutchinson (Ramstein Airbase Controller), E.E. Bell, Mark Thomson, Marciarose Shestack, Ren Hanami (Reporters), Suzanne Michaels (CNN Anchor), Boris Krutonog (MiG Leader), Alex Veadov (MiG Pilot), Allan Kolman (Kazak Soldier), Dan Barringer (USAF Jump Master), Jim Harley (Willis), Aleks Shaklin (Government Official), Igor N. Lobotsky (Russian Official), Koko Kiledjian (Russian Speaker), Gordon Michaels, Robert Peters, Kristian Sorensen (USAF Radio Specialists), Stuart Nixon (USAF Security), Marty Rosen (CIA Director), Lee Faranda (Russian Bad Guy), Mike Hambrick (CNN Reporter), Catherine T. Yang (Foreign TV Reporter), David MacIsaac (MC-130 Pilot), J. Scott Shonka, Paul Sklar (Pararescue Jumpers), David Permenter (Winch Recovery Master), David O'Donnell (Young Airman)

A terrorist group, demanding the release of a tyrannical Russian general, take the crew and passengers of Air Force One hostage, including the President of the United States. This film received Oscar nominations for film editing and sound.

© Columbia Pictures Industries

Glenn Close

Levani, Harrison Ford

Elaya Baskin

Jurgen Prochnow

Alan Woolf

Dean Stockwell

Wendy Crewson, Harrison Ford, Liesel Matthews

William H. Macy, Harrison Ford, Paul Guilfoyle

BOX OF MOONLIGHT

(TRIMARK) Producers, Marcus Viscidi, Thomas A. Bliss; Executive Producers, Michael Mendelsohn, Tom Rosenberg, Sigurjon Sighvatsson, Steven Sherman; Director/Screenplay, Tom DiCillo; Co-Producers, Meredith Zamsky, Taylor MacCrae; Photography, Paul Ryan; Designer, Therese DePrez; Editor, Camilla Toniolo; Costumes, Ellen Lutter; Music, Jim Farmer; Casting, Marcia Shulman; a Lakeshore Entertainment presentation of a Lemon Sky production; Dolby Stereo; Color; Rated R; 107 minutes; July release

CAST

Al Fountain	John Turturro
The Kid	Sam Rockwell
Floatie Dupre	Catherine Keener
Purlene Dupre	Lisa Blount
Deb Fountain	Annie Corley
Bobby Fountain	Alexander Goodwin
Wick	Dermot Mulroney
Doob	Mike Stanley
Doris	Rica Martens
Soapy	Ray Aranha
Dex	Robert Wightman
Taco	James Richardson
Elwood	Stephen Dupree
Lyle	Eugene Wolf
Luvven Coddle	Reathel Bean
Wynelle Coddle	Betty Wills Stephens
Curious Waitress	Linda Libby
Motel Clerk	Ernest R. Ogg
Earl Sykes	Gary Lowery
Willard Snarp	Bodi Soham
Barnett	Horace E. Smith
Stinky	Stuart Greer
Sheriff	John E. Davis
Newscasters	Gene Patterson, Kristin Hoke
Uncle Samson	Buddy Landel
Castroater	Chaz Warrington
Saddam Insane	Glenn Ruth

Questioning his life, electrical engineer Al Fountaine takes off on a journey of self-discovery where he befriends an offbeat dreamer named "The Kid" who lives by his own means in a trailer in the woods.

© Trimark Pictures

John Turturro, Sam Rockwell

Alexander Goodwin, John Turturro

Mike Stanley, Dermot Mulroney, Sam Rockwell,

Lisa Blount, Catherine Keener

AIR BUD

(WALT DISNEY PICTURES) Producers, William Vince, Robert Vince; Executive Producers, Michael Strange, Anne Vince, Bob Weinstein, Harvey Weinstein; Director, Charles Martin Smith; Screenplay, Paul Tamasy, Aaron Mendelsohn; Based on the character "Air Bud" created by Kevin DiCicco; Photography, Mike Southon; Designer, Elizabeth Wilcox; Music, Brahm Wenger; Editor, Alison Grace; Associate Producer, James A. Jusko; Line Producer, Michael Potkins; Buddy's Trainer, Kevin DiCicco; Casting, Abra Edelman, Elisa Goodman; a Robert Vince production presented in association with Keystone Pictures; Distributed by Buena Vista Pictures; Dolby Digital Stereo; Technicolor; Rated PG; 97 minutes; August release

CAST

Norm Snively	Michael Jeter
Josh Framm	Kevin Zegers
Jackie Framm	Wendy Makkena
Arthur Chaney	Bill Cobbs
Judge Cranfield	Eric Christmas
Referee 1	Jay Brazeau
Principal Pepper	Nicola Cavendish
Larry Willingham	Brendan Fletcher
Buck Willingham	Norman Browning
Coach Barker	Stephen E. Miller
Tom	Shayn Solberg
Greg	Chris Turner
Melissa	Christine Kennedy
Bailiff	Frank C. Turner
Reporter	Marian Dodd
Party Mom	Ursula Martin
Referee 2	Kevin DiCicco
Andrea Framm	Jessebel Mather, Kati Mather
Buddy/Air Bud	Buddy

A shy 12-year-old boy befriends a runaway dog who turns out to have an uncanny ability to play basketball. Sequel Air Bud: Golden Receiver was released in 1998 by Miramax with Kevin Zegers repeating his role.

Kevin Zegers, Buddy

Michael Jeter

Wendy Makkena

Kevin Zegers, Buddy

Kevin Zegers, Buddy

PICTURE PERFECT

Jay Mohr, Jennifer Aniston

(20TH CENTURY FOX) Producer, Erwin Stoff; Executive Producers, Williem Teitler, Molly Madden; Director, Glenn Gordon Caron; Screenplay, Arleen Sorkin, Paul Slansky, Glenn Gordon Caron; Story, Arleen Sorkin, Paul Slansky, May Quigley; Photography, Paul Sarossy; Designer, Larry Fulton; Editor, Robert Reitano; Costumes, Jane Robinson; Music, Carter Burwell; Casting, Mary Colquhoun; a 3 Arts production; Dolby Digital Stereo; Color; Rated PG-13; 100 minutes; August release

CAST

Kate Mosley ....Jennifer Aniston
Nick ....Jay Mohr
Sam Mayfair ....Kevin Bacon
Rita Mosley ....Olympia Dukakis
Darcy O'Neal ....Illeana Douglas
Mr. Mercer ....Kevin Dunn
Sela ....Anne Twomey
Mrs. Mercer ....Faith Prince
Jim Davenport ....John Rothman
Mrs. Davenport ....Margaret Gibson
Brad ....Paul Cassell
Ad Executives ....Ivar Brogger, Peter McRobbie, Bray Poor,
                                                      Daryl Edwards, Jenna Stern
Ad Agency Receptionist...Bellina Logan
Ad Agency Researcher..Sean Patrick Thomas
Pregnant Friend ....Andrea Bendewald
Rosie ....Marcia DeBonis
Darcy's Husband..Matthew Sussman
Anchor Person..Jim Ryan
Maitre D' ....Doug Easley
Snack Lady ....Ali Marsh
Watch Seller ....Richard Spore
Susan ....Amelia Campbell
The Maharishi ....Vimesh Thakar
Sajit ....Faran Tahir
Minister...David Cromwell
Bride..Jessica Cushman
Groom..Barry Del Sherman
Little Girl..Kaley Cuoco

When her friend invents a fiancee for Kate in order to impress her boss, Kate asks a wedding photographer named Nick to pose as her boyfriend to carry on the deception.

© Twentieth Century Fox

Kevin Bacon, Jennifer Aniston

Illeana Douglas, Jennifer Aniston

Olympia Dukakis, Jennifer Aniston

IN THE COMPANY OF MEN

Matt Malloy, Aaron Eckhart

(SONY CLASSICS) Producers, Mark Archer, Stephen Pevner; Director/Screenplay, Neil LaBute; Photography, Tony Hettinger; Editor, Joel Plotch; Music, Ken Williams, Karel Roessingh; Executive Producers, Toby Gaff, Mark Hart, Matt Malloy; Line Producer, Lisa Bartels; Designer, Julia Henkel; a Stephen Pevner/Atlantis Entertainment production in association with Fair and Square productions; Color; Rated R; 93 minutes; August release

CAST

Chad	Aaron Eckhart
Christine	Stacy Edwards
Howard	Matt Malloy
Co-Workers	Michael Martin, Chris Hayes
John	Mark Rector
Intern	Jason Dixie
Suzanne	Emily Cline

Two businessmen, frustrated at their recent failed relationships with women, decide to get revenge by romancing and then dumping a deaf temp in their office.

Jason Dixie, Aaron Eckhart

Aaron Eckhart, Matt Malloy

Stacy Edwards, Aaron Eckhart

Aaron Eckhart, Stacy Edwards

John Leguizamo, Martin Sheen

Michael Jai White

SPAWN

(NEW LINE CINEMA) Producer, Clint Goldman; Executive Producers, Todd McFarlane, Alan C. Blomquist; Director, Mark A.Z. Dippé; Screenplay, Alan McElroy; Screen Story, Alan McElroy, Mark A.Z. Dippé Based on the comic book by Todd McFarlane; Co-Executive Producers, Brian Witten, Adrianna AJ Cohen; Photography, Guillermo Navarro; Designer, Philip Harrison; Costumes, Dan Lester; Editor, Michael N. Knue; Visual Effects Supervisor, Steve "Spaz" Williams; ILM Animation Supervisor, Dennis Turner; Special Make-Up and Animatronic Creature Effects, Robert Kurtzman, Gregory Nicotero, Howard Berger; a Dippé Goldman Williams production, presented in association with Todd McFarlane Entertainment; SDDS Stereo; Fujicolor; Rated PG-13; 97 minutes; August release

CAST

Al Simmons/Spawn	Michael Jai White
Clown	John Leguizamo
Jason Wynn	Martin Sheen
Wanda	Theresa Randle
Cogliostro	Nicol Williamson
Terry Fitzgerald	D.B. Sweeney
Jessica Priest	Melinda Clarke
Zack	Miko Hughes
Cyan	Sydni Beaudoin
Zack's Dad	Michael Papajohn
Voice of The Devil Malebolgia	Frank Welker
XNN Reporter	Robia LaMorte
News Anchor	Caroline Gibson
African Liaisons	John Cothran, Jr., Tony Haney
Punks	Marc Robinson, Chris Coppola, Jay Caputo
Security Guard	Darryl Warren
Foreign Dignitaries	Mike Akrawi, Romeo Akrawi
Doctor	Jack Coleman
Angela	Laura Stepp
Anesthesiologist	Garrison Singer
Alley Bum	Todd McFarlane

Nicol Williamson   Michael Jai White

Five years after his murder Al Simmons makes a pact with the devil to return from the dead as the leader of Hell's Army in order that he might see his wife. Once on Earth he is torn between two different mysterious figures, one encouraging him to rebel against the devil and fight evil, the other prodding him to lead the Armageddon.

D.B. Sweeney

EVENT HORIZON

(PARAMOUNT) Producers, Lawrence Gordon, Lloyd Levin, Jeremy Bolt; Executive Producer, Nick Gillott; Director, Paul Anderson; Screenplay, Philip Eisner; Photography, Adrian Biddle; Designer, Joseph Bennett; Editor, Martin Hunter; Visual Effects Supervisor, Richard Yuricich; Costumes, John Mollo; Music, Michael Kamen; Casting, Deborah Aquila, Jane Shannon-Smith (US), John and Ros Hubbard (UK); a Lawrence Gordon presentation of a Golar production, in association with Impact Pictures; Dolby Digital Stereo; Panavision; Rank color; Rated R; 95 minutes; August release

Kathleen Quinlan, Laurence Fishburne

CAST

Captain Miller ....Laurence Fishburne
Dr. William Weir ....Sam Neill
Peters..Kathleen Quinlan
Starck...Joely Richardson
Cooper...Richard T. Jones
Justin...Jack Noseworthy
D.J..Jason Isaacs
Smith..Sean Pertwee
Kilpack ....Peter Marinker
Claire..Holley Chant
Denny...Barclay Wright
Burning Man..Noah Huntley
Rescue Technician...Robert Jezek

When Event Horizon, a prototype spaceship that had mysteriously disappeared, abruptly reappears seven years later, a USAC rescue team is sent to find out who is sending a signal from the ship.

Jack Noseworthy

Laurence Fishburne, Sam Neill, Kathleen Quinlan, Jason Isaacs

Robert De Niro, Sylvester Stallone, Harvey Keitel

Peter Berg, Arthur J. Nascarella

Arthur J. Nascarella, Michael Rapaport

Robert De Niro, Sylvester Stallone

Janeane Garofalo, Sylvester Stallone

COP LAND

Sylvester Stallone, Ray Liotta

(MIRAMAX) Producers, Cary Woods, Cathy Konrad, Ezra Swerdlow; Executive Producers, Bob Weinstein, Harvey Weinstein, Meryl Poster; Co-Producer, Kerry Orent; Director/Screenplay, James Mangold; Associate Producers, Christopher Goode, Kevin King, Richard Miller; Photography, Eric Edwards; Editor, Craig McKay; Designer, Lester Cohen; Costumes, Ellen Lutter; Music, Howard Shore; Casting, Todd Thaler; a Wood Entertainment production; Dolby Stereo; Color; Rated R: 105 minutes; August release

CAST

Freddy Heflin	Sylvester Stallone
Ray Donlan	Harvey Keitel
Gary Figgis	Ray Liotta
Moe Tilden	Robert De Niro
Joey Randone	Peter Berg
Deputy Cindy Betts	Janeane Garofalo
Jack Rucker	Robert Patrick
Murray Babitch	Michael Rapaport
Liz Randone	Annabella Sciorra
Deputy Bill Geisler	Noah Emmerich
Rose Donlan	Cathy Moriarty
Leo Crasky	John Spencer
PDA President Lassaro	Frank Vincent
Detective Carson	Malik Yoba
Frank Lagonda	Arthur J. Nascarella
Berta	Edie Falco
Russell	Victor J. Williams
Hector (Medic)	Paul Calderon
Lassaro's Aide	John Doman
Delores	Deborah Harry
Medic #2	Vincent Larseca
Black Man	Oliver Solomon
Black Woman	Terri Towns
Thin Cop	David Butler
Young Cop	Brad Beyer
TV Cyril Johns	Charles Dumas
News Anchor	John Johnson
Mayor	Frank Pellegrino
Officer B	Robert John Burke
Officer V	John Ventimiglia
Tony (Wincing Cop)	Terry Serpico
Shondel	Method Man
Other Cop	Sean Cullen
Game Operator	Paul Herman
Monica	Mel Gorham
Spanish Woman	Graciela Lecube
Gordon	Chris Conte
Young Freddy	Anthony Citro
Young Liz	Alexandra Adi

and Mark Cassella (Fireman), Timothy Stickney (Window Yeller), Father William Kalaidjian (Police Chaplain), Sean Runnette, Michael Gaston (IA Detectives), BEn Ellerni (Little Kid with Gordon), David Diaz (Funeral Reporter), Tracy O, Emory (Video Canera OP (News Segment)) Robert Castle (Chaplain at Joey's funeral), Bruce Altman (Counsel Burt Kandel), Carly Fordham (Liz'z Daughter), Tony Giorgio (Ceremonial Officer), Kevin O'Sullivan (Head Pall Bearer/Flag Holder), Louis D'Alto (Exiting Cop), Sylvia Khan (Deli Lady), Ronn Munro (Chief of Police), John Henry (Officer in Alleyway), Richard Lisi (Officer in Alleyway "Charlie"), Hans Moody (Sergeant in Alleyway), Garry Pastore (Core Cop "Johnny B"), Tony Sirico (Toy Torillo), Peter Wise, P.J. Brown, Manuel Corrado, Jeffrey Kaufman, Europe Harmon, Rene Ojeda (Plaza Cops)

Annabella Sciorra, Sylvester Stallone

Across the river from New York in the quiet New Jersey town of Garrison, sheriff Freddy Heflin discovers that a young NYPD officer, involved in a cover-up scandal and thought to be dead, is actually being hidden by his uncle, Ray Donlan, one of the many cops residing in Freddy's jurisdiction.

© Miramax Films

Harvey Keitel, Robert Patrick, Arthur J. Nascarella

Angel David, Demi Moore, Gregg Bello

G.I. JANE

(HOLLYWOOD PICTURES) Producers, Ridley Scott, Roger Birnbaum, Demi Moore, Suzanne Todd; Executive Producers, Danielle Alexandra, Julie Bergman Sender; Co-Producer, Nigel Wooll; Director, Ridley Scott; Screenplay, David Twohy, Danielle Alexandra; Story, Danielle Alexandra; Photography, Hugh Johnson; Designer, Arthur Max; Editor, Pietro Scalia; Costumes, Marilyn Vance; Music, Trevor Jones; Casting, Louis Di Giaimo, Brett Goldstein; a Roger Birnbaum/Scott Free/Moving Pictures production, presented in association with Scott Free and Largo Entertainment; Dolby Digital Stereo; Panavision; Technicolor; Rated R; 125 minutes; August release

CAST

Lt. Jordan O'Neil	Demi Moore
Command Master Chief John Urgayle	Viggo Mortensen
Lillian DeHaven	Anne Bancroft
Royce	Jason Beghe
Theodore Hayes	Daniel Von Bargen
Chief of Staff	John Michael Higgins
Instructor Pyro	Kevin Gage
Instructor Johns	David Warshofsky
Cortez	David Vadim
McCool	Morris Chestnut
Flea	Josh Hopkins
Slovnik	Jim Caviezel
Wickwire	Boyd Kestner
Newberry	Angel David
Stamm	Stephen Ramsey
Miller	Gregg Bello
C.O. Salem	Scott Wilson
Blondell	Lucinda Jenney
Flag Officers	Ted Sutton, Gary Wheeler
Yeoman Davis	Donn Swaby
Goldstein	Jack Gwaltney
Duty Officer	Neal Jones

and Rhonda Overby (Civilian Secretary), Stephen Mendillo (Admiral O'Connor), Dan DePaola (Cook Compliments), Susan Aston (Civilian Girl), John Seitz, Kent Lindsey (JAGS), Bob Moore (WNM Reporter), Harry Humphries (Artillery Instructor), Michael Currie (Commission Speaker), Steve Gonzales (Press Hound), Arthur Max (Barber), Billy Dowd (Photographer), Duffy Gaver, Scott Helvenston (Instructors), Phil Neilson (Hostile Rat), Dimitri Diatchenko, David Bruce, David Overton, Hashem Shaalan, Chris Soule (Trainees), Joseph Merzak Makkar (Libyan Sentry)

Lt. Jordan O'Neil is recruited as a test case to be the first woman to train for the Navy SEALs.

Anne Bancroft, Demi Moore

Demi Moore, Jason Beghe

Viggo Mortensen, Demi Moore

Chris Tucker, Paul Sorvino, Charlie Sheen

Chris Tucker

Chris Tucker, Heather Locklear, Charlie Sheen

MONEY TALKS

(NEW LINE CINEMA) Producers, Walter Coblenz, Tracy Kramer; Executive Producer, Co-Producer, Chris Tucker; Co-Producer, Art Schaefer; Director, Brett Ratner; Screenplay, Joel Cohen, Alec Sokolow; Co-Executive Producers, Jay Stern, Amy Henkels; Photography, Russell Carpenter, Robert Primes; Designer, Robb Wilson King; Editor, Mark Helfrich; Costumes, Sharen Davis; Music, Lalo Schifrin; Casting, Valerie McCaffrey; Dolby SDDS Stereo; Super 35 Widescreen; Deluxe color; Rated R; 95 minutes; August release

CAST

Franklin Hatchett	Chris Tucker
James Russell	Charlie Sheen
Guy Cipriani	Paul Sorvino
Grace Cipriani	Heather Locklear
Pickett	Paul Gleason
Paula	Elise Neal
Barklay	David Warner
Connie Cipriani	Veronica Cartwright
Roland	Larry Hankin
Mercedes Owner	Robertson Dean
News Cameraman	Nathan Anderson
Carmine	Damian Chapa
Detective at Carwash	Richard Noyce
Cellmate	Faizon Love
Raymond Villard	Gerard Ismael
Prison Bus Guard	Ralph Odum
Debray	Frank Bruynbroek
News Anchor	Doug Llewelyn
Diner Cops	Jeff Brockton, Gary Price
Officer Williams	Dan Roebuck
Cabby at Pier	Vahe Berberian
Red Camel Doorman	Jon Chardiet
Store Owner	Tom Huff
Aaron's Bodyguard	Rosey Brown
Aaron	Michael Wright
Detective at Precinct	Kevin Lowe

and Marty Levy, Mark Benninghofen, David McLain (Ticket Customers), Tawny Little (News Reporter), Viveca Paulin (Auctioneer), Mojoe Nicosia (Carmine's Driver), Dexter Tucker, Norris Tucker (Aaron's Boys), Matthew G. Brandstein (Cameraman #2), Rance Howard (Reverend)

A headline-grabbing newsman draws attention to a con artist who has been wrongly accused of killing police officers during a prison break.

© New Line Cinema

SUNDAY

(CFP) Producers, Jonathan Nossiter, Alix Madigan, Jed Alpert; Executive Producers, D.J. Paul, George Pezyos; Director, Jonathan Nossiter; Screenplay, James Lasdun, Jonathan Nossiter; Photography, Michael Barrow, John Foster; Editor, Madeleine Gavin; Designer, Deana Sidney; Casting, Mali Finn; from Goatworks Films; Ultra-Stereo; Color; Not rated; 93 minutes; August release

CAST

Matthew/Oliver	David Suchet
Madeleine Vesey	Lisa Harrow
Ray	Jared Harris
Ben Vesey	Larry Pine
Scotti Elster	Joe Grifasi
Andy	Arnold Barkus
Abram	Bahman Soltani
Selwyn	Willis Burks
Subalowsky	Joe Sirola
Sam	Henry Hayward
David	Kevin Thigpen

and Chen Tsun Kit, Jimmy Broadway (Themselves), Young Joo Kim (Suky Vesey), Fran Capo (Judy, Madeleine's Friend), Spencer Paterson (Johnnie O)

A struggling British actress living in Queens, and a recently laid off accountant living in a homeless shelter, meet when she mistakes him for a famous film director.

© CFP Distribution

John Travolta, Robin Wright Penn

Harry Dean Stanton, Sean Penn

David Suchet, Lisa Harrow

SHE'S SO LOVELY

(MIRAMAX) formerly *She's De Lovely*; Producer, Rene Cleitman; Executive Producers, John Travolta, Gerard Depardieu, Sean Penn, Bernard Bouix; Co-Executive Producers, Bob Weinstein, Harvey Weinstein; Director, Nick Cassavetes; Screenplay, John Cassavetes; Co-Producer, Avram Butch Kaplan; Photography, Thierry Arbogast; Designer, David Wasco; Costumes, Beatrix Aruna Pasztor; Editor, Petra Von Oelffen; Music, Joseph Vitarelli; Casting, Matthew Barry; a Hachette Premiere & Cie production, in association with Clyde Is Hungry Films; U.S.- French; Dolby Digital Stereo; Research PLC Widescreen; Color; Rated R; 100 minutes; August release

CAST

Eddie	Sean Penn
Maureen	Robin Wright Penn
Joey	John Travolta
Shorty	Harry Dean Stanton
Georgie	Debi Mazar
Miss Green	Gena Rowlands
Kiefer	James Gandolfini
Saul	David Thornton
Jeanie	Kelsey Mulrooney
Lucinda	Susan Traylor
Cooper	Bobby Cooper
Leonard	John Marshall Jones
Nancy Swearingen	Chloe Webb
Avi	James Soravilla
Interns	James Bozian, Paul Johansson
Ticket Taker	Justina Machado
Lead Singer	Tito Larriva
Band Member	Tony Marsico
Taxi Driver	Ilya Brodsky
Lorenzo	Burt Young
Mario	Neill Barry
Attendants	Clayton Landey, Jason O'Malley

and Dennis Fanning, John Cundari, Noon Orsatti (Cops), Nina Barry (Helen Caldwell), Chris Kinkade (Security Guard), Kristina Malota (Rosie), Nicollette Little (Dolly), Lester Matthews (Black Dude), and Talia Shire

A wild and unstable married couple, Eddie and Maureen, lead a life on the edge until Eddie is arrested and put away. When he is released years later he is stunned to find that Maureen has remarried. Based on a script by the late John Cassavetes, the father of the director, Nick Cassavetes. Nick's mother, Gena Rowlands, also appears in the film.

© Miramax Films

HOODLUM

(UNITED ARTISTS) Producer, Frank Mancuso, Jr.; Executive Producers, Bill Duke, Laurence Fishburne, Helen Sugland; Co-Producers, Paul Eckstein, Chris Brancato; Director, Bill Duke; Screenplay, Chris Brancato; Line Producer, Vikki Williams; Photography, Frank Tidy; Designer, Charles Bennett; Music, Elmer Bernstein; Editor, Harry Keramidas; Costumes, Richard Bruno; Casting, Amanda Mackey Johnson, Cathy Sandrich; a Frank Mancuso, Jr. production; Distributed by MGM Distribution; DTS Stereo; Deluxe color; Rated R; 130 minutes; August release

Laurence Fishburne, Andy Garcia

CAST

Ellsworth "Bumpy" Johnson ....Laurence Fishburne
Dutch Schultz...Tim Roth
Francine Hughes...Vanessa L. Williams
Lucky Luciano ....Andy Garcia
Stephanie St. Clair ....Cicely Tyson
Illinois Gordon ....Chi McBride
Bub Hewlett...Clarence Williams III
Captain Foley ....Richard Bradford
Thomas Dewey ....William Atherton
Pigfoot Mary ....Loretta Devine
Sulie...Queen Latifah
Albert Salke ....Mike Starr
Jules Salke ....Beau Starr
Whispers ....Paul Benjamin
Bo Weinberg ....Joe Guzaldo
Lulu Rosenkrantz ....Ed O'Ross
Calvin...J.W. Smith
Tee-Ninchy ....Eddie "Bo" Smith, Jr.
Vallie...John Toles-Bey
Johnny "Figures" DiPalmero ....David Darlow
Lucky's Henchman ....Steve Pickering
Undertaker...Ellis Foster
Mr. Redmond ....Bill Henderson
Enrique "Henry" Miro...Juan A. Ramirez
Waldo...Kevin Morrow
Dutch's Driver ....Tony Fitzpatrick
Hobo...Robert Cornelius
Willie Brunder...Tab Baker
and Joe Van Slyke (Warden), Daniel Bryant (Hep-Cat Man), Don James (Piano Man), Sulanya "Sue" Conway (Miss Philmore), Paul Eckstein (Dutch's Thug), Christian Payton (Jimmy), Jackie Taylor (Mrs. Andrews), Dick Gjonola (Owney Madden), David Nisbet (Man in Cotton Club), Nancy Nickel (Woman in Cotton Club), Ted Love, Kenya Cagle (Runners), Jim Saltouros (Lieutenant), Marc Vann (Dutch's Liquor Henchman), Cheridah Best (Prostitute), Colin Bradley Sylvester (Chee Chee), Iris Lieberman (Prison Guard), Leonard Roberts (Tyrone), John Watson, Sr. (Manager of Pool Hall), Lisa Botauzer (Dancer), Michael McCary (Osgood), Eric Kilpatrick (Security Guard), Demetrice O'Neal (Singer), Tony Powell (Rent Party Singer), Kevin Morrow (Church Conductor), Louis Price, Vernon Oliver Price (Church Singers), Laurnea Wilkerson (Cotton Club Singer), Tony Rich (Duke Ellington), Kim Adams (Show Girl), David A. Jansen (Doorman), Fred Nelson (Sideline Musician), Robert Keating, Charles Koysta, Joe Testa, Rocky McCord (Luciano's Mob Bosses)

Fictional look at the life of gangster Ellsworth "Bumpy" Johnson, who became king of the Harlem numbers racket during the 1930s.

Laurence Fishburne, Vanessa L. Williams

Laurence Fishburne, Cicely Tyson, Paul Benjamin, Eddie "Bo" Smith

EXCESS BAGGAGE

(COLUMBIA) Producers, Bill Borden, Carolyn Kessler; Director, Marco Brambilla; Screenplay, Max D. Adams, Dick Clement, Ian La Frenais; Photography, Jean Yves Escoffier; Designer, Missy Stewart; Editor, Stephen Rivkin; Co-Producer, B. Casey Grant; Music, John Lurie; Costumes, Beatrix Aruna Pasztor; Casting, Mike Fenton, Allison Cowitt; a First Kiss production; Dolby SDDS Stereo; Technicolor; Rated PG-13; 101 minutes; August release

CAST

Emily T. Hope	Alicia Silverstone
Vincent Roche	Benicio Del Toro
"Uncle" Ray Perkins	Christopher Walken
Alexander Hope	Jack Thompson
Greg Kistler	Harry Connick, Jr.
Stick	Nicholas Turturro
Gus	Michael Bowen
Detective Sims	Robert Wisden
Detective Barnaby	Leland Orser
Louise	Sally Kirkland
Jon	Hiro Kanagawa
Man on Pay Phone	Brendan Beiser
Surveillance Van Cop	Demetri Goritsas
Mini Mart Clerk	Jorge Vargas
Monique	Danielle Saklofsky
Car Showroom Receptionist	Stacy Grant
Motel Manager	Callum Rennie
Waitress at Diner	Carrie Cain Sparks
Waitress at Knotty Pines	Nicole Parker

and Bill Croft, C. Ernst Harth, Adrien Derval (Truckers), Claire Riley (Dream Reporter), Dean Wray (Barge Mate), Fulvio Cecere (Sharp Shooter), David Longworth (RV Gas Pumper)

Feeling neglected by her father, Emily Hope intends to fake her own kidnapping, only to be inadvertently abducted by professional car thief Vincent Roche.

Benicio Del Toro, Alicia Silverstone

LEAVE IT TO BEAVER

(UNIVERSAL) Producer, Robert Simonds; Executive Producers, Ben Myron, David Helpern, Lynn Arost; Director, Andy Cadiff; Screenplay, Brian Levant, Lon Diamond; Based on the tv series created by Bob Mosher and Joe Connelly; Photography, Thomas Del Ruth; Designer, Perry Andelin Blake; Editor, Alan Heim; Co-Producer, Kelly Van Horn; Associate Producer, Rita Smith; Costumes, Jean Pierre Dorleac; Music, Randy Edelman; Leave It to Beaver Theme (Toy Parade) by Dave Kahn and Melvyn Lenard; Casting, Joanna Colbert; a Robert Simonds production; DTS Stereo; Eastman color; Rated PG; 88 minutes; August release

CAST

Ward Cleaver	Christopher McDonald
June Cleaver	Janine Turner
Theodore "Beaver" Cleaver	Cameron Finley
Wally Cleaver	Erik von Detten
Eddie Haskell	Adam Zolotin
Aunt Martha	Barbara Billingsley
Eddie Haskell, Sr.	Ken Osmond
Karen Connelly	Erika Christensen
Frank	Frank Bank
Fred Rutherford	Alan Rachins
Larry Mondello	E.J. De La Pena
Lumpy	Justin Restivo
Coach Gordon	Geoff Pierson
Gilbert Bates	Louis Martin Braga III
Punk	Glenn Harris, Jr.
Miss Landers	Grace Phillips
Richard Rickover	Sam Gifaldi

and Brighton Hertford (Judy Hensler), Shirley Prestia (Claire Hensler), Brenda Song (Susan), Fran Bennett (Dr. Beaumont), Wendy Walsh (Reporter), Lindsay Boyd (Lusty Girl), Heather Lauren Olson (Tamara), Matthew Thomas Carey (Kyle), George Fisher (Bert the Pie Man), Kate C. Sklar (Cute Girl), Darryl Smith (Referee)

Beaver Cleaver sets his sights on getting a bicycle for his eighth birthday. Based on the ABC tv series that ran from 1958 to 1963 and starred Hugh Beaumont (Ward), Barbara Billingsley (June), Tony Dow (Wally), and Jerry Mathers (Beaver). The follow-up series, Still the Beaver/The New Leave It to Beaver ran on cable stations from 1986 to 1989 and was created by this film's writer, Brian Levant. Billingsley, Ken Osmond (the original Eddie Haskell), and Frank Bank (Lumpy Rutherford) from the original series also appear in this film.

Erik von Detten, Cameron Finley, Christopher McDonald, Janine Turner

MIMIC

(MIRAMAX) Producers, Bob Weinstein, B.J. Rack, Ole Bornedal; Executive Producer, Michael Phillips; Director, Guillermo Del Toro; Screenplay/Screen Story, Matthew Robbins, Guillermo Del Toro; Based on the short story by Donald A. Wolheim; Co-Producers, Gary Granat, Richard Potter, Andrew Rona, Scott Shiffman, Michael Zoumas; Photography, Dan Laustsen; Designer, Carol Spier; Editor, Patrick Lussier; Music, Marco Beltrami; Visual Effects Supervisor, Brian M. Jennings; Creatures Created by Rick Lazzarini/The Character Shop; Creature Designers, Rob Bottin, Tyruben Ellingson; Costumes, Marie-Sylvie Deveau; Casting, Billy Hopkins, Suzanne Smith, Kerry Barden; a Dimension Films presentation; Dolby Digital Stereo; Color; Rated R: 105 minutes; August release

Charles S. Dutton, Giancarlo Giannini, Mira Sorvino, Jeremy Northam

CAST

Susan Tyler	Mira Sorvino
Peter Mann	Jeremy Northam
Chuy	Alexander Goodwin
Manny	Giancarlo Giannini
Leonard	Charles S. Dutton
Josh	Josh Brolin
Remy	Alix Koromzay
Dr. Gates	F. Murray Abraham
Ricky	James Costa
Davis	Javon Barnwell
Jeremy	Norman Reedus
Preacher	Pak-Kwong Ho
Yang	Glen Bang
Chinese Woman	Margaret Ma
Bag Lady	Warna Fisher
Skeletal Bum	Alan Argue
Homeless Man	Charles Hayter
Workman	Julian Richings
Subway Repairman	James Kidnie
Homeless Woman	Eve English
Long John	Bill Lasovich, Doug Jones, Roger Clown

A pair of scientists, Susan Tyler and Peter Mann, successfully eradicate a life-threatening epidemic by coming up with a biological counteragent to the carrier of the disease. Years later they realize that they have inadvertently created a breed of giant insect-like creatures that are living under New York City.

Giancarlo Giannini, Jeremy Northam, Charles S. Dutton

Josh Brolin

Mira Sorvino

THE KEEPER

(KINO INTERNATIONAL) Producer, Jordi Torrent, Joe Brewster; Director/Screenplay, Joe Brewster; Co-Producer, Giancarlo Esposito; Executive Producers, Juan Amalbert, Forrest Murray; Co-Executive Producer, Marcia Shulman; Photography, Igor Sunara; Designer, Flavia Galuppo; Art Director, Tom Jarmusch; Music, John Petersen; Editor, Tom McArdle; a Rada Films production; Color; Not rated; 90 minutes; September release

CAST

Paul Lamont	Giancarlo Esposito
Angela Lamont	Regina Taylor
Jean Baptiste	Isaach De Bankole
Clarence Ross	Ron Brice
Ron Baker	O.L. Duke
Officer Jones	Alvaleta Guess
Officer Santana	Sam E. Wright
Majhid	Shiek Mahmud-Bey
Officer Corvino	Victor Colicchio
Jimmy Johnson	Arthur French
Captain Walker	Jude Ciccolella
Officer Melendez	Liza Colon

and Cory Glover (Martin), Sixto Ramos (Wilson), Curtis McClarin (Joseph), Laurence Mason (Tony), Michael Kirby (Michael), Mitchell Marchand (Horton), Kenshaka Ali (Officer Williams), Gordon Joseph Weiss (Police Officer Guido), Oni F. Lampley (Mrs. Grant), Novella Nelson (Mrs. Lamont), Emile St. Lot (Mr. Lamont), Aaron Griffin (Young Paul), Diego Lopez (Jose), Jewdyer Osborne (Officer Smith), Lionel Bernard, Constance Bernard (Haitian Musicians), Rocco Iacovone (Hospital Doctor)

A prison guard, moved by the plight of a Haitian immigrant wrongly accused of rape, invites the man to move in with him and his wife.

Bill Pullman, Andie MacDowell

Loren Dean, Traci Lind

Giancarlo Esposito

Isaach De Bankole

THE END OF VIOLENCE

(MGM) Producers, Deepak Nayar, Wim Wenders, Nicholas Klein; Executive Producers, Jean François Fonlupt, Ulrich Felsberg; Director, Wim Wenders; Screenplay, Nicholas Klein; Story, Nicholas Klein, Wim Wenders; Photography, Pascal Rabaud; Designer/Costumes, Patricia Norris; Editor, Peter Przygodda; Music, Ry Cooder; Casting, Heidi Levitt, Monika Mikkelsen; a Ciby 2000 presentation of a Ciby Pictures/Road Movies/Kintop Pictures co-production; Dolby Stereo; Super 35 Widescreen; Deluxe color; Rated R; 122 minutes; September release

CAST

Mike Max	Bill Pullman
Paige	Andie MacDowell
Ray Bering	Gabriel Byrne
Doc	Loren Dean
Cat	Traci Lind
Phelps	Daniel Benzali
Six O One	K. Todd Freeman
Lowell	John Diehl
Frank	Pruitt Taylor-Vince
Brian	Peter Horton
Zoltan	Udo Kier
Ramon	Enrique Castillo
Kenya	Nicole Parker
Claire	Rosalind Chao
Mathilda	Marisol Padilla Sanchez
Call	Marshall Bell
MacDermot	Frederic Forrest

and Chris Douridas (Technician), Richard Cummings (Tyler), Soledad St. Hilaire (Anita), Sam Fuller (Louis), Sal Lopez (Tito), Ulises Cuadra (Jose), Aymara De Llano (Florinda), Mili Avital, Kevin Chesley, Teresa De La Riva, Rick Edwards, Russell Gethering, Mark Hardisty, Daryl Hemmrich, Irene Hilleary, Chris Howell, Anne Nielsen, Ailinda Camile Pena, Kerry Rossal, Virgil Smith, Krist Thompson (Featured Background Performers)

Surveillance expert Ray Bering, testing a network of hidden cameras to cut down crime in Los Angeles, witnesses the abduction of successful film producer Mike Max who has made millions from movies that dwell on violence. This was the last film credit of director-actor Samuel Fuller who died on Oct. 30, 1997.

THE GAME

(POLYGRAM) Producers, Steve Golin, Céan Chaffin; Director, David Fincher; Screenplay/Co-Producers, John Brancato, Michael Ferris; Photography, Harris Savides; Designer, Jeffrey Beecroft; Editor, James Haygood; Music, Howard Shore; Costumes, Michael Kaplan; Executive Producer, Jonathan Mostow; Casting, Don Phillips; a Propaganda Films production; Dolby DTS Digital Stereo; Super 35 Widescreen; Technicolor; Rated R; 128 minutes; September release

Michael Douglas, Deborah Kara Unger

CAST

Nicholas Van Orton	Michael Douglas
Conrad Van Orton	Sean Penn
Christine	Deborah Kara Unger
Jim Feingold	James Rebhorn
Samuel Sutherland	Peter Donat
Ilsa	Carroll Baker
Elizabeth	Anna Katarina
Anson Baer	Armin Mueller-Stahl
Nicholas' Father	Charles Martinet
Young Nicholas	Scott Hunter McGuire
Nicholas' Mother	Florentine Mocanu
Maria	Elizabeth Dennehy
Maggie	Caroline Barclay
Himself	Daniel Schorr
Power Executive	John Aprea
Obsequious Executive	Harrison Young
Cynthia, CRS Receptionist	Kimberly Russell
CRS Data Collecting Technician	Joe Frank
James the Bartender	James Brooks
New Member Ted	Gerry Becker
New Member Victor	Jarlon Monroe
Solicitor/Taxi Driver	Tommy Flanagan
Tubercular Commuter	Bill Flannery
Rattle Gatherer	Kathryn Jean Harris
Man in Airport	John Cassini
Ankles	Harris Savides
City Club Waiter	Aaron Thomas Luchich
City Club Maitre D'	Victor Talmadge
City Club Waiter	Marc Siegler
Heart Attack Performer	André Brazeau
Officer Hicks	Keena Turner
Paramedic Graves	Carlos Hoy
Paramedic Stern	Edward Campbell
Paramedic Kirkland	Sean Lanthier
Ambulance EMT	Curtis Vanterpool
Triage Doctor	Jay Gordon
Officer Walker	Jeffrey Michael Young
Pickpocket	Owen Masterson

and Yuji Okumoto (Nikko Hotel Manager), Hideo Kimura (Nikko Hotel Bellhop), Rachel Schadt (Nikko Hotel Maid), Mark Boone Junior (Shady Private Investigator), Joy Ann Ryan (Kaleigh Baer), Peter Davidian (Mr. Garcia), Jack Kehoe (Lt. Sullivan), Christopher John Fields (Detective Boyle), Linda Manz (Christine's Roommate Amy), Victor Ferrerira (Assassin Mobubbi), Duffy Gaver (Assassin Brodi), Robert J. Stephenson (Assassin Kartmann), Sean Moloney (Assassin Rankin), John Hammil (U.S. Embassy Counselor), Rachel Steinberg (Sheraton Desk Clerk), George Maguire (Sheraton Manager), Trish Sommerville (Hot Waitress), Jason Kristopher (Teen Thug), Lily Soh Froelich (New Moon Cafe Manager), Tammy Koehler (Tammy Fisher), Michael Lynwood (Michael Fisher), Alex Lynwood (Alex Fisher), Charles Branklyn (CRS Guard), Spike Jonze (Airbag EMT Beltran), Michael Massee (Airbag EMT Galliano), Sara Davallou (Rachel), Stephen Cowee (Mel)

Sean Penn

Successful but stuffy businessman Nicholas Van Orton is signed up to be part of a "game" conducted by a mysterious organization and soon finds that his life is thrown into an uproar from which there appears to be no escape.

© PolyGram Films

Michael Douglas

Joan Cusack, Kevin Kline

Kevin Kline

IN & OUT

(PARAMOUNT) Producer, Scott Rudin; Executive Producer, Adam Schroeder; Director, Frank Oz; Screenplay, Paul Rudnick; Co-Producer, G. Mac Brown; Photography, Rob Hahn; Designer, Ken Adam; Editors, Dan Hanley, John Jympson; Costumes, Ann Roth; Music, Marc Shaiman; Casting, Margery Simkin; a Scott Rudin production, presented in association with Spelling Films; Dolby Digital Stereo; Deluxe color; Rated PG-13; 90 minutes; September release

CAST

Howard Brackett..Kevin Kline
Emily Montgomery ....Joan Cusack
Peter Malloy ....Tom Selleck
Cameron Drake..Matt Dillon
Berniece Brackett ....Debbie Reynolds
Frank Brackett ....Wilford Brimley
Tom Halliwell ....Bob Newhart
Walter Brackett ....Gregory Jbara
Sonya..Shalom Harlow
Jack..Shawn Hatosy
Mike ....Zak Orth
Vicky..Lauren Ambrose
Meredith..Alexandra Holden
Ed Kenrow ....Lewis J. Stadlen
Ava Blazer ....Deborah Rush
Trina Paxton ....J. Smith-Cameron
Aunt Becky ....Kate McGregor Stewart
Mrs. Lester ....Debra Monk
Aldo Hooper ....Ernie Sabella
Voice on "Be a Man" Tape ....John Cunningham
Danny ....Gus Rogerson
Military Attorney...Dan Hedaya
Father Tim ....Joseph Maher
Fred Mooney..William Parry
Emmett Wilson ....William Duell
Reverend Morgan ....Richard Woods
Carl Mickley ....Kevin Chamberlin
and Wally Dunn (Cousin Lenny), Larry Clarke (Cousin Ernie), June Squibb (Cousin Gretchen), Alice Drummond (Aunt Susan), Mary Diveny (Cousin Ellen), Anne Russell (Aunt Marge), Patrick Garner (Stan Forrest), Adam LeFevre, Bill Camp, Scott Robertson, John Christopher Jones, MacIntyre Dixon (Bachelor Party Guests), Joanna Wolff (Jennifer the Flower Girl), Chris I. McKenna, Mark Ballou, Charles Newmark, Andrew Levitas, Jonathan Michael Hershfield, Daniel Joseph, Seth Ullian, Greg Siff, Ryan Janis (Locker Room Guys), Jane Hoffman (Mrs. Baxter), Becky Ann Baker (Darlene), William P. Hoag (Bartender), Danny Canton (Cameraman), Selma Blair (Cousin Linda), Patricia Guinan (Billy's Mom), Nesbitt Blaisdell (Billy's Dad), Samantha Buck, Lauren Fox, Lizzy Mahon, Simone Marean, Michael McGruther, Niki Roma, Jacqueline Maloney, Patrick Mylod, Ginger R. Williams (Classroom Students), Joshua Wade Miller, Jill Horner, Lauren Ward, Julie Entwisle, Clare Kramer, Miranda Kent, Tara Carnes, Arden Myrin, Ian Sherwood, Kevin Keating, Kathy Lyn Cavanaugh (Students), Jo-Jo Lowe (Awards Event Model), Lisa Emery, Gary Dewitt Marshall (Classroom Reporters), Marla Sucharetza, Ronald Rand, Ross de Marco, Joanne DiMauro, Tony Jones, Grace DeSena, Bruce Bennetts, Tracy Appleton, Jim Taylor McNickle, Laura Caufield, Mimi Stuart, Dinah Gravel (School Reporters), Peter Barmonde (Wedding Photographer), Glenn Close, Whoopi Goldberg, Jay Leno (Themselves)

On the eve of his wedding, small town English teacher Howard Brackett finds himself the center of media attention when a former student "outs" him on national television at the Academy Awards ceremony. This film received an Oscar nomination for supporting actress (Joan Cusack).

Tom Selleck, Shalom Harlow, Matt Dillon

Kevin Kline, Bob Newhart

Kevin Kline

Kevin Kline

Kevin Kline, Tom Selleck

Wilford Brimley, Debbie Reynolds, Joan Cusack, Kevin Kline

GOING ALL THE WAY

(GRAMERCY) Producers, Tom Gorai, Sigurjon Sighvatsson; Executive Producers, Tom Rosenberg, Ted Tannebaum, Michael Mendelsohn; Director, Mark Pellington; Screenplay, Dan Wakefield, based upon his novel; Photography, Bobby Bukowski; Editor, Leo Trombetta; Designer, Therese Deprez; Costumes, Arianne Phillips; Music, Tomandandy; Line Producer, Mark Lipson; Casting, Ellen Chenoweth; a PolyGram Filmed Entertainment presentation of a Tom Gorai/Lakeshore Entertainment production; Dolby Stereo; Foto-Kem color; Rated R; 110 minutes; September release

CAST

Sonny Burns	Jeremy Davies
Gunner Casselman	Ben Affleck
Buddy Porter	Amy Locane
Gale Ann Thayer	Rose McGowan
Marty Pilcher	Rachel Weisz
Elwood Burns	John Lordan
Luke	Bob Swan
Alma Burns	Jill Clayburgh
Nina Casselman	Lesley Ann Warren
Conducter/Ticket Taker	Richard Gaeckle
Beautiful Young Girl	Teri Beitel
Wiater	Everett Greene
Religious Man	Jerry Panatieri
Blow Mahoney	Jeff Buelterman
Wilks	Nick Offerman

and Pat Daley, Charlie Webb (Meadowlark Residents), Wendy Carter (Deedee), Dave Webster (Crooner), Ted Steeg (Minister), Adrienne Reiswerg (Farmer's Wife), David Aikens, Dan Wakefield (Farmers), John Craig (Doctor), Cup a' Joe (Winkie the Dog)

Following military service, Sonny and Gunner, two decidely different young men, form an unlikely friendship as they begin to question the limitations life in Indianapolis has to offer them.

© Gramercy Pictures

Jeremy Davies, Ben Affleck

Rose McGowan, Jeremy Davies

Ben Affleck, Rachel Weisz

THE LONG WAY HOME

(SEVENTH ART) Producers, Rabbi Marvin Hier, Richard Trank; Director/Screenplay, Mark Jonathan Harris; Photography, Don Lenzer; Editor, Kate Amend; Music, Lee Holdridge; Associate Producer, Christo Brock; a Moriah Films of the Simon Wiesenthal Center presentation; Color; Not rated; 119 minutes; September release. Documentary the plight of the tens of thousands of Jewish refugees who survived the Holocaust; Narrated by Morgan Freeman; and featuring the voices of Edward Asner, Sean Astin, Martin Landau, Miriam Margolyes, David Paymer, Nina Siemaszko, Helen Slater, Michael York.

1997 Academy Award-winner for Best Feature Documentary.

©Seventh Art Releasing

THE MYTH OF FINGERPRINTS

(SONY PICTURES CLASSICS) Producers, Mary Jane Skalski, Tim Perell, Bart Freundlich; Executive Producers, James Schamus, Ted Hope; Director/Screenplay, Bart Freundlich; Photography, Stephen Kazmierski; Designer, Susan Bolles; Editors, Kate Williams, Ken J. Sackheim; Music, David Bridie, John Phillips; Associate Producers, Howard Bernstein, Anthony Bergman, Noah Wyle; Line Producer, Victoria McGarry; Costumes, Lucy W. Corrigan; Casting, Douglas Aibel, Christine Sheaks; a Good Machine production in association with Eureka Pictures; Dolby Stereo; Color; Rated R; 90 minutes; September release

CAST

Daphne	Arija Bareikis
Lena	Blythe Danner
Margaret	Hope Davis
Leigh	Laurel Holloman
Elliot	Brian Kerwin
Cezanne	James LeGros
Mia	Julianne Moore
Hal	Roy Scheider
Jake	Michael Vartan
Warren	Noah Wyle

and Randee Allen (Waitress), Justin Barreto (Young Jake), Chris Bauer (Jerry), Nicholas Bourgeois (Young Warren), Tom Cumler (Man at Train Station), Christopher Duva (Tom), Kelsey Gunn (Young Leigh), Polly Pelletier (Young Mia), Pamela Polhemus (Bookstore Woman), Michael Rupert (Warren's Psychiatrist)

Hal and Lena's grown-up children return home with their various partners for an uncomfortable Thanksgiving gathering that opens some old wounds.

© Sony Pictures Entertainment

Roy Scheider, Blythe Danner

Julianne Moore, Noah Wyle, Laurel Holloman, Michael Vartan

Donald Sutherland, Ben Kingsley, Aidan Quinn

THE ASSIGNMENT

(TRIUMPH) Producers, Tom Berry, Franco Battista; Executive Producers, David Saunders, Joseph Newton Cohen; Co-Producer, Stefan Wodoslawsky; Director, Christian Duguay; Screenplay, Dan Gordon, Sabi H. Shabtai; Photography, David Franco; Designer, Michael Joy; Editor, Yves Langlois; Music, Normand Corbeil; Digital Effects Supervisor, Richard Ostiguy; Casting, Mary Margiotta, Karen Margiotta, Lucie Robitaille; an Allegro Films production; Dolby SDDS Stereo; Color; Rated R; 115 minutes; September release

CAST

Annibal Ramirez/Carlos "The Jackal" Sanchez	Aidan Quinn
Jack Shaw (Henry Fields)	Donald Sutherland
Amos	Ben Kingsley
Maura Ramirez	Claudia Ferri
Carla	Céline Bonnier
KGB Head Officer	Vlasta Vrana
Agnieska	Liliana Komorowska
Koj	Von Flores
Carl Mickens—CIA	Al Waxman
Joey Ramirez	Mitchell David Rothpan
KGB Aide	Grégory Hlady
KGB Agents	Gabriel Marian Oseciuc, Frederic Desager
KGB Technician	Kliment Denchev

and Yonathan Gordon (Yoni), Ndiouga Sarr (Nigerian Oil Minister), Manuel Aranguiz (Venezuelan Oil Minister), Leni Parker (OPEC Receptionist), Jacques Lavallée (Du Foltiere—DST), David Francis (Naval Aide), Gouchy Boy, Tim Post (CIA Aides), Daniel Pilon (Admiral Crawford), Richard Jutras (Commander Scowcroft), Hisham Zayed (Libyan Customs Official), Ted Whittal (Norfolk Police Captain), Francis Delvecchio (Injured Paris Boy), Lisa Wegner (Berlin Lover), Lucie Laurier (Paris Lover), Neil Kroetsch (Ramirez' Father), Matthew Dupuis (Young Ramirez), Paul Stewart (Hospital Father), Claude Genest (Baseball Dad), Michael Caloz (Baseball Kid), David Franco (St. Martin Postman), Heinz Becker, Louis Bouchard, Mark Knoeffel, Andres Lange, Martin Morf (German Beerhall Singers)

Annibal Ramirez, a dead ringer for an illusive international terrorist called "The Jackal," is persuaded by two intelligence agents to impersonate his twin so that they can lay a trap and bring the killer out of hiding.

© TriStar Pictures

Jessica Lange, Michelle Pfeiffer, Jennifer Jason Leigh

A THOUSAND ACRES

(TOUCHSTONE) Producers, Marc Abraham, Lynn Arost, Steve Golin, Kate Guinzburg, Sigurjon Sighvatsson; Executive Producers, Armyan Bernstein, Thomas A. Bliss; Co-Producer, Diana Pokorny; Director, Jocelyn Moorhouse; Screenplay, Laura Jones; Based on the novel by Jane Smiley; Photography, Tak Fujimoto; Designer, Dan Davis; Editor, Maryann Brandon; Costumes, Ruth Myers; Music, Richard Hartley; Casting, Nancy Klopper; a Via Rosa/Prairie Films production, presented in association with Beacon Pictures and Propaganda Films; Distributed by Buena Vista Pictures; Dolby Digital Stereo; Panavision; Technicolor; Rated R; 104 minutes; September release

CAST

Rose Cook Lewis	Michelle Pfeiffer
Ginny Cook Smith	Jessica Lange
Larry Cook	Jason Robards
Caroline Cook	Jennifer Jason Leigh
Jess Clark	Colin Firth
Ty Smith	Keith Carradine
Peter Lewis	Kevin Anderson
Harold Clark	Pat Hingle
Ken LaSalle	John Carroll Lynch
Mary Livingstone	Anne Pitoniak
Charles Carter	Vyto Ruginis
Pammy	Michelle Williams
Linda	Elizabeth Moss
Marv Carson	Ray Toler
Doctor	Kenneth Tigar
Laren Clark	Steve Key
Henry Dodge	Dan Conway
Frank	Stan Cahill
Wallace Crockett	Ray Baker
Roberta	Beth Grant
Waitress	Andrea Nittoli

Larry Cook's decision to divide his thousand acre farm between his three daughters causes animosity within the family and brings some terrible past secrets to light.

Keith Carradine, Jessica Lange, Colin Firth

Jennifer Jason Leigh, Jason Robards, Keith Carradine

© ATA Films

THE EDGE

(20TH CENTURY FOX) Producer, Art Linson; Executive Producer, Lloyd Phillips; Director, Lee Tamahori; Screenplay, David Mamet; Photography, Donald M. McAlpine; Deisgner, Wolf Kroeger; Editor, Neil Travis; Music, Jerry Goldsmith; Costumes, Julie Weiss; Casting, Donna Isaacson; Bear Trainer, Doug Seus; an Art Linson production; Dolby Digital Stereo; Panavision; Deluxe color; Rated R; 117 minutes; September release

CAST

Charles Morse	Anthony Hopkins
Robert Green	Alec Baldwin
Mickey Morse	Elle Macpherson
Stephen	Harold Perrineau
Styles	L.Q. Jones
Ginny	Kathleen Wilhoite
James	David Lindstedt
Mechanic	Mark Kiely
Jet Pilot	Eli Gabay
Amphibian Pilot	Larry Musser
Reporters	Brian Arnold, Kelsa Kinsly, Bob Boyd
Jack Hawk	Gordon Tootoosis
Bear	Bart the Bear

Following a plane crash, billionaire Charles Morse finds himself stuck in the mountain wilderness with the man who has been carrying on with Morse's beautiful wife.

Anthony Hopkins, Bart

Alec Baldwin, Anthony Hopkins

Harold Perrineau, Alec Baldwin, Anthony Hopkins

Alec Baldwin, Elle Macpherson

(Standing) Vanessa L. Williams, Michael Beach, Jeffrey D. Sams, Vivica A. Fox, Morgan Méchelle Smith; (Seated) Irma P. Hall, Nia Long, Brandon Hammond, Mekhi Phifer

SOUL FOOD

(20TH CENTURY FOX) Producers, Tracey E. Edmonds; Executive Producer, Kenneth "Babyface" Edmonds; Director/Screenplay, George Tillman, Jr.; Photography, Paul Elliott; Designer, Maxine Shepard; Editor, John Carter; Music, Wendy Melvoin, Lisa Coleman; Co-Producer, Michael McQuarn; Line Producer, Llewellyn Wells; Costumes, Salvador Perez; Casting, Robi Reed-Humes; a Fox 2000 Pictures presentation of an Edmonds Entertainment production; Dolby Stereo; Deluxe color; Rated R; 114 minutes; September release

CAST

Teri	Vanessa L. Williams
Maxine	Vivica A. Fox
Bird	Nia Long
Miles	Michael Beach
Lem	Mekhi Phifer
Ahmad	Brandon Hammond
Kenny	Jeffrey D. Sams
Faith	Gina Ravera
Mother Joe	Irma P. Hall
Reverend Williams	Carl Wright
Simuel	Mel Jackson
Kelly	Morgan Méchelle Smith
Uncle Pete	John M. Watson, Sr.
Jada	M.T. Alexander
Harome	Lawrence Petty
Nicole	Marcia Wright
Dr. Benson	Bernard Mixon
Hamp	Hamp Clemons
Blimp	Theron Touché Lykes
Ahmad (age 4)	Martell Hill Edmond
Dread Man	Ras Majah Couzan

and James W. Boinski (Foreman), Mike Bacarella (Printing Company Owner), Joan Collaso (Choir Member #1), Donn C. Harper (Funeral Minister), George Brashear, Larry C. Tankson (Blimp's Henchmen), Austin Curtis (Family Member), Sylvester Phifer (Bartender), Malik Yoda (Studio Engineer), Kenneth "Babyface" Edmonds, Kevon Edmonds, Melvin Edmonds, Jo Jo Hailey, K-Ci Hailey, Simon Horrocks, Randy Walker (Band Members), Tamara Braun (Teri's Secretary)

The relationships of three sisters and their families are tested when their mother, who is instrumental in keeping them together, becomes ill.

Vanessa L. Williams, Nia Long, Vivica A. Fox

Nia Long, Mekhi Phifer

© Twentieth Century Fox

Vanessa L. Williams, Michael Beach

Irma P. Hall, Brandon Hammond

THE ICE STORM

Kevin Kline, Joan Allen

(FOX SEARCHLIGHT) Producers, Ted Hope, James Schamus, Ang Lee; Director, Ang Lee; Screenplay, James Schamus; Based on the novel by Rick Moody; Photography, Frederick Elmes; Designer, Mark Friedberg; Editor, Tim Squyres; Music, Mychael Danna; Costumes, Carol Oditz; Associate Producers, Alysse Bezahler, Anthony Bregman; Casting, Avy Kaufman; a Good Machine production; Dolby Stereo; Color; Rated R; 113 minutes; September release

CAST

Ben Hood	Kevin Kline
Elena Hood	Joan Allen
George Clair	Henry Czerny
Sandy Carver	Adam Hann-Byrd
Francis Davenport	David Krumholtz
Paul Hood	Tobey Maguire
Wendy Hood	Christina Ricci
Jim Carver	Jamey Sheridan
Mikey Carver	Elijah Wood
Janey Carver	Sigourney Weaver
Dorothy Franklin	Kate Burton
Ted Shackley	William Cain
Philip Edwards	Michael Cumpsty
Mrs. Gadd	Maia Danziger
Pharmacist	Michael Egerman
Marie Earle	Christine Farrell
Neil Conrad	Glenn Fitzgerald
Train Conductor	Tom Flagg
Ted Franklin	Jonathan Freeman
Weather Reporter	Babara Garrick
Stephen Earle	Dennis Gazomiros
Mark Boland	John Benjamin Hickey
Libbets Casey	Katie Holmes
Dot Halford	Allison Janney
Pierce Sawyer	Byron Jennings
Sari Steele	Colette Kilroy
Jack Moellering	Ivan Kronenfeld
Weatherman	Daniel McDonald
Mr. Gadd	Miles Marek
Maria Conrad	Donna Mitchell
Helen Wentworth	Barbara Neal
Claudia White	Nancy Opel
Dave Gorman	Larry Pine
Mikey's Teacher	Marcell Rosenblatt
Pharmacy Attendant	Wendy Scott
Woman in Pharmacy	Evelyn Solann
Marge	Jessica Stone
Beth	Sarah Thompson
Paul's Teacher	Scott Wentworth
Rob Halford	Rob Westenberg

Elijah Wood

In November of 1973 two families in suburban New Canaan, Connecticut experience the alienation and confusion of the sexual revolution as they loose communication with each other during an ice storm.

Christina Ricci, Tobey Maguire

Adam Hann-Byrd

Tobey Maguire, Joan Allen

Christina Ricci, Kevin Kline

Kevin Kline, Sigourney Weaver

Joan Allen, Jamey Sheridan

Sigourney Weaver

THE PEACEMAKER

(DREAMWORKS) Producers, Walter Parkes, Branko Lustig; Executive Producers, Michael Grillo, Laurie MacDonald; Director, Mimi Leder; Screenplay, Michael Schiffer; Photography, Dietrich Lohmann; Designer, Leslie Dilley; Editor, David Rosenbloom; Co-Executive Producer, John Wells; Costumes, Shelley Komarov; Music, Hans Zimmer; Co-Producers, Pat Kehoe, Leslie Cockburn, Andrew Cockburn; Casting, Risa Bramon Garcia, Randi Hiller; Dolby DTS Stereo; Super 35 Widescreen; Technicolor; Rated R; 122 minutes; September release

CAST

Thomas Devoe	George Clooney
Julia Kelly	Nicole Kidman
Dusan Gavrich	Marcel Iures
Alexsander Kodoroff	Alexander Baluev
Vlado Mirich	Rene Medvesek
Hamilton	Gary Werntz
Ken	Randall Batinkoff
General Garnett	Jim Haynie
Shummaker	Alexander Strobele
Appleton	Holt McCallany
CPN Beach	Michael Boatman
Senator Bevens	Joan Copeland
Santiago	Carlos Gomez
Dimitri Vertikoff	Armin Mueller-Stahl
Stevo	Slavko Juraga
Vassily	Alexander Peskov
Driver	Dejan Acimovic
Dr. Taraki	Harsh Nayyar
Alan	Matt Adler
Jody	Tamara Tunie
Russian Corporal	Alexander Yatsko
DOE Helo Tech	Bruce MacVittie
Pockman	Lubomir Paulovic
Branigan	Charles Dumas

and Ramsey Faragallah (Cabbie), Murphy Guyer (INS Agent), Leslie Dilley (Priest—NY), David Lomax, Blaise Corrigan, John Ottavio (FBI Agents), Adina Porter (NY Cop), Hubert Kramar (Kordech Guard), Alma Cuervo (UN Representative), Sabastian Roche (German Backpacker), Gordon Catlin (Gunner), Goran Visnjic (Bazta Sgt.), Jay Acovone (Cop), Hannah Werntz (Piano Student), James Colby (Limo Driver), Jean Rogers (CNN Rep—Sarajevo), Matt Winston (UN Official), Terry Serpico, Jerry Dixon (Snipers), Thom Mathews (Maj. Rich Numbers), David Lagle, Jerome Hardeman (Pilots), Lou Mustillo (Costello), Bozidar Smiljanic (Serb Minister), Michael Potts, Richard Poe (DOE Haz-mat Techs), Slobodan Dimitrijevic (Serb Official), Martin Nikodym (Polish IFOR Soldier), Charles Cavalier (Angry Motorist), David Hamilton Simonds (Philly Agent), Irmelin Mai Hoffer (Vienna Cafe Singer), Chuck Cooper (NYPD Cop), Jono Kouzouyan (Bazta Merchant), Jared Chandler (Marine), Evert Sooster (Praporshik), Branko Lustig (Man with Poodle), Matthew Sussman (National Guard Captain), Bill Christ (DOE Agent), William Hill (Agent), Bernie McInerney (Carey), Andrea Doven (Kelly Girl), James Dumont (Young Sniper), Mark Johnson (CIA Agent), Alexander Kuznetsov (Russian Controller), Ed Semenov (Radio Officer), Bruce Gray (CNN Newscaster), Endre Hules (Older Major)

Nicole Kidman, George Clooney

Marcel Iures

Armin Mueller-Stahl

A nuclear scientist and an army intelligence officer team up to track down the terrorists who have hijacked a nuclear weapon during a train crash. This film was the first release from DreamWorks Pictures.

George Clooney, Nicole Kidman

U TURN

(TRISTAR) Producers, Dan Halsted, Clayton Townsend; Director, Oliver Stone; Executive Producer/Screenplay, John Ridley, based on his book *Stray Dogs*; Photography, Robert Richardson; Designer, Victor Kempster; Editors, Hank Corwin, Thomas J. Nordberg; Music, Ennio Morricone; Costumes, Beatrix Aruna Pasztor; Co-Producer, Richard Rutowski; Casting, Mary Vernieu; a Phoenix Pictures presentation of an Illusion Entertainment Group production in association with Clyde is Hungry Films; Dolby SDDS Stereo; Technicolor; Rated R; 125 minutes; October release

CAST

Bobby Cooper...Sean Penn
Jake McKenna ....Nick Nolte
Grace McKenna...Jennifer Lopez
Darrell ....Billy Bob Thornton
Sheriff Virgil Potter..Powers Boothe
Jenny...Claire Danes
Toby N. Tucker ....Joaquin Phoenix
Blind Man ....Jon Voight
Bikers ....Abraham Benrubi, Richard Rutowski
Jamilla..Aida Linares
Boy in Grocery Store ....Sean Stone
Sergi ....Ilia Volokh
Mr. Arkady ....Valery Nikolaev
Boyd ....Brent Briscoe
Ed ....Bo Hopkins
Flo ....Julie Hagerty
Short Order Cook...Annie Mei-Ling Tien
Grace's Mother ....Sheri Foster
Bus Station Clerk ....Laurie Metcalf
Girl in Bus Station ....Liv Tyler

On his way to Vegas to pay off his gambling debts, Bobby Cooper's car breaks down in a dead end town called Superior, Arizona, where he unwittingly becomes involved with several of its strange inhabitants.

Jennifer Lopez, Sean Penn

Billy Bob Thornton

Nick Nolte

Jon Voight, Sean Penn

Joaquin Phoenix, Claire Danes

KISS THE GIRLS

Cary Elwes, Alex McArthur, Morgan Freeman

Morgan Freeman

(PARAMOUNT) Producers, David Brown, Joe Wizan; Executive Producer, C.O. Erickson; Director, Gary Fleder; Screenplay, David Klass; Based on the novel by James Patterson; Photography, Aaron Schneider; Designer, Nelson Coates; Editors, William Steinkamp, Harvey Rosenstock; Costumes, Abigail Murray; Music, Mark Isham; Casting, Deborah Aquila, Jane Shannon-Smith; a David Brown/Joe Wizan production, presented in association with Rysher Entertainment; Dolby Digital Stereo; Panavision; Deluxe color; Rated R; 119 minutes; October release

CAST

Alex Cross	Morgan Freeman
Kate Mctiernan	Ashley Judd
Nick Ruskin	Cary Elwes
Sikes	Alex McArthur
Will Rudolph	Tony Goldwyn
Kyle Craig	Jay O. Sanders
Sampson	Bill Nunn
Chief Hatfield	Brian Cox
Seth Samuel	Richard T. Jones
Dr. Ruocco	Roma Maffia
Henry Castillo	Jeremy Piven
Naomi Cross	Gina Ravera
Dr. Wick Sachs	William Converse-Roberts
Nana Cross	Helen Martin
Janell Cross	Tatyana M. Ali
Coty Pierce	Mena A. Suvari
Megan Murphy	Heidi Schanz
Sgt. Willard	Rick Warner
Instructor	Billy Blanks
Jennifer	Dianna Miranda

and Mary Major, Melinda Renna (TV Reporters), Angel Harper, Alan Wilder, Dan Cashman, Patrick T. O'Brien, Brenda Kincaid, Lonnie McCullough, Larry Cedar, Tresha Rodriguez, Caroline Case (Reporters), Loanne Bishop (Kate's Nurse), Tim Ahern (LAPD Sergeant), W. Earl Brown (Locksmith), Brian Brophy (Swim Team Manager), Michael J. Cutt (FBI Agent—Hospital), Meta Golding, Sadie Kratzig, Brandi Andres, Dana Atwood, Justina Vail, Nichole McAuley (Beautiful Girls), Tricia Vessey (Woman at Nepenthe Bar), John Cothran, Jr. (FBI Agent at Lair), Robert Peters (Agent on Robe), Jill Callaham (Reporter in Durham), Nancy Yee (Chinese Grandmother), Christina Ma (Chinese Mother), David Cowgill (Chief Resident), Weston Blakesley (Bellman), Joe Inscoe (Large Cop), Deborah Strang (Dianne Wainford), Robert Overmyer (Competitive Swimmer), Boise Holmes (Basketball Player)

When detective Alex Cross discovers that his niece has been abducted, he teams with Kate Mctiernan, who has escaped from the same kidnapper, to solve the mystery of the other victims' whereabouts.

© Paramount Pictures

Brian Cox, Cary Elwes, Morgan Freeman

Morgan Freeman, Ashley Judd

Jennifer Jason Leigh, Albert Finney

WASHINGTON SQUARE

(HOLLYWOOD PICTURES) Producers, Roger Birnbaum, Julie Bergman Sender; Director, Agnieszka Holland; Screenplay, Carol Doyle; Based on the novel by Henry James; Executive Producer, Randy Ostrow; Photography, Jerzy Zielinski; Designer, Allan Starski; Editor, David Siegel; Costumes, Anna Sheppard; Music, Jan A.P. Kaczmarek; Casting, Debra Zane; a Roger Birnbaum production in association with Ann Dubinet; Presented in association with Caravan Pictures; Distributed by Buena Vista Pictures; Dolby Digital Stereo; Technicolor; Rated PG; 115 minutes; October release

Ben Chaplin, Jennifer Jason Leigh

CAST

Catherine Sloper	Jennifer Jason Leigh
Dr. Austin Sloper	Albert Finney
Aunt Lavinia Penniman	Maggie Smith
Morris Townsend	Ben Chaplin
Mrs. Elizabeth Almond	Judith Ivey
Mr. Almond	Arthur Laupus
Marian Almond	Jennifer Garner
Arthur Townsend	Robert Stanton
Mrs. Montgomery	Betsy Brantley
Maureen (Maid)	Nancy Daly
Catherine Sloper (age 11)	Sara Ruzicka
Sarah Almond (age 16)	Rachel Layne Sacrey
Alice Almond (age 17)	Rachel Osborne
John Ludlow	Scott Jaeck
Jacob Webber/Notary	Peter Maloney
Edith	Lauren Hulsey
Therese (Maid)	Sara Constance Marshall
Paris Singer	Marissa Anna Muro
Midwife	Loretto McNally
Sloper's Cook	Eva Jean Berg
Engagement Party Pianist	David Hildebrand
Engagement Party Singer	James J. Waltz
Engagement Party Guest	Peter Klaus

Ben Chaplin, Albert Finney

Catherine Sloper, the plain and unpopular daughter of a wealthy physician, suddenly finds herself being courted by the handsome Morris Townsend who may or may not be wooing her for her fortune. Henry James' story was previously filmed by Paramount in 1949 as The Heiress (based on the stage play) and starred Olivia de Havilland (Catherine), Montgomery Clift (Morris), and Ralph Richardson (Dr. Sloper).

Ben Chaplin, Jennifer Jason Leigh, Maggie Smith

FAST, CHEAP & OUT OF CONTROL

(SONY PICTURES CLASSICS) Producer/Director, Errol Morris; Co-Producers, Julia Sheehan, Mark Lipson, Kathy Trustman; Executive Producer, Lindsay Law; Photography, Robert Richardson; Editors, Shondra Merrill, Karen Schmeer; Designer, Ted Bafaloukos; Music, Caleb Sampson; a Fourth Floor Productions, Inc. production in association with American Playhouse; Color/Black and White; Rated PG; 82 minutes; October release

CAST

Wild Animal Trainer	Dave Hoover
Topiary Gardner	George Mendonça
Mole-Rat Specialist	Ray Mendez
Robot Scientist	Rodney Brooks

A documentary that looks at the oddball pursuits and professions of four different men.

© Sony Pictures Entertainment, Inc.

Dave Hoover

George Mendoça

Kate Capshaw, Vince Vaughn

THE LOCUSTS

(ORION) Producers, Brad Krevoy, Steve Stabler, Bradley Thomas; Director/Screenplay, John Patrick Kelley; Executive Producers, Adam Duritz, Beth Holden, Charles B. Wessler, Cynthia Guidry; Photography, Phedon Papamichael; Designer, Sherman Williams; Editors, Kathryn Himoff, Erica Flaum; Music, Carter Burwell; Costumes, Gail McMullen; Co-Producers, Bruce Franklin, Marc Ezralow; Line Producer, Garrett Grant; a Brad Krevoy & Steve Stabler production; Dolby Digital Stereo; Super 35 Widescreen; Deluxe color; Rated R; 124 minutes; October release

CAST

Delilah Ashford Potts	Kate Capshaw
Flyboy	Jeremy Davies
Clay Hewitt	Vince Vaughn
Kitty	Ashley Judd
Earl	Paul Rudd
Joel	Daniel Meyer
Patsy	Jessica Capshaw
Ellen	Jessie Robertson
Cameron	Jimmy Pickens
Harlan	Jerry Haynes
Wrangler	Jason Davis

Clay Hewitt, a drifter trying to escape from his past, takes a job on a cattle ranch run by the dominant and sensual Mrs. Potts who is responsible for the state of her emotionally crippled son, Flyboy.

© MGM Distribution/ Orion Pictures

Jeremy Davies, Ashley Judd

SEVEN YEARS IN TIBET

(TRISTAR) Producers, Jean-Jacques Annaud, John H. Williams, Iain Smith; Executive Producers, Richard Goodwin, Michael Besman, David Nichols; Director, Jean-Jacques Annaud; Screenplay, Becky Johnston; Based on the book by Heinrich Harrer; Photography, Robert Fraisse; Designer, At Hoang; Editor, Noële Boisson; Costumes, Enrico Sabbatini; Music, John Williams; Cello Solos by Yo-Yo Ma; Casting, Priscilla John, Francine Maisler; a Mandalay Entertainment presentation of a Reperage and Vanguard Films/Applecross production; Dolby SDDS Stereo; Panavision; Technicolor; Rated PG-13; 131 minutes; October release

CAST

Heinrich Harrer	Brad Pitt
Peter Aufschnaiter	David Thewlis
Ngawang Jigme	B.D. Wong
Kungo Tsarong	Mako
Regent	Danny Denzongpa
Chinese "Amban"	Victor Wong
Ingrid Harrer	Ingeborga Dapkunaite
Dalai Lama (14 years)	Jamyang Jamtsho Wangchuk
Pema Lhaki	Lhakpa Tsamchoe
Great Mother	Jetsun Pema
Tashi	Ama Ashe Dongtse
Dalai Lama (8 years)	Sonam Wangchuk
Dalai Lama (4 years)	Dorjee Tsering
General Chang Jing Wu	Ric Young
Lord Chamberlain	Ven. Ngawang Chojor
British Officer	Duncan Fraser
Nazi Official	Benedick Blythe
Lutz Chicken	Tom Raudaschl
Hans Lobenhoffer	Wolfgang Tonninger
The Garpon	Samdup Dhargyal
Garpon's Agent	Chemchok
Declaration Monk Official	Ven. Tenzin Jangchub
Tibetan General	Major Angphurba Sherpa

and Tsering Wangdue, Yama Nugdup Cheshatsang (Burly Guides), Kalsang Dhundop Lungtok (Vendor Ice Skates), Sonam Bidhartsang (Jacket Vendor), Lama Champa Tsondu (Watch Vendor), Geshe Lobsang Nyma (Ling Rinpoche), Geshe Yeshi Tsultrim (Trijang Rinpoche), Lama Champa Chandu (Dalai Lama's Room Attendant), Pemba Norbu Sherpa (Young Sherpa), Karma Apo-Tsang (Messenger to Great Mother), Ven. Ngawang Tenzin Gyatso (Jokhang Monk Official), Choeden Tsering (Military Instructor), Lama Jampa Lekshe (Monk Head of Security), Lama Thupten Nugdup (Head of Security's Aide), Daniel Tedeschi (Marchese), Gerardo Ebert (Horst Immendorf), Sebastian Zevalia (Rolf Harrer—younger), Philipp Kriechbaum (Rolf Harrer—older), Lobsang Gendun Rinpoche, Tenzin Gyaltsen Rinpoche, Sharpa Tulku Rinpoche, Zongra Tulku Rinpoche (Additional Tibetan Roles)

The true story of how Austrian mountaineer Heinrich Harrer escaped from a British prisoner-of-war camp and ended up befriending the young Dalai Lama in the Tibetan city of Lhasa.

David Thewlis, Lhakpa Tsamchoe, Brad Pitt

B.D. Wong

Jamyang Jamtsho Wangchuk, Brad Pitt

David Thewlis, Brad Pitt

THE HOUSE OF YES

(MIRAMAX) Producers, Beau Flynn, Stefan Simchowitz; Executive Producer, Robert Berger; Director/Screenplay, Mark Waters; Based on the play by Wendy MacLeod; Co-Producers, Ron Wechsler, Jeffrey L. Davidson; Photography, Michael Spiller; Designer, Patrick Sherman; Editor, Pamela Martin; Costumes, Edi Giguere; Music, Rolfe Kent; Co-Executive Producer, Scott Silver; Associate Producer/Casting, Mary Vernieu; a Spelling Films presentation of a Bandeira Entertainment production; Dolby Digital Stereo; CFI color; Rated R; 89 minutes; October release

CAST

Jackie-O Pascal	Parker Posey
Marty Pascal	Josh Hamilton
Lesly	Tori Spelling
Anthony Pascal	Freddie Prinze, Jr.
Mrs. Pascal	Genevieve Bujold
Young Jackie-O	Rachael Leigh Cook
Voice of Young Marty	David Love

Marty Pascal brings his fiancee Lesly to meet his wildly unconventional family, including his disturbed sister Jackie-O who is obsessed with the Kennedy assassination.

Genevieve Bujold, Tori Spelling

Tori Spelling, Parker Posey, Josh Hamilton, Freddie Prinze Jr.

Keenen Ivory Wayans, Jon Voight

MOST WANTED

(NEW LINE CINEMA) Producer, Eric L. Gold; Executive Producers, Keenen Ivory Wayans, Tony Mark; Director, David Glenn Hogan; Screenplay, Keenen Ivory Wayans; Photography, Marc Reshovsky; Designer, Jean-Philippe Carp; Editors, Michael J. Duthie, Mark Helfrich; Costumes, Ileane Meltzer; Music, Paul Buckmaster; Casting, Valerie McCaffrey; an Ivory Way production; Dolby SDDS Stereo; Super 35 Widescreen; Deluxe color; Rated R; 99 minutes; October release

CAST

Sgt. James Dunn	Keenen Ivory Wayans
Gen. Adam Woodward/Lt. Col. Grant Casey	Jon Voight
Dr. Victoria Constantini	Jill Hennessy
CIA Deputy Director Rackmill	Paul Sorvino
Asst. Deputy Director Spencer	Eric Roberts
Donald Bickhart	Robert Culp
Capt. Steve Braddock	Wolfgang Bodison
Stephen Barnes	Simon Baker Denny
SWAT Leader	Michael Milhoan
Commander Goldstein	Lee DeBroux
TV Station Manager	David Groh
Police Captain	John Diehl
Sergeant	Thomas G. Waites
Omega 3	Michael Marich
Lt. Scruggs	Dave Oliver
Sgt. Peyton	Eddie Velez

and Robert Kotecki (Marine Lieutenant), Rick Cramer, Kenn Whitaker (Bus Guards), Donna Cherry (First Lady), Tucker Smallwood (Police Chief William Watson), Amanda Kravat (Charlie), Mario Vitale (Bartender), Ping Wu (Patrolman), Andy Hogan (Video Tech), Casey Lee (Randy), Richard Noyce, Jerry Rector (Policemen in Hospital), Chris Geier (Laundry Orderly), Sasha Foo (Newscaster), Karen Folkes (Checkpoint Officer), Martin Grimes (Hot Dog Vendor), Benny Moore (Man on Street), Kaye Wade (Grocery Woman), L.V. Sanders, Tito Larriva (Gangbangers), Michael D. Roberts (Homeless Man), Vernon P. Thompson (Homeless Camp Police Officer), David Basulto (Library Security Guard), Melanie Van Betten (VA Hospital Clerk), Mitchell Marchand, Antonio T. Arnold, Jr., Ernie Lee Banks (Card Players), Brian Macon (C.I.A. Agent), Christine Devine (Hearing's Reporter)

Awaiting execution for killing an officer in self-defense, Gulf War veteran James Dunn is recruited by a secret government assassination squad called the "Black Sheep" and made to particpate in the killing of a black market industrialist.

I KNOW WHAT YOU DID LAST SUMMER

(COLUMBIA) Producers, Neal H. Moritz, Erik Feig, Stokely Chaffin; Executive Producer, William S. Beasley; Director, Jim Gillespie; Screenplay, Kevin Williamson; Based on the novel by Lois Duncan; Photography, Denis Crossan; Designer, Gary Wissner; Editor, Steve Mirkovich; Music, John Debney; Costumes, Catherine Adair; Casting, Mary Vernieu; a Mandalay Entertainment presentation of a Neal H. Moritz production; Dolby SDDS Stereo; Panavision; Technicolor; Rated R; 100 minutes; October release

CAST

Julie James	Jennifer Love Hewitt
Helen Shivers	Sarah Michelle Gellar
Barry Cox	Ryan Phillippe
Ray Bronson	Freddie Prinze, Jr.
Benjamin Willis/Fisherman	Muse Watson
Elsa Shivers	Bridgette Wilson
Melissa Egan	Anne Heche
Max	Johnny Galecki
Officer	Stuart Greer
MC	J. Don Ferguson
Mrs. James	Deborah Hobart
Mrs. Cox	Mary McMillan
Deb	Rasool J'Han
Sheriff	Dan Albright
Pageant Official	Lynda Clark
Contestants	Shea Broom, Jennifer Bland
Old Man	John Bennes
Hank	William Neely
David Egan	Jonathan Quint
Band Members	Richard Dale Miller, Mary Neva Huff, David Lee Hartman

A year after four teenagers secretly dispose of the body of a man they hit during a driving accident, they are taunted and stalked by someone who knows about their dirty deed. 1998 sequel I Still Know What You Did Last Summer also featured Jennifer Love Hewitt and Freddie Prinze, Jr.

Freddie Prinze Jr., Jennifer Love Hewitt, Sarah Michelle Gellar, Ryan Phillippe

Sarah Michelle Gellar, Bridgette Wilson

Sarah Michelle Gellar, Ryan Phillippe, Jennifer Love Hewitt

Sarah Michelle Gellar, Ryan Phillippe, Jennifer Love Hewitt, Freddie Prinze Jr.

Jack Wallace, Ricky Jay, Nicole Ari Parker, Burt Reynolds, William H. Macy, Mark Wahlberg, Julianne Moore, John C. Reilly, Philip Seymour Hoffman

Burt Reynolds, William H. Macy

Mark Wahlberg

Julianne Moore, Mark Wahlberg

John C. Reilly, Mark Wahlberg

BOOGIE NIGHTS

(NEW LINE CINEMA) Producers, Lloyd Levin, Paul Thomas Anderson, John Lyons, Joanne Sellar; Executive Producer, Lawrence Gordon; Director/Screenplay, Paul Thomas Anderson; Co-Producer, Daniel Lupi; Photography, Robert Elswit; Designer, Bob Ziembicki; Editor, Dylan Tichenor; Costumes, Mark Bridges; Music, Michael Penn; Casting, Christine Sheaks; a Lawrence Gordon production in associatiowith Ghoulardi Film Company of a P.T. Anderson Picture; Dolby SDDS Stereo; Panavision; Deluxe color; Rated R; 152 minutes,October Realease

CAST

Buck Swope	Don Cheadle
Rollergirl	Heather Graham
Maurice TT Rodriguez	Luis Guzman
Floyd Gondolli	Philip Baker Hall
Scotty J	Philip Seymour Hoffman
Kurt Longjohn	Ricky Jay
Little Bill	William H. Macy
Rahad Jackson	Alfred Molina
Amber Waves	Julianne Moore
Becky Barnett	Nicole Ari Parker
Reed Rothchild	John C. Reilly
Jack Horner	Burt Reynolds
The Colonel	Robert Ridgely
Dirk Diggler (Eddie Adams)	Mark Wahlberg
Jessie St. Vincent	Melora Walters
Jerry	Stanley DeSantis
Eddie's Mother	Joanna Gleason
Little Bill's Wife	Nina Hartley
Sheryl Lynn	Laurel Holloman
Jerome	Michael Jace
Todd Parker	Thomas Jane
Mr. Brown	Howard Morris
Rocky	Jack Wallace
Bank Worker	Don Amendolia
Colonel's Limo Driver	Jason Andrews
Hot Traxx Chef	Samson Barkhordarian
Big Stud	Brad Braeden
Sheryl Lynn's Husband	Kevin Breznahan
Hot Traxx Waiter	Rico Bueno
Puerto Rican Kid	Jose Chaidez
Rahad's Asian Kid or Cosmo	Joe GM Chan
Donut Boy	Dustin Courtney
Watchers	Tom Dorfmeister, Jake Cross
Minister	Gregory Daniel
Thomas	John Doe
Recording Studio Manager	Robert Downey, Sr.

and Patricia Forte (Teacher), Jamielyn Gamboa (Colonel's Girlflriend at Hot Traxx), Goliath (Tyrone), Allan Graf (Man with Gun), Laura Greenwood (Angie), Vernon Guichard II (Jack's Bartender), Michael Raye Smith, Mike Gunther, Michael Scott Stencil (Surfer Punks), Veronica Hart (Judge), Lawrence Hudd (Eddie's Father), Amber Hunter (Colonel's O.D. Girlfriend), Ron Hyatt (Jail Guard), B. Philly Johnson (Rahad's Bodyguard), Israel Juarbe, George Anthony Rae (Maurice's Brothers), Raymond Laboriel (Hot Traxx Patron), Greg Lauren (Young Stud), Loren Lazerine (Police Officer), Henry Lee (Tailor), Lexi Leigh (Amateur Actress), Thomas Lenk (Tommy), Kai Lennox (High School Kid), Selwyn Emerson Miller (Hot Traxx DJ), Michael Penn (Recording Studio Engineer), Jonathan Quint (Johnny Doe), George Anthony Rae (Maurice's Brother #2), Leslie Redden (KC Sunshine), Jack Riley (Lawyer), Channon Roe (Surfer), Skye, Summer (Jacuzzi Girls), Alexander D. Slanger (Pete), Melissa Spell (Becky's Friend in Hot Traxx), Mike Stein (Super-Duper Customer), Tony Tedeschi (New Year's Eve Young Stud), Eric Winzenried (Doctor), Jody Wood (Pedestrian), Sharon Ferrol, Anne Fletcher, Scott Fowler, Melanie A. Gage, Eddie Garcia, Sebastian LaCause, Lance MacDonald, Diane Mizota, Nathan Frederic Prevost, Lisa E. Ratzin, Dee Dee Weathers, Darrel W. Wright (Hot Traxx Dancers)

In the late 1970's, during the height of the disco and drug era, naive Eddie Adams rises to the top as male porn star Dirk Diggler, helped by his unusually large physical endowment. This film received Oscar nominations for supporting actor (Burt Reynolds), supporting actress (Julianne Moore), and original screenplay.

Mark Wahlberg, Burt Reynolds

Heather Graham

Don Cheadle

PLAYING GOD

(TOUCHSTONE) Producers, Marc Abraham, Laura Bickford; Executive Producers, Armyan Bernstein, Thomas A. Bliss; Co-Producers, Melanie Greene, Nancy Rae Stone; Director, Andy Wilson; Screenplay, Mark Haskell Smith; Photography, Anthony B. Richmond; Designer, Naomi Shohan; Editor, Louise Rubacky; Music, Richard Hartley; Costumes, Mary Zophres; Casting, Johanna Ray, Elaine J. Huzzar; Presented in association with Beacon Pictures; Distributed by Buena Vista Pictures; Dolby Digital Stereo; Technicolor; Rated R: 93 minutes; October release

CAST

Dr. Eugene Sands	David Duchovny
Raymond Blossom	Timothy Hutton
Claire	Angelina Jolie
Gage	Michael Massee
Vladimir	Peter Stormare
Cyril	Andrew Tiernan
Yates	Gary Dourdan
Flick	John Hawkes
Perry	Will Foster Stewart
Casey	Philip Moon
Andrei	Pavel D. Lynchnikoff
Jim	Tracey Walter
Sue	Sandra Kinder
Jerry	Bill Rosier
Mr. Hsi	Keone Young
Digiacomo	Eric DaRe
Phelps	Gareth Williams
Adonis	Teo

and Stacey Travis (Nurse), Max Lazar (Dimitri), Frank Ensign (Len), Bob A. Jennings (Dr. Clifford), Ross Kettle (Resident Surgeon), Nikki Lee (Anaesthesiologist), John Roselius (Surgeon #1), Damon White (Winston), Dan Hildebrand, J.P. Jones, Jerry Sloan (Russian Thugs), Alphonse V. Walter (Isaac), Melvin Jones (Rasta Doorman), Mara Duronslet (Jessica), Ernest Garcia (Burt), Alex Desert (Bartender), Sarah Stavrou (Woman), Jesse Perez (Crack Dealer), Daniel Rey Silvas (Basketball Player), Michael Chong (Chinese Security Guard #2), Alexander Folk (South African Businessman), Stella Garcia (South American Businesswoman), Guy Siner (Dutch Businessman), Al Ahlf (FBI Agent)

A surgeon, stripped of his medical license, becomes the personal doctor of a ruthless criminal, treating associates of his who cannot risk being taken to a hospital.

Nick Stahl, Martha Plimpton

David Duchovny

Angelina Jolie, Timothy Hutton

EYE OF GOD

(CASTLE HILL) Producers, Wendy Ettinger, Michael Nelson; Director/Screenplay, Tim Blake Nelson; Photography, Russell Lee Fine; Designer, Patrick Geary; Editor, Kate Sanford; Music, David Van Tieghem; a Minnow Pictures presentation; Color; Not rated; 84 minutes; October release

CAST

Ainsley Dupree	Martha Plimpton
Jack Stillings	Kevin Anderson
Sheriff Rogers	Hal Holbrook
Tom Spencer	Nick Stahl
Willard Sprague	Richard Jenkins
Claire Spencer	Mary Kay Place
Les Hector	Chris Freihofer
Glen Briggs	Woody Watson
Dorothy	Margo Martindale
R.J. Prichard	Wally Welch
Jim Nutter	Larry Flynn
Janice	Maggie Moore
Fast Food Customer	Vernon Grote
Lee	Gary Ragland
Mrs. Rogers	Caroline Wickwire

and Toby Metcalf, Darryl Cox (Officers), Karen Carney (Mrs. Sprague), Robert Peters (Del), Lisa Benavides (Nurse), Gail Peister (Doctor)

Short order cook Ainsley Dupree agrees to marry ex-con Jack Stillings who has converted to Christianity while serving time in jail. In a parallel storyline, 14-year-old Tom Spencer has been discovered by the police wandering about in a state of shock after witnessing a violent crime.

TELLING LIES IN AMERICA

(BANNER ENTERTAINMENT) Producers, Ben Myron, Fran Kuzui; Executive Producers, Brian Swardstrom, Mickey Liddell, Naomi Eszterhas; Director, Guy Ferland; Screenplay, Joe Eszterhas; Co-Producer, Fred Caruso; Co-Executive Producer, Kaz Kazui; Photography, Reynaldo Villalobos; Designer, James Gelarden; Music, Nicholas Pike; Editor, Jill Savitt; Costumes, Laura Cunningham; Casting, Emily Schweber, Susan Brown; a Joe Eszterhas presentation in association with Kuzui Enterprises and Ben Myron productions; Dolby Stereo; Super 35 Widescreen; Color; Rated PG-13; 101 minutes; October release

Brad Renfro, Kevin Bacon

CAST

Billy Magic	Kevin Bacon
Karchy Jonas	Brad Renfro
Dr. Istvan Jonas	Maximilian Schell
Diney Majeski	Calista Flockhart
Father Norton	Paul Dooley
Kevin Boyle	Jonathan Rhys Meyers
Henry	Luke Wilson
Amos	Damen Fletcher
Andy "Croak" Stas	Jerry Swindall
Justine	K.K. Dodds
Cecil Simms	James Kisicki
The Blind Kid	J.J. Horna
Timmy Morelli	Ben Saypol
Danny Hogan	Tony Devon
Sgt. Disapri	Rohn Thomas
Det. Carpenter	Joe Baka
WHK Receptionist	Tuesday Knight
WHK Newscaster	Dave Buckel
Assistant D.A.	Matt Miller
Immigration Judge	Jack Skelley
Groupies	Jane Jean Miller, Wendy Waltz
Giggly Girl	Angelique Osborne
Old Man	Abdullah Bey
Driver	Kevin Willigham
School Kid	Patrick White

In early 1960's Cleveland, struggling high school student Karchy Jonas becomes the friend and protege of smooth radio DJ Billy Magic who introduces the impressionable young lad to the highly desirable world of music, cars, and women.

Brad Renfro, Calista Flockhart

© Banner Pictures

Brad Renfro, Maximilian Schell

Kevin Bacon

GATTACA

(COLUMBIA) Producers, Danny DeVito, Michael Shamberg, Stacey Sher; Director/Screenplay, Andrew Niccol; Photography, Slawomir Idziak; Designer, Jan Roelfs; Editor, Lisa Zeno Churgin; Costumes, Colleen Atwood; Music, Michael Nyman; Co-Producer, Gail Lyon; Casting, Francine Maisler; a Jersey Films production; Dolby SDDS Stereo; Super 35 Widescreen; Technicolor; Rated PG-13; 112 minutes; October release

Jude Law, Ethan Hawke

CAST

Vincent Freeman (Jerome)	Ethan Hawke
Irene	Uma Thurman
Detective Hugo	Alan Arkin
Jerome Eugene Morrow (Eugene)	Jude Law
Anton	Loren Dean
Director Josef	Gore Vidal
Caesar	Ernest Borgnine
Geneticist	Blair Underwood
Lamar	Xander Berkeley
German	Tony Shalhoub
Marie	Jayne Brook
Antonio	Elias Koteas
Delivery Nurse	Maya Rudolph
Head Nurse	Una Damon
Pre-School Teacher	Elizabeth Dennehy
Younger Vincent	Mason Gamble
Younger Anton	Vincent Nielson
Young Vincent	Chad Christ
Young Anton	William Lee Scott
Personnel Officer	Clarence Graham
Gattaca Hoover	Carlton Benbry

and Grace Sullivan (Sequencing Customer), Ken Marino (Sequencing Technician), Cynthia Martells (Cavendish), Gabrielle Reece (Gattaca Trainer), Ryan Dorin (Twelve Fingered Pianist), Dean Norris (Cop on the Beat), Russell Milton (Gattaca Detective), George Marshall Ruge (Beaten Detective), Steve Bessen (Blood Test Detective), Lindsey Lee Ginter (Mission Commander)

In the 21st Century, where people who were genetically designed are considered superior, Vincent Freeman, an "In-Valid" who was conceived in love, tries to hide his identity in order to become an astronaut. This film received an Oscar nomination for art direction.

Uma Thurman

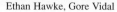

Ethan Hawke, Gore Vidal

Loren Dean, Alan Arkin

FAIRY TALE: A TRUE STORY

(PARAMOUNT) Producers, Wendy Finerman, Bruce Davey; Executive Producer, Paul Tucker; Director, Charles Sturridge; Screenplay, Ernie Contreras; Story, Albert Ash, Tom McLoughlin, Ernie Contreras; Photography, Michael Coulter; Designer, Michael Howells; Editor, Peter Coulson; Co-Producers, Selwyn Roberts, Tom McLouglin, Albert Ash; Visual Effects Supervisor, Tim Webber; Music, Zbigniew Preisner; Costumes, Shirley Russell; Casting, Mary Selway, Sarah Trevis; an Icon Productions/Wendy Finerman production; U.S.-British; Dolby Stereo; Deluxe color; Rated PG-13; 99 minutes; October release

Florence Hoath, Harvey Keitel

CAST

Elsie Wright...Florence Hoath
Frances Griffiths..Elizabeth Earl
Arthur Wright...Paul McGann
Polly Wright..Phoebe Nicholls
Sir Arthur Conan Doyle................................Peter O'Toole
Harry Houdini..Harvey Keitel
James Collins..Jason Salkey
Jean Doyle..Lara Morgan
Adrian Doyle...Adam Franks
Denis Doyle..Guy Witcher
Houdini's Assistant......................................Joseph May
Portly Gentleman...John Bradley
Peter Pan...Anna Chancellor
Stage Manager..Leonard Kavanagh
Wounded Corporal.......................................Anton Lesser
Harry Briggs..Bob Peck
Mrs. Thornton...Lynn Farleigh
Lucy..Sarah Marsden
Judith..Tara Marie
Margie..Alannah McGahan
Edward Gardner...Bill Nighy
John Ferret...Tim McInnerny
Sergeant Farmer...Peter Mullan
Albert, the Postman.....................................Jim Wiggins
Harold Snelling..David Calder
Geoffrey Hodson..Anthony Calf
and John Grillo (Mr. West), Benjamin Whitrow (Mr. Binley), Dick Brannick (News Vendor), Barbara Hicks (City Woman), Christopher Godwin (City Businessman), Andrew Cryer, Paul Popperwell (Soldiers), David Norman (O'Neill), Matilda Sturridge (Dorothy), Charlotte Champness (Alice), Anna Ramsey (Charlotte), Peter Wright (Newspaper Editor), Willie Ross (Old Print Worker), Ina Clough (Lady calling to Fairies), Carol Noakes (Station Photographer), Stephen Chapman (Boy in Hospital), Bill Stewart (Chess MC), Don Henderson (Sydney Chalker), Stewart Howson (Red-Faced Man), James Danaher (Joseph Wright), Martin Gent (Pushy Photographer), Anthony Collin (Older Photographer), Tom Georgeson, Angus Barnett (Reporters), Mel Gibson (Frances' Father); The Fairies: Suzy Barton (Lutey), Ali Bastian (Lull), Anna Brecon (Elabigathe), Sean Buckley (Mr. Bandylegs), Lindsey Butcher (Tib), Norma Cohen (Nanny Button Cap), Matt Costain (Prince Malekin), Philip Fowler (Fenoderee), Katie Gibbon (Pinket), Sophy Griffiths (Sib), Sara Li Gustafsson (Loireag), Tara Kemp (Gull), William Lawrance (Tom Cockle), Caleb Lloyd (Lob), Marianne Melhus (Florella), Genevieve Monastesse (Morgana), Simon Penman (Peerifool), Briony Plant (Yarthkins), Anna-Louise Plowman (Shellycoat), Jane Read-Wilson (Asrai), Isabel Rocamora (Queen Mab), Thomas Sturridge (Hob), Mark Tate (Habetrot), Hayley Tibbins (Patch)

In 1917 England cousins Frances Griffiths and Elsie Wright become the center of controversy after insisting that they have photographed actual fairies.

Elizabeth Earl

Elizabeth Earl, Florence Hoath, Peter O'Toole

RED CORNER

(MGM) Producers, Jon Avnet, Jordan Kerner, Charles B. Mulvehill, Rosalie Swedlin; Executive Producers, Wolfgang Petersen, Gail Katz; Director, Jon Avent; Screenplay, Robert King; Photography, Karl Walter Lindenlaub; Designer, Richard Sylbert; Editor, Peter E. Berger; Costumes, Albert Wolsky; Music, Thomas Newman; Co-Producers, Martin Huberty, Lisa Lindstrom; Casting, David Rubin; an Avnet/Kerner production; Dolby DTS Stereo; Deluxe color; Rated R; 122 minutes; October release

CAST

Jack Moore	Richard Gere
Shen Yuelin	Bai Ling
Bob Ghery	Bradley Whitford
Lin Dan	Byron Mann
David McAndrews	Peter Donat
Ed Pratt	Robert Stanton
Chariman Xu	Tsai Chin
Lin Shou	James Hong
Li Cheng	Tzi Ma
Gerhardt Hoffman	Ulrich Matschoss
Ambassador Reed	Richard Venture
Hong Ling	Jessey Meng
Huan Minglu	Roger Yuan
General Hong	Li Chi Yu

and Henry O. (Procurator General Yang), Li Jia Yao (Director Liu), Lu Yukun (Director Liu's Associate), Robert Lin (Director Liu's Interpreter), Steve Beebe (Disco DJ), Wei De Zhong, Grace Zhan (Beijing Opera Performers), Yvonne Wang (Disco Waitress), Gao Qiang (PSB Captain), Gao Xiao-Hua, Yao Wang (PSB Arresting Officers), Gu Xiao Yang, Hans Hanbo Cui (Prison Guards), Zong Ping (Captain Feng), Lei Yin (Feng's Assistant), Paul Chen (Visitor's Room Official), Jeffrey Dong (Prison Doctor), Jian Rui Chao (Yuelin's Aide), Daxing Zhang (Procurator Ma), Ding Yi Wang (Procurator Ma's Assistant), Lily L. Lin (People's Housewife Assessor), Mike Wu (People's Accountant Assessor), Bing Yang, Hua Wahrman (Court Interpreters), Ming Lo (Medical Examiner), Ken Leung (Peng), Liu Baifang (Chinese TV Reporter), Danny Wang (PSB Escort), Kenny Ki (Guard at Hotel Door), Jack C. Huang (Guard at Phone Center), Mei-Juin Chen (Phone Clerk), Jin Zheng Hui (Phone Center Supervisor), Kent Faulcon (Marine Guard)

Attorney Jack Moore, in China to close a deal for a large entertainment conglomerate, spends a night with a beautiful woman only to wake up accused of her murder.

© Metro-Goldwyn-Mayer Pictures Inc.

Richard Gere, Bai Ling

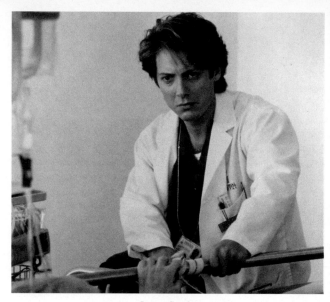

James Spader

CRITICAL CARE

(LIVE ENTERTAINMENT) Producers, Steven Schwartz, Sidney Lumet; Executive Producer, Don Carmody; Director, Sidney Lumet; Screenplay, Steven Schwartz; Based on the book by Richard Dooling; Executive in Charge of Production, Yalda Tehranian; Photography, David Watkin; Designer, Philip Rosenberg; Costumes, Dona Granata; Editor, Tom Swartwout; Music, Michael Convertino; Casting, Avy Kaufman; a LIVE Film and Mediaworks production, presented in association with Village Roadshow-ASQA Film Partnership; Dolby Digital Stereo; Color; Rated R; 109 minutes; October release

CAST

Dr. Werner Ernst	James Spader
Felicia Potter	Kyra Sedgwick
Stella	Helen Mirren
Nun	Anne Bancroft
Dr. Butz	Albert Brooks
Bed Two	Jeffrey Wright
Connie Potter	Margo Martindale
Furnaceman	Wallace Shawn
Dr. Hofstader	Philip Bosco
Wilson	Colm Feore
Robert Payne	Edward Herrmann
Poindexter	James Lally
Judge Fatale	Harvey Atkin
Sheldon Hatchett	Al Waxman
Hansen	Hamish McEwan
Mrs. Steckler	Jackie Richardson

and Barbara Eve Harris (E.R. Nurse), Conrad Coates (Dr. Miller), Bruno Dessler (Potter), Caroline Nielson (Luscious Nurse), Gladys O'Conner (Bed One), Kay Hawtry (Dr. Butz's Secretary), Don Carmody (Matire D'), Kim Roberts, Naomi Blicker (Interns), Merwin Mondesir (Head Injury), Bruce Hemmings (Orderly), Paul Brown (Insurance Man), Michael Colton (The Boy)

A young second-resident assigned to the Intensive Care Unit finds himself in the middle of a battle between two sisters over whether their father should be disconnected from his life support unit.

©LIVE Entertainment

SWITCHBACK

(PARAMOUNT) Producer, Gale Anne Hurd; Executive Producers, Keith Samples, Mel Efros, Jeb Stuart; Director/Screenplay, Jeb Stuart; Photography, Oliver Wood; Designer, Jeff Howard; Editor, Conrad Buff; Music, Basil Poledouris; Costumes, Betsy Heimann; Stunts, Jeff Habberstad; Casting, Pam Dixon Mickelson; a Rysher Entertainment presentation of a Pacific Western Production; Dolby Digital Stereo; Panavision; Deluxe color; Rated R; 121 minutes; October release

Jared Leto, Danny Glover

CAST

Bob Goodall	Danny Glover
Frank LaCrosse	Dennis Quaid
Lane Dixon	Jared Leto
Sheriff Buck Olmstead	R. Lee Ermey
Police Chief Jack McGinnis	William Fichtner
Deputy Sheriff Nate Booker	Ted Levine
Babysitter	Claudia Stedelin
Andy LaCrosse	Ian Nelson
Man on Porch	Brent Hinkley
Bud	Walt Goggins
Sim	Louis Schaefer
Rancher	Robert L. Somers
Rancher's Daughter	Lexie Stuart
Bartender	Ted Markland
Rick	Gregory Scott Cummins
Ben	Tommy Puett
Luke	Stuart Grant
Morgue Attendant	Ken Thorley
Highway Patrol Captain	Pat Mahoney
Deputy	Michael K. Osborn
Sally	Wendelin Harston
SWAT Leader	Dean Hallo
Saldez	Orville Stoeber
Police Captain	Robert Himber
Cook	Bill Rodgers

and Roy Yearby (Truck Driver), Allorah Creevay (Wiatress), Maggie Roswell (Fae), Gil Colon (Deputy), Allison Smith (Becky), Julio Oscar Mechoso (Jorge Martinez), Kevin Cooney (Montgomery), Leo Burmester (Shorty), Merle Kennedy (Betty), Donnie L. Betts (Patrolman), Stan Parks (FBI Agent), Ben Fuhrman (Captain Heber), Lois Hicks (Ruth), Gary Giem (Al), Mark Curry (Robby), Martin David Boyd (Hank), Kevin Bartlett (Tate), Vern Porter (Cubby), Leigh Reyburn (Woman in Bar), Lionel Douglas, Paul Parducci (Men in Shower), Kristin McCloskey (News Anchor), Trishia Springer (Reporter), Keith Hatten (Brakeman Ray), Sandy Ward (Tex), Silan Smith, Jim Clark (Engineers), Christopher Michael, Robert Peters (Colorado Troopers), Joe Alphasa (Small Mexican Man)

FBI agent Frank LaCrosse becomes determined to catch the person responsible for a cross-country murder spree after the suspect kidnaps LaCrosse's young son.

Dennis Quaid

Danny Glover, Jared Leto

Dennis Quaid

STARSHIP TROOPERS

Casper Van Dien

Patrick Muldoon

(TRISTAR) Producers, Jon Davison, Alan Marshall; Co-Producers, Phil Tippett, Ed Neumeier, Frances Doel, Stacy Lumbrezer; Director, Paul Verhoeven; Screenplay, Ed Neumeier; Based on the novel by Robert A. Heinlein; Designer, Allan Cameron; Editors, Mark Goldblatt, Caroline Ross; Costumes, Ellen Mirojnick; Music, Basil Poledouris; Special Visual Effects, Industrial Light & Magic; Spaceship Visual Effects Supervisor, Scott E. Anderson; ILM Visual Effects Supervisor, Scott Squires; Visual Effects Director of Photography, Alex Funke; Creature Visual Effects, The Tippet Studio; Spaceship Visual Effects, Sony Pictures Imageworks Inc.; Full Scale Creature Effects, Alec Gillis, Tom Woodruff Jr./Amalgamated Dynamics Inc.; Casting, Johanna Ray, Elaine J. Huzzar; a co-presentation of Touchstone Pictures, of a Jon Davison production; Dolby SDDS Stereo; Technicolor; Rated R; 129 minutes; November release

CAST

Johnny Rico ....Casper Van Dien
Dizzy Flores ....Dina Meyer
Carmen Ibanez ....Denise Richards
Ace Levy ....Jake Busey
Carl Jenkins...Neil Patrick Harris
Sgt. Zim ....Clancy Brown
Sugar Watkins ....Seth Gilliam
Zander Barcalow ....Patrick Muldoon
Jean Rasczak ....Michael Ironside
Biology Teacher ....Rue McClanahan
General Owen...Marshall Bell
Breckinridge ....Eric Bruskotter
Kitten Smith ....Matt Levin
Katrina ....Blake Lindsley
Shujimi ....Anthony Ruivivar
Captain Deladier ....Brenda Strong
Commanding Officer..Dean Norris
Mr. Rico ....Christopher Curry
Mrs. Rico..Lenore Kasdorf
Djana'D ....Tami-Adrian George
Corporal Bronski ....Teo
Lt. Willy ....Steven Ford
Corporal Birdie ....Ungela Brockman
Sgt. Gillespie...Curnal Aulisio
and Greg Travis (Net Correspondent), Bruce Gray (Sky Marshall Dienes), Denise Dowse (Sky Marshall Meru), John Cunningham (Fed Net Announcer), Julianna McCarthy, Timothy McNeil (Experts), Robert David Hall (Recruiting Sergeant), Brad Kane (Lanny), Amy Smart (Pilot Cadet), Timothy Omundson (Psychic), Patrick Bishop (Engineering Officer), Hunter Bodine (Young Cap Trooper), Travis Lowen (Little Boy Trooper), Patrick Wolff (Late Cadet), Mara Duronslet (Communications Officer), Dale A. Dye (General), Michael Stokey (Officer with Morita), Tyrone Tann (Student), Matt Entriken (Marco), Ronald L. Botchan (Jumpball Referee), Walter Adrian (Judge), Stephanie Erb (Young Mother), Alexi Lakatos, Nathaniel Marshall, Austin Sanderford, Rhiannon Vigil (Stomping Kids), Mylin Brooks, Armand Darius, Kai Lennox (Troopers)

In the distant future a group of young soldiers are trained to do battle with gigantic alien bugs, intent on wiping out the human race. This film received an Oscar nomination for visual effects.

© TriStar Pictures

Casper Van Dien, Denise Richards, Neil Patrick Harris

Lynn Whitfield, Debbi Morgan

Jake Smollett, Meagan Good, Lynn Whitfield, Jurnee Smollett

Jurnee Smollett, Samuel L. Jackson

EVE'S BAYOU

(TRIMARK) Producers, Caldecot Chubb, Samuel L. Jackson; Executive Producers, Eli Selden, Nick Wechsler, Julie Silverman Yorn; Director/Screenplay, Kasi Lemmons; Co-Executive Producers, Michael Bennett, Margaret Matheson; Co-Producers, Cevin Cathell, Jay Polstein, Cami Winikoff; Photography, Amy Vincent; Designer, Jeff Howard; Editor, Terilyn A. Shropshire; Costumes, Karyn Wagner; Music, Terence Blanchard; Casting, Jaki Brown-Karman, Robyn M. Mitchell; a Chubbco/Addis Wechsler production; Dolby SDDS Stereo; Color; Rated R; 109 minutes; November release

CAST

Eve Batiste	Jurnee Smollett
Cisely Batiste	Meagan Good
Louis Batiste	Samuel L. Jackson
Roz Batiste	Lynn Whitfield
Mozelle Batiste Delacroix	Debbi Morgan
Poe Batiste	Jake Smollett
Gran Mere	Ethel Ayler
Elzora	Diahann Carroll
Julian Grayraven	Vondie Curtis Hall
Lenny Mereaux	Roger Guenveur Smith
Matty Mereaux	Lisa Nicole Carson
Harry Delacroix	Branford Marsalis
Henrietta	Afonda Colbert
Lynette	Lola Dalferes
Hosea	Marcus Lyle Brown
Paige	Alverta Perkins Dunigan
Vendor	Ron Flagge
Hilary	Sharon K. London
Madame Renard	Carol Sutton
Stevie Hobbs	Victoria Rowell
Bus Driver	Oneal A. Isaac
Bartender	Julian Dalcour
Maynard	Leonard Thomas
Proprietor	Allen Toussaint
Ghost of Original Eve	Billie Neal
Narrator	Tamara Tunie

In a Louisiana backwater town of the 1960s, ten-year-old Eve Batiste sees her family being torn apart by her father's infidelities.

Jurnee Smollett, Diahann Carroll

© Trimark Pictures, Inc.

ANASTASIA

(20TH CENTURY FOX) Producers/Directors, Don Bluth, Gary Goldman; Executive Producer, Maureen Donley; Screenplay, Susan Gauthier, Bruce Graham, Bob Tzudiker, Noni White; Based on the play by Marcelle Maurette as adapted by Guy Bolton and the screenplay by Arthur Laurents; Animation Adaptation, Eric Tuchman; Music Score, David Newman; Songs by Lynn Ahrens (lyrics) and Stephen Flaherty (music); Casting, Brian Chavanne; Directing Animators, Len Simon, John Hill, Troy Saliba, Fernando Moro, Sandro Cleuzo, Paul Newberry; Color Key Styling, Richard C. Bentham, Kenneth Valentine Slevin; Character Layout & Design, Chris Schouten; Production Designer, Mike Peraza; Conceptual Artis, Suzanne Lemieux Wilson; Pre Production Design, John Lakey; Storyboard Artists, Larry Leker, Joe Oranntia, Chip Pace, Jay Schultz, Ferran Xalabarder; a Fox Family Films presentation; Dolby Digital Stereo; Cinemascope; Technicolor; Rated G; 90 minutes; November release

Dimitri, Anastasia, Vladimir

VOICE CAST

Anastasia ....Meg Ryan
Dimitri ....John Cusack
Vladimir ....Kelsey Grammer
Rasputin ....Christopher Lloyd
Bartok ....Hank Azaria
Sophie ....Bernadette Peters
Young Anastasia..Kirsten Dunst
Dowager Empress Marie...Angela Lansbury
Singing Voice of Anastasia ....Liz Callaway
Singing Voice of Young Anastasia..................................Lacey Chabert
Singing Voice of Rasputin ....Jim Cummings
Singing Voice of Dimitri ....Jonathan Dokuchitz
Czar Nicholas/Servant/ Revolutionary
Soldier/Ticket Agent ....Rick Jones
Phlegmenkoff/Old Woman ....Andrea Martin
Actress...Debra Mooney
Travelling Man/Major Domo ....Arthur Malet
Anastasia Impostor..Charity Jones

In 1920s Russia a pair of con-men hope to pass off a young girl as Anastasia, the surviving child of the murdered royal family. Previous film version was released by 20th Century-Fox in 1956 and starred Ingrid Bergman, Yul Brynner and Helen Hayes. This film received Oscar nominations for song ("Journey to the Past") and original musical or comedy score.

Rasputin, Bartok

Dimitri, Anastasia

THE JACKAL

(UNIVERSAL) Producers, James Jacks, Sean Daniel, Michael Caton-Jones, Kevin Jarre; Executive Producers, Terence Clegg, Hal Lieberman, Gary Levinsohn, Mark Gordon; Director, Michael Caton-Jones; Screen Story and Screenplay, Chuck Pfarrer; Based on the motion picture screenplay *The Day of the Jackal* by Kenneth Ross, from the novel by Frederick Forsythe; Photography, Karl Walter Lindenlaub; Designer, Michael White; Editor, Jim Clark; Costumes, Albert Wolsky; Music, Carter Burwell; Casting, Ellen Chenoweth; a Mutual Film Company presentation of an Alphaville production; Dolby DTS Stereo; Panavision; Deluxe color; Rated R; 123 minutes; November release

CAST

The Jackal	Bruce Willis
Declan Mulqueen	Richard Gere
Carter Preston	Sidney Poitier
Valentina Koslova	Diane Venora
Isabella	Mathilda May
Witherspoon	J.K. Simmons
McMurphy	Richard Lineback
Donald Brown	John Cunningham
Lamont	Jack Black
The First Lady	Tess Harper
Woolburton	Leslie Phillips
Douglas	Stephen Spinella
Jamaican Girl	Sophie Okonedo
Terek Murad	David Hayman
George Decker	Steve Bassett
Politovsky	Yuri Stepanov
Dennehey	Walt MacPherson
Ghazzi Murad	Ravil Isyanov
13 Year Old Girl	Maggie Castle
Speaker	Karen Kirschenbauer
Surgeon General	Terrence Currier
Akashi	Daniel Dae Kim
Man in Video	Michael Caton-Jones
Woman in Video	Laura Viederman
Vasilov	Peter Sullivan
General Belinko	Richard Cubison
Green Beret Colonel	Jim Grimshaw
Paramedic	Greg Miller
Ambassador Koldin	Bob Kingdom
NSC Rep	Murphy Guyer
Bored Teenage Clerk	Philip Le Maistre
Beaufres	Serge Houde

and James McCauley, Daniel Ziskie (CIA Reps), Terry Loughlin (Davis), Victor Sobchak (Doctor), Serge Christiaenssens (Immigration Officer), Boris Boscovic (Interrogator), Ewan Bailey (Prison Guard), Danette Alberico, Debra Gano (Women with Champagne), John Bland (Dave), Pamela Poitier (Law Clerk), Jonathan Aris (Alexander Radzinski), Eddie "Bo" Smith, Jr. (Washington Cop), Larry King (Himself), Gayle Jessup (Reporter), Bill Collins (Medic), David Gene Gibbs (Pilot), James M. Helkey (Co-Pilot)

The FBI enlists the aide of imprisoned underground operative Declan Mulqueen to help them track down a cold-blooded assassin named "The Jackal" and find out his intended target before it is too late. Previous version was the 1973 Universal release The Day of the Jackal which starred Edward Fox.

Richard Gere

Bruce Willis

Sidney Poitier, Richard Gere

ONE NIGHT STAND

(NEW LINE CINEMA) Producers, Mike Figgis, Annie Stewart, Ben Myron; Executive Producer, Robert Engelman; Co-Executive Producers, Michael DeLuca, Richard Saperstein; Director/Screenplay/Music, Mike Figgis; Photography, Declan Quinn; Designer, Waldemar Kalinowski; Editor, John Smith; Costumes, Laura Goldsmith, Enid Harris; Casting, Nancy Foy; a Red Mullet production; Dolby SDDS Stereo; Deluxe color; Rated R; 103 minutes; November release

CAST

Max Carlyle	Wesley Snipes
Karen	Nastassja Kinski
Mimi	Ming-Na Wen
Charlie	Robert Downey, Jr.
Vernon	Kyle MacLachlan
Young Charlie	Marcus Paulk
Saffron	Natalie Trott
Charlie's Father	John Calley
George	Glenn Plummer
Margaux	Amanda Donohoe
Mickey	Zoe Nathenson
Don	Thomas Haden Church
Nathan	Vincent Ward
Phil	John Ratzenberger
Merv	Thomas Kopache
Marie	Annabelle Gurwitch
Malinda	Susan Barnes
Malissa	Michelle Jonas
Receptionist	Margaret Makinen
Hotel Clerk	Mike Figgis
Nurse Chris	Julian Sands
Kevin	Donovan Leitch

and Edita Brychta, Hans Tester, Richard Paradise, Joe Drago (Karen's Business Associates), Johanna Torell (Doctor Olsson), Ione Skye, Xander Berkeley, Greta Gaines (Charlie's Friends), Crystal Pite (Title Dance Sequence and Featured Dancer), Christopher Bauer (Bartender), Anne Lambton, Nick Sandow (Muggers), Michela Zanchi, Tiffany Hecht (Armani Women), Bill Raymond (Gridlock Taxi Driver), Tracy Thorne (Helicopter Traffic Woman), Oscar Conlon, Ahmed Ben Larby (Delegates in Line), Saffron Burrows (Supermodel), Robie Yamamoto (Featured Male Model), Tracey Stockwell, Caroline Hepburn, Sheetel Bhagat, Jesus Yinh, Emily Hseih, Sabrina Van Tassel, Cleveland Mitchell, Lisa Ann Cabasa, Kort Anderson, Michael Pauldine, Karis Jagger, Johanna Torrel, Freeman White (Armani Models), Stacey Elder, Heidi Komarek, Nelle Dreyer, Michelle Merkin (Agency Models), Chris Edwards, Richard Caselnova, Jeffrey Howard Kaufman (Policemen), Joseph John Scott (Flower Vendor), Trula Marcus (Party Guest), Tava Smiley (Hotel Receptionist), David Acosta (Caterer), Aixa Maldonado (Caterer's Assistant), Nadira Hall (Middle Eastern Musician), Daniel Hawk Hicks, Lee Wells (Doormen), Xavier Urquieta (Pakastani Diplomat), Rachel Escalera (Nanny)

Max Carlyle tries to forget his adulterous one night stand with Karen until a return trip to New York to visit a dying friend brings the two together again.

© New Line Cinema

Natassja Kinski, Wesley Snipes

Kyle MacLachlan, Natassja Kinski, Wesley Snipes, Ming-Na Wen

SICK: THE LIFE AND DEATH OF BOB FLANAGAN, SUPERMASOCHIST

(CFP) Producer/Director, Kirby Dick; Photography, Jonathan Dayton, Kirby Dick, Sheree Rose, Geza Sinkovics; Editors, Kirby Dick, Dody Dorn; Co-Producer, Sheree Rose; Music, Blake Leyh; Interviewers, Kathe Burkhart, Kirby Dick, Rita Valencia; a Cinepix Film Properties presentation; Dolby Stereo; Color; Not rated; 89 minutes; November release. Documentary on performance artist Bob Flanagan who dealt in sado-masochism in order to cope with Cystic Fibrosis.

Bob Flanagan

ALIEN RESURRECTION

(20TH CENTURY FOX) Producers, Bill Badalato, Gordon Carroll, David Giler, Walter Hill; Director, Jean-Pierre Jeunet; Screenplay, Joss Whedon; Based on characters created by Dan O'Bannon and Ronald Shusett; Photography, Darius Khondji; Designer, Nigel Phelps; Editor, Herve Schneid; Visual Effects Supervisors, Pitof and Erik Henry; Alien Effects Designers/Creators, Alec Gillis, Tom Woodruff, Jr.; Costumes, Bob Ringwood; Music, John Frizzell; Casting, Rick Pagano; a Brandywine production; Dolby Digital Stereo; Super 35 Widescreen; Deluxe color; Rated R; 108 minutes; November release

CAST

Ripley	Sigourney Weaver
Call	Winona Ryder
Vriess	Dominique Pinon
Johner	Ron Perlman
Christie	Gary Dourdan
Elgyn	Michael Wincott
Hillard	Kim Flowers
General Perez	Dan Hedaya
Dr. Wren	J.E. Freeman
Gediman	Brad Dourif
Distephano	Raymond Cruz
Purvis	Leland Orser
Anesthesiologist	Carolyn Campbell
Scientist	Marlene Bush
Surgeon	David St. James

and Rodney Mitchell (Soldier with Glove), Robert Faltisco (Soldier Shot through Helmet), David Rowe (Frozen Soldier), Garrett House, Rod Damer, Mark Mansfield, Daniel Raymont, Chip Nuzzo (Soldiers), Steven Gilborn (Voice of "Father"), Robert Bastens, Rico Bueno, Alex Lorre, Ron Ramessar (Sleepers), Nicole Fellows (Young Ripley), Tom Woodruff, Jr. (Lead Alien), Joan LaBarbara, Archie Hahn (Newborn Vocals)

A team of scientists, interested in bringing together human and alien genes, resurrects Ripley in order to remove the alien embryo she is carrying inside of her. This is the fourth film in the series of 20th Century-Fox releases, following Alien (1979), Aliens (1986), and Alien3 (1992), all of which starred Sigourney Weaver.

Winona Ryder, Ron Perlman

Sigourney Weaver

Sigourney Weaver, Winona Ryder

Brad Dourif, Sigourney Weaver

Danny DeVito, Matt Damon

Mary Kay Place, Jon Voight

Claire Danes, Matt Damon

Matt Damon, Danny DeVito

John Grisham's
THE RAINMAKER

(PARAMOUNT) Producers, Michael Douglas, Steven Reuther, Fred Fuchs; Director/Screenplay, Francis Ford Coppola; Narration, Michael Herr; Based on the novel by John Grisham; Photography, John Toll; Designer, Howard Cummings; Editor, Barry Malkin; Costumes, Aggie Guerard Rodgers; Co-Producer, Georgia Kacandes; Casting, Linda Phillips-Palo; a Constellation Films presentation of a Douglas/Reuther production in association with American Zoetrope; Dolby Stereo; Panavision; Deluxe color; Rated PG-13; 134 minutes; November release

CAST

Rudy Baylor	Matt Damon
Deck Schifflet	Danny DeVito
Kelly Riker	Claire Danes
Leo F. Drummond	Jon Voight
Dot Black	Mary Kay Place
Judge Harvey Hale	Dean Stockwell
Miss Birdie	Teresa Wright
Jackie Lemancyzk	Virginia Madsen
Bruiser Stone	Mickey Rourke
Cliff Riker	Andrew Shue
Buddy Black	Red West
Donny Ray Black	Johnny Whitworth
Judge Tyrone Kipler	Danny Glover
Wilfred Keeley	Roy Scheider
Billy Porter	Randy Travis
Prince Thomas	Wayne Emmons
Butch	Adrian Roberts
Everett Lufkin	Michael Girardin
Jack Underhall	Randall King
F. Franklin Donaldson	Justin Ashforth
B. Bobby Shaw	Michael Keys Hall
J. Michael Floquet	James Cunningham
Mr. Van Landel	Frank Clem
Kermit Aldy	Alan Woolf
Delbert Birdsong	Sonny Shroyer
Vera Birdsong	Pamela Tice Chapman
Jewelry Saleswoman	Trula Marcus
Bruiser's Driver	Tony Dingman
Carl	Daniel O'Callaghan
Homicide Detectives	Tom Kagy, John Yancey
Jailer	Chris Gray
Jury Foreman	Verda Davenport
Courtroom Clerk	Johnetta Shearer
Court Reporter	Tammy Wendel
Mr. McKenzie	Nate Bynum

and James W. Redmond (CNN Reporter), John Gray (Hospital Volunteer), Sherry Sanford (Nurse), Billy Ray Reynolds, Mary Lester (Murder Scene Bystanders), Deborah Frazier (St. Peter's Receptionist), Vernon Newman (Great Benefit Salesman), Lynn Carthane (Newscaster), Rodney Peck (Rehab Center Desk Clerk), Bill Lunn (Himself), Terrance Stewart (Boy with Broken Arm), Bridget Brunner (Bruiser's Receptionist), Mike Cody (Tinley Britt Lawyer), Donald Polden (Legal Commentator), Eloise Dukes (Court Clerk), Katherine Morrow (Deposition Court Reporter), Alex Harvey (Bar Exam Proctor), Melissa Hurst (Waitress at Bar), Anasa Briggs-Graves, Ronnie Dee Blaire (Bailiffs)

While working for a sleazy Memphis lawyer, idealistic Rudy Baylor agrees to help a grief-stricken mother sue the insurance company that rejected the claim for her son who is dying of leukemia.

Matt Damon

Matt Damon, Mickey Rourke

Matt Damon, Virginia Madsen, Danny DeVito

FLUBBER

(WALT DISNEY PICTURES) Producers, John Hughes, Ricardo Mestres; Executive Producer, David Nicksay; Director, Les Mayfield; Screenplay, John Hughes, Bill Walsh; From the screenplay for The Absent Minded Professor by Bill Walsh, based on a story by Samuel W. Taylor; Photography, Dean Cundey; Designer, Andrew McAlpine; Editors, Harvey Rosenstock, Michael A. Stevenson; Costumes, April Ferry; Music (including The Flubber Mambo), Danny Elfman; Co-Producer, Michael Polaire; Visual Effects Supervisors, Peter Crosman, Tom Bertino, Douglas Hans Smith; Casting, Nancy Foy; Stunts, Freddie Hice; a Great Oaks production; Dolby SDDS Stereo; Panavision; Technicolor; Rated PG; 92 minutes; November release

CAST

Prof. Phillip Brainard	Robin Williams
Sara Jean Reynolds	Marcia Gay Harden
Wilson Croft	Christopher McDonald
Chester Hoenicker	Raymond Barry
Smith	Clancy Brown
Wesson	Ted Levine
Bennett Hoenicker	Wil Wheaton
Martha George	Edie McClurg
Voice of Weebo	Jodi Benson
Sylvia	Leslie Stefanson
Father	Malcolm Brownson
Window Boy	Benjamin Brock
Minister	Dakin Matthews
Teenage Boy	Zack Zeigler
Willy Barker	Samuel Lloyd
Dale Jepner	Scott Michael Campbell
Rutland Coach	Bob Sarlatte
Referee	Bob Greene
Medfield Basketball Player	Tom Barlow
Voice of Flubber	Scott Martin Gershin
Voice of Weebette	Julie Morrison
Secretary	Nancy Olsen

Absent-minded university professor Phillip Brainard creates a revolutionary substance, a flying rubber, that he dubs "flubber," and hopes to use to save his financially troubled school. Remake of the 1961 Disney film The Absent Minded Professor which starred Fred MacMurray, Nancy Olsen, Keenan Wynn, and Tommy Kirk.

Robin Williams

Wil Wheaton, Robin Williams, Raymond Barry, Marcia Gay Harden, Christopher McDonald

© Disney Enterprises

Robin Williams

Marcia Gay Harden, Robin Williams

OTHER VOICES, OTHER ROOMS

(ARTISTIC LICENSE) Producers, Peter Wentworth, David Rocksavage; Director, David Rocksavage; Screenplay, Sara Flanigan, David Rocksavage; Based on the novel by Truman Capote; Executive Producers, Robert C. Stigwood, Lili Mahtani; Photography, Paul Ryan; Designer, Amy McGary; Editor, Cynthia Scheider; Costumes, Jane Greenwood; Music, Chris Hajian; Casting, Hopkins, Barden, Smith; a Golden Eye Films presentation; U.S.-British; Color; Not rated; 98 minutes; December release

CAST

Randolph Skully	Lothaire Bluteau
Amy Skully	Anna Thomson
Joel Sansom	David Speck
Zoo	April Turner
Ed Sansom	Frank Taylor
Idabell Tompkins	Aubrey Dollar
Narrator	Robert Kingdom

13-year-old Joel, sent to a decaying plantation to be with his father, meets up with the house's mistress, Amy Skully, and her debauched cousin Randolph.

© Artistic Liscense

Kirstie Alley, Tim Allen

Tim Allen

Lothaire Bluteau, David Speck

FOR RICHER OR POORER

(UNIVERSAL) Producers, Sid, Bill and Jon Sheinberg; Executive Producers, Richard Baker, Rick Messina, Gayle Fraser Baigelman; Director, Bryan Spicer; Screenplay, Jana Howington, Steve Lukanic; Photography, Buzz Feitshans IV; Designer, Stephen Hendrickson; Editor, Russell Denove; Co-Producers, Michael S. Glick, Bruce Economou; Music, Randy Edelman; Costumes, Abigail Murray; Casting, Victoria Burrows; a co-presentation of The Bubble Factory of a Sheinberg production in association with Yorktown Productions; Dolby DTS Stereo; Super 35 Widescreen; Deluxe color; Rated PG-13; 115 minutes; December release

CAST

Brad Sexton	Tim Allen
Caroline Sexton	Kirstie Alley
Samuel Yoder	Jay O. Sanders
Phil Kleinman	Michael Lerner
Bob Lachman	Wayne Knight
Derek Lester	Larry Miller
Frank Hall	Miguel A. Nunez, Jr.
Levinia Yoder	Megan Cavanagh
Henner Lapp	John Pyper-Ferguson
Rebecca Yoder	Carrie Preston
Jerry	Ethan Phillips
Dave	John Caponera
Anna Yoder	Katie Moore
Samuel, Jr.	Bobby Steggert
Sammy	Michael Angarano
Grandma Yoder	Rosemary Knower
Grandpa Yoder	David Harscheid

and Hunter and Scout Stover (Baby Yoder), June Claman (Judge Northcutt), Marla Maples (Cynthia), Holly Rudkin (Mary), Crystal Bock (Penny), Monica Deeter (Hanna Yoder), Richard Pelzman (Jonathan Yoder), Madeline Mager (Sarah), Terrence Currier (Elder Joseph), Hal Handerson (Elder Thomas), Michael Howell (Bailiff), Johanna Cox (Emma Yoder), Stefan Aleksander (Jacob Yoder), Holly Atkinson (Teller), Emily Chamberlain (Evelyn), Anthony Azizi (Taxi Driver), David Maples (IRS Agent), Markus Flanagan (George), Wes Johnson (Tourist Man), Rick Foucheux (Tom), Drenda Spohnholtz (Waitress), Marla Sucharetza (Stacy)

A pair of bickering Manhattan socialites, on the run from the IRS, hide out in Amish country, passing themselves off as the long-lost relatives of a local farming family.

© Universal Studios/The Bubble Factory

137

GOOD WILL HUNTING

(MIRAMAX) Producer, Lawrence Bender; Executive Producers, Bob Weinstein, Harvey Weinstein, Jonathan Gordon, Su Armstrong; Co-Executive Producers, Kevin Smith, Scott Mosier; Director, Gus Van Sant; Screenplay, Ben Affleck, Matt Damon; Co-Producer, Chris Moore; Photography, Jean Yves Escoffier; Designer, Melissa Stewart; Editor, Pietro Scalia; Music, Danny Elfman; Song: Miss Misery by Elliott Smith; Costumes, Beatrix Aruna Pasztor; Casting, Billy Hopkins, Suzanne Smith, Kerry Barden; a Lawrence Bender production; Dolby Digital Stereo; Color; Rated R; 126 minutes; December release

CAST

Sean McGuire	Robin Williams
Will Hunting	Matt Damon
Chuckie	Ben Affleck
Skylar	Minnie Driver
Lambeau	Stellan Skarsgard
Morgan	Casey Affleck
Billy	Cole Hauser
Tom	John Mighton
Krystyn	Rachel Majowski
Cathy	Colleen McCauley
Girl on Street	Shannon Egleson
Carmine Scarpaglia	Rob Lyons
Carmine Friend #1	Steven Kozlowski
Lydia	Jennifer Deathe
Clark	Scott Williams Winters
Head Custodian	Philip Williams
Assistant Custodian	Patrick O'Donnell
Courtroom Guard	Kevin Rushton
Judge Malone	Jimmy Flynn
Prosecutor	Joe Cannons
Court Officer	Ann Matacunas
Psychologist	George Plimpton
Hypnotist	Francesco Clemente
Bunker Hill College Students	Jessica Morton, Barna Moricz
Toy Store Cashier	Libby Geller
M.I.T. Professor	Chas Lawther
Timmy	Richard Fitzpatrick
Marty	Patrick O'Donnell
NSA Agents	Bruce Hunter, Robert Talvano
Security Guard	James Allodi

and Matt Mercier, Ralph St. George, Bob Lynds, Dan Washington (Barbershop Quartet), Alison Folland, Derrick Bridgeman, Vic Sahay (M.I.T. Students), Frank Nakashima, Chris Britton, David Eisner (Executives)

Will Hunting, an M.I.T. janitor with exceptional mathematical abilities, is reluctant to accept a professor's suggestion that the boy seek a life beyond hanging out in Boston with his drinking buddies. 1997 Academy Award-winner for Best Supporting Actor (Robin Williams) and Original Screenplay. This film received additional Oscar nominations for picture, actor (Matt Damon), supporting actress (Minnie Driver), director, film editing, original dramatic score, and song ("Miss Misery").

Robin Williams, Matt Damon

Minnie Driver, Matt Damon

Ben Affleck, Matt Damon

Ben Affleck, Matt Damon

Matt Damon, Robin Williams

Robin Williams, Stellan Skarsgard

Minnie Driver, Matt Damon, Ben Affleck

Cole Hauser, Casey Affleck, Matt Damon, Ben Affleck

Morgan Freeman, Chiwetel Ejiofor, Matthew McConaughey, Daniel Von Bargen

Djimon Hounsou (c)

AMISTAD

(DREAMWORKS) Producers, Steven Spielberg, Debbie Allen, Colin Wilson; Executive Producers, Walter Parkes; Director, Steven Spielberg; Screenplay, David Franzoni; Photography, Janusz Kaminski; Designer, Rick Carter; Editor, Michael Kahn; Music, John Williams; Costumes, Ruth E. Carter; Associate Producers, Bonnie Curtis, Paul Deason; Co-Producer, Tim Shriver; Co-Executive Producer, Robert Cooper; Casting, Victoria Thomas; Presented in association with HBO Pictures; Dolby Digital Stereo; Widescreen; Technicolor; Rated R; 152 minutes; December release

CAST

Theodore Joadson	Morgan Freeman
Martin Van Buren	Nigel Hawthorne
John Quincy Adams	Anthony Hopkins
Cinque	Djimon Hounsou
Roger Baldwin	Matthew McConaughey
Secretary Forsyth	David Paymer
Holabird	Pete Postlethwaite
Lewis Tappan	Stellan Skarsgård
Yamba	Razaaq Adoti
Fala	Abu Bakaar Fofanah
Queen Isabella	Anna Paquin
Calderon	Tomas Milian
Ensign Covey	Chiwetel Ejiofor
Buakei	Derrick N. Ashong
Ruiz	Geno Silva
Montes	John Ortiz
Lieutenant Gedney	Ralph Brown
Lieutenant Meade	Darren Burrows
Judge Juttson	Allan Rich
Attorney	Paul Guilfoyle
Captain Fitzgerald	Peter Firth
Hammond	Xander Berkeley
Judge Coglin	Jeremy Northam
John C. Calhoun	Arliss Howard
Professor Gibbs	Austin Pendleton
Warden Pendelton	Daniel Von Bargen
Mrs. Pendelton	Rusty Schwimmer
General Espatero	Pedro Armendariz

and Frank T. Wells (Crier), Miles Herter (Sailor), Michael Massee (Pickney), Jake Weber (Mr. Wright), Victor Rivers (Captain Ferrar), Fay Masterson (Queen Victoria), Joseph Kosseh (Birmaja), Steve Passewe (Cinque's In-Law), Sherly Acosta Williams (Cinque's Wife), Amistad Africans: Willie Amakye (Folowa), Luc Assogba (Gbatui), Mariah Campbell (Masery), Habib Conteh (Bai), Stephen Conteh (Morlai), Monguehy Fanzy (Fabanna), Jimmy Fotso (Kwong), Adekunle Ilori (Kahei), Sheriff Kargbo (Almamy), Saye Lah (Kessebe), Sylvestre Massaquoi (Santigiie), Samson Odede (Kpona), Chike Okpala (Sorie), Willie Onafesso (Jina), Samuel Pieh (Suuleh), Lansana Sawi (Morlu), Abu Sidique (Tsukama), Elhadju Malik Sow (Golabu), Lamine Thiam (Mahmud); Matthew Sarles (Young Aide), John Sapiel (Old Abnaki Indian), George Gerdes (Marshal), Jerry Molen (Magistrate), Kevin J. O'Connor (Missionary), Robert Walsh (Guardsman), Sean McGuirk (Courier), Tony Owen (Farmer), William Young (Businessman), Michael Riley (British Officer), Frederic Kimball (William Harrison), James Warwick, Zanne Shaw (Aristocrats), Leon Singer (Don Pablo), Castulo Guerra (Spanish Priest), Jonathan Epstein (Second Lieutenant), Brian Smiar (Lieutenant Paine), Harry Groener (Tecora Captain), Father Ellwood Kieser C.S.P. (Priest), Hawthorne James (Creole Cook), Ingrid Walters (Woman Overboard with Baby), Harry A. Blackmun (Associate Justice Joseph Story); Additional Amistad Africans: Curtis Shields (Bassie), Charles Udoma (Kessebe), Tony Onafesso (Baa), Clarence Mobley (Kenei), Edward Appiah (Followolo), Paul Mwakutuya (Sessi), Samuel Orekhio (Fawni), Ransford Thomas (Alkali), Issac Mayanja (Sanpha), Roosevelt Flenoury (Njaooni), Carlos Spivey (Chike), Andrew L. Josiah (Tamba), Peter Mansaray (Kapr), Brian Macon (Yauai), Denver Dowridge (Kpau), Rory Burton (Vakina), Omo Lara Tosin (Kula), Juliette Darko (Teme), Charlean Isata Bangalie (Margru), M.S. Kaleiwo (Kaleiwo)

Off the coast of Cuba, a group of Africans aboard the slaveship Amistad reclaim their freedom only to discover that they must stand trial when they end up in American waters. This film received Oscar nominations for supporting actor (Anthony Hopkins), cinematography, costume design, and original dramatic score.

Morgan Freeman

Anthony Hopkins

Matthew McConaughey

DECONSTRUCTING HARRY

Woody Allen, Judy Davis

(FINE LINE FEATURES) Producer, Jean Doumanian; Executive Producer, J.E. Beaucaire; Director/Screenplay, Woody Allen; Co-Executive Producers, Jack Rollins, Charles H. Joffe, Letty Aronson; Co-Producer, Richard Brick; Photography, Carlo DiPalma; Designer, Santo Loquasto; Editor, Susan E. Morse; Costumes, Suzy Benzinger; Casting, Juliet Taylor; a Sweetland Films presentation of a Jean Doumanian production; Dolby Stereo; Color; Rated R: 93 minutes; December release

CAST

Doris	Caroline Aaron
Harry Block	Woody Allen
Joan	Kirstie Alley
Richard	Bob Balaban
Ken	Richard Benjamin
Burt	Eric Bogosian
Larry	Billy Crystal
Lucy	Judy Davis
Cookie	Hazelle Goodman
Beth Kramer	Mariel Hemingway
Jane	Amy Irving
Grace	Julie Kavner
Hilly	Eric Lloyd
Leslie	Julia Louis-Dreyfus
Harvey Stern	Tobey Maguire
Helen	Demi Moore
Fay	Elisabeth Shue
Paul Epstein	Stanley Tucci
Mel	Robin Williams
Max	Hy Anzel
Ms. Paley	Scotty Bloch
Professor Clark	Philip Bosco
Dolly	Shifra Lerer
Harry's Father	Gene Saks

and Judy Bauerlein (Actress), Joseph Reidy (First Assistant Director), Phyllis Burdoe (Script Supervisor), Barbara Hollander (Mel's Daughter), Adam Rose (Mel's Son), David S. Howard (Mel's Doctor), Amanda Barudin (Beth Kramer's Daughter), Juliet Gelfman-Randazzo (Baby Hilly), Floyd Resnick (Israeli Patient), Brian McConnachie (Dr. Reese), Peter Jacobson (Goldberg), Tracey Lynne Miller (Goldberg's Girlfriend), Jennifer Garner (Woman in Elevator), Irwin Charone (Bar Mitzvah Host), John Doumanian, Alexa Aronson, Kenneth Edelson (Bar Mitzvah Guests), Viola Harris (Elsie), Si Picker (Wolf Fishbein), Howard Spiegel (Mr. Farber), Eugene Troobnick (Professor Wiggins), Ray Aranha (Professor Aranha), Paul Giamatti (Professor Abbot), Marvin Chatinover (Professor Cole), Daniel Wolf (Professor Wolf), Waltrudis Buck (Dean of Adair University), Arden Myrin (Student Mary), Daisy Prince (Elevator Voice), Peter McRobbie (Damned Man), Dan Moran (Devil), Ray Garvey (Policeman on Campus), Linda Perri (Policewoman on Campus), Tony Sirico (Policeman at Jail)

Harry, suffering from writer's block, examines the various relationships in his life, many of which wound up in his stories, much to the discomfort of the real-life principles. This film received an Oscar nomination for original screenplay.

© Fine Line Features

Tobey Maguire

Stanley Tucci, Demi Moore

Julia Louis-Dreyfus

Woody Allen, Elisabeth Shue, Billy Crystal

Eric Lloyd, Mariel Hemingway, Woody Allen

Hazelle Goodman

Robin Williams, Julie Kavner

Kirstie Alley, Woody Allen

SCREAM 2

(DIMENSION) Producers, Cathy Konrad, Marianne Maddalena; Executive Producers, Bob Weinstein, Harvey Weinstein, Kevin Williamson; Director, Wes Craven; Screenplay, Kevin Williamson; Co-Producer, Daniel Lupi; Co-Executive Producers, Cary Granat, Richard Potter, Andrew Rona; Photography, Peter Deming; Editor, Patrick Lussier; Designer, Bob Ziembicki; Music, Marco Beltrami; *Cassandra Ari* by Danny Elfman; Costumes, Kathleen Detoro; Casting, Lisa Beach; a Konrad Pictures production in association with Craven/Maddalena Films; Distributed by Miramax Films; Dolby Digital Stereo; Panavision; Color; Rated R; 120 minutes; December release

Dewey Riley	David Arquette
Sidney Prescott	Neve Campbell
Gale Weathers	Courteney Cox
Cici	Sarah Michelle Gellar
Randy Meeks	Jamie Kennedy
Debbie Salt	Laurie Metcalf
Hallie	Elise Neal
Derek	Jerry O'Connell
Mickey	Timothy Olyphant
Maureen	Jada Pinkett
Cotton Weary	Liev Schreiber
Chief Hartley	Lewis Arquette
Joel	Duane Martin
Sorority Sister Lois	Rebecca Gayheart
Sorority Sister Murphy	Portia De Rossi
Phil	Omar Epps

and Paulette Patterson (Usher Giving out Costumes), Rasila Schroeder (Screaming Girl up Aisle), Heather Graham ("Stab" Casey), Roger L. Jackson ("The Voice"), Peter Deming (Popcorn Boy), Molly Gross (Theatre #1), Rebecca McFarland (Theatre #2), Kevin Williamson (Cotton's Interviewer), Sandy Heddings-Katulka (Girl in Dorm Hallway), Joe Washington, Angie Dillard, John Patrick, Stephanie Belt, Richard Doughty, Mark Oliver, Jennifer Weston, Shelly Benedict (Reporters), Craig Shoemaker (Artsy Teacher), Josh Jackson, Walter Franks (Film Class Guys), Nina Pertronzio (Film Class Mopey Girl), Jamie Kennedy (Randy Meeks), Marisol Nichols (Dawnie), Cornelia Kiss (Coroner at Cici's House), Lucy In (ER Doctor), Philip Pavel (Officer Andrews), Timothy T. Hillman (Captain Down), Nancy O'Dell (Tori's Interviewer), Tori Spelling (Herself), Luke Wilson ("Stab" Billy), David Warner (Drama Teacher Gus Gold), Greg Meiss (Zeus), Adam Shankman (Ghost Dancer), Jon Kriestien Andersson, Carmen M. Chavez, Anne Fletcher, Erik Hyler, Sebastan Lacause, Lance MacDonald, Sarah Christine Smith, Laurie Sposit, Ryan Lee Swanson (Dancers), Jack Baun (Tackled Cell Phoner), Corey Parker (Library Guy), Chris Doyle (Officer Richards), Jason Horgan, D.K. Arredondo, John Embry (Fraternity Brothers)

Two years after a series of killings in the town of Woodsboro, Stab, a movie based on the murders opens, prompting another killer to strike. Sequel to the 1996 Dimension/Miramax Films release Scream, with Neve Campbell, Jamie Kennedy, Courteney Cox, David Arquette, and Liev Schreiber repeating their roles.

Leslie Nielsen, Matt Keeslar

Timothy Olyphant, Jamie Kennedy, Neve Campbell, Jerry O'Connell, Elise Neal

MR. MAGOO

(WALT DISNEY PICTURES) Producer, Ben Myron; Executive Producers, Henry G. Saperstein, Andre Morgan, Robert L. Rosen; Director, Stanley Tong; Sreenplay, Pat Proft, Tom Sherohman; Based on the character from UPA Productions of America; Co-Producer, Justis Greene; Photography, Jingle Ma; Designer, John Willett; Editors, Stuart Pappé, David Rawlins, Michael R. Miller; Costumes, Tom Bronson; Music, Michael Tavera; Casting, Marcia Ross, Donna Morong; a Ben Myron production; Distributed by Buena Vista Pictures; Dolby Digital Stereo; Panavision; Eastman color; Rated PG; 87 minutes; December release

CAST

Quincy Magoo	Leslie Nielsen
Luanne	Kelly Lynch
Waldo	Matt Keeslar
Bob Morgan	Nick Chinlund
Agent Chuck Stupak	Stephen Tobolowsky
Agent Gus Anders	Ernie Hudson
Stacey Sampanahoditra	Jennifer Garner
Austin Cloquet	Malcolm McDowell
Ortega Peru	Miguel Ferrer
Schmitt	L. Harvey Gold
Gosha	Art Irizawa
Hebzinski	John Tierney
McManus	Terence Kelly
Molinaro	Rick Burgess
Javier	Jerry Wasserman
Museum Curator	Bill Dow
Ralston (Stage Manager)	Frank C. Turner
Rosita	Monique Rusu
Desk Clerk	Robert Metcalfe
Tenor	Danny Steele
Tourist	Dolores Drake
Newswoman	Claire Riley
Soprano	Pat Waldron

and Michael Puttonen (Security Guard), Pamela Diaz (Tour Guide), Chancz Perry (Train Station Porter), Marke Driesschen (Radio Announcer), Brenda MacDonald (Opera Patron), Joseph Davies (TV Trainer), Shaun MacDonald (Cook Show Host), David Neale (Fix It Guy), Carrie Cain Sparks (Rosita's Dresser), Kristie Yzerman, Kelly Kay, Yvette Jackson, Tara Mead, Dan Redford, Kirk Coatte (Snowboarders), David Mylrea (Baboon Performer), Greg Burson (Animated Magoo Voice)

When a precious stolen gem inadvertently lands in his possession, bumbling millionaire Quincy Magoo becomes the center of a dastardly plot to get the jewel back.

THE APOSTLE

(OCTOBER)Producer, Rob Carliner; Executive Producer/Director/Screenplay, Robert Duvall; Photography, Barry Markowitz; Designer, Linda Burton; Editor, Steve Mack; Co-Producer, Steven Brown; Music, David Mansfield; Costumes, Douglas Hall; Casting, Renee Rousselot, Ed Johston; a Butchers Run Films Production; Dolby Stereo; CFI color; Rated PG-13; 132 minutes; December release.

Robert Duvall

CAST

Euliss "Sonny" Dewey (The Apostle E.F.)	Robert Duvall
Jessie Dewey	Farrah Fawcett
Tossie	Miranda Richardson
Horace	Todd Allen
Brother Blackwell	John Beasley
Mrs. Dewey, Sr.	June Carter Cash
Sam	Walter Goggins
Joe	Billy Joe Shaver
Troublemaker	Billy Bob Thornton
Elmo	Rick Dial
Mother Blackwell	Mary Lynette Braxton
Sister Johnson	Zelma Loyd
Sister Jewell	Sister Jewell Jernigan
Bayou Man	William Atlas
Sonny Supporter	Lenore Banks
Helper	Brett Brock
Sister Johnsons Twins	Christopher Canady, Christian Canady
Singer	Elizabeth Chisholm
Preacher	Carl D. Cook
Scripture Reader	Naomi Craig
Liquor Store Preacher	Wayne Dehart
Texas State Trooper	Stuart Greer
Virgil	Emery Hopkins
Faith Healers	Brenda B. Jakcson, Vera Kemp
12 Year Old Sonny	Jay Robicheaux
"Amen" Men	Terrence Rosemore
Sister Delilah	Joyce Jolivet Starks
Jessie Jr.	Christina Stojanovich
Bobby	Nicholas Stojanovich

and Paul Baggett, Chili Graham, Bobby Green, Charles Johnson, Steve White, Fay Winn (Tag Team Preachers), Lenore Banks, John E. Hawkins, Jesse Walkrop (Sonny Supporters), Frank Collins, Jr., Joseph Lindsey, Melete Woods (Soloists), Hunter Hayes (Child Accordionist), Daniel Hickman (Flashback Preacher), Julie Johnson (Baptism Soloist), Sharon London (Church Woman), Fernie E. McMillan (Doctor), Jimmie J. Meaux (Church Member #2), L. Christian Mixon (The Bodyguard), Richard Nance, Graham Timbes (Church Men), Douglas Perry (LA State Trooper), Harold Portier, Sr. (Coronet George), Pat Ratliff (Accident Witness), Ronnie Stutes (Needy Receiver), Ruby Francis Terry (Choir Director), James B. Towry (Nosey Neighbor), Renee Victor (Latin Translator), Jerry H. Skelton (Organist) James Gammon

After attacking his wife's lover, Pentecostal preacher Sonny Dewey flees his Texas town, baptizes himself "The Apostle E.F." and settles down in a Louisiana bayou town to preach to the citizens. This film received an Oscar nomination for actor (Robert Duvall).

June Carter Cash, Farrah Fawcett, Christina Stojanovich

Robert Duvall, Billy Bob Thornton

The Mouse

Lee Evans, Nathan Lane

MOUSE HUNT

(DREAMWORKS) Producers, Alan Riche, Tony Ludwig, Bruce Cohen; Director, Gore Verbinski; Screenplay, Adam Rifkin; Photography, Phedon Papamichael; Designer, Linda DeScenna; Editor, Craig Wood; Costumes, Jill Ohanneson; Visual Effects Supervisor, Charles Gibson; Music, Alan Silvestri; Mouse and Cat Trainer, Boone's Animals for Hollywood; Casting, Denis Chamian; an Alan Riche/Tony Ludwig production; Dolby Digital Stereo; Technicolor; Rated PG; 97 minutes; December release

CAST

Christopher Walken

Ernie Smuntz	Nathan Lane
Lars Smuntz	Lee Evans
April Smuntz	Vicki Lewis
Alexander Falko	Maury Chaykin
The Lawyer	Eric Christmas
Quincy Thorpe	Michael Jeter
Ingrid	Debra Christofferson
Hilde	Camilla Soeberg
Auctioneer	Ian Abercrombie
Roxanne Atkins	Annabelle Gurwitch
The Banker	Eric Poppick
Maury	Ernie Sabella
Rudolf Smuntz	Wickey Hickey
Caesar	Christopher Walken
Mayor McKrinkle	Cliff Emmich
Mayor's Wife	Melanie MacQueen
Becky	Brianna Shebby
Betty	Danielle Shebby
Leslie Reinhart	Leslie Upson
Zeppco Suits	Mario Cantone, Peter Anthony Rocca
Lester Dinkus	Steve Bean
Waitress #1	Suzanne Krull
Mr. Texas	William Frankfather

and Pat Thomas (Construction Worker #1), Peter Gregory (Doctor), E.J. Callahan (Historical Clerk), Susan Blommaert (Ms. Park Avenue), Valorie Armstrong (Franklin's Wife), Michael Rae Sommers (Paramedic), Michael Ross (Cop), Jose Rey (Cuban Postal Worker), Carmen Filpi (Pallbearer#4), Harper Roisman, David Fresco (Factory Workers), Scott Smith (City Paramedic), Sarah Dampf (Crying Child), Orville Stoeber, David Weisenberg (Experts), Fred Pierce (Large Nosed Man), Clement E. Blake (Homeless Man), Saverio Carubia (Photographer), Pep Torres (Bus Boy)

Lee Evans, Nathan Lane

Having been left a dilapidated mansion by their late father, the Smuntz brothers are delighted to find out it is an architectural masterpiece worth millions. Unfortunately, their efforts to renovate the house and sell it are waylaid by a determined mouse who refuses to vacate the premises. This was the final film of actor William Hickey who died on June 29, 1997.

JACKIE BROWN

(MIRAMAX) Producer, Lawrence Bender; Executive Producers, Bob Weinstein, Harvey Weinstein, Richard N. Gladstein, Elmore Leonard; Director/Screenplay, Quentin Tarantino; Based on the novel *Rum Punch* by Elmore Leonard; Co-Producer, Paul Hellerman; Photography, Guillermo Navarro; Designer, David Wasco; Editor, Sally Menke; Costumes, Mary Claire Hannan; Casting, Jaki Brown, Robyn M. Mitchell; a Band Apart production; Dolby Digital Stereo; CFI color; Rated R; 158 minutes; December release

Michael Keaton, Pam Grier

CAST

Jackie Brown	Pam Grier
Ordell Robbie	Samuel L. Jackson
Max Cherry	Robert Forster
Melanie	Bridget Fonda
Ray Nicolette	Michael Keaton
Louis Gara	Robert De Niro
Mark Dargus	Michael Bowen
Beaumont Livingston	Chris Tucker
Sheronda	Lisa Gay Hamilton
Winston	Tommy "Tiny" Lister, Jr.
Simone	Hattie Winston
Public Defender	Denise Crosby
Judge	Sid Haig
Amy, Billingsley Sales Girl	Aimee Graham
Cockatoo Bartender	Ellis E. William
Billingsley Sales Girl #2	Tangie Ambrose
Raynelle, Ordell's Junkie Friend	T'Keyah Crystal Keymah
Cabo Flight Attendant	Venessia Valentino
Anita Lopez	Diana Uribe
Cocktail Waitress	Renee Kelly
Bartender at Sam's	Elizabeth McInerney
Girl at Security Gate	Colleen Mayne
Steakhouse Waitress	Laura Lovelace

and Christine Lydon M.D., Julia Ervin, Juliet Lon, Michelle Berube, Gillian Ilian-Waters (Chicks Who Love Guns), Candice Briese, Gary Man (The Deputies), Jeffrey Deedrick, Roy Nesvold, Herbert Hans Wilmsen (The Sheriffs), Quentin Tarantino (Voice on Answering Machine).

Jackie Brown, a stewardess who has been smuggling money into the country for gunrunner Ordell Robbie, is confronted by the federal authorities who ask her to help them bring Ordell to justice. This film received an Oscar nomination for supporting actor (Robert Forster).

Robert De Niro, Bridget Fonda

© Miramax Films

Robert De Niro, Samuel L. Jackson

Pam Grier, Robert Forster

Jack Nicholson, Helen Hunt

Helen Hunt, Greg Kinnear

Jack Nicholson, Cuba Gooding Jr., Greg Kinnear

AS GOOD AS IT GETS

(TRISTAR) formerly *Old Friends*; Producers, James L. Brooks, Bridget Johnson, Kristi Zea; Executive Producers, Richard Sakai, Laurence Mark, Laura Ziskin; Director, James L. Brooks; Screenplay, Mark Andrus, James L. Brooks; Story, Mark Andrus; Co-Producers, John D. Schofield, Richard Marks; Photography, John Bailey; Designer, Bill Brzeski; Editor, Richard Marks; Associate Producers, Aldric Porter, Maria Kavanaugh; Costumes, Molly Maginnis; Music, Hans Zimmer; Song: "Always Look on the Bright Side of Life," written by Eric Idle; Casting, Francine Maisler; a Gracie Films production; Dolby SDDS Stereo; Technicolor; Rated PG-13; 138 minutes; December release

CAST

Melvin Udall	Jack Nicholson
Carol Connelly	Helen Hunt
Simon Nye	Greg Kinnear
Frank Sachs	Cuba Gooding, Jr.
Vincent	Skeet Ulrich
Beverly	Shirley Knight
Jackie	Yeardley Smith
Nora	Lupe Ontiveros
Verdell	Jill
Supporting Dogs	Timer, Billy
Neighbor Woman	Bibi Osterwald
Carl	Ross Bleckner
Caterer	Bernadette Balagtas
Partygoers	Jaffe Cohen, Laurie Kilpatrick, Alice Vaughn
Handyman	Brian Doyle-Murray
Mother at Table	Kristi Zea
Daughter at Table	Annie Maginnis Tippe
Cafe 24 Waitresses	Patricia Childress, Rebekah Johnson, Missi Pyle, Leslie Stefanson, Tara Subkoff
Cafe 24 Manager	Shane Black
Man at Table	Peter Jacobson
Woman at Table	Lisa Edelstein
Cafe 24 Customer	Stan Bly
Carol's Date	Randall Batinkoff
Spencer Connelly	Jesse James
Street Hustlers	Jamie Kennedy, Justin Herwick
Policewoman	Maya Rudolph
Detective Ray	John F. O'Donohue
Hospital Doctor	David A. Kipper
Nurse Receptionist	Mary Elizabeth Still
Children at Cafe 24	Chloe Brooks, Cooper Brooks
Passersby	Sharon L. Alexander, Holly Denys
Dr. Green	Lawrence Kasdan
Psychiatric Patients	Alison Rose, Kathryn Morris
Cafe 24 Busboy	Wood Harris
Publisher	Linda Gehringer
Receptionist	Julie Benz
Dr. Bettes	Harold Ramis

Antonia Jones, (Nurse), Kaitlin Hopkins, (Woman in Lobby), Jimmy Workman, (Sean from the Bakery), Danielle Spencer, (Veterinarian), Todd Solondz, (Man on Bus), Tom McGowan (Maitre'd), Danielle Brisebois, (Singer), Matt Malloy, (Men's Store Salesman), Paul Greenberg, (Bar Waiter), Kirk Ringberg, (Food Waiter), Dave Hawthorne (Bartender)

Melvin Udall, an obsessive-compulsive romance novelist with an angry edge towards the human race, finds himself forming a bond with Carol, a single mother and waitress, and, more unexpectedly, Simon, a struggling artist whose gay lifestyle Melvin abhors. 1998 Academy Award-winner for Best Actor (Jack Nicholson) and Actress (Helen Hunt). This film received additional Oscar nominations for picture, original screenplay, supporting actor (Greg Kinnear), film editing, and original musical or comedy score.

© TriStar Pictures

Jack Nicholson, Greg Kinnear, Jill

Jill, Jack Nicholson

Yeardley Smith

Shirley Knight

Helen Hunt, Jack Nicholson

Greg Kinnear, Jack Nicholson, Helen Hunt

Dustin Hoffman, Anne Heche, Robert De Niro

Anne Heche, Robert De Niro, Dustin Hoffman

Robert De Niro, Dustin Hoffman

WAG THE DOG

(NEW LINE CINEMA) Producers, Jane Rosenthal, Robert De Niro, Barry Levinson; Executive Producers, Michael De Luca, Claire Rudnick Polstein, Ezra Swerdlow; Director, Barry Levinson; Screenplay, Hilary Henkin, David Mamet; Based on the book *American Hero* by Larry Beinhart; Photography, Robert Richardson; Designer, Wynn Thomas; Editor, Stu Linder; Costumes, Rita Ryack; Music, Mark Knopfler; Co-Producer, Eric McLeod; Special War & News Segments Producers, Steven Pollock, Ted Eccles; Casting, Ellen Chenoweth, Debra Zane; a Tribeca/Baltimore Pictures/Punch production; Dolby Digital Stereo; Technicolor; Rated R; 98 minutes; December release

Dustin Hoffman

CAST

Stanley Motss	Dustin Hoffman
Conrad Brean	Robert De Niro
Winifred Ames	Anne Heche
Sgt. William Schumann	Woody Harrelson
Fad King	Denis Leary
Johnny Green	Willie Nelson
Liz Butsky	Andrea Martin
President	Michael Belson
Amy Cain	Suzanne Cryer
John Levy	John Michael Higgins
Grace	Suzie Plakson
Tracy Lime	Kirsten Dunst
A.D.	Jason Cottle
Director	David Koechner
Pet Wrangler	Harland Williams
Bob Richardson	Sean Masterson
Mr. Young	William H. Macy
Technician	Bernard Hocke
Sharon	Jenny Byrne
Kid with Shoes	Maurkice Woods
Themselves	Pops Staples, Merle Haggard, Jim Belushi, Jay Leno
Co-Pilot	Phil Morris
Officer	Chris Ellis
Owner	Edwin T. Morgan
Pilot	J. Patrick McCormack
Teenage Girl	Jennifer Manley
Judge	Edrie Warner
Young Man/CIA	Richard Lawson
Gate Stewardess	Drena De Niro
Combine Driver	Alberto Vasquez

and Stephanie Kemp, Jack Esformes, John Cho, Michael Reid Davis (Aides), Brant Cotton (Sharon's Boyfriend), Kenneth Kern (Nashville Engineer), Michelle Levinson (Faye), Ron McCoy (Limo Driver), Derrick Morgan (CIA Agent), Garry R. Roleder (USAF Captain), George Gaynes (Senator Nole), Rick Scarry (White House Reporter), Cliff B. Howard (Ranger), Furley Lumpkin, Sean Fenton (Raking Dads), Nikki Crawford (Mom), John Franklin, Kevin Furlong (Jockeys), Lu Elrod (Southern Woman), Michael Villani (Commentator), Warren Wilson (Crossfire Interviewer), Terry Anzur (Announcer #3), Melissa Gardner (Chris Andrews Reporter), Giselle Fernandez (Press Person), Christine Devine, Richard Saxton (Chicago Newscasters), Geffrey Blake, Jerry Levine (Media Guys), Jack Shearer (Sklansky), Emmett Miller (News Break Reporter), Bill Handel (Reporter #7 - Andrew AFB), Arlene Afshangol (Albanian Girl), Hope Garber (Albanian Grandmother), Gina Menza (Press Room Reporter), Maggie Mellin (Mrs. Rose), Tom Murray (Aircraft Carrier Reporter), Shirley Prestia (Moderator Named Shirley), Ralph Tabakin (Southern Man), Marguerite Moreau (Teenage Girl in Audience), Nicole Avant, Tom Bähler, Allen Carter, Carmen Carter, Lance Eaton, Karen Geraghty, Jim Gilstrap, Jennifer Gross, Wendy Lou Halvorsen, Anthony Holiday, Brad Kalas, Billy Trudel, Mark Vieha, Julia Waters, Oren Waters, Maxine Waters ("American Dream" Singers), Craig T. Nelson

Robert De Niro, Anne Heche

Days before the election, the President of the United States is accused of making a pass at a girl scout. In order to take the media focus off of this event, a Washington troubleshooter enlists the aide of Hollywood producer Stanley Motss to create a fake "war" with Albania. This film received Oscar nominations for actor (Dustin Hoffman) and adapted screenplay.

Willie Nelson

Tulku Jamyang Kunga Tenzin, Lobsang Samten

Gyurme Tethong, Tashi Dhondup

Tenzin Thuthob Tsarong, Gyatso Lukhang

KUNDUN

(TOUCHSTONE) Producer, Barbara De Fina; Executive Producer, Laura Fattori; Director, Martin Scorsese; Screenplay/Co-Producer, Melissa Mathison; Photography, Roger Deakins; Designer/Costumes, Dante Ferretti; Editor, Thelma Schoonmaker; Music, Philip Glass; Casting, Ellen Lewis; a Cappa/De Fina production; Distributed by Buena Vista Pictures; Dolby Digital Stereo; Super 35 Widescreen; Technicolor; Rated PG-13; 134 minutes; December release

CAST

Dalai Lama (Adult) ....Tenzin Thuthob Tsarong
Dalai Lama (Age 12) ....Gyurme Tethong
Dalai Lama (Age 5) ....Tulku Jamyang Kunga Tenzin
Dalai Lama (Age 2) ....Tenzin Yeshi Paichang
Mother...Tencho Gyalpo
Lobsang (5-10) ....Tenzin Topjar
Father ....Tsewang Migyur Khangsar
Takster ....Tenzin Lodoe
Tsering Dolma..Tsering Lhamo
Lama of Sera..Geshi Yeshi Gyatso
The Messenger..Lobsang Gyatso
Reting Rinpoche..Sonam Phuntsok
Lord Chamberlain..Gyatso Lukhang
Master of the Kitchen..Lobsang Samten
Taktra Rinpoche...................................Tsewang Jigme Tsarong
Ling Rinpoche..Tenzin Trinley
Kashag/Noblemen.............................Ngawang Dorjee, Phinsto Thonden
Layman #1 ....Chewang Tsering Ngokhang
Norbu Thundrup...Jamyang Tenzin
Lobsang (Adult)...Tashi Dhondup
Nechung Oracle ....Jampa Lungtok
and Karma Wangchuck (Deformed Face Bodyguard), Ben Wang (General Chang Chin-Wu), Kim Chan (Second Chinese General), Henry Yuk (General Tan), Ngawang Kaldan (Prime Minister Lobsang Tashi), Jurme Wangda (Prime Minister Lukhangwa), Robert Lin (Chairman Mao), Selden Kunga (Tibetan Doctor), John Wong (Chinese Comrade), Gawa Youngdung (Old Woman), Tenzin Rampa (Tenzin Chonegyl—age 12), Vyas Ananthakrishnan (Indian Soldier)

The true story of the Tibetan boy who would be declared the 14th reincarnation of the Dalai Lama. This film received Oscar nominations for art direction, cinematography, costume design, and original dramatic score.

© Touchstone Pictures

AFTERGLOW

(SONY PICTURES CLASSICS) Producer, Robert Altman; Executive Producers, Ernst Stroh, Willi Baer; Director/Screenplay, Alan Rudolph; Co-Producer, James McLindon; Photography, Toyomichi Kurita; Editor, Suzy Elmiger; Designer, François Seguin; Costumes, Francois Barbeau; Music, Mark Isham; Associate Producer, Rebecca Morton; Casting, Lucie Robitaille; a Moonstone Entertaiment presentation of a Sandcastle 5 and Elysian Dreams production; U.S.-Canadian; Dolby Stereo; Color; Rated R; 113 minutes; December release

Nick Nolte, Julie Christie

CAST

Lucky Mann	Nick Nolte
Phyllis Mann	Julie Christie
Marianne Byron	Lara Flynn Boyle
Jeffrey Byron	Jonny Lee Miller
Donald Duncan	Jay Underwood
Helene Pelletier	Domini Blythe
Bernard Ornay	Yves Corbeil
Count Falco/Jack Dana	Alan Fawcett
Cassie	Genevieve Bissonnette
Isabel Marino	Michele-Barbara Pelletier
Gloria Marino	France Castel
Monica Bloom	Claudia Besso
Judy the Waitress	Ellen David
The Byrons' Concierge	Don Jordan
Pedro	Bill Rowat
Frederico	Cas Anvar
Falco's Butler	David Francis
Doctor	Ivan Smith
Derelict in Park	John Dunn-Hill
Chateau Lenore Pianist	Warren "Slim" Williams
Chateau Lenore Singer	Jean-François Sauvageau

and Bernard Tanguay (Maitre D'), Dave McKeown (Security Guard), Vanya Rose (Hotel Receptionist), Mark Camacho (Ritz-Carlton Bartender), Amy Kadawaki (Chinese Restaurant Hostess), Salvatore Agostino (Restaurant Owner)

Lara Flynn Boyle, Jonny Lee Miller

Lucky and his wife Phyllis find their already fragile marriage crumbling further apart when they become separately involved with a younger, equally unhappy couple, Marianne and her corporate-minded husband Jeffrey. This film received an Oscar nomination for actress (Julie Christie).

© Sony Pictures Entertainment, Inc.

Nick Nolte, Lara Flynn Boyle

Julie Christie

Louis Gossett Jr., Nigel Hawthorne in *Inside*   © *Strand Releasing*

INSIDE (Strand) Producer, Hilly Elkins; Executive Producers, Louis Gossett, Jr., Dan Paulson; Director, Arthur Penn; Screenplay, Bima Stagg; Photography, Jan Weincke; Designer, David Barkham; Editor, Suzanne Pillsbury; Music, Robert Levin; Casting, Moonyeenn Lee; a Showtime in association with Hallmark Entertainment/Elkin Entertainment and Logo Entertainment presentation; Ultra-Stereo; Color; Rated R; 94 minutes; January release. **CAST:** Eric Stoltz (Marty Strydom), Nigel Hawthorne (Col. Kruger), Louis Gossett, Jr. (Questioner), Ian Roberts (Guard Moolman), Ross Preller (Guard Potgieter), Jerry Mofokeng (Mzwaki), Louis Van Nickerk (J. Martin Strydom, Sr.), Patrick Shai (Bhambo), Janin Eser (Christie Malcolm), Joshua Lyndenberg (Guard Koos), Desmond Dube (Scabenga), Peter Suzman (Michael Radowsky), Nick Boraine (Robert Henderson), Gary Coppin (Big Policeman), Temba Indaba (Bakwana), Nandi Nyemba (Mzwaki's Wife). (Note: This film received its official premiere on Showtime in August of 1996).

SCREWED: AL GOLDSTEIN'S KINGDOM OF PORN (Cinema Village Features) Producers, Todd Phillips, Andrew Gurland; Director/Photography/Editor, Alexander Crawford; from Saint Dympna Prods.; Color; Not rated; 85 minutes; January release. Documentary on pornography mogul Al Goldstein, publisher of Screw magazine.

SPREAD THE WORD: THE PERSUASIONS (Independent) Producer/Director, Fred Parnes; No other credits available; Color; Not rated; 80 minutes; January release. Documentary of a cappella singing group The Persuasions.

KC Hall, Teri Driver in *Screwed* © St. Dympna Productions

SHADOW CONSPIRACY (Hollywood Pictures) Producer, Terry Collis; Executive Producers, Andrew G. Vajna, Buzz Feitshans IV; Director, George P. Cosmatos; Screenplay, Adi Hasak, Ric Gibbs; Photography, Buzz Feitshans IV; Designer, Joe Alves; Editor, Robert A. Ferretti; Co-Producer, Adi Hasak; Music, Bruce Broughton; Costumes, April Ferry; Casting, Karen Rae; an Andrew G. Vajna presentation of a Cinergi production; Distributed by Buena Vista Pictures; Dolby Digital Stereo; Panavision; Technicolor; Rated R; 103 minutes; January release. **CAST:** Charlie Sheen (Bobby Bishop), Linda Hamilton (Amanda Givens), Donald Sutherland (Conrad), Stephen Lang (The Agent), Sam Waterston (President), Ben Gazzara (Vice President Saxon), Henry Strozier (Treasury Secretary Murphy), Charles Cioffi (Gen. Blackburn), Stanley Anderson (Attorney Gen. Toyanbee), Nicholas Turturro (Grasso), Theodore Bikel (Prof. Pochenko), Dey Young (Janet), Reginald Davis, Johnny Newman, Antonio Todd (Basketball Players), Bobby Zajonc (Helicopter Pilot), Casey Biggs (Stokes), Richard Bauer (Grolier), Penny Fuller (Dr. Olson), Gore Vidal (Congressman Page), Tom Quinn (Reporter #1), Jonas Elmblad (Jergon), James A. Chory (Man), Paul Gleason (Blythe), Terry O'Quinn (Frank Ridell), Vicki Ross-Norris, Bob Child (News Reporters), Beverly Brigham (Cafe Waitress), Harold Surratt (Marine Colonel), Helen Carey (Tamara Yarshov), Walt MacPherson (Hickman), Scott Wesley Morgan (Agent Wyndham), F.T. Rea, James L. Byrd (Security Men), Thomas Shelton (Street Vendor), Jeffrey Thompson (Taxi Driver), Karen Bralove (First Lady), Katrina Tabori (Situation Room Assistant), Brian Smyj (Rawlings), Ralph Cosham (Driver), Ramon Estevez (Mr. Jones), Nicholas A. Puccio, Karyn V. Cody, Charles Bowen (Cabinet Members), Michael Cunningham (White House Desk Clerk), Oscar Pitts, Jr., Reginald C. Colbert, Dominick De Marco, J. Williams Midkiff, Jr. (Restaurant Patrons), Richard A. Mention III (Tech), Nick Olcott, Roy Bordon, Andreas Brandt (Secret Service), John Leisenring, Lawrence Leonard (Men in Accident), Richard Turner (Senator)

Sam Waterston, Charlie Sheen in *Shadow Conspiracy*
© *Cinergi Pictures*

VISITING DESIRE (Independent) Producer/Director/Photography/Screenplay, Beth B.; Editor, Melody London; Color; Not rated; 70 minutes; February release. **CAST:** Kembra Pfah, Lydia Lunch.

Lara Flynn Boyle in *Farmer and Chase* © Arrow/ J. Patrick Furden

FARMER & CHASE (Arrow) Producers, Scott Kalmbach, Julie Costanzo, Michael Seitzman; Executive Producer, Doug Humphreys; Director/Screenplay, Michael Seitzman; Photography, Michael Maley; Designer, Doug Freeman; Music, Tony Saunders; Editor, Doug Werby; Casting, Joan Marechal; a Red Sky Films presentation of a Kalmbach/Seitzman production; Color; Not rated; 97 minutes; February release. **CAST::** Ben Gazzara (Farer), Todd Field (Chase), Lara Flynn Boyle (Hillary), Ron Kael (JoJo), David Booth (Casey—FBI), Steven Anthony Jones (Ollie), George Maguire (Chet), Ted Draper (Check Cashing Clerk), Luis Oropeza (Check Cashing Guard), David Renaud (Pawn Shop Customer), Michael De Martini (Jimbo), Jack Byrne (Clarence), Pamela Dunham (Betty—Store Clerk), Yuri Lane (Steve—Store Clerk), Ira Steen (Bank Manager), Nellie Sciutto (Susan—Bank Hostage), Mike Girardin (Harold—Bank Hostage), Dixie Jenay, Leo Downey (Bank Hostages), Robert Ernst (Security Guard), Shamus Maley (Shamus), Warren White (Det. Smith), Lance Brady (Det. Bell), Denny Delk (Capt. Cornell), Jarion Moore (Detective), Danny Kovacs (Chicago Det.), Tom Dryden, Randall King (Snipers), Robert DeWalt (Taxi Driver), Walter Brown, Ed Hanson (Bank Police), Tommy Banks, Garrett Griffin, Steve Bakunas, Annie Combs (FBI Agents)

Benjamin Bratt, Steve Reevis, Calvin Levels, Jesse Borrego in *Follow Me Home* © New Millennia

FOLLOW ME HOME (New Millennia Films) Producers, Alan Renshaw, Irene Romero, Peter Bratt, Benjamin Bratt; Executive Producers, Bonnie Duran, Eduardo Duran, Jennifer Newell-Easton, Gary Rhine; Director/Screenplay, Peter Bratt; Photography, Garett Griffin; Designer, Katernia Keith; Music, Cyril Neville, Speech, Roy Finch; a Chacras Filmworks production in association with Amber Images and In

Pictures; Color; Not rated; 104 minutes; February release. **CAST:** Philmore Steele (Spirit Drummer), Steve Reevis (Freddy), Jesse Borrego (Tudee), Benjamin Bratt (Abel), Calvin Levels (Kaz), Noah Verduzco (Ricky), Cynthia Tinajero (Belinda), David Carrera (Loco), Salma Hayek (Veronica), Blair Renshaw (Michael), Robert Collins (The White Man), Kim McGuire (Pat the Waitress), Alfre Woodard (Evey), Tom Towles (The Cook), Rocky McMurray (Dead Brave & D.J. Voice), David Chase (Jimmy), David Denard (Hal), Ahimsa Stone (Little Girl), John Allen Nelson (Perry), Tom Bower (Larry), Kieran Mulroney (Farmer), Lei Maa (Woman in Painting), Casey Camp (Beckoning Spirit)

Ice Cube, Elizabeth Hurley in *Dangerous Ground* © *New Line Cinema*

DANGEROUS GROUND (New Line Cinema) Producers, Gillian Gorfil, Darrell Roodt; Director, Darrell James Roodt; Screenplay, Greg Latter, Darrell Roodt; Executive Producers, Ice Cube, Pat Charbonnet; Photography, Paul Gilpin; Designer, Dimitri Repanis; Music, Stanley Clarke; Costumes, Ruy Filipe; Editor, David Heitner; a Gillian Gorfil/Darrell Roodt production; Dolby SDDS Stereo; Deluxe color; Rated R; 95 minutes; February release. **CAST:** Ice Cube (Vusi), Elizabeth Hurley (Karen), Ving Rhames (Muki), Eric "Waku" Miyeni (Steven), Sechaba Morajele (Ernest), Thokozani Nkosi (Young Vusi), Ron Smerczac (Interrogation Policeman), Wilson Dunster (Heavy Policeman), Peter Kubheka (Igqira), Roslyn Morapedi (Vusi's Mother), Mabel Mafuya (Woman), Fana Mokoena, Maimela Motubatse, Nkululeko Mabandla (Youths), Robert Whitehead (Sandton Hotel Receptionist), Gresham Phet Jaulima (Bellboy), Toni Caprari (Bar Owner), Temsie Times (Hooker), Prophets of Da City (Band in Nightclub), Helge Janssen (Crack Dealer), Anthony Bishop, Ross Preller (Thugs), Greg Latter (Sam), Ernest Ndlovu, Ike Kanupi, Simo Mogwaza, Godrey Dzingeni, Eddy Msize, Isaac Mavimbela, Peter Nkwanyana, Ernest Mbanzi, Prosperous Ban, Eric Sulu (Muki's Men), Candy Jack Lee (Chinese Girl), Robin Smith (Iron Guard), Gys De Villiers (Det. Sgt.), Veronica Mitchell (Muki's Wife)

FLIPPING (Dove Entertainment) Producers, Gene Mitchell, David Amos; Executive Producer, Michael Woods; Director/Screenplay, Gene Mitchell; Photography, Phil Parmet; Editor, Kevin Krasny; Designer, Diane Hughes; Costumes, Nadine Reimer; Casting, Pat Melton, Paul G. Bens; a Mon Frere Motion Pictures production; Dolby Stereo; Deluxe color; Not rated; 102 minutes; February release. **CAST:** David Amos (Michael Moore), David Proval (Billy White), Gene Mitchell (Shot), Shant Benjamin (Hooker), Barry Primus (Joey), Paul Klar (Dennis), Tony Burton (Chuckie), Mike Starr (C.J.), Keith David (Leo Richards), Willem Keane (Gordie), Lynn Mitchell (Careen), Christine Harte (Melanie), Kim Meredith (Jolie), Gee Thomas (Sam), David Basulto (Nick), James Howell (Marilyn the Transvestite), Christina Fonteyn, Francois Pelligan, Fabrizio (Transvestites), Nick Dimitri (Tommy Barnett), Keith Lewis (Joseph's Cafe Maitre'd), Jon Paul Jones (Bodyguard), Ara Shahbazian (Wedding Band Leader), Peter Kalos (Wedding Maitre 'd), Walt Robles (Drunk in Nightclub), Ron Gilbert (Ray-Ray), Jack Leal, Matt Gallini (Ray-Ray's Friends), Christopher Kriesa (News Reporter Voice)

Troy Sostillio in *Raising Heroes* © Phaedra

RAISING HEROES (Phaedra) Producer/Director/Screenplay/Editor, Douglas Langway; Screenplay, Douglas Langway, Henry White, Edmond Sorel; Photography, Stephen Schlueter; a Doppelganger Films production; Color; Not rated; 84 minutes; February release. **CAST:** Troy Sostillio (Josh Sullivan), Henry White (Paul McEwen), Edmond Sorel (Victor), Stewart Groves (Stephen aka Vinny), Chandra Pointer (Nicole), Robert Zolli (Claudio), Greg Bodkin (Rocco Nappi), Constantine Nikos (Vito), Julian Safavi (Micheal), Nicolas Siljee (Nicki), Susan Silijee (Susan), James Pappas (Jimmy), Victor Barbella (Gerard), Chris Ferraro (Chris), Darrell Scott Rushton (Tom), David Matwijkow (Anthony), Bonnie Perlman (Barbara), Christina Burz (Julie), Douglas Langway (Angelo), Stephen Langway (Mark), Robert Karp (Doctor), Gloria Barber (Susan's Mother), David Zayas (Deli Clerk), Lenny Finelli (Boss' Waiter)

Unforgotten © Castle Hill

UNFORGOTTEN: TWENTY-FIVE YEARS AFTER WILLOW-BROOK (Castle Hill) Producer, Danny Fisher; Executive Producer, Katie Meskell; Director, Jack Fisher; Screenplay, Stuart Warmflash; Photography, Eric Lau, Mark Kroll, Alan McPheely, Richard Mauro; Music, Hayes Greenfield; Editors, Constantine Limperis, Matthew Mallinson, Shelly Toscano; Narrator, Danny Aiello; a City Lights International presentation in association with HeartShare; Color; Not rated; 60 minutes; February release. Documentary looks at the lives of some of the survivors of the notorious Staten Island institution for the mentally retarded, Willowbrook State School, the disgraceful living conditions of which were exposed 25 years earlier by TV reporter Geraldo Rivera.

GOOD LUCK (East West Film Partners) Producers, Richard Hahn, Shirley Honickman Hahn, Andrzej Kamrowski; Executive Producers, Bob Comfort, Richard Hahn; Director, Richard Labrie; Screenplay, Bob Comfort; Photography, Maximo Munzi; Designer, Jane Ann Stewart; Editor, Neal Grieve; Music, Tim Truman; a Richard Hahn production; Dolby DTS Stereo; Color; Rated R; 98 minutes; March release. **CAST:** Gregory Hines (Bernard "Bern" Lemley), Vincent D'Onofrio (Tony "Ole" Olezniak), James Earl Jones (James Bing), Max Gail (Farmer John), Joe Theismann, Roy Firestone (Themselves), Robert O'Reilly ("Bartender"), Jack Rader ("Drag Queen"), Ramsay Midwood ("Santa Claus"), Maria O'Brien (Peggy), Sara Trigger (Heidi), Ross Huffman-Kerr (Olsen), Kathryn Howell (Doris), William C. Simmonds (Steve), Doug Mace ("Clock Hat Man"), Jerry A. Basham ("Chicken Foot Man"), Kathleen Stefano (Rhonda, the Dealer), Doug Baldwin (Owner of the Trashed Car), Maureen McVerry (Joan Redack), Heath Lourwood, James Martin (Sons), Troy Bryant (Cop in Police Car), Joe Ivy (Detective), Garwood Perkins (Buzz), Dennis Dun (Chang), Diedre Kilgore (Topless Fan), Eric Tecosky (Stadium Fan), Charles Gould Taylor (Cop on the Street), Gary Budoff, Stephen Orloff, Aaron Daniel Haber, Brad Heffler, Barry Koff (Football Fans)

Jerry A. Basham, Gregory Hines in *Good Luck*
© East-West Film Partners

RHYME AND REASON (Miramax) Producers, Charles X Block, Peter Spirer, Daniel Sollinger; Executive Producer, Helena Echegoyen; Director, Peter Spirer; Co-Producer, Richard Spero; Photography, Peter Spirer, Daniel Sollinger, George Mitas, Sean Adair, Brennan McClean, Alex Rappaport, Adam Vardy, Antonio Ponti; Music, Benedikt Brydern; Music Supervisors, Happy Walters, Andrew Shack; Executive in Charge of Production, Shannon McIntosh; Editors, Andy Robertson, David Wilson; a City Block and Aslan Pictures production; Dolby Stereo; Color; Rated R; 90 minutes; March release. Documentary on hip hop and rap, featuring Busta Rhymes, A Tribe Called Quest, Pharcyde, The Fugees, The Alkoholiks, The Notorious B.I.G., Kurtis Blow and Crew, Heavy D, Grand Master Caz, Salt-N-Pepa, Speech, Biz Markie,

NAS in *Rhyme and Reason* © Miramax Films

Lords of the Underground, DAS EFX, Air Force Crew, Li'l Caesar, Wise Intelligent, Andre Charles, Chuck D, Erick Sermon, Craig Mack, LBC Crew, Redman, Diezzle Don, Mack 10, KRS-ONE, Cypress Hill, MC Eiht, Chaz Hays, Suave, Whodini, Guru, Spearhead, Ras Kass and Crew, Parrish Smith, Kris Kross, Xzibit, NAS, "Puffy" Combs, Paul Stewart, Sen Dog, Kid of Kid N' Play, The Luniz, Adario Strange, Keith Murray, Kool Herc, Red Alert, LL Cool J, Da Brat, Tupac, Spice 1, LV, Master P, Lost Boyz, Suga T, E-40, Too-Short, Melly Mel, Scorpio, Young MC, The Rza, Dogg Pound, Jermaine Dupri, Jay-Z, Homicide, Dr. Dre.

Spalding Gray in *Gray's Anatomy* © Northern Arts Entertainment

GRAY'S ANATOMY (Northern Arts Entertainment) Producer, John Hardy; Executive Producers, Jonathan Sehring, Caroline Kaplan, Kathleen Russo; Director, Steven Soderbergh; Screenplay, Spalding Gray; Based on his performance piece; Photography, Elliot Davis; Editor, Susan Littenberg; Music, Cliff Martinez; from Bait and Switch, Inc.; Color/Black and White; Not rated; 80 minutes; March release. A monologue by Spalding Gray.

Adrienne Shelly, Tim Guinee in *Sudden Manhattan* © Phaedra Cinema/Homegrown

SUDDEN MANHATTAN (Phaedra) Producer, Marcia Kirkley; Executive Producers, Paul D'Addario, Jeff Sine, Larry Lavine; Director/Screenplay, Adrienne Shelly; Photography, Jim Denault; Designer, Teresa Mastropierro; Costumes, Cherish Cullison; Editor, Jack Haigis; Music, Pat Irwin; a Homegrown Pictures production; Dolby Stereo; Color; Not rated; 85 minutes; March release. **CAST:** Adrienne Shelly (Donna), Tim Guinee (Adam), Roger Rees (Murphy), Louise Lasser (Dominga), Hynden Walch (Georgie), Jon Sklaroff (Alex), Paul Cassell (Ian), Chuck Montgomery (Bearded Man), David Simonds (Roses Man), Melinda Wade (Roses Woman), Pamela Gray (Bagel Business Woman), Brian Quirk (Playwright), C.C. Loveheart (Waitress), Shirl Bernheim, Elizabeth Newitt (Old Ladies), Garry Goodrow (Fainting Man), Bobby Caravella (Cop Kelly), Bill Boggs (Newscaster), Elaine Lang (Bunny Lady), Jan Leslie Harding (Crazy Diner Lady), Neil

John Randolph in *The Hotel Manor Inn* © Manor Films

Deodhar (Convenience Guy), Trish Hunter (Georgie's Mom), Kevin Cahoon (Georgie's Brother), Emily Cutler (Georgie's Friend), Kevin Hagan (Jim), Joey Golden (Bernie), Mark Blum (Louis), Gordana Roshovich (Barbara), Hugh Palmer (Joe), Harry Bugin (Gran'pa Pete).

THE HOTEL MANOR INN (Manor Films) Producer/Director/Screenplay, Wayne Chesler; Executive Producers, Robert Gillings, Damon Testaverde, Wayne Chesler; Photography, Michael McCurry; Designer, Pilar Turner; Music, Alan Schwartz; Color; Not rated; 92 minutes; March release. **CAST:** John Randolph (Gus), Sam Trammell (Nolan), Burke Moses (Brian Armor), Jennifer Corby (Kathy), Fred Norris (Pete), Richard Bright (Gregor), William Preston (Charlie), Jessica Dublin (Lucille), Lawrence Vincent (Ed), Herschel Sparber (Chief Farrell), Jack William Scott (Boney), Jane Strauss (Holly), Steve Roberts (Kiki), Dory Binyon (Tara), Jerome Richards (Pat), Robert Gillings (Rob King), Zabryna Guevara (Denise), Bill London (London Luge), Michael McCurry (Preston Press), Bob Greenberg (Marty), Joseph Haddock (Camera Man), Derek Chesler (Jimmy Horn), Kali LaBorne (Sally Horn), Kevin Cottrell (D.J.), Cary Schwartz (Chief Adel), Dan Moyer (Roger Wiley), Paul Pfeifer (Hilda the Builder), Matt Ross (Coffee Man), Tom Camarda (Ladder Man), Janie Chesler (Goldie), Alex Fong (Videotape Man), David Benullo (Joe Deak)

SUZANNE FARRELL: ELUSIVE MUSE (Seahorse Films) Producer, Anne Belle; Directors, Anne Belle, Deborah Dickson; Photography, Don Lenzer, Tom Hurwitz, Wolfgang Held; Editor, Deborah Dickson; Co-Producer, Catherine Tambini; Color; Not rated; 105 minutes; March release. Documentary on ballerina Suzanne Farrell, featuring Jacques d'Amboise, Maria Calegari, Arthur Mitchell, Heléne Alexopoulos, Paul Mejia, Maurice Béjart, Isabelle Guérin, Susan Jaffe, Peter Boal, Marie-Christine Mouis.

Suzanne Farrell in *Suzanne Farrell: Elusive Muse* © Seahorse Films

Nakia Burrise, Jason David Frank, Catherine Sutherland, Johnny Yong Bosch in *Turbo: A Power Rangers Movie* © Twentieth Century Fox

TURBO: A POWER RANGERS MOVIE (20th Century Fox) Producer, Jonathan Tzachor; Executive Producers, Haim Saban, Shuki Levy; Directors, David Winning, Shuki Levy; Screenplay, Shuki Levy, Shell Danielson; Photography, Ilan Rosenberg; Editors, Henry Richardson, B.J. Sears; Music, Shuki Levy; Designer, Yuda Ako; Costumes, Danielle Baker; a Saban Entertainment/Toei Co. production;U.S.-Japanese; Dolby Stereo; Color; Rated PG; 99 minutes; March release. **CAST:** Jason David Frank (Tommy/Red Ranger), Steve Cardenas (Rocky/Blue Ranger), Johnny Yong Bosch (Adam/Green Ranger), Catherine Sutherland (Katherine/Pink Ranger), Nakia Burrise (Tanya/Yellow Ranger), Blake Foster (Justin), Paul Schrier (Bulk), Jason Narvy (Skull), Austin St. John (Jason), Amy Jo Johnson (Kimberly), Hilary Shepard Turner (Divatox), Richard Genelle (Ernie), Jon Simanton (Lerigot), Ed Neil (Lord Zedd), Carla Pérez (Rita Repulsa), Jon Simanton (Lerigot), Gregg Bullock (Lt. Stone), Paul Schrier (Bulk)

DRUNKS (Northern Arts) Producers, Peter Cohn, Shireen Meistrich, Burtt Harris; Executive Producers, Larry Meistrich, John Hart, Tom Carouso; Director, Peter Cohn; Screenplay, Gary Lennon, based on his play *Blackout*; Photography, Peter Hawkins; Designer, Michael Shaw; Editor, Hughes Winborne; Costumes, Kim Druce; Casting, Lina Todd; a Seagoat Films and Kardana Films presentation of a Shooting Gallery production; Ultra-Stereo; Color; Rated R; 88 minutes; March release. **CAST:** Richard Lewis (Jim), Liza Harris (Melanie), Liam Ahern (Billy), George Martin (Marty), Sam Rockwell (Tony), Amanda Plummer (Shelley), Kevin Corrigan (Cam), Fanni Green (Jasmine), Parker Posey (Debbie), Dianne Wiest (Rachel), Billy Dove (Leo), Julie Halston (Carol), Faye Dunaway (Becky), Lisa Gay Hamilton (Brenda), Calista Flockhart (Helen), Annette Arnold (Kathy), Howard Rollins (Joseph), Oscar Koch

Christopher Lawford, Richard Lewis in *Drunks* © Northern Arts

(Dennis), Margaret Devine (Terry), Michael Medeiros (Charlie), Kevin Rendon (First Liquor Clerk), Burtt Harris (Harry), Laurie Taylor-Williams (Francine), Spalding Gray (Louis), Anna Thomson (Tanya), Zach Grenier (Al), Christopher Lawford (Rich), Michael Campbell (Ted), Abe Gurko (Huge Guy), David Drumgold (Chaka), Cisco Davis (Park Kid), Joey Arias (Ruby), Jonathan Cook (Freddie), Olga Merediz (Chairwoman), Judy Bauerlein (Lucy), Kevin Davis (Tom)(Note: This film made its debut on Showtime in November of 1996).

Cheryl Dunye, Guinevere Turner, Lisa Marie Bronson, Valarie Walker in *The Watermelon Woman* © First Run Features

THE WATERMELON WOMAN (First Run Features) Producers, Barry Swimar, Alexandra Juhasz; Executive Producer, Michael Light; Director/Screenplay, Cheryl Dunye; Photography, Michelle Crenshaw; Co-Producer, Cate Wilson; Co-Executive Producer/Editor, Annie Taylor; Color; Not rated; 80 minutes; March release. **CAST:** Cheryl Dunye (Cheryl), Guinevere Turner (Diana), Valarie Walker (Tamara), Camille Paglia (Herself), Lisa Marie Bronson (Fae Richards), Toshi Reagon, Cheryl Clarke, Sarah Schulman.

B*A*P*S (New Line Cinema) Producers, Mark Burg, Loretha Jones; Executive Producers, Michael De Luca, Jay Stern; Director, Robert Townsend; Screenplay, Troy Beyer; Photography, Bill Dill; Designer, Keith Brian Burns; Editor, Patrick Kennedy; Costumes, Ruth Carter; Music, Stanley Clarke; Casting, Valerie McCaffrey; an Island Pictures production; Dolby Digital Stereo; Deluxe color; Rated PG-13; 90 minutes; March release. **CAST:** Halle Berry (Nisi), Martin Landau (Mr. Blakemore), Ian Richardson (Manley), Natalie Desselle (Mickey), Troy Beyer (Tracy), Luigi Amodeo (Antonio), Jonathan Fried (Isaac), Pierre (Ali), A.J. Johnson (James), Bernie Mac (Mr. Johnson), Darrel Heath

Natalie Desselle, Halle Berry in *B*A*P*S* © New Line Cinema

Cameron Foord, Sam Trammell in *Childhood's End*
© Plainview/Open City

(Terrance), Vince Cooke (Z.Z.), Faizon Love (Tiger J), Rudy Ray Moore (Nate), Darrow Igus (Bartender), Debra Wilson (Flight Attendant), Robin Van Sharner (Airline Passenger), Jessica Page (Audition Dancer), Alex Thomas (Music Store Salesman), Eric Poppick (Vincent), Downtown Julie Brown, Heavy D, Idalis DeLeon, Howard Hewitt, LL Cool J, Leon, Dennis Rodman (Themselves)

CADILLAC RANCH (Legacy) Producers, J. Todd Harris, Harvey Kahn; Executive Producers, John Davis, Stephen Nemeth, Robert William Landaas, Chip Duncan; Director, Lisa Gottlieb; Screenplay, Jennifer Cecil; Photography, Bruce Douglas Johnson; Designer, John Huke; Editor, Dan Loewenthal; Costumes, Kari Perkins; Music, Christopher Tyng; Casting, Cathy Henderson; a Davis Entertainment Classics and Water Street Pictures presentation of a J. Todd Harris/Water Street Pictures production; Panavision; CFI color; Rated R ; 104 minutes; April release. **CAST:** Christopher Lloyd (Wood Grimes), Suzy Amis (CJ Crowley), Renee Humphrey (Mary Katherine Crowley), Caroleen Feeney (Frances Crowley), Linden Ashby (Beau), Jim Metzler (Travis Crowley), Joe Stevens (Leroy), Bill Wise (Hippie Artist), Ashley Coe (Young CJ), Renee Olstead (Young Mary Katherine), Hillary Van Scoy (Young Frances), Doyle Carter (Bailiff), William Earl Ray (Judge), Robert Fieldsteel (CJ's Attorney), Barbara Lasater (Mother), Jennifer Cecil (Bridal Shower Photographer), Brad Leland (Booking Deputy), Chamblee Ferguson (Cody Nolan), Sage Schlather (Jasmine), Ray Benson (Lou), Sarah Cecil (Woman Making Out), Charles Mooneyhan, Wally Welch (Men), Gary Carter (Sgt. Polk), Richard Dillard (Capt. Steadlin), Charles Solomon (Bartender), Ken Tigar (Clown)

LICENSED TO KILL (DeepFocus Prod.) Producer/Director/Screenplay/Editor, Arthur Dong; Photography, Robert Shepard; Music, Miriam Cutler; Associate Producer, Thomas G. Miller; "Leviticus: Faggot" written and performed by Me'Shell Ndegéocello; Color; Not rated; 80 minutes; April release. Documentary looking at the experiences of several men who have murdered homosexuals.

CHILDHOOD'S END (Plainview Pictures) Producers, Jason Kliot, Joana Vicente; Director/Screenplay, Jeff Lipsky; Photography, Victoria Ford; Designer, Wing Lee; Editor, Sabine Hoffman; Costumes, Angela Wendt; Casting, Diana Jaher; Color; Not rated; 90 minutes; April release. **CAST:** Cameron Foord (Evelyn), Heather Gottlieb (Rebecca), Sam Trammell (Greg), Colleen Werthmann (Denise), Bridget White (Chloe), Reiko Aylesworth (Laurie) Philip Coccioletti (Harvey), Georgia Creighton (Saleswoman), Edie Falco (Patty), Linda Larkin (Caroline), Joe Lisi (Mr. Meyer), Keith Primi (Mark), John Rothman (Bernard), Fay Rusli (Minako), Charlie Schiff (Sid), Maureen Silliman (Mrs. Meyer), Ellen Tobie (Miranda), Cody Tucker (Virginia)

GRIND (Castle Hill) Producer, Laura Lau; Executive Producer, Tom Staub; Director, Chris Kentis; Screenplay, Laura Lau, Christ Kentis; Co-Producer, Melissa Powell; Photography, Stephen Kazmierski; Designer, Therese Deprez; Costumes, Katherine Jane Bryant; Music, Brian Kelly; Casting, Laura Lau, Melissa Powell, Cassandra Han; a Kodiak Productions L.L.C. presentation; Dolby Stereo; Color; Not rated; 96 minutes; April release. **CAST:** Billy Crudup (Eddie), Adrienne Shelley (Janey), Paul Schulze (Terry), Frank Vincent (Nick), Saul Stein (Jack), Amanda Peet (Patty), Steven Beach (Jimmy), Jason Andrews (Joey), Arthur Nascarella (John), Nick Sandow (Lenny), Tim Williams (Scott), Angela Pupello (Pam), Lydia Radzull (Liz), Tim Devlin (Scully), Joe Pallister (J.J.)

Billy Crudup in *Grind*   © Castle Hill Prods. Inc.

SCHIZOPOLIS (Northern Arts) Producer, John Hardy; Director/Screenplay/Photography, Steven Soderbergh; Music, Cliff Martinez, Joseph Wilkins, Mark Mangini, Harry Garfield; Editor, Sarah Flack; Color; Not rated; 99 minutes; April release. **CAST:** Steven Soderbergh (Fletcher Munson), Betsy Brantley (Mrs. Munson/Attractive Woman #2), David Jensen (Elmo Oxygen), Eddie Jemison (Nameless Numberheadman), Scott Allen (Right Hand Man), Mike Malone (T. Azimuth Schwitters), Katherne LaNasa (Attractive Woman #1)

David Jensen in *Shizopolis*
© Northern Arts

Debra Messing, Dean Stockwell, French Stewart in *McHale's Navy*
© Universal Studios/Bubble Factory

McHALE'S NAVY (Universal) Producers, Sid Sheinberg, Bill Sheinberg, Jon Sheinberg; Executive Producers, Lance Hool, Perry Katz; Director, Bryan Spicer; Screenplay, Peter Crabbe; Story, Peter Crabbe, Andy Rose; Based on the ABC television series; Photography, Buzz Feitshans IV; Designer, Gene Rudolf; Editor, Russell Denove; Co-Producers, Tom Arnold, Conrad Hool; Costumes, Michael T. Boyd; Music, Dennis McCarthy; Casting, Lisa London, Catherine Stroud; The Bubble Factory presentation of a Sheinberg production; Dolby DTS Stereo; Eastman color; Rated PG; 109 minutes; April release. CAST: Tom Arnold (Lt. Cmmdr. Quinton McHale), Dean Stockwell (Capt. Wallace B. Binghampton), Debra Messing (Lt. Penelope Carpenter), David Alan Grier (Ens. Charles T. Parker), Tim Curry (Maj. Vladakov), Ernest Borgnine (Cobra), Bruce Campbell (Virgil), French Stewart (Happy), Danton Stone (Gruber), Brian Haley (Christy), Henry Cho (Willie), Anthony Jesse Cruz (Roberto), Honorato Magaloni (Castro), Guillermo Rios (Jose), Eduardo Lopez Rojas (Gonzalez), Tom Ayers (Henchman Carl), Scott Cleverdon (Henchman David), Robert Schuch (Boat Henchman), Tommy Chong (Armando/Ernesto), Paco Mauri (Doctor), Juan Rebolledo (Juan), Diego Vazquez (Rey), Lucy Moreno (Hermina), Mineko Mori (Mystic Woman), Luis Lemus (Sergeant), Alejandro Reyes (Manuel), Alex Cole (Guard), Joe Keyes (Officer), Tomas Leal (Monkey Owner), Luisa Huertas (Nurse), Joe Minjares (Pharmacist/Barber), Fima Noveck (Russian Leader), Eric Champnella (Stan), John Pyper Ferguson (Interrupting Henchman), Anthony Azizi (Bad News Henchman), Bryan Spicer (Unlucky Henchman)

Lauri Crook in *Without Air* © Phaedra Cinema

WITHOUT AIR (Phaedra Cinema) Producer, John Bick; Director/Screenplay/Photography, Neil Abramson; Editor, Suzanne Hines; Music, Kennard Ramsey; Designer, Paula Good; Black and white; Not rated; 88 minutes; April release. CAST: Lauri Cook (Shay), Jack May (Boyfriend), Leigh-Anne Potter (Angel), Nokie Taylor (Harry), Larry "Bait" Wiltsey (Sleazy Driver), Dennis Brockway (Donut Man), Trick Cantrell (Strip Joint DJ), Russell George (Bartender), Michelle McGlocklin, Vicky Tubbs, Angel Carpenter, Meresa Ferguson (Strip Joint Dancers), Kathy D. Bennett, Anthony R. Jackson (Arguing Couple), Christopher Rutherford (Kid), William Watson, Jimme Turner, Leon "Jelly Belly" Jeter (Men), Jimmy Ellis (Jimmy), Carrie Wilchie (Laundromat Woman), Pat Lawyer (Cajun Clyde), Vicky Alford (BBQ Counterperson), Gary Hardy (Hobo Joe), Mack Orr, Joe H. Hicks, Tony McKinney, James Bonner, Otto Carnes ("The Fieldstones")

Mary Tyler Moore, Eric Stoltz in *Keys To Tulsa*
© Gramercy Pictures

KEYS TO TULSA (Gramercy) Producers, Leslie Greif, Harley Peyton; Executive Producers, Michael Birnbaum, Peter Isacksen; Director, Leslie Greif; Screenplay, Harley Peyton; Based on the novel by Brian Fair Berkey; Line Producer, Elliot Rosenblatt; Co-Producer, Guy J. Louthan; Photography, Robert Fraisse; Music, Stephen Endelman; Designer, Derek R. Hill; Editors, Eric L. Beason, Louis F. Cioffi, Michael R. Miller; Costumes, Marie France; Casting, Fern Champion, Mark Paladini; from ITC Entertainment Group; CFI color; Rated R; 113 minutes; April release. CAST: Eric Stoltz (Richter Boudreau), James Spader (Ronnie Stover), Mary Tyler Moore (Cynthia Whitlow Boudreau Simpson Rawling), James Coburn (Harmon Shaw), Deborah Kara Unger (Vicky Michaels Stover), Joanna Going (Cherry), Michael Rooker (Keith Michaels), Peter Strauss (Chip Carlson), Randy Graff (Louise Brinkman), Cameron Diaz (Trudy), Dennis Letts (Preston Liddy), Josh Ridgway (Billy), Marco Perella (Bedford Shaw), George Greif (Bartender), Doran Ingrham (Tattoo Man), Alex Allen Morris (Policeman), Veron Grote (Desk Sergeant), Lauren Rochelle (Earla), Randy Stripling (Waiter), Randy Means (Victor Hill), Vicky Hutson, Lucia Reeves (News Reporters), Roger Burlage (Hills Friend), Debbie Bowman, Sanda Czapla, Marcella Mhall, Erin Swenson, Dawn Wagner (Sixty-Six Club Dancers)

NO ORDINARY LOVE (Phaedra Cinema) Producer, Eli Kabillio; Director/Screenplay, Doug Witkins; Executive Producer, Adam Fast; Photography, Armando Basulito; Music, Bob Christianson; Editor, John Orland; an Eli Kabillio production, 1995; Color; Not rated; 104 minutes; April release. CAST: Smith Forté (Kevin), Ericka Klein (Wendy), Robert Pecora (Andy), Mark S. Larson (Ben), Koing Kuoch (Vince), Dan Frank (Tom), Kathleen Gibson (Rona), Tymme Reitz (Ramon), Marina Palmier (Gloria), Alejandro Patino (Juan Pablo), Randy Brown (Ricky), Elizabeth Mehr (Tina), Alaina P. Pepito (Laurie), Alex Mercer (Cowboy Al), Srey Teang (Short Woman), David Vincent Holland (Transvestite), Rob Gibson

No Ordinary Love © Phaedra Cinema

Daisy Eagan, Monica Keena in *Ripe* ©Trimark Pictures

(Heavy Metal Guy), Lobo Sebastian (Carlos), Fred Blanco, Jose Angel Ceja, Jesus Covarrubias, Randy Guiting (Gangbangers), Mark Solum, T.J. Paolino (Uniformed Officers), Alexandria Nicole Finkelman (Baby Patrick), Susie Spear (Rachel Kingsley), Kelly O'Brien (Officer), Gary Perez (Detective), Eli Kabillio (Interrogator).

DEAD MEN CAN'T DANCE (LIVE Entertainment) Producer, Elaine Hastings Edell; Executive Producer, Leslie Grief; Co-Producer, Frank Hildebrand; Director, Stephen M. Anderson; Screenplay, Paul Sinor, Mark Sevi, Bill Kerby; Story, Paul Sinor; Photography, Levie Isaacks; Editor, Christopher Rouse; Designer, Gary Griffin Constable; Music, Richard Marvin; Color; Rated R; 97 minutes; April release. **CAST**: Kathleen York (Capt. Victoria Elliot), Michael Biehn (Hart), Adrian Paul (Shooter), Barbara Eve Harris (Sgt. Beverly Rhodes), Kelly Jo Minter (Chrissie Brooks), Hiep Thi Le (Min Yan Chun), Jennifer Blanc (Susie Warzenak), Wendy Gazelle (Lorraine Towers), Shawnee Smith (Addy Cooper), Joel Miller (Bear Claw), Rodney Eastman (David Porter), Grace Zabriskie (Gen. Burke), Yancey Arias (Sixkiller), Mark Edward Anderson (Wayne Northrop), Paul Perri (Maj. Shelby), John Carroll Lynch (Sgt. Plonder), R. Lee Ermey (Pullman T. Fowler), Denis Forest (Dennis Larson), Greg Joung Paik (Maj. Kang), Valerie Hastings (Sgt. Tripet), Patrick Newall (Instructor)

RIPE (Trimark) Producers, Suzy Landa, Tom Razzano; Executive Producers, Patrick Panzarella, Michael Chambers; Director/Screenplay, Mo Ogrodnik; Co-Producer, Richard Abramowitz; Photography, Wolfgang Held; Designer, Sally Petersen; Music, Anton Sanko; Editor, Sarah Durham; a C&P production; Ultra-Stereo; Color; Not rated; 93 minutes; May release. **CAST:** Monica Keena (Violet), Daisy Eagan (Rosie), Gordon Currie (Pete), Ron Brice (Ken), Karen Lynn Gorney (Janet Wuman), Vincent Laresca (Jimmy), Scott Sowers (Col. Wyman), Eric Jensen (Dave), Curtis McClarin (H), Donia Silver-Smith (Young Violet), Janna Silver-Smith (Young Rosie), Nurit Koppel (Fran), Bruce McCarty (Daniel), Candice Love (Maxine), Hollie Harper (Dell), Jennifer Chambers (Louise), Mary Leopard (Flag Lady), Zip Hannah (Drill Sergeant), Michael Chambers, Greg Bass, Jac Calabro, Matt Chiaravalle (The Phoids)

FETISHES (Cinema Village Features) Producers, Nick Broomfield, Michelle D'Acosta; Executive Producer, Sheila Nevins; Co-Producer, Jamie Ader-Brown; Director, Nick Broomfield; Photography, Christophe Lazenberg; Editors, Betty Burkhart, Nick Broomfield; Music, Jamie Muhoberac; Associate Producer, Nancy Abraham; Line Producer, S.J. Bloom; Color; Not rated; 90 minutes; May release. A look at the underground world of fetishism and sadomasochism at New York's infamous S&M parlor, Pandora's Box, featuring Mistress Natasha, Mistress Catherine, Mistress Delilah, and Mistress Raven.

Michael Biehn in *Dead Men Can't Dance* © LIVE Entertainment

Mistress Catherine (left) in *Fetishes*
© Susan Meiselas

Vincent Gallo, Kiefer Sutherland in *Truth or Consequences, N.M.*
© Triumph Films

TRUTH OR CONSEQUENCES, N.M. (Triumph) Producers, J. Paul Higgins, Kevin J. Messick, Hilary Wayne; Executive Producer, Phillip M. Goldfarb; Director, Kiefer Sutherland; Screenplay/Co-Producer, Brad Mirman; Photography, Ric Waite; Designer, Anne Stuhler; Editor, Lawrence Jordan; Costumes, Susan Bertram; Music, Jude Cole; Casting, Janet Hirshenson, Jane Jenkins; a Higgins/Messick/Wayne production; Dolby SDDS Stereo; Technicolor; Rated R; 106 minutes; May release. **CAST:** Vincent Gallo (Raymond Lembecke), Mykelti Williamson (Marcus Weans), Kiefer Sutherland (Curtis Freley), Kevin Pollak (Gordon Jacobson), Kim Dickens (Addy Monroe), Grace Phillips (Donna Moreland), James McDaniel (Frank Thompson), Rick Rossovich (Robert Boylan), John C. McGinley (Eddie Grillo), Max Perilch (Wayne), Rod Steiger (Tony Vago), Martin Sheen (Sir), Scott Christopher (Frank Pearson), Steve O'Neill (Detective), Marshall Bell (Police Lt.), Richard Clark (Don Severt), Mark Lonow (Alan Gryder), Jason Rodriguez, Jim Wilkey (Sir Men), Craig Cliver (Sheriff), Robert Peters (Market Clerk), Craig Clyde (Patrol Officer), Joan Robinson, Colin Patrick Lynch (Sheriffs), Peter Iacangelo (Wiseguy), James Verbois (Man on Hillside), Tim Parati (Cecil), Donre Sampson (Cecil's Man), Bill McIntosh, Perry Barndt, John Brimley (Warehouse Cops), Maurice Dunster (Dodge Owner), Dennis Bridwell, Richard Slaughter, Don Shanks (Vago Wiseguys), Chris Howell (Roadside Bar Fighter)

THE BLOODY CHILD (Mirage Releasing) Producer/Director/Photography, Nina Menkes; Screenplay/Editors, Nina Menkes, Tinka Menkes; a Menkesfilm production for the Independent Television Service; Color; Not rated; 85 minutes; May release. **CAST:** Tinka Menkes (Police Captain), Sherry Sibley (Murdered Wife), Russ Little (Sergeant), Robert Mueller (Murderer), Jack O'Hara (Enlisted Man)

Tina Menkes in *The Bloody Child* © Menkes Films

UNDERWORLD (Legacy) Producers, Robert Vince, William Vince; Executive Producers, Mark Amin, Michael Strange, Abra Edelman; Director, Roger Christian; Screenplay, Larry Bishop; Photography, Steven Bernstein; Designer, John Ebden; Editor, Robin Russell; Music, Anthony Marinelli; Casting, Abra Edelman, Elisa Goodman; a Keystone Pictures in association with Trimark Pictures presentation of a Robert Vince production; Color; Rated R; 95 minutes; May release. **CAST:** Denis Leary (Johnny Crown/Johnny Alt), Joe Mantegna (Frank Gavilan/Richard Essex), Annabella Sciorra (Dr. Leah), Larry Bishop (Ned Lynch), Abe Vigoda (Will Cassady), Robert Costanzo (Stan), Traci Lords (Anna), Jimmie F. Skaggs (Smilin' Phil Fox/Todd Streeb), James Otlkan (Dan "Iceberg" Eagan), Heidi Schanz (Simone/Joyce Alt), Christi Conaway (Julianne), Angela Jones (Janette), Michael David Simms (Mitch Reed), Amy Moon (Ava), Marc Baur (Leo), Michael Benyaer (Vince), Tracey Mannen (Stripper), Claudio De Victor (Bartender), Nino Caratozzolo (Billy Dax), Darcy Laurie (Buster Powell), Ken Roberts (Wild Man Palmer), Dave "Squatch" Ward (Slim Crawford), Dean Wray (Walt Clanton), Frank Ferrucci, L. Harvey Gold, Philip Granger, Sal Sortino (Villa Essex Man), Christine Anthony, Thomasina Grieve, Diana Vlaskalic (Showgirls)

Joe Mantegna, Annabella Sciorra, Denis Leary in *Underworld*
© UnderworldFilms

RUDYARD KIPLING'S THE SECOND JUNGLE BOOK: MOWGLI & BALOO (TriStar) Producer, Raju Patel; Executive Producers, Sharad Patel, Mark Damon; Co-Producer, Peter Shepherd; Co-Executive Producers, Stephen Monas, Mohammed Yusef; Director, Duncan McLachlan; Screenplay, Bayard Johnson, Matthew Horton; Based on characters from the novel *The Jungle Book* by Rudyard Kipling; Photography, Adolfo Bartoli; Designer, Errol Kelly; Music, John Scott; Editor, Marcus Manton; Casting, Don Pemrick, Dean Fronk, Jo Gilbert; an MDP Worldwide and Sharad Patel presentation of a Kiplinbook/Raju Patel production; Dolby Stereo; Technovision; Color; Rated PG; 88 minutes; May release. **CAST:** Jamie Williams (Mowgli), Bill Campbell (Harrison), Roddy McDowall (King Murphy), David Paul Francis (Chuchundra), Gulshan Grover (Buldeo), Cornelia Hayes O'Herlihy (Emily Reece), B.J. Hogg (Col. Reece), Amy Robbins (Molly Ward), Hal Fowler (Capt. Ward), Albert Moses (Conductor), Wijeratne Warakagoda (Engineer), Simon Barker (Train Official), EA Piyasena (Porter), Raja Sumanapala (Buldeo's Servant), Sunil Hettiarachchi (Rickshaw Man)

FRANK CAPRA'S AMERICAN DREAM (Columbia TriStar Television) Producer, Charles A. Duncombe, Jr.; Director/Screenplay, Kenneth Bowser; Photography, Richard Pendleton; Editor, Arnold Galssman; Music, John Hodian; Research, Richard Hutt; Presented in association with Frank Capra Prods., ZM Prods. and Sony Pictures High Definition Center; Color/Black and white; Not rated; 108 minutes; May release. Documentary on filmmaker Frank Capra, narrated by Ron Howard.

Jamie Williams, Timo in *The Second Jungle Book*
© TriStar Pictures

THE TURNING (Leo Films) formerly Home Fires Burning; Producers, William B. O'Boyle, L.A. Puopolo; Director, L.A. Puopolo; Screenplay, Chris Ceraso, L.A. Puopolo; Based on the play *Home Fires Burning* by Chris Ceraso; Photography, J. Michael McClary; Designer, Mike Moran; Costumes, Natasha Landau; Editor, Lesley Topping; Music, Herb Pilhofer; 1992; Color; Rated R; 91 minutes; May release. **CAST:** Karen Allen (Glory Lawson), Raymond J. Barry (Mark Harnish), Michael Dolan (Clifford Harnish), Tess Harper (Martha Harnish), Gillian Anderson (April Cavanaugh), Jim Simmons (Mayor), Madison Arnold (Mr. Cavanaugh), Tannis Benedict (Vivian Sinott), John Newton (Mr. Creasy), Bill O'Boyle (Pete Tarosky), Murphy Larson (Rita Smithson), Michael P. Moran (Jim McCutcheon)

JOE & JOE (Independent) Producers, Sean Patrick Brena, David Wall, David Wysocki; Director/Screenplay, David Wall; No other credits available; Color; Not rated; 80 minutes; May release. **CAST:** Sean Patrick Brennan, Tracy Griffith, David Wysocki.

Mario Yedidia, Doug Jones in *Warriors Of Virtue*
© IJL Creations/Law Bros. Ent.

WARRIORS OF VIRTUE (MGM) Producers, Dennis Law, Ronald Law, Christopher Law, Jeremy Law, Patricia Ruben; Executive Producer, Joseph Law; Director, Ronny Yu; Screenplay, Michael Vickerman, Hugh Kelley; Co-Producers, Peter Pau, Ronny Yu; Photography, Peter Pau; Editor, David Wu; Music, Don Davis; Make-up and Animatronic Character Effects, Tony Gardner & Alterian Studios; Action Choreographer, Siuming Tsui; Costumes, Shirley Chan; Visual Effects Supervisor, John Gajdecki; Line Producers, Ogden Gavanski, Hong-An

Jin, Nancy Rae Stone; a Law Brothers production; Digital DTS Stereo; Panavision; Deluxe color; Rated PG; 101 minutes; May release. **CAST:** Angus Macfadyen (Komodo), Mario Yedidia (Ryan), Marley Shelton (Elysia), Chao-Li Chi (Master Chung), Jack Tate (Yun), Doug Jones (Yee), Don W. Lewis (Lai), J. Todd Adams (Chi), Adrienne Corcoran (Tsun), Michael John Anderson (Mudlap), Tom Towles (Grillo), Lee Arenberg (Mantose), Dennis Dun (Ming), Roy Ceballos (Willy Beest), Jason Hamer (Mosely), Don W. Lewis (Mayor Keena), Rickey D'Shon Collins (Chucky), Michael Dubrow (Brad), Peter Abrahamson (Chila), Stuart Kingston (Dullard), Qu Ying (Barbarotious), Gill Butler, Victoria Schoenke (Villagers), Michael Vickerman (Dragoon Commander), Warren Moon (Coach), Teryl Rothery (Kathryn), Julie Patzwald (Tracey), Kimberly Warnat (Lisa), Adam Mills (Toby), Clay McRae, Hamish Allan-Headley (Football Pals), Lian-Yi Li (Chinese Cook), Tynehead's Dog "Rush" (Bravo)

MURDER AND MURDER (Zeitgeist) Producer/Director/Screenplay, Yvonne Rainer; Photography, Stephen Kazmierski; Designer, Stephen McCabe; Costumes, Linda Gui; Music, Frank London; Casting, Heidi Griffiths; Color; Nor rated; 113 minutes; June release. **CAST:** Joanna Merlin (Doris), Kathleen Chalfant (Mildred), Catherine Kellner (Young Mildred), Isa Thomas (Jenny), Yvonne Rainer (Herself), Alice Playten, Kendal Thomas, Rod McLachlan, Jennie Moreau, Sasha Martin, Barbara Haas, Rainn Wilson

Denise Faye, Rick Negron in *The Next Step*   © Phaedra Films

THE NEXT STEP (Phaedra) Producers, Aaron Reed, Hank Blumenthal; Director, Christian Faber; Screenplay, Aaron Reed; Photography, Zack Winestine; Editors, Judd Maslansky, David Codron; Music, Roni Skies, Mio Morales; Choreographer, Brian Otto; Designer, Elise Bennett; Costumes, Nancy Brous, Ivan Ingerman; Associate Producers, Taylor Nichols, Raphael Moreu; a Curb Entertainment presentation of a Wavelength production; Color; Not rated; 97 minutes; June release. **CAST:** Rick Negron (Nick), Kristin Moreu (Amy), Denise Faye (Heidi), Taylor Nichols (Peter), Gerry McIntyre (Sean), Aubrey Lynch (Steven), Michelle Pertier (Michelle), Donald Byrd (Austin), Fuschia Walker (Rolanda), Jane Edith Wilson (Greta), Barry McNabb (Owen), Yvonne Racz (Veronica), Jamie Bishton (Kevin), Michael Donaghy (Luis), Howard Wesson (Louie), Fredrick Deane (Scott), Richard Stegman (Agent), Chris Eigeman (David), Peter Reffie (Frankie), John Battista (Sal), Julio Munge (Ramon), Ted Neuhoff (Husband in Restaurant), Yvonne Trinkwater (Wife in Restaurant), Pamela Berkeley (Woman in Hotel), Mio Morales (Prem), David Turley (Beefcakes Waiter), Max Miller (Dr. Astin), Joan Ranquet (Woman in Bar), Thomas Gibson (Bartender), Star Reese (Videographer), Lisa Johnson (Dance Captain)

Rudolph Martin, Amanda De Cadenet in *Fall*
© Capella International

Connie Nelson, Dee Hennigan in *Late Bloomers*
© *Strand Releasing*

FALL (Capella Intl.) Producers, Eric Schaeffer, Terence Michael; Director/Screenplay, Eric Schaeffer; Photography, Joe De Salvo; Editor, Thom Zimny; Music, Amanda Kravat; a Five Minutes Before the Miracle presentation; Color; Not rated; 94 minutes; June release. **CAST**: Eric Schaeffer (Michael Shiver), Amanda DeCadenet (Sarah Easton), Rudolph Martin (Philippe), Francie Swift (Robin), Lisa Vidal (Sally), Roberta Maxwell (Joan Alterman), Jose Yenque (Scasse), Josip Kuchan (Zsarko)

TIMOTHY LEARY'S DEAD (Strand) Producers/Screenplay, Todd Easton Mills, Paul Davids; Director, Paul Davis; Photography, Paul Helling; Editors, David Wilson, Mark Deimel; Music, The Moody Blues, Ray Thomas; a Todd Easton Mills presentation; Color; Not rated; 80 minutes; June release. Documentary on former Harvard psychology professor Timothy Leary who became a guru and promoter of sixties counter-culture and psychedelic tripping; featuring Timothy Leary, Richard Alpert (Ram Dass), Frank DiPaola.

Timothy Leary in *Timothy Leary's Dead*   © Strand Releasing

LATE BLOOMERS (Strand) Producers, Gretchen Dyer, Stephen Dyer, Julia Dyer; Executive Producers, Jim Jerge, Martha Little; Director, Julia Dyer; Screenplay, Gretchen Dyer; Photography, Bill Schwarz; Designer, Michael McGarty; Editors, Julia Dyer, Gretchen Dyer; Costumes, Happy Yancey, Mattie O'Neal; Music, Ted Pine; Casting, Nancy Fine; a One Mind Productions Feature, Ultra-Stereo; Color; Not rated; 104 minutes; June release. **CAST**: Connie Nelson (Dinah Groshardt), Dee Hennigan (Carly Lumpkin), Gary Carter (Rom Lumpkin), Lisa Peterson (Val Lumpkin), Esteban Powell (Jamie Hooper), Joe Nemmers (Rick Musso), T.A. Taylor (Bill Boardway)

THE LAST TIME I COMMITTED SUICIDE (Kushner-Locke) Producers, Edward Bates, Louise Rosner; Executive Producers, Peter Abrams, Robert F. Levy, J.P. Guerin, Peter Locke, Donald Kushner, Lawrence Mortorff; Co-Executive Producers, Estelle Lasher, Elizabeth Robinson; Director/Screenplay, Stephen Kay; Photography, Bobby Bukowski; Designer, Amy B. Ancona; Editor, Dorian Harris; Music, Tyler Bates; from Tapestry Films; Dolby Stereo; Color; Rated R; 92 minutes; June release. **CAST**: Thomas Jane (Neal), Keanu Reeves (Harry), Tom Bower (Captain), Adrien Brody (Ben), John Doe (Lew), Claire Forlani (Joan), Marg Helgenberger (Lizzy), Alexandra Holden (Vicky), Lucinda Jenny (Rosie Trickle), Pat McNamara (Father Fletcher), Gretchen Mol (Cherry Mary), Christie Rose (Mrs. Greenway), Meadow Sisto (Sarah), Amy Smart (Jeananne), Kate Williamson (Nurse). (Note: This film premiered on cable television in early 1997).

HEAD ABOVE WATER (Fine Line Features) Producers, Jim Wilson, John M. Jacobsen; Executive Producers, Guy East, Tristan Whalley; Director, Jim Wilson; Screenplay, Theresa Marie; Based on a screenplay by Geir Eriksen, Eirik Ildahl; Photography, Richard Bowen; Designer, Jeffrey Beecroft; Editor, Michael R. Miller; Music, Christopher Young; Costumes, Colleen Atwood; Casting, Elisabeth Leustig; a Tig Productions/Majestic Films production; Dolby Digital Stereo; Super 35 Widescreen; Deluxe Color; Rated PG-13; 92 minutes; June release. **CAST**: Harvey Keitel (George), Cameron Diaz (Nathalie), Craig Sheffer (Lance), Billy Zane (Kent), Shay Duffin (Policeman), Mo (Mo). (Note: This film premiered on cable television in February 1997).

Thomas Jane in *The Last Time I Committed Suicide*
© Kushner Locke Int.

Cameron Diaz, Harvey Keitel in *Head Above Water*
© Tig Productions

END OF SUMMER (JGM Enterprises) Producer/Director/Linda Yellen; Executive Produces, Ted Swanson, Karen Goodwin; Screenplay, Jonathan Platnick, Linda Yellen; Photography, David Bridges; Designer, Bob Ziembicki; Music, Patrick Seymour; a Showtime presentation in association with Hallmark Entertainment; Ultra-Stereo; Deluxe Color; Rated R; 95 minutes; June release. **CAST**: Jacqueline Bisset (Christine Van Burne), Peter Weller (Theo Remmington), Julian Sands (Basil), Amy Locane (Alice), Elizabeth Shepherd (Vera), Michael Hogan (The General), Karyn Dwyer (Jenny), Janet-Laine Green (Lucie), Dennis O'Connor (Otto), Colin Fox (Ezra), Peter James Haworth (Brother), Lynne Cormack (Sister-in-Law), Susan Coyne (Supervisor), Polly Shannon (Maid), Don Allison (Hotel Manager), June Crowley (Romantic Singer), Stan Coles (Ezra's Doctor), Emma Corosky (Helena), Barry Flatman (Mr. Anderson), Caroline Yeager (Mrs. Anderson), Nolan Jennings (Theo's Doctor), Alan Jordan (Investor), Myles Dumont (Little Boy)

Sheryl Lee, Craig Sheffer in *Bliss*
© Triumph Films

BLISS (Triumph) Producer, Allyn Stewart; Executive Producer, Matthew O'Connor; Director/Screenplay, Lance Young; Photography, Mike Molloy; Editor, Allan Lee; Music, Jan A.P. Kaczmarek; Designers, John Willettt, David Lloyd Fischer; Co-Producer, Lisa Towers; Costumes, Jori Woodman; Casting, Glenn Daniels; a Stewart Pictures production, in association with Pacific Motion Pictures Corp.; Dolby SDDS Stereo; Technicolor; Rated R; 103 minutes; June release. **CAST**: Craig Sheffer (Joseph), Sheryl Lee (Maria), Terence Stamp (Baltazar Vincenza), Casey Siemaszko (Tanner), Spalding Gray (Alfred), Leigh Taylor Young

(Redhead), Lois Chiles (Eva), Blu Mankuma (Nick), Ken Camroux (Hank), Pamela Perry (Dottie), Eli Gabay (Carlos), Molly Parker (Connie), Hiro Kanagawa (Doctor), Merrilyn Gann (Motel Woman), Gillian Barber (Therapist), Peter Kelamis (Neighbor), Norman Armour (Patient), David Glyn-Jones (Priest), Quincy & Carson Welch (Boy), Serena Bodnar (Girl), Kristin Lehman (Scope/Steps Woman), Akesh Gill (Therapy Woman)

Waco: The Rules of Engagement © Somford Entertainment

WACO: THE RULES OF ENGAGEMENT (Somford Entertainment) Producers/Photography, William Gazecki, Rick Nyburg; Director/Editor, William Gazecki; Music, David Hamilton; Color; Not rated; 135 minutes; June release. Documentary on the 1993 events outside of Waco, Texas, during which four federal agents and 76 members of the Branch Davidians died. (This film received an Oscar nomination as feature-length documentary).

A LIFE APART: HASIDISM IN AMERICA (First Run Features) Producers/Directors, Menachem Daum, Oren Rudavsky; Executive Producer, Arnold Labaton; Screenplay, Menachem Daum, Bob Seidman; Photography, Oren Rudavsky; Music, Yale Strom; Editor, Ruth Schell; Narrators, Leonard Nimoy, Sarah Jessica Parker; Color; Not rated; 95 minutes; July release. Documentary on the creation of the Hasidic communities in America following the Holocaust.

A Life Apart: Hasidism in America © First Run Features

Anthony Barrile, Nick Scotti in *Kiss Me, Guido*
© Paramount Pictures

KISS ME, GUIDO (Paramount) Producers, Ira Deutchman, Christine Vachon; Executive Producers, Jane Barclay, Tom Carouso, Sharon Harel, Christopher Lawford; Director/Screenplay, Tony Vitale; Photography, Claudia Raschke; Designer, Jeffrey Rathaus; Costumes, Victoria Farrell; Editor, Alexander Hall; Line Producer, Katie Roumel; Casting, Hopkins, Smith and Barden; a Redeemable Features production, presented in association with Kardana/Swinsky Films and Capitol Films; Color; Rated R; 86 minutes; July release. **CAST:** Nick Scotti (Frankie Zito), Anthony Barrile (Warren), Anthony DeSando (Pino Zito), Craig Chester (Terry), Domenick Lombardozzi (Joey Chips), Molly Price (Meryl), Christopher Lawford (Dakota), David Deblinger ("#"), John Tormey (Patsy Zito), Antonia Rey (Josephina Zito), Irma St. Paule (Grandma), Jennifer Esposito (Debbie), Anthony Vitale, Frankie Dellarosa (Guidos), Rebecca Waxman (Wiggy), Tony Ray Rossi (Vinny the Fish), Dwight Ewell (Usher), Marcia Firesten (Real Estate Broker), Bryan Batt (Tino), Craig Archibald (Robbie), Guinevere Turner (Indignant Lesbian), Damien Achilles, Bruce Smolanoff (Tough Guys)

Princess Odette, Jean-Bob in *The Swan Princess* © Legacy

SHOOTING PORN (Caryn Horwitz Presents) Producers, Caryn Horwitz, Doug Lindeman; Director/Creator, Ronnie Larsen; Photography, Bruce McCarthy; Editor, James Lyons; Color; Not rated; 75 minutes; July release. Documentary on the gay porn industry featuring Gino Colbert, Chi Chi LaRue (Porn Directors), Blue Blake, Bryan Kidd, Adam Rom, Hunter Scott, Rip Stone, Adam Wilde (Porn Actors), Mickey Skee, David Widmer (Porn Critics-Reviewers)

THE SWAN PRINCESS: ESCAPE FROM CASTLE MOUNTAIN (Legacy) Producers, Richard Rich, Jared F. Brown; Executive Producers, Seldon O. Young, Jared F. Brown, K. Douglas Martin; Director, Richard Rich; Screenplay, Brian Nissen; Story, Richard Rich, Brian Nissen; Editor, James D. Koford; Songs, Lex de Azevedo, Clive Romney; Music, Lex de Azevedo; Character Design, Steve E. Gordon; Storyboard Artists, Steven E. Gordon, Bruce Woodside, Frank Paur; a Nest Entertainment/Seldon O. Young, Jared F. Brown, K. Douglas Martin presentation of a Rich Animation Studios production; Color; Rated G; 71 minutes; July release. **VOICE CAST:** Michelle Nicastro (Odette), Douglas Sills (Derek), Jake Williamson (Clavius), Christy Landers (Uberta), Donald Sage MacKay (Jean-Bob), Doug Stone (Speed), Steve Vinovich (Puffin), Joseph Medrano (Lord Rogers), James Arrinton (Chamberlain), Joey Camen (Knuckles), Owen Miller (Bromley), Rosie Mann (Bridget)

Shainee Gabel, Kristin Hahn in *Anthem*
© Zeitgeist Films

ANTHEM (Zeitgeist) Producers/Directors/Screenplay, Shainee Gabel, Kristin Hahn; Executive Producer, Jo Ann Fagan; Photography, Bill Brown; Editor, Lucas Platt; a Gabel/Hahn production; Color; Not rated; 124 minutes; July release. Documentation of a 1995 road trip by Shainee Gabel and Kristin Hahn as they set out across the country to interview some of America's people, with Jim Adkisson, Miguel Algarin, Jimmy Santiago Baca, John Perry Barlow, Dorothy Betts, Rev. Marvin Lewis Booker, Douglas Brinkley, Lisa "Suckdog" Carver, Chuck D, Rita Dove, Geraldine Ferraro, Dave Foreman, Jack Healey, Wes Jackson, Winona Laduke, George McGovern, Willie Nelson, Krist Novoselic, Robert Redford, Tom Robbins, Michael Spinola, George Stephanopoulos, Michael Stipe, Studs Terkel, Hunter S. Thompson, Micah Wagner, Rebecca Walker, John Waters.

THE WINNER (LIVE Entertainment) Producer, Kenneth Schwenker; Executive Producers, Mark Damon, Rebecca DeMornay; Director, Alex Cox; Screenplay, Wendy Riss; Based on her play *A Darker Purpose*; Co-Executive Producer, Andrew Pfeffer; Photography, Denis Maloney; Designer, Cecilia Montiel; Editor, Carlos Puente; Color; Not rated; 91 minutes; July release. **CAST:** Rebecca DeMornay (Louise), Vincent D'Onforio (Philip), Richard Edson (Frankie), Saverio Guerra (Paulie), Delroy Lindo (Kingman), Michael Madsen (Wolf), Billy Bob Thornton (Jack), Frank Whaley (Joey), Luis Contreras (Guy in Couple), Ed Pansullo (Man with Broken Arm), Sy Richardson (Bartender), Craig Vincent (Man), Bigg Yeager (Philip's Father), Del Zamora (Cellmate), Roger Jennings (Croupier), Alex Cox (Gaston). (This film made its U.S. premiere earlier in the year on cable television)

Rebecca DeMornay, Michael Madsen in *The Winner*
© LIVE Entertainment

CAFE SOCIETY (Northern Arts Entertainment) Producers, Steve Alexander, Elan Sassoon; Executive Producers, Carl-Jan Colpaert, Frederic Bouin, Jim Steele; Director/Screenplay, Raymond De Felitta; Photography, Michael Mayers; Editor, Suzy Elmiger; Music, Chris Guardino; a Cineville presentation in association with Skyline Entertainment and Daylight productions; Color/Black and whitw; Not rated; 107 minutes; July release. **CAST:** Peter Gallagher (Jack Kale), Frank Whaley (Mickey Jelke), Lara Flynn Boyle (Patricia Ward), John Spencer (Ray Davioni), Anna Thompson (Erica Steele), David Patrick Kelly (J. Roland Sala), Christopher Murney (Frank Frustinsky), Paul Guilfoyle (Anthony Liebler), Richard B. Shull (Samuel Segal), Cynthia Watros (Diane Harris), Alan Manson (Judge Valente), Alan North (Frank Hogan), Kelly Bishop (Mrs. Jelke), Zach Grenier (Milton Macka), Ivy DeFelitta (Dorothy Kilgallen), Marshall Efron (Moe Persky), Robert Whaley (Marco), Joshua Whiting (Arthur), Norman Douglas (Tux), Larry Weiss (Bartender), Bill McHugh (Richard Short), Kelly Reynolds (June Short), Arnold Sherman (Greenbaum), Beth Schakatt (The Stripper), Elaina Redmond (Cora), Steve Alexander (Reporter). (This film made its U.S. premiere on cable television in 1996)

Frank Whaley, Peter Gallagher in *Cafe Society*
© Northern Arts Entertainment

BEYOND BARBED WIRE (Tribute to Freedom Foundation) Producer/Screenplay, Terri DeBono; Executive Producers, Yukio Sumida, Sherry Lapham Thomas, Charles Richard Woodson; Director/Editor/Photography, Steve Rosen; Narrator, Noriyuki "Pat" Morita; a Mac and Ava film presented in association with Sunwood Entertainment; Color/Black and white; Not raed; 88 minutes; July release. Documentary on the Japanese-Americans who fought in World War II.

Scott Thompson, Mark Metcalf, Henry Thomas in *Hijacking Hollywood*
© Broken Twig Prods.

HIJACKING HOLLYWOOD (Broken Twig Prods.) Producer/Director, Neil Mandt; Screenplay, Neil Mandt, Jim Rossow; Executive Producer, Ann Mandt; Photography, Anton Floquet; Designer, Todd Cherniawsky; Editor, Charlie Webber; Music, Erik Lundmark; a Curb Entertainment/Broken Twig production; Ultra-Stereo; Color; Not rated; 91 minutes; July release. **CAST:** Henry Thomas (Kevin Conroy), Scott Thompson (Russell), Mark Metcalf (Michael Lawrence), Neil Mandt (Tad), Paul Hewitt (Harvey), Nicole Gian (Sarah), Art La Fleur (Eddie), Shirly Brener (Ginger), Helen Duffy (Mrs. Cohen), Mark Holton, Loren Lazerine (Officers), Hedy Popson (Sandy), J.F. Pryor (Shaft), Noella Akwiri (Receptionist), Chris Morris (Grip), Bobby Knoeral (P.A.), Steve Van Wormer (Tony), Joe Watson (Bicycler)

SOUL IN THE HOLE (Northern Arts) Producer, Lilibet Foster; Director, Danielle Gardner; Photography, Paul Gibson; Editor, Melissa Neidich; Associate Producer, Alise Allen; an Asphalt Films production; Color; Not rated; 90 minutes; August release. Documentary on the basketball street tournaments held on the playgrounds of Brooklyn, featuring Ed "Booger" Smith, Kenny Jones, Kenny's Kings.

Ed "Booger" Smith in *Soul in the Hole*
© Northern Arts

Charles Ingram (Gary Bloom), Ron Gephart (Ken Bloom), Kim Newman (Denise Bloom), Polly Edelstein (Debbie Bloom), Vanita Thomas (Bernice), Randall Reinke (Danny), Melissa Dunn (Tina Clifton), Erin Grills (Jacquie Clifton), Kate Davis (Gloria Clifton), Alluring Strange (Club Band), Mark Hyman (Club Bouncer), Michael Locke (Michael—Kid on Bike), Robert Hathaway (2nd Kid on Bike), Lamar Sorrento (Ted), Richard Daggett (Pick-up Driver), Anthony Isbell (Jerry—Man in Hotel), J.R. Crumpton (Joe), Patricia A. Gill (Joe's Wife), Moses J. Peace (Policeman), Nhan Van Dang (Minh's Roommate), Bay Thi Ho (Old Vietnamese Woman), Hoang N. Pham (Minh's Friend), Mai Ballard (Pool Hall Owner)

Natalie Desselle, Bill Bellamy, Mari
Morrow in *How To Be A Player* © Gramercy Pictures

DEF JAM'S HOW TO BE A PLAYER (Gramercy) Producers, Mark Burg, Todd Baker, Russell Simmons, Preston Holmes; Executive Producers, Robert Newmyer, Jeffrey Silver, Stan Lathan; Co-Producers, Joanne Milter, Rose Catherine Pinkney, Carrie Morrow; Director, Lionel C. Martin; Screenplay, Mark Brown, Demetria Johnson; Story, Mark Brown; Music, Darren Floyd; Editor, William Young; Casting, Jaki Brown-Karman; a PolyGram Filmed Entertainment presentation of an Island Pictures production, in association with Outlaw Productions; Dolby Stereo; Deluxe color; Rated R; 94 minutes; August release. **CAST**: Bill Bellamy (Drayton Jackson), Natalie Desselle (Jenny Jackson), Lark Voorhies (Lisa), Mari Morrow (Katrina), Pierre (David), Jermaine "Big Hugg" Hopkins (Kilo), A.J. Johnson (Spootie), Max Julien (Uncle Fred), Beverly Johnson (Robin), Gilbert Gottfried (Tony the Doorman), Bernie Mac (Buster), Stacii Jae Johnson (Sherri), Elise Neal (Nadine), J. Anthony Brown (Uncle Snook), Amber Smith (Amber), Devika Parikh (Barbara), Bebe Drake (Mama Jackson), Gillian Iliana Waters (Shante), Tara Davis (Cute Party Girl), Marta Boyett (C.C.), Jazsmin Lewis (Pookie), Licia Shearer (Nikki), Jerod Mixon, Jamal Mixon (Kids), D.D. Rainbow (Jealous Girl), Natashia Williams (Pink Bikini Girl), Edith Grant (Peaches), Jesse Collins (D.J.), Melissa Cross (Sales Girl), Claude "Pete" Bryant (Chess Player)

THE DELTA (Strand) Producer, Margot Bridger; Director/Screenplay, Ira Sachs; Photography, Benjamin P. Speth; Designer, Bernhard Blythe; Editor, Affonso Gonçalves; Music, Michael Rohatyn; Costumes, Stevan Lazich; a Charlie Guidance production; Technicolor; Not rated; 85 minutes; August release. **CAST**: Shayne Gray (Lincoln Bloom), Thang Chan (Minh Nguyen—John), Rachel Zan Huss (Monica), Colonius Davis (Ricky Little), Larry Reynolds (Man in Park), Angelique Owens (Donut Shop Clerk), Leigh Walden (Cece Bloom), Gene Crain (Sam Bloom),

Shayne Gray in *The Delta*
© Strand Releases

Lauren Holly, Greg Kinnear in
A Smile Like Yours © Paramount Pictures

A SMILE LIKE YOURS (Paramount) Producers, David Kirkpatrick, Tony Amatullo; Executive Producer, Robert Harling; Director, Keith Samples; Screenplay, Kevin Meyer, Keith Samples; Photography, Richard Bowen; Designer, Garreth Stover; Editor, Wayne Wahrman; Costumes, Jill Ohanneson; Music, William Ross; Title song by Diane Warren/performed by Natalie Cole; Casting, Jennifer Shull; a Rysher Entertainment presentation of a David Kirkpatrick production; Dolby Digital Stereo; Super 35 Widescreen; Deluxe color; Rated R; 99 minutes; August release. **CAST**: Greg Kinnear (Danny Robertson), Lauren Holly (Jennifer Robertson), Joan Cusack (Nancy Tellen), Jay Thomas (Steve Harris), Jill Hennessy (Lindsay Hamilton), Christopher McDonald (Richard Halstrom), Donald Moffat (Dr. Felber), France Nuyen (Dr. Chin), Marianne Muellerleile (Nurse Wheeler), Shirley MacLaine (Martha), Sheridan Samples (Holly), Barbara Larsen (Woman in Window/Woman on Plane), Tony Abou-Ganim, Nick Scoggin (Welders), Genee Nakashita (Karaoke Bar Owner), Lewis Brown, Nicholas Bearde, June Lomena, Latrice Sellers, Lynda Marie Sellers, Kirby Coleman, Dooney Jones, Bilal Muslim (Karaoke Acts), Steven Brown, Paul Ghiringhelli, Richard Thorn (Baseball Buddies), T. Michael Sutton (Pool Hall Guy), Ben Stein (Clinic Video Narrator), Meggan Kimberley, Jack Sharrar (Couple at Fertility Clinic), Nancy Carlin (Pregnant Mother), Tony Amatullo, Tim Helfet, Jeff Matloff, Brad Rivers (Surrell Board Members), Kevin Wiatt, Terri Orth-Pallavinci (Couple Entering Fertility Clinic), Craig Samples, Carol Samples, Jennifer Samples, Karen Samples, Ellen Samples (Baby Stroller Family), Michael Jang, Woody Jang, Tali Jang (Family with Camera), Ellen Hoberman, Sarah Hoberman (Mother and Daughter), Marianna Amatullo, Nicolas Amatullo (Pregnant Family), Kent Samples, Katie Samples, Brandon Samples (Reading Family), Michael Santo (Maitre D'), Jim Cranna (Guy on Plane), Charlie Holliday (Cab Driver), Marle Gaines (Perky Airline Representative), Helen Swee (Angry Flight Attendant), Joy Michiel (Woman on Plane), Jim Burke (Nancy Tellen's Groom), Christine Doherty, Kathryn Doherty, Matthew Doherty (The Robertsons' Triplets)

Kevin Sorbo in *Kull the Conqueror*
© Universal Studios ,Inc.

KULL THE CONQUEROR (Universal) Producer, Raffaella De Laurentiis; Co-Producer, Hester Hargett; Director, John Nicolella; Screenplay, Charles Edward Pogue; Based on the Worlds and the Characters Created by Robert E. Howard; Photography, Rodney Charters; Designer, Benjamin Fernandez; Editor, Dallas Puett; Music, Joel Goldsmith; Costumes, Thomas Casterline, Sibylle Ulsamer; Special Effects Supervisor, Kit West; Visual Effects Supervisor, Richard Malzahn; Associate Producer, Arthur M. Lieberman; Executive Producers, Beverlee Dean, Jeff Franklin, Steve Waterman; Casting, Jeffery Passero, Elizabeth Hayden-Passero; a Raffaella De Laurentiis production; DTS Stereo; Super 35 Widescreen; Deluxe color; Rated PG-13; 95 minutes; August release. **CAST:** Kevin Sorbo (Kull), Tia Carrere (Akivasha), Thomas Ian Griffith (Taligaro), Litefoot (Ascalante), Roy Brocksmith (Tu), Harvey Fierstein (Juba), Karina Lombard (Zaretta), Edward Tudor-Pole (Enaros), Douglas Henshall (Ducalon), Joe Shaw (Dalgar), Sven Ole Thorsen (King Borna), Terry O'Neill (Ship Captain), Pat Roach (Zuleki), John Hallam (Mandara), Peter Petruna, Boris Bacik (Slaves), Paul Kynman, Paul Weston (Dragon Legion Guards)

BUTCH CAMP (Billingsgate Prod.) Producers, Timothy E. Sabo, Steven Gellman; Executive Producer, Gary Metzger; Director/Screenplay, Alessandro De Gaetano; Photography, C. Brett Webster; Editors, Amy Harvey, Jeanne Bonansinga; Music, Conrad Pope; Color; Not rated; 103 minutes; August release. **CAST:** Judy Tenuta (Samantha Rottweiler), Paul Denniston (Matt Grabowski), Jason Terisi (Rod Cazzone), Jordan Roberts (Janet), Bill Ingraham (Danny), Duane Sharp, Joel Himelhoch, Richard Henzel, John Kimilcko, Sean Solan, Stephanie Ferrell.

Vincent Kartheiser, Patrick Stewart
in *Masterminds* © Columbia Pictures
Industries, Inc.

MASTERMINDS (Columbia) Producers, Robert Dudelson, Floyd Byars; Executive Producers, Matthew O'Connor, David Saunders; Director, Roger Christian; Screenplay, Floyd Byars; Story, Floyd Byars, Alex Siskin, Chris Black; Co-Executive Producer, Richard M. Heller; Photography, Nic Morris; Designer, Douglas Higgins; Editor, Robin Russell; Costumes, Monique Sanchez, Derek J. Baskerville; Music, Anthony Marinelli; Associate Producers, Patti Allen, T. Michael O'Connor; Casting, Andrea Stone; a Pacific Motion Pictures production; a Byars/Duddelson production; Dolby SDDS Stereo; Super 35 Widescreen; Deluxe color; Rated PG-13; 106 minutes; August release. **CAST:** Patrick Stewart (Rafe Bentley), Vincent Kartheiser (Ozzie Paxton), Brenda Fricker (Principal Claire Maloney), Brad Whitford (Miles Lawrence), Matt Craven (Jake Paxton), Annabelle Gurwitch (Helen Paxton), Jon Abrahams (K-Dog), Katie Stuart (Melissa Randall), Michael MacRae (Foster Deroy), Callum Keith Rennie (Ollie), Earl Pastko (Capt. Jankel), Jason Schombing (Marvin), Michael David Simms (Col. Duke), David Paul Grove (Ferret), Akiko Morison (Janet), Teryl Rothery (Ms. Saunders), Vanessa Morley (Gabby), Douglas Arthurs, Phillip Granger, Andrew Kavadas, Lauro Chartrand, Charles Andre, Alan Van Sprang, Nino Caratozzolo (Happy Boys), Bruce Pinard (Happy Boy Guard), April Telek (Sexy Girl), Steve Makaj (Capt. Majors), Jay Brazeau (Eliot), Douglas Newell (Science Teacher), Frank Cassini (Cop), Kimberly Unger (Flight Attendant), Pamela Martin, Merrett Green (TV Reporters), Andrew Wheeler (Bank Officer), Michael Benyaer (Taxi Driver)

Matthew Hennessey, Lee Holmes, Steve
Parlavecchio, Kevin Corrigan in
Bandwagon © CFP Distribution

BANDWAGON (CFP) Producers, Alyson Poole, John Schultz; Co-Producer, Michael Shevloff; Director/Screenplay, John Schultz; Photography, Shawn Maurer; Editor, John Pace; Music, Greg Kendall; a Lakeshore Entertainment and Pamlico Pictures presentation; Dolby Stereo; Color; Not rated; 99 minutes; September release. **CAST:** Kevin Corrigan (Wynn Knapp), Lee Holmes (Tony Ridge), Matthew Hennessey (Charlie Flagg), Steve Parlavecchio (Eric Ellwood), Doug MacMillan (Linus Tate)

CRACKING UP (Phaedra Cinema) Producer/Director/Editor, Matt Mitler; Screenplay, Matt Mitler, Theodore P. Lorusso; Photography, Mark Traver; Music, Arthur Rosen; Co-Producer, Lilli Mitler; Associate Producers, Robert Prichard, Jennifer Prichard, William Otterson; a Foolish Mortal Films production; Color; Not rated; 93 minutes; September release. **CAST**: Matt Mitler (Danny Gold), Carolyn McDermott (Carolyn Davis), Kevin Brown (Dack Waterbone), Kimberly Flynn (Kimberly Lane), Debra Wilson (Alliandra Burrel), Jason Brill (Jake Weinberg), Jeff Eyres (Cosmo), David Wells (Alan Malcolm), Jonathan Powers (Mr. Strong), Frank Senger (Mr. Kansy), Cynthia Rector (Head Shaved Girl), Chuck Montgomery (M.C. Lucky Jackson), Sherry Anderson, John Augustine (Philanthropic Couple), Todd Alcott, Gail Dennison (Themselves)

James Woods, Kevin Corrigan in
Kicked in the Head © October Films

KICKED IN THE HEAD (October Films) Producer, Barbara De Fina; Executive Producer, Martin Scorsese; Director, Matthew Harrison; Screenplay, Kevin Corrigan, Matthew Harrison; Photography, John Thomas, Howard Krupa; Editor, Michael Berenbaum; Music, Stephen Endelman; Designer, Kevin Thompson; Costumes, Nina Canter; Casting, Sheila Jaffe, Georgianne Walken; a De Fina/Cappa Production; Dolby Stereo; Color; Rated R; 88 minutes; September release. **CAST:** Kevin Corrigan (Redmond), Linda Fiorentino (Megan), Michael Rapaport (Stretch), James Woods (Uncle Sam), Burt Young (Jack), Lili Taylor (Happy), Olek Krupa (Borko), Elliot Cuker (Sheldon), David Deblinger (Escalator Man), Alan Davidson (Subway Gunman), Bianca Bakija (Pearl), Sol Frieder (Elderly Man), Matthew Harrison (Luau Man), Gary Perez (Dean), John Ventimiglia (Man at Party), Royale Watkins (Chicky), Lawton Paseka (Pilot), George Odom (Door Person), Nicole Baptiste (Cop)

Pamela Stewart, Tara Bellando in
100 Proof

100 PROOF (Independent-Film Forum) Producer/Editor, George Maranville; Executive Producer, Jay Faires; Director/Screenplay, Jeremy Horton; Photography, Harold Jarboe; Costumes, Peggy Watts; Designer, Patrick McNeese; Music, Michael Mossier; Color; Not rated; 94 minutes; September release. **CAST:** Pamela Stewart (Rae), Tara Bellando (Carla), Jack Stubblefield Johnson (Arco), Minnie Bates Yancy (Sissy), Larry Brown (Eddie), Kevin Hardesty (Roger), Jim Varney (Rae's Father), Loren Crawford (Trudy), Joe Ventura (Ted), Warren Ray (Tommy), Jeff Lycan (R.T.), Bobby Simmons (Toby), Peter Smith (Fryman), Buck Finley (Chester), Joe Gatton (Owen), Nick Ewan, Josh Barrett (Boys), Clint Voight, Brad K. Ingram (Policemen), Archie Borders, Evelyn Blythe (Yuppies), Ed Desiato (Chappy), Ben Daughtrey (Parkette Cook), Peggy Watts (Liquor Customer)

THE TOILERS AND THE WAYFARERS (Outsider Enterprises) Producers, Karen Manion, Ralf Schirg, Keith Froelich; Executive Producer, Marc Huestis; Director/Screenplay, Keith Froelich; Photography, Jim Tittle; Editors, Robb Harriss, Keith Froelich; Music, Chan Poling; Casting, Jessica Nelson; 1995; Black and White; Not rated; 75 minutes; September release. **CAST:** Matt Klemp (Dieter), Ralf Schirg (Udo), Andrew Woodhouse (Phillip), Jerome Samuelson (Helmut), Joan Wheeler (Anna), Michael Glen (Lt. Scallon), Ralph Jacobus (Carl)

Macky Alston, George DeGrafenreid
in *Family Name* © Opelika Pictures

FAMILY NAME (Opelika Pictures) Producer, Selina Lewis; Executive Producer, Nicholas Gottlieb; Director, Macky Alston; Narration Written by Macky Alston, Kay Gayner; Photography, Eliot Rockett; Editors, Sandra Marie Christie, Christopher White; Music, Camara Kambon; Color; Not rated; 89 minutes; September release. Filmmaker Macky Alston traces his lineage, discovering that his forebearers were North Carolina slaveholders.

JULIAN PO (Fine Line Features) Producers, Joseph Pierson, Jon Glascoe; Executive Producers, Allan Mindel, Denise Shaw; Director/Screenplay, Alan Wade; Photography, Bernd Heinl; Designer, Stephen McCabe; Editor, Jeffrey Wolf; Costumes, Juliet Polcsa; Music, Patrick Williams; Casting, Todd Thaler; Dolby Stereo; Color; Rated PG-13; 84 minutes; September release. **CAST:** Christian Slater (Julian Po), Robin Tunney (Sarah), Michael Parks (Vern), Cherry Jones (Lucy), Frankie R. Faison (Sheriff), Harve Presnell (Mayor), Allison Janney (Lilah), LaTanya Richardson (Darlene), Dina Spybey (Dee), Bruce Bohne (Pastor Bean), Roy Cooper (Tobias), Zeljko Ivanek (Potter), Io Tillett Wright (Walter)

Christian Slater, Robin Tunney in
Julian Po © Fine Line Features

Tony Tucci, Michael Parducci, Thomas
Brandise, Tom Malloy in *Gravesend*
© Island Digital Media

GRAVESEND (Island Digital Media) Producer/Director/Screenplay,
Salvatore Stabile; Executive Producers, Toni Ross, Mark Ross, Daniel
Edelman; Photography, Joseph Dell'Olio; Editors, Miranda Devin,
Salvatore Stabile; Music, Bill Laswell; Presented by Oliver Stone; Dolby
Stereo; Color; Rated R; 85 minutes; September release. **CAST**: Tony
Tucci (Zane), Michael Parducci (Ray), Tom Malloy (Chicken), Thomas
Brandise (Mikey), Macky Aquilino (JoJo the Junkie).

DELINQUENT (Beyond Films/Big Bad Prods.) Producer/Director/
Screenplay, Peter Hall; Photography, Todd Crockett; Music, Gang of Four;
Editor, Thom Zimny; Color; Not rated; 84 minutes; September release.
CAST: Desmond Devenish (Tim), Shawn Batten (Tracy DeLors), Jeff
Paul (Ben), Marisa Townshend (Mrs. Richman), Ian Eaton (Eddie),
Melissa Chalsma, Donald Christopher, Maraya Chase, Olga Matlin, Peter
Hall, Meg Myles, Ruby Mitchell.

Tom Gilroy, Neal Jones in *Ratchet*
© Phaedra Cinema

RATCHET (Phaedra Cinema) Producers, George Belshaw, John S.
Johnson; Executive Producer, Hank Blumenthal; Director/Screenplay,
John S. Johnson; Photography, Joaquin Baca-Asay; Designer, Debbie
Devilla; Costumes, Jana Rosenblatt; Music, Paul Schwartz; Editors, James
Lyons, Keith Reamer; Casting, Susan Shopmaker; from Ratchet
Productions LLC in association with Altar Rocks Films Inc.; Ultra-Stereo;
Color; Not rated; 114 minutes; September release. **CAST:** Tom Gilroy
(Elliott Callahan), Margaret Welsh (Catherine Ripley), Mitchell
Lichtenstein (Tim Greenleaf), Murit Koppel (Julia Webb), Matthew Dixon
(Henry Carver), Neal Jones (Sam O'Leary), Robert Whaley (Ed Deputy),
John A. Mackay (Chief Groves), David Dossey (Man in Airplane),
Isabelle Fortea (Kitty Webb), Anthony Greenleaf (Photographer), Timothy
Britton Parker (Jeffrey Kahn), Shari-Lyn Safir (Margaret Dickson)

LATIN BOYS GO TO HELL (Strand) Producer, Jurgen Bruning;
Executive Producer, Steve Gallagher; Co-Producers, Fernando Colomo
P.C., Beatriz de la Gandara; Director, Ela Troyano; Screenplay, Andre
Salas, Ela Troyano; Additional Soap Dialog, Carmelita Tropicana; Based
on the novel by Andre Salas; Photography, James Carman; Art Director,
Uzi Parnes; Editor, Brian A. Kates; Music, John Zorn; from Stance
Company/GM Films; Color; Not rated; 86 minutes; September release.
CAST: Irwin Ossa (Justin), John Bryant Davila (Angel), Jenifer Lee
Simard (Andrea), Alexis Artiles (Braulio), Mike Ruiz (Carlos), Annie
Lobst (Monica), Dashia (Jackie), Norma Maldonado (Mrs. Vega), Jehad
Nga (Sylvano), Guinevere Turner (Sombra), Rebecca Bugos (Luz),
Umberto Gonzalez (Rodrigo), Yvonne Washington (Gladys), Reynier
Molenaar (Eduardo), Iris Prado Salas (Braulio's Mom), J.R. Valdes,
William Gonzalez (Bartenders), Adrian Sanchez (Italian Guy), Fil
Fernandez (Cashier), Ari Gold (Trash Popstar), Pepper Burns, Veronica
Fox (Gender Illusionists), Jose Munoz (Mr. Bully), Carmelita Tropicana
(Mrs. Bully)

Mike Ruiz in *Latin Boys Go To Hell*
© Strand Releasing

RIDING THE RAILS (Artistic License) Producers/Directors/
Screenplay, Michael Uys, Lexy Lovell; Photography, Samuel Henriques;
Editor, Howard Sharp; Music, Jay Sherman-Godfrey; an Out of the
Blue/American History Project production; DuArt color; Not rated; 72
minutes; September release. Documentary on teenage freight-train riders
during the Great Depression, featuring Clarence Lee, Bob "Guitar
Whitey" Symmonds, John Fawcett, Jim Mitchell, Charley Bull, Rene
Champion, Peggy De Hart.

Riding the Rails © National Archives

Robert Englund, Kane Hodder, Tony
Todd in *Wishmaster* © Live Entertainment

WISHMASTER (LIVE Entertainment) Producers, Pierre David, Clark Peterson, Noel A. Zanitsch; Executive Producer, Wes Craven; Director, Robert Kurtzman; Screenplay, Peter Atkins; Photography, Jacques Haitkin; Designers, Dorian Vernaccio, Deborah Raymond; Music, Harry Manfredini; Co-Producer, David Tripet; Editor, David Handman; Line Producer, Russ Markowitz; Costumes, Karyn Wagner; Visual Effects Supervisor, Thomas C. Rainone; Special Make-Up Effects, Robert Kurtzman, Greg Nicotero, Howard Berger; Casting, Cathy Henderson-Martin, Dori Zuckerman; a Pierre David production; Dolby Digital Stereo; Eastman color; Rated R; 90 minutes; September release. **CAST:** Tammy Lauren (Alexandra Amberson), Andrew Divoff (The Djinn/Nathaniel Demarest), Robert Englund (Raymond Beaumont), Tony Todd (Johnny Valentine), Wendy Benson (Shannon Amberson), Tony Crane (Josh Aickman), Chris Lemmon (Nick Merritt), Jenny O'Hara (Wendy Derlith), Angus Scrimm (Narrator), Ari Barak (Zoroaster), Jake McKinnon (Skeleton Man), Greg Funk (Snake Man), Richard Assad (Persian King), Ted Raimi (Ed Finney), Danny Hicks (Customs Official), Josef Pilato (Mickey Torelli), Tom Kendall (Etchison), John Byner (Doug Clegg), Ashley Power (Sierra), Verne Troyer, Walter Phelan (Creature Stages), Ricco Ross (Lt. Nathanson), Buck Flower (Homeless Man), Reggie Banister (Pharmacist), Peter Liapis, Frank Nicotero (Pharmacy Customers), Brian Klugman (Medical Student), Gretchen Palmer (Ariella), Jean St. James (Customer), Azita Azar (Student with Mask), Joe Svezia (Uniformed Cop), Kane Hodder (Merritt's Guard), Dennis Hayden (Security Guard), Betty McGuire (Mrs. Merritt), Renee Faia (Insurance Assistant), Cyndi Pass (Glass Woman), Howard Berger, Robert Jacob (Party Guards), Brad Mead (Cop at Blackwood)

Toshiya Nagasawa, Eugene Nomura,
Nick Feyz in *Sleepy Heads* © Phaedra Cinema

THE LAY OF THE LAND (Northern Arts) Producers, Jonathan D. Krane, Sally Kellerman; Executive Producers, Edward Oleschak, Ralph Clemente; Director, Larry Arrick; Screenplay, Mel Shapiro; Co-Producer, Mary Hinton; Photography, Frederic Goodich; Designer, Clare Brown; Editor, Richard Brummer; Costumes, Judy B. Schwartz, Beverly Safire; Music, Jeff Lass; Casting, Carol Lefko; a JKG Production presentation of a Jonathan D. Krane production; Color; Rated R; 94 minutes; September release. **CAST:** Sally Kellerman (M.J. Dankworth), Ed Begley, Jr. (Harvey Dankworth), Sandra Taylor (Muriel Johanson), Stuart Margolin (Carmine Ficcone), Tyne Daly (Dr. Guttmacher), Rance Howard (Dr. Brown), Avery Schreiber (Dean Bill Whittier), April Shawhan (Erma Whittier), Tom Nowicki (Bob Chambers), Elisabeth Redford (Blanche Cafferty), Timothy McLoughlin (Gordon Dimitri), Patrick Desmond (Dr. Smith), Avis-Marie Barnes (Secretary), Riley Gelwicks (Jack Dankworth), Jesse Zeigler (Timmy Dankworth), David Sollberg (Leslie), Cyndi Vicino (Gunshop Saleslady), Richard Bassett (Bookshop Salesman), Bobbi Spencer (Landlady), Frank Eugene Matthews Jr., Dennis Wood (Janitors), Suzanne Shepherd (Alice), Claire Kellerman, Densi Van Gerena, Scott Graham, Mikki McKeever (Students)

James Belushi, Dennis Quaid, Tupac
Shakur in *Gang Related* © MGM DistributingCo.

SLEEPY HEADS (Phaedra Cinema) Producers, Yuko Yoshikawa, Shunji Okada, Yoshifumi Hosoya; Director/Photography, Yoshifumi Hosoya; Screenplay, Yoshifumi Hosoya, Nick Feyz, Christo Assefi, Edwin Baker; Editor, Keiko Deguchi; Designer, Mark Helmuth; Music, Joshua Stone; an Elephant Studio/Zazou Productions presentation; Dolby; Color; Not rated; 86 minutes; September release. **CAST:** Eugene Nomura (Hiro), Toshiya Nagasawa (Ken), Takahiro "Engin" Fujita (Akira), Nick Feyz (B.J.), Sayuri Higuchi Emerson (Akiko), Snakey Mao (Shun), Mariko H. Fusillo (Haruka), Yuki Nishida (Keiko), Masayuki Nakanishi (Daisuke), Ron Contawe (Gang Leader)

GANG RELATED (Orion) Producers, Brad Krevoy, Steve Stabler, John Bertolli; Executive Producer, Lynn Bigelow-Kouf; Director/Screenplay, Jim Kouf; Photography, Brian J. Reynolds; Designer, Charles Breen; Costumes, Shari Feldman; Editor, Todd Ramsay; Music, Mickey Hart; Co-Producer, Jeffrey D. Ivers; Line Producer, Jeffrey Downer; Casting, Carol Lewis; a Brad Krevoy & Steve Stabler production; Super 35 Widescreen; DTS Stereo; Deluxe color; Rated R; 112 minutes; October release. **CAST:** James Belushi (Divinci), Tupac Shakur (Rodriguez), Lela Rochon (Cynthia), Dennis Quaid (William), James Earl Jones (Arthur Baylor), David Paymer (Elliot Goff), Wendy Crewson (Helen Eden), Gary Cole (Richard Simms), T.C. Carson (Manny Ladrew), Brad Greenquist (Richard Stein), James Handy (Capt. Henderson), Kool Moe Dee (Lionel Hudd), Victor Love (Hooper), Robert LaSardo (Sarkasian), Perry Anzilotti (Vic), Gregory Scott Cummins (Clyde), Tiny Lister Jr. (Cutless Supreme), Thomas Mills (Patrolman Mahoney), Rick LaFond (Desk Officer), Anthony C. Hall (James), Catero Colbert (Cortez), Steve Wilcox (Dave), Alexander Folk (Reverend), Paul Gold (Lineup Suspect), Douglas Bennet

(Guard), David Weisenberg (Doctor), Will Jeffries (Dunner Attorney), Jason Bagby (Young Man), Chris Hendrie (Judge Weinberg), Bob Apisa (Dunner Bailiff), Terrance Ellis (Gun Seller), Todd Patrick Breaugh (Steven J. Allen), Yuri Ogawa (Jury Foreperson), Joseph Hieu (Asian Man), Deborah Rennard (Caroline Divinci), Edward Edwards (Sgt. Gardner), Fred Ornstein (Officer), Taylor Anderson (Butler), Tom Ormeny (Nathan McCall), Tony Perez (Judge Pine), Ron Cummins (Bailiff), Elizabeth Maynard (Newscaster), Charlene Simpson (Manny's Secretary), Jimmie F. Skaggs (Duncan), Leonard O. Turner (Guard at Cynthia's Jail), Andrea C. Robinson, Dafidd McCracken, Nellie Sciutto (Reporters), Donald Craig (Sinclair), Lisa Dinkins (Nurse), Teddy Lane Jr. (Guard at County), Reginald W. Miller, George Christy, Jesse J. Donnelly (Detectives), Peter Navy Tuiasosopo (Bob the Bouncer), Myles DeRussy III (Officer)

KISS AND TELL (FilmWorks) Producer, David R. Kappes; Executive Producers, Mitchell Galin, Richard P. Rubinstein; Director, Andy Wolk; Screenplay/Story, David Birke; Photography, Paul Maibaumn; Designer, Michael Helmy; Editor, Lauren A. Schaffer; Music, Tim Truman; Color; Not rated; 90 minutes; October release. **CAST:** Cheryl Ladd (Jean McAvoy), John Terry (Eric McAvoy), Derin Altay (Arlane), John Bedford Lloyd (Dan Turman), C.K. Bibby (Dr. Hayes), Michael Burgess (E.R. Doctor), Barry Corbin (George Reed), Diana De Garmo (Cindy), Aubrey Dollar (Candy Stripper), David Forrester (Cop), Randell Haynes (Psychiatrist), J. Michael Hunter (Ted Wallace), Gen. Fermon Judd, Jr. (Bartender), Chuck Kinlaw (Father), Lorri Lindberg (Molly), Leslie Riley (Sue), Francie Swift (Kelly Krieger), Nello Tare (Tour Guide), Marty Terry (Elderly Lady), Caitlin Clarke, Jack Gilpin

Keelin Curnuck in *Wonderland*
© Fox Lorber

PLAN B (Puny But Loud Prods.) Producer, Lulu Baskins-Leva; Executive Producers, Elizabeth Joslin, Burr Joslin, Shelly Leva; Director/Screenplay, Gary Leva; Photography, Yoram Astrakhan; Music, Andrew Rose; Designer, Carol Strober; Editor, Jane Allison Fleck; Dolby Stereo; Color; Rated R; 102 minutes; October release. **CAST:** Jon Cryer (Stuart Winer), Lisa Darr (Clare Sadler), Lance Guest (Jack Sadler), Mark Matheisen (Ricky Stone), Sara Mornell (Gina Ferris), Clauda Carey (Marie), Donna Wieczorkowski (Liz), Staey Katzin, Ilia Volokh, John Kozeluh, Annie Grindlay, Candace DeSarro, Justin Ross, Nicole Chamberlain, Christine Mitges, Jose Heredia, Heather Harris, Roger La Page.

WONDERLAND (Fox Lorber) Producer/Director/Photography/Editor, John O'Hagan; Executive Producers, Ted Hope, James Schamus, David Linde; Associate Producers, Sheri Bylander, Gabrielle Kelly, Anne Carey; Co-Producer, Mary Janes Skalski; DuArt color; Not rated; 80 minutes; October release. Documentary celebrating the 50th Anniversary of America's first mass-produced, planned suburb, Levittown, New York; featuring Eddie Money, Bill Griffith, Keelin Curnuck, and various residents of Levittown past and present.

Director Jim Jarmusch, Neil Young in
Year Of The Horse © October Films

YEAR OF THE HORSE (October) Producer, L.A. Johnson; Executive Producers, Bernard Shakey, Elliot Rabinowitz; Director, Jim Jarmusch; Photography, L.A. Johnson, Jim Jarmusch; Editor, Jay Rabinowitz; Music, Neil Young & Crazy Horse; a Shakey Pictures production; Dolby Digital Stereo; Color; Rated R; 107 minutes; October release. Documentary on Neil Young and his band Crazy Horse in concert, featuring Ralph Molina, Frank "Poncho" Sampedro, Billy Talbot, Neil Young.

THE TWILIGHT OF THE GOLDS (Avalanche) Producers, Paul Colichman, Mark R. Harris, John Davimos; Executive Producer, Garry Marshall; Director, Ross Marks; Screenplay, Jonathan Tolins, Seth Bass; Based upon the play by Jonathan Tolins; Co-Producer/Casting, Valorie Massalas; Line Producers, John Schouweiler, Lisa Levy; Photography, Tom Richmond; Music, Lee Holdridge; Editor, Dana Congdon; a Showtime presentation of a Regent Entertainment/Below the Belt productions and Hallmark Entertainment; Color; Rated PG-13; 93 minutes; October release. **CAST:** Jennifer Beals (Suzanne Stein), Jon Tenney (Rob Stein), Faye Dunaway (Phyllis Gold), Brendan Fraser (David Gold), Garry Marshall (Walter Gold), Rosie O'Donnell (Jackie), Sean O'Bryan (Steven), Patrick Bristow (Brandon), John Schlesinger (Adrian Lodge), Phil Reeves (Suzanne's Doctor), Lucas Richman (Brik), Robert Barry Fleming (Randy), Kathleen Marshall (Debby Klein), Mark Medoff (Mr. Klein). (This film originally premiered on the Showtime Cable Network in March of 1997.)

Garry Marshall, Brendan Fraser in
The Twilight of the Golds © Avalanche/ CFD

Harland Williams, Raven in
Rocketman © Disney Enterprises

ROCKETMAN (Walt Disney Pictures) Producer, Roger Birnbaum; Director, Stuart Gillard; Screenplay, Craig Mazin, Greg Erb; Story, Oren Aviv, Craig Mazin, Greg Erb; Photography, Steven Poster; Designer, Roy Forge Smith; Editor, William D. Gordean; Costumes, Daniel Orlandi; Executive Producers, Jon Turteltaub, Oren Aviv, Jonathan Glickman; Co-Executive Producer, Richard H. Prince; Co-Producers, Jamie Masada, Peter Safran; Music, Michael Tavera; Casting, Rick Montgomery, Dan Parada; a Roger Birnbaum/Gold/Miller production, presented in association with Caravan Pictures; Distributed by Buena Vista Pictures; Dolby Digital Stereo; Eastman color; Rated PG; 93 minutes; October release. **CAST:** Harland Williams (Fred Z. Randall), Jessica Lundy (Julie Ford), William Sadler ("Wild Bill" Overbeck), Jeffrey DeMunn (Paul Wick), James Pickens, Jr. (Ben Stevens), Beau Bridges (Bud Nesbitt), Peter Onorati (Gary Hackman), Don Lake (Flight Surgeon), William Arthur Jenkins, Ken Farmer (Mission Controllers), Blake Boyd (Gordon A. Peacock), Brandon Kaplan (Young Fred), Paxton Whitehead (British Reporter), Don Armstrong (Anchorman), Pamela West, Marjorie Carroll (Nuns), Claire Birnbaum (School Kid #1), Sean Tweedley (NASA Lab Tech), Cindy Hogan, Felicia Griffin (Reporters), Lidia Porto (Gary's Nurse), Richard Dillard (The President), Gil Glasgow (Bartender), Raven (Ulysses), Shelley Duvall (Fred's Mom)

LOVE ALWAYS (Legacy) Producer, Isaac Artenstein; Executive Producers, Ken Branson, Coop Cooprider; Director, Jude Pauline Eberhard; Screenplay, Jude Pauline Eberhard, Sharlene Baker; Based on the novel Finding Signs by Sharlene Baker; Photography, Xavier Perez Grobet; Editor, Joel Goodman; Music, Jamie Valle, Anton Sanko; a Persistence of Vision Films presentation of an Isaac Artenstein production.

Nick Sutton, Jacob Reynolds in
Gummo © Fine Line Features

Color; Rated R; 93 minutes; October release. **CAST:** Marisa Ryan (Julia Bradshaw), Moon Zappa (Mary Ellen), Beverly D'Angelo (Miranda), Michael Reilly Burke (Mark Righetti), Mick Murray, Tracy Fraim, Beth Grant, Doug Hutchison, Jerry O'Donnell, Vareli Arizmendi.

GUMMO (Fine Line Features) Producer, Cary Woods; Director/Screenplay, Harmony Korine; Co-Producers, Robin O'Hara, Scott Macaulay; Photography, Jean Yves Escoffier; Editor, Christopher Tellefsen; Designer, Dave Doernberg; Costumes, Chloe Sevigny; an Independent Pictures production; Dolby Stereo; Color; Rated R; 95 minutes; October release. **CAST:** Jacob Reynolds (Solomon), Nick Sutton (Tummler), Jacob Sewell (Bunny Boy), Darby Dougherty (Darby), Chloe Sevigny (Dot), Carisa Bara (Helen), Linda Manz (Solomon's Mom), Max Perlich (Cole)

THE LOVEMASTER (Rocket Pictures) Producer, Tom Coleman; Executive Producers, Alan David, Mark Breen; Co-Producer, Holly MacConkey; Director, Michael Goldberg; Screenplay, Craig Shoemaker, Michael Goldberg; Based on a story by Craig Shoemaker; Photography, Phil Parmet, Jeff Zimmerman; Editors, Richard Currie, Jeremy Kasten; Music, Michael Skloff, Giorgio Bertuccelli; Designer, Gary Randall; Costumes, Maud Kersnowski; Casting, Robyn Ray; Foto-Kem color; Rated R; 84 minutes; October release. **CAST:** Craig Schoemaker (Craig), Farrah Fawcett (The Date), Courtney Thorne-Smith (Deb Memet), Harley Jane Kozak (Karen), Esther Auerbach (Nana), Karen Witter (Marie), Kurt Rambis (Kurt), George Wendt (Therapist), Robert Steinberg (Steiny)

Dan Haggerty, Dylan Haggerty in
Grizzly Mountain © Mega Comm., Inc.

TIMELESS (Phaedra Cinema) Producer, Patricia Bice; Director/Screenplay/Editor, Chris Hart; Co-Producer, Joe Hart; Photography, Chris Norr; Music, Joseph Hart, Sr.; Color; Not rated; 90 minutes; October release. **CAST:** Peter Byrne (Terry), Melissa Duge (Lyrica), Michael Griffiths (Tommy), Joe Hart (Flood), Thomas Grube (Bill), Jim Cronin (Dix), Larry Robinson (Max), Marilise Tronto (Grace), Tony Kruk (Manny Gould), Arnold Merkitch (Bartender), Ann Parker (Manny Gould's Secretary), Frank McMahon (Max's Friend), Robin Farbman, Jodi Salmond (Couple Shopping), Marta Bukowski (Flood's Girl), Jerry Kocka (Mickie the Bartender), Joseph Tudisco (Trucker Driver), Gerald Del Sol (Shop Foreman), Robert Van Lindt (Bill's Boss), Clinton Lee Reeves (Man in Bar)

GRIZZLY MOUNTAIN (Legacy) Producers, Anthony Dalesandro, Peter White; Executive Producers, Eric Parkinson, Nicholas Konstant, George Furla; Executive in Charge of Production, Michael Slifkin; Director, Jeremy Haft; Screenplay, Jeremy Haft, Peter White; Story, Eric Parkinson; Photography, Andy Parke; Music, Jon McCallum; Editors, Richard Westover, Anthony Dalesandro; a Mega Communications, Inc. in association with Napor Kids presentation of a Parkinson/Konstant/Furla production; Ultra-Stereo; Color; Rated G; 96 minutes; October release. **CAST:** Dan Haggerty (Jeremiah), Dylan Haggerty (Dylan), Nicole Lund (Nicole), Kim Morgan Greene (Betty), Perry Stephens (Boss Man/Burts), Robert Patteri (Roscoe), Andrew Craig (Bailey), Robert Budaska (Jones),

E.E. "Ed" Bell (Mayor), Martin Kove (Marshall Jackson), Don Borza (Bill Marks), Marguerite Hickey (Karen Marks), Megan Haggerty (Megan Marks), Gil Revilla (Chief), Mark Abbott (Tukayoo)

THE DELI (Golden Monkey Pictures) Producers, Sylvia Caminer, John Dorrian; Director, John Andrew Gallagher; Screenplay, John Dorrian, John Andrew Gallagher; Photography, Bob Lechterman; Designer, Lisa Frantz; Costumes, Melissa Toth; Music, Ernie Mannix; Editor, Sue Blainey; Color; Not rated; 96 minutes; November release. **CAST**: Mike Starr (Johnny), Matt Keeslar (Andy), Judith Malina (Vincenza Amico), Brian Vincent (Pinky), Michael Badalucco (Eric), Heavy D (Bo), Ice-T (Phil), Iman (Avocado Lady), Michael Imperioli (Matty), David Johansen (The Cabbie), Heather Matarazzo (Sabrina), Debi Mazar (Teresa), William McNamara (Kevin), Gretchen Mol (Mary), Christopher Noth (Sal), Tony Sirico (Tony), Jerry Stiller (Petey), Frank Vincent (Tommy), Burt Young (J.C.)

Michael Imperioli, Mike Starr in
The Deli © Golden Monkey Pictures

HABIT (Glass Eye Pix/Passport Cinemas) Producer, Dayton Taylor; Director/Screenplay/Editor, Larry Fessenden; Photography, Frank DeMarco; Associate Producer, Susan A. Stover; Costumes, Loren Bevans; Music, Geoffrey Kidde; Color; Not rated; 112 minutes; November release. **CAST**: Larry Fessenden (Sam), Meredith Snaider (Anna), Aaron Beall (Nick), Patricia Coleman (Rae), Heather Woodbury (Liza), Jesse Hartman (Lenny), Marcus A. Miranda (Segundo), Herb Rogers (Slimma), Hart Fessenden (Sam's Dad), Lon Waterford (Mr. Lyons), Alan Bandit (Norman in Bridgehampton), Dale Cameron (Sandy in Bridgehampton), Whitney Alexandra McGann (Kid in Bridgehampton), Helene Weintraub (Liza's Nosy Neighbor), Michael Buscemi (Liza's Friend Dave), Rebecca Moore (Liza's Friend Susan), Jack Dingas (Harry at the Party), Kelly Reichardt (Partygirl on Phone), Cain Berlinger (Carrot Man), Ginny Hack (What's with That Guy Patron), Tom Hale (Record Executive on Cellular Phone), Derek Davis (Kid Hurt in Accident), Erc Vesbit (Halloween Delivery Man), Danilo Randjic Coleman (Devil Boy), Beverly Washington (Segundo's Wife), Christopher Reyes (Segundo's Son), Jain V. Alonso (Segundo's Daughter), John Gaddy (Departing Tenant at Liza's)

NEVER MET PICASSO (Turbulent Arts) Producers, Patrick Cunningham, Stephen Kijak; Executive Producer, Jennifer Ryan; Director/Screenplay, Stephen Kijak; Photography, David Tames; Designers, Humberto Cordero, Julie Lupien; Costumes, Kathleen Chisholm; Editor, Angelica Brisk; Music, Kristin Hersh, Bill Lee; a Mighty Reel production; Color; Not rated; 90 minutes; November release. **CAST**: Alexis Arquette (Andrew Magnus), Georgia Ragsdale (Lucy), Margot Kidder (Genna Magnus), Don McKellar (Jerry), Keith David (Larry), Alvin Epstein (Uncle Alfred), Omewenne (Ingrid), Diane Beckett (Mailwoman), Craig Hickman (Poetry Slammer), David Levine (Jack), John O'Callaghan (Paul), Jody O'Neil (Marc), Eddie Rutkowski (Young David/Mailperson), Ursula Ryan (Nurse), Richard Snee (Thomas Magnus), Adrienne Starrs (Diane), Suzanne Crosby, Lanie Fischera (Art Critics), Lakia Norwood, Verna Turbulence, Stephanie Whyte (Drag Queens)

Meredith Snaider, Larry Fessenden
in *Habit* © GlassEys/ Passport

COLD AROUND THE HEART (20th Century Fox) Producers, Craig Baumgarten, Dean Halsted, Adam Merims; Executive Producer, Richard Rutowski; Director/Screenplay, John Ridley; Photography, Malik Hassan Sayeed; Designer, Kara Lindstrom; Music, Mason Daring; Costumes, Sara Jane Slotnick; Editor, Eric L. Beason; a Baumgarten-Prophet Entertainment/Illusion Entertainment/Kushner-Locke productions; Super 35 Wiidescreen; Color; Rated R; 96 minutes; November release. **CAST**: David Caruso (Ned Tash), Kelly Lynch (Jude), Stacey Dash (Bec Rosenberg), Christopher Noth (T), John Spencer (Uncle Mike), Pruitt Taylor Vince (Johnny "Cokebottles" Costello), Richard Kind (Nabbish), Kirk Baltz (Detective Argan), Jennifer Jostyn (Inez), Tom McGowan (Gun Store Man), Mark Boone Junior (Angry Man), Jack Brind (Motel Man), Tracey Ross (Nurse Woman), Gareth Williams (Car Dealer Man), Richard Arquette (Gas Station Man), Jack Wallace (Police Captain Man), Viggis Knittridge (Himself)

Nicole Prescott, Kevin Thigpen in
Tar © Mongrel Films

TAR (Mongrel Movies) Producer, Abigail Hunt; Director, Goetz Grossmann; Screenplay, Goetz Grossmann, James A. Pearson, Gilbert Giles; Photography, Lloyd Handwerker; Designer, Pavel Salek; Costumes, Robin Newland; Editor, Sabine Krayenbuhl; Music, John Hill, Billy Bourne; Casting, Caroline Sinclair; Color; Not rated; 90 minutes; November release. **CAST**: Kevin Thigpen (Curtis), Nicole Prescott (Tracy), Seth Gilliam (Tyrone), Ron Brice (Jamal), Frank Minucci (Hank), Chris McKinney, Tracie Jade, Bo Rucker, Danny Johnson, John Henry Cox, Robert Colston, Ernestine Johnson, John Carter, Achilles Lavidis, Ann Gartland, Charlie Smith, Kieve Gitlin, Kesean Gardner, Evan Parke, David Maxwell

John Savage in *The Mouse*
© Strand Releasing

Peter Greene, Darling Narita in *Bang*
© Panorama Entertainment

THE MOUSE (Strand) Producers, Hank Blumenthal, Harris Tulchin, John Savage; Co-Producer, Matt Janes; Director/Screenplay, Daniel Adams; Executive Producers, Richard Segedin, Charlie Irish, Jimmy Walter; Photography, Denise Brassard; Designer, Gay Studebaker; Editor, Victoria Street; Costumes, Deborah Newhall; Music, Jonathon Edwards; Casting, Sheila Jaffe, Georgianne Walken; an Early Morning Films presentation; Color; Not rated; 98 minutes; November release. **CAST:** John Savage (Bruce "The Mouse" Strauss), Angelica Torn (Mary Lou Strauss), Rip Torn (Trucker - God), Charles Bailey-Gates (Joe), Irina Cashen (Jamie Strauss), Tim Williams (Frank "Gator" Lux), Edward Lynch (Ron "Butcher" Stander), Rhasaan Orange, Gary Galone, Danny Venezia (Shamsters), Burt Young, Randall "Tex" Cobb, Vinny Pazienza, Sean O'Grady, Danny Campbell, Jim Tunney, Kip Diggs, Dick Ryan (Themselves), Ray "Boom Boom" Mancini (Larry), Richard Segedin (Sammy), Vito Antuofermo (Trainer), Tommy Makem (Commissioner Adams), Dominic Chianese (Al the Trainer), Keena Keel (Ann), Gerald Orange (Pete), Verdell Smith (Marty McCormick), Jack Celli (Flashback Promoter), Mario Cianfione (Lopez), John Nacco (Bernie), Ed Begine (Don the Promoter), Steve Brito (Dead Boxer), Frank Gio (Commissioner Brennan), Charlie Irisih (Drunk), Michael A. Biase (Ear Doctor), George Van Voorhis (Dead Boxer Trainer), Frank "The Gator" Lux (Lopez Newscaster), Ron "The Butcher" Stander (Bar Patron), Bruce "The Mouse" Strauss (Angelo), Rebecca Rae Adams (Ginny), Mitch Fennel (Ryan Trainer), Daniel Welch (Flashback), Susan Youngs, Michael Campbell, Edward Biggine (McCormick Hecklers), Randy Gordon (Fan), Guy Strauss (Finger Referee), Richard Pitts-Wiley (McCormick Referee), Nick Hasomeris (Flasback Referee), Bill Galvin, Tim Miller, James Paul Ludwig (Lopez Reporters), Wendy Adams, Tonya Jeria (Round Card Girls), Tom Kemp (Commissioner Collins), Lance Norris (Bear Bartender), Burke Carroll (Bear), William J. Devany (McCormick Trainer), Bernie Barry (Lopez Referee)

NICK AND JANE (Avalanche) Producer, Bill McCutchen III; Co-Producer/Director, Rich Mauro; Screenplay, Rich Mauro, Peter Quigley, Neil William Alumkal; Photography, Chris Norr; Music, Mark Suozzo; Editors, Wendey Stanzler, Rich Mauro; Line Producer, Kirsten Bates-Renaud; Casting, Eve Battaglia; a Prophecy Pictures Inc. presentation of an Emeralde Productions in association with Mira Vista Films and Cobalt Films production; Dolby Stereo; Color; Rated R; 96 minutes; November release. **CAST:** Dana Wheeler-Nicholson (Jane), James McCaffrey (Nick), Dave Johansen (Carter), Gedde Watanabe (Enzo), John Dossett (John), Lisa Gay Hamilton (Vick), Saundra Santiago (Stephanie), Clinton Leupp (Miss CoCo), George Coe (Mr. Morgan), Siobhan Fallon (Julie), Dianne Brill (Celine), Ron Parady (Mr. Phillips), Jim Bigwood (Prof. Garrett), Jin Kameno (Restaurant Manager)

BANG (Panorama Entertainment) Producers, Daniel M. Berger, Ladd Vance; Executive Producers, Tomy E. Drissi, Ziggi Golding, Sean B. Kelly, Jude Narita; Director/Screenplay, Ash; Photography, Dave Gasperik; Designer, Daniel M. Berger; Editors, Ash, Daniel M. Berger; an Eagle Eye Films Inc. presentation; Ultra-Stereo; Color; Not rated; 98 minutes; November release. **CAST:** Darling Narita (The Girl), Peter Greene (Adam), Michael Newland (Officer Rattler), Eric Schrody (Pimp), Michael Arturo (Officer Trotter), James Sharpe (Officer Ham), Luis Guizar (Jesus), Art Cruz (Juan), David Allen Graff (The Producer), Stanley Herman (Landlord), Donald "Notorious" D (O.G. on Rooftop), Noble James (Rooftop Dealer), Eric Kirkpatrick (Tucker), Wandi Herman (Piwi on Roof), David Conner (Ivan), Stephanie Martini (Joy), Jason Pepper (Newscaster/TV Cop), Lucy Lui (Hooker), David Preston (Cook), Paul Saucido (Drive by Cholo), Tom Prisco (Addict), Claudia Kareem (Waitress), Daniel Berger (Man on Bus), Pamela Tomasetti (Housewife), Roberta Rodman (Audition Model), Rowen Kerr (Golfer), Darren Lane (Businessman), Juanita Salinas (Latina Woman),

Dana Wheeler-Nicholson, James
McCaffrey in *Nick and Jane* © CFP

RonReaco Lee, Deanna Davis in
How I Spent My Summer Vacation © Cinema Guild

Robin Shou, Sandra Hess, Irina Pantaeva,
Lynn Red Williams in *Mortal Kombat : Annihilation*
© New Line Cinema Inc.

Molly Gross, Marisa Ryan, Claudia Rossi,
Natasha La Ferriere in *Slaves To The Underground*
© Overseas Filmgroup

HOW I SPENT MY SUMMER VACATION (Cinema Guild)
Producers, Alan James Gay, Christopher Mills; Director/Screenplay, John Fisher; Photography, Charles Mills; Art Director, Tim Dempsey; Music, Johnny Barrow; Editors, Norman Todd, Alan James Gay; Costumes, D'Carol Randle, Wayne Van Nuygen; Casting, Shay Bentley-Griffin; a Castleway Entertainment presentation of an Alan James Gay production; Color; Not rated; 75 minutes; November release. **CAST:** RonReaco Lee (Perry), Deanna Davis (Stephanie), E. Roger Mitchell (Joseph), Mike Ngaujah (D'Angelo), Jade Janise Dixon (Tammy), Darren Law (Nolan), Maude Bond (Monica), T'Erica Jenks (Kim), Angela Thigpen (Rachel), Parish German (Young Lady in Parking Lot), Kee McKinney (Donna), Deborah Duke (Mace Lady), Nevaina Graves (Tina), Amil Gibbs (Rude Guy), Derrell Keith Lester (Buster), Maisha Dyson (Rhonda), Felice Monteith (Helen), John Fisher (Voice Over Questioning Stephanie)

MORTAL KOMBAT: ANNIHILATION (New Line Cinema) Producer,
Lawrence Kasanoff; Executive Producers, Alison Savitch, Carla Fry, Brian Witten; Director, John R. Leonetti; Screenplay, Brent V. Friedman, Bruce Zabel; Story, Lawrence Kasanoff, Joshua Wexler, John Tobias; Based on the videogame created by Ed Boon & John Tobias; Co-Producer, Kevin Reidy; Photography, Matthew F. Leonetti; Designer, Charles Wood; Editor, Peck Prior; Music, George S. Clinton; Costumes, Jennifer J. Parsons; Visual Effects Supervisors, Chuck Comisky, Alison Savitch; Stunts, Pat Johnson, Eddie Stacey; Fight Choreographer, Robin Shou; Casting, Fern Champion, Mark Paladini; a Lawrence Kasanoff/Threshold Entertainment production; Dolby SDDS Stereo; Fotokem color; Rated PG-13; 93 minutes; November release. **CAST:** Robin Shou (Liu Kang), Talisa Soto (Kitana), James Remar (Rayden), Sandra Hess (Sonya Blade), Lynn Red Williams (Jax), Brian Thompson (Shao-Kahn), Reiner Schoene (Shinnok), Musetta Vander (Sindel), Irina Pantaeva (Jade), Deron McBee (Motaro), Marjean Holden (Sheeva), Litefoot (Nightwolf), Chris Conrad (Johnny Cage), John Medlen (Ermac), J.J. Perry (Cyrax/Scorpion), Tyrone Wiggins (Rain), Dennis Keiffer (Baraka), Ridley Tsui Po Wah (Smoke), Keith Cooke Hirabayashi (Sub-Zero), Lance LeGault, Carolyn Seymour (Elder Gods), Dana Hee (Mileena)

ILL GOTTEN GAINS (Spats Films) Director/Screenplay, Joel B.
Marsden; Photography, Ben Kufrin; Designer, Stacie B. London; Music, Mike Baum; Editor, David Schaufele; Color; Rated R; 101 minutes; November release. **CAST:** Djimon Hounsou (Fyah), Akosua Busia (Fey), De'aundre Bonds (Pop), Eartha Kitt (The Wood), Reg E. Cathey (Nassor), Tom Fitzpatrick (Jeremiah), Mario Gardner (Barc), Clabe Hartley (Skinner), Jamillah Nicole (Fa), Tom Taglang (Cowlie), Tony Torn (The Vet), Peter Navy Tuiasosopo (Cooper), Claudia Robinson (Femi)

SLAVES TO THE UNDERGROUND (First Look Pictures) Producers,
Kristine Peterson, Bill Cody, Raquel Caballes Maxwell; Executive Producers, Joel Soisson, Jeffrey Thal, Judy Friend; Director, Kristine Peterson; Screenplay, Bill Cody; Photography, Zoran Hochstatter; Designer, Michael Moran; Editor, Eric Vizents; Music, Mike Martt; a Neo Motion Pictures production; Dolby Stereo; Color; Rated R; 94 minutes;

November release. **CAST:** Molly Gross (Shelly), Marisa Ryan (Suzy), Jason Bortz (Jimmy), Bob Neuwirth (Big Phil), Natacha La Ferriere (Zoe), Claudia Rossi (Brenda), James Garver (Brian), Peter Szumlas (Dale)

THE SELLER (Proletariat Pictures) Producers, Craig Schlattman,
Juliet Bashore; Director/Screenplay, Craig Schlattman; Photography, Wes Llewellyn, Bubba Bukowski; Eidtors, Lester Fatt, Victor Livingston; Music, Garic Cargi; Art Director, J. Lyons; Dolby; Color; Not rated; 113 minutes; December release. **CAST:** Brian Brophy (Bartholomew Trust), Kathy Morozova (Melissa Barnstead), Arthur Roberts (Derrick Murdock), Adam Paul (Dwight Lately), Andre Marquis (Quinton Bendick), Mink Stole (Aunt Betty), David Alexander (Jimbo Carvelton), Jeffrey von Meyer (Robert Barnstead), Nancy van Iderstine (Carla Barnstead Normack), T.J. Castronovo (Herman), Craig Schlattman (Bartender), Jim Boyce (TV Announcer), Bob Van Rossum (Cowboy), Dan Frank (Don), John Smith, Franklin Youri (Valets)

DOGS: THE RISE AND FALL OF AN ALL-GIRL BOOKIE JOINT
(Phaedra Cinema) Executive Producer, Marcia Kirkley; Director/Screenplay, Eve Annenberg; Co-Producers, Heather D'Adamo, Eve Annenberg; Photography, Joe Foley, Wolfgang Held; Designer, Miro Bazac; Editor, Jack Haigis; Music, John Gunter, Richard Thompson; Color; Not rated; 80 minutes; December release. CAST: Toby Huss (Sammy Cybernowski), Pam Columbus (Leila), Pam Gray (Stephanie), Leo Marks (Arnie), Amadeo D'Adamo (Bruce), Melody Beale (Amina), Eve Annenberg (Gypsy)

Melody Beal, Pamela Gray, Eve Annenberg
in *Dogs* © Phaedra Cinema

Anthony Crivello, David Norona in
Twisted © Leisure Time Features

TWISTED (Leisure Time Features) Producer, Adrian Agromonte; Executive Producers, Bernard Arbit, Barry Witz, Mark Weiner; Director/Screenplay, Seth Michael Donsky; Photography, Hernan Toro; Editors, Tom McArdle, Seth Michael Donsky; Designer, Scott Bailey; Music, Q Lazzarus, Danny Z; Costumes, Rosemary Ponzo; a Dons Quixote Production in association with Miravista Films; Color; Not rated; 100 minutes; December release. CAST: David Norona (Angel), Keiven McNeil Graves (Lee), William Hickey (Andre), Anthony Crivello (Eddie), Jean Loup (Fine Art), Billy Porter (Shiniqua), Elizabeth Franz (Social Worker), Ray Aranha (Can Man)

RUNNING TIME (Panoramic Pictures) Producers, Josh Becker, Jane Goe; Director/Screenplay, Josh Becker; Story, Peter Y. Choi; Photography, Kurt Rauf; Music, Joseph LoDuca; Editor, Kaye Davis; Black and white; Not rated; 79 minutes; December release. CAST: Bruce Campbell (Carl), Jeremy Roberts (Patrick), Anita Barone (Janie), Stan Davis (Buzz), Gordon Jennison (Donny), Art LaFleur (Warden), Dana Craig (Mr. Mueller), Bidget Hoffman (Receptionist)

HOME ALONE 3 (20th Century Fox) Producers, John Hughes, Hilton Green; Executive Producer, Ricardo Mestres; Director, Raja Gosnell; Screenplay, John Hughes; Photography, Julio Macat; Designer, Henry Bumstead; Music, Nick Glennie-Smith; Costumes, Jodie Tillen; Editors, Bruce Green, Malcolm Campbell, David Rennie; Casting, Billy Hopkins, Suzanne Smith, Kerry Barden, Jennifer McNamara; a John Hughes production; Dolby Digital Stereo; Deluxe color; Rated PG; 102 minutes; December release. CAST: Alex D. Linz (Alex), Olek Krupa (Beaupre), Rya Kihlstedt (Alice), Lenny Von Dohlen (Jernigan), David Thornton (Unger), Haviland Morris (Karen), Kevin Kilner (Jack), Marian Seldes

Olek Krupa, Alex D. Linz in *Home Alone 3* © Twentieth Century Fox

(Mrs. Hess), Seth Smith (Stan), Scarlett Johansson (Molly), Christopher Curry (Agent Stuckey), Baxter Harris (Police Captain), James Saito (Chinese Mob Boss), Kevin Gudahl (Techie), Richard Hamilton (Cab Driver), Freeman Coffey (Recruiting Officer), Krista Lally (Dispatcher), Neil Flynn, Tony Mockus Jr., James L. Chisem (Police Officers), Pat Healy (Agent Rogers), Darwin L. Harris (Photographer), Adrianne Duncan (Flight Attendant), Sharon Sachs (Annoying Woman), Joseph L. Caballero (Security Guard), Larry C. Tankson (Cart Driver), Jennifer Daley (Police Photographer #2), Darren T. Knaus (Voice of Parrot)

Sean Penn, Malcolm McDowell in
Hugo Pool © BMG / Northern Arts

HUGO POOL (Northern Arts/BMG Independents) Producer, Barbara Ligeti; Executive Producers, Douglas Berquist, Michael Frislev, Chad Oakes, Iren Koster, Lawrence Steven Meyers; Director, Robert Downey; Screenplay, Robert Downey, Laura Downey; Photography, Joseph Montgomery; Editor, Joe D'Augustine; Music, Danilo Perez; Designer, Lauren Gabor; Costumes, Jocelyn F. Wright; a Nomadic Pictures presentation of a Downey/Ligeti production; Dolby Stereo; Color; Rated R; 93 minutes; December release. CAST: Patrick Dempsey (Floyd Gaylen), Robert Downey, Jr. (Franz Mazur), Richard Lewis (Chic Chicalini), Malcolm McDowell (Henry Dugay), Alyssa Milano (Hugo Dugay), Cathy Moriarty (Minerva), Sean Penn (The Leprechaun), Mark Boone Junior (Pool Supply Man), Brendan B. Dawson (Man with Truck), Sean Glenn (Andy), Bert Remsen (Sad Old Man), Kevin Dornan (Bad Advice Father), Michael Mazzola (Kid), Chuck Barris (Irwin), Jim Shield (Lifeguard), Ann Magnuson (Drowning Matron), Eddie Perez (Gardener), Lora Gomez Eastwood, Pablo Ferro, Helen Hewitt Garb (Merengue Dancers), Domingo Ambriz (Spanish Husband), Paul Herman (Rabbi), Joanne Dearing (Extra's Mother), Michael Goldman (Extra's Father), Michael Bolger (One Man Band), Aaron Cuhr, Jacob James Hanft, N. Dylan Pfeifer (Party Waiters), Larry Kaplan (Man at Track), Brian David Zola (Guard at Track), Barbara Ligeti (Radio Newscaster) (Cable premiere: 11/97)

OFFICE KILLER (Strand) Producers, Christine Vachon, Pamela Koffler; Executive Producers, Tom Carouso, John Hart, Ted Hope, James Schamus; Director, Cindy Sherman; Screenplay, Elise MacAdam, Tom Kalin; Story, Cindy Sherman, Elise MacAdam; Additional Dialogue, Todd Haynes; Photography, Russell Fine; Editor, Merril Stern; Designer, Kevin Thompson; Music, Evan Lurie; Special Effects Makeup, Rob Benevides; Casting, Billy Hopkins, Suzanne Smith, Kerry Barden; a prresentation in association with Good Machine and Kardana/Swinsky Films of a Good Fear film; Color; Not rated; 81 minutes; December release. CAST: Carol Kane (Dorine Douglas), Molly Ringwald (Kim Poole), Jeanne Tripplehorn (Norah Reed), Barbara Sukowa (Virginia Wingate), Michael Imperioli (Daniel Birch), David Thornton (Gary Michaels), Mike Hodge (Mr. Landau), Alice Drummond (Carlotta Douglas), Florina Rodov (Receptionist), Jason Brill (Delivery Man), Eddie Malavarca (Brian the Mailboy), Doug Barron (Ted), Linda Powell (Naomi), Albert Macklin (Brad), Michelle Hurst (Kate), Paula Cale (Paula), Harvey Kaplan (Steve), Marla Sucharetza (Mrs. Gary Michaels), Rachel Aviva (Young Dorine), Marceline Hugot (Young Carlotta), Wayne Maxwell (Jimmy the Homeless

Man), Julia McIlvaine (Linda the Girl Scout), Cleopatra St. John (Girl Scout #2), Danny Morgenstern (Ted's Secretary), Timothy D. Stikney, Christopher Tracy (Paramedics)

THE EDUCATION OF LITTLE TREE (Paramount) Producer, Jake Eberts; Director/Screenplay, Richard Friedenberg; Based on the novel by Forrest Carter; Co-Producers, Lenny Young, Louise Gendron; Photography, Anastas Michos; Designer, Dan Bishop; Editor, Wayne Wahrman; Music, Mark Isham; Costumes, Renée April; Casting, Vera Miller, René Haynes; a Jake Eberts production, presented in association with Allied Films/Lightmotive; Color; Rated PG; 117 minutes; December release. **CAST**: James Cromwell (Granpa), Tantoo Cardinal (Granma), Joseph Ashton (Little Tree), Graham Green (Willow John), Leni Parker (Martha), Rebecca Dewey (Dolly), William Rowat (Henry), Robert Daviau (Ralph), Christopher Heyerdahl (Pine Billy), Norris Domingue (Mr. Jenkins), Mika Boorem (Little Girl), Mark Jeffrey Miller (Preacher), Gordon Masten (Politician), Howard Rosenstein (Calf's Owner), Teddy-Lee Dillon, James Rae, Alain Goulem (Revenuers), Griffith Brewer (Church Man), Dawn Ford (Church Woman), Lisa Bronwyn Moore (Elizabeth), Larry Day (Mr. Lane), Dean Hagopian (Joe Taylor), Jonathan Stark (Girl's Father), Pauline Little (Mrs. Higgenbotham), Peter Colvey (Proctor #1), Michel Perron (Headmaster), Chris Fennell (Wilburn), Victoria Barkoff (Teacher), Karentiio Phillips (Older Boy), Pierre Boudreau (Pilgrim), Richard Jutras (Indian), Jeff Jeffcoat (Voice of Older Little Tree)

VEGAS VACATION (Jerry Weintraub Productions) Producer, Jerry Weintraub; Executive Producers, Matty Simmons, Susan Ekins; Director, Stephen Kessler; Screenplay, Elisa Bell; Story, Elisa Bell, Bob Ducsay; Photography, William A. Fraker; Designer, David L. Snyder; Editor, Seth Flaum; Music, Joel McNeely; Distributed by WB; Dolby; Technicolor; Rated PG-13; 95 minutes; February release. **CAST**: Chevy Chase (Clark Griswold), Beverly D'Angelo (Ellen Griswold), Randy Quaid (Cousin Eddie), Ethan Embry (Rusty Griswold), Marisol Nichols (Audrey Griswold), Miriam Flynn (Cousin Catherine), Shae D'Lyn (Cousin Vickie), Wayne Newton (Himself), Siegfried and Roy (Themselves), Wallace Shawn (Marty), Sid Caesar (Old Guy), Julio Oscar Mechoso (Limo Driver), Sly Smith (Mirage Security Guard), Julia Sweeney (Mirage Reception Person), Corinna Harney Jones (Girl at Blackjack Table), Joe Armeno (Roulette Stickman), Christie Brinkley (Woman in Ferrari), Juliette Brewer (Cousin Ruby-Sue), Zach Moyes (Cousin Denny), John Finnegan (Hoover Dam Guide), Seth Walker (Bellman), Howard Platt (Maitre 'd), Elizabeth Illia (Woman at Concert), Wayne Brown, Gary Devaney (Croupiers), Maria Cina (Mirage Cashier), Wendy Kaufman (Wendy), Joe LaCoco (Riviera Bartender), David L. Garoutte (Riviera Security Guard), C.C. Costigan (Kelli), Peter George (Marcus), Frank Mendonga (Kurt), Daniel Steven Lopez (Kyle), Shannah Laumeister (Mariah), Aki (Aki), Bud Ekins (O'Shea's Security Guard), Jerry Weintraub (Jilly), Bernie Yuman (Doc Sandy), Paul Kessler (Silent Al), S.A. Griffin (Pit Boss), Lou DiMaggio (Casino Host), Ruth Gillis (Saleswoman), Samuel J. Marber (Painter), Antonio Mitchell (Larry), Jason Stuart (Buffet Guy), Nick Mazzola (War Dealer), Jim Migliore (Rock Paper Scissors Dealer), Reno Nichols (Coin Tosser), Frank Washko, Jr. (Guess Which Hand Dealer), Ken Michelman (Pick a Number Dealer), Clinton Brandhagen (Valet), Hayley Mortison (Girl in Hot Tub), Gene Ellison Jones (Mirage Guard at Party), Steve "Biscuit" Walker (Bouncer), Rusty Meyers (Club Manager), Roxy Swaney (Keno Caller), Billy Morrissette, Sharon Mendel (Paramedics), Larry Hankin (Preacher)

ROSEWOOD (Peters Entertainment) Producer, Jon Peters; Executive Producer, Tracy Barone; Director, John Singleton; Screenplay, Gregory Poirier; Photography, Johnny E. Jensen; Designer, Paul Sylbert; Editor, Bruce Cannon; Co-Producer, Penelope L. Foster; Music, John Williams; Costumes, Ruth E. Carter; Casting, Marion Dougherty; a Peters Entertainment production in association with New Deal Productions; Distributed by WB; Dolby; Panavision; Technicolor; Rated R; 142 minutes; February release. **CAST**: Jon Voight (John Wright), Ving Rhames (Mann), Don Cheadle (Sylvester), Bruce McGill (Duke Purdy), Loren Dean (James Taylor), Esther Rolle (Aunt Sarah), Elise Neal (Scrappie), Robert Patrick (Lover), Michael Rooker (Sheriff Walker), Catherine Kellner (Fanny Taylor), Akosua Busia (Jewel), Paul Benjamin (James

Jeanne Tripplehorn in *Office Killer*
© Strand Releasing

Carrier), Kevin Jackson (Sam Carter), Mark Boone Junior (Poly), Muse Watson (Henry Andrews), Badja Djola (John Bradley), Kathryn Meisle (Mary Wright), Jaimz Woolvett (Deputy Earl), James Edward Coleman II (Arnett), Tristan Hook (Emmett Purdy), Benea Ousley (Philomena), Isabell Monk (Emma), Bridgid Coulter (Gertrude), Gabie Chavis (Minnie), Vanessa Baden (Lee Ruth), Marcus Barrington (Denny), Matthew Davison (Timothy), Brett Rice (William Bryce), Ric Reitz (John Bryce), Ken Sagoes (Big Baby), Phil Moore (Aaron Carrier), Lowell Fenner (Judge Johnson), Andrew "J.R." Tarver (Preacher), Harold G. Crawford (Clevus), Marc Macaulay (Bobby), Clarence Thomas (Lemuel), Blaine Farmer (Michael Wright), Valerie Herald, Susan Gallagher (Women), Steven Tyler (Little Ronnie), Danny Hanemann (White Brother), Eldrid Foye (Blackman), Michael Galloway (Cracker #2), Macon McCalman (Governor Hardee), Tom Schuster (Kid's Redneck Dad), Peggy Sheffield (Mrs. Ellis Walker), Steve Raulerson (Sheriff of Bronson), Henry Laurence (Man #2)

SELENA (Q Productions Inc.—Esparza/Katz Prod.) Producers, Moctesuma Esparza, Robert Katz; Executive Producer, Abraham Quintanilla; Co-Executive Producer, David Wisnievitz; Co-Producer, Peter Lopez; Director/Screenplay, Gregory Nava; Photography, Edward Lachman; Designer, Cary White; Editor, Nancy Richardson; Music, Dave Grusin; Costumes, Elisabetta Beraldo; Casting, Roger Mussenden; Distributed by WB; Dolby; Super 35 Widescreen; Technicolor; Rated PG; 130 minutes; March release. **CAST**: Jennifer Lopez (Selena Quintanilla), Edward James Olmos (Abraham Quintanilla), Jon Seda (Chris Perez), Constance Marie (Marcella Quintanilla), Jacob Vargas (Abie Quintanilla),

Graham Greene, Joseph Ashton in
The Education of Little Tree © Paramount Pictures

179

Lupe Ontiveros (Yolanda Saldivar), Jackie Guerra (Suzette Quintanilla), Alexandra Meneses (Sara), Peter Astrudillo, Ricky Vela (Themselves), Ruben Gonzalez (Joe Ojeda), Don Shelton (Stage Dancer), Richard Emanuele (Concert Reporter), Panchito Gomez (Young Abraham—Dinos 1961), Richard Coca (Bobby—Dinos 1961), George Perez (Seff—Dinos 1961), Brian Fallteen (Club Owner), Carmen Martinez, Elisabeth Gonzalez, Richard Iglesias (Irate Club Goers), Everett Sifuentes (Lerma's Club Owner), Gil Glasgow (Police Officer—1961), Rebecca Lee Meza (Young Selena), Victoria Elena Flores (Young Suzette), Rafael Tamayo (Young Abie), Carl William Holler (Neighbor), Bel Hernandez (Dolores Quintanilla), Gail Cronauer (Customer), Elia Ortiz (Waitress), Fernando Cubillas (Eddie Quintanilla), Sal Lopez (Juan Luis), Richard Williams Hughes (MC), Erick Carrillo, Frank Mendez (Cholos), Seidy Lopez (Deborah), Francisco J. De La Fuente, Keith Kaslow (Hotel Managers), Don Cass (Security Guard), Peter P. Montejano, Michael Guerrero, Ronald Gonzales, Chris Doughten (Chris' Friends), Leon Singer (Concert Promoter), Martha Flores, Terry Elena Ordaz (Monterrey Reporters), Marcos Padilla (Concert Official), Valerio Longoria, Sr. (Accordian Player), Philip Raybourn (Bungie Jump Attendant), Mark Carrillo (Manuel), Darline Tigrett (Mexico City Reporter), Donnie Neubauer (Record Executive), John Verea (Jose Behar), Joe Stevens (Record Producer), Marika Baca, Michelle McManus (Pedicurists), Barbara Petricini-Buxton (Saleslady), Leonardo Martinez (Boutique Worker), Molly Moroney (Store Manager), Desi McGill (Blonde Teenager), Tom Christopher (Grammy Presenter), Cora Cardona (Head Seamstress), Amin Mery (Paramedic)

CATS DON'T DANCE (Turner Feature Animation)
Producers, David Kirschner, Paul Gertz; Executive Producers, David Steinberg, Charles L. Richardson, Sandy Russell Gartin; Director, Mark Dindal; Screenplay, Roberts Gannaway, Cliff Ruby, Elana Lesser, Theresa Pettengill; Story, Rick Schneider, Robert Lence, Mark Dindal, Brian McEntee, David Womersley, Kelvin Yasuda; Co-Producers, Jim Katz, Barry Weiss; Art Director, Brian McEntee; Music, Steve Goldstein; Songs, Randy Newman; Editor, Dan Molina; Casting, Judy Taylor, Lynda Gordon; Storyboard, Rich Schneider, Mark Dindal; Layout, David Womersley; Background, Jim Hickey; Clean-Up, Don Parmele; Effects and Computer Graphics Imagery, Mark Myer; a David Kirschner production; Distributed by WB; Dolby; Color; Rated G; 75 minutes; March release. **VOICE CAST**: Scott Bakula (Danny), Jasmine Guy (Sawyer—speaking), Natalie Cole (Sawyer—singing), Ashley Peldon (Darla Dimple—speaking), Lindsay Ridgeway (Darla Dimple—singing), Kathy Najimy (Tillie), John Rhys-Davies (Woolie), George Kennedy (L.B. Mammoth), Rene Auberjonois (Flanigan), Hal Holbrook (Cranston), Don Knotts (T.W.), Betty Lou Gerson (Francis), Matthew Herried (Pudge), Frank Welker (Farley Wink), David Johansen (Bus Driver), Mark Dindal (Max)

MURDER AT 1600 (Regency Enterprises)
Producers, Arnold Kopelson, Arnon Milchan; Executive Producers, Anne Kopelson, Michael Nathanson, Stephen Brown; Director, Dwight Little; Screenplay, Wayne Beach, David Hodgin; Co-Producer, Ralph S. Singleton; Photography, Steven Bernstein; Designer, Nelson Coates; Editors, Billy Weber, Leslie Jones; Music, Christopher Young; Costumes, Denise Cronenberg; Casting, Amanda Mackey Johnson, Cathy Sandrich; an Arnold Kopelson production; Presented in association with Regency Enterprises; Distributed by WB; Dolby; Technicolor; Rated R; 107 minutes; April release. **CAST**: Wesley Snipes (Det. Regis), Diane Lane (Nina Chance), Daniel Benzali (Spikings), Dennis Miller (Det. Stengel), Alan Alda (Jordan), Ronny Cox (Pres. Jack Neil), Diane Baker (Kitty Neil), Tate Donovan (Kyle Neil), Harris Yulin (Gen. Clark Tully), Nicholas Pryor (Paul Moran), Charles Rocket (Jeffrey), Nigel Bennett (Burton Cash), Tamara Gorski (Young Woman in Bar), Douglas O'Keeffe (Assassin—John Kerry), Tony Nappo (Luchessi), Mary Moore (Carla Town), George R. Robertson (Mack Falls), Ho Chow (Tepper), James Millington (Lt. Marty Dill), John Bourgeois (Capt. Farr), Peter James Haworth, Aron Tager (Treasury Guards), David Gardner (Speaker of the House), Cliff McMullen (Sniper—Carl), Keith Williams (Lawyer Randy Queeg), Grace Armas (Screaming Cleaning Woman), David Fraser (Brack Electronics), George Sperdakos (Reporter—Last Press), Sandra Caldwell (Mrs. Wallace), Frank Moore (Capt. Ford Gibbs), Richard Blackburn (Coroner Jimmy Foley), James Gallanders (Law Student), Victor Ertmanis (Cop Bartender),

Richard Fitzpatrick (Law Professor), Michael Ricupero (Landlord), Chris Gillett (V.P. Gordon Dylan), J. Craig Sandy (FBI Agent #1), Robert Bidaman (V.P. Aide), Carol Anderson (Capt. Farr's Asst.), Christopher Kennedy (Techy), Mike Kinney (Reporter—Jail), Michael Hambrick, Dan Duran, Sandi Stahlbrand (CNN Reporters), Jackie Bensen, Maureen Bunyan, Kathryn Klvana (TV Reporters), Sheldon Turcott (CNN Newscaster #1), Tom Urich (CNN News Anchor), Tino Monte (Local Newscaster), Raven Dauda (Waitress), Michael Dyson (Treasury Drone), Doris E. McMillon, Lewis Grenville (Network Reporters), Moe Kelso (Gorgeous Woman), Junior Williams (Medic), Howard Hoover, Bryan Renfro, Markus Parilo, Leight E. Brinkman, Len Wagner, Peter Ellery, Ray Paisley, Brian King (Suits), Donald Jones (Reporter C), Marco Bianco, Matt Birman, Eric Bryson, Walter Masko, Branko Racki, Mike Shute, Anton Tyukodi (Secret Service)

LEO TOLSTOY'S ANNA KARENINA (Icon Prod.)
Producer, Bruce Davey; Executive Producer, Stephen McEveety; Director/Screenplay, Bernard Rose; Based on the novel by Leo Tolstoy; Photography, Daryn Okada; Designer, John Myhre; Editor, Victor Du Bois; Costumes, Maurizio Millenotti; Casting, Marion Dougherty; Distributed by WB; Dolby Stereo; Panavision; Technicolor; Rated R; 108 minutes; April release. **CAST**: Sophie Marceau (Anna Karenina), Sean Bean (Vronsky), Alfred Molina (Levin), Mia Kirshner (Kitty), James Fox (Karenin), Fiona Shaw (Lydia), Danny Huston (Stiva), Phyllida Law (Vronskaya), David Schofield (Nikolai), Saskia Wickham (Dolly), Jennifer Hall (Betsy), Anna Calder Marshall (Shcherbatskaya), Valerie Braddell (Ambassador's Wife), Niall Buggy (Doctor), Anthony Calf (Serpuhovsky), Vernon Dobtcheff (Pestov), Hamish Falconer (Seriozha), Stefan Gryff (Korsunsky), Barbara Horne (Miss Edwards), Larissa Kousnetsova (Agatha), Jeremy Sheffield (Boris), Justine Waddell (Nordston), Mikail Hmelev (Mahotin), Ksenia Rappoport (Maria), Peter Sholohov (Kapitonich), Julia Krasnova (Annushka), Ludmila Kurepova (Sorokina), German Maximov (Priest), Tatiana Zaharova (Midwife), Sergei Scherbina (Korney), Gelena Ivleva (Lizaveta), Father Vadim Sadovnikov (Inn Priest), Sergei Parshin (Doctor's Doorman), Valery Kukhareshen (Specialist Doctor), Nora Griakalova (Myagkaya), Oleg Kosminsky (Titus), Victor Guiranov, Leonty Varenstov (Peasants), Igor Efimov (Servant), Konstantin Lukashov (Moscow Railway Worker), Alexandra Lavrova (Young Anna)

FATHERS' DAY (Silver Pictures)
Producers, Joel Silver, Ivan Reitman; Executive Producers, Joe Medjuck, Daniel Goldberg, Francis Veber; Director, Ivan Reitman; Screenplay, Lowell Ganz, Babaloo Mandel; Based on the film Les Comperes by Francis Veber; Photography, Stephen H. Burum; Designer, Thomas Sanders; Editors, Sheldon Kahn, Wendy Greene Bricmont; Co-Producers, Gordon Webb, Karyn Fields; Music, James Newton Howard; Songs "Young Boy" and "The World Tonight" written and performed by Paul McCartney; Costumes, Rita Ryack; Casting, Bonnie Timmermann, Michael Chinich; a Silver Pictures production in association with Northern Lights Entertainment; Distributed by WB; Dolby; Panavision; Technicolor; Rated PG-13; 98 minutes; May release. **CAST**: Robin Williams (Dale Putley), Billy Crystal (Jack Lawrence), Julia Louis-Dreyfus (Carrie Lawrence), Nastassja Kinski (Collette Andrews), Charlie Hofheimer (Scott Andrews), Bruce Greenwood (Bob Andrews), Dennis Burkley (Calvin), Haylie Johnson (Nikki), Charles Rocket (Russ Trainor), Patti D'Arbanville (Shirley Trainor), Jared Harris (Lee), Louis Lombardi (Matt), Mark McGrath, Craig Bullock, Charles Stan Frazier, Matthew Murphy Karges, Rodney Sheppard (Sugar Ray Band), Alan Berger (Rex), Tom Verica (Peter), Jennifer Crystal (Rose), David Ripley, Ryan "Rhino" Michaels (Roadies), Jason Reitman (Wrong Kid in Alley), William Hall (Hotel Clerk), Ricky Harris (Bellhop), Paul Herman (Mr. Barmore), Christopher Jaymes (Gas Station Guy), Catherine Reitman (Victoria), Claudette Wells (Ms. Tweesbury), Susan Traylor (Flight Attendant), Dana Gould (Room Service Waiter), Meagen Fay (Megan), Mary Gillis (Slot Machine Lady), Mindy Seeger (Nurse), Jennifer Echols (Ball Park Vendor), Marc Glimcher (Cashier), Geoffrey Infeld (Mime), Harry E. Northup (Cop—Reno Jail), Tamara Zook (Waitress—Francene), Frank Medrano (Mechanic), Elston Ridgle (Security Guard), Kim Shattuck, Ronnie Barnett, Roy McDonald (The Muffs), Caroline Reitman (Lost Girl), Lee Weaver (Airline Passenger), Jose "Esau" Pena (Boat Painter), Andre Zotoff (Doorman), Kay Ford (Woman in Lobby), Jasmine Rose (Nosering Girl), Mel Gibson (Pierced Guy)

ADDICTED TO LOVE (Outlaw Production/Miramax) Producers, Jeffrey Silver, Bobby Newmyer; Executive Producers, Bob Weinstein, Harvey Weinstein; Director, Griffin Dunne; Screenplay, Robert Gordon; Photography, Andrew Dunn; Designer, Robin Standefer; Editor, Elizabeth Kling; Co-Producers, Caroline Baron, Johanna Demetrakas; Music, Rachel Portman; Costumes, Renee Ehrlich Kalfus; Casting, Amanda Mackey Johnson, Cathy Sandrich; Distributed by WB; Dolby; Technicolor; Rated R; 100 minutes; May release. **CAST:** Meg Ryan (Maggie), Matthew Broderick (Sam), Kelly Preston (Linda), Tcheky Karyo (Anton), Maureen Stapleton (Nana), Nesbitt Blaisdell (Ed Green), Remak Ramsay (Prof. Wells), Lee Wilcof (Carl), Dominick Dunne (Matheson), Susan Forristal (Cecile), Larry Pine (Street Comic), Debbon Ayer (Gwen), Maurizio Benazzo (Euro-Chic Man), Paolo Calamari (French Bartender), Helmar Augustus Cooper (Bus Driver), Tom Forrest (Astronomer), Shoshana Gleich (School Teacher), Jacqueline Heinze (Bald Girl), Mike Hodge (Linda's Doorman), Daniel Dae Kim (Undergrad Assist.), Bill Kux (Desk Clerk), Steve McAuliff (Business Man), Conrad McLaren (Motorcycle Man), Bill Timoney (Restaurant Patron)

BATMAN & ROBIN (Joel Schumacher Film) Producer, Peter MacGregor-Scott; Executive Producers, Benjamin Melniker, Michael E. Uslan; Director, Joel Schumacher; Screenplay, Akiva Goldsman; Based upon Batman characters created by Bob Kane and published by DC Comics; Photography, Stephen Goldblatt; Designer, Barbara Ling; Editor, Dennis Virkler; Visual Effects, John Dykstra; Music, Elliot Goldenthal; Costumes, Ingrid Ferrin, Robert Turturice; Co-Producer, William M. Elvin; Casting, Mali Finn; Distributed by WB; Dolby; Technicolor; Rated PG-13; 130 minutes; June release. **CAST:** Arnold Schwarzenegger (Mr. Freeze/Dr. Victor Fries), George Clooney (Batman/Bruce Wayne), Chris O'Donnell (Robin/Dick Grayson), Uma Thurman (Poison Ivy/Dr. Pamela Isley), Alicia Silverstone (Batgirl/Barbara Wilson), Michael Gough (Alfred Pennyworth), Pat Hingle (Commissioner Gordon), John Glover (Dr. Jason Woodrue), Elle MacPherson (Julie Madison), Vivica A. Fox (Ms. B. Haven), Vendela K. Thommessen (Nora Fries), Jeep Swenson (Bane), Elizabeth Sanders (Gossip Gerty), John Fink (Aztec Museum Guard), Michael Reid MacKay (Antonio Diego), Eric Lloyd (Young Bruce Wayne), Jon Simmons (Young Alfred), Christian Boeving, Stogie Kenyatta, Andy LaCombe (Snowy Cones Thugs), Joe Sabatino (Frosty), Michael Paul Chan (Observatory Scientist), Kimberly Scott (Observatory Associate), Jay Luchs, Roger Nehls (Observatory Reporters), Anthony E. Cantrell (Observatory Press), Alex Daniels, Peter Navy Tuiasosopo (Observatory Guards), Harry Van Gorkum (M.C.), Sandra Taylor, Elizabeth Guber (Debutantes), Jack Betts, Marc Glimcher, Mark P. Leahy, Jim McMullan (Party Guests), Senator Patrick Leahy (Himself), Jesse Ventura, Ralf Moeller (Arkham Asylum Guards), Doug Hutchison (Golum), Tobias Jelinek, Greg Lauren, Dean Cochran (Motorcycle Gang), Coolio (Banker), Nicky Katt (Spike), Lucas Berman (Tough Boy Biker), Uzi Gal, Howard Velasco (Cops), Bruce Roberts (Handsome Cop), John Ingle (Doctor), Azikiwee Anderson, Michael Bernardo, Steve Blalock, Steve Boyles, Dave Cardoza, Christopher Caso, Mark Chadwick, Danny Costa, Stephan Desjardins, Todd Grossman, James Hardy, Steven Ito, Dennis Keiffer, James Kim, Simon Kim, Dennis Lefevre, Jean Luc Martin, Cory M. Miller, Chris Mitchell, Christopher Nelson, Jim Palmer, Jeff Podgurski, Robert Powell, Chris Sayour, Don Sinnar, Paul Sklar, Takis Triggelis (Ice Thugs)

WILD AMERICA (Morgan Creek Prod.) Producers, James G. Robinson, Irby Smith, Mark Stouffer; Executive Producers, Gary Barber, Steve Tisch, Bill Todman, Jr.; Director, William Dear; Screenplay, David Michael Wieger; Photography, David Burr; Designer, Steven Jordan; Editor, O. Nicholas Brown; Music, Joel McNeely; Costumes, Mary McLeod; Casting, Pam Dixon Mickelson; a James G. Robinson presentation of a Morgan Creek production in association with the Steve Tisch Company; Dolby; Clairmont-Scope; Color; Rated PG; 106 minutes; July release. **CAST:** Jonathan Taylor Thomas (Marshall), Devon Sawa (Mark), Scott Bairstow (Marty), Frances Fisher (Agnes), Jamie Sheridan (Marty Sr.), Tracey Walter (Leon), Don Stroud (Stango), Zack Ward (D.C.), Claudia Stedelin (Annie), Anastasia Spivey (Donna Jo), Leighanne Wallace (Tanna), Amy Lee Douglas (Julie Anne), Sonny Shroyer (Bud), Rachel Fowler (Sarah), Jennifer Crumbley (Betsy), Maggie Blackkettle (Old Native Woman), Larry Reese (Dr. Pierce), Susan Dear (Donna

Pierce), Nadine Browning (Woman at Gravesite), Norman Taber (D.C. Gang Member), Devon Dear, Jennifer Mikelson, Emily Messmer (Swoon Girls), Danny Glover (Mountain Man)

CONTACT (South Side Amusement Co.) Producers, Robert Zemeckis, Steve Starkey; Executive Producers, Joan Bradshaw, Lynda Obst; Director, Robert Zemeckis; Screenplay, James V. Hart, Michael Goldenberg; Based on the novel by Carl Sagan; Co-Producers/Based on the story by Carl Sagan, Ann Druyan; Photography, Don Burgess; Designer, Ed Verreaux; Editor, Arthur Schmidt; Music, Alan Silvestri; Costumes, Joanna Johnston; Senior Visual Effects Supervisor, Ken Ralston; Casting, Victoria Burrows; Distributed by WB; Dolby; Panavision; Technicolor; Rated PG; 150 minutes; July release. **CAST:** Jodie Foster (Ellie Arroway), Matthew McConaughey (Palmer Joss), James Woods (Michael Kitz), John Hurt (S.R. Hadden), Tom Skerritt (David Drumlin), Angela Bassett (Rachel Constantine), Jena Malone (Young Ellie), David Morse (Ted Arroway), Rob Lowe (Richard Rank), Jake Busey (Joseph), Geoffrey Blake (Fisher), William Fichtner (Kent), SaMi Chester (Vernon), Timothy McNeil (Davio), Laura Elena Surillo (Cantina Woman), Henry Strozier (Minister), Michael Chaban (Hadden Suit), Maximilian Martini (Willie), Thomas Garner (Ian Broderick), Conroy Chino (KOB—TV Reporter), Dan Gifford (Jeremy Roth), Vance Valencia (Senator Valencia), Behrooz Afrakhan (Middle Eastern Anchor), Saemi Nakamura (Japanese Anchor), Maria Celeste Arraras (Latina Anchor), Ian Whitcomb (British Anchor), Michael Albala (Decryption Hacker), Ned Netterville (Decryption Expert), Leo Lee (Major Domo), William Jordan (Chairman of Joint Chiefs), David St. James (Joint Chief), Haynes Brooke (Drumlin Aid), Steven Ford (Major Russell), Alex Zemeckis (Major Russell's Son), Janie Peterson (Major Russell's Daughter), Phillip Bergeron (French Committee Member), Jennifer Balgobin (Dr. Patel), Anthony Fife Hamilton (British Committee Member), Rebecca T. Beucler (NASA Public Relations), Marc Macaulay (NASA Technician), Pamela Wilsey (Voice of NASA), Tucker Smallwood (Mission Director), Jeff Johnson (Mechanical), Yuji Okumoto (Electrical), Gerry Griffin, Kristoffer Ryan Winters (Dynamics), Brian Alston (Communications), Rob Elk (Pad Leader), Mark Thomason (Security), José Rey (Controller #8), Todd Patrick Breaugh (New VLA Technician), Alex Veadov (Russian Cosmonaut), Alice Kushida (Scientist), Robin Gammell (Project Official), Richardson Morse (Mission Doctor), Seiji Okamura (Japanese Ensign), Mak Takano, Tom Tanaka (Japanese Techs), Catherine Dao (Life Support), Valorie Armstrong (Senator), Jim Hild, Bill Thomas (Reporters), Diego Montoya (School Boy), Larry King, Donna J. Kelley, Leon Harris, Claire Shipman, Tabitha Soren, Geraldo Rivera, Jay Leno, Natalie Allen, Robert D. Novak, Geraldine A. Ferraro, Ann Druyan, Kathleen Kennedy, Jill Dougherty, John Holliman, Bobbie Battista, Dee Dee Myers, Bryant Gumbel, Linden Soles, Bernard Shaw (Themselves)

CONSPIRACY THEORY (Silver Pictures) Producers, Joel Silver, Richard Donner; Executive Producer, Jim Van Wyck; Director, Richard Donner; Screenplay, Brian Helgeland; Photography, John Schwartzman; Designer, Paul Sylbert; Editors, Frank J. Urioste, Kevin Stitt; Co-Producers, Dan Cracchiolo, J. Mills Goodloe, Rick Solomon; Music, Carter Burwell; Costumes, Ha Nguyen; Casting, Marion Dougherty; a Silver Pictures production in association with Shuler Donner/Donner productions; Distributed by WB; Dolby; Panavision; Technicolor; Rated R; 135 minutes; August release. **CAST:** Mel Gibson (Jerry Fletcher), Julia Roberts (Alice Sutton), Patrick Stewart (Dr. Jonas), Cylk Cozart (Agent Lowry), Stephen Kahan (Wilson), Terry Alexander (Flip), Alex McArthur (Cynic), Rod McLachlan, Michael Potts, Jim Sterling (Justice Guards), Rich Hebert (Public Works Man), Brian J. Williams (Clarke), G.A. Aguilar (Piper), Cece Neber Labao (Finch's Secretary), Saxon Trainor (Alice's Secretary), Claudia Stedelin (Wilson's Secretary), Leonard Jackson (Old Man—Bookstore), Donal Gibson (Doctor—Roosevelt Hospital), Joanna Sanchez (Nurse—Roosevelt Hospital), Michael Shamus Wiles, Mik Scriba (Cops—Roosevelt Hospital), Patrick Wild (Intern in Jerry's Room), Mushond Lee, Kevin Kindlin, Troy Garity (Interns), J. Mills Goodloe (Jonas' Aide), Michael Kurtz (Well Dressed Man), Pete Koch (Fire Captain), Kevin Jackson, Nick Kusenko, Karl Makinen (CIA Agents), Darren Peel (Geronimo Cleet), Marian Collier (Geronimo Cook), John Harms (Agent Murphy), Christine Toy Johnson (Bookstore Clerk), David Koch, Danny Smith, Juan Riojas (Techs), Paul Tuerpé Dean Winters (Cleets), Jose Ramon Rosario, Louis Cantarini (Angry Vendors), Sean

Patrick Thomas, Peter Jacobson (Surveillance Operators), Edita Brychta (Finch's Receptionist), Sage Allen (Grouchy Nurse), Thomas McCarthy (Helicopter Spotter), K.T. Vogt (Woman in Mental Hospital), Joshua Fardon (Hospital Guard), Joan Lunden (TV Announcer), Charles McDaniel (Bureaucrat), Matte Osian, David Hamilton Simonds (Operatives), Rick Hoffman (Night Security—Federal Building), Edward J. Rosen (Old Man—Diner), Bert Remsen (Alice's Father), Lincoln Simonds (Cop by Laundry Chute), Bill Henderson (Hospital Security), Jay Fiondella (Patient), James Louis Oliver (Man in Justice Department), Kerry Palmisano, Victory Grace Palmisano, Kate Bayley (Nurses' Aides), Irene Hilleary (Justice Department Receptionist), Stephen Liska (Hospital Orderly), Don Stanley (Justice Department Guard), Lorna R. Millen (Charge Nurse), Brad Rea, Jim Van Wyck, Jayson Merrill, Dan Cracchiolo (Spotters), John Schwartzman (Sniper), Raymond King, Jared Crawford (Bucket Drummers), Jeremy A. Graham, Chad Santiago (Rappers), Christo Morse (Taxi Patron), H. Clay Dear, Daniel Nugent (Traffic Cops), Andrew Lauren, Tom Schanley, Kenneth Tigar, Judy Woodbury (Lawyers), Maureen Lauder (Lady with Dog)

FREE WILLY 3: THE RESCUE (Regency Enterprises) Producer, Jennie Lew Tugend; Executive Producers, Lauren Shuler Donner, Richard Donner, Arnon Milchan; Director, Sam Pillsbury; Screenplay, John Mattson; Photography, Tobias Schliessler; Designer, Brent Thomas; Editor, Margie Goodspeed; Music, Cliff Eidelman; Co-Producers, Douglas C. Merrifield, Mark Marshall; Costumes, Maya Mani; Casting, Judy Taylor, Lynne Carrow; a Shuler Donner/Donner production presented in association with Regency Enterprises; Distributed by WB; Dolby; Clairmont-scope; Technicolor; Rated PG; 86 minutes; August release. **CAST:** Jason James Richter (Jesse), August Schellenberg (Randolph), Annie Corley (Drew), Vincent Berry (Max), Patrick Kilpatrick (Wesley), Tasha Simms (Mary), Peter Lacroix (1st Mate Sanderson), Stephen E. Miller (Dineen), Ian Tracey (Kron), Matthew Walker (Capt. Drake), Roger R. Cross (1st Mate Stevens), Rick Burgess (Smiley), Roman Danylo (Pizza Kid)

FIRE DOWN BELOW (Seagal/Nasso Production) Producers, Steven Seagal, Julius R. Nasso; Executive Producers, William S. Gilmore, Jeb Stuart; Director, Felix Enriquez Alcalá; Screenplay, Jeb Stuart, Philip Morton; Story, Jeb Stuart; Co-Producer, Ronald G. Smith; Photography, Tom Houghton; Music, Nick Glennie-Smith; Designer, Joe Alves; Editor, Robert A. Ferretti; Costumes, Rosanna Norton; Casting, Shari Rhodes, Joseph Middleton; Distributed by WB; Dolby; Technicolor; Rated R; 105 minutes; September release. **CAST:** Steven Seagal (Jack Taggert), Marg Helgenberger (Sarah Kellogg), Stephen Lang (Earl), Brad Hunt (Orin, Jr.), Kris Kristofferson (Orin, Sr.), Harry Dean Stanton (Cotton), Levon Helm (Rev. Goodall), Mark Collie (Hatch), Alex Harvey (Sims), Ed Bruce (Lloyd), Amelia Neighbors (Edie), Richard Masur (Pratt), Newell Alexander, Michael Krawic (FBI Agents), Clay Jeter (Walter), Yvonne Pollard (Mother), Peggy Lynn (Betsy Hamill), Patsy Lynn (Patsy Hamill), John Diehl (Frank Elkins), Michael Mattison (Walter's Father), Dennis Letts (Dr. Schultz), Melodie Past (Store Clerk), Petrice Jordan (Natalie), Ellaraino (Judge), John Prosky, Dan O'Donahue (Aides), Gina Mari (Darlene), Scott L. Schwartz (Pimple), Rick Johnson, Joe Basile, Brian Leckner (Security), Andy Stahl (EPA Agent), Robert Ridgely (Simon), Lana Vassie (Amber), Randy Travis (Ken Adams), Ernie Lively (Todd), Lisa Coles (Beauty), David Brisbin (Lawyer), Blue Deckert (Chick Larsen), James Mathers (Marshal), Michelle von Flotow (Waitress), Charley J. Epling (Alberta), Ginger Carroll (Receptionist), Dan Beene (Dilbert/Grocer), Kimberly Cole, Brett Mellon, Randall R. Roberts, Kennita Collins, Benjamin Mays, LeAndra Arrowood, Ben Greer (Townspeople), Marty Stuart, Travis Tritt (Themselves), Julius R. Nasso (Actor), Aaron Chadwick, Michael Crosby, Jan Eddy (Pot Growers), John R. Gulino (Joey Chips), Nicky Julius (Casino Patron), Bruce Benson (Helicopter Pilot), William H. Greer (Choir Minister), Julie Dawn Mullins (Christine), Lonnie Duran Tackett, Mackie Richerson (Minors)

L.A. CONFIDENTIAL (Regency Enterprises) Producers, Arnon Milchan, Curtis Hanson, Michael Nathanson; Executive Producers, David L. Wolper, Dan Kolsrud; Director, Curtis Hanson; Screenplay, Brian Helgeland, Curtis Hanson; Based on the novel by James Ellroy; Photography, Dante Spinotti; Designer, Jeannine Oppewall; Editor, Peter Honess; Co-Producer, Brian Helgeland; Costumes, Ruth Myers; Music, Jerry Goldsmith; Casting, Mali Finn; a Regency Enterprises presentation of an Arnon Milchan/David L. Wolper production; Dolby; Super 35 Widescreen; Technicolor; Rated R; 136 minutes; September release. CAST: Kevin Spacey (Jack Vincennes), Russell Crowe (Bud White), Guy Pearce (Ed Exley), James Cromwell (Dudley Smith), Kim Basinger (Lynn Bracken), Danny DeVito (Sid Hudgens), David Strathairn (Pierce Patchett), Ron Rifkin (D.A. Ellis Loew), Matt McCoy ("Badge of Honor" Star Brett Chase), Paul Guilfoyle (Mickey Cohen), Paolo Seganti (Johnny Stompanato), Elisabeth Granli, Sandra Taylor (Mickey Cohen's Mambo Partners), Steve Rankin (Officer Arresting Mickey Cohen), Graham Beckel (Dick Stensland), Allan Graf (Wife Beater), Precious Chong (Wife), Symba Smith (Jack's Dancing Partner), Bob Clendenin (Reporter at Hollywood Station), Lennie Loftin (Photographer at Hollywood Station), Will Zahrn (Liquor Store Owner), Amber Smith (Susan Lefferts), Darrell Sandeen (Buzz Meeks), Michael Warwick (Sid's Assistant), Simon Baker Denny (Matt Reynolds), Shawnee Free Jones (Tammy Jordan), Matthew Allen Bretz (Officer Escorting Mexicans), Thomas Rosales, Jr. (First Mexican), Shane Dixon, Norman Howell, Brian Lally, Don Pulford, Chris Short (Officers/Detectives at Hollywood Station), John Mahon (Police Chief), Tomas Arana (Breuning), Michael McCleery (Carlisle), George Yager (Gangster at Victory Motel), Jack Conley (Vice Captain), Ginger Slaughter (Secretary in Vice), Jack Knight (Detective at Detective Bureau), John H. Evans (Patrolman at Nite Owl Cafe), Gene Wolande (Forensic Chief), Brian Bossetta (Forensic Officer), Michael Chieffo (Coroner), Gwenda Deacon (Mrs. Lefferts), Mike Kennedy (Bud's Rejected Partner), Ingo Neuhaus (Jack's Rejected Partner), Robert Harrison (Pierce Patchett's Bodyguard), Jim Metzler (City Councilman), Robert Barry Fleming (Boxer), Jeremiah Birkett (Ray Collins), Salim Grant (Louis Fontaine), Karreem Washington (Ty Jones), Noel Evangelisti (Stenographer), Marisol Padilla Sanchez (Inez Soto—Rape Victim), Jeff Sanders (Sylvester Fitch), Steve Lambert (Roland Navarette), Jordan Marder (Officer at Detective Bureau), Gregory White (Mayor), April Breneman, Lisa Worthy (Look-Alike Dancers), Beverly Sharpe (Witness on "Badge of Honor"), Colin Mitchell (Reporter at Hospital), John Slade (Photographer at Hospital), Brenda Bakke (Lana Turner), Kevin Maloney (Frolic Room Bartender), Patrice Walters, Rebecca Jane Klingler (Police File Clerks), Irene Roseen (D.A. Ellis Loew's Secretary), Scott Eberlein (West Hollywood Sheriff's Deputy), David St. James (Detective at Hush-Hush Office), Bodie Newcomb (Officer at Hush-Hush Office), Jeff Austin, Henry Meyers, Robert Foster, Michael Ossman, Kevin Kelly, Dick Stilwell, Henry Marder, Jess Thomas, Monty McKee, Samuel Thompson, Jody Wood (Detectives)

THE DEVIL'S ADVOCATE (Regency Enterprises) Producers, Arnon Milchan, Arnold Kopelson, Anne Kopelson; Executive Producers, Taylor Hackford, Michael Tadross, Erwin Stoff, Barry Bernardi, Steve White; Director, Taylor Hackford; Screenplay, Jonathan Lemkin, Tony Gilroy; Based on the novel by Andrew Neiderman; Photography, Andrzej Bartkowiak; Designer, Bruno Rubeo; Editor, Mark Warner; Music, James Newton Howard; Demons Designer/Creator, Rick Baker; Visual Effects, Richard Greenberg; Costumes, Judianna Makovsky; Casting, Nancy Klopper, Mary Colquhoun; a Kopelson Entertaiment production in association with Regency Enterprises; Distributed by WB; Dolby; Panavision; Technicolor; Rated R; 144 minutes; October release. **CAST:** Keanu Reeves (Kevin Lomax), Al Pacino (John Milton), Charlize Theron (Mary Ann Lomax), Jeffrey Jones (Eddie Barzoon), Judith Ivey (Mrs. Lomax), Connie Nielsen (Christabella), Craig T. Nelson (Alexander Cullen), Tamara Tunie (Jackie Heath), Ruben Santiago-Hudson (Leamon Heath), Debra Monk (Pam Garrety), Vyto Ruginis (Weaver), Laura Harrington (Melissa Black), Pamela Gray (Diana Barzoon), George Wyner (Meisel), Christopher Bauer (Gettys), Connie Embesi (Mrs. Gettys), Jonathan Cavallary (Gettys' Son), Heather Matarazzo (Barbara), Murphy Guyer

(Barbara's Father), Leo Burmester (Florida Prosecutor), Bill Moor (Florida Judge), Neal Jones (Florida Reporter), Eddie Aldridge (Florida Bailiff), Mark Deakins (Florida Lawyer #1), Rony Clanton (Junkie), George Gore II (Boy), Alan Manson (Judge Sklar), Brian Poteat (Pie Face), Daniel Oreskes (Metro D.A.), Kim Chan (Chinese Man), Caprice Benedetti (Menage a Trois Woman), Don King (Himself), Ray Garvey, Rocco Musacchia (Fight Fans), Susan Kellermann (Joyce Rensaleer), James Saito (Takaori Osumi), Harsh Nayyar (Parvathi Resh), M.B. Ghaffari (Bashir Toabal), Nicki Cochrane (Multi-Lingual Party Guest), Fenja Klaus (Female #1), Gino Lucci (Limo Driver), Novella Nelson (Botanica Woman), Vincent Laresca, Benny Nieves (Big Guys), Franci Leary (Babs Coleman), Gloria L. Henry (Tiffany), Jorge Navarro (Spanish Restaurant Manager), Jose Fernandes Torres (Flamenco Guitarist), Antonio Vargas Cortes (Flamenco Singer), Elena Camunez Andujar (Flamenco Dancer), Monica Keena (Allesandra), Linda Atkinson (Therapist), William Hill (Feeney), Juan Hernandez (Paparazzi), Wei Mei (Gizelle), E. Katherine Kerr (Judge), Liza Harris, Bill Boggs, Bo Rucker (Reporters), Michael Lombard (Judge Poe), Marc Manfro, J. Nester (Bailiffs), John Rothman (Broygo), George Sperdakos (Technician), Hollis Granville, Edward Seamon (Old Men), Patrick Joseph Byrnes, Gregory Lichtenson (Joggers), Socorro Santiago, Marcia DeBonis (Nurses), Marie Stuart Vassallo (Patient Marie), Tom Riis Farrell (Priest), Harold Surratt (Orderly #1), Senator Alfonse D'Amato, Ambassador Charles Gagano, Lou Rudin, Ernie Grunseld, Alan Grubman (Themselves), Cadillac Moon (Band), Delroy Lindo (Animal Sacrifice Practioner)

MAD CITY (Arnold Kopelson Production) Producers, Arnold Kopelson, Anne Kopelson; Director, Costa Gavras; Screenplay, Tom Matthews; Story, Tom Matthews, Eric Williams; Executive Producers, Wolfgang Glattes, Stephen Brown, Jonathan D. Krane; Photography, Patrick Blossier; Designer, Catherine Hardwicke; Editor, Francoise Bonnot; Music, Thomas Newman; Costumes, Deborah Nadoolman; Casting, Amanda Mackey Johnson, Cathy Sandrich; an Arnold Kopelson production in association with Punch Productions, Distributed by WB; Dolby; Super 35 Widescreen; Technicolor; Rated PG-13; 114 minutes; November release. **CAST:** John Travolta (Sam), Dustin Hoffman (Brackett), Mia Kirshner (Laurie), Alan Alda (Hollander), Robert Prosky (Lou Potts), Blythe Danner (Mrs. Banks), William Atherton (Dohlen), Ted Levine (Lemke), Tammy Lauren (Miss Rose), William O'Leary (CTN Junior Executive), Raymond J. Barry (Dobbins), Lucinda Jenney (Jenny), Akosua Busia (Diane), Ebbe Roe Smith (Bartholomew), Bingwa (Nat Jackson), Chris Byrne (KXBD Cameraman), Bobby Brewer, Max Becker, Philip David Robinson, Milton Davis Jr., Jeremy Espinoza, Nicole Fellows, Victoria Gregson, Molly Hager, Sarah Haney, Kyla Pratt, Paige Tamada, Hannah Vaughan (The Kids), Dyllan Christopher (Sam's Son), Kiersten Nally (Cliff's Daughter), Sylvia Short (Mrs. Baily), Scanlon Gail (Bob), Charlie Holliday (Banker), Kevin Cooney (Principal), John Landis (Doctor), Susan Segal (Tabloid Reporter), Jenna Byrne (Reporter KMUR), Jason Cottle (Hollander's Assistant), Randall Batinkoff (CTN Junior Executive), Julian Wall (British Reporter), Laura Davis (Hollander's Producer), Nick Scoggin (Statz), Julio Oscar Mechoso (Air Force Sergeant), Rueben Grundy (Reporter Reuben), David Clennon (Street Preacher), Jay Leno (Himself), Stephen E. Kaufman (Hollander's Lawyer), Richard Portnow (Brackett's Agent), Bill Rafferty (Bill Gottsegen), Kurt Johnson (Macho Parent), Susan Burig (Stage Manager), Pastor D. Seifert (Minister), J.P. Bumstead (Fisherman), Sean O'Kane (Lemke's Assistant), Donal O'Sullivan (Policeman), Lee Ann Manley (Rachel's Mother), Velina Brown (Bonnie's Mother), Michelle Pelletier (Max's Mother), Patricia Smith (Jenny's Mother), Adina Goldman (Lou's Assistant), Roger Shamas (Hollander's Driver), Stephen Brown (Hollander's Associate), Richard Gross (FBI Agent), Adam M. Koppekin (Assistant), Aaron Lucich (Sniper), Caryn Matchinga (Mother), Tom Fridley (Young Man), Christopher Michael Moore, Dirk Blocker (Bowlers), Pamela S. Laws, John Halbleib, Shannon L. Linke (Folk Singers), Eric Wycoff, Norman Berry, Chad Russell, Steven Lazaneo, Omar Lima (Rap Singers), Bill Nunn

THE MAN WHO KNEW TOO LITTLE (Regency Enterprises) Producers, Arnon Milchan, Michael Nathanson, Mark Tarlov; Executive Producers, Elisabeth Robinson, Joe Caracciolo, Jr.; Director, Jon Amiel; Screenplay, Robert Farrar, Howard Franklin; Based on the novel Watch That Man by Robert Farrar; Photography, Robert Stevens; Designer, Jim Clay; Editor, Pamela Power; Music, Chris Young; Co-Producer, Madeline Warren; Costumes, Janty Yates; Casting, Michelle Guish, Hopkins Smith & Barden; a Regency Enterprises presentation of an Arnon Milchan/Polar production; Distributed by WB; Dolby; Color; Rated PG-13; 94 minutes; November release. **CAST:** Bill Murray (Wallace Ritchie), Peter Gallagher (James Ritchie), Joanne Whalley (Lori), Alfred Molina (Boris), Richard Wilson (Daggenhurst), John Standing (Embleton), Simon Chandler (Hawkins), Geraldine James (Dr. Ludmilla Kropotkin), Anna Chancellor (Barbara Ritchie), Nicholas Woodeson (Sergei), Cliff Parisi (Uri), John Thomson (Dimitri), Janet Henfrey (Ms. Goldstein), Terry O'Neill (Spenser), Isabel Hernandez (Consuela), Donald Pickering (Sir Duncan), Venetia Barrett (Sir Duncan's Wife, Felicity), Terence Harvey (Herr Schuster), Cate Fowler (Frau Schuster), Richard Dixon (Rupert), Sarah Crowden (Sylvia/Fiona), Barnaby Kay (Swat Team Leader/PC in James), David Hounslow (Wilkie), Adam Fogerty (Newman), Jacqueline Phillips (Annabel), Inday Ba (Des), Dexter Fletcher (Otto), Josephine Gradwell (WPC—Wendy), Linda Broughton (Middle-Aged Woman), David Boyce (Middle-Aged Man), Jo Dow (Hotel Manager), Bob Holmes (Husband in Hotel Room), Paul Shearer (TV Reporter), Yoshinori Yamamoto (Japanese Man), Toshie Ogura (Japanese Woman), Charles Simon (Aged Desk/Night Clerk), Roger Morlidge (PC Cochrane), Ashley Gunstock (2nd Policeman in Car), Judith Dawson (TV Newscaster), David Michaels (MI5 Agent), Damian Myerscough (Stage Manager), Jason Round (Policeman), Andrew Woodall (Det. Sgt. Malloy), Malcolm Storry (Chief Ins. Cockburn), Eddie Marsan, Tat Whalley (Muggers), Fred Whitham (Toastmaster), Daryll Kay, Linzi Lazlo-Carr (Liveried Children), Richard Cubison (Immigration Officer), Sarah Greene, Mike Smith (TV Presenters), Je Freeman (CIA Man), Maxwell Caulfield (British Agent), Mike Justus (Waiter)

MIDNIGHT IN THE GARDEN OF GOOD AND EVIL (Malpaso/Silver Pictures) Producers, Clint Eastwood, Arnold Stiefel; Director, Clint Eastwood; Executive Producer, Anita Zuckerman; Screenplay, John Lee Hancock; Based on the book by John Berendt; Co-Producer, Tom Rooker; Photography, Jack N. Green; Designer, Henry Bumstead; Music, Lennie Niehaus; Editor, Joel Cox; Casting, Phyllis Huffman; Distributed by WB; Dolby; Panavision; Technicolor; Rated R; 155 minutes; November release. **CAST:** John Cusack (John Kelso), Kevin Spacey (Jim Williams), Jack Thompson (Sonny Seiler), Irma P. Hall (Minerva), Jude Law (Billy Hanson), Alison Eastwood (Mandy Nicholls), Paul Hipp (Joe Odom), The Lady Chablis (Chablis Deveau), Dorothy Loudon (Serena Dawes), Anne Haney (Margaret Williams), Kim Hunter (Betty Harty), Geoffrey Lewis (Luther Driggers), Richard Herd (Henry Skerridge), Leon Rippy (Det. Boone), Bob Gunton (Finley Largent), Michael O'Hagan (Geza von Habsburg), Gary Anthony Williams (Bus Driver), Tim Black (Jeff Braswell), Muriel Moore (Mrs. Baxter), Sonny Seiler (Judge White), Terry Rhoads (Assistant D.A.), Victor Brandt (Bailiff), Patricia Herd (Juror #1), Nick Gillie (Juror #20), Patrika Darbo (Sara Warren), J. Patrick McCormack (Doctor), Emma Kelly (Herself), Tyrone Lee Weaver (Ellis), Gregory Goossen (Prison Cell Lunatic), Shannon Eubanks (Mrs. Hamilton), Virginia Duncan, Rhoda Griffis, Judith Robinson (Card Club Women), JoAnn Pflug (Cynthia Vaughn), James Moody (Mr. Glover), John Duncan (Gentleman in Park), Bess S. Thompson (Pretty Girl), Jin Hi Soucy (Receptionist), Michael Rosenbaum (George Tucker), Dan Biggers (Harry Cram), Georgia Allen (Lucille Wright), Collin Wilcox Paxton (Woman at Party), Charles Black (Alpha), Aleta Mitchell (Alphabette), Michael "Kevin" Harry (Phillip), Dorothy Kingery (Jim Williams' Sister), Amanda Kingery (Jim Williams' Niece Amanda), Susan Kingery (Jim Williams' Niece Susan), Ted Manson (Passer-by), Margaret R. Davis (Ruth), Danny Nelson (Senator), Bree Luck (Woman at Club), Ann Cusack (Delivery Woman), Jerry Spence (Hair Dresser)

STEEL (Quincy Jones-David Salzman Entertainment) Producers, Quincy Jones, David Salzman, Joel Simon; Executive Producers, Shaquille O'Neal, Leonard Armato, Bruce Binkow; Director/Screenplay, Kenneth Johnson; Based upon characters published by DC Comics; "Steel" created by Louise Simonson, Jon Bogdanove; Photography, Mark Irwin; Designer, Gary Wissner; Editor, John F. Link; Co-Producer, Mark Allan; Music, Mervyn Warren; Steel's Suit by Greg Cannom; Costumes, Catherine Adair; Casting, Shana Landsburg, Laura Adler; Distributed by WB; Dolby; Clairmont Scope; Technicolor; Rated PG-13; 97 minutes; August release. **CAST:** Shaquille O'Neal (John Henry Irons), Annabeth Gish (Sparky), Judd Nelson (Nathaniel Burke), Richard Roundtree (Uncle Joe), Irma P. Hall (Grandma Odessa), Ray J. (Martin), Charles Napier (Col. David), Kerrie Keane (Senator), Eric Pierpoint (Major), Tembi Locke (Norma), Thom Barry (Senior Cop), Gary Graham (Detective), Eric Saiet (Young Cop), Hill Harper (Slats), George Lemore (Cutter), Joseph Palmer (Holdecker), Eric Poppick (Mr Hunt "Mugging Victim"), Rutanya Alda (Mrs. Hunt), John Hawkes (Mugger), Steve Mattila (Big Willy Daniels), Claire Stansfield (Duvray), Kevin Grevioux (Singer), Tim deZarn, Michael Shamus Wiles (Skinheads), Kamau Holloway, Norris Young (Skins), Maurice Chasse (French Mercenary), Josh Cruze (Columbian), Harvey Silver (Lamont), Nancy Wolfe (American Overlord), Danny Hartigan (Chauffer), Rick Worthy (Swat Man), Marabina Jaimes (Swat Woman), Scotch Ellis Loring (Swat Officer), Ben Martin (District Attorney), Dirk Wallace Craft (Officer Craft), Jacquelyn Houston (Soldier), John F. O'Donohue (Federal Reserve Guard), Patrick Hayes, Manner "Mooky" Washington (Pre-Teens), Cyd Strittmatter (Lieutenant), John Donohue (Crewman #1), Jody Fasanella (Matronly Secretary), Kevin Sifuentes (Reef Driver), Joe Wandell (Reef Gunman), Joshua G. Adams, Zane Graham (Basketball Kids)

ONE EIGHT SEVEN (Icon Prod.) Producers, Bruce Davey, Stephen McEveety; Director, Kevin Reynolds; Screenplay, Scott Yagemann; Photography, Ericson Core; Designer, Stephen Storer; Editor, Stephen Semel; Costumes, Darryle Johnson; Music Supervisor, Chris Douridas; Casting, Marion Dougherty; an Icon Production; Distributed by WB; Dolby; Deluxe color; Rated R; 119 minutes; July release. **CAST:** Samuel L. Jackson (Trevor Garfield), John Heard (Dave Childress), Kelly Rowan (Ellen Henry), Clifton Gonzalez Gonzalez (Cesar), Tony Plana (Garcia), Karina Arroyave (Rita), Lobo Sebastian (Benny), Jack Kehler (Hyland), Jonah Rooney (Stevie), Demetrius Navarro (Paco), Ebony Monique Solomon (Lakesia), Yannis Borgis (Barsek), Dominic Hoffman (Victor), Martha Velez (Mrs. Chacon), Method Man (Dennis Broadway), Sage Allen (Teacher), Kathryn Leigh Scott (Anglo Woman), Donal Gibson

(Animal Regulation Officer), Liza Del Mundo (Asian Girl), Vic Polizos (Asst. Coroner), Leonard L. Thomas (N.Y. Asst. Principal), Antwon Tanner (Augie), Gannon Brown (Tywan), Larry Costales (Hispanic Man), David Reyes (Investigator), Joanna Sanchez (Iris), Richard Riehle (Walter), Harry James (Librarian), Esther Scott (Mrs. Ford), Esther "Tita" Mercado (Mrs. Santana), Chase A. Garland (Struggling Student), Guy Torry (Voice in Crowd), Anthony Aguilar (Chicano Tagger)

THE POSTMAN (Tig Prod.) Producers, Jim Wilson, Steve Tisch, Kevin Costner; Director, Kevin Costner; Screenplay, Eric Roth, Brian Helgeland; Based on the novel by David Brin; Photography, Stephen Windon; Designer, Ida Random; Editor, Peter Boyle; Music, James Newton Howard; Song: "You Didn't Have to Be So Nice" by John Sebastian and Steve Boone/performed by Amy Grant and Kevin Costner; Costumes, John Bloomfield; Casting, Mindy Marin; a Tig Production; Distributed by WB; Dolby; Panavision; Technicolor; Rated R; 177 minutes; December release. **CAST:** Kevin Costner (The Postman), Will Patton (Bethlehem), Larenz Tate (Ford), Olivia Williams (Abby), James Russo (Idaho), Daniel von Bargen (Sheriff Briscoe), Tom Petty (Bridge City Mayor), Scott Bairstow (Luke), Giovanni Ribisi (Bandit #20), Roberta Maxwell (Irene March), Joe Santos (Getty), Ron McLarty (Old George), Peggy Lipton (Ellen March), Brian Anthony Wilson (Woody), Todd Allen (Gibbs), Rex Linn (Mercer), Shawn Hatosy (Billy), Ryan Hurst (Eddie), Charles Esten (Michael), Anne Costner (Ponytail), Ty O'Neal (Drew), Kirk Fox (Gangly Recruit), Ken Linhart (Disappointed Conscript), Korey Scott Pollard (Thin Recruit), Kayla Lambert (Shakespeare Girl), Austin Howard Early (Shakespeare Boy), Ellen Geer (Mrs. Thompson), Randle Mell (Village Mayor), Cooper Taylor (Tony), Dylan Haggerty (Slow Recruit), Michael Milgrom (Holnist Projectionist), Keith C. Howell (Holnist Scout), H.P. Evetts (Holnist Soldier), Jeff Johnson, Jeff McGrail (Rope Bridge Soldiers), Lily Costner (Lily March), Gregory Avellone (Pineview Man), Susan Brightbill, Elisa Daniel, Jenny Buchanan, Ann Manning (Pineview Women), Andy Garrison (Pineview Sentry), Rusty Hendrickson (Pineview Minister), Marvin Winton (Pineview Old Man), Jono Manson, John J. Coinman, Veron T. Williams, Mark Clark, Blair Forward, Robyn Pruitt-Hamm, Michelle Ramminger (Pineview Band), Tom Novak, Richard Joel (Benning Gatekeepers), George Wyner (Benning Mayor), Brooke Becker, Eva Gayle Six (Benning Women), Todd Lewis (Benning Man), Joe Costner (Letter Boy), Kathi Sheehan (Mother of Letter Boy), Amy Weinstein, Betty Moyer (Elvis Women), Joseph McKenna (Holnist Captain), Neal Preston Coon (Bridge City Boy), Rick Wadkins (Bridge City Man), Shiree Porter (Bridge City Woman), Anthony Guidera (Bridge City Guard), Jade Herrera (Carrier), Greg Serano (California Carrier), Derk Cheetwood (Carrier Twelve), Mark Thomason (Adult Letter Boy), Mary Stuart Masterson (Hope—Grown-up)

Kate Winslet, Leonardo DiCaprio

Titanic © Paramount Pictures/ Twentieth Century Fox

Leonardo DiCaprio, Kate Winslet

Kathy Bates, Frances Fisher

Bill Paxton, Gloria Stuart, Suzy Amis

TITANIC

(PARAMOUNT/20TH CENTURY FOX) Producers, James Cameron, Jon Landau; Executive Producer, Rae Sanchini; Director/Screenplay, James Cameron; Photography, Russell Carpenter; Designer, Peter Lamont; Editors, Conrad Buff, James Cameron, Richard A. Harris; Costumes, Deborah L. Scott; Visual Effects Supervisor, Robert Legato; Music, James Horner; Song: "My Heart Will Go On" by James Horner (music) and Will Jennings (lyric)/performed by Celine Dion; Co-Producers, Al Giddings, Grant Hill, Sharon Mann; Casting, Mali Finn; a Lightstorm Entertainment production; Dolby Digital Stereo; Panavision; Deluxe color; Rated PG-13; 193 minutes; December release

CAST

Jack Dawson ....Leonardo DiCaprio
Rose DeWitt Bukater ....Kate Winslet
Cal Hockley ....Billy Zane
Molly Brown ....Kathy Bates
Ruth DeWitt Bukater ....Frances Fisher
Old Rose ....Gloria Stuart
Brock Lovett ....Bill Paxton
Captain E.J. Smith...Bernard Hill
Spicer Lovejoy...David Warner
Thomas Andrews ....Victor Garber
Bruce Ismay ....Jonathan Hyde
Lizzy Calvert ....Suzy Amis
Lewis Bodine...Lewis Abernathy
Bobby Buell...Nicholas Cascone
Anatoly Milkailavich ....Dr. Anatoly M. Sagalevitch
Fabrizio ....Danny Nucci
Tommy Ryan ....Jason Barry
1st Officer Murdoch...Ewan Stewart
Fifth Officer Lowe ....Ioan Gruffudd
2nd Officer Lightoller ....Johnny Phillips
Chief Officer Wilde...Mark Lindsay Chapman
Quartermaster Rowe ....Richard Graham
Quartermaster Hichens ....Paul Brightwell
Master at Arms ....Ron Donachie
John Jacob Astor ....Eric Braeden
Madeleine Astor..Charlotte Chatton
Col. Archibald Gracie ....Bernard Fox
and Michael Ensign (Benjamin Guggenheim), Fannie Brett (Madame Aubert), Jenette Goldstein (Irish Mommy), Camilla Overbye Roos (Helga Dahl), Linda Kerns (3rd Class Woman), Amy Gaipa (Trudy Bolt), Martin Jarvis (Sir Duff Gordon), Rosalind Ayres (Lady Duff Gordon), Rochelle Rose (Countess of Rothes), Jonathan Evans-Jones (Wallace Hartley), Brian Walsh (Irish Man), Rocky Taylor (Bert Cartmell), Alexandre Owens (Cora Cartmell), Simon Crane (4th Officer Boxhall), Edward Fletcher (6th Officer Moody), Scott G. Anderson (Frederick Fleet), Martin East (Lookout Lee), Craig Kelly (Harold Bride), Gregory Cooke (Jack Phillips), Liam Tuohy (Chief Baker Joughin), James Lancaster (Father Byles), Elsa Raven (Ida Straus), Lew Palter (Isidor Straus), Reece P. Thompson III (Irish Little Boy), Laramie Landis (Irish Little Girl), Amber and Alison Waddell (Cal's Crying Girl), Mark Rafael Truitt (Yaley), John Walcutt (1st Class Husband), Terry Forrestal (Chief Engineer Bell), Derek Lea (Leading Stoker Barrett), Richard Ashton (Carpenter John Hutchinson), Sean M. Nepita (Elevator Operator), Brendan Connolly (Scotland Road Steward), David Cronnelly (Crewman), Garth Wilton (1st Class Waiter), Martin Laing (Promenade Deck Steward), Richard Fox, Nick Meaney, Kevin Owers, Mark Capri (Stewards), Marc Cass, Paul Herbert (Hold Stewards), Emmett James (1st Class Steward), Christopher Byrne (Stairwell Steward), Oliver Page (Steward Barnes), James Garrett (Titanic Porter), Erik Holland (Olaf Dahl), Jari Kinnunen (Bjorn Gunderson), Anders Falk (Olaus Gunderson), Martin Hub (Slovakian Father), Seth Adkins (Slovakian 3 Year Old Boy), Barry Dennen (Praying Man), Vern Urich (Man in Water), Rebecca Jane Klingler (Mother at Stern), Tricia O'Neil (Woman), Kathleen Dunn (Woman in Water), Romeo Francis (Syrian Man), Mandana Marino (Syrian Woman), Van Ling (Chinese Man), Bjørn (Olaf), Dan Pettersson (Sven), Shay Duffin (Pubkeeper), Greg Ellis (Carpathia Steward), Diana Morgan (News Reporter), I Salonisti (Titanic Orchestra), Gaelic Storm (Steerage Band)

(Clockwise from bottom left) Leonardo DiCaprio, Rochelle Rose, Jonathan Hyde, Bernard Fox, Fannie Brett, Michael Ensign, Rosalind Ayres, Martin Jarvis, Billy Zane, Kate Winslet, Victor Garber, Kathy Bates

Billy Zane, Kate Winslet

After a drawing of her is found in the wreckage of the Titanic, one-hundred-year-old Rose recounts the story of how she fell in love with steerage passenger Jack Dawson aboard the ill-fated vessel on its maiden voyage in 1912. 1998 Academy Award-winner for Best Picture, Director, Cinematography, Art Direction, Costume Design, Film Editing, Original Dramatic Score, Song ("My Heart Will Go"), Sound, Sound Effects Editing, and Visual Effects. This film received additional Oscar nominations for actress (Kate Winslet), supporting actress (Gloria Stuart), and makeup. Its eleven awards tied it with Ben-Hur (MGM, 1959) for the Academy record, as had its fourteen nominations that tied it with All About Eve (20th Century Fox, 1950). This film became the biggest box-office hit of 1997 and the highest grossing motion picture of all time. Previous films on the Titanic include Titanic (20th Century Fox, 1953), starring Clifton Webb and Barbara Stanwyck; and A Night to Remember (1958), starring Kenneth More.

©Paramount Pictures/ Twentieth Century Fox

Kate Winslet, Leonardo DiCaprio

JACK NICHOLSON
in *As Good As It Gets*
© TriStar Pictures
ACADEMY AWARD FOR BEST ACTOR OF 1997

HELEN HUNT
in *As Good As It Gets*
© TriStar Pictures
ACADEMY AWARD FOR BEST ACTRESS OF 1997

ROBIN WILLIAMS
in *Good Will Hunting*
© Miramax Films
ACADEMY AWARD FOR BEST SUPPORTING ACTOR OF 1997

KIM BASINGER
for *L.A. Confidential*
ACADEMY AWARD FOR BEST SUPPORTING ACTRESS OF 1997

ACADEMY AWARD NOMINEES FOR BEST ACTOR

Matt Damon in *Good Will Hunting*

Robert Duvall in *The Apostle*

Peter Fonda in *Uiee's Gold*

Dustin Hoffman in *Wag the Dog*

ACADEMY AWARD NOMINEES FOR BEST ACTRESS

Helena Bonham Carter in *The Wings of the Dove*

Julie Christie in *Afterglow*

Judi Dench in *Mrs. Brown*

Kate Winslet in *Titanic*

ACADEMY AWARD NOMINEES FOR BEST SUPPORTING ACTOR

Robert Forster in *Jackie Brown*

Anthony Hopkins in *Amistad*

Greg Kinnear in *As Good As It Gets*

Burt Reynolds in *Boogie Nights*

ACADEMY AWARD NOMINEES FOR BEST SUPPORTING ACTRESS

Joan Cusack in *In & Out*

Minnie Driver in *Good Will Hunting*

Julianne Moore in *Boogie Nights*

Gloria Stuart in *Titanic*

Jan Decleir

CHARACTER

(SONY PICTURE CLASSICS) Producer, Laurens Geels; Director, Mike van Diem; Screenplay, Mike van Diem, Laurens Geels, Rund van Megen; Photography, Rogier Stoffers; Art Directors, Jelier & Schief; Editor, Jessica de Kooning; Music, Het Paleis van Boem; Casting, Jeannette Snik; Netherlands; Dolby Stereo; Color; Rated R; 125 minutes; March 1998 release

CAST

Katadreuffe	Fedja van Huet
Deverhaven	Jan Decleir
Joba	Betty Schuurman
De Gankelaar	Victor Low
Lorna te George	Tamar van de Dop
Jan Maan	Hans Kesting
Retenstein	Lou Landre
Stroomkoning	Bernhard Droog
De Bree	Frans Vortsman
Schuwagt	Fred Goessens

A young lawyer, arrested for the murder of Rotterdam's most feared bailiff, proclaims his innocence and recounts the series of ecents in his life leading up to the time od the crime.

Fedja van Huet, Betty Schuurman

Fedja van Huet, Victor Low, Tamar van de Dop

Fedja van Huet, Victow Low

ACADEMY AWARD WINNER FOR BEST FOREIGN LANGUAGE FILM

PROMISING NEW ACTORS OF 1997

Joey Lauren Adams
(Chasing Amy)

Ben Affleck
(Chasing Amy, Going All the Way, Good Will Hunting)

Aaron Eckhart
(In the Company of Men)

Stacy Edwards
(In the Company of Men)

Lee Evans
(Mouse Hunt, The Fifth Element)

Jennifer Lopez
(Blood and Wine, Selena, Anaconda, U Turn)

Debbi Morgan
(Eve's Bayou)

Jude Law
(Gattaca; I Love You, I Love You Not; Midnight in the Garden of Good and Evil)

Tobey Maguire
(The Ice Storm, Deconstructing Harry)

Sarah Polley
(The Sweet Hereafter)

Angelina Jolie
(Playing God)

Freddie Prinze, Jr.
(The House of Yes, I Know What You Did Last Summer)

TOP 100 BOX OFFICE FILMS OF 1997

1. Titanic (Par-20th/Dec) $600,770,000
2. Men in Black (Col/Jul) $250,100,000
3. The Lost World: Jurassic Park (Univ/May) $229,100,000
4. Liar Liar (Univ/Mar) $181,420,000
5. Air Force One (Col/Jul) $172,630,000
6. As Good As It Gets (TriS/Dec) $147,660,000
7. Good Will Hunting (Mir/Dec) $138,410,000
8. Star Wars (reissue) (20th/Jan) $138,200,000
9. My Best Friend's Wedding (TriS/Jun) $126,710,000
10. Tomorrow Never Dies (MGM-UA/Dec) $124,690,000

Leonardo DiCaprio, Kate Winslet in *Titanic*
© Paramount Pictures/Twentieth Century Fox

11. Face/Off (Par/Jun) $112,300,000
12. Batman and Robin (Jun) $107,310,000
13. George of the Jungle (BV/Jul) $105,200,000
14. Con Air (BV/Jun) $101,100,000
15. Contact (Jul) $100,900,000
16. Scream 2 (Mir/Dec) $100,320,000
17. Hercules (BV/Jun) $99,100,000
18. Flubber (BV/Nov) $92,830,000
19. Conspiracy Theory (Aug) $76,100,000
20. I Know What You Did Last Summer (Col/Oct) $72,240,000

Gary Oldman in *Air Force One*
© Columbia Pictures Industries, Inc.

21. The Empire Strikes Back (reissue) (20th/Feb) $67,600,000
22. Dante's Peak (Univ/Feb) $67,200,000
23. Anaconda(Col/Apr) $65,900,000
24. L.A. Confidential (Sept) $64,430,000
25. The Fifth Element (Col/May) $63,800,000
26. In & Out(Par/Sep) $63,100,000
27. Mouse Hunt (DW/Dec) $61,850,000
26. The Saint(Par/Apr) $61,400,000
29. The Devil's Advocate (Oct) $60,800,000
30. Kiss the Girls (Par/Oct) $60,160,000
31. Jungle 2 Jungle (BV/Mar) $59,900,000
32. Anastasia(20th/Nov) $58,300,000
33. Spawn (NLC/Aug) $55,100,000
34. The Jackal (Univ/Nov) $54,700,000
35. Starship Troopers (TriS/Nov) $54,200,000
36. Austin Powers: Intl. Man of Mystery (NLC/May) $53,900,000
37. Breakdown (Par/May) $50,150,000
38. Absolute Power (Col/Feb) $50,110,000

Hercules, Pegasus in *Hercules*
© Disney Enterprises, Inc.

39. The Game (Poly/Sep) $48,300,000
40. G.I. Jane(BV/Aug) $48,200,000
41. Speed 2: Cruise Control (20th/Jun) $47,600,000
42. Alien Resurrection (20th/Nov) $47,540,000
43. Volcano (20th/Apr) $47,500,000
44. The Full Monty (Fox S/Aug) $45,890,000
45. John Grisham's The Rainmaker (Par/Nov) $45,820,000
46. Return of the Jedi (reissue) (20th/Mar) $45,500,000
47. Bean (Gram/Nov) $44,910,000
48. Cop Land(Mir/Aug) $44,900,000
49. Nothing to Lose (BV/Jul) $44,500,000
50. Soul Food (20th/Sep) $43,600,000

51. Amistad (DW/Dec) $43,270,000
52. Wag the Dog (NLC/Dec) $42,980,000
53. The Devil's Own (Col/Mar) $42,900,000
54. Donnie Brasco (TriS/Feb) $42,100,000
55. The Peacemaker (DW/Sep) $41,300,000
56. Private Parts (Par/Mar) $41,200,000
57. Money Talks (NLC/Aug) $41,100,000
58. Jackie Brown (Mir/Dec) $39,480,000
59. Seven Years in Tibet (TriS/Oct) $37,870,000
60. Vegas Vacation (Feb) $36,500,000
61. Mortal Kombat: Annihilation (NLC/Nov) $35,900,000
62. Selena (Mar) $35,500,000
63. Addicted to Love (May) $34,700,000
64. The Relic (Par/Jan) $33,900,000
65. Metro (BV/Jan) $32,100,000

Vivica A. Fox, Vanessa L. Williams, Nia Long in *Soul Food*
© Twentieth Century Fox

81. Air Bud (BV/Aug) $24,610,000
82. Hoodlum (MGM/Aug) $23,300,000
83. Good Burger (Par/Jul) $22,860,000
84. Red Corner (MGM/Oct) $21,870,000
85. Mr. Magoo (BV/Dec) $21,280,000
86. The Apostle (Oct/Dec) $20,720,000
87. Booty Call (Col/Feb) $19,490,000
88. Gone Fishin' (BV/May) $19,270,000
89. Event Horizon (Par/Aug) $17,800,000
90. That Darn Cat (BV/Feb) $17,100,000
91. That Old Feeling (Univ/Apr) $15,810,000
92. Fire Down Below (Sep) $15,800,000
93. Rocketman (BV/Oct) $15,100,000
94. Eve's Bayou (Tri/Nov) $14,840,000
95. The Sixth Man (BV/Apr) $14,730,000

Freddie Prinze Jr., Jennifer Love Hewitt in
I Know What You Did Last Summer
© Mandalay Entertainment

66. For Richer or Poorer (Univ/Dec) $31,540,000
67. Beverly Hills Ninja (TriS/Jan) $31,500,000
68. Picture Perfect (20th/Aug) $31,400,000
69. Fools Rush In (Col/Feb) $29,500,000
70. Home Alone 3 (20th/Dec) $29,390,000
71. Romy & Michele's High School Reunion (BV/Apr) $29,220,000
72. Out to Sea (20th/Jul) $29,100,000
73. Fathers' Day (May) $28,900,000
74. Grosse Pointe Blank (BV/Apr) $28,100,000
75. The Edge (20th/Sep) $27,800,000
76. Boogie Nights (NLC/Oct) $26,330,000
77. An American Werewolf in Paris (BV/Dec) $26,320,000
78. Murder at 1600 (Apr) $25,800,000
79. Mimic (Mir/Aug) $25,430,000
80. Midnight in the Garden of Good & Evil (Nov) $24,680,000

Johnny Depp in *Donnie Brasco*
© Mandalay Entertainment

96. The Postman (Dec) $14,300,000
97. Excess Baggage (Col/Aug) $14,100,000
98. Def Jam's How to Be a Player (Gram/Aug) $13,870,000
99. Wishmaster (Tri/Sep) $13,730,000
100. The Wings of the Dove (Mir/Nov) $13,670,000

FOREIGN FILMS RELEASED IN THE U.S. IN 1997

Sergei Bodrov, Jr.

Oleg Menshikov

Susanna Mekhralieva

PRISONER OF THE MOUNTAINS

(ORION CLASSICS) Producers, Boris Giller, Sergei Bodrov; Director, Sergei Bodrov; Screenplay, Arif Aliev, Sergei Bodrov, Boris Giller; Photography, Pavel Lebeshev; Editors, Olga Grinshpun, Vera Kruglova, Alan Baril; Art Director, Valery Kostrin; Music, Leonid Desyatnikov; a Caravan Co. and BG Production with the Russian State Film Commission; Russian, 1996; Dolby Stereo; Color; Rated R; 99 minutes; January release

CAST

Sacha...Oleg Menshikov
Vania ....Sergei Bodrov, Jr.
Abdoul-Mourat...Djemal Sikharulidze
Dina..Susanna Mekhralieva
The Captain..Alexei Jharkov
The Mother..Valentina Fedotova

Abdoul-Mourat captures two Russian soldiers and holds them for ransom in his isolated Muslim community. This film was nominated for an Oscar in the foreign-lanuage film category for 1996.

Djemal Sikharulidze

JACKIE CHAN'S FIRST STRIKE

(NEW LINE CINEMA) Producer, Barbie Tung; Executive Producer, Leonard Ho; Director, Stanley Tong; Screenplay, Stanley Tong, Nick Tramontane, Greg Mellott, Elliot Tong; Photography, Jingle Ma; Designer, Oliver Wong; Editors, Peter Cheung, Chi Wai Yau; Music, J. Peter Robinson; Hong Kong 1996; a Raymond Chow/Golden Harvest production; Dolby Stereo; Technovision; Color; Rated PG-13; 110 minutes; January release

CAST

Jackie	Jackie Chan
Tsui	Jackson Lou
Annie	Chen Chun Wu
Uncle Bill	Bill Tung
Col. Gregor Yegorov	Jouri Petrov
Natasha	Grishajeva Nonna
Mark	John Eaves
Uncle Seven	Terry Woo
Commander Korda	Kristoff Kaczmarek

and Ailen Sit, Chan Man Ching, Rocky Lai, Chan Wai To (Golden Dragon Club Members), Brett Arthur, Mark French, Damien Gates, Mark Gilks, Nathan Jones, Mathew Walker Kininmonth, John Langmead, Steve Livingstone, Steve Morris (Hit Men), Brenton Heeren, Steve Jones (Snipers), Jennifer Hung, Doris Lam, Shirley Mak, Wella Shieh (Annie's Relatives), Symantha Liu (Channel 7 Reporter), Gary Wilkinson (News Anchorman), Low Houi Kang (H.K. Policeman), Esmond Ren, Jim Hsin (C.I.A. Members), Igro Guleen (USS Agent), N. Leshcinkov (Gen. Gudanov), Rusean Scripnik (Strike Force Leader), Alexander Ustichenko (Major Majenko)

A Hong Kong police officer is contracted by both the CIA and Russian intelligence in hopes that he can locate a stolen Ukranian nuclear warhead.

© New Line Cinema

Jackie Chan

ULYSSES' GAZE

(FOX LORBER) Producer/Director, Theo Angelopoulos; Screenplay, Theo Angelopoulos, Tonino Guerra, Petros Markaris; Photography, Yorgos Arvanitis; Editor, Yannis Tsitsopoulos; Music, Eleni Karaindrou; Designer, Yorgos Patsas, Mile Nicolic; Costumes, Yorgos Ziakas; a Theo Angelopoulos Films Prods.-Greek Film Center (Athens)/Paradis Films-La Generale d'Images-La Sept Cinema (Paris)/Basic Cinematografica-Istituto Luce-RAI (Rome) co-production in association with Tele Munchen, Concorde Films, Channel 4; Greek-French-Italian, 1995; Dolby Stereo; Color; Not rated; 177 minutes; January release

CAST

A	Harvey Keitel
Naomi Levy and the "Wives"	Maïa Morgenstern
Library Curator	Erland Josephson
Taxi Driver	Thanassis Vengos
Nikos	Yorgos Michalakopoulos
Old Woman	Dora Volanaki

and Mania Papadimitriou, Angel Ivanof, Ljuba Tadic, Gert Llanaj, Agni Vlahou, Giannis Zavradinos, Vangelis Kazan

A movie director returns to Greece after a 35-year absence to make a documentary about a family of pioneering filmmakers.

© Fox Lorber

Harvey Keitel

Jacqueline McKenzie, John Lynch

ANGEL BABY

(CFP) Producers, Timothy White, Jonathan Shteinman; Director/Screenplay, Michael Rymer; Photography, Ellery Ryan; Designer, Chris Kennedy; Editor, Danny Cooper; Costumes, Kerri Mazzocco; Casting, Alison Barrett Casting, Trish McAskill; a Stamen/Meridian Films production; a presentation of the Australian Film Finance Corporation; Australian 1995; Dolby Stereo; Color; Not rated; 105 minutes; January release

John Lynch, Jacqueline McKenzie

CAST

Harry	John Lynch
Kate	Jacqueline McKenzie
Morris	Colin Friels
Louise	Deborra-Lee Furness
Sam	Daniel Daperis
Dave	David Argue
Rowan	Geoff Brooks
Frank	Humphry Bower

Harry, a young man troubled by periods of psychosis, meets and falls in love with the similarly disturbed Kate at one of his group therapy sessions.

© CFP Distribution

John Lynch, Colin Friels

MARGARET'S MUSEUM

(CFP) Producers, Mort Ransen, Christopher Zimmer, Claudio Luca, Steve Clark-Hall; Director, Mort Ransen; Screenplay, Gerald Wexler, Mort Ransen; Based on The Glace Bay Miner's Museum and other stories by Sheldon Currie; Photography, Vic Sarin; Editor, Rita Roy; Designers, William Fleming, David McHenry; Costumes, Nicoletta Massone; Music, Milan Kymlicka; Casting, Stuart Aikins, Anne Tait; a Cabin Fever Entertainment presentation/a Malofilm Communications presentation of a Ranfilm/Imagex/Télé-Action/Skyline production; Canadian-1995; Color; Rated R; 118 minutes; February release

Helena Bonham Carter, Clive Russell

CAST

Margaret MacNeil	Helena Bonham Carter
Neil Currie	Clive Russell
Jimmy	Craig Olejnik
Catherine	Kate Nelligan
Angus	Kenneth Welsh
Marilyn	Andrea Morris
Grandfather	Peter Boretski
Mr. Campbell	Barry Dunn
Mrs. Campbell	Norma Dell'Agnese

and Glenn Wadman (Willy), Elizabeth Richardson (Sister), Ida Donovan (Sarah), Gordon Joe (Hum Sing), Wayne Reynolds (Fraser), Murdoch MacDonald (Clerk), Yow Wah Chee (Chinese Cook), Terry O'Keefe (Miner), Liam Hussey (Peter), Mary Alvena Poole (Woman), Carol Kennedy (Tourist Woman), Bruce MacLeod (Mountie), Peter Maclean, Malcolm "Maxi" MacNeil, Alec MacDougall, Alan MacLeod (Old Men), Emma Fahey (Alma McLaren), Sam White (Young Man), Amy Jo Lamb (Young Margaret), Ian Mugford, Billy Fraser (Little Boys), David B. Lamb (Roddie MacKenzie), Aaron Schneider (Tourist Man), Peter Marinker (Hiring Man), Paul Young, Sean Hewitt, Matt Zimmerman (Doctors)

In a mining town in 1940s Nova Scotia, Margaret MacNeil, who relishes being an outcast and has sworn she will not marry, finds herself falling in love with a charismatic roustabout, Neil Currie.

© CFP Distribution

Kate Nelligan

BOYFRIENDS

(FIRST RUN FEATURES) Producers/Directors/Screenplay, Neil Hunter, Tom Hunsinger; Photography, Richard Tisdall; Editor, John Trumper; Art Director, James Dearlove; an Essex Features presentation; British, 1996; Color; Not rated; 82 minutes; February release

CAST

Paul	James Dreyfus
Matt	Michael Urwin
Will	David Coffey
Ben	Mark Sands
Owen	Andrew Ableson
Adam	Darren Petrucci
James	Michael McGrath

Three gay couples spend a weekend in the country where they examine the status of their relationships.

Michael Urwin, Andrew Ableson, Darren Petrucci

SMILLA'S SENSE OF SNOW

(FOX SEARCHLIGHT) Producers, Bernd Eichinger, Martin Moszkowicz; Director, Bille August; Screenplay, Ann Biderman; Based on the novel Miss Smilla's Feeling for Snow by Peter Hoeg; Photography, Jorgen Persson; Designer, Anna Asp; Editor, Janus Billeskov Jansen; Costumes, Barbara Baum; Music, Hans Zimmer, Harry Gregson Williams; a Bernd Eichinger production; British-German-Swedish-Danish; Dolby Digital Stereo; Panavision; Color; Rated R; 121 minutes; February release

Julia Ormond

CAST

Smilla Jaspersen	Julia Ormond
The Mechanic	Gabriel Byrne
Tork Hviid	Richard Harris
Elsa Lubing	Vanessa Redgrave
Moritz Jaspersen	Robert Loggia
Lagermann	Jim Broadbent
Sigmund Lukas	Mario Adorf
Ravn	Bob Peck
Dr. Loye	Tom Wilkinson
Benja	Emma Croft
Lander	Peter Capaldi
Jakkelsen	Jürgen Vogel
Isaiah	Clipper Miano
Juliane	Agga Olsen
Hansen	Erik Holmey

and Claire Skinner

Smilla Jaspersen, convinced that an Inuit boy's fall from a rooftop was not accidental, begins an investigation that uncovers a link to a powerful mining company.

© Twentieth Century Fox

Richard Harris

Gabriel Byrne, Julia Ormond

KAMA SUTRA: A TALE OF LOVE

(TRIMARK) Producers, Mira Nair, Lydia Dean Pilcher; Executive Producer, Michiyo Yoshizaki; Director, Mira Nair; Screenplay, Helena Kriel, Mira Nair; Co-Producer, Caroline Baron; Photography, Declan Quinn; Designer, Mark Friedberg; Editor, Kristina Boden; Costumes, Eduardo Castro; Music, Mychael Danna; an NDF International Ltd., Pony Canyon Inc., and Pandora Films, in association with Channel Four Films presentation of a Mirabai Production; Indian-British 1996; Dolby Stereo; Color; Not rated; 115 minutes; February release

Pascal Duquenne, Daniel Auteuil

CAST

Maya	Indira Varma
Tara	Sarita Choudhury
Jai Kumar	Ramon Tikaram
Raj Singh	Naveen Andrews
Rasa Devi	Rekha
Biki	Khalik Tyabji
Annabi	Arundhati Rao
Young Maya	Surabhi Bhansali
Young Tara	Garima Dhup
Maham Anga	Pearl Padamsee
Dilki	Kusum Haidar
Doctor Mani	Harish Patel
Babu	Ranjit Chowdhry
Rupa	Achla Sachdev
Bashir	Arjun Sajnani
Vazir	Avijit Dutt

and Anjum Rajabali (Madho Singh), Anand Kumar (Prem. Siddharth), Debi Basu (Dance Teacher), Rahul Vohra (Royal Messenger), Manize Boga (Aunt Laila), Prabeen Singh (Praveen), Sinia Jain (Begum Para), Urvashi Nair (Rich Friend), Bhanumathi Rao (Old Woman), Vasudeo Bhatt (Astrologer), Moneeka Misra Tanvir (Madame), Shubha Mudgal (Singer)

During the 16th century Tara, a princess, and Maya, her servant, approach sexuality in a variety of different ways, using the teachings of "The Kama Sutra."

© Trimark Pictures

Naveen Andrews, Indira Varma

Pascal Duquenne, Daniel Auteuil

THE EIGHTH DAY

(GRAMERCY) Producer, Philippe Godeau; Director/Screenplay, Jaco Van Dormael; Photography, Walther Vanden Ende; Set Deisnger, Hubert Pouille; Costumes, Yan Tax; Editor, Susana Rossberg; Music, Pierre Van Dormael; a PolyGram Filmed Entertainment presentation of a co-production of Pan-Européenne production, Homemade Films, TF1 Films production, RTL TV1, Working Title and D.A. Films; French-Belgian, 1996; Dolby Digital Stereo; Super 35 Widescreen; Color; Not rated; 114 minutes; March release

CAST

Harry	Daniel Auteuil
Georges	Pascal Duquenne
Julie	Miou-Miou
Georges' Mother	Isabelle Sadoyan
Company Director	Henri Garcin
Nathalie	Michèle Maes
Luis Mariano	Laszlo Harmati
Julie's Mother	Hélène Roussel
Fabienne	Fabienne Loriaux
Fabienne's Husband	Didier De Neck

A salesman whose personal life has fallen to ruin befriends a young man named Georges who is challenged with Down's Syndrome.

© Gramercy Pictures

CRASH

(FINE LINE FEATURES) Producer/Director/Screenplay, David Cronenberg; Based on the book by J.G. Ballard; Executive Producers, Jeremy Thomas, Robert Lantos; Co-Executive Producers, Andras Hamori, Chris Auty; Co-Producers, Stephane Reichel, Marilyn Stonehouse; Photography, Peter Suschitzky; Designer, Carol Spier; Costumes, Denise Cronenberg; Editor, Ronald Sanders; Music, Howard Shore; Casting, Deirdre Bowen; a Robert Lantos and Jeremy Thomas presentation of an Alliance Communications production; Canadian, 1996; Dolby Stereo; Color; Rated NC-17; 98 minutes; March release

Deborah Unger, James Spader

CAST

James Ballard	James Spader
Helen Remington	Holly Hunter
Vaughan	Elias Koteas
Catherine Ballard	Deborah Unger
Gabrielle	Rosanna Arquette
Colin Seagrave	Peter MacNeill
Airport Hooker	Yolande Julian
Vera Seagrave	Cheryl Swarts
Salesman	Judah Katz
Tattooist	Nicky Guadagni
A.D.	Ronn Sarosiak
Grip	Boyd Banks
Man in Hanger	Markus Parilo
Camera Girl	Alice Poon
Trask	John Stoneham, Jr.

TV producer James Ballard and Dr. Helen Remington find themselves be-coming involved in a bizarre cult in which people get erotic thrills through car crashes.

© Fine Line Features

Elias Koteas

James Spader, Deborah Unger

James Spader, Holly Hunter

THE QUIET ROOM

(FINE LINE FEATURES) Producers, Domenico Procacci, Rolf de Heer; Co-Producers, Giuseppe Pedersoli, Sharon Jackson, Fiona Paterson; Director/Screenplay, Rolf de Heer; Photography, Tony Clark; Editor, Tania Nehme; Music, Graham Tardif; Designer, Fiona Paterson; a Vertigo/Fandango production, presented in association with Domenico Procacci; Australian, 1996; Dolby Stereo; Color; Rated PG; 91 minutes; March release

CAST

Mother	Celine O'Leary
Father	Paul Blackwell
Girl (Age 7)	Chloe Ferguson
Girl (Age 3)	Phoebe Ferguson
Babysitter	Kate Greetham
Workman	Todd Telford
Carpet Cleaners	Peter Ferris, Peter Green

In response to her parents' growing marital difficulties, a 7-year-old girl stops talking altogether.

Chloe Ferguson, Paul Blackwell, Celine O'Leary

LOVE AND OTHER CATASTROPHES

(FOX SEARCHLIGHT) Producer, Stavros Andonis Efthymiou; Director, Emma-Kate Croghan; Screenplay, Yael Bergman, Emma-Kate Croghan, Helen Bandis; Story, Stavros Andonis Efthymiou; Photography, Justin Brickle; Editor, Ken Sallows; Co-Producers, Helen Bandis, Yael Bergman; Music, Oleh Witer, Daryl McKenzie; a Beyond Films presentation; Australian, 1996; Dolby Stereo; Color; Rated R; 76 minutes; March release

CAST

Alice	Alice Garner
Mia	Frances O'Connor
Ari	Matthew Dyktynski
Michael	Matt Day
Danni	Radha Mitchell
Savita	Suzi Dougherty
Professor Leach	Kim Gyngell
Dr. Russell	Suzanne Dowling
Toby	Torquil Neilson
Susan	Christine Stephen-Daly
Zac	Dominic McDonald
Alvin	Alvin Chong
Myles	Myles Collins
Tony	Anthony Neate
Brigid	Brigid Kelly
Emma	Emma de Clario
Shanti	Shanti Gudgeon

and Maurie Annese (Computer Geek), Nicholas Crawford Smith (Nick), Adrian Martin (Himself), Leroy Ryan (Nazi), Sanjot Kaur Sekhon (Sanjot), Caroline Lloyd (Carol), Kate Croghan (Office Worker), Joyce Yuen (Lecturer), Paul Harris (Professor Novak)

Comedy follows a day in the life of five university students.

Frances O'Connor, Radha Mitchell, Matthew Dyktynski,
Matt Day, Alice Garner

GENTLEMEN DON'T EAT POETS

(LIVE ENTERTAINMENT) aka *The Grotesque*, and *Grave Indiscretions;* Producer, Trudie Styler; Executive Producer, Stephen Evans; Director, John-Paul Davidson; Screenplay, Patrick McGrath, John Paul-Davidson; Based on the novel *The Grotesque* by Patrick McGrath; Photography, Andrew Dunn; Designer, Jan Roelfs; Associate Producer, Anita Sumner; Costumes, Colleen Atwood, Graham Churchyard; Editor, Tariq Anwar; Music, Anne Dudley; Casting, Joyce Nettles; a Trudie Styler production, presented in association with J&M Entertainment and Xingu Films; British, 1995; Dolby Stereo; Color; Rated R; 97 minutes; March release

CAST

Sir Hugo Coal	Alan Bates
Lady Harriet Coal	Theresa Russell
Fledge	Sting
Sir Edward Cleghorn	John Mills
Cleo Coal	Lena Headey
Mrs. Giblet	Anna Massey
Sidney Giblet	Steven Mackintosh
George Lecky	Jim Carter
Lavinia Freebody	Maria Aitken
Inspector Limp	James Fleet
Doris Fledge	Trudie Styler
John Lecky	Chris Barnes
Harbottle	Timothy Kightley
Sykes-Herring	Richard Durden
Hubert Cleggie	Nick Lucas
Connie Babblehump	Annette Badland
Freddy Hough	David Henry

and Bob Goody (Father Pin), Edward Jewesbury (Sir Edward Tome), David Killick (Sir Humphrey Stoker), Geoffrey Freshwater (Jury Foreman), Jeffry Wickham (Justice Congreve), Michael Cronin (Dr. Walter Dendrite), Eleanor Church (Nurse)

A coniving butler takes a job at the Coal estate and proceeds to seduce most of the household members. Sting and Trudie Styler are real-life husband and wife.

© LIVE Entertainment

Martin Donovan, Ian Hart

Alan Bates, Sting

HOLLOW REED

(CFP) Producer, Elizabeth Karlsen; Executive Producers, Nik Powell, Stephen Woolley; Director, Angela Pope; Screenplay, Paula Milne; Photography, Remi Adefarasin; Designer, Stuart Walker; Editor, Sue Wyatt; Music, Anne Dudley; Co-Executive Producers, Andres Vicente Gomez, Finola Dwyer, Neville Bolt, Hanno Huth; Costumes, Pam Downe; Casting, Susie Figgis; a Scala, Senator Films and Channel Four Films presentation; British-German, 1996; Dolby Stereo; Color; Not rated; 106 minutes; April release

CAST

Martyn Wyatt	Martin Donovan
Hannah Wyatt	Joely Richardson
Tom Dixon	Ian Hart
Frank Donally	Jason Flemyng
Oliver Wyatt	Sam Bould
Doctor Razmu	Shaheen Khan
Jamie's Mother	Kelly Hunter
Site Foreman	Tim Crouch
Record Shop Girl	Jane Hill
Unemployed Youth	Glen Hammond
Mr. Bugler	Simon Chandler
School Nurse	Dilys Hamlett
Doctor Ian Slater	Andy Rashleigh
Martyn's Lawyer	David Calder
Sgt. Curtis	Maeve Murphy
Court Welfare Officer	Victoria Scarborough
Hannah's Lawyer	Roger Lloyd Pack
High Court Welfare Officer	Kenneth Anderson
Martyn's Barrister	Annette Badland
Hannah's Barrister	Douglas Hodge
High Court Judge	Edward Hardwicke

Having left his wife for another man, Martyn Wyatt now fights to get his son away from his ex-wife's abusive boyfriend.

© CFP Distribution

210

PARADISE ROAD

(FOX SEARCHLIGHT) Producers, Sue Milliken, Greg Coote; Executive Producers, Andrew Yap, Graham Burke; Director/Screenplay, Bruce Beresford; Based on a story by David Giles, Martin Meader; Photography, Peter James; Designer, Herbert Pinter; Editor, Tim Wellburn; Music, Ross Edwards; Costumes, Terry Ryan; a Village Roadshow Pictures/YTC Pictures production, in association with Planet Pictures; Australian-U.S.; Dolby Stereo; Panavision; Color; Rated R; 115 minutes; April release

Glenn Close, Julianna Margulies

CAST

Adrienne Pargiter	Glenn Close
Margaret Drummond	Pauline Collins
Susan Macarthy	Cate Blanchett
Dr. Verstak	Frances McDormand
Topsy Merritt	Julianna Margulies
Rosemary Leighton-Jones	Jennifer Ehle
Mrs. Roberts	Elizabeth Spriggs
Sister Wilhelminia	Joanna Ter Steege
Mrs. Dickson	Wendy Hughes
Mrs. Tippler	Pamela Rabe
Edna	Lisa Hensley
Mrs. Pike	Penne Hackforth-Jones
Wing	Pauline Chan
Celia Roberts	Tessa Humphries
Bett	Anita Hegh
Oggi	Susie Porter
Helen Van Praagh	Marta Dusseldorp
Mrs. O'Riorden	Lia Scallon
Mrs. Cronje	Marijke Mann
The Snake	Clyde Kusatsu
Colonel Hiroyo	Sab Shimono
Captain Tanaka	Stan Egi
Interpreter	David Chung
Singer at Raffles	Julie Anthony
Bill Seary	Aden Young
Dennis	Paul Bishop
William Pargiter	Stephen O'Rourke
Mr. Dickson	Vincent Ball
Marty Merritt	Nicholas Hammond
Robbie Rober	Noel Ferrier
Major-General Downes	Robert Grubb
Westmacott	Steven Grives

Glenn Close, Pauline Collins

During World War II a disparate group of women survive the bombing of their ship as it flees Singapore only to be captured by the Japanese and placed in a prison camp.

© Twentieth Century Fox

Frances McDormand, Cate Blanchett

Tessa Humphries, Elizabeth Spriggs, Julianna Margulies, Anita Hegh, Jennifer Ehle

KISSED

(GOLDWYN) Producers, Dean English, Lynne Stopkewich; Executive Producer, John Pozer; Director, Lynne Stopkewich; Screenplay, Angus Fraser, Lynne Stopkewich; Based on the short story "We So Seldom Look on Love" by Barbara Gowdy; Photography, Gregory Middleton; Editors, John Pozer, Peter Roeck, Lynne Stopkewich; Designer, Eric McNab; Music, Don MacDonald; Casting, Wendy O'Brien Livingstone; a Boneyard Film Company production, produced in association with British Columbia Film; Canadian, 1996; Dolby Stereo; Color; Not rated; 73 minutes; April release

CAST

Sandra Larson	Molly Parker
Matt	Peter Outerbridge
Mr. Wallis	Jay Brazeau
Young Sandra	Natasha Morley
Carol	Jessie Winter Mudie
Jan	James Timmons
Biology Teacher	Joe Maffei
Detective	Robert Thurston
Mother Larson	Annabel Kershaw
Father Larson	Tim Dixon
Lisa Brown	Amber Warnat
Minister	Bill Finck
Mourner	Janet Craig
Embalming Professor	Edward Davey

and Hamish Wilson (Gurney Goner), Valerie Boeke (Cancer Corpse), Jeff Richards (Tony the Torso), Noel Boulanger (Prep Room Demo), Debra L. Huntley (Dead Madonna), John Pozer (Class Carcass), Raul Inglis (Lucky Stiff), Andrew Guy (Coffin Deceased), David Lone (Long Gone)

Sandra's childhood obsession with dead animals develops into a bizarre desire to make love to the corpses at the funeral home where she works.

Peter Outerbridge, Molly Parker

James Frain, Ian Hart

NOTHING PERSONAL

(TRIMARK) Producers, Jonathan Cavendish, Tracy Seaward; Executive Producer, James Mitchell; Director, Thaddeus O'Sullivan; Screenplay, Daniel Mornin, based on his novel All Our Fault; Photography, Dick Pope; Designer, Mark Geraghty; Editor, Michael Parker; Costumes, Consolata Boyle; Music, Philip Appleby; Casting, Ros & John Hubbard; a Channel Four Films with the participation of Bord Scannan na hEireann—The Irish Film Board—British Screen and Little Bird Productios; Irish; Dolby Digital Stereo; Color; Not rated; 86 minutes; April release

CAST

Ginger	Ian Hart
Liam	John Lynch
Kenny	James Frain
Leonard	Michael Gambon
Eddie	Gary Lydon
Tommy	Ruaidhri Conroy
Ann	Maria Doyle Kennedy
Kathleen	Jeni Courtney
Cecil	Gerard McSorley
Michael	Gareth O'Hare
Young Liam	Ciaran Fitzgerald
Malachy	Antony Brophy
Jake	BJ Hogg
Billy	Jim Duran
Lizzie	Cathy White
Gloria	Lynne James
Joe	Joe Rea
Susan	Amanda Maguire

and Robbie Doolin (Drunk Fella), Oliver Maguire (Marty), Andrew Roddy (Lizzie's Husband), Frank McCusker (1st Man), Seamus Ball (Jimmy), Danny McElhinney (Pub Bomber), Janet Moran (Waitress), Lydia Courtney (Penelope), Noah Eli Davis (Scruffy Young Man), Alan Burke (Ginger's Brother), Colm O'Brien (Young Kenny)

Kenny, a vengeful Protestant Loyalist squad leader, is stunned by the orders of a cease fire between the Protestants and the Catholics and the wishes of his superior that Kenny kill his violent friend Ginger as a sort of peace offering to the enemy.

A CHEF IN LOVE

(SONY PICTURES CLASSICS) Producer, Marc Ruscart; Director, Nana Djordjadze; Screenplay, Irakli Kvirikadze; Adaptation, Andre Grall; Photography, Guiorgui Beridze; Designer, Vakhtang Rouroua, Teimour Chmaladze; Music, Goran Bregovic; Editors, Vessela Martschewski, Guili Grigoriani; a Les Films du Rivage, Studios Adam et Eve, La Sept Cinema, Studio Babelsberg, CMC, Sotra, Innova co-production; French-Georgian, 1996; Dolby Stereo; Color; Rated PG-13; 100 minutes; April release

CAST

Pascal Ichac..Pierre Richard
Marcelle Ichac...Micheline Presle
Cecilia Abachidze...Nino Kirtadze
Zigmund Gogoladze ....Teimour Kahmhadze
Anton Gogoladze ....Jean-Yves Gautier
and Ramaz Tchkhikvadze

In 1995 Paris a painter is given a manuscript which describes his mother's relationship with a famous French chef. This film received an Oscar nomination in the foreign-language film category for 1996.

© Sony Pictures Entertainment

Maggie Cheung

FLAMENCO

(NEW YORKER) Producer, Juan Lebrón; Director, Carlos Saura; Executive Producer, José López Rodero; Photography, Vittorio Storaro; Designers, José Lopéz, Carlos Regidor; Costumes, Rafael Palmero; Editor, Pablo del Amo; Music Producer and Director, Isidro Muñoz; Spanish, 1995; Color; Not rated; 100 minutes; April release. Documentary on the variations of the flamenco dance featuring Paco de Lucía, Manolo Sanlúcar, Lole y Manuel, Joaquín Cortés, Farruco, Farruquito, Mario Maya, Matilde Coral, Enrique Morente, José Mercé, José Menese, Merche Esmeralda, Manuela Carrasco, La Paquera de Jerez, Carmen Linares, Paco Toronjo, Fernanda de Utrera, Chocolate, Paco Del Gastor.

© New Yorker Films

Nino Kirtadze, Pierre Richard

IRMA VEP

(ZEITGEIST) Producer, Georges Benayoun; Executive Producer, Françoise Guglielmi; Director/Screenplay, Olivier Assayas; Photography, Eric Gautier; Designer, Francoise-Renaud Labarthe; Editor, Luc Barnier; Costumes, Francoise Clavel, Jessica Doyle; a Dacia Films production; French, 1996; Color; Not rated; 96 minutes; April release

CAST

Maggie ....Maggie Cheung
Rene Vidal ....Jean-Pierre Leaud
Zoe ....Nathalie Richard
Mireille ....Bulle Ogier
Jose Murano...Lou Castel
American Woman...Arsinee Khanjian
Journalist ....Antonie Basler
Laure ....Nathalie Boutefeu
Desormeaux..Alex Descas
Maite ....Dominique Faysse
Markus..Bernard Nissile
Ferdinand/Moreno ....Olivier Torres

Hong Kong action star Maggie Cheung comes to France to appear as "Irma Vep," the head of a band of vampires, in director Rene Vidal's remake of the silent seral "Les Vampires."

© Zeitgeist Films

CHILDREN OF THE REVOLUTION

(MIRAMAX) Producer, Tristram Miall; Director/Screenplay, Peter Duncan; Photography, Martin McGrath; Designer, Roger Ford; Editor, Simon Martin, Music, Nigel Westlake; Costumes, Terry Ryan; Associate Producer, Greg Ricketson; a presentation of the Australian Film Finance Corporation; Australian, 1996; Dolby Digital Stereo; Color; Rated R; 101 minutes; May release

CAST

Joan Fraser	Judy Davis
Nine	Sam Neill
Josef Stalin	F. Murray Abraham
Joe	Richard Roxburgh
Anna	Rachel Griffiths
Welch	Geoffrey Rush
Barry	Russell Kiefel
Dr. Wilf Wilke	John Gaden
Young Joe	Ben McIvor
Brendan Shaw	Marshall Napier
Bernard Shaw	Ken Radley
Mavis	Fiona Press
Yuri	Alex Menglet
Colin Slansky	Rowan Woods
Police Commissioner	Harold Hopkins
Mrs. Savage	Heather Mitchell
Beria	Paul Livingstone
Malenkov	Stephen Abbott
Khrushchev	Dennis Watkins
Allan Miles	Ron Haddrick
Ted	Barry Langrishe
Minister	Robbie McGregor
Police Sergeant	Roy Billing

Communist Joan Fraser looks back on how her infatuation with Josef Stalin led to her having his child.

F. Murray Abraham, Judy Davis

Judy Davis, Geoffrey Rush

BROKEN ENGLISH

(SONY CLASSICS) Producer, Robin Scholes; Executive Producer, Timothy White; Director, Gregor Nicholas; Screenplay, Gregor Nicholas, Johanna Pigott, Jim Salter; Photography, John Toon; Editor, David Coulson; Music, Murray Grindlay, Murray McNabb; Designer, Michael Kane; Casting, Fiona Edgar; a Village Roadshow Pictures Worldwide presentation of a Communicado Production in association with the New Zealand Film Commission and New Zealand on Air; New Zealand, 1996; Dolby Stereo; Color; Rated NC-17; 90 minutes; May release

CAST

Ivan	Rade Serbedzija
Nina	Aleksandra Vujcic
Eddie	Julian Arahanga
Darko	Marton Csokas
Mira	Madeline McNamara
Vanya	Elizabeth Mavric
Clara	Jing Zhao
Wu	Yang Li

Nina, having fled with her family to New Zealand from war-torn Croatia, finds herself falling in love with a handsome Maori boy much to the displeasure of her overly-protective father.

Aleksandra Vujcic, Madeline McNamara, Marton Csokas, Rade Serbedzija, Elizabeth Mavric

THE DESIGNATED MOURNER

(FIRST LOOK PICTURES) Producers, Donna Grey, David Hare; Executive Producers, Mark Shivas, Simon Curtis; Director, David Hare; Screenplay, Wallace Shawn, based on his play; Photography, Oliver Stapleton; Designer, Bob Crowley; Music, Richard Hartley; Editor, George Akers; a BBC Films presentation of a Greenpoint Film; British; Dolby Stereo; Color; Rated R; 93 minutes; May release

CAST

Jack ....Mike Nichols
Judy...Miranda Richardson
Howard ....David de Keyser

Jack, mourning the passing of his stepfather, a famous poet, reflects on the death of intellectualism and compassion. Director Mike Nichols makes his theatrical film debut as an actor.

© First Line Pictures

Jérémie Renier

DIARY OF A SEDUCER

(LEISURE TIME FEATURES) Producer, Philippe Saal; Executive Producer, Paulo Branco; Director/Screenplay, Daniele Dubroux; Photography, Laurent Machuel; Editor, Jean-Francois Naudon; Music, Jean-Marie Senia; Art Director, Patrick Durand; Costumes, Anne Schotte; a production of Gemini Films with the participation of the National Center of Cinematography and Canal+; French; Color; Not rated; 95 minutes; May release

CAST

Claire Conti ....Chiara Mastroianni
Gregoire Moreau ....Melvil Poupaud
Hubert Markus...Hubert Saint Macary
Sebastien ....Mathieu Amalric
Anne, Claire's Mother ....Daniele Dubroux
Hugo ....Jean-Pierre Leaud
Diane ....Micheline Presle
Robert ....Serge Merlin
Charlotte ....Karen Viard

A copy of Kierkegaard's Diary of a Seducer turns anyone who comes into contact with the book into a romantic fool.

© Leisure Time Features

Miranda Richardson, Mike Nichols

LA PROMESSE

(NEW YORKER) Producers, Luc Dardenne, Hassen Daldoul; Directors/Screenplay, Jean-Pierre Dardenne, Luc Dardenne; Photography, Alain Marcoen, Benoit Dervaux; Associate Producers, Jacqueline Pierreux, Claude Waringo; Set Designer, Igor Gabriel; Costumes, Monic Parelle; Editor, Marie-Helene Dozo; Music, Jean-Marie Billy, Denis M'Punga; a presentation of Luc and Jean-Pierre Dardenne—Les Films du Fleuve—Hassen Daldoul—Touza Productions & Touza Films—Claude Waringo—Samsa Film—Jacqueline Pierreux—RTBF (Belgian Television); French-Belgian-Luxembourgian-Tunisian, 1996; Dolby Digital Stereo; Color; Not rated; 93 minutes; May release

CAST

Igor ....Jérémie Renier
Roger...Olivier Gourmet
Assita ....Assita Ouedraogo
Hamidou...RasmanéOuedraogo
Ibrahim...R. Amrani
Nicolai ....I. Tanaru

15 year-old Igor is forced to accept his father's illegal way of making a living by exploiting illegal immigrants until a young African laborer is killed on the job, causing Igor to try to help the man's widow

© New Yorker Films

Jean-Pierre Leaud, Chiara Mastroianni

THE FIFTH ELEMENT

Bruce Willis

(COLUMBIA) Producer, Patrice Ledoux; Director/Story, Luc Besson; Screenplay, Luc Besson, Robert Mark Kamen; Photography, Thierry Arbogast; Designer, Dan Weil; Editor, Sylvie Landra; Co-Producer, Iain Smith; Special Visual Effects Supervisor, Mark Stetson; Costumes, Jean-Paul Gaultier; Music, Eric Serra; Stunts, Marc Boyle; Casting, Lucinda Syson; a Gaumont Production; French; Dolby SDDS Stereo; Super 35 Widescreen; Eastman color; Rated PG-13; 127 minutes; May release

CAST

Korben Dallas	Bruce Willis
Zorg	Gary Oldman
Cornelius	Ian Holm
Leeloo	Milla Jovovich
Ruby Rhod	Chris Tucker
Billy	Luke Perry
General Munro	Brion James
President Lindberg	Tommy "Tiny" Lister, Jr.
Fog	Lee Evans
David	Charlie Creed Miles
Right Arm	Tricky
General Staedert	John Neville
Professor Pacoli	John Bluthal
Mugger	Mathieu Kassovitz
Mactilburgh	Christopher Fairbank
Thai	Kim Chan
Neighbor	Richard Leaf
Major Iceborg	Julie T. Wallace
General Tudor	Al Matthews
Diva	Maïwenn Le Besco
Priest	John Bennett
Left Arm	Ivan Heng
President's Aide	Sonita Henry
Scientist's Aide	Tim McMullan
Munro's Captain	Hon Ping Tang
Head Scientist	George Khan
Head of Military	John Hughes
Omar	Roberto Bryce
Aziz	Said Talidi

Chris Tucker

and Justin Lee Burrows, Richard Ashton, Jerome Blake, Kevin Molloy (Mondoshawan), Bill Reimbold (Mactilburgh's Assistant), Colin Brooks (Staedert's Captain), Anthony Chinn (Mactilburgh's Technicians), Sam Douglas (Chief NY Cop), Derek Ezenagu (NY Cop), David Kennedy, David Barrass, Roger Monk, Mac McDonald, Mark Seaton, Jean Luc Caron, Riz Meedin, Jerry Ezekiel (Flying Cops), Indra Ove, Nicole Merry, Stacey McKenzie (VIP Stewardesses), Rachel Willis, Genevieve Maylam, Josie Perez, Natasha Brice (Stewardesses), Sophia Goth (Check In Attendant), Martin McDougall (Warship Captain), Peter Dunwell (Diva's Manager), Paul Priestley, Jason Salkey (Cops), Stewart Harvey Wilson, Dave Fishley, Carlton Chance (Ruby Rhod Assistants), Gin Clarke (Diva's Assistant), Vladimir McCrary (Human Aknot), Clifton Lloyd Bryan (Mangalore Aknot/Airport Guard), Aron Paramor (Mangalore Akanit), Alan Ruscoe (Mangalore Kino), Christopher Adamson (Airport Cop), Eve Salvail (Tawdry Girl), Kaleem Janjua (Shuttle Pilot), Tyrone Tyrell (Shuttle Co-Pilot), Kevin Brewerton (Shuttle Mechanic), Kevin Molloy, Vince Pellegrino (Ground Crew), Ian Beckett (Baby Ray), Sonny Caldinez (Emperor Kodar Japhet), Zeta Graff (Princess Achen), Eddie Ellwood (Roy Von Bacon), Yui, Laura DePalma (Fhloston Hostesses), Michael Culkin (Hefty Man), Lenny McLean (Police Chief), Robert Oates (Fhloston Commander), John Sharian (Fhloston Captain), Fred Williams (Hotel Manager), Sibyl Buck (Zorg's Secretary), Sarah Carrington, Grant James, Ali Yassine, Sean Buckley (Scientists), Dane Messam, Roger Monk, Nathan Hamlett, Cecil Cheng (Military Technicians), Scott Woods, Leon Dekker (Lab Guards), David Garvey, Stanley Kowalski, Omar Hibbert Williams (Staedert's Technicians), Robert Clapperton (Robot Barman), Robert Alexander (Warship Technician), Mia Frye (TV Stewardess), Leo Williams, Keith Martin (Power Operators), J.D. Dawodu, Patrick Nicholls, Shaun Davis, Roy Garcia Singh, Alex Georgijev (Zorg's Men), Marie Guillard, Renee Montemayor, Stina Richardson (Burger Assistants)

Tiny Lister, Jr. (c)

In 23rd Century New York cab driver Korben Dallas rescues Leeloo, a strange being who is the key element needed to save the earth from cosmic anti-life forces. This film received an Oscar nomination for sound effects editing.

© Columbia Pictures Industries

Maïwenn LeBesco

Gary Oldman

Charlie Creed Miles, Milla Jovovich, Ian Holm

PONETTE

(ARROW) Producer, Alain Sarde; Director/Screenplay, Jacques Doillon; Photography, Caroline Champetier; Costumes, Astrid Traissac; Set Designer, Henri Berthon; Editor, Jacqueline Fano (Leconte); Music, Philippe Sarde; Co-Produced by Les Films Alain Sarde, Rhone-Alpes Cinema with the participation of La Region Rhone Alpes, Centre National de la Cinematographie and Canal+; French, 1996; Dolby Stereo; Color; Not rated; 97 minutes; May release

CAST

Ponette	Victoire Thivisol
Ponette's Cousins	Matiaz Bureau, Delphine Schiltz
The Mother	Marie Trintignant
The Father	Xavier Beauvois
The Aunt	Claire Nebout
Aurélie	Aurelie Verillon
Ada	Leopoldine Serre
The Teacher	Henri Berthon
Carla	Carla Ibled
Luce	Luckie Royer
Antoine	Antoine Du Merle
Marianne	Marianne Favre

Surviving a car crash which has killed her mother, 4-year-old Ponette deals with the tragedy by clinging to the notion that her mother will somehow come back to her.

© Arrow Releasing

Victoire Thivisol

Xavier Beauvois, Victoire Thivisol

BROTHERS IN TROUBLE

(FIRST RUN FEATURES) Producer/Screenplay, Robert Buckler; Executive Producer, George Faber; Director, Udayan Prasad; Photography, Alan Almond; Designer, Chris Townsend; Editor, Barrie Vince; Music, Stephen Warbeck; Casting, Lucinda Syson; a BBC Film presentation of a Renegade Films production, in association with Kinowelt Film Produktion and Mikado Film; British, 1995; Dolby Digital Stereo; Color; Not rated; 102 minutes; May release

CAST

Hussein Shah	Om Puri
Mary	Angeline Ball
Amir	Pavan Malhotra
Sakib	Pravesh Kumar
Irshad	Ahsen Bhatti
Old Ram	Badi Uzzaman
Gholam	Bhasker
The Agent	Kulvinder Ghir
Prostitute	Lesley Clare O'Neill

Amir smuggles himself into England only to find that living and working conditions for himself and seventeen other illegal Pakistani immigrants with whom he resides, is no easier than it was back home.

© First Run Features

Om Puri (left)

Pavan Malhotra

BRASSED OFF

(MIRAMAX) Producer, Steve Abbott; Co-Producer, Olivia Stewart; Director/Screenplay, Mark Herman; Photography, Andy Collins; Designer, Don Taylor; Editor, Mike Ellis; Costumes, Amy Roberts; Music, Trevor Jones; Brass Music Performed by The Grimethorpe Colliery Band; Casting, Priscilla John, Julia Duff; a Channel Four Films presentation of a Steve Abbott/Prominent Features production; British, 1996; Dolby Stereo; Color; Rated R; 101 minutes; May release

Ewan McGregor, Tara Fitzgerald, Pete Postlethwaite

CAST

Danny	Pete Postlethwaite
Gloria	Tara Fitzgerald
Andy	Ewan McGregor
Phil	Stephen Tompkinson
Harry	Jim Carter
Jim	Philip Jackson
Ernie	Peter Martin
Vera	Sue Johnston
Ida	Mary Healey
Rita	Lill Roughley
Sandra	Melanie Hill
Simmo	Peter Gunn
McKenzie	Stephen Moore
Greasley	Ken Colley
Mrs. Foggan	Olga Grahame
Gary	Toni Garlacki
Kylie	Sky Ingram
Shane	Luke McGann
Craig	Christopher Tetlow
Chapman	Bernard Wrigley
Heavies	Ken Kitson, Adrian Hood
Ward Sister	Sally Adams
Bus Driver	Tubby Andrews
Nurse	Katherine Dow Beyton

and Adam Fogerty (Miner), Jacqueline Naylor, Vanessa Know-Mawer (Mothers), Sally Ann Matthews (Waitress), Bob Rodgers (Halifax Judge), Max Smith (Night Watchman), Ronnie Stevens (Albert Hall Judge), Peter Wallis (Elderly Man)

Tara Fitzgerald, Ewan McGregor

In the Yorkshire village of Grimley, the town's brass band tries to concentrate on rehearsing for the National Championships while facing the almost certain closure of the mine and the resulting loss of employment for all the band's members.

© Miramax Films

Pete Postlethwaite

Stephen Tompkinson, Pete Postlethwaite

THE VAN

(FOX SEARCHLIGHT) Producer, Lynda Miles; Executive Producer, Mark Shivas; Co-Producer/Screenplay, Roddy Doyle, based on his novel; Director, Stephen Frears; Photography, Oliver Stapleton; Designer, Mark Geraghty; Costumes, Consolata Boyle; Editor, Mick Audsley; Music, Eric Clapton, Richard Hartley; Presented in association with BBC Films; a Deadly Films production in association with Beacon Pictures; British, 1996; Dolby Stereo; Color; Rated R; 105 minutes; May release

CAST

Larry	Colm Meaney
Bimbo	Donal O'Kelly
Maggie	Ger Ryan
Mary	Caroline Rothwell
Diane	Neili Conroy
Kevin	Ruaidhri Conroy
Weslie	Brendan O'Carroll
Sam	Stuart Dunne

Bimbo, favoring unemployment after being fired from his bakery job, hits on the idea of running a fast-food truck with his friend Larry as his business partner.

© Twentieth Century Fox

Yoshi Oida

Ewan McGregor, Vivian Wu

Ger Ryan, Colm Meaney, Ruaidhri Conroy

THE PILLOW BOOK

(CFP) Producer, Kees Kasander; Executive Producers, Terry Glinwood, Jean Louis Piel, Denis Wigman; Director/Screenplay, Peter Greenaway; Photography, Sacha Vierny; Designers, Wilbert van Dorp, Andree Putnam, Emi Wada; Costumes, Dien van Straalen, Koji Tatsuno, Martin Margiela, Emi Wada; Editors, Chris Wyatt, Peter Greenaway; Calligraphy, Brody Neuenschwander, Yukki Yaura; from Channel Four Films/Studio Canal+/Delux Productions, with the support of The Eurimages Fund of the Council of Europe/Nederlands Fonds Voor de Film; British-Netherlands-French, 1996; Dolby Stereo; Super 35 Widescreen; Color; Not rated; 126 minutes; June release

CAST

Nagiko	Vivian Wu
The Publisher	Yoshi Oida
The Father	Ken Ogata
The Aunt & The Maid	Hideko Yoshida
Jerome	Ewan McGregor
The Mother	Judy Ongg
The Husband	Ken Mitsuishi
Hoki	Yutaka Honda
Jerome's Mothe	Barbara Lott
The Book of the Innocent	Wichert Dromkert
The Book of the Idiot	Martin Tukker
The Book of Old Age	Wu Mei
The Book of the Exhibitionist	Tom Kane
The Book of the Seducer	Kheim Lam
The Book of Youth	Daishi Hori
The Book of Secrets	Kinya Tsuruyama
The Book of the Betrayer	Eiichi Tanaka
The Book of Silence	Rick Waney
The Book of Birth & Beginnings	Masaru Matsuda
The Book of the Dead	Wataru Murofush

and Miwako Kawai, Chizurur Ohnishi, Shiho Takmatsu, Aki Ishimaru (Young Nagikos), Hisashi Hidaka, Dehong Chen, Ham Cham Luong, Akihiro Nishida, Kentaro Matsuo, Nguyen Duc Nhan, Augusto Aristotle, Roger To Thanh Hien, Chris Bearne (Calligraphers), Ronald Guttman (Lecturer), Ryuko Azuma (Grandmother), Seitaro Koyama, Tatsuya Kimura (Nephew), Yoshihiko Nagata, Atsushi Miura (Husband's Friends), Kazushi Ishimaru (Baby Nagiko), Hikari Abe (Nagiko's Baby), Ai Kanafuji, Yoshino Yoshioka, Yuki Nou, Masami Nishio, Satomi Kimura, Michiko Matsuo (Nagiko's Friends), Arnita Swanson (Edele), Jim Adhi Limas (Man in Lift), Miho Tanaka, Fabienne De Marco, Tania De Jaeger (Model Friends at Cafe Typo), Lu Jinhua (Wife of Calligrapher), Tien Sing Wang, Chau, See Wah Leung, Kha (Intruders), Kumi Komino (Elderly Secretary), Yuki Hayashi, Maskai Taketani (Young Secretaries), Mr. and Mrs. Lo (Old Servant and Wife), See Yan Leung (Bookshop Manager), Francois Van Den Bergen (Book of Seducer)

Having been painted on by her father for each birthday, Nagiko searches for a lover to fulfill her fetish for being drawn on.

© CFP Distribution

WHEN THE CAT'S AWAY

Garance Clavel

(SONY CLASSICS) Producers, Aissa Djabri, Farid Lahouassa, Manuel Munz; Director/Screenplay, Cédric Klapisch; Photography, Benoit Delhomme; Editor, Francine Sandberg; Costumes, Pierre Yves Gayraud; Designer, Francois Emmanuelli; a co-production of Vertigo Productions and France2 Cinema with the participation of Canal+; French; Dolby Stereo; Color; Rated R; 95 minutes; June release

CAST

Chloé	Garance Clavel
Jamel	Zinedine Soualem
Madame Renée	Renée Le Calm
Michel	Olivier Py
Gris-Gris	Arapimou
Rambo	Rambo
Drummer	Romain Duris
Photographer's Assistant	Nicolas Koretzky
Madame Dubois	Andrée Damant
Flo the Hair Stylist	Estelle Larrivaz
Victoire	Camille Japy
Stylist	Marina Tomé
Models	Marine Delterme, Helene De Fougerolles, Liane Leroy, Jane Bradbury
Publicist	Marie Riva
Photographer	Frederic Aufray
Assistant Stylist	Philippe Garcia
Carlos	Simon Abkarian
Drunk Guy	Antoine Chappey
Madame Henriette	Jacqueline Jehanneuf
Woman Who Gets Lost	Madeleine Marie
Baker	Coraly Zahonero
African Worker	Eriq Ebouaney
Bartender	Aurélia Petit
Bouncer	Jean-Marc Truong
Agressive Guys	Francis Renaud, Franck Bussi
Michel's First Boyfriend	Michel Glasko
Michel's Second Boyfriend	Franck Manzoni
Eleven of Spades Militant	Eric Savin
Mover/Painter	Pascal Chardin
Bel Canto, the Painter	Joel Brisse
Denis	Denis Falgoux

and Danielle Hoisnard (Madame Verligodin), Suzanne Plasson (Odile), Marcelle Dupuy (Pipelette), Marthe Fouquet (Madame Vilchenu), Aline Chantal (Madame Doubrowsky), Gisele Laquit (Gisele), Olympe Brugeille (Madame Brugeille), Jean-Marie and Lila (Owners of the Bar des Taillandiers), Felipe Moya (Troude), P'Tit Louis (Homeless Guy), Kristelle (Kristelle), Paola Ramirez, Carlos Donoso (Salsa Dancers), Marilyne Canto (Cop)

Garance Clavel, Arapimou

When Chloé returns from vacation she discovers that the absent-minded Madame Renée, entrusted with watching her cat, has lost the animal, leading the two on a picaresque series of misaventures as they search for the missing feline.

© Sony Pictures Entertainment, Inc.

Zinedine Soualem, Renée Le Calm, Garance Clavel

TEMPTRESS MOON

(MIRAMAX) Producers, Tong Cunlin, Hsu Feng; Executive Producer, Sunday Sun; Director, Chen Kaige; Screenplay, Shu Kei; Story, Chen Kaige, Wang Anyi; Photography, Christopher Doyle; Art Director, Huang Qiagui; Costumes, William Chang Suk-ping, Chen Changmin; Music, Zhao Jiping; Editor, Pei Xiaonan; Hong Kong, 1996; Color; Rated R; 115 minutes; June release

CAST

Yu Zhongliang	Leslie Cheung
Pang Ruyi	Gong Li
Pang Duanwu	Kevin Lin
Yu Xiuyi (Zhongliang's Sister)	He Saifei
Li Niangjiu	Zhang Shi
Pang An	Lin Lianqun
Elder Qi	Ge Xiangting
Boss	Xie Tian
Jingyun	David Wu
"The Woman of Heavenly Lane"	Zhou Jie
Pang Zhengda	Zhou Yemang
Yu Zhongliang (Child)	Ren Lei
Pang Ruyi (Child)	Wang Ying
Pang Duanwu (Child)	Ge Lin

Young Zhongliang, raised as a servant at the decadent Pang family estate, grows up and ventures to pre-Communist era Shanghai where he becomes a gigolo.

© Miramax Films

Rupert Graves

Annabella Sciorra

Gong Li

THE INNOCENT SLEEP

(CASTLE HILL) Producers, Scott Michell, Matthew Vaughn; Executive Producer, Rod Mitchell; Director, Scott Michell; Screenplay, Ray Villis, Derek Trigg; Photography, Alan Dunlop; Editor, Derek Trigg; Costumes, Stephanie Collie; Designer, Eve Mavrakis; Music, Mark Ayres; Casting, Simone Ireland; British, 1996; Dolby Stereo; Super 35 Widescreen; Color; Rated R; 90 minutes; June release

CAST

Alan Terry	Rupert Graves
Billie Hayman	Annabella Sciorra
Matheson	Michael Gambon
Cavani	Franco Nero
James	John Hannah
George	Graham Crowden
Lusano	Oliver Cotton
Thorn	Tony Bluto
Pelham	Paul Brightwell
Mac	Campbell Morrison
Sheila Terry	Hilary Crowson
Police Constable	Sean Gilder
Police Sergeant	Biran Lipson
Willie	Dermot Kerrigan

and Kieran Smith (Newspaper Vendor), Dermot Keaney (Driver), Alex Richardson (Thugs), Chris Jury (News Photographer), Laura Berkeley (Glamorous Blonde), Hugh Walters (Lewis), Crispin Redman (Simon, C.I.D.), Katy Carr (Alice), Chris Armstrong (C.I.D. Man), Lehla Eldridge (Morgue Attendant), Struan Rodger (Peter Samson), Stephen Yardley (Drago), Ken Ratcliffe (Stephens), Carmen de Venere (Cavani's Aide), Paul Gregory (Newsreader), Robert James (Hopkin), Susan Gilmore (News Programme Presenter), Peter Cartwright (Gerald Phillips), Julian Rivett (Bike Courier), Patrick Duggan (Landlord), Hilary Waters, Riz Abbasi, Martin Biltcliffe, James Peck (Journalists), Peter Howell (Sir Frank), Ben de Saumserez (Assassin)

Alan Terry, a homeless man living on the streets of London, fears for his life after witnessing the brutal murder of a high-profile businessman.

© Castle Hill Prods.

EAST SIDE STORY

(KINO) Producer, Andrew Horn; Director, Dana Ranga; Screenplay, Dana Ranga, Andrew Horn; Translations, Sergei Grimalschi, Irina Goldstein, Karin Beck; Photography, Mark Daniels; Editor, Guido Krajewski; Costumes, Suse Brown; Produced by ANDA Films/WDR/DocStar/Canal+; German-French; Color/Black and White; Not rated; 77 minutes; June release. A look at the socialist movie musicals made behind the Iron Curtain during Communist rule; featuring Andrea Schmidt, Brit Kruger, Barbara Harnisch (Communist Party Girls); interviews with Karin Schröder, Brigitte Ulbrich, Helmut Hanke, Hans-Joachim Wallstein, Maya Turorskaya, Maragarita Andrushkevitch, Chris Doerk, Frank Schöbel. Featuring musicals numbers from the films Hard Work, Happy Holiday (GDR, 1950), The Antique Coin (Bulgaria/GDR, 1965), Adventure in Marienstadt (Poland, 1954), A Handful of Notes (GDR, 1962), New Year's Punch (GDR, 1960), Vacation on the Black Sea (Romania, 1963), I Don't Want to Marry (Romania, 1961), The Jolly Fellows (USSR, 1934), Volga Volga (USSR, 1938), The Swineherd and the Shepherd (USSR, 1941), Tractor Drivers (USSR, 1939), Cossacks of the Kuban River (USSR, 1946), The Bright Path (USSR, 1940), At 6PM at the End of the War (USSR, 1944), Ernest Thalmann—Class Leader (GDR, 1955), My Wife Wants to Sing (GDR, 1958), Midnight Revue (GDR, 1962), The Lovable White Mouse (GDR, 1964), Hot Summer (GDR, 1968), No Cheating Darling (GDR, 1973), Woman on the Rails (Czechoslovakia, 1965), Carnvial Night (USSR, 1957)

GABBEH

(NEW YORKER) Producers, Khalil Doroudt-Chi, Khalil Mahmoudi; Executive Producer, Mustafa Mirza-Khani; Director/Screenplay/Art Director/Editor, Mohsen Makhmalbaf; Photography, Mahmoud Kalari; Music, Hossein Alizadeh; a co-production of Sanayeh Dasti of Iran and MK2 (France); Iranian-French, 1996; Color; Not rated; 75 minutes; June release

CAST

Gabbeh	Shaghayegh Djodat
The Uncle	Abbas Sayahi
The Old Man	Hossein Moharami
The Old Woman	Roghieh Moharami

A woman named Gabbeh arises from a carpet to tell an old woman and her husband the story of how she is being pursued by a horseman who wishes to marry her.

Shaghayegh Djodat

FOR ROSEANNA

(FINE LINE FEATURES) formerly *Roseanna's Grave*; Producers, Paul Trijbits, Alison Owen, Dario Poloni; Executive Producers Ruth Vitale, Mark Ordesky, Jonathan Weisgel, Miles Donnelly; Director, Paul Weiland; Screenplay, Paul Tureltaub; Line Producer, Chris Thompson; Photography, Henry Brahm; Designer, Rod McLean; Editor, Martin Walsh; Music, Trevor Jones; Costumes, Annie Hardinge; Casting, Nina Gold; Presented in association with Spelling FIlms, of a Hungry Eye Trijbits/Worrell production; British-Italian; Dolby SDDS Stereo; Panavision; Technicolor, Rated PG-13; 98 minutes; June release

Mercedes Ruehl, Jean Reno

CAST

Marcello	Jean Reno
Roseanna	Mercedes Ruehl
Cecilia	Polly Walker
Antonio	Mark Frankel
Father Bramilla	Giuseppe Cederna
Dr. Benvenuto	Renato Scarpa
Capestro	Luigi Dilberti
Rossi	Roberto Della Casa
Iaccoponi	Trevor Peacock
Francesca	Fay Ripley
Sgt. Baggio	George Rossi
Umberto	Romano Ghinin
Enzo	Giovanni Pallavicino
Salvatore	Jorge Krimer
Nunzio	Daniele Ferretti
Pavone	Paul Müller
Gianna	Lucia Guzzardi

and Lidia Biondi (Signora Aprea), Anna Mazzotti (Claudia), Giuseppe Paplia (Dino), Luis C. Garcia (Pasquale), Mario Donatone (Old Gaurd), Peter Gunn, Pietro Bontempo (Cops), Alfred Varelli (Shoe Shop Owner), Gisella Mathews (Sister), Franco Odoardi (Patient), Julia Hine (Secretary), Luciana De Falco (Gigi), Stefani Stella (Hooker), Francesco Gabrielle (Maristrate), Zita Perczel (Old Woman in Court)

Marcello, determined to fulfill his dying wife Roseanna's wish that she be buried in one of the few remaining plots in the village cemetary, goes out of his way to make sure that nobody in town dies before her.

Mirtha Ibarra

Jean Reno

GUANTANAMERA!

(CFP) Producer, Gerardo Herrer; Executive Producer, Camilo Vives; Directors, Tomás Gutiérrez Alea, Juan Carlos Tabio; Screenplay, Eliseo Alberto Diego, Tomás Gutiérrez Alea, Juan Carlos Tabio; Photography, Hans Burmann; Art Director, Onelia Larralde; Music, José Nieto; Editor, Carmen Frias; Cuban; Dolby Digital Stereo; Color; Not rated; 101 minutes; July release

CAST

Adolfo	Carlos Cruz
Georgina	Mirtha Ibarra
Candido	Raúl Eguren
Mariano	Jorge Perugorria
Ramon	Pedro Fernández
Tony	Luis Alberto Garcia Novoa
Aunt Yoyita	Conchita Brando
Iku	Suset Pérez Malberti

Returning to the town of Guantanamera after a fifty year absence, Yoyita finds herself reunited with her former lover, Candido.

ALIVE AND KICKING

(FIRST LOOK PICTURES) a.k.a. *Indian Summer*; Producer, Martin Pope; Director, Nancy Meckler; Screenplay, Martin Sherman; Photography, Chris Seager; Designer, Cecelia Brereton; Editor, Rodney Holland; Music, Peter Salem; Associate Producer, Lorraine Goodman; Costumes, Monica Howe; Choreographer, Liz Ranken; Casting, Janey Fothergill; a Channel Four Films presentation of an M-P production; British; Dolby Stereo; Color; Rated R; 100 minutes; July release

CAST

Tonio	Jason Flemyng
Jack	Antony Sher
Luna	Dorothy Tutin
Ramon	Anthony Higgins
Tristan	Bill Nighy
Duncan	Philip Voss
Millie	Diane Parish
Vincent	Aiden Waters
Catherine	Natalie Roles
Luke	Freddy Douglas
Howard	Kenneth Tharp
Alan	Michael Keegan-Dolan
Night Nurse	Ruth Lass
Doctor	Linda Bassett
Nurse	Hilary Reynolds
Muggers	Dickon Tolson

and David Ashton, Annabel Leventon (Paris Mourners), David Phelan (Mourner), Dugald Bruce Lockhart (Man at Club), Ian Abbey (T-Shirt Man), John Baxter (Man at Bar), Jason Cheater (Smoking Man), Ellen Van Schuylenburch (Dance Teacher), Marty Cruickshank (Woman at Party), Allan Corduner (Therapist), Richard Hope (Karaoke Doctor), Martin Sherman (Man at Pub), Sakuntala Ramanee (Hospital Doctor), Frank Boyce (Man in Park), Frank Bock, Odette Hughes, Michelle Levi, Ulala Yamamoto, Stephen Houghton (Dancers)

Tonio, a narcissistic dancer, and Jack, a therapist, begin an unlikely romance.

© First Look Pictures

Jason Flemyng, Antony Sher

Anthony Higgins, Jason Flemyng

Jason Flemyng

Dorothy Tutin

Koji Yakusho

SHALL WE DANCE?

(MIRAMAX) Producers, Yasuyoshi Tokuma, Shoji Masui, Yuji Ogata; Executive Producers, Hiroyuki Kato, Seiji Urushido, Shigeru Ohno, Kazuhiro Igarashi, Testuya Ikeda; Director/Screenplay, Masayuki Suo; Photography, Naoki Kayano; Designer, Kyoko Heya; Music, Yoshikazu Suo; Shall We Dance? performed by Taeko Ohnuki; Editor, Junichi Kikuchi; a Daiea, NTV, Hakuhodo and Nippan presentation of an Altamira Pictures production; Japanese, 1996; Dolby Stereo; Super 35 Widescreen; Color; Rated PG; 118 minutes; July release

CAST

Shohei Sugiyama..Koji Yakusho
Mai Kishikawa..Tamiyo Kusakari
Tomio Aoki..Naoto Takenaka
Toyoko Takahashi ....Eriko Watanabe
Toru Miwa ....Akira Emoto
Tokichi Hattori..Yu Tokui
Masahiro Tanaka..Hiromasa Taguchi
Tamako Tamura..Reiko Kusamura
Masako Sugiyama..Hideko Hara
Ryou Kishikawa..Syuichiro Moriyama
Hiromasa Kimoto ....Masahiro Motoki
Natsuko ....Misa Shimizu

An average middle-aged businessman finds his life changing for the better when he signs up for a ballroom dancing class.

© Miramax Films

Tamiyo Kusakari, Koji Yakusho

Reiko Kusamura, Yu Tokui, Hiromasa Taguchi, Koji Yakusho

Hideko Hara, Koji Yakusho

Tamiyo Kusakari

Koji Yakusho, Tamiyo Kusakari, Reiko Kusamura

Billy Connolly, Judi Dench

Judi Dench, Billy Connolly

Billy Connolly, Judi Dench

Judi Dench

MRS. BROWN

(MIRAMAX) Producer, Sarah Curtis; Executive Producers, Douglas Rae, Andrea Calderwood, Rebecca Eaton, Nigel Warren-Green; Director, John Madden; Screenplay, Jeremy Brock; Photography, Richard Greatrex; Designer, Martin Childs; Music, Stephen Warbeck; Costumes, Deirdre Clancy; Editor, Robin Sales; Make Up Designer, Lisa Westcott; Associate Producer, Paul Sarony; Casting, Michelle Guish; a BBC Films and WGBH/Mobil Masterpiece Theatre in association with Irish Screen presentation of an Ecosse Films production; British-Irish; Dolby Stereo; Color; Rated PG; 103 minutes; July release

Billy Connolly, Judi Dench

CAST

Queen Victoria	Judi Dench
John Brown	Billy Connolly
Henry Ponsonby	Geoffrey Palmer
Benjamin Disrael	Antony Sher
Archie Brown	Gerard Butler
Doctor Jenner	Richard Pasco
Bertie, Prince of Wales	David Westhead
Lady Ely	Bridget McConnel
Lady Churchill	Georgie Glen
Lady in Waiting	Catherine O'Donnell
Princess Alexandria	Sara Stewart
Princess Helena	Finty Williams
Princess Louise	Clair Nicolson
Princess Alice	Hattie Ladburty
Prince Alfred	Oliver Kent
Prince Arthur	Alex Menzies
Prince Leopold	Simon McKerrell
Bertie's Valet	Rupert Farley
Mrs. Grant	Elaine Collins
Mr. Grant	Jimmy Chisholm
Lord Stanley	Jason Morell
Assistant Dresser	Rebecca Charles
Mary Ann Disraeli	Cherith Mellor
Speaker of the House	George Hall
Commons Counter	Robin Marchal
Dean of Windsor	Oliver Ford Davies

and Patrick Hannaway, John Ramsay (Journalists), Delia Lindsay (Society Lady), James Vaughan (Sir Charles Dilke), Brendan O'Hea (Barney), Theo Steele (Footman)

Antony Sher, Judi Dench

Still overcome by grief three years after the death of her husband, Queen Victoria places herself in self-exile until Scotsman John Brown coaxes her back into the world. This film received Oscar nominations for actress (Judi Dench) and makeup.

Judi Dench, Billy Connolly

Billy Connolly

OPERATION CONDOR

(DIMENSION) formerly *Armour of God II: Operation Condor*; Producer, Leonard Ho; Executive Producer, Raymond Chow; Director, Jackie Chan; Screenplay, Jackie Chan, Edward Tang; English Dialogue, Maggie Dickie; Photography, Wong Ngok Tai; Art Directors, Oliver Wong, Eddie Ma, Lo Ka Yiu; Music, Stephen Endelman; Editor, Cheung Yiu Chung; Special Effects, Cinefax Workshop Co. Ltd., Unlimited Effects (HK) Ltd.; a Media Asia Distribution presentation 1991; Distributed by Miramax Films; Dolby SDDS Stereo; Technovision; Color; Rated PG-13; 92 minutes; July release

CAST

Jackie (Condor)	Jackie Chan
Ada	Carol Cheng
Elsa	Eva Cobo De Garcia
Momoko	Shoko Ikeda
Adolf	Alfred Brel Sanchez
Tasza	Jonathan Isgar
Amon	Daniel Mintz
Duke Scapio	Bozidar Smiljanic

and Ken Goodman, Gregory Tartaglia, Lyn Percival, Bruce Fontaine, Archer Wayne, Brandon Charles, Low Houi Kang, Peter Klimenko, Christian Perrochaud (Adolf's Guards), Mark King, Bryan Baker (Duke's Guards), Charles Yeomans (Man with Stolen Clothes)

The United Nations sends secret agent Condor to stop a group of international terrorists who have discovered the whereabouts of a fortune in stolen gold that they plan to use for evil means.

Anthony LaPaglia, Rebecca Gibney

Anthony LaPaglia, Gia Carides

Jackie Chan, Carol Cheng

PAPERBACK ROMANCE

(GOLDWYN) Producer, Bob Weis; Director/Screenplay, Ben Lewin; Co-Producer, Judi Levine; Photography, Vince Monton; Editor, Peter Carrodus; Designer, Peta Lawson; Costumes, Anna Borghesi; Music, Paul Grabowsky; Casting, Liz Mulinar Consultants; an Australian Film Finance Corporation in association with Generation Films, Lewin Films and Pandora Cinema presentation; Australian, 1994; Dolby Digital Stereo; Color; Rated R; 89 minutes; August release

CAST

Sophie	Gia Carides
Eddie	Anthony LaPaglia
Gloria	Rebecca Gibney
Yuri	Jacek Koman
Kate	Sioban Tuke
Bruce Wrightman	Lewis Fiander
Anne-Marie LePine	Robyn Nevin
George LePine	Marshall Napier
Myra	Mary-Anne Fahey
Benny	Michael Edward-Stevens
Nicholas	Steady Eddy
Det. Sgt. Scott	Michael Vietch
Det. Tyrone	Russell Fletcher
Sophie's Doctor	Nicholas Bell
Ernst	Kurt Ludescher
Diamond Cutter	Max Bruch
Library Clerk	Lynda Gibson

and David Watson (Professor-type at Party), Kirk Alexander (Celebrant), Paul Karo (Defence Lawyer), Terry Norris (Judge), Alvin Chong (Chinese Doctor), Ernie Grey (Doctor at Wedding), Agnieszka Perepeczko (Woman at Wedding), Carolyn Bock (Hotel Hospitality Lady), Maggie Stevens (Mrs. Wrightman), Cliff Ellen (Airline Porter), Alexandra Lewin (Music Student), Paul Wishart (Courier), Mandy Bowden (Marjorie), Alan Levy (Wrong Man at Party), Geoff Lipton (Taxi Driver), Suzanne Chamberlain (Woman in Hotel Lobby), Petru Gheorghiu (Party Host), Phillipa Lee (Woman at Party), Teresa Blake (Woman on Greek Island), Pandora Finch (Madelaine), Eli Yanay (Man on Greek Island), Karen Davitt (Artist), Tasilimn Emiabata (Artist's Model), Teresa Blake (Catburglar)

Sophie, a romance novelist, is overheard spinning the erotic details of her latest work by Eddie, a jewelry dealer, who finds himself drawn to her sexual tastes.

TROJAN EDDIE

(CASTLE HILL) Producer, Emma Burge; Executive Producers, Rod Stoneman, Alan J. Wands, Kevin Menton, Nigel Warren-Green; Director, Gillies MacKinnon; Screenplay, Billy Roche; Co-Producer, Seamus Byrne; Photography, John deBorman; Designer, Frank Conway; Costumes, Consolata Boyle; Editor, Scott Thomas; Music, John Keane; Casting, Hubbard Casting; a Channel Four Films presentation with the participation of Bord Scannan na hEireann/The Irish Film Board; an Initial Films production in association with Irish Screen; British-Irish, 1996; Dolby Stereo; Color; Not rated; 105 minutes; August release

Richard Harris, Aislin McGuckin

CAST

Trojan Eddie	Stephen Rea
John Power	Richard Harris
Dermot	Stuart Townsend
Kathleen	Aislin McGuckin
Ginger	Brendan Gleeson
Raymie	Sean McGinley
Shirley	Angeline Ball
Carol	Angela O'Driscoll
Betty	Brid Brennan
Patsy McDonagh	Jason Gilroy
Rosy	Maria McDermottroe
Gerry	Sean Lawlor
Lady Cash	Britta Smith
Matt	Pat Laffan
Reg	Jimmy Keogh
Eddie's Mother	Gladys Sheehan
Arthur	Noel Donovan

and Aoife MacEoin (Landlady), Pecker Dunne (Traveller), Linda Quinn (Travelling Woman), Dolores Keane (Red-Haired Traveller), Orla Charlton (Young Woman), Billy Roche (Man), Des Cave (Priest), Michael Collins (Second Traveller), Aisling O'Flanagan (Daughter #1—Jenny), Roisin O'Flanagan (Daughter #2—Rebecca), Eugene O'Brien (Lady Cash's Son), Charlotte Bradley (Farmer's Wife)

Eddie, just released from prison, sets up a business selling items from the back of a van with partner Dermot, the son of the head of a band of Gaelic gypsies who covets the same woman as Dermot.

© Castle Hill Productions

Stephen Rea

Dominique Valadié, Anouk Grinberg

MON HOMME

(ARTIFICIAL EYE) Producer, Alain Sarde; Director/Screenplay, Bertrand Blier; Photography, Pierre Lhomme; Set Designer, Willy Holt, Georges Glon; Editor, Claudine Merlin; Costumes, Christian Gasc; Music, Barry White, Henryk Mikolaji Gorecki; Casting, Gérard Moulévrier; Produced by Les Films Alain Sarde—Plateau A—Studio Images 2, with the participation of Canal+; French, 1996; Dolby Digital Stereo; Panavision; Color; Not rated; 95 minutes; August release

CAST

Marie	Anouk Grinberg
Jeannot	Gérard Lanvin
Sanguine	Valéria Bruni Tedeschi
Jean-François	Olivier Martinez
Bérangère	Sabine Azéma
Gilberte	Dominique Valadié
First Client	Mathieu Kassovitz
Second Client	Jacques François
Third Client	Michel Galabru
Mélissa	Dominique Lollia
Personnel Director	Bernard Fresson
Inspecteur Marvier	Bernard Le Coq
Monsieur Claude	Jean-Pierre Léaud

Marie, a good-hearted prostitute, takes in Jeannot, a homeless man, who becomes her lover and her pimp.

© Artificial Eye Film Company Inc.

THE FULL MONTY

(FOX SEARCHLIGHT) Producer, Uberto Pasolini; Director, Peter Cattaneo; Screenplay, Simon Beaufoy; Photography, John de Borman; Designer, Max Gottlieb; Costumes, Jill Taylor; Co-Producers, Polly Leys, Paul Bucknor; Associate Producer, Lesley Stewart; Music, Anne Dudley; Choreographer, Suzanne Grand; Casting, Susie Figgis; a Redwave Films production; British; Dolby Stereo; Metrocolour London; Rated R; 95 minutes; August release

William Snape, Robert Carlyle

CAST

Gaz	Robert Carlyle
Gerald	Tom Wilkinson
Dave	Mark Addy
Jean	Lesley Sharp
Mandy	Emily Woof
Lomper	Steve Huison
Horse	Paul Barber
Guy	Hugo Speer
Linda	Deirdre Costello
Reg	Bruce Jones
Nathan	William Snape
Barry	Paul Butterworth
Alan	Dave Hill
Terry	Andrew Livingstone
Sharon	Vinny Dhillon
Bee	Kate Layden
Sheryl	Joanna Swain
Louise	Diane Lane
Dole Clerk	Kate Rutter
Lomper's Mum	June Broughton
Police Inspector	Glenn Cunningham
Duty Sergeant	Chris Brailsford
Policeman	Steve Garti
Job Club Manager	Malcolm Pitt
Director	Dennis Blanch
Social Worker	Daryl Fishwick
Repossession Man	David Lonsdale
Horse's Mum	Muriel Hunt
Beryl	Fiona Watts
Horse's Sisters	Theresa Maduemezia, Fiona Nelson
Brass Band	The British Steel Stocksbridge Band

Robert Carlyle

A group of men, unable to find work since the closing of their steelmill, hit upon the outrageous idea of earning money by starting a striptease act. 1997 Academy Award winner for Best Original Musical or Comedy Score. This film received additional Oscar nominations for picture, director, and screenplay.

© Twentieth Century Fox

Paul Barber

Hugo Speer

Tom Wilkinson, Hugo Speer, Paul Barber, Robert Carlyle

Tom Wilkinson, William Snape, Robert Carlyle, Steve Huison, Hugo Speer, Paul Barber, Mark Addy

William Snape, Mark Addy, Robert Carlyle, Steve Huison, Tom Wilkinson

Mark Benton, Lynda Steadman

Katrin Cartlidge, Joe Tucker

Lynda Steadman, Katrin Cartlidge

CAREER GIRLS

(OCTOBER) Producer, Simon Channing-Williams; Director/Screenplay, Mike Leigh; Photography, Dick Pope; Music, Marianne Jean-Baptiste, Tony Remy; Editor, Robin Sales; Designer, Eve Stewart; a Channel Four Films presentation of a Thin Man production; British; Dolby Stereo; Color; Rated R: 87 minutes; August release

Katrin Cartlidge

CAST

Hannah ....Katrin Cartlidge
Annie ....Lynda Steadman
Claire ....Kate Byers
Ricky ....Mark Benton
Mr. Evans ....Andy Serkis
Adrian ....Joe Tucker
Ricky's Nan ....Margo Stanley
Lecturer..Michael Healy

Annie and Hannah, who have not seen each other in the six years since they attended University, reunite for a weekend together, one that results in a re-evaluation of their friendship.

Katrin Cartlidge, Lynda Steadman

LOVE SERENADE

(MIRAMAX) Producer, Jan Chapman; Director/Screenplay, Shirley Barrett; Photography, Mandy Walker; Designer, Steven Jones-Eveans; Costumes, Anna Borghesi; Editor, Denise Haratzis; Casting, Alison Barrett; Presented in association with Australian Film Finance Corporation; Australian, 1996; Dolby Stereo; Super 35 Widescreen; Color; Rated R; 101 minutes; August release

CAST

Dimity Hurley	Miranda Otto
Vicki-Ann Hurley	Rebecca Frith
Ken Sherry	George Shevtsov
Albert Lee	John Alansu
Deborah	Jessica Napier
Curler Victim	Jill McWilliam
Boy on Ride	Ryan Jackson
Beautiful Baby	Sabrina Norris

In a small Australian town a pair of sisters, both of whom feel that life is passing them by, set their sights on a newly arrived disc jockey, causing a rift between them.

© Miramax Films

Max von Sydow, Ernst Jacobi

FIRE

(ZEITGEIST) Producers, Bobby Bedi, Deepa Mehta; Executive Producers, Suresh Bhalla, David Hamilton; Director/Screenplay, Deepa Mehta; Photography, Giles Nuttgens; Editor, Barry Farrell; Designer, Aradhana Seth; Music, A.R. Rahman; Line Producer, Anne Masson; Canadian-Indian, 1996; Ultra-Stereo; Color; Not rated; 104 minutes; August release

CAST

Radha	Shabana Azmi
Sita	Nandita Das
Ashok	Kulbushan Kharbanda
Jatin	Jaaved Jaaferi
Mundu	Ranjit Chowdhry
Biji	Kushal Rekhi

Radha, an obedient New Delhi housewife, finds solace from her loveless marriage when her brother-in-law's new wife, Sita becomes part of the household.

Rebecca Frith, Miranda Otto

HAMSUN

(FIRST RUN FEATURES) Producer, Erik Crone; Director/Photography, Jan Troell; Screenplay, Per Olov Enquist; Based on the book *Processen mod Hamsun* by Thorkild Hansen; Editors, Ghita Beckendorff, Jan Troell; Music, Arvo Part, Johann Strauss, Richard Wagner; Swedish-Danish-Norwegian-German, 1996; Color; Not rated; 160 minutes; August release

CAST

Knut Hamsun	Max von Sydow
Marie Hamsun	Ghita Nørby
Ellinor Hamsun	Anette Hoff
Cecilia Hamsun	Asa Söderling
Arild Hamsun	Gard B. Eidsvold
Tore Hamsun	Eindride Eidsvold
Vidkun Quisling	Sverre Anker Ousdal
Adolf Hitler	Ernst Jacobi
Psychiatrist	Erik Hivju

The true story of how Noble Prize-winning Norwegian novelist Knut Hamsun fell from his position of fame and power after blindly supporting the Nazi cause during World War II.

© First Run Features

Shabana Azmi, Ranjit Chowdhry

235

THE DISAPPEARANCE OF GARCIA LORCA

(TRIUMPH) formerly *Death in Granada*; Producer, Marcos Zurinaga, Enrique Cerezo; Executive Producers, Moctesuma Esparza, Robert Katz; Director, Marcos Zurinaga; Screenplay, Marcos Zurinaga, Juan Antonio Ramos, Neil Cohen; Based on the books *The Assassination of Federico Garcia Lorca* and *Federico Garcia Lorca: A Life* by Ian Gibson; Photography, Juan Ruiz Anchia; Editor, Carole Kravetz; Designer, Gil Parrondo; Costumes, Leon Revuelta; Associate Producers, Carolyn Caldera, Palmy Carballido; a Miramar Films-Esparza/Katz co-production with Enrique Cerezo, P.C.; Spanish-Puerto Rican-U.S.; Dolby Stereo; Panavision; Color; Rated R; 114 minutes; September release

CAST

Federico Garcia Lorca	Andy Garcia
Ricardo	Esai Morales
Lozano	Edward James Olmos
Colonel Aguirre	Jeroen Krabbe
Taxi	Giancarlo Giannini
Centeno	Miguel Ferrer
Maria Eugenia	Marcela Walerstein
Vicente Fernandez	Eusebio Lazaro
Nacha Montero	Marina Saura
Mercedes	Teresa Jose Berganza
Clotilde	Azucena De La Fuente
Gabino	Emilio Munoz

and Naim Thomas (Ricardo—14 years old), Gonzalo Penche (Jorge Aguirre), Alicia Borrachero (Lydia), Jose Coronado (Nestor Gonzalez), Ivonne Coll (Angelina Gonzalez), Miriam Tubert (Gonzalez's Mother), Jill Ramez (Carlota), Willie Marquez (Lorca's Father), Carmen Zapata (Lorca's Mother), Palmy Carballido (Concha Garcia Lorca), Simon Andreu (General Velez), Lara Dominguez (Lydia—11 years old), Ellea Ratier (Maria Eugenia—11 years old), Blaki (Aguirre's Servant), Perico Duran (Concierge), Concha Gomez Conde (Concierge's Wife), Gelian Cotto (Ricardo's Daughter), George Lian Cotto (Ricardo's Son), Jesus Daniel, Luis Gutierrez, Freddie De Arce, John Garcia (Thugs)

Ricardo, a journalist settled in San Juan, decides to investigate the mysterious events around the murder of his idol, poet Federico Garcia Lorca.

Mathieu Kassovitz, Anouk Grinberg

Andy Garcia

A SELF MADE HERO

(STRAND) Producer, Patrick Godeau; Director, Jacques Audiard; Screenplay, Alain Le Henry, Jacques Audiard; Based on the novel by Jean-François Deniau; Photography, Jean-Marc Fabre; Designer, Michel Vandestien; Costumes, Caroline De Vivaise; Editor, Juliette Welfling; Music, Alexandre Desplat; Presented in association with Alicelo - Lumiere - France 3 Cinema - M6 Films - Initial Groupe co-production with Cofimage 7 - Studio Images 2 - Canal+ - The Centre National de la Cinematographie and the support of Procirep; French; Dolby Stereo; Color; Not rated; 105 minutes; September release

CAST

Albert Dehousse	Mathieu Kassovitz
Servane	Anouk Grinberg
Yvette	Sandrine Kiberlain
Dionnet	Albert Dupontel
Older Albert	Jean-Louis Trintignant
Madame Louvier/Madame Revuz/The Général's Wife	Nadia Barentin
Ernst	Bernard Bloch
Louvier	François Chattot
Caron	Philippe Duclos
Man "English Girls"	Armand de Baudry D'Asson
Nervoix	Wilfred Benaiche
Monsieur Jo	François Berleand
Leguen	Philippe Berodot

and Gilles Del Frate (The Partisan), Stéfan Elbaum, Christophe Kourotchkine ("Little Versailles" Men), Marc Ernotte (De Vaincourt), Jérôme Floch (Etienne), Isabelle Gruault (Lutétia Young Woman), Donatien Guillot (Knickerbocker), Philippe Harel (Information Officer), Philippe Lehembre (Maître Becquard), François Levantal (Delavelle), Patrick Ligardes (Malbert), Clotilde Mollet (Odette), Philippe Mahon (The Général), Yann Pradal (FF1 1), Bruno Putzulu (Meyer), Georges Siatidis (Bauchamps), Laurent Vacher (Maldoror Man), Yves Verhoeven (Boutin), David Fernandes (Albert, child), Xavier Arcache (Jean Caron, child), Eléonore Godeau (Little Girl at Kiosk), Thomas Vindevogel (Lout)

Albert Dehousse, a life-long liar, creates a past for himself as a member of the French Resistance during World War II.

DIFFERENT FOR GIRLS

(FIRST LOOK PICTURES) Producer, John Chapman; Executive Producers, George Faber, Laura Gregory; Director, Richard Spence; Screenplay, Tony Marchant; Line Producer, Barney Reisz; Photography, Sean Van Hales; Designer, Grenville Horner; Editor, David Gamble; Music, Stephen Warbeck; Costumes, Susannah Buxton; Make-Up Designer, Fae Hammond; a BBC Films in association with CiBy Sales Limited and Maurice Marciano/Great Guns presentation of an X Pictures Film; British; Dolby Stereo; Color; Rated R; 92 minutes; September release

Rupert Graves, Steven Mackintosh

CAST

Paul Prentice ....Rupert Graves
Kim Foyle...Steven Mackintosh
Pamela...Miriam Margolyes
Jean...Saskia Reeves
Alison..Charlotte Coleman
Neil ....Neil Dudgeon
Angela ....Nisha K. Nayar
Defense Solicitor ....Lia Williams
Recovery Agent..Ian Dury
DS Cole...Robert Pugh
Taxi Driver ....Philip Davis
PC Ken...Rick Warden
PC Alan ....Kevin Allen
Sergeant Harry ....Gerard Horan
Prosecuting Solicitor...Edward Tudor-Pole
Mike Rendell...Adrian Rawlins
Barry Stapleton ....Peter-Hugo Daly
Biker Jim ....Shend
and Llewella Gideon (Receptionist), Charles De'Ath (Young Man at Gig), Robert Demeger (Magistrate), Malcolm Shields (Soldier), Graham Fellows (Dispatch Manager), Ruth Sheen (Nosey Woman), Christie Jennings (Waitress), Stephen Walker (Karl Foyle), Blake Ritson (Young Prentice), James D. White (Finer), Colin Ridgewell (Shrimp), Jamie Leyser (Matthew Payne)

Rupert Graves, Steven Mackintosh

Paul Prentice, an aging London bike messenger, meets up with Kim Foyle who, prior to her sex change operation, had been Paul's taunted schoolmate, Karl.

Rupert Graves

Nisha K. Nayar, Rupert Graves

INTIMATE RELATIONS

(FOX SEARCHLIGHT) Producers, Angela Hart, Lisa Hope, Jon Slan; Executive Producer, Gareth Jones; Director/Screenplay, Philip Goodhew; Line Producers, Simon Hardy, Simon Scotland; Photography, Andrés Garréton; Designer, Caroline Greville-Morris; Music, Lawrence Shragge; Editor, Pia Di Ciaula; Casting, Susan Forrest, Maximilian Boxer; a Handmade Films presentation of a Boxer Films and Paragon Entertainment Corporation production; British-Canadian, 1996; Dolby Stereo; Color; Rated R; 102 minutes; September release

Rupert Graves, Julie Walters

CAST

Marjorie Beasley	Julie Walters
Harold Guppy	Rupert Graves
Stanley Beasley	Matthew Walker
Joyce Beasley	Laura Sadler
Deirdre	Holly Aird
Maurice Guppy	Les Dennis
Iris Guppy	Elizabeth McKechnie
George	James Aidan
Mr. Pugh	Michael Bertenshaw
Mrs. Fox-Davies	Judy Clifton
Deirdre's Baby	Christopher Cook
Pauline	Candace Hallinan

and Charles Hart (Hotel Receptionist), George Hart (Car Vendor), Amanda Holden (Pamela), Nicholas Hoult (Bobby), Annie Keller (Jean), Elsie Kelly (Enid), Max (Princess Margaret), Gary Meredith (Mr. Jarvis), Sarah-Jane McKechnie (Mrs. Latimer), Lucy Rivers (Valerie), Sonya Sadler (Mrs. Clitherow), Leanne Summers (Girl at Swimming Pool)

In a small town in 1954 England, Marjorie Beasley, a seemingly content housewife in her early fifties, makes it her goal to seduce the younger man who has moved into her family's home as a lodger.

© Twentieth Century Fox

Julie Walters, Rupert Graves

Julie Walters, Rupert Graves, Laura Sadler

CAPITAINE CONAN

Philippe Torreton

(KINO) Producers, Alain Sarde, Frederic Bourboulon; Director, Bertrand Tavernier; Screenplay, Bertrand Tavernier, Jean Cosmos; Based on the novel by Roger Vercel; Photography, Alain Choquart; Art Director, Guy-Claude Francois; Editors, Luce Grunenwaldt, Laure Blancherie, Khadicha Bariha-Simsolo; Costumes, Jacqueline Moreau, Agnes Evein; Music, Oswald D'Andrea; Produced by Les Films Alain Sarde/Little Bear Films/TF1 Films Production, with the participation of Canal+ and Studio Images 2; French, 1996;Widescreen; Color; Not rated; 132 minutes; September release

CAST

Conan	Philippe Torreton
Norbert	Samuel Le Bihan
De Scève	Bernard Le Coq
Beuillard	Laurent Schilling
Rouzic	Jean-Yves Roan
Grenais	Phillipe Helies
Caboulet	Tonio Descanville
Corporal Armurier	Eric Savin
Mahut	Olivier Loustau
Lethore	Jean-Marie Juan
Madeline Erlane	Catherine Rich
Commandant Bouvier	Francois Berleand
General Pitard de Lauzier	Claude Rich

and Andre Falcon (Colonel Voirin), Claude Brosset (Pere Dubreuil), Crina Muresan (Ilyana), Cecile Vassort (Georgette), Francois Levantal (Forgeol), Pierre Val (Jean Erlane), Roger Knobelspiess (Major Cuypene), Frederic Pierrot (Train Officer), Jean-Claude Calon (Officer Greffier Loisy)

Following World War I, Capitaine Conan and his troops are ordered to stay behind in the Balkans to act as border patrol, an assignment that leads to the arrest of two of the soldiers in connection to the murder of two women.

© Kino International

Alice Houri

Gregoire Colin

NENETTE AND BONI

(STRAND) Producer, Georges Benayoun; Executive Producer, Francoise Guglielmi; Director, Claire Denis; Screenplay, Jean-Pol Fargeau, Claire Denis; Photography, Agnes Godard; Set Designer, Arnaud de Moleron; Costumes, Elisabeth Tavernier; Editor, Yann Dedet; Music, Tindersticks; French, 1996; Dolby Stereo; Color; Not rated; 103 minutes; October release

CAST

Boni	Gregoire Colin
Nenette	Alice Houri
The Baker Woman	Valeria Bruni-Tedeschi
The Baker	Vincent Gallo
Mr. Luminaire	Jacques Nolot
The Uncle	Gerard Meylan
The Gynecologist	Alex Descas
The Wise Woman	Jamila Farah

and Sebastien Pons, Mounir Aissa, Christophe Carmona, Djellali El'Ouzeri, Malek Sultan (Boni's Friends)

Boni, a lonely young man who works as a pizza maker, finds his life disrupted by the arrival of his pregnant fifteen-year-old sister Nenette.

© Strand Releasing

A LIFE LESS ORDINARY

Cameron Diaz, Ewan McGregor

(20TH CENTURY FOX) Producer, Andrew MacDonald; Director, Danny Boyle; Screenplay, John Hodge; Photography, Brian Tufano; Designer, Kave Quinn; Editor, Masahiro Hirakubo; Costumes, Rachael Fleming; Music Supervisor, Randall Poster; Line Producer, Margaret Hilliard; Choreographer, Adam Shankman; Casting, Donna Isaacson; Music, David Arnold; a Figment Film, developed and supported by Channel 4 Films; British; Dolby Digital Stereo; Super 35 Widescreen; Deluxe color; Rated R; 103 minutes; October release

CAST

Robert	Ewan McGregor
Celine	Cameron Diaz
O'Reilly	Holly Hunter
Jackson	Delroy Lindo
Mr. Naville	Ian Holm
Mayhew	Ian McNeice
Elliot	Stanley Tucci
Al	Tony Shalhoub
Gabriel	Dan Hedaya
Ted	Frank Kanig
Frank	Mel Winkler
Ms. Gesteten	Anne Cullimore Decker
Lily	K.K. Dodds
Walt	Christopher Gorham
Tod	Maury Chaykin
Hiker	Timothy Olyphant
Karaoke Cowboy	Robert Kellogg
Felix	David Stifel
Attendant	Duane Stephens
Cashier	Jayceen Craven
Bank Tellers	Crystal Martinez, Kitty Brunson
Customer	Jan Hanks
Bank Daughter	Mary-Cristina Schaub
Client	Chuck Gowdy
Celine's Mom	Judith Ivey
Secretary	Toni Lynn Byrd

Bored and beautiful Celine is delighted when Robert, one of her father's disgruntled employees, decides to kidnap her and hold her for ransom.

© Twentieth Century Fox

Delroy Lindo, Holly Hunter

Ewan Mc Gregor, Cameron Diaz

Cameron Diaz

I LOVE YOU, I LOVE YOU NOT

(AVALANCHE) Producers, Joe Caracciolo Jr., John Fiedler, Mark Tarlov; Executive Producers, Cameron McCracken, Bob Weinstein, Harvey Weinstein; Co-Producer, Frank Henschke, Pierre Novat; Director, Billy Hopkins; Screenplay Wendy Kesselman; Photography, Maryse Alberti; Designers, Bill Barclay, Gudrun Roscher; Editors, Paul Karasick, Jim Clark; Costumes, Sabine Boebbis, Candice Donnelly; a Polar Enterainment/Die Hauskunst & Romb/Chrysalis Films Intl/Canal+/Filmstifung North Phine Westphalia production; French-German-British-U.S. 1996; Color; Not rated; 89 minutes; October release

CAST

Daisy	Claire Danes
Nana	Jeanne Moreau
Ethan Wells	Jude Law
Mr. Gilman	Jerry Tanklow
Jane	Carrie Slaza
Chris	Josiah A. Mayo
Jessica	Emily Burkes-Nossiter
Hope	Natasha Wolff
Tony	James Van Der Beek
Seth	Kris Park
Alison	Lauren Fox
Angel of Death	Robert Sean Leonard

Daisy, a shy intelligent teenager who feels alienated from her classmates, find sanctuary in her weekend visits to her grandmother, a Holocaust survivor with whom she shares a deep bond.

© CFP Distribution

Jude Law, Claire Danes

Claire Danes, Jeanne Moreau

Danny Gilmore, Jason Cadieux

Danny Gilmore, Jason Cadieux

LILIES

(TURBULENT ARTS) Producers, Anna Stratton, Robin Cass, Arnie Gelbart; Director, John Greyson; Screenplay, Michel Marc Bouchard; Photography, Daniel Jobin; Designer, Sandra Kybartas; Costumes, Linda Muir; Editor, Andre Corriveau; Music, Mychael Danna; a Triptych Media Inc./Galafilm Inc. co-production; Canadian, 1996; Color; Not rated; 95 minutes; October release

CAST

The Countess	Brent Carver
The Bishop	Marcel Sabourin
Older Simon	Aubert Pallascio
Simon	Jason Cadieux
Vallier	Danny Gilmore
Young Bilodeau	Matthew Ferguson
Lydie-Anne	Alexander Chapman
The Baroness	Remy Girard
The Baron	Robert Lalonde
Chaplain/Father St. Michael	Ian D. Clark
Timothee	Gary Farmer

The prisoners at a federal penitentiary kidnap a visiting Catholic bishop and force him to watch a reenactment of an event that took place between him and one of the inmates forty years earlier.

© Turbulent Arts

Nicol Williamson, Steve Coogan, Eric Idle

THE WIND IN THE WILLOWS

(COLUMBIA) Producers, John Goldstone, Jake Eberts; Director/Screenplay, Terry Jones; Based on the novel by Kenneth Grahame; Photography, David Tattersall; Designer/Costumes, James Acheson; Music/Songs, John Du Prez, Terry Jones, Andre Jacquemin, Dave Howman; Music, John Du Prez; Editor, Julian Doyle; Make-Up Design, Jan Sewell; Casting, Irene Lamb; Choreographer, Arlene Phillips; Visual Effects, Peter Chiang, Peter Hutchinson; an Allied Filmmakers presentation of a John Goldstone production; British; Color; Rated PG; 83 minutes; October release

CAST

Mole	Steve Coogan
Rat	Eric Idle
Toad	Terry Jones
Chief Weasel	Antony Sher
Badger	Nicol Williamson
Mr. Toad's Lawyer	John Cleese
Judge	Stephen Fry
Engine Driver	Bernard Hill
The Sun	Michael Palin
Car Salesman	Nigel Planer
Jailer's Daughter	Julia Sawalha
Tea-Lady	Victoria Wood
St. John Weasel	Robert Bathurst
Sentry	Don Henderson
Geoffrey Weasel/Mole's Clock	Richard James
Clarence Weasel	Keith Lee Castle
Prosecution Counsel	Roger Ashton-Griffiths
Clerk of the Court	Bernard Padden
Samantha	Sarah Crowden
Justi	Hugo Blick
Policeman	William Lawrance
Guard	Richard Ridings
Detectives	Peter Whitfield, John Levitt
Elderly Gentleman	John Boswall
Booking Clerk	David Hatton
Drunken Weasel	Graham McTavish

The peaceful riverside animals find their land being seized by the Wild Wood weasels who intend to build a factory and slaughterhouse. The novel was previously featured as part of the animated Walt Disney film The Adventures of Ichabod and Mr. Toad (1949).

© Columbia Pictures Industries Inc.

Terry Jones

John Cleese

Eric Idle, Steve Coogan

HAPPY TOGETHER

(KINO) Producer/Director/Screenplay, Wong Kar-Wai; Executive Producer, Chan Ye-Cheng; Photography, Christopher Doyle; Associate Producers, Hiroko Shinohara, T.J. Chung, Christophe Tseng Ching-Chao; Designer, William Chang Suk-Ping; Editors, William Chang Suk-Ping, Wong Ming-Lam; Music, Danny Chung; a Block 2 Pictures Inc. in association with Prenom H Co., Ltd., a Seowoo Film Col. Ltd. presentation of a Jet Tone Production; Hong Kong/Chinese; Dolby Stereo; Color/Black and White; Not rated; 97 minutes; October release

CAST

Lai Yiu-Fai	Tony Leung Chiu-Wai
Ho Po-Wing	Leslie Cheung Kwok-Wing
Chang	Chang Chen

Leslie Cheung, Tony Leung

Believing it will help their floundering relationship, Ho Po-Wing and his lover Lai Yiu-Fai move to Buenos Aires, only to find themselves breaking up.

© Kino International Corp.

Matt Day, Frances O'Connor

Frances O'Connor, Matt Day, Barry Otto

Matt Day, Frances O'Connor

KISS OR KILL

(OCTOBER) Producers, Bill Bennett, Jennifer Bennett; Co-Producer, Corrie Soeterboek; Executive Producers, Mikael Borglund, Gary Hamilton; Director/Screenplay, Bill Bennett; Photography, Malcolm McCulloch; Designer, Andrew Plumer; Editor, Henry Dangar; a Bill Bennett Production in association with the Australian Film Finance Corporation; Australian; Dolby Stereo; Color; Rated R; 93 minutes; November release

CAST

Nikki	Frances O'Connor
Al	Matt Day
Hummer	Chris Haywood
Adler Jones	Barry Otto
Crean	Andrew S. Gilbert
Zipper Doyle	Barry Langrishe
Stan	Max Cullen
Bel	Jennifer Bennett

Nikki and Al, a pair of grifters who make their money by robbing businessmen, are forced to flee when one of the men accidentally dies leaving them with a suitcase containing an incriminating video tape.

© October Films

243

BEAN

Rowan Atkinson, Peter MacNicol

(GRAMERCY) Producers, Peter Bennett-Jones, Eric Fellner, Tim Bevan; Executive Producer, Richard Curtis; Director, Mel Smith; Screenplay, Richard Curtis, Robin Driscoll; Based on the character devised by Rowan Atkinson and Richard Curtis; Co-Producer, Rebecca O'Brien; Photography, Francis Kenny; Designer, Peter Larkin; Editor, Christopher Blunden; Costumes, Hope Hanafin; Music, Howard Goodall; Casting, Ronnie Yeskel, John and Ros Hubbard; a PolyGram Filmed Entertainment presentation of a Working Title production in association with Tiger Aspect Films; British; Dolby Stereo; Technicolor; Rated PG-13; 90 minutes; November release

CAST

Mr. Bean	Rowan Atkinson
David Langley	Peter MacNicol
Alison Langley	Pamela Reed
George Grierson	Harris Yulin
General Newton	Burt Reynolds
Stingo Wheelie	Johnny Galecki
Kevin Langley	Andrew J. Lawrence
Jennifer Langley	Tricia Vessey
Lord Walton	Peter Egan
Chairman	Sir John Mills
Gareth	Peter Capaldi
Delilah	June Brown
Dr. Rosenblum	Peter James
Dr. Cutler	Clive Corner
Dick Journo	Rob Brownstein
Phyllis Quill	Julia Pearlstein
Elmer	Larry Drake
Walter Merchandise	Tom McGowan
Bernice Schimmel	Sandra Oh
Stewardess Nicely	Alison Goldie
Passenger Tucker	Dakin Matthews
Timmy Pewker, Jr.	Scott Charles
Officer Stubbles	Thomas Mills
Mrs. Goodwoman	Ronnie Yeskel
Lieutenant Brutus	Richard Gant

and Chris Ellis (Detective Butler), Priscilla Shanks (Sylvia Grierson), Richard Hicks (Kart Pusherman), Danny Goldring (Security Buck), Gigi Fields (Nurse Desking), Lela Ivey (Nurse Pots), David Doty (Dr. Jacobson), Robert Curtis-Brown (Doctor Frowning), April Grace (Nurse Pans), Perry Anzilotti (Dr. Squeaking), Janni Brenn (Nurse Dyper), Annette Helde (Nurse Gripes)

Rowan Atkinson

Mr. Bean, a bumbling employee of London's National Art Gallery, is sent to America to accompany the masterpiece Whistler's Mother, which is to be exhibited in Los Angeles.

© Gramercy Pictures

Andrew Lawrence, Peter MacNicol, Tricia Vessey,
Pamela Reed, Rowan Atkinson

Peter MacNicol, Rowan Atkinson

BENT

(GOLDWYN) Producers, Michael Solinger, Dixie Linder; Executive Producers, Sarah Radclyffe, Hisami Kuroiwa; Director, Sean Mathias; Screenplay, Martin Sherman, based on his play; Photography, Yorgos Arvanitis; Designer, Stephen Brimson Lewis; Co-Producers, Sean Mathias, Martin Sherman; Editor, Isabel Lorente; Music, Philip Glass; Costumes, Stewart Meachem; Casting, Andy Pryor; a Channel Four Films and Goldwyn Entertainment Company presentation in association with NDF Inc., Ask Kodansha Co. Ltd. and the Arts Council of England; Distributed by MGM Distribution Co.; British; Dolby Stereo; Rank color; Rated NC-17; 105 minutes; November release

Clive Owen, Lothaire Bluteau

CAST

Horst	Lothaire Bluteau
Max	Clive Owen
Rudy	Brian Webber
Uncle Freddie	Ian McKellen
Greta	Mick Jagger
Wolf	Nikolaj Waldau
Stormtrooper	Jude Law
Waiter	Gresby Nash
Half-Woman, Half-Man	Suzanne Bertish
Gestapo Man	David Meyer
SS Captain	Stefan Marling
SS Guards	Richard Laing, Crispian Belfrage
Muttering Woman	Johanna Kirby
Fluff in Park	David Phelan
Officer on Train	Rupert Graves
Guards on Train	David Stark, Charlie Watts
Girl on Train	Holly Davidson
Guard on Road	Rupert Penry Jones
Corporal	Paul Kynman
Captain	Paul Bettany

and Claire Cunningham, Shira Haviv, Filip Van Huffel, Sacha Lee, Ben Maher, Jane Mason (Random Dance Company), Nat (Flame Throwing Man), Packer (Happy Sad Man), Ernesto (Leaping Man), Myer Taub (Rudy's Dresser), Geraldine Sherman, Rachel Weisz (Prostitutes), Mary Davidson, Sadie Frost, Lou Gish, Simon Hammerstein, Johan Johnstone, Chris Karlitz, Mark Misauer, Howard Sacks, Mandy Stone, William Stone, Daisy de Villeneuve, Poppy de Villeneuve, Jane de Villeneuve, Helen Whitehouse, Zed (Max's Friends)

Mick Jagger

Max's promiscuous Berlin nightlife is disrupted when the SS decides to wipe out Germany's gay community, sending Max and his lover Rudy on the run. Ian McKellen, who plays Uncle Rudy, appeared as Max in the original 1979 London production.

© MGM Distribution

Brian Webber, Clive Owen

Clive Owen, Ian McKellen

Alison Elliott, Alex Jennings, Helena Bonham Carter

Charlotte Rampling, Helena Bonham Carter

Linus Roache, Alison Elliott

Alison Elliott, Helena Bonham Carter, Linus Roache

THE WINGS OF THE DOVE

(MIRAMAX) Producers, Stephen Evans, David Parfitt; Executive Producers, Bob Weinstein, Harvey Weinstein, Paul Feldsher; Director, Iain Softley; Screenplay, Hossein Amini; Based on the novel by Henry James; Photography, Eduardo Serra; Designer, John Beard; Editor, Tariq Anwar; Music, Ed Shearmur; Costumes, Sandy Powell; Casting, Michelle Guish; a Renaissance Films production; British; Dolby Digital Stereo; Super 35 Widescreen; Fujicolor; Rated R; 101 minutes; November release

CAST

Kate Croy	Helena Bonham Carter
Merton Densher	Linus Roache
Millie Theale	Alison Elliott
Aunt Maude	Charlotte Rampling
Susan	Elizabeth McGovern
Kate's Father	Michael Gambon
Lord Mark	Alex Jennings
Journalists	Ben Miles, Philip Wright
Butler	Alexander John
Opium Den Lady	Shirley Chantrell
Merton's Party Companion	Diana Kent
Eugenio	Georgio Serafini
Concierge	Rachele Crisafulli

Told she will be disinherited if she continues her relationship with journalist Merton Densher, Kate Croy plots to have Merton romance and wed the fatally ill heiress Millie Theale. This film received Oscar nominations for actress (Helena Bonham Carter), cinematography, costume design, and adapted screenplay.

© Miramax Films

Alison Elliott, Linus Roache, Helena Bonham Carter

Linus Roache, Helena Bonham Carter

Helena Bonham Carter, Linus Roache

Alison Elliott, Linus Roache, Helena Bonham Carter

WELCOME TO SARAJEVO

Stephen Dillane, Woody Harrelson

Marisa Tomei

Emira Nusevic, Stephen Dillane

(MIRAMAX) Producers, Graham Broadbent, Damian Jones; Director, Michael Winterbottom; Screenplay, Frank Cottrell Boyce; Based on the book *Natasha's Story* by Michael Nicholson; Photography, Daf Hobson; Designer, Mark Geraghty; Costumes, Janty Yates; Editor, Trevor Waite; Music, Adrian Johnston; Line Producer, Paul Sarony; Casting, Simone Ireland, Vanessa Pereira; a Channel Four Films presentation of a Dragon Pictures production; British; Dolby Digital Stereo; Super 35 Widescreen; Color; Rated R; 100 minutes; November release

CAST

Michael Henderson	Stephen Dillane
Flynn	Woody Harrelson
Nina	Marisa Tomei
Emira	Emira Nusevic
Jane Carson	Kerry Fox
Risto	Goran Visnjic
Gregg	James Nesbitt
Annie McGee	Emily Lloyd
Jacket	Igor Dzambazov
Mrs. Savic	Gordana Gadzic
Helen Henderson	Juliet Aubrey
Zeljko	Drazen Sivak
Munira	Vesna Orel
Dragan	Davor Janjic
Emira's Uncle	Vladimir Jokanovic
Lucky Strike	Izudina Brutus
Sanja	Labina Mitevska
Alma	Sanja Buric
Altar Boy	Haris Secic
UN Convoy Official	Kerry Shale
Baker	Majda Tusar
Baker's Husband	Miralem Zupcevic
UN V.I.P.	Peter Kelly
Nina Co-Worker	Dijana Bolanca
Zivko	Nino Levi
Road Runner	Berina Salijevic
Christopher Henderson	Frank Dillane
Jane Henderson	Paige Brogan-Smith

and Petar Arsovski (Joey), Viktorija Peceva (Ajsha), Nikolina Kujaca (Bride), Joana Popovska (Bride's Mother), Natali Rajinovska (Bride's Sister), Brankica Jankoska (Hairdresser), Dragan Marinkovic (Chetnik Leader), Senad Basic (Black Marketeer Leader), Ines Hadzovic (Hospital Girl), Cesir Adi (Child on Bus), Milan Plistina (Beauty Contest Compere), Ines Fancovic (Woman Shouting at Bread Queue), Haris Sarvan, Pejdah Dzevad (Black Marketeers)

British news correspondent Michael Henderson is sent to cover the 1992 siege in Sarajevo where he hopes to bring attention to the plight of the orphans left behind by the carnage.

Stephen Dillane, Dragan Marinkovic

THE SWEET HEREAFTER

(FINE LINE FEATURES) Producers, Atom Egoyan, Camelia Frieberg; Director/Screenplay, Atom Egoyan; Based on the novel by Russell Banks; Executive Producers, Robert Lantos, Andras Hamori; Photography, Paul Sarossy; Designer, Phillip Barker; Costumes, Beth Pasternak; Editor, Susan Shipton; Music, Mychael Danna; Associate Producer, David Webb; Line Producer, Sandra Cunningham; an Alliance Communications presentation of an Ego Film Arts production; Canadian; Dolby Digital Stereo; Panavision; Eastman color; Rated R; 110 minutes; November release

Earl Pastko, Arsinée Khanjian

CAST

Mitchell Stephens	Ian Holm
Nicole Burnell	Sarah Polley
Billy Ansell	Bruce Greenwood
Sam Burnell	Tom McCamus
Dolores Driscoll	Gabrielle Rose
Wanda Otto	Arsinée Khanjian
Risa Walker	Alberta Watson
Wendell Walker	Maury Chaykin
Mary Burnell	Brooke Johnson
Hartley Otto	Earl Pastko
Abbott Driscoll	David Hemblen
Alison	Stephanie Morgenstern
Zoe Stephens	Caerthan Banks
Stewardess	Kirsten Kieferle
Bear	Simon Baker
Jessica	Sarah Rosen Fruitman
Mason	Marc Donato
Sea	Devon Finn
Klara	Fides Krucker
Young Zoe	Magdalena Sokoloski
Young Mitchell	James D. Watts
Jenny	Allegra Denton
Schwartz	Peter Donaldson
Dr. Robeson	Russell Banks

Attorney Mitchell Stephens arrives in a remote town in British Columbia to investigate the details behind a devestating school bus accident in which nearly two dozen children were killed. The film received Oscar nominations for director and adapted screenplay.

© Fine Line Features

Ian Holm

Sarah Rosen Fruitman, Sarah Polley, Marc Donato

Alberta Watson, Bruce Greenwood

THE TANGO LESSON

(SONY PICTURES CLASSICS) Producer, Christopher Sheppard; Co-Producers, Oscar Kramer, Christian Keller Sarmiento (Argentina), Simona Benzakein (France); Director/Screenplay/Music, Sally Potter; Photography, Robby Müller; Designer, Carlos Conti; Costumes, Paul Minter; Editor, Herve Schneid; Choreographer, Pablo Veron; Casting, Irene Lamb; an Adventure Pictures presentation; Argentinian-French; Dolby Digital Stereo; Black and white/color; Rated PG; 101 minutes; November release

Sally Potter, Pablo Veron

CAST

Sally	Sally Potter
Pablo	Pablo Veron
Red Model	Morgane Maugran
Yellow Model	Geraldine Maillet
Blue Model	Katernia Mechera
Fashion Designer	David Toole
Photographer	George Yiasoumi
Pablo's Partner	Carolina Iotti
Man at Tea Dance	Howard Lee
Builder	Heathcoat Williams
Waiter	Juan Jose Czalkin
Gustavo	Gustavo Naveira
Fabian	Fabian Salas
Carlos	Carlos Copello
Olga	Olga Besio

and Michele Parent, Claudine Mavros, Monique Couturier (Seamstresses), Matthew Hawkins, Simon Worgan (Bodyguards), Zobeida, Orazio Massaro, Anne Fassio, Guillaume Gallienne, Michel Andre, Flaminio Corcos (Pablo's Friends), Horacio Marassi (Shoe Man), David Derman, Oscar Dante Lorenzo, Omar Vega (Salon Dancers), Cantilo Pena (Hotel Porter), Maria Noel, Fabian Stratas, Gregory Dayton (Movie Executives), Peter Eyre (English Tango Fan), Emmanuelle Tertipis (Woman in Dressing Room), Ruben Orlando Di Napoli (Master of Ceremonies), Tito Haas (Taxi Driver), Alicia Monti (Carlos' Partner), Maria Fernanda Lorences (Woman Opening Door), Luis Sturla, Amanda Beita (Couple Opening Door), Marcos Woinski (Man Opening Door), Eduardo Rojo (Janitor), Oscar Arribas (Man at Synagogue)

A filmmaker, having trouble with her next script, becomes the pupil of an Argentinian tango dancer under the condition that he star in her next film.

Pablo Veron, Carolina Iotti

WILL IT SNOW FOR CHRISTMAS?

(ZEITGEIST) Producer, Humbert Balsan; Director/Screenplay, Sandrine Veysset; Photography, Hélène Louvart; Art Director, Jack Dubus; Editor, Nelly Quettier; Costumes, Nathalie Raoul; a production of Ognon Pictures with the participation of the Centre National de la Cinématographie and Canal+ and the participation of the Caisse Centrale D'Activités Sociales du Personnel des Industries Électrique et Gazière; French, 1996; Dolby Stereo; Color; Not rated; 90 minutes; December release

CAST

Mother	Dominique Reymond
Father	Daniel Duval
Jeanne	Jessica Martinez
Bruno	Alexandre Roger
Pierrot	Xavier Colonna
Marie	Fanny Rochetin
Blandine	Flavia Chimènes
Paul	Jérémy Chaix
Rémi	Guillaume Mathonnet

and Éric Huyard (Yvan), Leys Cappatti (Bernard), Marcel Guilloux-Delaunay (Schoolteacher), Bouaza Annab, Bouziane Bouakline (Arab Workers), Julie Peysson, Irène Galitzine (Students)

A young mother, living in a stone farmhouse in southern France, tries to fill the lives of her seven illegitimate children with hope and small pleasures

Dominique Reymond

Phyllida Law, Emma Thompson

Emma Thompson

Phyllida Law, Sean Biggerstaff

THE WINTER GUEST

(FINE LINE FEATURES) Producers, Ken Lipper, Edward R. Pressman; Executive Producers, Ruth Vitale, Jonathan Weisgal, Emma Clarke; Co-Producer, Steve Clark-Hall; Director, Alan Rickman; Screenplay, Sharman MacDonald, Alan Rickman; Adapted from the play by Sharman MacDonald; Photography, Seamus McGarvey; Editor, Scott Thomas; Costumes, Joan Bergin; Music, Michael Kamen; Designer, Robin Cameron Don; Visual Effects Supervisor, Steve Rundell; Associate Producer, Alan J. Wands; Casting, Joyce Nettles; a Pressman Lipper production presented in association with Capitol Films, Channel Four Films and the Scottish Arts Council National Lottery Fund; British; Dolby Stereo; Technicolor; Rated R; 110 minutes; December release

CAST

Elspeth	Phyllida Law
Frances	Emma Thompson
Lily	Sheila Reid
Chloe	Sandra Voe
Nita	Arlene Cockburn
Alex	Gary Hollywood
Tom	Sean Biggerstaff
Sam	Douglas Murphy
Minister	Tom Watson
Cafe Proprietor	Jan Shand
Passer-by	Sandy Neilson
Bus Driver	Billy McElhaney
Woman in Tea Shop	Helen Devon
Boy in Tea Shop	Harry Welsh
Young Man in Church	Christian Zanone
Jamie	Ross Lewis

In a seaside Scottish town on the coldest day of winter, Elspeth decides to visit her daughter Frances who is still suffering from the recent loss of her husband. This marked the directorial and screenwriting debut of actor Alan Rickman. Law and Thompson are real-life mother and daughter.

Pierce Brosnan, Michelle Yeoh

Pierce Brosnan, Michelle Yeoh

Desmond Llewelyn, Pierce Brosnan

Pierce Brosnan

Michelle Yeoh, Jonathan Pryce, Götz Otto

Michelle Yeoh

TOMORROW NEVER DIES

(UNITED ARTISTS) Producers, Michael G. Wilson, Barbara Broccoli; Director, Roger Spottiswoode; Screenplay, Bruce Feirstein; Photography, Robert Elswit; Designer, Allan Cameron; Music, David Arnold; Title song by Sheryl Crow and Mitchell Froom/performed by Sheryl Crow; Editors, Dominique Fortin, Michel Arcand; Costumes, Lindy Hemming; Special Effects Supervisor, Chris Corbould; Main Title Designer, Daniel Kleinman; Line Producer, Anthony Waye; Stunts/2nd Unit Director, Vic Armstrong; Casting, Debbie McWilliams; an Albert R. Broccoli's Eon Productions Limited presentation; Distributed by MGM Distribution Co.; Dolby DTS Stereo; Panavision; Deluxe color; Rated PG-13; 119 minutes; December release

CAST

James Bond	Pierce Brosnan
Elliot Carver	Jonathan Pryce
Wai Lin	Michelle Yeoh
Paris Carver	Teri Hatcher
Henry Gupta	Ricky Jay
Stamper	Götz Otto
Wade	Joe Don Baker
Dr. Kaufman	Vincent Schiavelli
M	Judi Dench
Q	Desmond Llewelyn
Moneypenny	Samantha Bond
Robinson	Colin Salmon
Admiral Roebuck	Geoffrey Palmer
Minister of Defence	Julian Fellowes
General Bukharin	Terence Rigby
Professor Inga Bergstrom	Cecilie Thomsen
Tamara Steel	Nina Young
PR Lady	Daphne Deckers
Dr. Dave Greenwalt	Colin Stinton
Master Sergeant 3	Al Matthews
Stealth Boat Captain	Mark Spalding

and HMS Chester: Bruce Alexander (Captain), Anthony Green (Firing Officer); HMS Devonshire: Christopher Bowen (Commander Richard Day), Andrew Hawkins (Lt. Commander Peter Hume), Dominic Shaun (Lt. Commander), Julian Rhind-Tutt (Yeoman), Gerard Butler (Leading Seaman), Adam Barker (Sonar); HMS Bedford: Michael Byrne (Admiral Kelly), Pip Torrens (Captain), Hugh Bonneville (Air Warfare Officer), Jason Watkins (Principal Warfare Officer), Eoin McCarthy (Yeoman), Brendan Coyle (Leading Seaman); and David Ashton (First Sea Lord), William Scott-Masson, Laura Brattan (Staff Officers), Nadia Cameron (Beth Davidson), Liza Ross (Mary Golson), Hugo Napier (Jeff Hobbs), Rolf Saxon (Philip Jones), Vincent Wang (Mig Pilot), Philip Kwok (General Chang)

James Bond tries to stop a power-hungry media billionaire who plots domination of the world's news bureaus by manufacturing his own series of crises. This marks the 18th official installment of the James Bond series from United Artists, the second featuring Brosnan (Bond), Judi Dench (M), and Samantha Bond (Moneypenny) and the sixteenth for Desmond Llewelyn (Q).

© Danjaq, LLC and United Artists Pictures

Pierce Brosnan

Michelle Yeoh

Teri Hatcher

Pierce Brosnan, Michelle Yeoh

AN AMERICAN WEREWOLF IN PARIS

Julie Delpy, Tom Everett Scott

Tom Everett Scott, Julie Delpy

Phil Buckman, Vince Vieluf, Tom Everett Scott

(HOLLYWOOD PICTURES) Producer, Richard Claus; Executive Producer/Director, Anthony Waller; Screenplay, Tim Burns, Tom Stern, Anthony Waller; Based on characters created by John Landis in the film An American Werewolf in London; Co-Producer, Alexander Buchman; Photography, Egon Werdin; Designer, Matthias Kammermeier; Editor, Peter R. Adam; Music, Wilbert Hirsch; Visual Effects, Santa Barbara Studios; Line Producer, Patricia McMahon; Visual Effects Supervisors, John Grower, Bruce Walters; Werewolf Design/Visual Effects Art Director, Peter Lloyd; Costumes, Maria Schicker; Animatronic and Prosthetic Effects Creators, Magicon & Crawley Creatures; Animatronic and Prosthetic Effects Supervisors, Joachim Grueninger, Jez Harris; Casting, Gail Levin; a Richard Claus production; Presented in association with Cometstone Pictures and J&M Entertainment; Distributed by Buena Vista Pictures; British-Dutch-Luxembourgian-U.S.-French; Dolby Digital Stereo; Widescreen; Color; Rated R; 97 minutes; December release

CAST

Andy McDermott ....Tom Everett Scott
Serafine ....Julie Delpy
Brad ....Vince Vieluf
Chris ....Phil Buckman
Amy ....Julie Bowen
Claude ....Pierre Cosso
Dr. Pigot ....Thierry Lhermitte
Inspector Leduc...Tom Novembre
Chief Bonnet ....Maria Machado
Detective Ben Bou ....Ben Salem Bouabdallah
Officer with Flashlight..Serge Basso
Bouncer...Charles Maquignon
First Lycanthrope ....Jochen Schneider
Second Lycanthrope ....Alan McKenna
Third Lycanthrope ....Herve Sogne
Fourth Lycanthrope..Edgar Kohn
Professor Martin ....Jean-Claude Deret
Serafine's Mother ....Isabelle Costantini
Nightclub Visitor...Davis Freeman
Surgeon...Chris Bearne
and Pierre Bodry (Waiter on Train), Peter Riemens (Waiter in Restaurant), Emile Cappachione (Bodybuilder), Serge Hugel (French Car Driver), John Waller (British Car Driver), Anthony Waller (Metro Driver)

Andy, an American college student on vacation in Paris, meets a mysterious woman who happens to be a werewolf. A follow-up to the 1981 Universal release An American Werewolf in London which starred David Naughton and Jenny Agutter.

© Stonewood Communications,/Hollywood Pictures

Tom Everett Scott, Pierre Cosso

MA VIE EN ROSE
(MY LIFE IN PINK)

(SONY PICTURES CLASSICS) Producer, Carole Scotta; Director, Alain Berliner; Screenplay, Chris vander Stappen, Alain Berliner; Photography, Yves Cape; Set Designer, Veronique Melery; Costumes, Karen Muller Serreau; Editor, Sandrine Deegen; Special Effects, Sparx; Make-up, Kaatje Van Damme; Co-Producers, John McGrath, Jacqueline Pierraux; Co-produced by WFE, RTBF (Belgium), Haut et Court, La Sept Cinema, TF1 Film production (France), Freeway Films (U.K.), with the participation of Belgique European, Coproduction Fund and Eurimages, Canal+, Cofimage 8, Avance Surrecettes/CNC, Centre du Cinema et de l'Audiovisual de la Communaute Francaise; Belgian-French-British; Dolby Stereo; Color; Rated R; 88 minutes; December release

Hélène Vincent, Georges Du Fresne, Michèle Laroque

CAST

Ludovic	Georges Du Fresne
Hanna	Michèle Laroque
Pierre	Jean-Philippe Ecoffey
Elisabeth	Hélène Vincent
Jerome	Julien Riviere
Zoe	Cristina Barget
Thom	Gregory Diallo
Jean	Erik Cazals De Fabel
Albert	Daniel Hanssens
Lisette	Laurence Bibot
Jeannot	Jean-Francois Gallotte
Monique	Caroline Baehr
Schoolteacher	Anne Cossens
Chris	Raphaelle Santini
Chid Psychologist	Marie Bunel

Julien Riviere, Georges Du Fresne

Seven-year-old Ludovic sends his family into an uproar when the boy announces that he is one day destined to be a girl.

© Sony Pictures Entertainment Inc.

Georges Du Fresne, Jean-Philippe Ecoffey,
Cristina Barget, Michèle Laroque

Georges Du Fresne

THE BOXER

(UNIVERSAL) Producers, Jim Sheridan, Arthur Lappin; Director, Jim Sheridan; Screenplay, Jim Sheridan, Terry George; Photography, Chris Menges; Designer, Brian Morris; Editor, Gerry Hambling; Music, Gavin Friday, Maurice Seezer; Associate Producer, Nye Heron; Boxing Consultant, Barry McGuigan; Costumes, Joan Bergin; Casting, Nuala Moiselle; a Hell's Kitchen production; Irish; Dolby DTS Stereo; Technicolor; Rated R; 107 minutes; December release

Daniel Day-Lewis, Emily Watson

CAST

Danny Flynn	Daniel Day-Lewis
Maggie	Emily Watson
Joe Hamill	Brian Cox
Ike Weir	Ken Stott
Harry	Gerard McSorley
Patsy	Eleanor Methven
Liam	Ciaran Fitzgerald
Matt Maguire	Kenneth Cranham
Prison Officers	Daragh Donnelly, Frank Coughlan, Sean Kearns
Bride	Lorraine Pilkington
Groom	Niall Shanahan
Priest	Father John Wall
Betty	Maria McDermottro
Prison Governor	Oliver Maguire
Sean	David McBlain
Cake Decorator	Sandra Corbally
Pianist	Tess Sheridan
Joe Hamill's Aide	David Hayman
Singer	Josie Doherty
Agnes' Son	Joseph Rea
Agnes	Joan Sheehy
Peter Mallon	Peter Sheridan
Old Man in Shelter	Larry Byrne
Car Bomb Driver	Joe Gallagher
Boy on Bicycle	Sean Brunett
Bomb Victim	James Hayes
Sean's Helper	Richie Piggott
Soldier on Roof	Jack Waters
Doorman at Gym	Padraic O'Neill
Old Men in Gym	Mark Mulholland, John Cowley, Don Foley
Caretaker of Gym	Tim McDonnell
Boxer on Pads	Philip Sutcliffe
Mrs. Boots	Britta Smith
Bootsy	Gavin Kennedy

Ciaran Fitzgerald, Emily Watson

and Eamon Brown (Referee-1st Fight), Martin Lynch (Journalist), Gavin Brown Liam's Opponent), Noel O'Donovan (Timekeeper-1st Fight), Joe Colgan (Danny's Cornerman), Damien Denny (Eddie Carrol), Nye Heron (Eddi's Trainer), Paul Ronan (Eddie's Corneman), Carol Scanlan, Kate Perry, Andrea Irvine, Joan McGarry, Theresa McComb, Catherine Dunne, Kerrie Duggan, Sharon Dunne, Derbhla McClelland (Wedding Guests), Paul Sheridan, John Sheridan, Pat Mulryan, Peter O'Donoghue, Martin Dunne, Tommy O'Neil (IRA Men), Liam Carney (Mr. Walsh), Veronica Duffy (Mrs. Walsh), Des Braiden (Mr. Orr), Joan Brosnan Walsh (Mrs. Orr), Sean Donaghy (Mickey), Brian Milligan (Ned), Vinny Murphy, Mick Nolan, Berts Folan (Danny's Supporters), Juliet Cronin (Cardgirl-1st Fight), Kirsten Sheridan (Girl with Drinks), Mickey Tohill (Billy Patterson), Ian McElhinney (Reggie Bell), Conor Bradford (TV Announcer), Anna Meegan (Woman at 2nd Fight), Al Morris (Referee —2nd Fight), Ian Thompson (Child at 2nd Fight), Paul Wesley (Danny's Sparring Partner), Michael James Ford (Head Waiter), John Cooke (Toastmaster), Cornelius Carr, Norman Kelly (London Fighters), Gerry Storey (Cornerman), Fred Tiedt (Referee—London Fight), Clayon Stewart (Akim), Jery O'Leary (Timekeeper—London Fight), Jules Kingelesi, Dennis Mika (Akim's Corner), David Heap (Maitre D'), John Hewitt (Ike's Drinking Buddy), Janine McGuinness (Cardgirl—London Fight), Tom Maguire (Policeman at Checkpoint)

Danny Flynn, a former IRA member, released from a fourteen year stint in prison, begins an affair with Maggie, the wife of a currently imprisoned organization member, much to the disapproval of the IRA.

Brian Cox, Emily Watson

Cate Blanchett, Ralph Fiennes

Ralph Fiennes

Cate Blanchett

OSCAR AND LUCINDA

(FOX SEARCHLIGHT) Producers, Robin Dalton, Timothy White; Director, Gillian Armstrong; Screenplay, Laura Jones; Based on the novel by Peter Carey; Photography, Geoffrey Simpson; Designer, Luciana Arrighi; Music, Thomas Newman; Editor, Nicholas Beauman; Associate Producer, Mark Turnbull; Costumes, Janet Patterson; Casting, Alison Barrett, Kathleen Mackie; a Dalton Films production, presented in association with the Australian Film Finance Corporation and the New South Wales Film and Television Office; Australian; Color; Panavision; Rated R; 132 minutes; December release

CAST

Oscar Hopkins	Ralph Fiennes
Lucinda Leplastrier	Cate Blanchett
Reverend Dennis Hasset	Ciaran Hinds
Hugh Stratton	Tom Wilkinson
Mr. Jeffris	Richard Roxburgh
Theophilus	Clive Russell
Percy Smith	Bille Brown
Miriam Chadwick	Josephine Byrnes
Wardley-Fish	Barnaby Kay
Jimmy D'Abbs	Barry Otto
Betty Stratton	Linda Bassett
Narrator	Geoffrey Rush
Young Lucinda	Polly Cheshire
Elizabeth Leplastrier	Gillian Jones
Abel Leplastrier	Robert Menzies
Young Oscar	Adam Hayes
13-year-old Oscar	James Tingey
Mrs. Williams	Matyelok Gibs
Fanny Drabble	Sonia Ritter

and Will Barton, Jonathan Markwood, Nicholas Tennant, Sam Newman, Nicholas Fordham (College Students), Peter Whitford (Mr. Ahearn), Lynette Curran (Mrs. Ahearn), Ron Blanchard (Steamer Captain), Colin Taylor (Frazer), Michelle Doake (Hotel Maid), Karen Vickery, Elspeth MacTavish (Society Gossips) Andrea Moore (Miss Shaddock), Leverne McDonnell (Miss Malcolm), Geoff Morrell (Charley Fig), Christian Manon (Mr. Tomasetti)

Oscar, a somewhat emotionally unbalanced minister with a penchant for picking winning race horses, finds himself joining forces with Lucinda, a wealthy Australian who owns a glass works in Sydney. This film received an Oscar nomination for costume design.

© Twentieth Century Fox

Cate Blanchett, Ralph Fiennes

Julie Epstein, Max Epstein, Willie Epstein in *A Tickle in the Heart*
© Kino International

Johnny Peterson (c) in *Saint Clara*
© Kino International

A TICKLE IN THE HEART (Kino) Producers, Edward Rosenstein, Martin Hagemann, Thomas Kufus; Director, Stefan Schwietert; Based on an idea by Joel Rubin, Rita Ottens; Photography, Robert Richman; Editor, Arpad Bondy; Music, The Epstein Brothers; Produced by Zero Film/Ö Film/Neapel Film; German, 1996; Black and white; Not rated; 84 minutes; January release. Documentary about the Kings of Klezmer, Max, Willie and Julie Epstein, featuring Peter Solokow, Harriet Goldstein Darr, Pat Merola, Harry Kolstein, Joel Rubin.

THE JEW (First Run Features) Producer, Antonio da Cunha Telles; Director, Jom Tob Azulay; Screenplay, Millor Fernandes, Geraldo Carneiro, Gilvan Pereira; Photography, Eduardo Serra; Music, Rui Luis Pereira; Editors, José Manuel Lopes, Pedro Ribeiro, Ruy Guerra; Portuguese-Brazilian, 1995; Color; Not rated; 85 minutes; January release. **CAST:** Felipe Pinheiro (António José da Silva), Dina Sfat (Lourença Coutinho), Mário Viegas (King João V), Edwin Luisi (Alexandre), JoséNeto (Priest)

ANGEL DUST (Northern Arts) Producers, Taro Maki, Kenzo Horikoshi, Eiji Izumi; Director, Sogo Ishii; Screenplay, Yorozu Ikuta, Sogo Ishii; Photography, Norimichi Kasamatsu; Music, Hiroyuki Nagashima; Editors, Hiroshi Matsuo, Sogo Ishii; a Twins Japan Inc./Euro Space production; Japanese, 1994; Dolby Stereo; Color; Not rated; 116 minutes; January release. **CAST:** Kaho Minami (Setsuko Suma), Takeshi Wakamatsu (Rei Aku), Etsushi Toyokawa (Tomoo), Ryoko Takizawa (Yuki Takei)

OUT OF THE PRESENT (Independent) Director, Andrei Ujica; No other credits available; Russian; Color; Not rated; 96 minutes; January release. Documentary using footage from four different space missions to the Mir space station.

SAINT CLARA (Kino) Producers, Marek Rozenbaum, Uri Sabag; Directors/Screenplay, Ari Folman, Ori Sivan; Based on the novel by Pavel Kohout; Original Story, Jelena Machinova; Photography, Valentin Belanogov; Designer, Ariel Glaser; Music, Barry Saharov; Israeli, 1996; Color; Not rated; 85 minutes; January release. **CAST:** Lucy Dubinchik (Clara Chanov), Halil Elohev (Eddie Tikel), Johnny Peterson (Rosy Rosenthal), Maya Mayron (Libby), Israel Damidov (Elvis Chanov), Yigal Naor (Headmaster Tissona), Maya De Fries (Eleanor Galash), Tal Feignboim (Galit Biron), Tal Ben Bina (Tikel's Mother), Menashe Noy (Tikel's Father), Jenia Doudina (Clara's Mother), Ronald Hairlovsky (Clara's Father), Joseph El Dror (Teacher Mounitz), Orly Zilberschatz-Banai (TV Reporter), Ronny Bachar (Vered Rosenthal), Tomer Patlock (Asthma), Divan Sivan (Baby Chanov), Helena Zoubtov (Seismographic Engineer)

RATS IN THE RANKS (Film Australia/Arundel Films) Producers/Directors, Bob Connolly, Robin Anderson; Executive Producer, Chris Oliver; Photography, Bob Connolly; Editors, Ray Thomas, Bob Connolly; Produced in association with the Australian Broadcasting Corporation, Channel Four and La Sept ARTE; Australian; Color; Not rated; 98 minutes; February release. **CAST:** Larry Hand (Himself)

Kaho Minami in *Angel Dust*
© Northern Arts

Larry Hand in *Rats in the Ranks*
© Film Australia

Simon Bossell, Saffron Burrows, Aden Young in *Hotel de Love*
© Live Entertainment

Ulf Friberg, Max von Sydow in *Jerusalem*
© Overseas Filmgroup

HOTEL DE LOVE (LIVE Entertainment) Producers, Michael Lake, David Parker; Director/Screenplay, Craig Rosenberg; Executive Producers, Peter Heller, Alex Waislitz, Heloise Waislitz; Photography, Stephen Windon; Editor, Bill Murphy; Music, Brett Rosenberg; Designer, Simon Dobbin; Costumes, Bruce Finlayson; Casting, Maura Fay & Associates, Lou Mitchell; a Village Roadshow Pictures and Pratt Films production; Australian; Dolby Stereo; Color; Rated R; 95 minutes; February release. **CAST:** Aden Young (Rick Dunne), Saffron Burrows (Melissa Morrison), Simon Bossell (Stephen Dunne), Pippa Grandison (Alison Leigh), Ray Barrett (Jack Dunne), Julia Blake (Edith Dunne), Peter O'Brien (Norman), Belinda McClory (Janet), Caleb Cluff (Bruce), Cassandra Magrath (Suzy), Andrew Bibby (Matt), Alan Hopgood (Ronnie), Raelee Hill (Emma Andrews), Margaret Hoctor (Bridesmaid), Bayard Templin (Melissa's Father), Robert Lowe (Priest), Leo Faust (Brett), Alan Stone (Minister), Sally Lightfoot (Maid), Barbara Burder (Mrs. Fielding), Robert Tuttleby (Mr. Fielding), Craig Gillespie (Young Man), Madonna Munasinha (Young Woman—Eleanor), Michelle Twigden (Young Girl—Nail Biter), Cameron Nugent (Young Man She Kisses), Paul Crossley (Handsome Guy), Bettina Petrone (Handsome Guy's Girlfriend), Stephanie Turner, Andrew Russell (Lovers)

SALUT COUSIN! (Seventh Art) Producer, Jacques Bidou; Director, Merzak Allouache; Screenplay, Merzak Allouache, Caroline Thivel; Photography, Pierre Aim; Editor, Pierre Abela; Music, Safy Boutella; French-Algerian, 1996; Color; Not rated; 102 minutes; February release. **CAST:** Gad Elmaleh (Alilo), Mess Hattou (Mok), Magaly Berdy (Fatoumata), Ann Gisel Glass (Laurence), Jean Benguigui (Maurice), Xavier Maly (Claude), Cheik Doukoure (Voisin Ivoirien), Dalia Renuault (Malika), Fatiha Cheriguene (The Aunt), Malek Kates (Uncle), Mohamed Ourdach (Rachid), Mostefa Djadam (Said), Arno Chevrier (Gonrand), Mosefa Stiti (Father of the Bride), Isaac Sharry (Isaac the Actor)

JERUSALEM (First Look Pictures) Producer, Ingrid Dahlberg; Director/Screenplay, Bille August; Based on the novel by Selma Lagerlöf; Photography, Jörgen Persson; Editor, Janus Billeskov-Jansen; Music, Stefan Nilsson; Designer, Anna Asp; Costumes, Ann-Margret Fyregård; Swedish-Danish, 1996; Dolby Stereo; Color; Not rated; 166 minutes; March release. **CAST:** Ulf Friberg (Ingmar), Maria Bonnevie (Gertrud), Pernilla August (Karin), Reine Brynolfsson (Tim), Lena Endre (Barbro), Jan Mybrand (Gabriel), Sven-Bertil Taube (Hellgum), Björn Granath (Storm), Viveka Seldahl (Stina), Mona Malm (Eva Gunnarsdotter), Hans Alfredson (Mats Hök), Torsten Sjöholm (Gunnar Hok), Max von Sydow (The Vicar), Olympia Dukakis (Mrs. Gordon), Annika Borg (Gunhild), Johan Rabaeus (Eljas), Sven Wollter (Big Ingmar), Mats Dahlbäck (Hans Berger), Anders Nyström (Sven Persson), Douglas Johansson (Lars Tipers), Nils Eklund (The Landlord), Lars Engstrom (The Doctor), Viktor Friberg (The Sawmilworker), Stina von Sydow (The Maid), André Beinö (Young Ingmar), Stina Wargert (Young Gertrud), Amanda Steen (Greta), Jan Sjödin (Gabriel's Father), Eva Stellby (Gabriel's Mother), Michael Nyqvist, Lasse Almebäck (Carpenters), Rolf Jenner, Christer Flodin (Big Men), John Gunnarsson ("Jesus"), Claes Esphagen (Forest Administrator), Fredrik Ohlsson (The Lawyer), Mel Cobb, Sydnee Blake, Katherne Kjellgren (Americans)

TANGO FEROZ (Tara) Producers, Claudio Pustelnik, Katrina Bayonas; Director, Marcelo Piñeyro; Screenplay, Aida Bortnik, Marcelo Piñeyro; Photography, Alfredo F. Mayo; Editor, Miguel Perez; Art Director, Jorge Ferrari; Argentinian; Dolby Stereo; Color; Not rated; 125 minutes; March release. **CAST:** Hector Alterio (Lobo), Imanol Arias (Angel), Cecilia Dopazo (Mariana), Fernan Miras (Tango)

Ann Gisel Glass, Mess Hattou in *Salut Cousin!*
© Seventh Art Releasing

Fernan Miras, Cecilia Dopazo in *Tango Feroz*
© Tara Releasing

Barry Otto, Toni Cotllette, Paul Chubb in *Cosi*
© Miramax Films

Michael Muller, Susanne Birkemose Konsgaard in *Portland*
© Zentropa

A MONGOLIAN TALE (New Yorker) Producer, Ma Fung-kwok, Wellington Fung; Executive Producer, Jin Ji-wu, Du Yong-ling; Director, Xie Fei; Screenplay, Zhang Cheng-zhi, based on his novel *Black Steed*; Photography, Fu Jing-sheng; Editors, Xie Fei, Zhao Xiu-qin; Music, Tengger; a Media Asia Films and Beijing Youth Film Studio presentation; Mongolian, 1995; Color; Not rated; 103 minutes; April release. **CAST:** Tengger (Beiyinpalica), Naranhua (Someyer), Dalarsurong (Nai Nai)

COSI (Miramax) Producers, Richard Brennan, Timothy White; Executive Producer, Phaedon Vass; Director, Mark Joffe; Screenplay, Louis Nowra; Photography, Ellery Ryan; Designer, Chris Kennedy; Editor, Nicholas Beuman; Associate Producer, Lynn Gailey; Casting, Alison Barret; Australian, 1996;; Color; Rated R; 100 minutes; April release. **CAST:** Ben Mendelsohn (Lewis), Toni Collette (Julie), Barry Otto (Roy), Pamela Rabe (Ruth), Jacki Weaver (Cherry), Colin Hay (Zac), David Wenham (Doug), Paul Chubb (Henry), Colin Friels (Errol), Rachel Griffiths (Lucy), Aden Young (Nick), Tony Llewellyn-Jones (Kirner), Kerry Walker (Sandra), Robin Ramsay (Minister for Health), Henry Maas (Bernard Goldman), Raymond Walsh (Air Wrestler), Lawrence Woodward (Electrician), Brian Ellison (Rigger), Tamara Kuldin (Seamstress), Dennis Allard (Carpenter), Toni Moran (Painter), David Anthony (Knucklehead), Skye Wansey (Ms. Spock), Samantha McDeed (Pink Lady)

TO HAVE (OR NOT) (Cinema Parallel) Producers, Francois Cuel, George Benayoun; Director/Screenplay, Laetitia Masson; Photography, Caroline Champetier; Editor, Yann Dedet; Music, Marianne Faithfull, Nick Drake, Cheb Mami; a co-production of CLP-Dacia Films/National Center for Cinematography et Canal+ presented in association with Fabiano Canosa; French; Color; Not rated; 90 minutes; April release. **CAST:** Sandrine Kiberlain (Alice), Arnaud Giovaninetti (Bruno), Roschdy Zem (Night Porter)

Russell Crowe, Bridget Fonda in *Rough Magic*
© Rysher Entertainment

THE SADNESS OF SEX (Tara) Director, Rupert Wainwright; Screenplay, Barry Yourgrau, based on his book; Photography, AndréPienaar; Music, Tomandandy (Tom Hajdu, Andy Milburn); Designer, Franco De Cotiis; Costumes, Mariska M. Nicholson; Editor, Brian Berdan; from Skyvision Partners; Canadian, 1995; Ultra-Stereo; Color; Not rated; 87 minutes; April release. **CAST**: Barry Yourgrau (The Host), Peta Wilson (Girl of His Dreams), Mark Benesh (Son), Richard Bulley (Dad), Dianne Zeust (Mom)

PORTLAND (Zentropa) Producer, Peter Aalbaek Jensen; Director/Screenplay, Niels Arden Oplev; Photography, Henrik Jongdahl; Editor, Henrik Fleischer; Music, Sons of Cain; Danish, 1996; Color; Not rated; 103 minutes; May release. **CAST:** Anders Wodskou Berthelsen (Janus), Michael Muller (Jakob), Ulrich Thomsen (Lasse), Iben Hjejle (Eva), Birthe Neumann (Mother), Baard Owe (Kaj), Edith Thrane (Mrs. Eriksen), Helle Charotte Dolleris (Irene), Susanne Birkemose Konsgaard (Minna), Karsten Geisnæs (Kenneth), Preben Raunsbjerg (Johny), René Johnsen (Peter), Allan Johansen (Hans), Peter Heidemann Jørgensen (Jens), Jens Albinus (Carsten), Hans Henrik Voetmann (Suicide)

ROUGH MAGIC (Goldwyn) Producers, Laurie Parker, Declan Baldwin; Executive Producers, Yves Attal, Jonathan Taplin, Andrew Karsch; Director, Clare Peploe; Screenplay, Robert Mundy, William Brookfield, Clare Peploe; Based upon the novel *Miss Shumway Waves a Wand* by James Hadley Chase; Photography, John J. Campbell; Designer, Waldemar Kalinowski; Editor, Suzanne Fenn; Music, Richard Hartley; Costumes, Richard Hornung; Casting, Elisabeth Leustig; a UGC Images and Recorded Picture Company presentation in association with Martin Scorsese; French-British, 1995; Dolby Stereo; Foto-Kem color; Rated PG-13; 104 minutes; May release. **CAST:** Bridget Fonda (Myra Shumway), Russell Crowe (Alex Ross), Jim Broadbent (Doc Ansell), D.W. Moffett (Cliff Wyatt), Kenneth Mars (Magician), Paul Rodriguez (Diego), Andy Romano (Clayton), Richard Schiff (Wiggins), Euva Anderson (Diego's Wife/Tojola), Michael Ensign (Powerbroker), Gabriel Pingarron (Telegraph Man), Santos Morales, Rene Pereyra (Policemen), Gregory Avellone (Burly Usher), Mark Del Castillo (Clayton's Assistant), Chris Otto (Mechanic), Jose Escandon (Waiter), Ana Cristina Vasquez (Maid), Barkley (Dog)

MONDO (Shadow Distribution/Upstate Films) Producer, Michèle Ray-Gavras; Director/Screenplay, Tony Gatliff; Story, J.M.G. Le Clezio; Photography, Eric Guichard; Editor, Nicole D.V. Berckmans; a production of K.G. Productions with the participation of Canal+ and the Centre National de Cinemtographie; French; Color; Not rated; 80 minutes; May release. **CAST**: Ovidiu Balan (Mondo), Philippe Petit (The Magician), Pierette Fesch (Thi-Chin), Schahla Aalam (The Magician's Companion), Jerry Smith (Dadi), Maurice Maurin (Giordan the Fisherman), Catherine Brun (Church Solist/The Woman in the Elevator)

Llyr Evans, Rhys Ifans in *Twin Town*
© Gramercy Pictures

Tetsuo II: Body Hammer   © Manga Entertainment

TWIN TOWN (Gramercy) Producer, Peter McAleese; Executive Producers, Andrew MacDonald, Danny Boyle; Director, Kevin Allen; Screenplay, Kevin Allen, Paul Durden; Photography, John Mathieson; Designer, Pat Campbell; Music, Mark Thomas; Editor, Oral Norrie Ottey; Costumes, Rachel Fleming; Casting, Nina Gold; a PolyGram Filmed Entertainment presentation of a Figment Films production in association with Agenda; British; Dolby Digital Stereo; Color; Not rated; 99 minutes; May release. **CAST:** Llyr Evans (Julian), Rhys Ifans (Jeremy), Dorien Thomas (Greyo), Dougray Scott (Terry), Biddug Williams (Mrs. Mort), Ronnie Williams (Mr. Mort), Huw Ceredig (Fatty), Rachel Scorgie (Adie), Di Botcher (Jean), Mary Allen (Olive), Paul Durden (Taxi Driver), David Hayman (Dodgy), Kevin Allen (TV Presenter), Brian Hibbard (Dai Rees), Morgan Hopkins (Chip), Sion Tudor Owen (Dewi), William Thomas (Bryn), Denny Durden (Kazoo Player), Jenny Evans (Bonny), Helen Griffith (Lynette), Royston John (Ivor), Julie Davies (Madeline), Gillian Elise (Pat), Steffan Rhodri (Hunky), Nicholas McGaughey (Chunky), Brian Hancock (Drunk in Toilet), Martin Ace (Rocking Sikh), Bhasker Patel (Renjit), Michael Cunningham (Mr. Waldron), Boyd Clack (Vicar), Keith Allen (Emrya), Charlie (Cantona), Snowy (Fergie)

GAMERA: GUARDIAN OF THE UNIVERSE (A.D. Vision) Producer, Yasuyoshi Tokuma; Director, Shusuke Kaneko; Screenplay, Kazunori Ito; Photography, Junichi Tozawa, Kenji Takama; Music, Koh Ohtani; Special Effects, Shinji Higuchi; Japanese, 1995; Dolby Stereo; Color; Not rated; 92 minutes; April release. **CAST:** Tsuyosi Ihara (Yoshinari Yonemori), Akira Onodera (Naoya Kusanagi), Ayako Fujitani (Asagi Kusanagi), Shinobu Nakayama (Mayumi Nagamine)

Gayaos, Gamera in *Gamera: Gaurdian of the Universe*

CHRONICLE OF A DISAPPEARANCE (Intl. Film Circuit) Producer, Elia Suleiman, Dhat Productions; Director/Screenplay, Elia Suleiman; Photography, Marc Andre Batigne; Editor, Anna Ruiz; Music, Alla, Abed Azrie, Leonard Cohen, Natacha Atlas; Casting, Ula Tabari; Palestine, 1996; Dolby Stereo; Color; Not rated; 88 minutes; May release. **CAST:** Elia Suleiman (E.S.), Ula Tabari (Adan), Nazira Suleiman (Mother), Fuad Suleiman (Father), Jamal Daher (Owner of the Holyland Shop)

TETSUO II: BODY HAMMER (Manga) Producers, Fuminori Shishido, Fumio Kurokawa, Nobuo Takeuchi, Hiromi Aihara; Executive Producers, Hiroshi Koizumi, Shinya Tsukamoto; Director/Screenplay/Photography/Art Director/Editor, Shinya Tsukamoto; Music, Chu Ishikawa, Tomoyasu Hotei; Special Make-up & Effects, Takashi Oda, Kan Takahama, Akira Fukaya; Japanese, 1991; Stereo; Color; Not rated; 83 minutes; June release. **CAST:** Tomoroh Taguchi (Tomoo Taniguchi), Nobu Kanaoka (Kana), Shinya Tsukamoto (Guy), Sujin Kim (Taniguchi's Father), Hideaki Tezuka (Punk—Big Brother), Nobuo Asada (Punk—Young Brother), Toraemon Utazawa (Dr. Arita), Min Iwata (Taniguchi's Mother)

DUST OF LIFE (Swift) Producer, Jean Brehat; Executive Producer, Charles Wang; Director, Rachid Bouchareb; Screenplay, Bernard Gesbert, Rachid Bouchareb; Adapted from the book *Fanta Hill* by Duyen Anh; Photography, Youcef Sahraoui; Music, Safy Boutella; Editor, Hélène Ducret; from 3B Productions; French-Algerian, 1994; Color; Widescreen; Not rated; 87 minutes; June release. **CAST:** Daniel Guyant (Son), Gilles Chitlaphone (Bob), Leon Outtrabady (Shrimp), Jéhan Pagès (Little Hai), Eric Nguyen (One-Two), Siu Lin Lam (Greaser), Yann Roussel (Steel Muscles), William Low (Commander)

Gilles Chitlaphone, Daniel Guyant, Leon Outtrabady in
Dust of Life   © Swift

Ghalia Lacroix in *For Ever Mozart*
© New Yorker Films

Yondejunai, Tseded in *Molom*
© Lung Ta-Compagnie Des Films

FOR EVER MOZART (New Yorker) Producers, Ruth Waldburger, Alain Sarde; Executive Producer/Director, Jean-Luc Godard; Photography, Christophe Pollack; Designer, Ivan Niclass; Music, David Darling, Ketil Bjornstad, Ben Harper, Gyorgi Kurtag; Produced by Vega Film/Aventura Films/Périphéria/ECM; Swiss-French, 1996; Color; Not rated; 85 minutes; July release. CAST: Madeleine Assas, Ghalia Lacroix, Bérangère Allaux, Vicky Messica, Frédéric Pierrot.

LOVE'S DEBRIS (In Pictures) Producers, Wieland Schultz-Keil, Jean-Pierre Bailly, Christoph Meyer-Wiel; Director, Werner Schroeter; Based on an idea by Werner Schroeter, Claire Alby; Photography, Elfi Mikesch, Editor, Juliane Lorez; Designer/Costumes, Alberte Bersaqc; an MC4 and Imalyre/VTCOM production; German-French; Dolby Stereo; Color; Not rated; 120 minutes; July release. A documentary on opera, featuring Carole Bouquet, Isabelle Huppert, Anita Cerquetti, Martha Modl, Rita Gorr, Katherine and Kristine Ciesinski, Laurence Dale, Jenny Drivala, Gail Gilmore, Serguei Larin, Trudeliese Schmidt.

BRILLIANT LIES (Castle Hill) Producers, Richard Franklin, Sue Farrelly; Director, Richard Franklin; Screenplay, Peter Fitzpatrick, Richard Franklin; Photography, Geoff Burton; Designer, Tracy Watt; Editor, David Pulbrook; Costumes, Roger Kirk; Casting, Greg Apps; Australian, 1996; Dolby Stereo; Color; Not rated; 93 minutes; July release. CAST: Gia Carides (Susy Connor), Anthony La Paglia (Gary Fitzgerald), Zoe Carides (Katy Connor), Ray Barrett (Brian Connor), Michael Veitch (Paul Connor), Catherine Wilkin (Marion Lee), Neil Melville (Vince Williams), Jennifer Jarman Walker (Ruth Miller), Grant Tilly (Steve Lovett), Beverley Dunn (President), Brad Lindsay (Registrar), Barry Friedlander (Mr. Buxton), Iain Murton (Mr. Hall), Tim Elston (Young Brian), Nathalie Gauchi (Young Katy), Emily-Jane Romig (Young Susy), Daniel Holten (Young Paul), Lisa Aldenhoven (Stephanie Fitzgerald)

CONSPIRATORS OF PLEASURE (Zeitgeist) Producers, Jaromir Kallista, Jan Svankmajer; Co-Producer, P. Assouline, Keith Griffiths; Director/Screenplay/Set Designer, Jan Svankmajer; Photography, Miroslav Spala; Puppet Designer, Eva Svankmajer; Animation, Bedrich Glaser, Martin Kublak; Editor, Marie Zemanova; Czech-British; Dolby Stereo; Color; Not rated; 83 minutes; August release. CAST: Petr Meissel, Anna Wetlinska, Gabriela Wilhelmova, Jiri Labus, Barbora Hrzanova, Pavel Novy

MOLOM: A LEGEND OF MONGOLIA (Norkat Company) Executive Producer, Fabien Quaki; Producer/Director/Screenplay, Marie Jaoul De Poncheville; Music, John McLaughlin, Trilok Gurtu; Photography, Jacques Besse; Editor, Danielle Anezin; Line Producer, Vincent Roget; a Lung Ta production with the participation of Canal+/France 2/Centre National de la Cinematographie/Ministre de la Culture de la Francophonie/Foundation Elf/Foundation Gan pour le Cinema; Mongolian-French; Color; Not rated; 93 minutes; August release. CAST: Tseded (Molom), Yondejunai (Yonden)

LISBON STORY (Fox Lorber) Producers, Ulrich Felsberg, Paulo Branco, Wim Wenders; Executive Producer, Joao Canijo; Director/Screenplay, Wim Wenders; Photography, Liza Rinzler; Designer, ZéBranco; Editors, Peter Przygodda, Anne Schnee; a Road Movies Filmproduktion/Madragoa Films, in collaboration with LISBOA 94 and WDR; Portuguese, 1995; Dolby Stereo; Color; Not rated; 100 minutes; August release. CAST: Rudiger Vogler (Phillip Winter), Patrick Bauchau (Friedrich Monroe), Vasco Sequeira (The Van Driver), Canto E. Castro (The Barber), Viriato JoséDa Silva (The Cobbler), Joao Canijo (The Swindler), Ricardo Colares (Ricardo), Joel Ferreira (Zé), Sofia Bénard De Costa (Sofia), Vera Cunha Rocha (Vera), Elisabete Cunha Rocha (Beta)

PIPPI LONGSTOCKING (Legacy) Producers, Hasmi Giakoumis, Merle-Anne Ridley; Executive Producers, Michael Hirsch, Patrick Loubert, Clive Smith; Co-Executive Producer, David Ferguson; Director, Clive Smith; Art Director, Clive Powsey; Animation Directors, Robin Budd, Bill Giggie; Screenplay, Catharina Stackelberg, Susie Snooks, Ken Sobol, Frank Nissen, Clive Smith; Based on the books by Astrid Lindgren; Character Design, Frank Nissen; Design Supervisors, Paul Riley, Dermot Walshe; Editor, Noda Tsamardos; a co-production of AB Svensk Filmindustri, Idunafilm, Trickompany and Nelvana; Canadian-Swedish-German; Dolby Stereo; Color; Rated G; 75 minutes; August release. VOICE CAST: Melissa Altro (Pippi Longstocking), Catherine O'Hara (Mrs. Prysselius), Carole Pope (The Teacher), Dave Thomas (Thunder-Karlsson), Gordon Pinsent (Captain Longstocking)

Pippi Longstocking   © Idvna/TFC/Nelvana/SF

Lou Castel, Johanna Ter Steege in *The Birth of Love*
© Courtesy Noon Pictures

Thierry Lhermite, Philippe Noiret in *Ripoux Contre Ripoux*
© Interama

AARON'S MAGIC VILLAGE (CFP) Producers, Dora Benousilio, Peter Volkle; Director, Albert Hanan Kaminski; Screenplay, Albert Hanan Kaminski, Jacqueline Galia Benousilio; Adapted from Isaac Bashevis Singer's Stories for Children; Music, Michel Legrand; Songs, Michel Legrand, Sheldon Harnick; an Albert Kaminski Film and a Benousilio-Volkle production; French-German, 1995; Color; Rated G; 80 minutes; September release. **VOICE CAST:** Fyvush Finkel (Narrator), Tommy Michaels (Aaron), Tovah Feldshuh (Aunt Sarah/Zlateth the Goat/The Matchmaker), Ronn Carroll (Uncle Shlemiel), Harry Goz (Gronam Ox), Steve Newman (The Sorcerer), Ivy Austin (The Lantuch), Lee Wilkof, Chip Zien, Lewis J. Stadlen.

THE BIRTH OF LOVE (Noon Pictures) Producers, Christian Paumier, Martine Cassinelli, Cyrille Bragnier, Rossella Ragazzi, Pierre-Alain Schatzmann, Claudia Sontheim; Director, Philippe Garrel; Screenplay, Philippe Garrel, Marc Cholodenko, Muriel Cerf; Photography, Raoul Coutard; Music, John Cale; Editors, Sophie Coussein, Yann Dedet, Nathalie Hubert, Alexandra Strauss; French, 1993; Black and white; Not rated; 94 minutes; September release. **CAST:** Lou Castel (Paul), Jean-Pierre Leaud (Marcus), Johanna Ter Steege (Ulrika), Domonique Reymond (Helene), Marie-Paule Laval (Fanchon)

MY SEX LIFE ... OR HOW I GOT INTO AN ARGUMENT (Zeitgeist) Producers, Pascal Caucheteux, Gregoire Sorlet; Director, Arnaud Desplechin; Screenplay, Arnaud Desplechin, Emmanuel Bourdieu; Photography, Eric Gautier, Stéphane Fontaine, Dominique Perrier-Royer; Designer, Antoine Platteau; Music, Krishna Lévy; Costumes, Claire Gérard-Hirne, Delphine Hayat; Editors, François

Jeanne Balibar, Mathieu Amalric in
My Sex Life , or How I Got into an Argument   © Zeitgeist Films

Gédigier, Laurence Briaud; French, 1996; Not rated; 178 minutes; September release. **CAST:** Mathieu Amalric (Paul), Emmanuelle Devos (Esther), Emmanuel Salinger (Nathan), Marianne Denicourt (Sylvia), Jeanne Balibar (Valérie), Chiara Mastroianni (Patricia), Thibault de Montalembert (Bob), Denis Podalydès (Jean-Jacques), Fabrice Desplechin (Ivan), Michel Vuillermoz (Frédéric Rabier), Hélène Lapiower (Le Mérou), Roland Amstutz (Chernov), Marion Cotillard (Student Ivan), Solenn Jarniou (Pascale), Philippe Duclos (Spiritual Guide), Elisabeth Maby ("Tatie"), Paule Annen (Madame Chernov), Anne-Katerine Normant (Esther's Friend), Vincent Nemeth (Friend), David Gabison (Representative of the Diocese)

RIPOUX CONTRE RIPOUX (MY NEW PARTNER AT THE RACES) (Interama) Producers, Bertrand de la Fontaine, Claude Zidi; Director, Claude Zidi; Screenplay, Simon Michael, Claude Zidi; Photography, Jean-Jacques Tarbes; Editor, Nicole Saunier; Music, Frances Lai; a Films 7 - Orly Films -Sedif - TF1 Films production; French, 1989; Color; Not rated; 107 minutes; September release. **CAST:** Philippe Noiret (René, Thierry Lhermite (Francois), Guy Marchand (Inspector Brisson), Line Renaud (Simone), Grace De Capitani (Natacha), Michel Aumont (Commissaire Bloret), Jean-Pierre Castaldi (Inspector Portal), Jean-Claude Brialy (Le Banquier), Jean Benguigui (Cesarini), Christian Bouillette (Le Bijoutier), Roger Jendly (Albert le Fourgue), Georges Montillier (Le Marchand de Fringues), RenéMorard (Fernand), Alain Mottet (Le Préfet), Bernard Freyd (Guichard), Tadie Huene (Le Marabout), Patricia Karim (La Boutiquiére), Michel Cremades (Le Braquerur)

MOUTH TO MOUTH (BOCA A BOCA) (Miramax) Producers, César Benítez, Joaquín Oristrell, Manuel Gómez Pereira; Director, Manuel Gomez Pereira; Screenplay, Joaquín Oristrell, Juan Luis Iborra, Naomi Wise, Manuel Gómez Pereira; Executive Producers, César Benítez, Fernando Garcillán; Photography, Juan Amorós; Music, Bernardo Bonezzi; Editor, Guillermo Represa; Costumes, Nereida Bonmatí; for Sogetel/Bocaboca Prouccienes, S.A./Star Line Productions, S.L.; Spanish, 1996; Dolby Digital Stereo; Color; Rated R; 105 minutes; September release. **CAST**: Javier Bardem (Victor), Josep María Flotats (Ricardo), Aitana Sánchez-Gijón (Amanda), María Barranco (Angela), Myriam Mézières (Sheila), Jordi Bosch (Thug), Sam Makenzie (Oswaldo), Fernando Guillén-Cuervo (Raul), Amparo Baró (Margot), Candela Peña (Tanya)

MY MOTHER'S COURAGE (National Center for Jewish Film) Producer/Director/Screenplay, Michael Verhoeven; Based on the novel by George Tabori; Photography, Michael Epp, Theo Bierkens; Music, Juliann Nott, Simon Verhoeven; Editor, David Freeman; Designer, Wolfgang Hundhammer; German-British, 1995; Dolby Stereo; Cinemascope; Color; Not rated; 88 minutes; September release. **CAST:** George Tabori (Himself), Pauline Collins (Elsa Tabori), Ulrich Tukur (SS Officer), Natalie Morse (Maria), Robert Giggenbach (Cornelius Tabori), Heribert Sasse (Kelemen), Günter Bothur ("Moustache"), Simon Verhoeven

Javier Bardem, Aitana Sanchez-Gijon in *Mouth to Mouth*
© Miramax Films

Pauline Collins, Natalie Morse in *My Mother's Courage*

(Young SS Man), Buddy Elias (Rabbi), Peter Radtke (German Teacher "Wireless"), Otto Grünmandl (Julius), Hana Frejkova (Martha), Jens Harzer (Young Man in Pyjamas), Tatjana Vilhelmova (Olga), Istvan Iglodi (Usicky), Eddi Arent (Klapka), Wolfgang Gasser (Igoldi), Johanna Mertinz (Tram Conductor), Jindrich Bonaventura (Greenshirt with Chalk), Jiri Knot (German Bookkeeper)

YO SOY, DEL SON A LA SALSA (RMM FilmWorks)
Producer/Director, Rigoberto Lopez; Screenplay, Rigoberto Lopez, Leonardo Padura; Photography, Luis Garcia, Jose M. Riera; Editor, Miriam Talavera; Cuban; Color; Not rated; 100 minutes; September release. Documentary on Caribbean dance music with Celia Cruz, Tito Puente, Oscar D'Leon, Cheo Feliciano, Fania All-Stars, Eddie Palmieri, Johnny Pacheco, El Gran Combo, Marc Anthony, Andy Montanez, Gilberto Santa Rosa, Larry Harlow, Issac Delgado, Tito Gomez, Papo Lucca, Dave Valentin, Tite Curet Alonso, Israel Loperz "Cachao", Joe Cuba, Chucho Valdes, Los Van Van, Adalberto Alvarez, Yoruba Andabo, Grupo Changui, Lazaro Herrera , Rudy Calzado.

STAG (CFP)
Producers, John Duning, Michael Paseornek; Executive Producers, Gabrielle Kelly, Jeff Sackman, Andre Link; Director, Gavin Wilding; Screenplay, Evan Tylor, Pat Bermel; Story, Jason Schombing; Photography, Maryse Alberti; Editor, Mark Sanders; Music, Paul J. Zaza; Designer, Phyllis Cedar; Costumes, Ane Crabtree; Casting, Tom McSweeney; a Rampage Entertainment production; Color; Not rated; 92 minutes; September release. **CAST:** Andrew McCarthy (Peter), John Stockwell (Victor), Kevin Dillon (Dan), Taylor Dayne (Serena), Mario Van Peebles (Michael), Ben Gazzara (Frank), Mark Blum, Gerald Anthony, William McNamara, John Henson, Gregalan Williams, Jennifer Miller, William Prael, Jerry Stiller. (This film made its U.S. debut on HBO in June of 1997).

TAXI LISBOA (Wolf Gauditz)
Producer/Director/Screenplay, Wolf Gauditz; Photography, Claus Langer, Rodger Hinrichs; Editor, André Bendocchi-Alves; Music, Gert Wilden, Jr.; a Solofilm/München, in co-production with BR, München/SR, Saarbrücken; Portuguese-German-Italian; Dolby Stereo; Color; Not rated; 86 minutes; October release. **CAST:** Augusto Macedo, Antonio Torchiaro, Josefina Lind, Leonore Mau, Ana-Teresa Sousa, Gerard Samaan.

DANCEHALL QUEEN (Island Digital Media)
Producers, Carolyn Pfeiffer, Carl Bradshaw; Executive Producers, Chris Blackwell, Dan Genetti; Directors, Don Letts, Rick Elgood; Screenplay, Suzanne Fenn, Ed Wallace, Don Letts; Based on an idea by Ed Wallace, Carl Bradshaw; Photography, Louis Mulvey; Editor, Suzanne Fenn; an Island Jamaica Films presentation in association with Hawk's Nest productions; Color; Not rated; 94 minutes; October release. **CAST:** Audrey Reid (Marcia), Carl Davis ("Uncle" Larry), Paul Campbell (Priest), Pauline Stone-Myrie (Mrs. Gordon), Cherine Anderson, Mark Danvers, Patrice Harrison, Anika Grason, Donald Thompson, Henry Brown, Carl Bradshaw, Michael London, Beenie Man, Lady Saw, Anthony B, Chevelle Franklyn.

PRETTY VILLAGE, PRETTY FLAME (Fox Lorber)
Producers, Goran Bjelogrlic, Dragan Bjelogrlic, Nikola Kojo; Executive Producer, Milko Josifov; Director, Srdjan Dragojevic; Screenplay, Vanja Bulic, Srdjan Dragojevic, Nikola Pejakovic; Photography, Dusan Joksimovic; Editor, Petar Markovic; Music, Laza Ristovski; a Cobra Film Department presentation in association with MCRS and RTS; Yugoslav, 1996; Color; Not rated; 125 minutes; October release. **CAST:** Dragan Bjelogrlic (Milan), Nikola Kojo (Velja), Velimir-Bata Zivojinovic (Gvozden), Dragan Maksimovic (Petar), Zoran Cvijanovic (Brzi), Nikola Pejakovic (Halil), Dragan Petrovic (Laza), Milorad Mandic (Gavra).

LIKE A BRIDE (Atara Releasing)
Executive Producer, Tita Lombardo; Director, Guita Schyfter; Screenplay, Hugo Hiriart; Based on the book by Rosa Nissan; Photography, Toni Kuhn; Editor, Carlos Bolado; Art Director, Tere Pecanins; Music, Joaquin Guitierrez; Mexican, 1993; Color; Not rated; 115 minutes; October release. **CAST:** Claudette Maille (Oshinica Mataraso), Angelica Aragon (Sara), Maya Mishalska (Rifke Groman), Ernesto Laguardia (Saavedra).

FOREIGN LAND (Riofilme/Videofilmes)
Executive Producer, Flávio R. Tambellini; Directors, Walter Salles, Daniela Thomas; Screenplay, Daniela Thomas, Marcos Bernstein, Walter Salles, Millôr Fernandes; Photography, Walter Carvalho; Art Director, Daniela Thomas; Editors, Walter Salles, Felipe Lagerda; Music, Jose Miguel Wisnik; Costumes, Cristina Camargo; Portuguese; Color; Not rated; 100 minutes; October release. **CAST:** Fernanda Torres (Alex), Fernando Alves Pinto (Paco), Luis Melo (Igor), Alexandre Borges (Miguel), Laura Cardoso (Manuela), João Lagarto (Pedro), Tcheky Karyo (Kraft)

Dragan Bjelogrlic in *Pretty Village, Pretty Flame*
© Fox Lorber

BEAUMARCHAIS THE SCOUNDREL (New Yorker) Producer, Charles Gassot; Director, Edouard Molinaro; Screenplay, Edouard Molinaro, Jean-Claude Brisville; Inspired by an unpublished work by Sacha Guitry; Photography, Michael Epp; Executive Producer, Dominique Brunner; Editor, Veronique Parnet; Costumes, Sylvie De Segonzac; Set Designer, Jean-Marc Kerdelhue; Music, Jean-Claude Petit; a co-production of Téléma, Le Studio Canal+, France 2 Cinema, France 3 Cinema, with the participation of Canal+ and the assistance of Procirep/Investimage 4/Sofiarp 2; French, 1996; Panavision; Color; Not rated; 100 minutes; October release. **CAST:** Fabrice Luchini (Beaumarchais), Manuel Blanc (Gudin), Sandrine Kiberlain (Marie-Therese), Michel Serrault (Louis XV), Jacques Weber (Duc de Chaulnes), Michel Piccoli (Prince de Conti), Jean-François Balmer (Sartine), Florence Thomassin (Marion Menard), Isabelle Carré (Rosine), Claire Nebout (The Knight of Éon), Jean Yanne (Goezman), Martin Lamotte (Comte De La Blache), Jean-Claude Brialy (The Abbot), Dominique Besnehard (Louis XVI), Axelle Laffont (Mariette Lejay), Murray Head (Lord Rochford), Patrick Bouchitey (Monsieur Lejay), José Garcia (Figaro), François Morel (Peasant at Court), Alain Chabat (Courtier at Versailles), Pierre Gérard (Comte De Provence), Judith Godrèche (Marie-Antoinette), Evelyne Bouix (Madame Vigee-Lebrun), Michel Aumont (Baron De Breteuil), Jean-Marc Besset (Desfontaines), Roland Blanche (Thevenot De Morande), Jeff Nuttall (Benjamin Franklin)

DEEP CRIMSON (New Yorker) Producers, Miguel Necoechea, Paolo Barbachano; Executive Producer, Tita Lombardo; Director, Arturo Ripstein; Screenplay, Paz Alicia Garciadiego; Photography, Guillermo Granillo; Designers, Macarena Folache, Marisa Pecanins, Monica Chirinos; Editor, Rafael Castanedo; Music, David Mansfield; a co-production of Ivania Films/MK2/Wanda Films/Institute Mexicano de Cinematographia/TVE; Mexican-French-Spanish, 1996; Color; Not rated; 109 minutes; October release. **CAST:** Regina Orozco (Coral Fabre), Daniel Gimenez Cacho (Nicolas Estrella), Marisa Paredes (Irene Gallardo), Patricia Reyes Espindola (The Widow Ruelas), Juanita Norton (Julieta Egurrola), Rosa Furman (The Widow Morrison), Veronica Merchant (Rebecca San Pedro), Sherlyn Gonzales (Teresa), Giovanni Florido (Carlitos), Bianca Flordio (Mercedes)

THE KNOWLEDGE OF HEALING (In Pictures) Producer, Marcel Hoehn; Director/Screenplay, Franz Reichle; Photography, Pio Corradi; Editors, Myriam Flury, Franz Reichle; a T&C Film AG production; Tibetan; Color; Not rated; 90 minutes; November release. Documentary on Tibetan medicine featuring H.H. Tenzin Gyatso XIV Dalai Lama of Tibet, Tenzin Choedrak, Chimit-Dorzhi Dugarov, Karl Lutz, Alfred Hassig, Herbert Schwabl, Herbert Klima, Alexander P. Nechunayev, Dashinima D. Ayusheyev, Isaac Ginsburg, Lobsang Dolker, Tenzin Choedon, Nikita B. Maglayev, Viktoria Tsyrengarmayeva, Dolgor B. Linkovoin, Fritz Sterki.

A COUCH IN NEW YORK (Northern Arts) Producers, Régine Konckier, Jean-Luc Ormieres; Executive Producer, Robin O'Hara; Director, Chantal Akerman; Screenplay, Chantal Akerman, Jean-Louis Benoit; Photography, Dietrich Lohmann; Editor, Claire Atherton; Music, Paolo Conte, Sonia Atherton; Designer, Christian Marti; a Les Films Balengicaga, France 2 Cinema M6 Films (Paris)/Paradise Films, RTBF-Television Belge (Brussels)/Babelsberg Film Produktion (Berlin) production, with the participation of Canal+, Film Board Berlin Brandenburg; French-Belgian-German, 1996; Dolby Stereo; Color; Not rated; 109 minutes; November release. **CAST:** William Hurt (Henry Harriston), Juliette Binoche (Béatrice Saulnier), Paul Guilfoyle (Dennis), Stephanie Buttle (Anne), Richard Jenkins (Campton), Kent Broadhurst (Tim), Henry Bean (Stein), Barbara Garrick (Lisbeth Honeywell), Bernard Breuse (Jerome), Matthew Burton (Wood), Henry Burton (Stein), Bernard Breuse (Jérome), Adam LeFevre (Patron), Tiffany Frazer (Julie), Wendy Way (Airport Employee), Jean-Baptiste Filleau (Julien), Lysako Karunga (Martin), Blaise Chakir (Thomas). (This film made its U.S. debut on cable television in July of 1996).

BUGIS STREET (Margin Films) Produced by Jaytex Prods.; Director, Fan Yon; Screenplay, Yuo Chan, Fan Yon; Photography, Jacky Tang; Editor, Ma Kam; Singapore-Cantonese, 1994; Color; Not rated; 100 minutes; November release. **CAST:** Michael Lam, Hiep Thi Le. No other credits available.

Birdo Lucci, Napoleon in *Napoleon*
© MGM Distribution

NAPOLEON (Goldwyn) Producers, Michael Bourchier, Mario Andreacchio; Director, Mario Andreacchio; Screenplay, Michael Bourchier, Mario Andreacchio, Mark Saltzman; Executive Producers, Masato Hara, Ron Saunders; Producer for Herald Ace, Naonori Kawamura; Producer for the Samuel Goldwyn Company, Mark Saltzman; Photography, Roger Dowling; Designer, Vicki Niehus; Music, Bill Conti; Editor, Edward McQueen-Mason; Line Producer, John Wild; Dog & Bird Handler/Trainer, The Cuong Truong; a Herald Ace Inc. presentation in association with Nippon Herald Films/Fuji Television & Pony Canyon of a Film Australia/Herald Ace and Furry Feature Films production; Distributed by MGM Distribution; Australian; Dolby Digital; Color; Rated G; 82 minutes; October release. **VOICE CAST:** Jamie Croft (Napoleon), Philip Quast (Birdo), Susan Lyons (Napoleon's Mom/Wallaby), Coralie Sawade (Kid's Mother), Brenton Whittle (Owl/Frog/Wombat/Wallaby/Desert Mouse), Anne Lambert (Spider/Earless Wallaby), Carole Skinner (Cat), Catherine Lambert, Tracey Canini, Annabel Sims, Neusa Timms, Debbie Horn (Lorikeets/Rabbits), Lucia Mastrantone (Lone Lorikeet), Frank Whitton (Koala), Fiona Press (Wallaby/Mother Dingo), Steven Vidler (Snake/Desert Mouse/Turtle), David Argue (Frill Necked Lizard), Edward McQueen-Mason (Echidna), Stuart Pankin (Perenti Lizard/Father Penguin), Mignon Kent (Nancy), Michael Wilkop (Sid), Barry Humphries (Kangaroo), Casey Siemaszko (Conan), Joan Rivers (Mother Penguin), Stuart Zagnit, Carolyn Sloan (Penguins)

Fabrice Luchini, Sandrine Kiberlain in *Beaumarchais the Scoundrel*
© New Yorker Films

Daniel Gimenez Cacho, Regina Orozco in *Deep Crimson*
© New Yorker Films

Bryan Brown in *Dead Heart*
© Fox Lorber

DEAD HEART (Fox Lorber) Producers, Bryan Brown, Helen Watts; Director/Screenplay, Nicholas Parsons; Photography, James Bartle; Designer, Brian Edmonds; Costumes, Edie Kurzer; Australian; Color; Not rated; 106 minutes; November release. **CAST:** Bryan Brown (Ray), Ernie Dingo (David), Angie Milliken (Kate), Aaron Pedersen (Tony), Gnarnay Yarrahe Waitaire (Poppy), Lewis Fitzgerald (Les), Anne Tenney (Sarah), John Jarratt (Charlie), Lafe Charlton (Billy), Djunawong Stanley Mirindo (Tjulpu), Peter Francis (Mannga)

THE WITMAN BOYS (Bunyik Entertainment) Producer, Ferenc Kardos; Director, Janos Szasz; Screenplay, Geza Csath, Janos Szasz; Photography, Tibor Mathe; Editor, Anna Kornis; Designer, Jozsef Romvary; a Budapest Filmstudio-MTM Kommunikacios-47eme Parallele-StudioFilmowe Zebra-Mafilm co-production; Hungarian-French-Polish; Color; Not rated; 92 minutes; November release. **CAST:** Alpar Fogarassi (Janos Witman), Szaboles Gergely (Erno Witman), Maia Morgenstern (Mrs. Witman), Dominika Ostalowska (Iren), Peter Andorai (Talloi), Lajos Kovacs (Denes Witman)

O AMOR NATURAL (First Run Features/Icarus) Producer, Pieter van Huystee; Director/Screenplay, Heddy Honigmann; Editor, Marc Nolens; a Pieter van Huystee Film & TV/NPS TV production; Dutch-Portuguese; Color; Not rated; 76 minutes; December release. Documentary celebrating the erotic poetry of Brazil's Carlos Drummond.

WE FREE KINGS (I Magi Randagi) **(Independent)** Producer, Francesco Torelli; Director/Screenplay, Sergio Citti; Photography, Franco Di Giacomo; Music, Ennio Morricone; Art Director, Danilo Donati; Editor, Ugo De Rossi; a co-production of I.P.S. S.r.l. (Rome)—Journal Film (Berlin)—Films Sans Frontieres (Paris); Italian-French-German; Color; Not rated; 94 minutes; December release. **CAST:** Silvio Orlando, Patrick Bauchau, Rolf Zacher, David Grieco, Michele Salimbeni, Nanni Tamma, Laura Betti, Franco Citti, Ninetto Davoli, Gastone Moschin.

LA RENCONTRE (Artistic License) Conceived and Directed by Alain Cavalier; from Les Films de l'Astrophone; French, 1996; Not rated; 76 minutes; December release. The filmmaker's visual diary of objects that remind him of a woman he loved.

GUY (Gramercy) Producers, Vincent D'Onofrio, Warren Robert Jason, Renee Missel; Director, Michael Lindsay-Hogg; Screenplay, Kirby Dick; Photography, Arturo Smith; Music, Geoffrey Beal; Editor, Dody Dorn; produced by KRRWH Inc. aka GUY Prods./North Rhine Westfalia Filmfund/Pandora Film/PolyGram Filmed Entertainment; British-German, 1996; Color; Rated R; 91 minutes; December release. **CAST:** Vincent D'Onofrio (Guy), Hope Davis, Kimber Riddle

Juliette Binoche, William Hurt in *A Couch in New York*
© Northern Arts

Silvio Orlando, Patrick Bauchau, Rolf Zacher in *We Free Kings*

Danny Aiello

Jennifer Aniston

Dan Aykroyd

Kevin Bacon

Biographical Data

(Name, real name, place and date of birth, school attended)

AAMES, WILLIE (William Upton): Los Angeles, CA, July 15, 1960.
AARON, CAROLINE: Richmond, VA, Aug. 7, 1954. Catholic U.
ABBOTT, DIAHNNE: NYC, 1945.
ABBOTT, JOHN: London, June 5, 1905.
ABRAHAM, F. MURRAY: Pittsburgh, PA, Oct. 24, 1939. UTx.
ACKLAND, JOSS: London, Feb. 29, 1928.
ADAMS, BROOKE: NYC, Feb. 8, 1949. Dalton.
ADAMS, CATLIN: Los Angeles, Oct. 11, 1950.
ADAMS, DON: NYC, Apr. 13, 1926.
ADAMS, EDIE (Elizabeth Edith Enke): Kingston, PA, Apr. 16, 1927. Juilliard, Columbia.
ADAMS, JULIE (Betty May): Waterloo, IA, Oct. 17, 1926. Little Rock, Jr. College.
ADAMS, MASON: NYC, Feb. 26, 1919. UWi.
ADAMS, MAUD (Maud Wikstrom): Lulea, Sweden, Feb. 12, 1945.
ADJANI, ISABELLE: Germany, June 27, 1955.
AFFLECK, BEN: Berkeley, CA, Aug. 15, 1972.
AGAR, JOHN: Chicago, IL, Jan. 31, 1921.
AGUTTER, JENNY: Taunton, England, Dec. 20, 1952.
AIELLO, DANNY: NYC, June 20, 1933.
AIMEE, ANOUK (Dreyfus): Paris, France, Apr. 27, 1934. Bauer-Therond.
AKERS, KAREN: NYC, Oct. 13, 1945, Hunter College.
ALBERGHETTI, ANNA MARIA: Pesaro, Italy, May 15, 1936.
ALBERT, EDDIE (Eddie Albert Heimberger): Rock Island, IL, Apr. 22, 1908. U of Minn.
ALBERT, EDWARD: Los Angeles, Feb. 20. 1951. UCLA.
ALBRIGHT, LOLA: Akron, OH, July 20, 1925.
ALDA, ALAN: NYC, Jan. 28, 1936. Fordham.

ALEANDRO, NORMA: Buenos Aires, Dec. 6, 1936.
ALEJANDRO, MIGUEL: NYC, Feb. 21, 1958.
ALEXANDER, JANE (Quigley): Boston, MA, Oct. 28, 1939. Sarah Lawrence.
ALEXANDER, JASON (Jay Greenspan): Newark, NJ, Sept. 23, 1959. Boston U.
ALICE, MARY: Indianola, MS, Dec. 3, 1941.
ALLEN, DEBBIE (Deborah): Houston, TX, Jan. 16, 1950. Howard U.
ALLEN, JOAN: Rochelle, IL, Aug. 20, 1956. EastIllU.
ALLEN, KAREN: Carrollton, IL, Oct. 5, 1951. UMd.
ALLEN, NANCY: NYC, June 24, 1950.
ALLEN, REX: Wilcox, AZ, Dec. 31, 1922.
ALLEN, STEVE: NYC, Dec. 26, 1921.
ALLEN, TIM: Denver, CO, June 13, 1953. W. MI. Univ.
ALLEN, WOODY (Allan Stewart Konigsberg): Brooklyn, Dec. 1, 1935.
ALLEY, KIRSTIE: Wichita, KS, Jan. 12, 1955.
ALLYSON, JUNE (Ella Geisman): Westchester, NY, Oct. 7, 1917.
ALONSO, MARIA CONCHITA: Cuba, June 29, 1957.
ALT, CAROL: Queens, NY, Dec. 1, 1960. HofstraU.
ALVARADO, TRINI: NYC, Jan. 10, 1967.
AMIS, SUZY: Oklahoma City, OK, Jan. 5, 1958. Actors Studio.
AMOS, JOHN: Newark, NJ, Dec. 27, 1940. Colo. U.
ANDERSON, KEVIN: Waukeegan, IL, Jan. 13, 1960.
ANDERSON, LONI: St. Paul, MN, Aug. 5, 1946.
ANDERSON, MELISSA SUE: Berkeley, CA, Sept. 26, 1962.
ANDERSON, MELODY: Edmonton, Canada, 1955. Carlton U.

ANDERSON, MICHAEL, JR.: London, England, Aug. 6, 1943.
ANDERSON, RICHARD DEAN: Minneapolis, MN, Jan. 23, 1950.
ANDERSSON, BIBI: Stockholm, Sweden, Nov. 11, 1935. Royal Dramatic Sch.
ANDES, KEITH: Ocean City, NJ, July 12, 1920. Temple U., Oxford.
ANDRESS, URSULA: Bern, Switzerland, Mar. 19, 1936.
ANDREWS, ANTHONY: London, Dec. 1, 1948.
ANDREWS, JULIE (Julia Elizabeth Wells): Surrey, England, Oct. 1, 1935.
ANGLIM, PHILIP: San Francisco, CA, Feb. 11, 1953.
ANISTON, JENNIFER: Sherman Oaks, CA, Feb. 11, 1969.
ANN-MARGRET (Olsson): Valsjobyn, Sweden, Apr. 28, 1941. Northwestern U.
ANSARA, MICHAEL: Lowell, MA, Apr. 15, 1922. Pasadena Playhouse.
ANSPACH, SUSAN: NYC, Nov. 23, 1945.
ANTHONY, LYSETTE: London, 1963.
ANTHONY, TONY: Clarksburg, WV, Oct. 16, 1937. Carnegie Tech.
ANTON, SUSAN: Yucaipa, CA, Oct. 12, 1950. Bemardino College.
ANTONELLI, LAURA: Pola, Italy, Nov. 28, 1941.
ANWAR, GABRIELLE: Lalehaam, England, Feb. 4, 1970
APPLEGATE, CHRISTINA: Hollywood CA, Nov. 25, 1972.
ARCHER, ANNE: Los Angeles, Aug. 25, 1947.
ARCHER, JOHN (Ralph Bowman): Osceola, NB, May 8, 1915. USC.
ARDANT, FANNY: Monte Carlo, Mar 22, 1949
ARKIN, ADAM: Brooklyn, NY, Aug. 19, 1956.
ARKIN, ALAN: NYC, Mar. 26, 1934. LACC.

Scott Bakula

ATKINSON, ROWAN: England, Jan. 6, 1955. Oxford.
ATTENBOROUGH, RICHARD: Cambridge, England, Aug. 29, 1923. RADA.
AUBERJONOIS, RENE: NYC, June 1, 1940. Carnegie Tech.
AUDRAN, STEPHANE: Versailles, France, Nov. 8, 1932.
AUGER, CLAUDINE: Paris, France, Apr. 26, 1942. Dramatic Cons.
AULIN, EWA: Stockholm, Sweden, Feb. 14, 1950.
AUMONT, JEAN PIERRE: Paris, France, Jan. 5, 1909. French Nat'l School of Drama.
AUTRY, GENE: Tioga, TX, Sept. 29, 1907.
AVALON, FRANKIE (Francis Thomas Avallone): Philadelphia, PA, Sept. 18, 1939.
AYKROYD, DAN: Ottawa, Canada, July 1, 1952.
AZNAVOUR, CHARLES (Varenagh Aznourian): Paris, France, May 22, 1924.
AZZARA, CANDICE: Brooklyn, NY, May 18, 1947.
BACH, CATHERINE: Warren, OH, Mar. 1, 1954.
BACALL, LAUREN (Betty Perske): NYC, Sept. 16, 1924. AADA.
BACH, BARBARA: Queens, NY, Aug. 27, 1946.
BACKER, BRIAN: NYC, Dec. 5, 1956. Neighborhood Playhouse.
BACON, KEVIN: Philadelphia, PA, July 8, 1958.
BAIN, BARBARA: Chicago, IL, Sept. 13, 1934. U Ill.
BAIO, SCOTT: Brooklyn, NY, Sept. 22, 1961.
BAKER, BLANCHE: NYC, Dec. 20, 1956.
BAKER, CARROLL: Johnstown, PA, May 28, 1931. St. Petersburg, Jr. College.
BAKER, DIANE: Hollywood, CA, Feb. 25, 1938. USC.
BAKER, JOE DON: Groesbeck, TX, Feb.12, 1936.
BAKER, KATHY: Midland, TX, June 8, 1950. UC Berkley.
BAKULA, SCOTT: St. Louis, MO, Oct. 9, 1955. KansasU.
BALABAN, BOB: Chicago, IL, Aug. 16, 1945. Colgate.
BALDWIN, ADAM: Chicago, IL, Feb. 27, 1962.
BALDWIN, ALEC: Massapequa, NY, Apr. 3, 1958. NYU.
BALDWIN, STEPHEN: Long Island, NY, 1966.
BALDWIN, WILLIAM: Massapequa, NY, Feb. 21, 1963.
BALE, CHRISTIAN: Pembrokeshire, West Wales, Jan. 30, 1974.
BALLARD, KAYE: Cleveland, OH, Nov. 20, 1926.
BANCROFT, ANNE (Anna Maria Italiano): Bronx, NY, Sept. 17, 1931. AADA.
BANDERAS, ANTONIO: Malaga, Spain, Aug. 10, 1960.
BANERJEE, VICTOR: Calcutta, India, Oct. 15, 1946.
BANES, LISA: Chagrin Falls, OH, July 9, 1955. Juilliard.
BANNEN, IAN: Airdrie, Scotland, June 29, 1928.
BARANSKI, CHRISTINE: Buffalo, NY, May 2, 1952. Juilliard.
BARBEAU, ADRIENNE: Sacramento, CA, June 11, 1945. Foothill College.

William Baldwin

BARDOT, BRIGITTE: Paris, France, Sept. 28, 1934.
BARKIN, ELLEN: Bronx, NY, Apr. 16, 1954. Hunter College.
BARNES, BINNIE (Gitelle Enoyce Barnes): London, Mar. 25, 1906.
BARNES, CHRISTOPHER DANIEL: Portland, ME, Nov. 7, 1972.
BARR, JEAN-MARC: San Diego, CA, Sept. 1960.
BARRAULT, JEAN-LOUIS: Vesinet, France, Sept. 8, 1910.
BARRAULT, MARIE-CHRISTINE: Paris, France, Mar. 21, 1944.
BARREN, KEITH: Mexborough, England, Aug. 8, 1936. Sheffield Playhouse.
BARRETT, MAJEL (Hudec): Columbus, OH, Feb. 23. Western Reserve U.
BARRIE, BARBARA: Chicago, IL, May 23, 1931.
BARRY, GENE (Eugene Klass): NYC, June 14, 1919.
BARRY, NEILL: NYC, Nov. 29, 1965.
BARRYMORE, DREW: Los Angeles, Feb. 22, 1975.
BARRYMORE, JOHN DREW: Beverly Hills, CA, June 4, 1932. St. John's Military Academy.
BARTEL, PAUL: Brooklyn, NY, Aug. 6, 1938. UCLA.
BARTY, BILLY: (William John Bertanzetti) Millsboro, PA, Oct. 25, 1924.

Jacqueline Bisset

ARMSTRONG, BESS: Baltimore, MD, Dec. 11, 1953.
ARNAZ, DESI, JR.: Los Angeles, Jan. 19, 1953.
ARNAZ, LUCIE: Hollywood, July 17, 1951.
ARNESS, JAMES (Aurness): Minneapolis, MN, May 26, 1923. Beloit College.
ARQUETTE, DAVID: Sept. 8, 1971.
ARQUETTE, PATRICIA: NYC, Apr. 8, 1968.
ARQUETTE, ROSANNA: NYC, Aug. 10, 1959.
ARTHUR, BEATRICE (Frankel): NYC, May 13, 1924. New School.
ASHER, JANE: London, Apr. 5, 1946.
ASHLEY, ELIZABETH (Elizabeth Ann Cole): Ocala, FL, Aug. 30, 1939.
ASHTON, JOHN: Springfield, MA, Feb. 22, 1948. USC.
ASNER, EDWARD: Kansas City, KS, Nov. 15, 1929.
ASSANTE, ARMAND: NYC, Oct. 4, 1949. AADA.
ASTIN, JOHN: Baltimore, MD, Mar. 30, 1930. U Minn.
ASTIN, MacKENZIE: Los Angeles, May 12, 1973.
ASTIN, SEAN: Santa Monica, Feb. 25, 1971.
ATHERTON, WILLIAM: Orange, CT, July 30, 1947. Carnegie Tech.
ATKINS, CHRISTOPHER: Rye, NY, Feb. 21, 1961.
ATKINS, EILEEN: London, June 16, 1934.

Alec Baldwin

BARYSHNIKOV, MIKHAIL: Riga, Latvia, Jan. 27, 1948.

BASINGER, KIM: Athens, GA, Dec. 8, 1953. Neighborhood Playhouse.

BASSETT, ANGELA: NYC, Aug. 16, 1958.

BATEMAN, JASON: Rye, NY, Jan. 14, 1969.

BATEMAN, JUSTINE: Rye, NY, Feb. 19, 1966.

BATES, ALAN: Allestree, Derbyshire, England, Feb. 17, 1934. RADA.

BATES, JEANNE: San Francisco, CA, May 21, 1918. RADA.

BATES, KATHY: Memphis, TN, June 28, 1948. S. Methodist U.

BAUER, STEVEN (Steven Rocky Echevarria): Havana, Cuba, Dec. 2, 1956. U Miami.

BAXTER, KEITH: South Wales, England, Apr. 29, 1933. RADA.

BAXTER, MEREDITH: Los Angeles, June 21, 1947. Intelochen Acad.

BAYE, NATHALIE: Mainevile, France, July 6, 1948

BEACHAM, STEPHANIE: Casablanca, Morocco, Feb. 28, 1947.

BEALS, JENNIFER: Chicago, IL, Dec. 19, 1963.

BEAN, ORSON (Dallas Burrows): Burlington, VT, July 22, 1928.

BEAN, SEAN: Sheffield, Yorkshire, England, Apr. 17, 1958.

BEART, EMMANUELLE: Gassin, France, Aug. 14, 1965.

BEATTY, NED: Louisville, KY, July 6, 1937.

BEATTY, WARREN: Richmond, VA, Mar. 30, 1937.

BECK, JOHN: Chicago, IL, Jan. 28, 1943.

BECK, MICHAEL: Memphis, TN, Feb. 4, 1949. Millsap College.

BECKINSALE, KATE: England, July 26, 1974.

BEDELIA, BONNIE: NYC, Mar. 25, 1946. Hunter College.

BEGLEY, ED, JR.: NYC, Sept. 16, 1949.

BELAFONTE, HARRY: NYC, Mar. 1, 1927.

BEL GEDDES, BARBARA: NYC, Oct. 31, 1922.

BELL, TOM: Liverpool, England, 1932.

BELLER, KATHLEEN: NYC, Feb. 10, 1957.

BELLWOOD, PAMELA (King): Scarsdale, NY, June 26, 1951.

BELMONDO, JEAN PAUL: Paris, France, Apr. 9, 1933.

BELUSHI, JAMES: Chicago, IL, June 15, 1954.

BELZER, RICHARD: Bridgeport, CT, Aug. 4, 1944.

BENEDICT, DIRK (Niewoehner): White Sulphur Springs, MT, March 1, 1945. Whitman College.

BENEDICT, PAUL: Silver City, NM, Sept. 17, 1938.

BENIGNI, ROBERTO: Tuscany, Italy, Oct. 27, 1952.

BENING, ANNETTE: Topeka, KS, May 29, 1958. SFSt. U.

BENJAMIN, RICHARD: NYC, May 22, 1938. Northwestern U.

BENNENT, DAVID: Lausanne, Sept. 9, 1966.

BENNETT, ALAN: Leeds, England, May 9, 1934. Oxford.

BENNETT, BRUCE (Herman Brix): Tacoma, WA, May 19, 1909. U Wash.

Ruben Blades

Diahann Carroll

Cher

BENNETT, HYWEL: Garnant, So. Wales, Apr. 8, 1944.

BENSON, ROBBY: Dallas, TX, Jan. 21, 1957.

BERENGER, TOM: Chicago, IL, May 31, 1950, U Mo.

BERENSON, MARISA: NYC, Feb. 15, 1947.

BERG, PETER: NYC, 1964. Malcalester College.

BERGEN, CANDICE: Los Angeles, May 9, 1946. U PA.

BERGEN, POLLY: Knoxville, TN, July 14, 1930. Compton, Jr. College.

BERGER, HELMUT: Salzburg, Austria, May 29, 1942.

BERGER, SENTA: Vienna, Austria, May 13, 1941. Vienna Sch. of Acting.

BERGER, WILLIAM: Austria, Jan. 20, 1928. Columbia.

BERGERAC, JACQUES: Biarritz, France, May 26, 1927. Paris U.

BERGIN, PATRICK: Dublin, Feb. 4, 1951.

BERKLEY, ELIZABETH: Detroit, MI, July 28, 1972.

BERKOFF, STEVEN: London, England, Aug. 3, 1937.

BERLE, MILTON (Berlinger): NYC, July 12, 1908.

BERLIN, JEANNIE: Los Angeles, Nov. 1, 1949.

BERLINGER, WARREN: Brooklyn, Aug. 31, 1937. Columbia.

BERNHARD, SANDRA: Flint, MI, June 6, 1955.

BERNSEN, CORBIN: Los Angeles, Sept. 7, 1954. UCLA.

BERRI, CLAUDE (Langmann): Paris, France, July 1, 1934.

BERRIDGE, ELIZABETH: Westchester, NY, May 2, 1962. Strasberg Inst.

BERRY, HALLE: Cleveland, OH, Aug. 14, 1968.

BERRY, KEN: Moline, IL, Nov. 3, 1933.

BERTINELLI, VALERIE: Wilmington, DE, Apr. 23, 1960.

BEST, JAMES: Corydon, IN, July 26, 1926.

BETTGER, LYLE: Philadelphia, PA, Feb. 13, 1915. AADA.

BEY, TURHAN: Vienna, Austria, Mar. 30, 1921.

BEYMER, RICHARD: Avoca, IA, Feb. 21, 1939.

BIALIK, MAYIM: San Diego, CA, Dec. 12, 1975.

BIEHN, MICHAEL: Anniston, AL, July 31, 1956.

BIKEL, THEODORE: Vienna, May 2, 1924. RADA.

BILLINGSLEY, PETER: NYC, Apr. 16, 1972.

BINOCHE, JULIETTE: Paris, France, Mar. 9, 1964.

BIRKIN, JANE: London, Dec. 14, 1947

BIRNEY, DAVID: Washington, DC, Apr. 23, 1939. Dartmouth, UCLA.

BIRNEY, REED: Alexandria, VA, Sept. 11, 1954. Boston U.

BISHOP, JOEY (Joseph Abraham Gotllieb): Bronx, NY, Feb. 3, 1918.

BISHOP, JULIE (Jacqueline Wells): Denver, CO, Aug. 30, 1917. Westlake School.

BISSET, JACQUELINE: Waybridge, England, Sept. 13, 1944.

BLACK, KAREN (Ziegler): Park Ridge, IL, July 1, 1942. Northwestern.

Margaret Colin

Robbie Coltrane

Sean Connery

Richard Crenna

BLACKMAN, HONOR: London, Aug. 22, 1926.

BLADES, RUBEN: Panama City, July 16, 1948. Harvard.

BLAIR, BETSY (Betsy Boger): NYC, Dec. 11, 1923.

BLAIR, JANET (Martha Jane Lafferty): Blair, PA, Apr. 23, 1921.

BLAIR, LINDA: Westport, CT, Jan. 22, 1959.

BLAKE, ROBERT (Michael Gubitosi): Nutley, NJ, Sept. 18, 1933.

BLAKELY, SUSAN: Frankfurt, Germany, Sept. 7, 1950. U TX.

BLAKLEY, RONEE: Stanley, ID, 1946. Stanford U.

BLETHYN, BRENDA: Ramsgate, Kent, Eng., Feb. 20, 1946.

BLOOM, CLAIRE: London, Feb. 15, 1931. Badminton School.

BLOOM, VERNA: Lynn, MA, Aug. 7, 1939. Boston U.

BLOUNT, LISA: Fayettville, AK, July 1, 1957. UAk.

BLUM, MARK: Newark, NJ, May 14, 1950. UMinn.

BLYTH, ANN: Mt. Kisco, NY, Aug. 16, 1928. New Waybum Dramatic School.

BOCHNER, HART: Toronto, Canada, Oct. 3, 1956. U San Diego.

BOCHNER, LLOYD: Toronto, Canada, July 29, 1924.

BOGARDE, DIRK: London, Mar. 28, 1921. Glasgow & Univ. College.

BOGOSIAN, ERIC: Woburn, MA, Apr. 24, 1953. Oberlin College.

BOHRINGER, RICHARD: Paris, France, Jan. 16, 1941.

BOLKAN, FLORINDA (Florinda Soares Bulcao): Ceara, Brazil, Feb. 15, 1941.

BOLOGNA, JOSEPH: Brooklyn, NY, Dec. 30, 1938. Brown U.

BOND, DEREK: Glasgow, Scotland, Jan. 26, 1920. Askes School.

BONET, LISA: San Francisco, CA, Nov. 16, 1967.

BONHAM-CARTER, HELENA: London, England, May 26, 1966.

BONO, SONNY (Salvatore): Detroit, MI, Feb. 16, 1935.

BOONE, PAT: Jacksonville, FL, June 1, 1934. Columbia U.

BOOTHE, JAMES: Croydon, England, Dec.19, 1930

BOOTHE, POWERS: Snyder, TX, June 1, 1949. So. Methodist U.

BORGNINE, ERNEST (Borgnino): Hamden, CT, Jan. 24, 1917. Randall School.

BOSCO, PHILIP: Jersey City, NJ, Sept. 26, 1930. CatholicU.

BOSLEY, TOM: Chicago, IL, Oct. 1, 1927. DePaul U.

BOSTWICK, BARRY: San Mateo, CA, Feb. 24, 1945. NYU.

BOTTOMS, JOSEPH: Santa Barbara, CA, Aug. 30, 1954.

BOTTOMS, SAM: Santa Barbara, CA, Oct. 17, 1955.

BOTTOMS, TIMOTHY: Santa Barbara, CA, Aug. 30, 1951.

BOULTING, INGRID: Transvaal, So. Africa, 1947.

BOUTSIKARIS, DENNIS: Newark, NJ, Dec. 21, 1952. CatholicU.

BOWIE, DAVID (David Robert Jones): Brixton, South London, England, Jan. 8, 1947.

BOWKER, JUDI: Shawford, England, Apr. 6, 1954.

BOXLEITNER, BRUCE: Elgin, IL, May 12, 1950.

BOYLE, LARA FLYNN: Davenport, IA, Mar. 24, 1970.

BOYLE, PETER: Philadelphia, PA, Oct. 18, 1933. LaSalle College.

BRACCO, LORRAINE: Brooklyn, NY, 1955.

BRACKEN, EDDIE: NYC, Feb. 7, 1920. Professional Children's School.

BRAEDEN, ERIC (Hans Gudegast): Kiel, Germany, Apr. 3, 1942.

BRAGA, SONIA: Maringa, Brazil, June 8, 1950.

BRANAGH, KENNETH: Belfast, No. Ireland, Dec. 10, 1960.

BRANDAUER, KLAUS MARIA: Altaussee, Austria, June 22, 1944.

BRANDIS, JONATHAN: CT, Apr. 13, 1976.

BRANDO, JOCELYN: San Francisco, Nov. 18, 1919. Lake Forest College, AADA.

BRANDO, MARLON: Omaha, NB, Apr. 3, 1924. New School.

BRANDON, CLARK: NYC, Dec. 13, 1958.

BRANDON, MICHAEL (Feldman): Brooklyn, NY.

BRANTLEY, BETSY: Rutherfordton, NC, Sept. 20, 1955. London Central Sch. of Drama.

BRENNAN, EILEEN: Los Angeles, CA, Sept. 3, 1935. AADA.

BRIALY, JEAN-CLAUDE: Aumale, Algeria, 1933. Strasbourg Cons.

BRIDGES, BEAU: Los Angeles, Dec. 9, 1941. UCLA.

BRIDGES, JEFF: Los Angeles, Dec. 4, 1949.

BRIDGES, LLOYD: San Leandro, CA, Jan. 15, 1913.

BRIMLEY, WILFORD: Salt Lake City, UT, Sept. 27, 1934.

BRINKLEY, CHRISTIE: Malibu, CA, Feb. 2, 1954.

BRITT, MAY (Maybritt Wilkins): Sweden, Mar. 22, 1936.

BRITTANY, MORGAN (Suzanne Cupito): Los Angeles, Dec. 5, 1950.

BRITTON, TONY: Birmingham, England, June 9, 1924.

BRODERICK, MATTHEW: NYC, Mar. 21, 1962.

BROLIN, JAMES: Los Angeles, July 18, 1940. UCLA.

BROMFIELD, JOHN (Farron Bromfield): South Bend, IN, June 11, 1922. St. Mary's College.

BRON, ELEANOR: Stanmore, England, 1934.

BRONSON, CHARLES (Buchinsky): Ehrenfield, PA, Nov. 3, 1920.

BROOKES, JACQUELINE: Montclair, NJ, July 24, 1930. RADA.

BROOKS, ALBERT (Einstein): Los Angeles, July 22, 1947.

BROOKS, MEL (Melvyn Kaminski): Brooklyn, NY, June 28, 1926.

BROSNAN, PIERCE: County Meath, Ireland. May 16, 1952.

BROWN, BLAIR: Washington, DC, Apr. 23, 1947. Pine Manor.

Alan Cumming

John Cusack

Tim Daly

Judy Davis

BROWN, BRYAN: Panania, Australia, June 23, 1947.

BROWN, GARY (Christian Brando): Hollywood, CA, 1958.

BROWN, GEORG STANFORD: Havana, Cuba, June 24, 1943. AMDA.

BROWN, JAMES: Desdemona, TX, Mar. 22, 1920. Baylor U.

BROWN, JIM: St. Simons Island, NY, Feb. 17, 1935. Syracuse U.

BROWNE, LESLIE: NYC, 1958.

BROWNE, ROSCOE LEE: Woodbury, NJ, May 2, 1925.

BUCHHOLZ, HORST: Berlin, Germany, Dec. 4, 1933. Ludwig Dramatic School.

BUCKLEY, BETTY: Big Spring, TX, July 3, 1947. TxCU.

BUJOLD, GENEVIEVE: Montreal, Canada, July 1, 1942.

BULLOCK, SANDRA: Arlington, VA, July 26, 1964.

BURGHOFF, GARY: Bristol, CT, May 24, 1943.

BURGI, RICHARD: Montclair, NJ, July 30, 1958.

BURKE, PAUL: New Orleans, July 21, 1926. Pasadena Playhouse.

BURNETT, CAROL: San Antonio, TX, Apr. 26, 1933. UCLA.

BURNS, CATHERINE: NYC, Sept. 25, 1945. AADA.

BURNS, EDWARD: Valley Stream, NY, Jan. 28, 1969.

BURROWS, DARREN E.: Winfield, KS, Sept. 12, 1966

BURSTYN, ELLEN (Edna Rae Gillhooly): Detroit, MI, Dec. 7, 1932.

BURTON, LeVAR: Los Angeles, CA, Feb. 16, 1958. UCLA.

BUSCEMI, STEVE: Brooklyn, NY, Dec. 13, 1957.

BUSEY, GARY: Goose Creek, TX, June 29, 1944.

BUSFIELD, TIMOTHY: Lansing, MI, June 12, 1957. E. Tenn. St. U.

BUTTONS, RED (Aaron Chwatt): NYC, Feb. 5, 1919.

BUZZI, RUTH: Westerly, RI, July 24, 1936. Pasadena Playhouse.

BYGRAVES, MAX: London, Oct. 16, 1922. St. Joseph's School.

BYRNE, DAVID: Dumbarton, Scotland, May 14, 1952.

BYRNE, GABRIEL: Dublin, Ireland, May 12, 1950.

BYRNES, EDD: NYC, July 30, 1933.

CAAN, JAMES: Bronx, NY, Mar. 26,1939.

CAESAR, SID: Yonkers, NY, Sept. 8, 1922.

CAGE, NICOLAS (Coppola): Long Beach, CA, Jan.7, 1964.

CAINE, MICHAEL (Maurice Micklewhite): London, Mar. 14, 1933.

CAINE, SHAKIRA (Baksh): Guyana, Feb. 23, 1947. Indian Trust College.

CALHOUN, RORY (Francis Timothy Durgin): Los Angeles, Aug. 8, 1922.

CALLAN, MICHAEL (Martin Calinieff): Philadelphia, Nov. 22, 1935.

CALLOW, SIMON: London, June 15, 1949. Queens U.

CALVERT, PHYLLIS: London, Feb. 18, 1917. Margaret Morris School.

CALVET, CORRINE (Corinne Dibos): Paris, France, Apr. 30, 1925. U Paris.

CAMERON, KIRK: Panorama City, CA, Oct. 12, 1970.

CAMP, COLLEEN: San Francisco, CA, 1953.

CAMPBELL, BILL: Chicago, IL, July 7, 1959.

CAMPBELL, GLEN: Delight, AR, Apr. 22, 1935.

CAMPBELL, NEVE: Guelph, Ontario, Canada, Oct. 3, 1973.

CAMPBELL, TISHA: Oklahoma City, OK, Oct. 13, 1968.

CANALE, GIANNA MARIA: Reggio Calabria, Italy, Sept. 12, 1927.

CANNON, DYAN (Samille Diane Friesen): Tacoma, WA, Jan. 4, 1937.

CAPERS, VIRGINIA: Sumter, SC, Sept. 25, 1925. Juilliard.

CAPSHAW, KATE: Ft. Worth, TX, Nov. 3, 1953. UMo.

CARA, IRENE: NYC, Mar. 18, 1958.

CARDINALE, CLAUDIA: Tunis, N. Africa. Apr. 15, 1939. College Paul Cambon.

CAREY, HARRY, JR.: Saugus, CA, May 16, 1921. Black Fox Military Academy.

CAREY, PHILIP: Hackensack, NJ, July 15, 1925. U Miami.

CARIOU, LEN: Winnipeg, Canada, Sept. 30, 1939.

CARLIN, GEORGE: NYC, May 12, 1938.

CARLYLE, ROBERT: Glasgow, Scotland, Apr. 14, 1961.

CARMEN, JULIE: Mt. Vernon, NY, Apr. 4, 1954.

CARMICHAEL, IAN: Hull, England, June 18, 1920. Scarborough College.

CARNE, JUDY (Joyce Botterill): Northampton, England, 1939. Bush-Davis Theatre School.

CARNEY, ART: Mt. Vernon, NY, Nov. 4, 1918.

CARON, LESLIE: Paris, France, July 1, 1931. Nat'l Conservatory, Paris.

CARPENTER, CARLETON: Bennington, VT, July 10, 1926. Northwestern.

CARRADINE, DAVID: Hollywood, Dec. 8, 1936. San Francisco State.

CARRADINE, KEITH: San Mateo, CA, Aug. 8, 1950. Colo. State U.

CARRADINE, ROBERT: San Mateo, CA, Mar. 24, 1954.

CARREL, DANY: Tourane, Indochina, Sept. 20, 1936. Marseilles Cons.

CARRERA, BARBARA: Managua, Nicaragua, Dec. 31, 1945.

CARREY, JIM: Jacksons Point, Ontario, Canada, Jan. 17, 1962.

CARRIERE, MATHIEU: Hannover, West Germany, Aug. 2, 1950.

CARROLL, DIAHANN (Johnson): NYC, July 17, 1935. NYU.

CARROLL, PAT: Shreveport, LA, May 5, 1927. Catholic U.

CARSON, JOHN DAVID: California, Mar. 6, 1952. Valley College.

CARSON, JOHNNY: Corning, IA, Oct. 23, 1925. U of Neb.

CARSTEN, PETER (Ransenthaler): Weissenberg, Bavaria, Apr. 30, 1929. Munich Akademie.

CARTER, NELL: Birmingham, AL, Sept. 13, 1948.

Julie Delpy

Leonardo DiCaprio

Matt Dillon

CARTWRIGHT, VERONICA: Bristol, England, Apr. 20, 1949.

CARUSO, DAVID: Forest Hills, NY, Jan. 7, 1956.

CARVEY, DANA: Missoula, MT, Apr. 2, 1955. SFST.CoI.

CASELLA, MAX: Washington D.C, June 6, 1967

CASEY, BERNIE: Wyco, WV, June 8, 1939.

CASS, PEGGY (Mary Margaret Cass): Boston, MA, May 21, 1924.

CASSAVETES, NICK: NYC, 1959, Syracuse U, AADA.

CASSEL, JEAN-PIERRE: Paris, France, Oct. 27, 1932.

CASSEL, SEYMOUR: Detroit, MI, Jan. 22, 1935.

CASSIDY, DAVID: NYC, Apr. 12, 1950.

CASSIDY, JOANNA: Camden, NJ, Aug. 2, 1944. Syracuse U.

CASSIDY, PATRICK: Los Angeles, CA, Jan. 4, 1961.

CATES, PHOEBE: NYC, July 16, 1962.

CATTRALL, KIM: Liverpool, England, Aug. 21, 1956. AADA.

CAULFIELD, MAXWELL: Glasgow, Scotland, Nov. 23, 1959.

CAVANI, LILIANA: Bologna, Italy, Jan. 12, 1937. U Bologna.

CAVETT, DICK: Gibbon, NE, Nov. 19, 1936.

CHAKIRIS, GEORGE: Norwood, OH, Sept. 16, 1933.

CHAMBERLAIN, RICHARD: Beverly Hills, CA, March 31, 1935. Pomona.

CHAMPION, MARGE (Marjorie Belcher): Los Angeles, Sept. 2, 1923.

CHAN, JACKIE: Hong Kong, Apr. 7, 1954

CHANNING, CAROL: Seattle, WA, Jan. 31, 1921. Bennington.

CHANNING, STOCKARD (Susan Stockard): NYC, Feb. 13, 1944. Radcliffe.

CHAPIN, MILES: NYC, Dec. 6, 1954. HB Studio.

CHAPLIN, GERALDINE: Santa Monica, CA, July 31, 1944. Royal Ballet.

CHAPLIN, SYDNEY: Los Angeles, Mar. 31, 1926. Lawrenceville.

CHARISSE, CYD (Tula Ellice Finklea): Amarillo, TX, Mar. 3, 1922. Hollywood Professional School.

CHARLES, WALTER: East Strousburg, PA, Apr. 4, 1945. Boston U.

CHASE, CHEVY (Cornelius Crane Chase): NYC, Oct. 8, 1943.

CHAVES, RICHARD: Jacksonville, FL, Oct. 9, 1951. Occidental College.

CHAYKIN, MAURY: Canada, July 27, 1954

CHEN, JOAN (Chen Chung): Shanghai, Apr. 26, 1961. CalState.

CHER (Cherilyn Sarkisian): El Centro, CA, May 20, 1946.

CHILES, LOIS: Alice, TX, Apr. 15, 1947.

CHONG, RAE DAWN: Vancouver, Canada, Feb. 28, 1962.

CHONG, THOMAS: Edmonton, Alberta, Canada, May 24, 1938.

CHRISTIAN, LINDA (Blanca Rosa Welter): Tampico, Mexico, Nov. 13, 1923.

CHRISTIE, JULIE: Chukua, Assam, India, Apr. 14, 1941.

CHRISTOPHER, DENNIS (Carrelli): Philadelphia, PA, Dec. 2, 1955. Temple U.

CHRISTOPHER, JORDAN: Youngstown, OH, Oct. 23, 1940. Kent State.

CILENTO, DIANE: Queensland, Australia, Oct. 5, 1933. AADA.

CLAPTON, ERIC: London, Mar. 30, 1945.

CLARK, CANDY: Norman, OK, June 20, 1947.

CLARK, DANE: NYC, Feb. 18, 1915. Cornell, Johns Hopkins U.

CLARK, DICK: Mt. Vernon, NY, Nov. 30, 1929. Syracuse U.

CLARK, MATT: Washington, DC, Nov. 25, 1936.

CLARK, PETULA: Epsom, England, Nov. 15, 1932.

CLARK, SUSAN: Sarnid, Ont., Canada, Mar. 8, 1943. RADA.

CLAY, ANDREW DICE (Andrew Silverstein): Brooklyn, NY, Sept. 29, 1957, Kingsborough College.

CLAYBURGH, JILL: NYC, Apr. 30, 1944. Sarah Lawrence.

CLEESE, JOHN: Weston-Super-Mare, England, Oct. 27, 1939, Cambridge.

CLOONEY, ROSEMARY: Maysville, KY, May 23, 1928.

CLOSE, GLENN: Greenwich, CT, Mar. 19, 1947. William & Mary College.

COBURN, JAMES: Laurel, NB, Aug. 31, 1928. LACC.

COCA, IMOGENE: Philadelphia, Nov. 18, 1908.

CODY, KATHLEEN: Bronx, NY, Oct. 30, 1953.

COFFEY, SCOTT: HI, May 1, 1967.

COLE, GEORGE: London, Apr. 22, 1925.

COLEMAN, GARY: Zion, IL, Feb. 8, 1968.

COLEMAN, DABNEY: Austin, TX, Jan. 3, 1932.

COLEMAN, JACK: Easton, PA, Feb. 21, 1958. Duke U.

COLIN, MARGARET: NYC, May 26, 1957.

COLLET, CHRISTOPHER: NYC, Mar. 13, 1968. Strasberg Inst.

COLLINS, JOAN: London, May 21, 1933. Francis Holland School.

COLLINS, PAULINE: Devon, England, Sept. 3, 1940.

COLLINS, STEPHEN: Des Moines, IA, Oct. 1, 1947. Amherst.

COLON, MIRIAM: Ponce, PR., 1945. UPR.

COLTRANE, ROBBIE: Ruthergien, Scotland, Mar. 30, 1950.

COMER, ANJANETTE: Dawson, TX, Aug. 7, 1942. Baylor, Tex. U.

CONANT, OLIVER: NYC, Nov. 15, 1955. Dalton.

CONAWAY, JEFF: NYC, Oct. 5, 1950. NYU.

CONNELLY, JENNIFER: NYC, Dec. 12, 1970

CONNERY, SEAN: Edinburgh, Scotland, Aug. 25, 1930.

CONNERY, JASON: London, Jan. 11, 1963.

CONNICK, HARRY, JR.: New Orleans, LA, Sept. 11, 1967.

CONNOLLY, BILLY: Glasgow, Scotland, Nov. 24, 1942.

CONNORS, MIKE (Krekor Ohanian): Fresno, CA, Aug. 15, 1925. UCLA.

CONRAD, ROBERT (Conrad Robert Falk): Chicago, IL, Mar. 1, 1935. Northwestern U.

CONSTANTINE, MICHAEL: Reading, PA, May 22, 1927.

CONTI, TOM: Paisley, Scotland, Nov. 22, 1941.

CONVERSE, FRANK: St. Louis, MO, May 22, 1938. Carnegie Tech.

Stephen Dorff

Robert Downey, Jr.

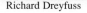
Richard Dreyfuss

Minnie Driver

CONWAY, GARY: Boston, Feb. 4, 1936.
CONWAY, KEVIN: NYC, May 29, 1942.
CONWAY, TIM (Thomas Daniel): Willoughby, OH, Dec. 15, 1933. Bowling Green State.
COOGAN, KEITH (Keith Mitchell Franklin): Palm Springs, CA, Jan. 13, 1970.
COOPER, BEN: Hartford, CT, Sept. 30, 1930. Columbia U.
COOPER, CHRIS: Kansas City, MO, July 9, 1951. UMo.
COOPER, JACKIE: Los Angeles, Sept. 15, 1921.
COPELAND, JOAN: NYC, June 1, 1922. Brooklyn College, RADA.
CORBETT, GRETCHEN: Portland, OR, Aug. 13, 1947. Carnegie Tech.
CORBIN, BARRY: Dawson County, TX, Oct. 16, 1940. Texas Tech. U.
CORBY, ELLEN (Hansen): Racine, WI, June 13, 1913.
CORCORAN, DONNA: Quincy, MA, Sept. 29, 1942.
CORD, ALEX (Viespi): Floral Park, NY, Aug. 3, 1931. NYU, Actors Studio.
CORDAY, MARA (Marilyn Watts): Santa Monica, CA, Jan. 3, 1932.
COREY, JEFF: NYC, Aug. 10, 1914. Fagin School.
CORNTHWAITE, ROBERT: St. Helens, OR, Apr. 28, 1917. USC.
CORRI, ADRIENNE: Glasgow, Scot., Nov. 13, 1933. RADA.
CORT, BUD (Walter Edward Cox): New Rochelle, NY, Mar. 29, 1950. NYU.
CORTESA, VALENTINA: Milan, Italy, Jan. 1, 1924.
COSBY, BILL: Philadelphia, PA, July 12, 1937. Temple U.
COSTER, NICOLAS: London, Dec. 3, 1934. Neighborhood Playhouse.
COSTNER, KEVIN: Lynwood, CA, Jan. 18, 1955. CalStaU.
COURTENAY, TOM: Hull, England, Feb. 25, 1937. RADA.
COURTLAND, JEROME: Knoxville, TN, Dec. 27, 1926.

COX, BRIAN: Dundee, Scotland, June 1, 1946. LAMDA.
COX, COURTENEY: Birmingham, AL, June 15, 1964.
COX, RONNY: Cloudcroft, NM, Aug. 23, 1938.
COYOTE, PETER (Cohon): NYC, Oct. 10, 1941.
CRAIG, MICHAEL: Poona, India, Jan. 27, 1929.
CRAIN, JEANNE: Barstow, CA, May 25, 1925.
CRAVEN, GEMMA: Dublin, Ireland, June 1, 1950.
CRAWFORD, MICHAEL (Dumbel-Smith): Salisbury, England, Jan. 19, 1942.
CREMER, BRUNO: Paris, France, 1929.
CRENNA, RICHARD: Los Angeles, Nov. 30, 1926. USC.
CRISTAL, LINDA (Victoria Moya): Buenos Aires, Feb. 25, 1934.
CROMWELL, JAMES: Los Angeles, CA, Jan. 27, 1940.
CRONYN, HUME (Blake): Ontario, Canada, July 18, 1911.
CROSBY, DENISE: Hollywood, CA, Nov. 24, 1957.
CROSBY, HARRY: Los Angeles, CA, Aug. 8, 1958.
CROSBY, MARY FRANCES: Los Angeles, CA, Sept. 14, 1959.
CROSS, BEN: London, Dec. 16, 1947. RADA.
CROSS, MURPHY (Mary Jane): Laurelton, MD, June 22, 1950.
CROUSE, LINDSAY: NYC, May 12, 1948. Radcliffe.
CROWE, RUSSELL: New Zealand, Apr. 7, 1964.
CROWLEY, PAT: Olyphant, PA, Sept. 17, 1932.
CRUISE, TOM (T. C. Mapother, IV): July 3, 1962, Syracuse, NY.
CRYER, JON: NYC, Apr. 16, 1965, RADA.
CRYSTAL, BILLY: Long Beach, NY, Mar. 14, 1947. Marshall U.

CULKIN, MACAULAY: NYC, Aug. 26, 1980.
CULLUM, JOHN: Knoxville, TN, Mar. 2, 1930. U Tenn.
CULLUM, JOHN DAVID: NYC, Mar. 1, 1966.
CULP, ROBERT: Oakland, CA, Aug. 16, 1930. U Wash.
CUMMING, ALAN: Perthshire, Scotland, 1964.
CUMMINGS, CONSTANCE: Seattle, WA, May 15, 1910.
CUMMINGS, QUINN: Hollywood, Aug. 13, 1967.
CUMMINS, PEGGY: Prestatyn, N. Wales, Dec. 18, 1926. Alexandra School.
CURRY, TIM: Cheshire, England, Apr. 19, 1946. Birmingham U.
CURTIN, JANE: Cambridge, MA, Sept. 6, 1947.
CURTIS, JAMIE LEE: Los Angeles, CA, Nov. 22, 1958.
CURTIS, KEENE: Salt Lake City, UT, Feb. 15, 1925. U Utah.
CURTIS, TONY (Bernard Schwartz): NYC, June 3, 1924.
CUSACK, JOAN: Evanston, IL, Oct. 11, 1962.
CUSACK, JOHN: Chicago, IL, June 28, 1966.
CUSACK, SINEAD: Dalkey, Ireland, Feb. 18, 1948
DAFOE, WILLEM: Appleton, WI, July 22, 1955.
DAHL, ARLENE: Minneapolis, Aug. 11, 1928. U Minn.
DALE, JIM: Rothwell, England, Aug. 15, 1935.
DALLESANDRO, JOE: Pensacola, FL, Dec. 31, 1948.
DALTON, TIMOTHY: Colwyn Bay, Wales, Mar. 21, 1946. RADA.
DALTREY, ROGER: London, Mar. 1, 1944.
DALY, TIM: NYC, Mar. 1, 1956. Bennington College.
DALY, TYNE: Madison, WI, Feb. 21, 1947. AMDA.

Robert Duvall

Ethan Embry

Rupert Everett

Dennis Farina

DAMON, MATT: Cambridge, MA, Oct. 8, 1970.

DAMONE, VIC (Vito Farinola): Brooklyn, NY, June 12, 1928.

DANCE, CHARLES: Plymouth, England, Oct. 10, 1946.

DANES, CLAIRE: New York, NY, Apr. 12, 1979.

D'ANGELO, BEVERLY: Columbus, OH, Nov. 15, 1953.

DANGERFIELD, RODNEY (Jacob Cohen): Babylon, NY, Nov. 22, 1921.

DANIELS, JEFF: Athens, GA, Feb. 19, 1955. EMichSt.

DANIELS, WILLIAM: Brooklyn, NY, Mar. 31, 1927. Northwestern.

DANNER, BLYTHE: Philadelphia, PA, Feb. 3, 1944. Bard College.

DANNING, SYBIL (Sybille Johanna Danninger): Vienna, Austria, May 4, 1949.

DANSON, TED: San Diego, CA, Dec. 29, 1947. Stanford, Carnegie Tech.

DANTE, MICHAEL (Ralph Vitti): Stamford, CT, 1935. U Miami.

DANZA, TONY: Brooklyn, NY, Apr. 21, 1951. UDubuque.

D'ARBANVILLE-QUINN, PATTI: NYC, 1951.

DARBY, KIM (Deborah Zerby): North Hollywood, CA, July 8, 1948.

DARCEL, DENISE (Denise Billecard): Paris, France, Sept. 8, 1925. U Dijon.

DARREN, JAMES: Philadelphia, PA, June 8, 1936. Stella Adler School.

DARRIEUX, DANIELLE: Bordeaux, France, May 1, 1917. Lycee LaTour.

DAVENPORT, NIGEL: Cambridge, England, May 23, 1928. Trinity College.

DAVID, KEITH: NYC, June 4, 1954. Juilliard.

DAVIDOVICH, LOLITA: Toronto, Ontario, Canada, July 15, 1961.

DAVIDSON, JAYE: Riverside, CA, 1968.

DAVIDSON, JOHN: Pittsburgh, Dec. 13, 1941. Denison U.

DAVIS, CLIFTON: Chicago, IL, Oct. 4, 1945. Oakwood College.

DAVIS, GEENA: Wareham, MA, Jan. 21, 1957.

DAVIS, JUDY: Perth, Australia, Apr. 23, 1955.

DAVIS, MAC: Lubbock, TX, Jan. 21,1942.

DAVIS, NANCY (Anne Frances Robbins): NYC, July 6, 1921. Smith College.

DAVIS, OSSIE: Cogdell, GA, Dec. 18, 1917. Howard U.

DAVIS, SAMMI: Kidderminster, Worcestershire, England, June 21, 1964.

DAVISON, BRUCE: Philadelphia, PA, June 28, 1946.

DAWBER, PAM: Detroit, MI, Oct. 18, 1954.

DAY, DORIS (Doris Kappelhoff): Cincinnati, Apr. 3, 1924.

DAY, LARAINE (Johnson): Roosevelt, UT, Oct. 13, 1917.

DAY LEWIS, DANIEL: London, Apr. 29, 1957. Bristol Old Vic.

DAYAN, ASSI: Israel, Nov. 23, 1945. U Jerusalem.

DEAKINS, LUCY: NYC, 1971.

DEAN, JIMMY: Plainview, TX, Aug. 10, 1928.

DEAN, LOREN: Las Vegas, NV, July 31, 1969.

DeCAMP, ROSEMARY: Prescott, AZ, Nov. 14, 1913.

DeCARLO, YVONNE (Peggy Yvonne Middleton): Vancouver, B.C., Canada, Sept. 1, 1922. Vancouver School of Drama.

DEE, FRANCES: Los Angeles, Nov. 26, 1907. Chicago U.

DEE, JOEY (Joseph Di Nicola): Passaic, NJ, June 11, 1940. Patterson State College.

DEE, RUBY: Cleveland, OH, Oct. 27, 1924. Hunter College.

DEE, SANDRA (Alexandra Zuck): Bayonne, NJ, Apr. 23, 1942.

DeHAVEN, GLORIA: Los Angeles, July 23, 1923.

DeHAVILLAND, OLIVIA: Tokyo, Japan, July 1, 1916. Notre Dame Convent School.

DELAIR, SUZY (Suzanne Delaire): Paris, France, Dec. 31, 1916.

DELANY, DANA: NYC, March 13, 1956. Wesleyan U.

DELPY, JULIE: Paris. Dec, 21, 1969.

DELON, ALAIN: Sceaux, France, Nov. 8, 1935.

DELORME, DANIELE: Paris, France, Oct. 9, 1926. Sorbonne.

DeLUISE, DOM: Brooklyn, NY, Aug. 1, 1933. Tufts College.

DeLUISE, PETER: NYC, Nov. 6, 1966.

DEMONGEOT, MYLENE: Nice, France, Sept. 29, 1938.

DeMORNAY, REBECCA: Los Angeles, Aug. 29, 1962. Strasberg Inst.

DEMPSEY, PATRICK: Lewiston, ME, Jan. 13, 1966.

DeMUNN, JEFFREY: Buffalo, NY, Apr. 25, 1947. Union College.

DENCH, JUDI: York, England, Dec. 9, 1934.

DENEUVE, CATHERINE: Paris, France, Oct. 22, 1943.

DeNIRO, ROBERT: NYC, Aug. 17, 1943. Stella Adler.

DENISON, MICHAEL: Doncaster, York, England, Nov. 1, 1915. Oxford.

DENNEHY, BRIAN: Bridgeport, CT, Jul. 9, 1938. Columbia.

DENVER, BOB: New Rochelle, NY, Jan. 9, 1935.

DEPARDIEU, GERARD: Chateauroux, France, Dec. 27, 1948.

DEPP, JOHNNY: Owensboro, KY, June 9, 1963.

DEREK, BO (Mary Cathleen Collins): Long Beach, CA, Nov. 20, 1956.

DEREK, JOHN: Hollywood, Aug. 12, 1926.

DERN, BRUCE: Chicago, IL, June 4, 1936. UPA.

DERN, LAURA: Los Angeles, Feb. 10, 1967.

DeSALVO, ANNE: Philadelphia, Apr. 3.

DEVANE, WILLIAM: Albany, NY, Sept. 5, 1939.

DeVITO, DANNY: Asbury Park, NJ, Nov. 17, 1944.

DEXTER, ANTHONY (Walter Reinhold Alfred Fleischmann): Talmadge, NB, Jan. 19, 1919. U Iowa.

DEY, SUSAN: Pekin, IL, Dec. 10, 1953.

DeYOUNG, CLIFF: Los Angeles, CA, Feb. 12, 1945. Cal State.

DIAMOND, NEIL: NYC, Jan. 24, 1941. NYU.

DIAZ, CAMERON: Long Beach, CA, Aug. 30, 1972.

DiCAPRIO, LEONARDO: Hollywood, CA, Nov.11, 1974.

DICKINSON, ANGIE (Angeline Brown): Kulm, ND, Sept. 30, 1932. Glendale College.

DILLER, PHYLLIS (Driver): Lima, OH, July 17, 1917. Bluffton College.

DILLMAN, BRADFORD: San Francisco, Apr. 14, 1930. Yale.

DILLON, KEVIN: Mamaroneck, NY, Aug. 19, 1965.

DILLON, MATT: Larchmont, NY, Feb. 18, 1964. AADA.

DILLON, MELINDA: Hope, AR, Oct. 13, 1939. Goodman Theatre School.

DIXON, DONNA: Alexandria, VA, July 20, 1957.

DOBSON, KEVIN: NYC, Mar. 18, 1944.

DOBSON, TAMARA: Baltimore, MD, May 14, 1947. MD Inst. of Art.

DOHERTY, SHANNEN: Memphis, TN, Apr. 12, 1971.

DOLAN, MICHAEL: Oklahoma City, OK, June 21, 1965.

DOMERGUE, FAITH: New Orleans, June 16, 1925.

DONAHUE, TROY (Merle Johnson): NYC, Jan. 27, 1937. Columbia U.

DONAT, PETER: Nova Scotia, Jan. 20, 1928. Yale.

DONNELLY, DONAL: Bradford, England, July 6, 1931.

D'ONOFRIO, VINCENT: Brooklyn, NY, June 30, 1959.

DONOHOE, AMANDA: London, June 29 1962.

DONOVAN, TATE: NYC, Sept. 25, 1963.

DOOHAN, JAMES: Vancouver, BC, Mar. 3, 1920. Neighborhood Playhouse.

DOOLEY, PAUL: Parkersburg WV, Feb. 22, 1928. U WV.

DORFF, STEPHEN: CA, July 29, 1973.

DOUGLAS, DONNA (Dorothy Bourgeois): Baywood, LA, Sept. 26, 1935.

DOUGLAS, ILLEANA: MA, July 25, 1965.

DOUGLAS, KIRK (Issur Danielovitch): Amsterdam, NY, Dec. 9, 1916. St. Lawrence U.

DOUGLAS, MICHAEL: New Brunswick, NJ, Sept. 25, 1944. U Cal.

DOUGLASS, ROBYN: Sendai, Japan, June 21, 1953. UCDavis.

DOURIF, BRAD: Huntington, WV, Mar. 18, 1950. Marshall U.

DOWN, LESLEY-ANN: London, Mar. 17, 1954.

DOWNEY, ROBERT, JR.: NYC, Apr. 4, 1965.

DRAKE, BETSY: Paris, France, Sept. 11, 1923.

DRESCHER, FRAN: Queens, NY, Sept. 30, 1957.

DREW, ELLEN (formerly Terry Ray): Kansas City, MO, Nov. 23, 1915.

DREYFUSS, RICHARD: Brooklyn, NY, Oct. 19, 1947.

DRILLINGER, BRIAN: Brooklyn, NY, June 27, 1960. SUNY/Purchase.

DRIVER, MINNIE (Amelia Driver): London, Jan. 31, 1971.

DUCHOVNY, DAVID: NYC, Aug. 7, 1960. Yale.

DUDIKOFF, MICHAEL: Torrance, CA, Oct. 8, 1954.

DUGAN, DENNIS: Wheaton, IL, Sept. 5, 1946.

DUKAKIS, OLYMPIA: Lowell, MA, June 20, 1931.

DUKE, BILL: Poughkeepsie, NY, Feb. 26, 1943. NYU.

Sally Field

Ralph Fiennes

Linda Fiorentino

DUKE, PATTY (Anna Marie): NYC, Dec. 14, 1946.

DUKES, DAVID: San Francisco, June 6, 1945.

DULLEA, KEIR: Cleveland, NJ, May 30, 1936. SF State College.

DUNAWAY, FAYE: Bascom, FL, Jan. 14, 1941, Fla. U.

DUNCAN, SANDY: Henderson, TX, Feb. 20, 1946. Len Morris College.

DUNNE, GRIFFIN: NYC, June 8, 1955. Neighborhood Playhouse.

DUPEREY, ANNY: Paris, France, 1947.

DURBIN, DEANNA (Edna): Winnipeg, Canada, Dec. 4, 1921.

DURNING, CHARLES S. : Highland Falls, NY, Feb. 28, 1923. NYU.

DUSSOLLIER, ANDRE: Annecy, France, Feb. 17, 1946.

DUTTON, CHARLES: Baltimore, MD, Jan. 30, 1951. Yale.

DUVALL, ROBERT: San Diego, CA, Jan. 5, 1931. Principia College.

DUVALL, SHELLEY: Houston, TX, July 7, 1949.

DYSART, RICHARD: Brighton, ME, Mar. 30, 1929.

DZUNDZA, GEORGE: Rosenheim, Germ., July 19, 1945.

EASTON, ROBERT: Milwaukee, WI, Nov. 23, 1930. U Texas.

EASTWOOD, CLINT: San Francisco, May 31, 1931. LACC.

EATON, SHIRLEY: London, 1937. Aida Foster School.

EBSEN, BUDDY (Christian, Jr.): Belleville, IL, Apr. 2, 1910. U Fla.

ECKEMYR, AGNETA: Karlsborg, Sweden, July 2. Actors Studio.

EDELMAN, GREGG: Chicago, IL, Sept. 12, 1958. Northwestern U.

EDEN, BARBARA (Huffman): Tucson, AZ, Aug. 23, 1934.

EDWARDS, ANTHONY: Santa Barbara, CA, July 19, 1962. RADA.

EGGAR, SAMANTHA: London, Mar. 5, 1939.

EICHHORN, LISA: Reading, PA, Feb. 4, 1952. Queens Ont. U RADA.

EIKENBERRY, JILL: New Haven, CT, Jan. 21, 1947.

EILBER, JANET: Detroit, MI, July 27, 1951. Juilliard.

EKBERG, ANITA: Malmo, Sweden, Sept. 29, 1931.

EKLAND, BRITT: Stockholm, Sweden, Oct. 6, 1942.

ELDARD, RON: Long Island, NY, Feb. 20, 1965.

ELIZONDO, HECTOR: NYC, Dec. 22, 1936.

ELLIOTT, CHRIS: NYC, May 31, 1960.

ELLIOTT, PATRICIA: Gunnison, CO, July 21, 1942. UCol.

ELLIOTT, SAM: Sacramento, CA, Aug. 9, 1944. U Ore.

ELWES, CARY: London, Oct. 26, 1962.

ELY, RON (Ronald Pierce): Hereford, TX, June 21, 1938.

EMBRY, ETHAN (Ethan Randall): Huntington Beach, CA, June 13, 1978.

ENGLUND, ROBERT: Glendale, CA, June 6, 1949.

ERDMAN, RICHARD: Enid, OK, June 1, 1925.

ERICSON, JOHN: Dusseldorf, Ger., Sept. 25, 1926. AADA.

ERMEY, R. LEE (Ronald): Emporia, KS, Mar. 24, 1944.

ESMOND, CARL (Willy Eichberger): Vienna, June 14, 1906. U Vienna.

ESPOSITO, GIANCARLO: Copenhagen, Denmark, Apr. 26, 1958.

ESTEVEZ, EMILIO: NYC, May 12, 1962.

ESTRADA, ERIK: NYC, Mar. 16, 1949.

EVANS, DALE (Francis Smith): Uvalde, TX, Oct. 31, 1912.

EVANS, GENE: Holbrook, AZ, July 11, 1922.

EVANS, JOSH: NYC, Jan. 16, 1971.

EVANS, LINDA (Evanstad): Hartford, CT, Nov. 18, 1942.

EVERETT, CHAD (Ray Cramton): South Bend, IN, June 11, 1936.

EVERETT, RUPERT: Norfolk, England, 1959.

EVIGAN, GREG: South Amboy, NJ, Oct. 14, 1953.

FABARES, SHELLEY: Los Angeles, Jan. 19, 1944.

FABIAN (Fabian Forte): Philadelphia, Feb. 6, 1943.

FABRAY, NANETTE (Ruby Nanette Fabares): San Diego, Oct. 27, 1920.

FAHEY, JEFF: Olean, NY, Nov. 29, 1956.

FAIRBANKS, DOUGLAS, JR.: NYC, Dec. 9, 1907. Collegiate School.

FAIRCHILD, MORGAN (Patsy McClenny): Dallas, TX, Feb. 3, 1950. UCLA.

FALK, PETER: NYC, Sept. 16, 1927. New School.

FARENTINO, JAMES: Brooklyn, NY, Feb. 24, 1938. AADA.

FARGAS, ANTONIO: Bronx, NY, Aug. 14, 1946.

FARINA, DENNIS: Chicago, IL, Feb. 29, 1944.

FARINA, SANDY (Sandra Feldman): Newark, NJ, 1955.

FARNSWORTH, RICHARD: Los Angeles, Sept. 1, 1920.

FARR, FELICIA: Westchester, NY, Oct. 4, 1932. Penn State College.

FARROW, MIA (Maria): Los Angeles, Feb. 9, 1945.

FAULKNER, GRAHAM: London, Sept. 26, 1947. Webber-Douglas.

FAWCETT, FARRAH: Corpus Christie, TX, Feb. 2, 1947. TexU.

FAYE, ALICE (Ann Leppert): NYC, May 5, 1912.

FEINSTEIN, ALAN: NYC, Sept. 8, 1941.

FELDMAN, COREY: Encino, CA, July 16, 1971.

FELDON, BARBARA (Hall): Pittsburgh, Mar. 12, 1941. Carnegie Tech.

FELDSHUH, TOVAH: NYC, Dec. 27, 1953. Sarah Lawrence College.

FELL, NORMAN: Philadelphia, PA, Mar. 24, 1924.

FELLOWS, EDITH: Boston, May 20, 1923.

FENN, SHERILYN: Detroit, MI, Feb. 1, 1965.

FERRELL, CONCHATA: Charleston, WV, Mar. 28, 1943. Marshall U.

FERRER, MEL: Elbeton, NJ, Aug. 25, 1912. Princeton U.

FERRER, MIGUEL: Santa Monica, CA, Feb. 7, 1954.

FERRIS, BARBARA: London, 1943.

FIEDLER, JOHN: Plateville, WI, Feb. 3, 1925.

FIELD, SALLY: Pasadena, CA, Nov. 6, 1946.

FIELD, SHIRLEY-ANNE: London, June 27, 1938.

FIENNES, RALPH: Suffolk, England, Dec. 22, 1962. RADA.

FIERSTEIN, HARVEY: Brooklyn, NY, June 6, 1954. Pratt Inst.

FINCH, JON: Caterham, England, Mar. 2, 1941.

FINLAY, FRANK: Farnworth, England, Aug. 6, 1926.

FINNEY, ALBERT: Salford, Lancashire, England, May 9, 1936. RADA.

FIORENTINO, LINDA: Philadelphia, PA, Mar. 9, 1960.

FIRTH, COLIN: Grayshott, Hampshire, England, Sept. 10, 1960.

FIRTH, PETER: Bradford, England, Oct. 27, 1953.

FISHBURNE, LAURENCE: Augusta, GA, July 30, 1961.

FISHER, CARRIE: Los Angeles, CA, Oct. 21, 1956. London Central School of Drama.

FISHER, EDDIE: Philadelphia, PA, Aug. 10, 1928.

FISHER, FRANCES: Orange, TX, 1952.

FITZGERALD, TARA: London, Sept. 17, 1968.

FITZGERALD, GERALDINE: Dublin, Ireland, Nov. 24, 1914. Dublin Art School.

FLAGG, FANNIE: Birmingham, AL, Sept. 21, 1944. UAl.

FLANNERY, SUSAN: Jersey City, NJ, July 31, 1943.

FLEMING, RHONDA (Marilyn Louis): Los Angeles, Aug. 10, 1922.

FLEMYNG, ROBERT: Liverpool, England, Jan. 3, 1912. Haileybury College.

FLETCHER, LOUISE: Birmingham, AL, July 22 1934.

FOCH, NINA: Leyden, Holland, Apr. 20, 1924.

FOLLOWS, MEGAN: Toronto, Canada, Mar. 14, 1968.

FONDA, BRIDGET: Los Angeles, Jan. 27, 1964.

FONDA, JANE: NYC, Dec. 21, 1937. Vassar.

FONDA, PETER: NYC, Feb. 23, 1939. U Omaha.

FONTAINE, JOAN: Tokyo, Japan, Oct. 22, 1917.

FOOTE, HALLIE: NYC, 1953. UNH.

FORD, GLENN (Gwyllyn Samuel Newton Ford): Quebec, Canada, May 1, 1916.

FORD, HARRISON: Chicago, IL, July 13, 1942. Ripon College.

FOREST, MARK (Lou Degni): Brooklyn, NY, Jan. 1933.

FORREST, FREDERIC: Waxahachie, TX, Dec. 23, 1936.

FORREST, STEVE: Huntsville, TX, Sept. 29, 1924. UCLA.

FORSLUND, CONNIE: San Diego, CA, June 19, 1950. NYU.

FORSTER, ROBERT (Foster, Jr.): Rochester, NY, July 13, 1941. Rochester U.

FORSYTHE, JOHN (Freund): Penn's Grove, NJ, Jan. 29, 1918.

FORSYTHE, WILLIAM: Brooklyn, NY, June 7, 1955

FOSSEY, BRIGITTE: Tourcoing, France, Mar. 11, 1947.

Laurence Fishburne

Richard Gere

Danny Glover

Cuba Gooding, Jr.

David Marshall Grant

Andy Griffith

Linda Hamilton

Ed Harris

FOSTER, JODIE (Ariane Munker): Bronx, NY, Nov. 19, 1962. Yale.

FOSTER, MEG: Reading, PA, May 14, 1948.

FOX, EDWARD: London, Apr. 13, 1937. RADA.

FOX, JAMES: London, May 19, 1939.

FOX, MICHAEL J.: Vancouver, BC, June 9, 1961.

FOXWORTH, ROBERT: Houston, TX, Nov. 1, 1941. Carnegie Tech.

FRAKES, JONATHAN: Bethlehem, PA, Aug. 19, 1952. Harvard.

FRANCIOSA, ANTHONY (Papaleo): NYC, Oct. 25, 1928.

FRANCIS, ANNE: Ossining, NY, Sept. 16, 1932.

FRANCIS, ARLENE (Arlene Kazanjian): Boston, Oct. 20, 1908. Finch School.

FRANCIS, CONNIE (Constance Franconero): Newark, NJ, Dec. 12, 1938.

FRANCKS, DON: Vancouver, Canada, Feb. 28, 1932.

FRANKLIN, PAMELA: Tokyo, Feb. 4, 1950.

FRANZ, ARTHUR: Perth Amboy, NJ, Feb. 29, 1920. Blue Ridge College.

FRANZ, DENNIS: Chicago, IL, Oct. 28, 1944.

FRASER, BRENDAN: Indianapolis, IN, Dec. 3, 1968.

FRAZIER, SHEILA: NYC, Nov. 13, 1948.

FRECHETTE, PETER: Warwick, RI, Oct. 1956. URI.

FREEMAN, AL, JR.: San Antonio, TX, Mar. 21, 1934. CCLA.

FREEMAN, KATHLEEN: Chicago, IL, Feb. 17, 1919.

FREEMAN, MONA: Baltimore, MD, June 9, 1926.

FREEMAN, MORGAN: Memphis, TN, June 1, 1937. LACC.

FREWER, MATT: Washington, DC, Jan. 4, 1958, Old Vic.

FRICKER, BRENDA: Dublin, Ireland, Feb. 17, 1945.

FRIELS, COLIN: Glasgow, Sept. 25, 1952.

FRY, STEPHEN: Hampstead, London, Eng., Aug. 24, 1957.

FULLER, PENNY: Durham, NC, 1940. Northwestern U.

FUNICELLO, ANNETTE: Utica, NY, Oct. 22, 1942.

FURLONG, EDWARD: Glendale, CA, Aug. 2, 1977.

FURNEAUX, YVONNE: Lille, France, 1928. Oxford U.

GABLE, JOHN CLARK: Los Angeles, Mar. 20, 1961. Santa Monica College.

GABOR, ZSA ZSA (Sari Gabor): Budapest, Hungary, Feb. 6, 1918.

GAIL, MAX: Derfoil, MI, Apr. 5, 1943.

GAINES, BOYD: Atlanta, GA, May 11, 1953. Juilliard.

GALLAGHER, PETER: NYC, Aug. 19, 1955. Tufts U.

GALLIGAN, ZACH: NYC, Feb. 14, 1963. ColumbiaU.

GAM, RITA: Pittsburgh, PA, Apr. 2, 1928.

GAMBON, MICHAEL: Dublin, Ireland, Oct. 19, 1940.

GANZ, BRUNO: Zurich, Switzerland, Mar. 22, 1941.

GARBER, VICTOR: Montreal, Canada, Mar. 16, 1949.

GARCIA, ANDY: Havana, Cuba, Apr. 12, 1956. FlaInt.

GARFIELD, ALLEN (Allen Goorwitz): Newark, NJ, Nov. 22, 1939. Actors Studio.

GARFUNKEL, ART: NYC, Nov. 5, 1941.

GARLAND, BEVERLY: Santa Cruz, CA, Oct. 17, 1926. Glendale College.

GARNER, JAMES (James Baumgarner): Norman, OK, Apr. 7, 1928. Okla. U.

GAROFALO, JANEANE: Newton, NJ, Sept. 28, 1964.

GARR, TERI: Lakewood, OH, Dec. 11, 1949.

GARRETT, BETTY: St. Joseph, MO, May 23, 1919. Annie Wright Seminary.

GARRISON, SEAN: NYC, Oct. 19, 1937.

GARY, LORRAINE: NYC, Aug. 16, 1937.

GASSMAN, VITTORIO: Genoa, Italy, Sept. 1,1922. Rome Academy of Dramatic Art.

GAVIN, JOHN: Los Angeles, Apr. 8, 1935. Stanford U.

GAYLORD, MITCH: Van Nuys, CA, Mar. 10, 1961. UCLA.

GAYNOR, MITZI (Francesca Marlene Von Gerber): Chicago, IL, Sept. 4, 1930.

GAZZARA, BEN: NYC, Aug. 28, 1930. Actors Studio.

GEARY, ANTHONY: Coalsville, UT, May 29, 1947. UUt.

GEDRICK, JASON: Chicago, IL, Feb. 7, 1965. Drake U.

GEESON, JUDY: Arundel, England, Sept. 10, 1948. Corona.

GEOFFREYS, STEPHEN: Cincinnati, OH, Nov. 22, 1964. NYU.

GEORGE, SUSAN: West London, England, July 26, 1950.

GERARD, GIL: Little Rock, AR, Jan. 23, 1940.

GERE, RICHARD: Philadelphia, PA, Aug. 29, 1949. U Mass.

GERROLL, DANIEL: London, Oct. 16, 1951. Central.

GERTZ, JAMI: Chicago, IL, Oct. 28, 1965.

GETTY, BALTHAZAR: Los Angeles, CA, Jan. 22, 1975.

GETTY, ESTELLE: NYC, July 25, 1923. New School.

GHOLSON, JULIE: Birmingham, AL, June 4, 1958.

GHOSTLEY, ALICE: Eve, MO, Aug. 14, 1926. Okla U.

GIANNINI, GIANCARLO: Spezia, Italy, Aug. 1, 1942. Rome Acad. of Drama.

GIBB, CYNTHIA: Bennington, VT, Dec. 14, 1963.

GIBSON, HENRY: Germantown, PA, Sept. 21, 1935.

GIBSON, MEL: Peekskill, NY, Jan. 3, 1956. NIDA.

GIELGUD, JOHN: London, Apr. 14, 1904. RADA.

GIFT, ROLAND: Birmingham, England, May 28 1962.

GILBERT, MELISSA: Los Angeles, CA, May 8, 1964.

GILES, NANCY: NYC, July 17, 1960. Oberlin College.

GILLETTE, ANITA: Baltimore, MD, Aug. 16, 1938.

GILLIAM, TERRY: Minneapolis, MN, Nov. 22, 1940.

GILLIS, ANN (Alma O'Connor): Little Rock, AR, Feb. 12, 1927.

GINTY, ROBERT: NYC, Nov. 14, 1948. Yale.

Ethan Hawke

GIRARDOT, ANNIE: Paris, France, Oct. 25, 1931.

GISH, ANNABETH: Albuquerque, NM, Mar. 13, 1971. DukeU.

GIVENS, ROBIN: NYC, Nov. 27, 1964.

GLASER, PAUL MICHAEL: Boston, MA, Mar. 25, 1943. Boston U.

GLASS, RON: Evansville, IN, July 10, 1945.

GLEASON, JOANNA: Winnipeg, Canada, June 2, 1950. UCLA.

GLEASON, PAUL: Jersey City, NJ, May 4, 1944.

GLENN, SCOTT: Pittsburgh, PA, Jan. 26, 1942. William and Mary College.

GLOVER, CRISPIN: NYC, Sept 20, 1964.

GLOVER, DANNY: San Francisco, CA, July 22, 1947. SFStateCol.

GLOVER, JOHN: Kingston, NY, Aug. 7, 1944.

GLYNN, CARLIN: Cleveland, Oh, Feb. 19, 1940. Actors Studio.

GOLDBERG, WHOOPI (Caryn Johnson): NYC, Nov. 13, 1949.

GOLDBLUM, JEFF: Pittsburgh, PA, Oct. 22, 1952. Neighborhood Playhouse.

GOLDEN, ANNIE: Brooklyn, NY, Oct. 19, 1951.

GOLDSTEIN, JENETTE: Beverly Hills, CA, 1960.

GOLDTHWAIT, BOB: Syracuse, NY, May 1, 1962.

GOLDWYN, TONY: Los Angeles, May 20, 1960. LAMDA.

GOLINO, VALERIA: Naples, Italy, Oct. 22, 1966.

GONZALEZ, CORDELIA: Aug. 11, 1958, San Juan, PR. UPR.

GONZALES-GONZALEZ, PEDRO: Aguilares, TX, Dec. 21, 1926.

GOODALL, CAROLINE: London, Nov. 13, 1959. BristolU.

GOODING, CUBA, JR.: Bronx, N.Y., Jan. 2, 1968.

GOODMAN, DODY: Columbus, OH, Oct. 28, 1915.

GOODMAN, JOHN: St. Louis, MO, June 20, 1952.

GORDON, KEITH: NYC, Feb. 3, 1961.

GORMAN, CLIFF: Jamaica, NY, Oct. 13, 1936. NYU.

GORSHIN, FRANK: Pittsburgh, PA, Apr. 5, 1933.

GORTNER, MARJOE: Long Beach, CA, Jan. 14, 1944.

GOSSETT, LOUIS, JR.: Brooklyn, NY, May 27, 1936. NYU.

GOULD, ELLIOTT (Goldstein): Brooklyn, NY, Aug. 29, 1938. Columbia U.

GOULD, HAROLD: Schenectady, NY, Dec. 10, 1923. Cornell.

GOULD, JASON: NYC, Dec. 29, 1966.

GOULET, ROBERT: Lawrence, MA, Nov. 26, 1933. Edmonton.

GRAF, DAVID: Lancaster, OH, Apr. 16, 1950. OhStateU.

GRAFF, TODD: NYC, Oct. 22, 1959. SUNY/Purchase.

GRAHAM, HEATHER: Milwaukee, WI, Jan. 29, 1970.

GRANGER, FARLEY: San Jose, CA, July 1, 1925.

GRANT, DAVID MARSHALL: Westport, CT, June 21, 1955. Yale.

GRANT, HUGH: London, Sept. 9, 1960. Oxford.

GRANT, KATHRYN (Olive Grandstaff): Houston, TX, Nov. 25, 1933. UCLA.

GRANT, LEE: NYC, Oct. 31, 1927. Juilliard.

GRANT, RICHARD E: Mbabane, Swaziland, May 5, 1957. Cape Town U.

GRAVES, PETER (Aurness): Minneapolis, Mar. 18, 1926. U Minn.

GRAVES, RUPERT: Weston-Super-Mare, England, June 30, 1963.

GRAY, CHARLES: Bournemouth, England, 1928.

GRAY, COLEEN (Doris Jensen): Staplehurst, NB, Oct. 23, 1922. Hamline.

GRAY, LINDA: Santa Monica, CA, Sept. 12, 1940.

GRAY, SPALDING: Barrington, RI, June 5, 1941.

GRAYSON, KATHRYN (Zelma Hedrick): Winston-Salem, NC, Feb. 9, 1922.

GREEN, KERRI: Fort Lee, NJ, Jan. 14, 1967. Vassar.

GREENE, ELLEN: NYC, Feb. 22, 1950. Ryder College.

GREENE, GRAHAM: Six Nations Reserve, Ontario, June 22, 1952

GREER, JANE: Washington, DC, Sept. 9, 1924.

Samuel L.Jackson

GREER, MICHAEL: Galesburg, IL, Apr. 20, 1943.

GREIST, KIM: Stamford, CT, May 12, 1958.

GREY, JENNIFER: NYC, Mar. 26, 1960.

GREY, JOEL (Katz): Cleveland, OH, Apr. 11, 1932.

GREY, VIRGINIA: Los Angeles, Mar. 22, 1917.

GRIECO, RICHARD: Watertown, NY, Mar. 23, 1965.

GRIEM, HELMUT: Hamburg, Germany, Apr. 6, 1932. HamburgU.

GRIER, DAVID ALAN: Detroit, MI, June 30, 1955. Yale.

GRIER, PAM: Winston-Salem, NC, May 26, 1949.

GRIFFITH, ANDY: Mt. Airy, NC, June 1, 1926. UNC.

GRIFFITH, MELANIE: NYC, Aug. 9, 1957. Pierce College.

GRIMES, GARY: San Francisco, June 2, 1955.

GRIMES, SCOTT: Lowell, MA, July 9, 1971.

GRIMES, TAMMY: Lynn, MA, Jan. 30, 1934. Stephens College.

GRIZZARD, GEORGE: Roanoke Rapids, NC, Apr. 1, 1928. UNC.

GRODIN, CHARLES: Pittsburgh, PA, Apr. 21, 1935.

Anne Heche

James Earl Jones

Nicole Kidman

GROH, DAVID: NYC, May 21, 1939. Brown U, LAMDA.
GROSS, MARY: Chicago, IL, Mar. 25, 1953.
GROSS, MICHAEL: Chicago, IL, June 21, 1947.
GUEST, CHRISTOPHER: NYC, Feb. 5, 1948.
GUEST, LANCE: Saratoga, CA, July 21, 1960. UCLA.
GUILLAUME, ROBERT (Williams): St. Louis, MO, Nov. 30, 1937.
GUINNESS, ALEC: London, Apr. 2, 1914. Pembroke Lodge School.
GULAGER, CLU: Holdenville, OK, Nov. 16 1928.
GUTTENBERG, STEVE: Massapequa, NY, Aug. 24, 1958. UCLA.
GUY, JASMINE: Boston, Mar. 10, 1964.
HAAS, LUKAS: West Hollywood, CA, Apr. 16, 1976.
HACK, SHELLEY: Greenwich, CT, July 6, 1952.
HACKETT, BUDDY (Leonard Hacker): Brooklyn, NY, Aug. 31, 1924.
HACKMAN, GENE: San Bernardino, CA, Jan. 30, 1930.
HAGERTY, JULIE: Cincinnati, OH, June 15, 1955. Juilliard.

HAGMAN, LARRY (Hageman): Weatherford, TX, Sept. 21, 1931. Bard.
HAID, CHARLES: San Francisco, June 2, 1943. CarnegieTech.
HAIM, COREY: Toronto, Canada, Dec. 23, 1972.
HALE, BARBARA: DeKalb, IL, Apr. 18, 1922. Chicago Academy of Fine Arts.
HALEY, JACKIE EARLE: Northridge, CA, July 14, 1961.
HALL, ALBERT: Boothton, AL, Nov. 10, 1937. Columbia.
HALL, ANTHONY MICHAEL: Boston, MA, Apr. 14, 1968.
HALL, ARSENIO: Cleveland, OH, Feb. 12, 1959.
HALL, HUNTZ: Boston, MA, Aug. 15, 1920.
HAMEL, VERONICA: Philadelphia, PA, Nov. 20, 1943.
HAMILL, MARK: Oakland, CA, Sept. 25, 1952. LACC.
HAMILTON, CARRIE: NYC, Dec. 5, 1963.
HAMILTON, GEORGE: Memphis, TN, Aug. 12, 1939. Hackley.
HAMILTON, LINDA: Salisbury, MD, Sept. 26, 1956.
HAMLIN, HARRY: Pasadena, CA, Oct. 30, 1951.
HAMPSHIRE, SUSAN: London, May 12, 1941.
HAMPTON, JAMES: Oklahoma City, OK, July 9, 1936. NTexasStU.
HAN, MAGGIE: Providence, RI, 1959.
HANDLER, EVAN: NYC, Jan. 10, 1961. Juillard.
HANKS, TOM: Concord, CA, Jul. 9, 1956. CalStateU.
HANNAH, DARYL: Chicago, IL, Dec. 3, 1960. UCLA.
HANNAH, PAGE: Chicago, IL, Apr. 13, 1964.
HARDIN, TY (Orison Whipple Hungerford, II): NYC, June 1, 1930.
HAREWOOD, DORIAN: Dayton, OH, Aug. 6, 1950. U Cinn.
HARMON, MARK: Los Angeles, CA, Sept. 2, 1951. UCLA.
HARPER, JESSICA: Chicago, IL, Oct. 10, 1949.
HARPER, TESS: Mammoth Spring, AK, 1952. SWMoState.
HARPER, VALERIE: Suffern, NY, Aug. 22, 1940.
HARRELSON, WOODY: Midland, TX, July 23, 1961. Hanover College.
HARRINGTON, PAT: NYC, Aug. 13, 1929. Fordham U.
HARRIS, BARBARA (Sandra Markowitz): Evanston, IL, July 25, 1935.
HARRIS, ED: Tenafly, NJ, Nov. 28, 1950. Columbia.
HARRIS, JULIE: Grosse Point, MI, Dec. 2, 1925. Yale Drama School.
HARRIS, MEL (Mary Ellen): Bethlehem, PA, 1957. Columbia.
HARRIS, RICHARD: Limerick, Ireland, Oct. 1, 1930. London Acad.
HARRIS, ROSEMARY: Ashby, England, Sept. 19, 1930. RADA.
HARRISON, GEORGE: Liverpool, England, Feb. 25, 1943.
HARRISON, GREGORY: Catalina Island, CA, May 31, 1950. Actors Studio.
HARRISON, NOEL: London, Jan. 29, 1936.

Natassja Kinski

HARROLD, KATHRYN: Tazewell, VA, Aug. 2, 1950. Mills College.
HARRY, DEBORAH: Miami, IL, July 1, 1945.
HART, ROXANNE: Trenton, NJ, 1952, Princeton.
HARTLEY, MARIETTE: NYC, June 21, 1941.
HARTMAN, DAVID: Pawtucket, RI, May 19, 1935. Duke U.
HARTMAN, PHIL: Ontario, Canada, Sept. 24, 1948.
HASSETT, MARILYN: Los Angeles, CA, Dec. 17, 1947.
HATCHER, TERI: Sunnyvale, CA, Dec. 8, 1964.
HAUER, RUTGER: Amsterdam, Holland, Jan. 23, 1944.
HAVER, JUNE: Rock Island, IL, June 10, 1926.
HAVOC, JUNE (Hovick): Seattle, WA, Nov. 8, 1916.
HAWKE, ETHAN: Austin, TX, Nov. 6, 1970.
HAWN, GOLDIE: Washington, DC, Nov. 21, 1945.
HAWTHORNE, NIGEL: Coventry, Eng., Apr. 5, 1929.
HAYEK, SALMA: Coatzacoalcos, Veracruz, Mexico, Sept. 2, 1968.

Harvey Keitel

Kevin Kline

Bruno Kirby

Nathan Lane

John Leguizamo

Robert Sean Leonard

HAYES, ISAAC: Covington, TN, Aug. 20, 1942.

HAYS, ROBERT: Bethesda, MD, July 24, 1947, SD State College.

HEADLY, GLENNE: New London, CT, Mar. 13, 1955. AmCollege.

HEALD, ANTHONY: New Rochelle, NY, Aug. 25, 1944. MIStateU.

HEARD, JOHN: Washington, DC, Mar. 7, 1946. Clark U.

HEATHERTON, JOEY: NYC, Sept. 14, 1944.

HECHE, ANNE: Aurora, OH, May 25, 1969.

HECKART, EILEEN: Columbus, OH, Mar. 29, 1919. Ohio State U.

HEDAYA, DAN: Brooklyn, NY, July 24, 1940.

HEDISON, DAVID: Providence, RI, May 20, 1929. Brown U.

HEDREN, TIPPI (Natalie): Lafayette, MN, Jan. 19, 1931.

HEGYES, ROBERT: Metuchen, NJ, May 7, 1951.

HELMOND, KATHERINE: Galveston, TX, July 5, 1934.

HEMINGWAY, MARIEL: Ketchum, ID, Nov. 22, 1961.

HEMMINGS, DAVID: Guilford, England, Nov. 18, 1941.

HEMSLEY, SHERMAN: Philadelphia, PA, Feb. 1, 1938.

HENDERSON, FLORENCE: Dale, IN, Feb. 14, 1934.

HENDRY, GLORIA: Jacksonville, FL, 1949.

HENNER, MARILU: Chicago, IL, Apr. 6, 1952.

HENRIKSEN, LANCE: NYC, May 5, 1940.

HENRY, BUCK (Henry Zuckerman): NYC, Dec. 9, 1930. Dartmouth.

HENRY, JUSTIN: Rye, NY, May 25, 1971.

HEPBURN, KATHARINE: Hartford, CT, May 12, 1907. Bryn Mawr.

HERMAN, PEE-WEE (Paul Reubenfeld): Peekskill, NY, Aug. 27, 1952.

HERRMANN, EDWARD: Washington, DC, July 21, 1943. Bucknell, LAMDA.

HERSHEY, BARBARA (Herzstein): Hollywood, CA, Feb. 5, 1948.

HESSEMAN. HOWARD: Lebanon, OR, Feb. 27, 1940.

HESTON, CHARLTON: Evanston, IL, Oct. 4, 1922. Northwestern U.

HEWITT, JENNIFER LOVE: Waco, TX, Feb. 21, 1979.

HEWITT, MARTIN: Claremont, CA, Feb. 19, 1958. AADA.

HEYWOOD, ANNE (Violet Pretty): Birmingham, England, Dec. 11, 1932.

HICKMAN, DARRYL: Hollywood, CA, July 28, 1933. Loyola U.

HICKMAN, DWAYNE: Los Angeles, May 18, 1934. Loyola U.

HICKS, CATHERINE: NYC, Aug. 6, 1951. Notre Dame.

HIGGINS, ANTHONY (Corlan): Cork City, Ireland, May 9, 1947. Birmingham Sch. of Dramatic Arts.

HIGGINS, MICHAEL: Brooklyn, NY, Jan. 20, 1926. AmThWing.

HILL, ARTHUR: Saskatchewan, Canada, Aug. 1, 1922. U Brit. College.

HILL, BERNARD: Manchester, England, Dec. 17, 1944.

HILL, STEVEN: Seattle, WA, Feb. 24, 1922. U Wash.

HILL, TERRENCE (Mario Girotti): Venice, Italy, Mar. 29, 1941. U Rome.

HILLER, WENDY: Bramhall, Cheshire, England, Aug. 15, 1912. Winceby House School.

HILLERMAN, JOHN: Denison, TX, Dec. 20, 1932.

HINES, GREGORY: NYC, Feb.14, 1946.

HINGLE, PAT: Denver, CO, July 19, 1923. Tex. U.

HIRSCH, JUDD: NYC, Mar. 15, 1935. AADA.

HOBEL, MARA: NYC, June 18, 1971.

HODGE, PATRICIA: Lincolnshire, England, Sept. 29, 1946. LAMDA.

HOFFMAN, DUSTIN: Los Angeles, Aug. 8, 1937. Pasadena Playhouse.

HOGAN, JONATHAN: Chicago, IL, June 13, 1951.

HOGAN, PAUL: Lightning Ridge, Australia, Oct. 8, 1939.

HOLBROOK, HAL (Harold): Cleveland, OH, Feb. 17, 1925. Denison.

HOLLIMAN, EARL: Tennesas Swamp, Delhi, LA, Sept. 11, 1928. UCLA.

HOLM, CELESTE: NYC, Apr. 29, 1919.

HOLM, IAN: Ilford, Essex, England, Sept. 12, 1931. RADA.

HOMEIER, SKIP (George Vincent Homeier): Chicago, IL, Oct. 5, 1930. UCLA.

HOOKS, ROBERT: Washington, DC, Apr. 18, 1937. Temple.

HOPE, BOB (Leslie Townes Hope): London, May 26, 1903.

HOPKINS, ANTHONY: Port Talbot, So. Wales, Dec. 31, 1937. RADA.

HOPPER, DENNIS: Dodge City, KS, May 17, 1936.

HORNE, LENA: Brooklyn, NY, June 30, 1917.

HORSLEY, LEE: Muleshoe, TX, May 15, 1955.

HORTON, ROBERT: Los Angeles, July 29, 1924. UCLA.

HOSKINS, BOB: Bury St. Edmunds, England, Oct. 26, 1942.

HOUGHTON, KATHARINE: Hartford, CT, Mar. 10, 1945. Sarah Lawrence.

HOUSER, JERRY: Los Angeles, July 14, 1952. Valley, Jr. College.

HOWARD, ARLISS: Independence, MO, 1955. Columbia College.

HOWARD, KEN: El Centro, CA, Mar. 28, 1944. Yale.

HOWARD, RON: Duncan, OK, Mar. 1, 1954. USC.

HOWARD, RONALD: Norwood, England, Apr. 7, 1918. Jesus College.

HOWELL, C. THOMAS: Los Angeles, Dec. 7, 1966.

HOWELLS, URSULA: London, Sept. 17, 1922.

HOWES, SALLY ANN: London, July 20, 1930.

HOWLAND, BETH: Boston, MA, May 28, 1941.

HUBLEY, SEASON: NYC, May 14, 1951.

HUDDLESTON, DAVID: Vinton, VA, Sept. 17, 1930.

HUDSON, ERNIE: Benton Harbor, MI, Dec. 17, 1945.

HUGHES, BARNARD: Bedford Hills, NY, July 16, 1915. Manhattan College.

HUGHES, KATHLEEN (Betty von Gerkan): Hollywood, CA, Nov. 14, 1928. UCLA.

HULCE, TOM: Plymouth, MI, Dec. 6, 1953. N.C. Sch. of Arts.

HUNNICUT, GAYLE: Ft. Worth, TX, Feb. 6, 1943. UCLA.

HUNT, HELEN: Los Angeles, June 15, 1963.

HUNT, LINDA: Morristown, NJ, Apr. 1945. Goodman Theatre.

HUNT, MARSHA: Chicago, IL, Oct. 17, 1917.

HUNTER, HOLLY: Atlanta, GA, Mar. 20, 1958. Carnegie-Mellon.

HUNTER, KIM (Janet Cole): Detroit, Nov. 12, 1922.

HUNTER, TAB (Arthur Gelien): NYC, July 11, 1931.

HUPPERT, ISABELLE: Paris, France, Mar. 16, 1955.

HURLEY, ELIZABETH: Hampshire, Eng., June 10, 1965.

HURT, JOHN: Lincolnshire, England, Jan. 22, 1940.

HURT, MARY BETH (Supinger): Marshalltown, IA, Sept. 26, 1948. NYU.

HURT, WILLIAM: Washington, DC, Mar. 20, 1950. Tufts, Juilliard.

HUSSEY, RUTH: Providence, RI, Oct. 30, 1917. U Mich.

HUSTON, ANJELICA: Santa Monica, CA, July 9, 1951.

HUTTON, BETTY (Betty Thornberg): Battle Creek, MI, Feb. 26, 1921.

HUTTON, LAUREN (Mary): Charleston, SC, Nov. 17, 1943. Newcomb College.

HUTTON, TIMOTHY: Malibu, CA, Aug. 16, 1960.

HYER, MARTHA: Fort Worth, TX, Aug. 10, 1924. Northwestern U.

ICE CUBE (O'Shea Jackson): Los Angeles, June 15, 1969.

IDLE, ERIC: South Shields, Durham, England, Mar. 29, 1943. Cambridge.

INGELS, MARTY: Brooklyn, NY, Mar. 9, 1936.

IRELAND, KATHY: Santa Barbara, CA, Mar. 8, 1963.

IRONS, JEREMY: Cowes, England, Sept. 19, 1948. Old Vic.

IRVING, AMY: Palo Alto, CA, Sept. 10, 1953. LADA.

IRWIN, BILL: Santa Monica, CA, Apr. 11, 1950.

ISAAK, CHRIS: Stockton, CA, June 26, 1956. UofPacific.

IVANEK, ZELJKO: Lujubljana, Yugo., Aug. 15, 1957. Yale, LAMDA.

IVEY, JUDITH: El Paso, TX, Sept. 4, 1951.

JACKSON, ANNE: Alleghany, PA, Sept. 3, 1926. Neighborhood Playhouse.

JACKSON, GLENDA: Hoylake, Cheshire, England, May 9, 1936. RADA.

JACKSON, JANET: Gary, IN, May 16, 1966.

JACKSON, KATE: Birmingham, AL, Oct. 29, 1948. AADA.

JACKSON, MICHAEL: Gary, IN, Aug. 29, 1958.

JACKSON, SAMUELL.: Atlanta, Dec. 21, 1948.

JACKSON, VICTORIA: Miami, FL, Aug. 2, 1958.

JACOBI, DEREK: Leytonstone, London, Oct. 22, 1938. Cambridge.

JACOBI, LOU: Toronto, Canada, Dec. 28, 1913.

JACOBS, LAWRENCE-HILTON: Virgin Islands, Sept. 14, 1953.

JACOBY, SCOTT: Chicago, IL, Nov. 19, 1956.

JAGGER, MICK: Dartford, Kent, England, July 26, 1943.

JAMES, CLIFTON: NYC, May 29, 1921. Ore. U.

JARMAN, CLAUDE, JR.: Nashville, TN, Sept. 27, 1934.

JASON, RICK: NYC, May 21, 1926. AADA.

JEAN, GLORIA (Gloria Jean Schoonover): Buffalo, NY, Apr. 14, 1927.

JEFFREYS, ANNE (Carmichael): Goldsboro, NC, Jan. 26, 1923. Anderson College.

JEFFRIES, LIONEL: London, June 10, 1926. RADA.

JERGENS, ADELE: Brooklyn, NY, Nov. 26, 1922.

JETER, MICHAEL: Lawrenceburg, TN, Aug. 26, 1952. Memphis St.U.

JILLIAN, ANN (Nauseda): Cambridge, MA, Jan. 29, 1951.

JOHANSEN, DAVID: Staten Island, NY, Jan. 9, 1950.

JOHN, ELTON (Reginald Dwight): Middlesex, England, Mar. 25, 1947. RAM.

JOHNS, GLYNIS: Durban, S. Africa, Oct. 5, 1923.

JOHNSON, DON: Galena, MO, Dec. 15, 1950. UKan.

JOHNSON, PAGE: Welch, WV, Aug. 25, 1930. Ithaca.

JOHNSON, RAFER: Hillsboro, TX, Aug. 18, 1935. UCLA.

JOHNSON, RICHARD: Essex, England, July 30, 1927. RADA.

JOHNSON, ROBIN: Brooklyn, NY, May 29, 1964.

JOHNSON, VAN: Newport, RI, Aug. 28, 1916.

JONES, CHRISTOPHER: Jackson, TN, Aug. 18, 1941. Actors Studio.

JONES, DEAN: Decatur, AL, Jan. 25, 1931. Actors Studio.

JONES, GRACE: Spanishtown, Jamaica, May 19, 1952.

JONES, JACK: Bel-Air, CA, Jan. 14, 1938.

JONES, JAMES EARL: Arkabutla, MS, Jan. 17, 1931. U Mich.

JONES, JEFFREY: Buffalo, NY, Sept. 28, 1947. LAMDA.

JONES, JENNIFER (Phyllis Isley): Tulsa, OK, Mar. 2, 1919. AADA.

JONES, L.Q. (Justice Ellis McQueen): Aug 19, 1927.

JONES, SAM J.: Chicago, IL, Aug. 12, 1954.

JONES, SHIRLEY: Smithton, PA, March 31, 1934.

JONES, TERRY: Colwyn Bay, Wales, Feb. 1, 1942.

JONES, TOMMY LEE: San Saba, TX, Sept. 15, 1946. Harvard.

Laura Linney

Michael Madsen

Stephen Mailer

Dylan McDermott

JOURDAN, LOUIS: Marseilles, France, June 19, 1920.

JOY, ROBERT: Montreal, Canada, Aug. 17, 1951. Oxford.

JUDD, ASHLEY: Los Angeles, CA, Apr. 19, 1968.

JURADO, KATY (Maria Christina Jurado Garcia): Guadalajara, Mex., Jan. 16, 1927.

KACZMAREK, JANE: Milwaukee, WI, Dec. 21, 1955.

KAHN, MADELINE: Boston, MA, Sept. 29, 1942. Hofstra U.

KANE, CAROL: Cleveland, OH, June 18, 1952.

KAPLAN, MARVIN: Brooklyn, NY, Jan. 24, 1924.

KAPOOR, SHASHI: Calcutta, India, Mar. 18, 1938.

KAPRISKY, VALERIE (Cheres): Paris, France, Aug. 19, 1962.

KARRAS, ALEX: Gary, IN, July 15, 1935.

KATT, WILLIAM: Los Angeles, CA, Feb. 16, 1955.

KAUFMANN, CHRISTINE: Lansdorf, Graz, Austria, Jan. 11, 1945.

KAVNER, JULIE: Burbank, CA, Sept. 7, 1951. UCLA.

KAZAN, LAINIE (Levine): Brooklyn, NY, May 15, 1942.

KAZURINSKY, TIM: Johnstown, PA, March 3, 1950.

KEACH, STACY: Savannah, GA, June 2, 1941. U Cal., Yale.

KEATON, DIANE (Hall): Los Angeles, CA, Jan. 5, 1946. Neighborhood Playhouse.

KEATON, MICHAEL: Coraopolis, PA, Sept. 9, 1951. KentStateU.

KEDROVA, LILA: Leningrad, 1918.

KEEL, HOWARD (Harold Leek): Gillespie, IL, Apr. 13, 1919.

KEITEL, HARVEY: Brooklyn, NY, May 13, 1939.

KEITH, DAVID: Knoxville, TN, May 8, 1954. UTN.

KELLER, MARTHE: Basel, Switzerland, 1945. Munich Stanislavsky Sch.

KELLERMAN, SALLY: Long Beach, CA, June 2, 1936. Actors Studio West.

KELLEY, DeFOREST: Atlanta, GA, Jan. 20, 1920.

KEMP, JEREMY (Wacker): Chesterfield, England, Feb. 3, 1935. Central Sch.

KENNEDY, GEORGE: NYC, Feb. 18, 1925.

KENNEDY, LEON ISAAC: Cleveland, OH, 1949.

KENSIT, PATSY: London, Mar. 4, 1968.

KERR, DEBORAH: Helensburg, Scotland, Sept. 30, 1921. Smale Ballet School.

KERR, JOHN: NYC, Nov. 15, 1931. Harvard, Columbia.

KERWIN, BRIAN: Chicago, IL, Oct. 25, 1949.

KEYES, EVELYN: Port Arthur, TX, Nov. 20, 1919.

KHAMBATTA, PERSIS: Bombay, Oct. 2, 1950.

KIDDER, MARGOT: Yellow Knife, Canada, Oct. 17, 1948. UBC.

KIDMAN, NICOLE: Hawaii, June 20, 1967.

KIEL, RICHARD: Detroit, MI, Sept. 13, 1939.

KIER, UDO: Koeln, Germany, Oct. 14, 1944.

KILEY, RICHARD: Chicago, IL, Mar. 31, 1922. Loyola.

Bette Midler

Julianne Moore

Rob Morrow

KILMER, VAL: Los Angeles, Dec. 31, 1959. Juilliard.

KINCAID, ARON (Norman Neale Williams, III): Los Angeles, June 15, 1943. UCLA.

KING, ALAN (Irwin Kniberg): Brooklyn, NY, Dec. 26, 1927.

KING, PERRY: Alliance, OH, Apr. 30, 1948. Yale.

KINGSLEY, BEN (Krishna Bhanji): Snaiton, Yorkshire, England, Dec. 31, 1943.

KINNEAR, GREG: Logansport, IN, June 17, 1963.

KINSKI, NASTASSJA: Berlin, Ger., Jan. 24, 1960.

KIRBY, BRUNO: NYC, Apr. 28, 1949.

KIRK, TOMMY: Louisville, KY, Dec.10 1941.

KIRKLAND, SALLY: NYC, Oct. 31, 1944. Actors Studio.

KITT, EARTHA: North, SC, Jan. 26, 1928.

KLEIN, ROBERT: NYC, Feb. 8, 1942. Alfred U.

KLEMPERER, WERNER: Cologne, Mar. 22, 1920.

KLINE, KEVIN: St. Louis, MO, Oct. 24, 1947. Juilliard.

KLUGMAN, JACK: Philadelphia, PA, Apr. 27, 1922. Carnegie Tech.

KNIGHT, MICHAEL E.: Princeton, NJ, May 7, 1959.

KNIGHT, SHIRLEY: Goessel, KS, July 5, 1937. Wichita U.

KNOX, ELYSE: Hartford, CT, Dec. 14, 1917. Traphagen School.

KOENIG, WALTER: Chicago, IL, Sept. 14, 1936. UCLA.

KOHNER, SUSAN: Los Angeles, CA, Nov. 11, 1936. U Calif.

KORMAN, HARVEY: Chicago, IL, Feb. 15, 1927. Goodman.

KORSMO, CHARLIE: Minneapolis, MN, July, 1978.

KORVIN, CHARLES (Geza Korvin Karpathi): Czechoslovakia, Nov. 21, 1907. Sorbonne.

KOTEAS, ELIAS: Montreal, Quebec, Canada, 1961. AADA.

KOTTO, YAPHET: NYC, Nov. 15, 1937.

KOZAK, HARLEY JANE: Wilkes-Barre, PA, Jan. 28, 1957. NYU.

KRABBE, JEROEN: Amsterdam, The Netherlands, Dec. 5, 1944.

KREUGER, KURT: St. Moritz, Switzerland, July 23, 1917. U London.

KRIGE, ALICE: Upington, So. Africa, June 28, 1955.

KRISTEL, SYLVIA: Amsterdam, The Netherlands, Sept. 28, 1952.

KRISTOFFERSON, KRIS: Brownsville, TX, June 22, 1936, Pomona College.

KRUGER, HARDY: Berlin, Germany, April 12, 1928.

KUDROW, LISA: Encino, CA, July 30, 1963.

KURTZ, SWOOSIE: Omaha, NE, Sept. 6, 1944.

KWAN, NANCY: Hong Kong, May 19, 1939. Royal Ballet.

LaBELLE, PATTI: Philadelphia, PA, May 24, 1944.

LACY, JERRY: Sioux City, IA, Mar. 27, 1936. LACC.

LADD, CHERYL (Stoppelmoor): Huron, SD. July 12, 1951.

LADD, DIANE (Ladner): Meridian, MS, Nov. 29, 1932. Tulane U.

Viggo Mortensen

LAHTI, CHRISTINE: Detroit, MI, Apr. 4, 1950. U Mich.

LAKE, RICKI: NYC, Sept. 21, 1968.

LAMARR, HEDY (Hedwig Kiesler): Vienna, Sept. 11, 1913.

LAMAS, LORENZO: Los Angeles, Jan. 28, 1958.

LAMBERT, CHRISTOPHER: NYC, Mar. 29, 1958.

LANDAU, MARTIN: Brooklyn, NY, June 20, 1931. Actors Studio.

LANDRUM, TERI: Enid, OK, 1960.

LANE, ABBE: Brooklyn, NY, Dec. 14, 1935.

LANE, DIANE: NYC, Jan. 22, 1963.

LANE, NATHAN: Jersey City, NJ, Feb. 3, 1956.

LANG, STEPHEN: NYC, July 11, 1952. Swarthmore College.

LANGE, HOPE: Redding Ridge, CT, Nov. 28, 1931. Reed College.

LANGE, JESSICA: Cloquet, MN, Apr. 20, 1949. U Minn.

LANGELLA, FRANK: Bayonne, NJ, Jan. 1, 1940. SyracuseU.

LANSBURY, ANGELA: London, Oct. 16, 1925. London Academy of Music.

LaPAGLIA, ANTHONY: Adelaide, Australia. Jan 31, 1959.

LARROQUETTE, JOHN: New Orleans, LA, Nov. 25, 1947.

LASSER, LOUISE: NYC, Apr. 11, 1939. Brandeis U.

LATIFAH, QUEEN (Dana Owens): East Orange, NJ, 1970.

LAUGHLIN, JOHN: Memphis, TN, Apr. 3.

LAUGHLIN, TOM: Minneapolis, MN, 1938.

LAUPER, CYNDI: Astoria, Queens, NYC, June 20, 1953.

LAURE, CAROLE: Montreal, Canada, Aug. 5, 1951.

LAURIE, HUGH: Oxford, Eng., June 11, 1959.

LAURIE, PIPER (Rosetta Jacobs): Detroit, MI, Jan. 22, 1932.

LAUTER, ED: Long Beach, NY, Oct. 30, 1940.

LAVIN, LINDA: Portland, ME, Oct. 15 1939.

LAW, JOHN PHILLIP: Hollywood, CA, Sept. 7, 1937. Neighborhood Playhouse, U Hawaii.

LAW, JUDE: Lewisham, Eng., Dec. 29, 1972.

LAWRENCE, BARBARA: Carnegie, OK, Feb. 24, 1930. UCLA.

LAWRENCE, CAROL (Laraia): Melrose Park, IL, Sept. 5, 1935.

LAWRENCE, VICKI: Inglewood, CA, Mar. 26, 1949.

LAWRENCE, MARTIN: Frankfurt, Germany, Apr. 16, 1965.

LAWSON, LEIGH: Atherston, England, July 21, 1945. RADA.

LEACHMAN, CLORIS: Des Moines, IA, Apr. 30, 1930. Northwestern U.

LEARY, DENIS: Boston, MA, Aug. 18, 1957.

LEAUD, JEAN-PIERRE: Paris, France, May 5, 1944.

LeBLANC, MATT: Newton, MA, July 25, 1967.

LEDERER, FRANCIS: Karlin, Prague, Czech., Nov. 6, 1906.

LEE, CHRISTOPHER: London, May 27, 1922. Wellington College.

LEE, MARK: Australia, 1958.

LEE, MICHELE (Dusiak): Los Angeles, June 24, 1942. LACC.

LEE, PEGGY (Norma Delores Egstrom): Jamestown, ND, May 26, 1920.

LEE, SPIKE (Shelton Lee): Atlanta, GA, Mar. 20, 1957.

LEGROS, JAMES: Minneapolis, MN, Apr. 27, 1962.

LEGUIZAMO, JOHN: Columbia, July 22, 1965. NYU.

LEIBMAN, RON: NYC, Oct. 1l, 1937. Ohio Wesleyan.

LEIGH, JANET (Jeanette Helen Morrison): Merced, CA, July 6, 1926. ColofPacific.

LEIGH, JENNIFER JASON: Los Angeles, Feb. 5, 1962.

LeMAT, PAUL: Rahway, NJ, Sept. 22, 1945.

LEMMON, CHRIS: Los Angeles, Jan. 22, 1954.

LEMMON, JACK: Boston, Feb. 8, 1925. Harvard.

LENO, JAY: New Rochelle, NY, Apr. 28, 1950. Emerson College.

LENZ, KAY: Los Angeles, Mar. 4, 1953.

LENZ, RICK: Springfield, IL, Nov. 21, 1939. U Mich.

LEONARD, ROBERT SEAN: Westwood, NJ, Feb. 28, 1969.

LERNER, MICHAEL: Brooklyn, NY, June 22, 1941.

LESLIE, BETHEL: NYC, Aug. 3, 1929. Brearley School.

Armin Mueller-Stahl

LESLIE, JOAN (Joan Brodell): Detroit, Jan. 26, 1925. St. Benedict's.

LESTER, MARK: Oxford, England, July 11, 1958.

LEVELS, CALVIN: Cleveland. OH, Sept. 30, 1954. CCC.

LEVIN, RACHEL: NYC, 1954. Goddard College.

LEVINE, JERRY: New Brunswick, NJ, Mar. 12, 1957, Boston U.

LEVY, EUGENE: Hamilton, Canada, Dec. 17, 1946. McMasterU.

LEWIS, CHARLOTTE: London, Aug.7, 1967.

LEWIS, GEOFFREY: San Diego, CA, Jan. 1, 1935.

LEWIS, JERRY (Joseph Levitch): Newark, NJ, Mar. 16, 1926.

LEWIS, JULIETTE: Los Angeles CA, June 21, 1973.

LIGON, TOM: New Orleans, LA, Sept. 10, 1945.

LINCOLN, ABBEY (Anna Marie Woolridge): Chicago, IL, Aug. 6, 1930.

LINDEN, HAL: Bronx, NY, Mar. 20, 1931. City College of NY.

LINDSAY, ROBERT: Ilketson, Derbyshire, England, Dec. 13, 1951, RADA.

LINN-BAKER, MARK: St. Louis, MO, June 17, 1954, Yale.

Joe Morton

Dermot Mulroney

LINNEY, LAURA: New York, NY, Feb. 5, 1964.

LIOTTA, RAY: Newark, NJ, Dec. 18, 1955. UMiami.

LISI, VIRNA: Rome, Nov. 8, 1937.

LITHGOW, JOHN: Rochester, NY, Oct. 19, 1945. Harvard.

LLOYD, CHRISTOPHER: Stamford, CT, Oct. 22, 1938.

LLOYD, EMILY: London, Sept. 29, 1970.

LOCKE, SONDRA: Shelbyville, TN, May 28, 1947.

LOCKHART, JUNE: NYC, June 25, 1925. Westlake School.

LOCKWOOD, GARY: Van Nuys, CA, Feb. 21, 1937.

LOGGIA, ROBERT: Staten Island, NY, Jan. 3, 1930. UMo.

LOLLOBRIGIDA, GINA: Subiaco, Italy, July 4, 1927. Rome Academy of Fine Arts.

LOM, HERBERT: Prague, Czechoslovakia, Jan. 9, 1917. Prague U.

LOMEZ, CELINE: Montreal, Canada, May 11, 1953.

LONDON, JULIE (Julie Peck): Santa Rosa, CA, Sept. 26, 1926.

LONE, JOHN: Hong Kong, Oct 13, 1952. AADA.

LONG, SHELLEY: Ft. Wayne, IN, Aug. 23, 1949. Northwestern U.

LOPEZ, JENNIFER: Bronx, NY, July 24, 1970.

LOPEZ, PERRY: NYC, July 22, 1931. NYU.

LORD, JACK (John Joseph Ryan): NYC, Dec. 30, 1928. NYU.

LOREN, SOPHIA (Sophia Scicolone): Rome, Italy, Sept. 20, 1934.

LOUIS-DREYFUS, JULIA: NYC, Jan. 13, 1961.

LOUISE, TINA (Blacker): NYC, Feb. 11, 1934, Miami U.

LOVE, COURTNEY (Love Michelle Harrison): San Francisco, July 9, 1965.

LOVETT, LYLE: Klein, TX, Nov. 1, 1957.

LOVITZ, JON: Tarzana, CA, July 21, 1957.

LOWE, CHAD: Dayton, OH, Jan. 15, 1968.

LOWE, ROB: Charlottesville, VA, Mar. 17, 1964.

LOWITSCH, KLAUS: Berlin, Apr. 8, 1936, Vienna Academy.

LUCAS, LISA: Arizona, 1961.

LUCKINBILL, LAURENCE: Fort Smith, AK, Nov. 21, 1934.

LUFT, LORNA: Los Angeles, Nov. 21, 1952.

LULU (Marie Lawrie): Glasgow, Scotland, Nov. 3, 1948.

LUNA, BARBARA: NYC, Mar. 2, 1939.

LUNDGREN, DOLPH: Stockolm, Sweden, Nov. 3, 1959. Royal Inst.

LuPONE, PATTI: Northport, NY, Apr. 21, 1949, Juilliard.

LYDON, JAMES: Harrington Park, NJ, May 30, 1923.

LYNCH, KELLY: Minneapolis, MN, Jan. 31, 1959.

LYNLEY, CAROL (Jones): NYC, Feb. 13, 1942.

LYON, SUE: Davenport, IA, July 10, 1946.

MacARTHUR, JAMES: Los Angeles, Dec. 8, 1937. Harvard.

MACCHIO, RALPH: Huntington, NY, Nov. 4, 1961.

MacCORKINDALE, SIMON: Cambridge, England, Feb. 12, 1953.

MacDOWELL, ANDIE (Rose Anderson MacDowell): Gaffney, SC, Apr. 21, 1958.

MacGINNIS, NIALL: Dublin, Ireland, Mar. 29, 1913. Dublin U.

MacGRAW, ALI: NYC, Apr. 1, 1938. Wellesley.

MacLACHLAN, KYLE: Yakima, WA, Feb. 22, 1959. UWa.

MacLAINE, SHIRLEY (Beaty): Richmond, VA, Apr. 24, 1934.

MacLEOD, GAVIN: Mt. Kisco, NY, Feb. 28, 1931.

MacNAUGHTON, ROBERT: NYC, Dec. 19, 1966.

MACNEE, PATRICK: London, Feb. 1922.

MacNICOL, PETER: Dallas, TX, Apr. 10, 1954. UMN.

MacPHERSON, ELLE: Sydney, Australia, 1965.

MACY, W. H. (William): Miami, FL, Mar. 13, 1950. Goddard College.

MADIGAN, AMY: Chicago, IL, Sept. 11, 1950. Marquette U.

MADONNA (Madonna Louise Veronica Cicone): Bay City, MI, Aug. 16, 1958. UMi.

MADSEN, MICHAEL: Chicago, IL, Sept. 25, 1958.

MADSEN, VIRGINIA: Winnetka, IL, Sept. 11, 1963.

MAGNUSON, ANN: Charleston, WV, Jan. 4, 1956.

MAGUIRE, TOBEY: Santa Monica, CA, June 27, 1975.

MAHARIS, GEORGE: Astoria, NY, Sept. 1, 1928. Actors Studio.

MAHONEY, JOHN: Manchester, England, June 20, 1940, WUIll.

MAILER, STEPHEN: NYC, Mar. 10, 1966. NYU.

MAJORS, LEE: Wyandotte, MI, Apr. 23, 1940. E. Ky. State College.

MAKEPEACE, CHRIS: Toronto, Canada, Apr. 22, 1964.

MAKO (Mako Iwamatsu): Kobe, Japan, Dec. 10, 1933. Pratt.

MALDEN, KARL (Mladen Sekulovich): Gary, IN, Mar. 22, 1914.

MALKOVICH, JOHN: Christopher, IL, Dec. 9, 1953, IllStateU.

MALONE, DOROTHY: Chicago, IL, Jan. 30, 1925.

MANN, TERRENCE: KY, 1945. NCSchl Arts.

MANOFF, DINAH: NYC, Jan. 25, 1958. CalArts.

MANTEGNA, JOE: Chicago, IL, Nov. 13, 1947. Goodman Theatre.

MANZ, LINDA: NYC, 1961.

MARAIS, JEAN: Cherbourg, France, Dec. 11, 1913, St. Germain.

MARCHAND, NANCY: Buffalo, NY, June 19, 1928.

MARCOVICCI, ANDREA: NYC, Nov. 18, 1948.

MARIN, CHEECH (Richard): Los Angeles, July 13, 1946.

MARIN, JACQUES: Paris, France, Sept. 9, 1919. Conservatoire National.

MARINARO, ED: NYC, Mar. 31, 1950. Cornell.

MARS, KENNETH: Chicago, IL, 1936.

MARSH, JEAN: London, England, July 1, 1934.

MARSHALL, E. G.: Owatonna, MN, June 18, 1910. U Minn.

MARSHALL, KEN: NYC, 1953. Juilliard.

MARSHALL, PENNY: Bronx, NY, Oct. 15, 1942. UN. Mex.

MARSHALL, WILLIAM: Gary, IN, Aug. 19, 1924. NYU.

MARTIN, ANDREA: Portland, ME, Jan. 15, 1947.

MARTIN, DICK: Battle Creek, MI Jan. 30, 1923.

MARTIN, GEORGE N.: NYC, Aug. 15, 1929.

MARTIN, MILLICENT: Romford, England, June 8, 1934.

MARTIN, PAMELA SUE: Westport, CT, Jan. 15, 1953.

MARTIN, STEVE: Waco, TX, Aug. 14, 1945. UCLA.

MARTIN, TONY (Alfred Norris): Oakland, CA, Dec. 25, 1913. St. Mary's College.

MASON, MARSHA: St. Louis, MO, Apr. 3, 1942. Webster College.

MASSEN, OSA: Copenhagen, Denmark, Jan. 13, 1916.

MASSEY, DANIEL: London, Oct. 10, 1933. Eton and King's Coll.

MASTERS, BEN: Corvallis, OR, May 6, 1947. UOr.

MASTERSON, MARY STUART: Los Angeles, June 28, 1966, NYU.

MASTERSON, PETER: Angleton, TX, June 1, 1934. Rice U.

MASTRANTONIO, MARY ELIZABETH: Chicago, IL, Nov. 17, 1958. UIll.

MASUR, RICHARD: NYC, Nov. 20, 1948.

MATHESON, TIM: Glendale, CA, Dec. 31, 1947. CalState.

MATHIS, SAMANTHA: NYC, May 12, 1970.

MATLIN, MARLEE: Morton Grove, IL, Aug. 24, 1965.

MATTHAU, WALTER (Matuschanskayasky): NYC, Oct. 1, 1920.

MATTHEWS, BRIAN: Philadelphia, Jan. 24. 1953. St. Olaf.

MATURE, VICTOR: Louisville, KY, Jan. 29, 1915.

MAY, ELAINE (Berlin): Philadelphia, Apr. 21, 1932.

MAYO, VIRGINIA (Virginia Clara Jones): St. Louis, MO, Nov. 30, 1920.

MAYRON, MELANIE: Philadelphia, PA, Oct. 20, 1952. AADA.

MAZURSKY, PAUL: Brooklyn, NY, Apr. 25, 1930. Bklyn College.

MAZZELLO, JOSEPH: Rhinebeck, NY, Sept. 21, 1983.

McCALLUM, DAVID: Scotland, Sept. 19, 1933. Chapman College.

McCAMBRIDGE, MERCEDES: Jolliet, IL, Mar. 17, 1918. Mundelein College.

McCARTHY, ANDREW: NYC, Nov. 29, 1962, NYU.

McCARTHY, KEVIN: Seattle, WA, Feb. 15, 1914. Minn. U.

McCARTNEY, PAUL: Liverpool, Eng- land, June 18, 1942.

McCLANAHAN, RUE: Healdton, OK, Feb. 21, 1934.

McCLORY, SEAN: Dublin, Ireland, Mar. 8, 1924. U Galway.

McCLURE, MARC: San Mateo, CA, Mar. 31, 1957.

McCLURG, EDIE: Kansas City, MO, July 23, 1950.

McCOWEN, ALEC: Tunbridge Wells, England, May 26, 1925. RADA.

Liam Neeson

Leslie Nielsen

Nick Nolte

Al Pacino

McCRANE, PAUL: Philadelphia, PA, Jan. 19. 1961.

McCRARY, DARIUS: Walnut, CA, May 1, 1976.

McDERMOTT, DYLAN: Waterbury, CT, Oct. 26, 1962. Neighborhood Playhouse.

McDONNELL, MARY: Wilkes Barre, PA, Apr. 28, 1952.

McDORMAND, FRANCES: Illinois, June 23, 1957.

McDOWALL, RODDY: London, Sept. 17, 1928. St. Joseph's.

McDOWELL, MALCOLM (Taylor): Leeds, England, June 19, 1943. LAMDA.

McENERY, PETER: Walsall, England, Feb. 21, 1940.

McENTIRE, REBA: McAlester, OK, Mar. 28, 1955. SoutheasternStU.

McGAVIN, DARREN: Spokane, WA, May 7, 1922. College of Pacific.

McGILL, EVERETT: Miami Beach, FL, Oct. 21, 1945.

McGILLIS, KELLY: Newport Beach, CA, July 9, 1957. Juilliard.

McGINLEY, JOHN C.: NYC, Aug. 3, 1959. NYU.

McGOOHAN, PATRICK: NYC, Mar. 19, 1928.

McGOVERN, ELIZABETH: Evanston, IL. July 18, 1961. Juilliard.

McGOVERN, MAUREEN: Youngstown, OH, July 27, 1949.

McGREGOR, EWAN: Perth, Scotland, March 31, 1971

McGUIRE, BIFF: New Haven, CT, Oct. 25. 1926. Mass. Stale College.

McGUIRE, DOROTHY: Omaha, NE, June 14, 1918.

McHATTIE, STEPHEN: Antigonish, NS, Feb. 3. Acadia U AADA.

McKAY, GARDNER: NYC, June 10, 1932. Comell.

McKEAN, MICHAEL: NYC, Oct. 17, 1947.

McKEE, LONETTE: Detroit, MI, July 22, 1955.

McKELLEN, IAN: Burnley, England, May 25, 1939.

McKENNA, VIRGINIA: London, June 7, 1931.

McKEON, DOUG: Pompton Plains, NJ, June 10, 1966.

McKERN, LEO: Sydney, Australia, Mar. 16, 1920.

McKUEN, ROD: Oakland, CA, Apr. 29, 1933.

McLERIE, ALLYN ANN: Grand Mere, Canada, Dec. 1, 1926.

McMAHON, ED: Detroit, MI, Mar. 6, 1923.

McNAIR, BARBARA: Chicago, IL, Mar. 4, 1939. UCLA.

McNAMARA, WILLIAM: Dallas, TX, Mar. 31, 1965.

McNICHOL, KRISTY: Los Angeles. CA, Sept. 11, 1962.

McQUEEN, ARMELIA: North Carolina, Jan. 6, 1952. Bklyn Consv.

McQUEEN, CHAD: Los Angeles, CA, Dec. 28, 1960. Actors Studio.

McRANEY, GERALD: Collins, MS, Aug. 19, 1948.

McSHANE, IAN: Blackburn, England, Sept. 29, 1942. RADA.

MEADOWS, JAYNE (formerly Jayne Cotter): Wuchang, China, Sept. 27, 1924. St. Margaret's.

MEARA, ANNE: Brooklyn, NY, Sept. 20, 1929.

MEAT LOAF (Marvin Lee Aday): Dallas, TX, Sept. 27, 1947.

MEDWIN, MICHAEL: London, 1925. Instut Fischer.

MEKKA, EDDIE: Worcester, MA, June 14, 1952. Boston Cons.

MELATO, MARIANGELA: Milan, Italy, 1941. Milan Theatre Acad.

MEREDITH, LEE (Judi Lee Sauls): Oct. 22, 1947. AADA.

MERKERSON, S. EPATHA: Saganaw, MI, Nov. 28, 1952. Wayne St. Univ.

MERRILL, DINA (Nedinia Hutton): NYC, Dec. 29, 1925. AADA.

METCALF, LAURIE: Edwardsville, IL, June 16, 1955., IIIStU.

METZLER, JIM: Oneonda, NY, June 23. Dartmouth.

MICHELL, KEITH: Adelaide, Australia, Dec. 1, 1926.

MIDLER, BETTE: Honolulu, HI, Dec. 1, 1945.

MILANO, ALYSSA: Brooklyn, NY, Dec. 19, 1972.

MILES, JOANNA: Nice, France, Mar. 6, 1940.

MILES, SARAH: Ingatestone, England, Dec. 31, 1941. RADA.

MILES, SYLVIA: NYC, Sept. 9, 1934. Actors Studio.

MILES, VERA (Ralston): Boise City, OK, Aug. 23, 1929. UCLA.

MILLER, ANN (Lucille Ann Collier): Chireno, TX, Apr. 12, 1919. Lawler Professional School.

MILLER, BARRY: Los Angeles, CA, Feb. 6, 1958.

MILLER, DICK: NYC, Dec. 25, 1928.

MILLER, JASON: Long Island City, NY, Apr. 22, 1939. Catholic U.

MILLER, LINDA: NYC, Sept. 16, 1942. Catholic U.

MILLER, PENELOPE ANN: Santa Monica, CA, Jan. 13, 1964.

MILLER, REBECCA: Roxbury, CT, 1962. Yale.

MILLS, DONNA: Chicago, IL, Dec. 11, 1945. UIl.

MILLS, HAYLEY: London, Apr. 18, 1946. Elmhurst School.

MILLS, JOHN: Suffolk, England, Feb. 22, 1908.

MILLS, JULIET: London, Nov. 21, 1941.

MILNER, MARTIN: Detroit, MI, Dec. 28, 1931.

MIMIEUX, YVETTE: Los Angeles, Jan. 8, 1941. Hollywood High.

MINNELLI, LIZA: Los Angeles, Mar. 19, l946.

MIOU-MIOU (Sylvette Henry): Paris, France, Feb. 22, 1950.

MIRREN, HELEN (Ilynea Mironoff): London, July 26, 1946.

MITCHELL, JAMES: Sacramento, CA, Feb. 29, 1920. LACC.

MITCHELL, JOHN CAMERON: El Paso, TX, Apr. 21, 1963. NorthwesternU.

MITCHUM, JAMES: Los Angeles, CA, May 8, 1941.

MODINE, MATTHEW: Loma Linda, CA, Mar. 22, 1959.

Gwyneth Paltrow

David Paymer

Sean Penn

Ryan Phillippe

MOFFAT, DONALD: Plymouth, England, Dec. 26, 1930. RADA.

MOFFETT, D. W.: Highland Park, IL, Oct. 26, 1954. Stanford U.

MOHR, JAY: New Jersey, Aug. 23, 1971.

MOKAE, ZAKES: Johannesburg, So. Africa, Aug. 5, 1935. RADA.

MOLINA, ALFRED: London, May 24, 1953. Guildhall.

MOLL, RICHARD: Pasadena, CA, Jan. 13, 1943.

MONTALBAN, RICARDO: Mexico City, Nov. 25, 1920.

MONTGOMERY, BELINDA: Winnipeg, Canada, July 23, 1950.

MONTGOMERY, GEORGE (George Letz): Brady, MT, Aug. 29, 1916. U Mont.

MOODY, RON: London, Jan. 8, 1924. London U.

MOOR, BILL: Toledo, OH, July 13, 1931. Northwestern.

MOORE, CONSTANCE: Sioux City, IA, Jan. 18, 1919.

MOORE, DEMI (Guines): Roswell, NM, Nov. 11, 1962.

MOORE, DICK: Los Angeles, Sept. 12, 1925.

MOORE, DUDLEY: Dagenham, Essex, England, Apr. 19, 1935.

MOORE, JULIANNE (Julie Anne Smith): Fayetteville, NC, Dec. 30, 1960.

MOORE, KIERON: County Cork, Ireland, 1925. St. Mary's College.

MOORE, MARY TYLER: Brooklyn, NY, Dec. 29, 1936.

MOORE, ROGER: London, Oct. 14, 1927. RADA.

MOORE, TERRY (Helen Koford): Los Angeles, Jan. 7, 1929.

MORALES, ESAI: Brooklyn, NY, Oct. 1, 1962.

MORANIS, RICK: Toronto, Canada, Apr. 18, 1954.

MOREAU, JEANNE: Paris, France, Jan. 23, 1928.

MORENO, RITA (Rosita Alverio): Humacao, P.R., Dec. 11, 1931.

MORGAN, HARRY (HENRY) (Harry Bratsburg): Detroit, Apr. 10, 1915. U Chicago.

MORGAN, MICHELE (Simone Roussel): Paris, France, Feb. 29, 1920. Paris Dramatic School.

MORIARTY, CATHY: Bronx, NY, Nov. 29, 1960.

MORIARTY, MICHAEL: Detroit, MI, Apr. 5, 1941. Dartmouth.

MORISON, PATRICIA: NYC, Mar. 19, 1915.

MORITA, NORIYUKI "PAT": Isleton, CA, June 28, 1932.

MORRIS, GARRETT: New Orleans, LA, Feb. 1, 1937.

MORRIS, HOWARD: NYC, Sept. 4, 1919. NYU.

MORROW, ROB: New Rochelle, NY, Sept. 21, 1962.

MORSE, DAVID: Hamilton, MA, Oct. 11, 1953.

MORSE, ROBERT: Newton, MA, May 18, 1931.

MORTENSEN, VIGGO: New York, NY, 1958.

MORTON, JOE: NYC, Oct. 18, 1947. Hofstra U.

MOSES, WILLIAM: Los Angeles, Nov. 17, 1959.

MOSTEL, JOSH: NYC, Dec. 21, 1946. Brandeis U.

MOUCHET, CATHERINE: Paris, France, 1959. Ntl. Consv.

MUELLER-STAHL, ARMIN: Tilsit, East Prussia, Dec. 17, 1930.

MULDAUR, DIANA: NYC, Aug. 19, 1938. Sweet Briar College.

MULGREW, KATE: Dubuque, IA, Apr. 29, 1955. NYU.

MULHERN, MATT: Philadelphia, PA, July 21, 1960. Rutgers Univ.

MULL, MARTIN: N. Ridgefield, OH, Aug. 18, 1941. RISch. of Design.

MULLIGAN, RICHARD: NYC, Nov. 13, 1932.

MULRONEY, DERMOT: Alexandria, VA, Oct. 31, 1963. Northwestern.

MUMY, BILL (Charles William Mumy, Jr.): San Gabriel, CA, Feb. 1, 1954.

MURPHY, EDDIE: Brooklyn, NY, Apr. 3, 1961.

MURPHY, MICHAEL: Los Angeles, CA, May 5, 1938. UAz.

MURRAY, BILL: Wilmette, IL, Sept. 21, 1950. Regis College.

MURRAY, DON: Hollywood, CA, July 31, 1929.

MUSANTE, TONY: Bridgeport, CT, June 30, 1936. Oberlin College.

MYERS, MIKE: Scarborough, Canada, May 25, 1963.

NABORS, JIM: Sylacauga, GA, June 12, 1932.

NADER, GEORGE: Pasadena, CA, Oct. 19, 1921. Occidental College.

NADER, MICHAEL: Los Angeles, CA, 1945.

NAMATH, JOE: Beaver Falls, PA, May 31, 1943. UAla.

NAUGHTON, DAVID: Hartford, CT, Feb. 13, 1951.

NAUGHTON, JAMES: Middletown, CT, Dec. 6, 1945.

NEAL, PATRICIA: Packard, KY, Jan. 20, 1926. Northwestern U.

NEESOM, LIAM: Ballymena, Northern Ireland, June 7, 1952.

NEFF, HILDEGARDE (Hildegard Knef): Ulm, Germany, Dec. 28, 1925. Berlin Art Acad.

NEILL, SAM: No. Ireland, Sept. 14, 1947. U Canterbury.

NELL, NATHALIE: Paris, France, Oct. 1950.

NELLIGAN, KATE: London, Ont., Canada, Mar. 16, 1951. U Toronto.

NELSON, BARRY (Robert Nielsen): Oakland, CA, Apr. 16, 1920.

NELSON, CRAIG T.: Spokane, WA, Apr. 4, 1946.

NELSON, DAVID: NYC, Oct. 24, 1936. USC.

NELSON, JUDD: Portland, ME, Nov. 28, 1959, Haverford College.

NELSON, LORI (Dixie Kay Nelson): Santa Fe, NM, Aug. 15, 1933.

NELSON, TRACY: Santa Monica, CA, Oct. 25, 1963.

NELSON, WILLIE: Abbott, TX, Apr. 30, 1933.

NEMEC, CORIN: Little Rock, AK, Nov. 5, 1971.

NERO, FRANCO (Francisco Spartanero): Parma, Italy, Nov. 23, 1941.

NESMITH, MICHAEL: Houston, TX, Dec. 30, 1942.

NETTLETON, LOIS: Oak Park, IL, 1931. Actors Studio.

NEWHART, BOB: Chicago, IL, Sept. 5, 1929. Loyola U.

NEWLEY, ANTHONY: Hackney, London, Sept. 24, 1931.

Lou Diamond Phillips

Brad Pitt

Martha Plimpton

Parker Posey

NEWMAN, BARRY: Boston, MA, Nov. 7, 1938. Brandeis U.

NEWMAN, LARAINE: Los Angeles, Mar. 2, 1952.

NEWMAN, NANETTE: Northampton, England, 1934.

NEWMAN, PAUL: Cleveland, OH, Jan. 26, 1925. Yale.

NEWMAR, JULIE (Newmeyer): Los Angeles, Aug. 16, 1933.

NEWTON-JOHN, OLIVIA: Cambridge, England, Sept. 26, 1948.

NGUYEN, DUSTIN: Saigon, Vietnam, Sept. 17, 1962.

NICHOLAS, DENISE: Detroit, MI, July 12, 1945.

NICHOLAS, PAUL: London, 1945.

NICHOLS, NICHELLE: Robbins, IL, Dec. 28, 1933.

NICHOLSON, JACK: Neptune, NJ, Apr. 22, 1937.

NICKERSON, DENISE: NYC, 1959.

NICOL, ALEX: Ossining, NY, Jan. 20, 1919. Actors Studio.

NIELSEN, BRIGITTE: Denmark, July 15, 1963.

NIELSEN, LESLIE: Regina, Saskatchewan. Canada, Feb. 11, 1926. Neighborhood Playhouse.

NIMOY, LEONARD: Boston, MA, Mar. 26, 1931. Boston College, Antioch College.

NIXON, CYNTHIA: NYC, Apr. 9, 1966. Columbia U.

NOBLE, JAMES: Dallas, TX, Mar. 5, 1922. SMU.

NOIRET, PHILIPPE: Lille, France, Oct. 1, 1930.

NOLAN, KATHLEEN: St. Louis, MO, Sept. 27, 1933. Neighborhood Playhouse.

NOLTE, NICK: Omaha, NE, Feb. 8, 1940. Pasadena City College.

NORRIS, CHRISTOPHER: NYC, Oct. 7, 1943. Lincoln Square Acad.

NORRIS, CHUCK (Carlos Ray): Ryan, OK,Mar. 10, 1940.

NORTH, HEATHER: Pasadena, CA, Dec. 13, 1950. Actors Workshop.

NORTH, SHEREE (Dawn Bethel): Los Angeles. Jan. 17, 1933. Hollywood High.

NORTHAM, JEREMY: Cambridge, Eng., Dec. 1, 1961.

NORTON, EDWARD: Boston, MA, Aug. 18, 1969.

NORTON, KEN: Jacksonville, Il, Aug. 9, 1945.

NOURI, MICHAEL: Washington, DC, Dec. 9, 1945.

NOVAK, KIM (Marilyn Novak): Chicago, IL, Feb. 13, 1933. LACC.

NOVELLO, DON: Ashtabula, OH, Jan. 1, 1943. UDayton.

NUYEN, FRANCE (Vannga): Marseilles, France, July 31, 1939. Beaux Arts School.

O'BRIAN, HUGH (Hugh J. Krampe): Rochester, N,. Apr. 19, 1928. Cincinnati U.

O'BRIEN, CLAY: Ray, AZ, May 6, 1961.

O'BRIEN, MARGARET (Angela Maxine O'Brien): Los Angeles, Jan. 15, 1937.

O'BRIEN, VIRGINIA: Los Angeles, Apr. 18, 1919.

O'CONNELL, JERRY (Jeremiah O'Connell): New York, NY, Feb. 17, 1974.

O'CONNOR, CARROLL: Bronx, NY, Aug. 2, 1924. Dublin National Univ.

O'CONNOR, DONALD: Chicago, IL, Aug. 28, 1925.

O'CONNOR, GLYNNIS: NYC, Nov. 19, 1955. NYSU.

O'DONNELL, CHRIS: Winetka, IL, June 27, 1970.

O'DONNELL, ROSIE: Commack, NY, March 21, 1961.

O'HARA, CATHERINE: Toronto, Canada, Mar. 4, 1954.

O'HARA, MAUREEN (Maureen Fitz-Simons): Dublin, Ireland, Aug. 17, 1920.

O'HERLIHY, DAN: Wexford, Ireland, May 1, 1919. National U.

O'KEEFE, MICHAEL: Larchmont, NY, Apr. 24, 1955. NYU, AADA.

OLDMAN, GARY: New Cross, South London, England, Mar. 21, 1958.

OLIN, KEN: Chicago, IL, July 30, 1954. UPa.

OLIN, LENA: Stockholm, Sweden, Mar. 22, 1955.

OLMOS, EDWARD JAMES: Los Angeles, Feb. 24, 1947. CSLA.

O'LOUGHLIN, GERALD S.: NYC, Dec. 23, 1921. U Rochester.

OLSON, JAMES: Evanston, IL, Oct. 8, 1930.

OLSON, NANCY: Milwaukee, WI, July 14, 1928. UCLA.

O'NEAL, GRIFFIN: Los Angeles, 1965.

O'NEAL, RON: Utica, NY, Sept. 1, 1937. Ohio State.

O'NEAL, RYAN: Los Angeles, Apr. 20, 1941.

O'NEAL, TATUM: Los Angeles, Nov. 5, 1963.

O'NEIL, TRICIA: Shreveport, LA, Mar. 11, 1945. Baylor U.

O'NEILL, ED: Youngstown, OH, Apr. 12, 1946.

O'NEILL, JENNIFER: Rio de Janeiro, Feb. 20, 1949. Neighborhood Playhouse.

ONTKEAN, MICHAEL: Vancouver, B.C., Canada, Jan. 24, 1946.

O'QUINN, TERRY: Newbury, MI, July 15, 1952.

ORBACH, JERRY: Bronx, NY, Oct. 20, 1935.

O'SHEA, MILO: Dublin, Ireland, June 2, 1926.

O'SULLIVAN, MAUREEN: Byle, Ireland, May 17, 1911. Sacred Heart Convent.

O'TOOLE, ANNETTE (Toole): Houston, TX, Apr. 1, 1953. UCLA.

O'TOOLE, PETER: Connemara, Ireland, Aug. 2, 1932. RADA.

OVERALL, PARK: Nashville, TN, Mar. 15, 1957. Tusculum College.

OZ, FRANK (Oznowicz): Hereford, England, May 25, 1944.

PACINO, AL: NYC, Apr. 25, 1940.

PACULA, JOANNA: Tamaszow Lubelski, Poland, Jan. 2, 1957. Polish Natl. Theatre Sch.

PAGET, DEBRA (Debralee Griffin): Denver, Aug. 19, 1933.

PAIGE, JANIS (Donna Mae Jaden): Tacoma, WA, Sept. 16, 1922.

PALANCE, JACK (Walter Palanuik): Lattimer, PA, Feb. 18, 1920. UNC.

PALIN, MICHAEL: Sheffield, Yorkshire, England, May 5, 1943, Oxford.

PALMER, BETSY: East Chicago, IN, Nov. 1, 1926. DePaul U.

PALMER, GREGG (Palmer Lee): San Francisco, Jan. 25, 1927. U Utah.

PALMINTERI, CHAZZ (Calogero Lorenzo Palminteri): New York, NY, May 15, 1952.

PAMPANINI, SILVANA: Rome, Sept. 25, 1925.

PANEBIANCO, RICHARD: NYC, 1971.

PANKIN, STUART: Philadelphia, Apr. 8, 1946.

287

PANTOLIANO, JOE: Jersey City, NJ, Sept. 12, 1954.

PAPAS, IRENE: Chiliomodion, Greece, Mar. 9, 1929.

PAQUIN, ANNA: Winnipeg, Manitoba, Canada, July, 24, 1982.

PARE, MICHAEL: Brooklyn, NY, Oct. 9, 1959.

PARKER, COREY: NYC, July 8, 1965. NYU.

PARKER, ELEANOR: Cedarville, OH, June 26, 1922. Pasadena Playhouse.

PARKER, FESS: Fort Worth, TX, Aug. 16, 1925. USC.

PARKER, JAMESON: Baltimore, MD, Nov. l8, 1947. Beloit College.

PARKER, JEAN (Mae Green): Deer Lodge, MT, Aug. 11, 1912.

PARKER, MARY-LOUISE: Ft. Jackson, SC, Aug. 2, 1964. Bard College.

PARKER, NATHANIEL: London, 1963.

PARKER, SARAH JESSICA: Nelsonville, OH, Mar. 25, 1965.

PARKER, SUZY (Cecelia Parker): San Antonio, TX, Oct. 28, 1933.

PARKER, TREY: Auburn, AL, May 30, 1972.

PARKINS, BARBARA: Vancouver, Canada, May 22, 1943.

PARKS, MICHAEL: Corona, CA, Apr. 4, 1938.

PARSONS, ESTELLE: Lynn, MA, Nov. 20, 1927. Boston U.

PARTON, DOLLY: Sevierville, TN, Jan. 19, 1946.

PATINKIN, MANDY: Chicago, IL, Nov. 30, 1952. Juilliard.

PATRIC, JASON: NYC, June 17, 1966.

PATRICK, DENNIS: Philadelphia, Mar. 14, 1918.

PATTERSON, LEE: Vancouver, Canada, Mar. 31, 1929. Ontario College.

PATTON, WILL: Charleston, SC, June 14, 1954.

PAULIK, JOHAN: Prague, Czech., 1975.

PAVAN, MARISA (Marisa Pierangeli): Cagliari, Sardinia, June 19, 1932. Torquado Tasso College.

PAXTON, BILL: Fort Worth, TX, May. 17, 1955.

PAYMER, DAVID: Long Island, NY, Aug. 30, 1954.

PAYS, AMANDA: Berkshire, England, June 6, 1959.

PEACH, MARY: Durban, S. Africa, 1934.

PEARCE, GUY: England, Oct. 5, 1967.

PEARSON, BEATRICE: Dennison, TX, July 27, 1920.

PECK, GREGORY: La Jolla, CA, Apr. 5, 1916. U Calif.

PEÑA, ELIZABETH: Cuba, Sept. 23, 1961.

PENDLETON, AUSTIN: Warren, OH, Mar. 27, 1940. Yale U.

PENHALL, BRUCE: Balboa, CA, Aug. 17, 1960.

PENN, SEAN: Burbank, CA, Aug. 17, 1960.

PEREZ, JOSE: NYC, 1940.

PEREZ, ROSIE: Brooklyn, NY, Sept. 6, 1964.

PERKINS, ELIZABETH: Queens, NY, Nov. 18, 1960. Goodman School.

PERKINS, MILLIE: Passaic, NJ, May 12, 1938.

PERLMAN, RHEA: Brooklyn, NY, Mar. 31, 1948.

Jonathan Pryce

Bill Pullman

Kathleen Quinlan

PERLMAN, RON: NYC, Apr. 13, 1950. UMn.

PERREAU, GIGI (Ghislaine): Los Angeles, Feb. 6, 1941.

PERRINE, VALERIE: Galveston, TX, Sept. 3, 1943. U Ariz.

PERRY, LUKE (Coy Luther Perry, III): Fredricktown, OH, Oct. 11, 1966.

PESCI, JOE: Newark, NJ. Feb. 9, 1943.

PESCOW, DONNA: Brooklyn, NY, Mar. 24, 1954.

PETERS, BERNADETTE (Lazzara): Jamaica, NY, Feb. 28, 1948.

PETERS, BROCK: NYC, July 2, 1927. CCNY.

PETERS. JEAN (Elizabeth): Caton, OH, Oct. 15, 1926. Ohio State U.

PETERSEN, PAUL: Glendale, CA, Sept. 23, 1945. Valley College.

PETERSEN, WILLIAM: Chicago, IL, Feb. 21, 1953.

PETERSON, CASSANDRA: Colorado Springs, CO, Sept. 17, 1951.

PETTET, JOANNA: London, Nov. 16, 1944. Neighborhood Playhouse.

PETTY, LORI: Chattanooga, TN, 1964.

PFEIFFER, MICHELLE: Santa Ana, CA, Apr. 29, 1958.

PHILLIPPE, RYAN (Matthew Phillippe): New Castle, DE, Sept. 10, 1975.

PHILLIPS, LOU DIAMOND: Phillipines, Feb. 17, 1962, UTx.

PHILLIPS, MacKENZIE: Alexandria, VA, Nov. 10, 1959.

PHILLIPS, MICHELLE (Holly Gilliam): Long Beach, CA, June 4, 1944.

PHILLIPS, SIAN: Bettws, Wales, May 14, 1934. UWales.

PHOENIX, JOAQUIN: Puerto Rico, Oct. 28, 1974.

PICARDO, ROBERT: Philadelphia, PA, Oct. 27, 1953. Yale.

PICERNI, PAUL: NYC, Dec. 1, 1922. Loyola U.

PIGOTT-SMITH, TIM: Rugby, England, May 13, 1946.

PINCHOT, BRONSON: NYC, May 20, 1959. Yale.

PINE, PHILLIP: Hanford, CA, July 16, 1920. Actors' Lab.

PISCOPO, JOE: Passaic. NJ, June 17, 1951.

PISIER, MARIE-FRANCE: Vietnam, May 10, 1944. U Paris.

PITILLO, MARIA: Mahwah, NJ, 1965.

PITT, BRAD (William Bradley Pitt): Shawnee, OK, Dec. 18, 1963.

PIVEN, JEREMY: NYC, July 26, 1965.

PLACE, MARY KAY: Tulsa OK, Sept. 23, 1947. U Tulsa.

PLAYTEN, ALICE: NYC, Aug. 28, 1947. NYU.

PLESHETTE, SUZANNE: NYC, Jan. 31, 1937. Syracuse U.

PLIMPTON, MARTHA: NYC, Nov. 16, 1970.

PLOWRIGHT, JOAN: Scunthorpe, Brigg, Lincolnshire, England, Oct. 28, 1929. Old Vic.

PLUMB, EVE: Burbank, CA, Apr. 29, 1958.

PLUMMER, AMANDA: NYC, Mar. 23, 1957. Middlebury College.

PLUMMER, CHRISTOPHER: Toronto, Canada, Dec. 13, 1927.

PODESTA, ROSSANA: Tripoli, June 20, 1934.

POITIER, SIDNEY: Miami, FL, Feb. 27, 1927.

POLANSKI, ROMAN: Paris, France, Aug. 18, 1933.

POLITO, JON: Philadelphia, PA, Dec. 29, 1950. Villanova U.

POLITO, LINA: Naples, Italy, Aug. 11, 1954.

POLLACK, SYDNEY: South Bend, IN, July 1, 1934.

POLLAK, KEVIN: San Francisco, Oct. 30, 1958.

POLLAN, TRACY: NYC, June 22, 1960.

POLLARD, MICHAEL J.: Passaic, NJ, May 30, 1939.

POSEY, PARKER: Baltimore, MD, Nov. 8, 1968.

POSTLETHWAITE, PETE: London, Feb. 7, 1945.

POTTS, ANNIE: Nashville, TN, Oct. 28, 1952. Stephens College.

POWELL, JANE (Suzanne Burce): Port-land, OR, Apr. 1, 1928.

POWELL, ROBERT: Salford, England, June 1, 1944. Manchester U.

POWER, TARYN: Los Angeles, CA, Sept. 13, 1953.

POWER, TYRONE, IV: Los Angeles, CA, Jan. 22, 1959.

POWERS, MALA (Mary Ellen): San Francisco, CA, Dec. 29, 1921. UCLA.

POWERS, STEFANIE (Federkiewicz): Hollywood, CA, Oct. 12, 1942.

PRENTISS, PAULA (Paula Ragusa): San Antonio, TX, Mar. 4, 1939. Northwestern U.

PRESLE, MICHELINE (Micheline Chassagne): Paris, France, Aug. 22, 1922. Rouleau Drama School.

PRESLEY, PRISCILLA: Brooklyn, NY, May 24, 1945.

PRESNELL, HARVE: Modesto, CA, Sept. 14, 1933. USC.

PRESTON, KELLY: Honolulu, HI, Oct. 13, 1962. USC.

PRESTON, WILLIAM: Columbia, PA, Aug. 26, 1921. PaStateU.

PRICE, LONNY: NYC, Mar. 9, 1959. Juilliard.

PRIESTLEY, JASON: Vancouver, Canada, Aug, 28, 1969.

PRIMUS, BARRY: NYC, Feb. 16, 1938. CCNY.

PRINCE (P. Rogers Nelson): Minneapolis, MN, June 7, 1958.

PRINCIPAL, VICTORIA: Fukuoka, Japan, Jan. 3, 1945. Dade, Jr. College.

PROCHNOW, JURGEN: Berlin, June 10, 1941.

PROSKY, ROBERT: Philadelphia, PA, Dec. 13, 1930.

PROVAL, DAVID: Brooklyn, NY, May 20, 1942.

PROVINE, DOROTHY: Deadwood, SD, Jan. 20, 1937. U Wash.

PRYCE, JONATHAN: Wales, UK, June 1, 1947, RADA.

PRYOR, RICHARD: Peoria, IL, Dec. 1, 1940.

PULLMAN, BILL: Delphi, NY, Dec. 17, 1954. SUNY/Oneonta, UMass.

PURCELL, LEE: Cherry Point, NC, June 15, 1947. Stephens.

PURDOM, EDMUND: Welwyn Garden City, England, Dec. 19, 1924. St. Ignatius College.

QUAID, DENNIS: Houston, TX, Apr. 9, 1954.

Vanessa Redgrave

Burt Reynolds

Christina Ricci

QUAID, RANDY: Houston, TX, Oct. 1, 1950. UHouston.

QUINLAN, KATHLEEN: Mill Valley, CA, Nov. 19, 1954.

QUINN, AIDAN: Chicago, IL, Mar. 8, 1959.

QUINN, ANTHONY: Chihuahua, Mex., Apr. 21, 1915.

RAFFERTY, FRANCES: Sioux City, IA, June 16, 1922. UCLA.

RAFFIN, DEBORAH: Los Angeles, Mar. 13, 1953. Valley College.

RAGSDALE, WILLIAM: El Dorado, AK, Jan. 19, 1961. Hendrix College.

RAILSBACK, STEVE: Dallas, TX, 1948.

RAINER, LUISE: Vienna, Austria, Jan. 12, 1910.

RALSTON, VERA (Vera Helena Hruba): Prague, Czech., July 12, 1919.

RAMIS, HAROLD: Chicago, IL, Nov. 21, 1944. WashingtonU.

RAMPLING, CHARLOTTE: Surmer, England, Feb. 5, 1946. U Madrid.

RAMSEY, LOGAN: Long Beach, CA, Mar. 21, 1921. St. Joseph.

RANDALL, TONY (Leonard Rosenberg): Tulsa, OK, Feb. 26, 1920. Northwestern U.

RANDELL, RON: Sydney, Australia, Oct. 8, 1920. St. Mary's College.

RAPP, ANTHONY: Chicago, Oct. 26, 1971.

RASCHE, DAVID: St. Louis, MO, Aug. 7, 1944.

RAYMOND, GENE (Raymond Guion): NYC, Aug. 13, 1908.

REA, STEPHEN: Belfast, No. Ireland, Oct. 31, 1949.

REAGAN, RONALD: Tampico, IL, Feb. 6, 1911. Eureka College.

REASON, REX: Berlin, Ger., Nov. 30, 1928. Pasadena Playhouse.

REDDY, HELEN: Melbourne, Australia, Oct. 25, 1942.

REDFORD, ROBERT: Santa Monica, CA, Aug. 18, 1937. AADA.

REDGRAVE, CORIN: London, July 16, 1939.

REDGRAVE, LYNN: London, Mar. 8, 1943.

REDGRAVE, VANESSA: London, Jan. 30, 1937.

REDMAN, JOYCE: County Mayo, Ireland, 1919. RADA.

REED, OLIVER: Wimbledon, England, Feb. 13, 1938.

REED, PAMELA: Tacoma, WA, Apr. 2, 1949.

REEMS, HARRY (Herbert Streicher): Bronx, NY, 1947. U Pittsburgh.

REES, ROGER: Aberystwyth, Wales, May 5, 1944.

REESE, DELLA: Detroit, MI, July 6, 1932.

REEVE, CHRISTOPHER: NYC, Sept. 25, 1952. Cornell, Juilliard.

REEVES, KEANU: Beiruit, Lebanon, Sept. 2, 1964.

REEVES, STEVE: Glasgow, MT, Jan. 21, 1926.

REGEHR, DUNCAN: Lethbridge, Canada, Oct. 5, 1952.

REID, ELLIOTT: NYC, Jan. 16, 1920.

REID, TIM: Norfolk, VA, Dec. 19, 1944.

REILLY, CHARLES NELSON: NYC, Jan. 13, 1931. UCt.

REINER, CARL: NYC, Mar. 20, 1922. Georgetown.

REINER, ROB: NYC, Mar. 6, 1947. UCLA.

James Russo

Greta Scacchi

Annabella Sciorra

Kyra Sedgwick

REINHOLD, JUDGE (Edward Ernest, Jr.): Wilmington, DE, May 21, 1957. NCSchool of Arts.

REINKING, ANN: Seattle, WA, Nov. 10, 1949.

REISER, PAUL: NYC, Mar. 30, 1957.

REMAR, JAMES: Boston, MA, Dec. 31, 1953. Neighborhood Playhouse.

REMSEN, BERT: Glen Cove, NY, Feb. 25, 1925. Ithaca.

RENFRO, BRAD: Knoxville, TN, July 25, 1982.

RENO, JEAN (Juan Moreno): Casablanca, Morocco, July 30, 1948.

REVILL, CLIVE: Wellington, NZ, Apr. 18, 1930.

REY, ANTONIA: Havana, Cuba, Oct. 12, 1927.

REYNOLDS, BURT: Waycross, GA, Feb. 11, 1935. Fla. State U.

REYNOLDS, DEBBIE (Mary Frances Reynolds): El Paso, TX, Apr. 1, 1932.

RHOADES, BARBARA: Poughkeepsie, NY, Mar. 23, 1947.

RHODES, CYNTHIA: Nashville, TN, Nov. 21, 1956.

RHYS-DAVIES, JOHN: Salisbury, England, May 5, 1944.

RIBISI, GIOVANNI: Los Angeles, CA, Mar. 31, 1976.

RICCI, CHRISTINA: Santa Monica, CA, Feb. 12, 1980.

RICHARD, CLIFF (Harry Webb): India, Oct. 14, 1940.

RICHARDS, MICHAEL: Culver City, CA, July 14, 1949.

RICHARDSON, JOELY: London, Jan. 9, 1965.

RICHARDSON, LEE: Chicago, IL, Sept. 11, 1926.

RICHARDSON, MIRANDA: Southport, England, Mar. 3, 1958.

RICHARDSON, NATASHA: London, May 11, 1963.

RICKLES, DON: NYC, May 8, 1926. AADA.

RICKMAN, ALAN: Hammersmith, England, Feb. 21, 1946.

RIEGERT, PETER: NYC, Apr. 11, 1947. U Buffalo.

RIFKIN, RON: NYC, Oct. 31, 1939.

RIGG, DIANA: Doncaster, England, July 20, 1938. RADA.

RINGWALD, MOLLY: Rosewood, CA, Feb. 16, 1968.

RITTER, JOHN: Burbank, CA, Sept. 17, 1948. US. Cal.

RIVERS, JOAN (Molinsky): Brooklyn, NY, NY, June 8, 1933.

ROBARDS, JASON: Chicago, IL, July 26, 1922. AADA.

ROBARDS, SAM: NYC, Dec. 16, 1963.

ROBBINS, TIM: NYC, Oct. 16, 1958. UCLA.

ROBERTS, ERIC: Biloxi, MS, Apr. 18, 1956. RADA.

ROBERTS, JULIA: Atlanta, GA, Oct. 28, 1967.

ROBERTS, RALPH: Salisbury, NC, Aug. 17, 1922. UNC.

ROBERTS, TANYA (Leigh): Bronx, NY, Oct. 15, 1954.

ROBERTS, TONY: NYC, Oct. 22, 1939. Northwestern U.

ROBERTSON, CLIFF: La Jolla, CA, Sept. 9, 1925. Antioch College.

ROBERTSON, DALE: Oklahoma City, July 14, 1923.

ROBINSON, CHRIS: West Palm Beach, FL, Nov. 5, 1938. LACC.

ROBINSON, JAY: NYC, Apr. 14, 1930.

ROBINSON, ROGER: Seattle, WA, May 2, 1940. USC.

ROCHEFORT, JEAN: Paris, France, 1930.

ROCK, CHRIS: Brooklyn, NY, Feb. 7, 1966.

ROGERS, CHARLES "BUDDY": Olathe, KS, Aug. 13, 1904. U Kan.

ROGERS, MIMI: Coral Gables, FL, Jan. 27, 1956.

ROGERS, ROY (Leonard Slye): Cincinnati, Nov. 5, 1912.

ROGERS, WAYNE: Birmingham, AL, Apr. 7, 1933. Princeton.

ROLLE, ESTHER: Pompano Beach, FL, Nov. 8, 1922.

ROMAN, RUTH: Boston, Dec. 23, 1922. Bishop Lee Dramatic School.

RONSTADT, LINDA: Tucson, AZ, July 15, 1946.

ROOKER, MICHAEL: Jasper, AL, Apr. 6, 1955.

ROONEY, MICKEY (Joe Yule, Jr.): Brooklyn, NY, Sept. 23, 1920.

ROSE, REVA: Chicago, IL, July 30, 1940. Goodman.

ROSEANNE (Barr): Salt Lake City, UT, Nov. 3, 1952.

ROSS, DIANA: Detroit, MI, Mar. 26, 1944.

ROSS, JUSTIN: Brooklyn, NY, Dec. 15, 1954.

ROSS, KATHARINE: Hollywood, Jan. 29, 1943. Santa Rosa College.

ROSSELLINI, ISABELLA: Rome, June 18, 1952.

ROSSOVICH, RICK: Palo Alto, CA, Aug. 28, 1957.

ROTH, TIM: London, May 14, 1961.

ROUNDTREE, RICHARD: New Rochelle, NY, Sept. 7, 1942. Southern Ill.

ROURKE, MICKEY (Philip Andre Rourke, Jr.): Schenectady, NY, Sept. 16, 1956.

ROWE, NICHOLAS: London, Nov. 22, 1966, Eton.

ROWLANDS, GENA: Cambria, WI, June 19, 1934.

RUBIN, ANDREW: New Bedford, MA, June 22, 1946. AADA.

RUBINEK, SAUL: Fohrenwold, Germany, July 2, 1948.

RUBINSTEIN, JOHN: Los Angeles, CA, Dec. 8, 1946. UCLA.

RUCKER, BO: Tampa, FL, Aug. 17, 1948.

RUDD, PAUL: Boston, MA, May 15, 1940.

RUDD, PAUL: Passaic, NJ, Apr. 6, 1969.

RUDNER, RITA: Miami, FL, Sept. 17, 1955.

RUEHL, MERCEDES: Queens, NY, Feb. 28, 1948.

RULE, JANICE: Cincinnati, OH, Aug. 15, 1931.

RUPERT, MICHAEL: Denver, CO, Oct. 23, 1951. Pasadena Playhouse.

RUSH, BARBARA: Denver, CO, Jan. 4, 1927. U Calif.

RUSH, GEOFFREY: Toowoomba, Queensland, Australia, July 6, 1951. Univ. of Queensland.

RUSSELL, JANE: Bemidji, MI, June 21, 1921. Max Reinhardt School.

RUSSELL, KURT: Springfield, MA, Mar. 17, 1951.

RUSSELL, THERESA (Paup): San Diego, CA, Mar. 20, 1957.

RUSSO, JAMES: NYC, Apr. 23, 1953.

RUTHERFORD, ANN: Toronto, Canada, Nov. 2, 1920.

RYAN, JOHN P.: NYC, July 30, 1936. CCNY.

RYAN, MEG: Fairfield, CT, Nov. 19, 1961. NYU.

RYAN, TIM (Meineslschmidt): Staten Island, NY, 1958. Rutgers U.

RYDER, WINONA (Horowitz): Winona, MN, Oct. 29, 1971.

SACCHI, ROBERT: Bronx, NY, 1941. NYU.

SÄGEBRECHT, MARIANNE: Starnberg, Bavaria, Aug. 27, 1945.

SAINT, EVA MARIE: Newark, NJ, July 4, 1924. Bowling Green State U.

SAINT JAMES, SUSAN (Suzie Jane Miller): Los Angeles, Aug. 14, 1946. Conn. College.

ST. JOHN, BETTA: Hawthorne, CA, Nov. 26, 1929.

ST. JOHN, JILL (Jill Oppenheim): Los Angeles, Aug. 19, 1940.

SALA, JOHN: Los Angeles, CA, Oct. 5, 1962.

SALDANA, THERESA: Brooklyn, NY, Aug. 20, 1954.

SALINGER, MATT: Windsor, VT, Feb. 13, 1960. Princeton, Columbia.

SALT, JENNIFER: Los Angeles, Sept. 4, 1944. Sarah Lawrence College.

SAMMS, EMMA: London, Aug. 28, 1960.

SAN GIACOMO, LAURA: Orange, NJ, Nov. 14, 1961.

SANDERS, JAY O.: Austin, TX, Apr. 16, 1953.

SANDLER, ADAM: Bronx, NY, Sept. 9, 1966.

SANDS, JULIAN: Yorkshire, England, Jan 15, 1958.

SANDS, TOMMY: Chicago, IL, Aug. 27, 1937.

SAN JUAN, OLGA: NYC, Mar. 16, 1927.

SARA, MIA (Sarapocciello): Brooklyn, NY, June 19, 1967.

SARANDON, CHRIS: Beckley, WV, July 24, 1942. U WVa., Catholic U.

SARANDON, SUSAN (Tomalin): NYC, Oct. 4, 1946. Catholic U.

SARRAZIN, MICHAEL: Quebec City, Canada, May 22, 1940.

SAVAGE, FRED: Highland Park, IL, July 9, 1976.

SAVAGE, JOHN (Youngs): Long Island, NY, Aug. 25, 1949. AADA.

SAVIOLA, CAMILLE: Bronx, NY, July 16, 1950.

SAVOY, TERESA ANN: London, July 18, 1955.

SAXON, JOHN (Carmen Orrico): Brooklyn, NY, Aug. 5, 1935.

SBARGE, RAPHAEL: NYC, Feb. 12, 1964.

SCACCHI, GRETA: Milan, Italy, Feb. 18, 1960.

SCALIA, JACK: Brooklyn, NY, Nov. 10, 1951.

SCARWID, DIANA: Savannah, GA, Aug. 27, 1955, AADA. Pace U.

SCHEIDER, ROY: Orange, NJ, Nov. 10, 1932. Franklin-Marshall.

SCHEINE, RAYNOR: Emporia, VA, Nov. 10. VaCommonwealthU.

SCHELL, MARIA: Vienna, Jan. 15, 1926.

SCHELL, MAXIMILIAN: Vienna, Dec. 8, 1930.

SCHLATTER, CHARLIE: Englewood, NJ, May 1, 1966. Ithaca College.

SCHNEIDER, JOHN: Mt. Kisco, NY, Apr. 8, 1960.

SCHNEIDER, MARIA: Paris, France, Mar. 27, 1952.

SCHREIBER, LIEV: San Francisco, CA, Oct. 4, 1967.

SCHRODER, RICK: Staten Island, NY, Apr. 13, 1970.

SCHUCK, JOHN: Boston, MA, Feb. 4, 1940.

SCHULTZ, DWIGHT: Milwaukee, WI, Nov. 10, 1938. MarquetteU.

SCHWARZENEGGER, ARNOLD: Austria, July 30, 1947.

SCHWIMMER, DAVID: Queens, NY, Nov. 12, 1966.

SCHYGULLA, HANNA: Katlowitz, Germany, Dec. 25, 1943.

SCIORRA, ANNABELLA: NYC, Mar. 24, 1964.

SCOFIELD, PAUL: Hurstpierpoint, England, Jan. 21, 1922. London Mask Theatre School.

SCOGGINS, TRACY: Galveston, TX, Nov. 13, 1959.

SCOLARI, PETER: Scarsdale, NY, Sept. 12, 1956. NYCC.

SCOTT, CAMPBELL: South Salem, NY, July 19, 1962. Lawrence.

SCOTT, DEBRALEE: Elizabeth, NJ, Apr. 2, 1953

SCOTT, GEORGE C.: Wise, VA, Oct. 18, 1927. U Mo.

SCOTT, GORDON (Gordon M. Werschkul): Portland, OR, Aug. 3, 1927. Oregon U.

SCOTT, LIZABETH (Emma Matso): Scranton, PA, Sept. 29, 1922.

SCOTT, MARTHA: Jamesport, MO, Sept. 22, 1914. U Mich.

SCOTT THOMAS, KRISTIN: Redruth, Cornwall, Eng., May 24, 1960.

SEAGAL, STEVEN: Detroit, MI, Apr. 10, 1951.

SEARS, HEATHER: London, Sept. 28, 1935.

SECOMBE, HARRY: Swansea, Wales, Sept. 8, 1921.

SEDGWICK, KYRA: NYC, Aug. 19, 1965. USC.

SEGAL, GEORGE: NYC, Feb. 13, 1934. Columbia.

SELBY, DAVID: Morganstown, WV, Feb. 5, 1941. UWV.

SELLARS, ELIZABETH: Glasgow, Scotland, May 6, 1923.

SELLECK, TOM: Detroit, MI, Jan. 29, 1945. USCal.

SERNAS, JACQUES: Lithuania, July 30, 1925.

SERRAULT, MICHEL: Brunoy, France. Jan. 24, 1928. Paris Consv.

SETH, ROSHAN: New Delhi, India. 1942.

Rufus Sewell

Charlie Sheen

Craig Sheffer

SEWELL, RUFUS: Twickenham, Eng., Oct. 29, 1967.

SEYMOUR, JANE (Joyce Frankenberg): Hillingdon, England, Feb. 15, 1952.

SHALHOUB, TONY: Oct. 7, 1953.

SHARIF, OMAR (Michel Shalhoub): Alexandria, Egypt, Apr. 10, 1932. Victoria College.

SHANDLING, GARRY: Chicago, IL, Nov. 29, 1949.

SHATNER, WILLIAM: Montreal, Canada, Mar. 22, 1931. McGill U.

SHAVER, HELEN: St. Thomas, Ontario, Canada, Feb. 24, 1951.

SHAW, STAN: Chicago, IL, 1952.

SHAWN, WALLACE: NYC, Nov. 12, 1943. Harvard.

SHEA, JOHN: North Conway, NH, Apr. 14, 1949. Bates, Yale.

SHEARER, HARRY: Los Angeles, Dec. 23, 1943. UCLA.

SHEARER, MOIRA: Dunfermline, Scotland, Jan. 17, 1926. London Theatre School.

SHEEDY, ALLY: NYC, June 13, 1962. USC.

SHEEN, CHARLIE (Carlos Irwin Estevez): Santa Monica, CA, Sept. 3, 1965.

SHEEN, MARTIN (Ramon Estevez): Dayton, OH, Aug. 3, 1940.

SHEFFER, CRAIG: York, PA, Apr. 23, 1960. E. StroudsbergU.

SHEFFIELD, JOHN: Pasadena, CA, Apr. 11, 1931. UCLA.

SHELLEY, CAROL: London, England, Aug. 16, 1939.

SHEPARD, SAM (Rogers): Ft. Sheridan, IL, Nov. 5, 1943.

SHEPHERD, CYBILL: Memphis, TN, Feb. 18, 1950. Hunter, NYU.

SHER, ANTONY: England, June 14, 1949.

SHERIDAN, JAMEY: Pasadena, CA, July 12, 1951.

SHIELDS, BROOKE: NYC, May 31, 1965.

SHIRE, TALIA: Lake Success, NY, Apr. 25, 1946. Yale.

SHORT, MARTIN: Toronto, Canada, Mar. 26, 1950. McMasterU.

SHOWALTER, MAX (formerly Casey Adams): Caldwell, KS, June 2, 1917. Pasadena Playhouse.

SHUE, ELISABETH: S. Orange, NJ, Oct. 6, 1963. Harvard.

SHULL, RICHARD B.: Evanston, IL, Feb. 24, 1929.

SIDNEY, SYLVIA: NYC, Aug. 8, 1910. Theatre Guild School.

SIEMASZKO, CASEY: Chicago, IL, March 17, 1961.

SIKKING, JAMES B.: Los Angeles, Mar. 5, 1934.

SILVA, HENRY: Brooklyn, NY, 1928.

SILVER, RON: NYC, July 2, 1946. SUNY.

SILVERMAN, JONATHAN: Los Angeles, CA, Aug. 5, 1966. USC.

SIMMONS, JEAN: London, Jan. 31, 1929. Aida Foster School.

SIMON, PAUL: Newark. NJ, Nov. 5, 1942.

SIMON, SIMONE: Bethune, France, Apr. 23, 1910.

SIMPSON, O. J. (Orenthal James): San Francisco, CA, July 9, 1947. UCLA.

SINATRA, FRANK: Hoboken, NJ, Dec. 12, 1915.

SINBAD (David Adkins): Benton Harbor, MI, Nov. 10, 1956.

SINCLAIR, JOHN (Gianluigi Loffredo): Rome, Italy, 1946.

SINDEN, DONALD: Plymouth, England, Oct. 9, 1923. Webber-Douglas.

SINGER, LORI: Corpus Christi, TX, May 6, 1962. Juilliard.

SINISE, GARY: Chicago, Mar. 17. 1955.

SKARSGÅRD, STELLAN: Gothenburg, Vastergotland, Sweden, June 13, 1951.

SKERRITT, TOM: Detroit, MI, Aug. 25, 1933. Wayne State U.

SKYE, IONE (Leitch): London, England, Sept. 4, 1971.

SLATER, CHRISTIAN: NYC, Aug. 18, 1969.

SLATER, HELEN: NYC, Dec. 15, 1965.

SMITH, CHARLES MARTIN: Los Angeles, CA, Oct. 30, 1953. CalState U.

SMITH, JACLYN: Houston, TX, Oct. 26, 1947.

SMITH, JADA PINKETT: Baltimore, MD, Sept. 18, 1971.

SMITH, KEVIN: Red Bank, NJ, Aug. 2, 1970.

SMITH, KURTWOOD: New Lisbon, WI, Jul. 3, 1942.

SMITH, LANE: Memphis, TN, Apr. 29, 1936.

SMITH, LEWIS: Chattanooga, TN, 1958. Actors Studio.

SMITH, LOIS: Topeka, KS, Nov. 3, 1930. U Wash.

SMITH, MAGGIE: Ilford, England, Dec. 28, 1934.

SMITH, ROGER: South Gate, CA, Dec. 18, 1932. U Ariz.

SMITH, WILL: Philadelphia, PA, Sept. 25, 1968.

SMITHERS, WILLIAM: Richmond, VA, July 10, 1927. Catholic U.

SMITS, JIMMY: Brooklyn, NY, July 9, 1955. Cornell U.

SNIPES, WESLEY: NYC, July 31, 1963. SUNY/Purchase.

SNODGRESS, CARRIE: Chicago, IL, Oct. 27, 1946. UNI.

SOLOMON, BRUCE: NYC, 1944. U Miami, Wayne State U.

SOMERS, SUZANNE (Mahoney): San Bruno, CA, Oct. 16, 1946. Lone Mt. College.

SOMMER, ELKE (Schletz): Berlin, Germany, Nov. 5, 1940.

SOMMER, JOSEF: Greifswald, Germany, June 26, 1934.

SORDI, ALBERTO: Rome, Italy, June 15, 1920.

SORVINO, MIRA: Tenafly, NJ, Sept. 28, 1967.

SORVINO, PAUL: NYC, Apr. 13, 1939. AMDA.

SOTHERN, ANN (Harriet Lake): Valley City, ND, Jan. 22, 1909.

SOTO, TALISA (Miriam Soto)**:** Brooklyn, NY, Mar. 27, 1967.

SOUL, DAVID: Chicago, IL, Aug. 28, 1943.

SPACEK, SISSY: Quitman, TX, Dec. 25, 1949. Actors Studio.

SPACEY, KEVIN: So. Orange, NJ, July 26, 1959. Juilliard.

SPADE, DAVID: Birmingham, MS, July 22, 1964.

SPADER, JAMES: Buzzards Bay, MA, Feb. 7, 1960.

SPANO, VINCENT: Brooklyn, NY, Oct. 18, 1962.

SPENSER, JEREMY: Ceylon, 1937.

SPRINGFIELD, RICK (Richard Spring Thorpe): Sydney, Australia, Aug. 23, 1949.

Elisabeth Shue

Jada Pinkett Smith

Mira Sorvino

Kevin Spacey

Mary Steenburgen

Madeleine Stowe

Meryl Streep

Sharon Stone

STACK, ROBERT: Los Angeles, Jan. 13, 1919. USC.
STADLEN, LEWIS J.: Brooklyn, NY, Mar. 7, 1947. Neighborhood Playhouse.
STAHL, NICK: Dallas, TX, Dec. 5, 1979.
STALLONE, FRANK: NYC, July 30, 1950.
STALLONE, SYLVESTER: NYC, July 6, 1946. U Miami.
STAMP, TERENCE: London, July 23, 1939.
STANG, ARNOLD: Chelsea, MA, Sept. 28, 1925.
STANLEY, KIM (Patricia Reid): Tularosa, NM, Feb. 11, 1925. U Tex.
STANTON, HARRY DEAN: Lexington, KY, July 14, 1926.
STAPLETON, JEAN: NYC, Jan. 19, 1923.
STAPLETON, MAUREEN: Troy, NY, June 21, 1925.
STARR, RINGO (Richard Starkey): Liverpool, England, July 7, 1940.
STEEL, ANTHONY: London, May 21, 1920. Cambridge.
STEELE,BARBARA: England, Dec. 29, 1937.
STEELE, TOMMY: London, Dec. 17, 1936.
STEENBURGEN, MARY: Newport, AR, 1953. Neighborhood Playhouse.
STEIGER, ROD: Westhampton, NY, Apr. 14, 1925.
STERLING, JAN (Jane Sterling Adriance): NYC, Apr. 3, 1923. Fay Compton School.
STERLING, ROBERT (William Sterling Hart): Newcastle, PA, Nov. 13, 1917. UPittsburgh.
STERN, DANIEL: Bethesda, MD, Aug. 28, 1957.
STERNHAGEN, FRANCES: Washington, DC, Jan. 13, 1932.
STEVENS, ANDREW: Memphis, TN, June 10, 1955.
STEVENS, CONNIE (Concetta Ann Ingolia): Brooklyn, NY, Aug. 8, 1938. Hollywood Professional School.
STEVENS, FISHER: Chicago, IL, Nov. 27, 1963. NYU.
STEVENS, STELLA (Estelle Eggleston): Hot Coffee, MS, Oct. 1, 1936.
STEVENSON, PARKER: Philadelphia, PA, June 4, 1953. Princeton.

STEWART, ALEXANDRA: Montreal, Canada, June 10, 1939. Louvre.
STEWART, ELAINE (Elsy Steinberg): Montclair, NJ, May 31, 1929.
STEWART, MARTHA (Martha Haworth): Bardwell, KY, Oct. 7, 1922.
STEWART, PATRICK: Mirfield, England, July 13, 1940.
STIERS, DAVID OGDEN: Peoria, IL, Oct. 31, 1942.
STILLER, BEN: NYC, Nov. 30, 1965.
STILLER, JERRY: NYC, June 8, 1931.
STING (Gordon Matthew Sumner): Wallsend, England, Oct. 2, 1951.
STOCKWELL, DEAN: Hollywood, Mar. 5, 1935.
STOCKWELL, JOHN (John Samuels, IV): Galveston, TX, Mar. 25, 1961. Harvard.
STOLER, SHIRLEY: Brooklyn, NY, Mar. 30, 1929.
STOLTZ, ERIC: Whittier, CA, Sept. 30, 1961. USC.
STONE, DEE WALLACE (Deanna Bowers): Kansas City, MO, Dec. 14, 1948. UKS.
STORM, GALE (Josephine Cottle): Bloomington, TX, Apr. 5, 1922.
STOWE, MADELEINE: Eagle Rock, CA, Aug. 18, 1958.
STRAIGHT, BEATRICE: Old Westbury, NY, Aug. 2, 1916. Dartington Hall.
STRASBERG, SUSAN: NYC, May 22, 1938.
STRASSMAN, MARCIA: New Jersey, Apr. 28, 1948.
STRATHAIRN, DAVID: San Francisco, Jan. 26, 1949.
STRAUSS, PETER: NYC, Feb. 20, 1947.
STREEP, MERYL (Mary Louise): Summit, NJ, June 22, 1949. Vassar, Yale.
STREISAND, BARBRA: Brooklyn, NY, Apr. 24, 1942.
STRITCH, ELAINE: Detroit, MI, Feb. 2, 1925. Drama Workshop.
STROUD, DON: Honolulu, HI, Sept. 1, 1937.
STRUTHERS, SALLY: Portland, OR, July 28, 1948. Pasadena Playhouse.
SUMMER, DONNA (LaDonna Gaines): Boston, MA, Dec. 31, 1948.
SUTHERLAND, DONALD: St. John, New Brunswick, Canada, July 17, 1935. U Toronto.

SUTHERLAND, KIEFER: Los Angeles, CA, Dec. 18, 1966.
SVENSON, BO: Goreborg, Sweden, Feb. 13, 1941. UCLA.
SWAYZE, PATRICK: Houston, TX, Aug. 18, 1952.
SWEENEY, D. B. (Daniel Bernard Sweeney): Shoreham, NY, Nov. 14, 1961.
SWINBURNE, NORA (Elinore Johnson): Bath, England, July 24, 1902. RADA.
SWIT, LORETTA: Passaic, NJ, Nov. 4, 1937, AADA.
SYLVESTER, WILLIAM: Oakland, CA, Jan. 31, 1922. RADA.
SYMONDS, ROBERT: Bistow, AK, Dec. 1, 1926. TexU.
SYMS, SYLVIA: London, June 1, 1934. Convent School.
SZARABAJKA, KEITH: Oak Park, IL, Dec. 2, 1952. UChicago.
T, MR. (Lawrence Tero): Chicago, IL, May 21, 1952.
TABORI, KRISTOFFER (Siegel): Los Angeles, Aug. 4, 1952.
TAKEI, GEORGE: Los Angeles, CA, Apr. 20, 1939. UCLA.
TALBOT, NITA: NYC, Aug. 8, 1930. Irvine Studio School.
TAMBLYN, RUSS: Los Angeles, Dec. 30, 1934.
TARANTINO, QUENTIN: Knoxville, TN, Mar. 27, 1963.
TATE, LARENZ: Chicago, IL, Sept. 8, 1975.
TAYLOR, DON: Freeport, PA, Dec. 13, 1920. Penn State U.
TAYLOR, ELIZABETH: London, Feb. 27, 1932. Byron House School.
TAYLOR, LILI: Glencoe, IL, Feb. 20, 1967.
TAYLOR, RENEE: NYC, Mar. 19, 1935.
TAYLOR, ROD (Robert): Sydney, Aust., Jan. 11, 1929.
TAYLOR-YOUNG, LEIGH: Washington, DC, Jan. 25, 1945. Northwestern.
TEEFY, MAUREEN: Minneapolis, MN, 1954, Juilliard.
TEMPLE, SHIRLEY: Santa Monica, CA, Apr. 23, 1927.
TENNANT, VICTORIA: London, England, Sept. 30, 1950.

Donald Sutherland

Quentin Tarentino

Lili Taylor

Henry Thomas

TERZIEFF, LAURENT: Paris, France, June 25, 1935.

TEWES, LAUREN: Braddock, PA, Oct. 26, 1954.

THACKER, RUSS: Washington, DC, June 23, 1946. Montgomery College.

THAXTER, PHYLLIS: Portland, ME, Nov. 20, 1921. St. Genevieve.

THELEN, JODI: St. Cloud, MN, 1963.

THERON, CHARLIZE: Benoni, So. Africa, Aug. 7, 1975.

THEWLIS, DAVID: Blackpool, Eng., 1963.

THOMAS, HENRY: San Antonio, TX, Sept. 8, 1971.

THOMAS, JAY: New Orleans, July 12, 1948.

THOMAS, MARLO (Margaret): Detroit, Nov. 21, 1938. USC.

THOMAS, PHILIP MICHAEL: Columbus, OH, May 26, 1949. Oakwood College.

THOMAS, RICHARD: NYC, June 13, 1951. Columbia.

THOMPSON, EMMA: London, England, Apr.15, 1959. Cambridge.

THOMPSON, FRED DALTON: Laurenceberg, TN, Aug. 19, 1942

THOMPSON, JACK (John Payne): Sydney, Australia, Aug. 31, 1940.

THOMPSON, LEA: Rochester, MN, May 31, 1961.

THOMPSON, REX: NYC, Dec. 14, 1942.

THOMPSON, SADA: Des Moines, IA, Sept. 27, 1929. Carnegie Tech.

THORNTON, BILLY BOB: Hot Spring, AR, Aug. 4, 1955.

THORSON, LINDA: Toronto, Canada, June 18, 1947. RADA.

THULIN, INGRID: Solleftea, Sweden, Jan. 27, 1929. Royal Drama Theatre.

THURMAN, UMA: Boston, MA, Apr. 29, 1970.

TICOTIN, RACHEL: Bronx, NY, Nov. 1, 1958.

TIERNEY, LAWRENCE: Brooklyn, NY, Mar. 15, 1919. Manhattan College.

TIFFIN, PAMELA (Wonso): Oklahoma City, OK, Oct. 13, 1942.

TIGHE, KEVIN: Los Angeles, Aug. 13, 1944.

TILLY, JENNIFER: Los Angeles, CA, Sept. 16, 1958.

TILLY, MEG: Texada, Canada, Feb. 14, 1960.

TOBOLOWSKY, STEPHEN: Dallas, Tx, May 30, 1951. So. Methodist U.

TODD, BEVERLY: Chicago, IL, July 1, 1946.

TODD, RICHARD: Dublin, Ireland, June 11, 1919. Shrewsbury School.

TOLKAN, JAMES: Calumet, MI, June 20, 1931.

TOMEI, MARISA: Brooklyn, NY, Dec. 4, 1964. NYU.

TOMLIN, LILY: Detroit, MI, Sept. 1, 1939. Wayne State U.

TOPOL (Chaim Topol): Tel-Aviv, Israel, Sept. 9, 1935.

TORN, RIP: Temple, TX, Feb. 6, 1931. UTex.

TORRES, LIZ: NYC, Sept. 27, 1947. NYU.

TOTTER, AUDREY: Joliet, IL, Dec. 20, 1918.

TOWSEND, ROBERT: Chicago, IL, Feb. 6, 1957.

TRAVANTI, DANIEL J.: Kenosha, WI, Mar. 7, 1940.

TRAVIS, NANCY: Astoria, NY, Sept. 21, 1961.

TRAVOLTA, JOEY: Englewood, NJ, 1952.

TRAVOLTA, JOHN: Englewood, NJ, Feb. 18, 1954.

TREMAYNE, LES: London, Apr. 16, 1913. Northwestern, Columbia, UCLA.

TREVOR, CLAIRE (Wemlinger): NYC, March 8, 1909.

TRINTIGNANT, JEAN-LOUIS: Pont-St. Esprit, France, Dec. 11, 1930. DullinBalachova Drama School.

TSOPEI, CORINNA: Athens, Greece, June 21, 1944.

TUBB, BARRY: Snyder, TX, 1963. AmConsv Th.

TUCCI, STANLEY: Katonah, NY, Jan. 11, 1960.

TUCKER, MICHAEL: Baltimore, MD, Feb. 6, 1944.

TUNE, TOMMY: Wichita Falls, TX, Feb. 28, 1939.

TURNER, JANINE (Gauntt): Lincoln, NE, Dec. 6, 1963.

TURNER, KATHLEEN: Springfield, MO, June 19, 1954. UMd.

TURNER, TINA (Anna Mae Bullock): Nutbush, TN, Nov. 26, 1938.

TURTURRO, JOHN: Brooklyn, NY, Feb. 28, 1957. Yale.

TUSHINGHAM, RITA: Liverpool, England, Mar. 14, 1940.

TUTIN, DOROTHY: London, Apr. 8, 1930.

TWIGGY (Lesley Hornby): London, Sept. 19, 1949.

TWOMEY, ANNE: Boston, MA, June 7, 1951. Temple U.

TYLER, BEVERLY (Beverly Jean Saul): Scranton, PA, July 5, 1928.

TYLER, LIV: Portland, ME, July 1, 1977.

TYRRELL, SUSAN: San Francisco, 1946.

TYSON, CATHY: Liverpool, England, June 12, 1965. Royal Shake. Co.

TYSON, CICELY: NYC, Dec. 19, 1933. NYU.

UGGAMS, LESLIE: NYC, May 25, 1943. Juilliard.

ULLMAN, TRACEY: Slough, England, Dec. 30, 1959.

ULLMANN, LIV: Tokyo, Dec. 10, 1938. Webber-Douglas Acad.

ULRICH, SKEET (Bryan Ray Ulrich): North Carolina, Jan. 20, 1969.

UMEKI, MIYOSHI: Otaru, Hokaido, Japan, Apr. 3, 1929.

UNDERWOOD, BLAIR: Tacoma, WA, Aug. 25, 1964. Carnegie-Mellon U.

URICH, ROBERT: Toronto, Canada, Dec. 19, 1946.

USTINOV, PETER: London, Apr. 16, 1921. Westminster School.

VACCARO, BRENDA: Brooklyn, NY, Nov. 18, 1939. Neighborhood Playhouse.

VALANDREY, CHARLOTTE (Anne Charlone Pascal): Paris, France, 1968.

VALLI, ALIDA: Pola, Italy, May 31, 1921. Academy of Drama.

VALLONE, RAF: Riogio, Italy, Feb. 17, 1916. Turin U.

VAN ARK, JOAN: NYC, June 16, 1943. Yale.

VAN DAMME, JEAN-CLAUDE (J-C Vorenberg): Brussels, Belgium, Apr. 1, 1960.

VAN DE VEN, MONIQUE: Netherlands, 1952.

VAN DEVERE, TRISH (Patricia Dressel): Englewood Cliffs, NJ, Mar. 9, 1945. Ohio Wesleyan.

VAN DOREN, MAMIE (Joan Lucile Olander): Rowena SD, Feb. 6, 1933.

VAN DYKE, DICK: West Plains, MO, Dec. 13, 1925.

VANITY (Denise Katrina Smith): Niagara, Ont., Can, Jan. 4, 1959.

VAN PALLANDT, NINA: Copenhagen, Denmark, July 15, 1932.

Uma Thurman

Marisa Tomei

Christopher Walken

Denzel Washington

VAN PATTEN, DICK: NYC, Dec. 9, 1928.
VAN PATTEN, JOYCE: NYC, Mar. 9, 1934.
VAN PEEBLES, MARIO: NYC, Jan. 15, 1958. Columbia U.
VAN PEEBLES, MELVIN: Chicago, IL, Aug. 21, 1932.
VANCE, COURTNEY B.: Detroit, MI, Mar. 12, 1960.
VARNEY, JIM: Lexington, KY, June 15, 1949.
VAUGHN, ROBERT: NYC, Nov. 22, 1932. USC.
VAUGHN, VINCE: Minneapolis, MN, Mar. 28, 1970.
VEGA, ISELA: Mexico, 1940.
VELJOHNSON, REGINALD: NYC, Aug. 16, 1952.
VENNERA, CHICK: Herkimer, NY, Mar. 27, 1952. Pasadena Playhouse.
VENORA, DIANE: Hartford, CT, 1952. Juilliard.
VERDON, GWEN: Culver City, CA, Jan. 13, 1925.
VERNON, JOHN: Montreal, Canada, Feb. 24, 1932.

VEREEN, BEN: Miami, FL, Oct. 10, 1946.
VICTOR, JAMES (Lincoln Rafael Peralta Diaz): Santiago, D.R., July 27, 1939. Haaren HS/NYC.
VINCENT, JAN-MICHAEL: Denver, CO, July 15, 1944. Ventura.
VIOLET, ULTRA (Isabelle Collin-Dufresne): Grenoble, France, 1935.
VITALE, MILLY: Rome, Italy, July 16, 1928. Lycee Chateaubriand.
VOHS, JOAN: St. Albans, NY, July 30, 1931.
VOIGHT, JON: Yonkers, NY, Dec. 29, 1938. Catholic U.
VON DOHLEN, LENNY: Augusta, GA, Dec. 22, 1958. UTex.
VON SYDOW, MAX: Lund, Sweden, July 10, 1929. Royal Drama Theatre.
WAGNER, LINDSAY: Los Angeles, June 22. 1949.
WAGNER, NATASHA GREGSON: Los Angeles, CA, Sept. 29, 1970.
WAGNER, ROBERT: Detroit, Feb. 10, 1930.
WAHL, KEN: Chicago, IL, Feb. 14, 1953.
WAITE, GENEVIEVE: South Africa, 1949.
WAITE, RALPH: White Plains, NY, June 22, 1929. Yale.
WAITS, TOM: Pomona, CA, Dec. 7, 1949.
WALKEN, CHRISTOPHER: Astoria, NY, Mar. 31, 1943. Hofstra.
WALKER, CLINT: Hartfold, IL, May 30, 1927. USC.
WALLACH, ELI: Brooklyn, NY, Dec. 7, 1915. CCNY, U Tex.
WALLACH, ROBERTA: NYC, Aug. 2, 1955.
WALLIS, SHANI: London, Apr. 5, 1941.
WALSH, J.T.: San Francisco,. CA. Sept. 28, 1943.
WALSH, M. EMMET: Ogdensburg, NY, Mar. 22, 1935. Clarkson College, AADA.
WALSTON, RAY: New Orleans, Nov. 22, 1917. Cleveland Playhouse.
WALTER, JESSICA: Brooklyn, NY, Jan. 31, 1944 Neighborhood Playhouse.
WALTER, TRACEY: Jersey City, NJ, Nov. 25, 1942.
WALTERS, JULIE: London, Feb. 22, 1950.
WALTON, EMMA: London, Nov. 1962. Brown U.
WARD, BURT (Gervis): Los Angeles, July 6, 1945.
WARD, FRED: San Diego, CA, Dec. 30, 1942.

WARD, RACHEL: London, Sept. 12, 1957.
WARD, SELA: Meridian, MS, July 11, 1956.
WARD, SIMON: London, Oct. 19, 1941.
WARDEN, JACK (Lebzelter): Newark, NJ, Sept. 18, 1920.
WARNER, DAVID: Manchester, England, July 29, 1941. RADA.
WARNER, MALCOLM-JAMAL: Jersey City, NJ, Aug. 18, 1970.
WARREN, JENNIFER: NYC, Aug. 12, 1941. U Wisc.
WARREN, LESLEY ANN: NYC, Aug. 16, 1946.
WARREN, MICHAEL: South Bend, IN, Mar. 5, 1946. UCLA.
WARRICK, RUTH: St. Joseph, MO, June 29, 1915. U Mo.
WASHINGTON, DENZEL: Mt. Vernon, NY, Dec. 28, 1954. Fordham.
WASSON, CRAIG: Ontario, OR, Mar. 15, 1954. UOre.
WATERSTON, SAM: Cambridge, MA, Nov. 15, 1940. Yale.
WATLING, JACK: London, Jan. 13, 1923. Italia Conti School.

Sigourney Weaver

Michael York

WATSON, EMILY: London, Jan. 14, 1967.

WAYANS, DAMON: NYC, Sept. 4, 1960.

WAYANS, KEENEN, IVORY: NYC, June 8, 1958. Tuskegee Inst.

WAYNE, PATRICK: Los Angeles, July 15, 1939. Loyola.

WEATHERS, CARL: New Orleans, LA, Jan. 14, 1948. Long Beach CC.

WEAVER, DENNIS: Joplin, MO, June 4, 1924. U Okla.

WEAVER, FRITZ: Pittsburgh, PA, Jan. 19, 1926.

WEAVER, SIGOURNEY (Susan): NYC, Oct. 8, 1949. Stanford, Yale.

WEBER, STEVEN: March 4, 1961.

WEDGEWORTH, ANN: Abilene, TX, Jan. 21, 1935. U Tex.

WELCH, RAQUEL (Tejada): Chicago, IL, Sept. 5, 1940.

WELD, TUESDAY (Susan): NYC, Aug. 27, 1943. Hollywood Professional School.

WELDON, JOAN: San Francisco, Aug. 5, 1933. San Francisco Conservatory.

WELLER, PETER: Stevens Point, WI, June 24, 1947. AmThWing.

WENDT, GEORGE: Chicago, IL, Oct. 17, 1948.

WEST, ADAM (William Anderson): Walla Walla, WA, Sept. 19, 1929.

WETTIG, PATRICIA: Cincinatti, OH, Dec. 4, 1951. TempleU.

WHALEY, FRANK: Syracuse, NY, July 20, 1963. SUNY/Albany.

WHALLEY-KILMER, JOANNE: Manchester, England, Aug. 25, 1964.

WHEATON, WIL: Burbank, CA, July 29, 1972.

WHITAKER, FOREST: Longview, TX, July 15, 1961.

WHITAKER, JOHNNY: Van Nuys, CA, Dec. 13, 1959.

WHITE, BETTY: Oak Park, IL, Jan. 17, 1922.

WHITE, CHARLES: Perth Amboy, NJ, Aug. 29, 1920. Rutgers U.

WHITELAW, BILLIE: Coventry, England, June 6, 1932.

WHITMAN, STUART: San Francisco, Feb. 1, 1929. CCLA.

WHITMORE, JAMES: White Plains, NY, Oct. 1, 1921. Yale.

WHITNEY, GRACE LEE: Detroit, MI, Apr. 1, 1930.

WHITTON, MARGARET: Philadelphia, PA, Nov, 30, 1950.

WIDDOES, KATHLEEN: Wilmington, DE, Mar. 21, 1939.

WIDMARK, RICHARD: Sunrise, MN, Dec. 26, 1914. Lake Forest.

WIEST, DIANNE: Kansas City, MO, Mar. 28, 1948. UMd.

WILBY. JAMES: Burma, Feb. 20, 1958.

WILCOX, COLIN: Highlands, NC, Feb. 4, 1937. U Tenn.

WILDER, GENE (Jerome Silberman): Milwaukee, WI, June 11, 1935. UIowa.

WILLIAMS, BILLY DEE: NYC, Apr. 6, 1937.

WILLIAMS, CARA (Bernice Kamiat): Brooklyn, NY, June 29, 1925.

WILLIAMS, CINDY: Van Nuys, CA, Aug. 22, 1947. KACC.

WILLIAMS, CLARENCE, III: NYC, Aug. 21, 1939.

WILLIAMS, ESTHER: Los Angeles, Aug. 8, 1921.

WILLIAMS, JOBETH: Houston, TX, Dec 6, 1948. Brown U.

WILLIAMS, PAUL: Omaha, NE, Sept. 19, 1940.

WILLIAMS, ROBIN: Chicago, IL, July 21, 1951. Juilliard.

WILLIAMS, TREAT (Richard): Rowayton, CT, Dec. 1, 1951.

WILLIAMS, VANESSA L.: Tarrytown, NY, Mar. 18, 1963.

WILLIAMSON, FRED: Gary, IN, Mar. 5, 1938. Northwestern.

WILLIAMSON, NICOL: Hamilton, Scotland, Sept. 14, 1938.

WILLIS, BRUCE: Penns Grove, NJ, Mar. 19, 1955.

WILLISON, WALTER: Monterey Park, CA, June 24, 1947.

WILSON, DEMOND: NYC, Oct. 13, 1946. Hunter College.

WILSON, ELIZABETH: Grand Rapids, MI, Apr. 4, 1925.

WILSON, FLIP (Clerow Wilson): Jersey City, NJ, Dec. 8, 1933.

WILSON, LAMBERT: Paris, France, 1959.

WILSON, SCOTT: Atlanta, GA, 1942.

WINCOTT, JEFF: Toronto, Canada, May 8, 1957.

WINCOTT, MICHAEL: Toronto, Canada, Jan. 6, 1959. Juilliard.

WINDE, BEATRICE: Chicago, IL, Jan. 6.

WINDOM, WILLIAM: NYC, Sept. 28, 1923. Williams College.

WINDSOR, MARIE (Emily Marie Bertelson): Marysvale, UT, Dec. 11, 1924. Brigham Young U.

WINFIELD, PAUL: Los Angeles, May 22, 1940. UCLA.

WINFREY, OPRAH: Kosciusko, MS, Jan. 29, 1954. TnStateU.

WINGER, DEBRA: Cleveland, OH, May 17, 1955. Cal State.

WINKLER, HENRY: NYC, Oct. 30, 1945. Yale.

WINN, KITTY: Washington, D.C., Feb, 21, 1944. Boston U.

WINNINGHAM, MARE: Phoenix, AZ, May 6, 1959.

WINSLET, KATE: Reading, Eng., Oct. 5, 1975.

WINSLOW, MICHAEL: Spokane, WA, Sept. 6, 1960.

WINTER, ALEX: London, July 17, 1965. NYU.

WINTERS, JONATHAN: Dayton, OH, Nov. 11, 1925. Kenyon College.

WINTERS, SHELLEY (Shirley Schrift): St. Louis, Aug. 18, 1922. Wayne U.

WITHERS, GOOGIE: Karachi, India, Mar. 12, 1917. Italia Conti.

WITHERS, JANE: Atlanta, GA, Apr. 12, 1926.

WITHERSPOON, REESE (Laura Jean Reese Witherspoon): Nashville, TN, Mar. 22, 1976.

WONG, B.D.: San Francisco, Oct. 24,1962.

WONG, RUSSELL: Troy, NY, 1963. SantaMonica College.

WOOD, ELIJAH: Cedar Rapids, IA, Jan 28, 1981.

WOODARD, ALFRE: Tulsa, OK, Nov. 2, 1953. Boston U.

WOODLAWN, HOLLY (Harold Ajzen-berg): Juana Diaz, PR, 1947.

WOODS, JAMES: Vernal, UT, Apr. 18, 1947. MIT.

WOODWARD, EDWARD: Croyden, Surrey, England, June 1, 1930.

WOODWARD, JOANNE: Thomasville, GA, Feb. 27, 1930. Neighborhood Playhouse.

WORONOV, MARY: Brooklyn, NY, Dec. 8, 1946. Cornell.

WORTH, IRENE (Hattie Abrams): Nebraska, June 23, 1916. UCLA.

WRAY, FAY: Alberta, Canada, Sept. 15, 1907.

WRIGHT, AMY: Chicago, IL, Apr. 15, 1950.

WRIGHT, MAX: Detroit, MI, Aug. 2, 1943. WayneStateU.

WRIGHT, ROBIN: Dallas, TX, Apr. 8, 1966.

WRIGHT, TERESA: NYC, Oct. 27, 1918.

WUHL, ROBERT: Union City, NJ, Oct. 9, 1951. UHouston.

WYATT, JANE: NYC, Aug. 10, 1910. Barnard College.

WYMAN, JANE (Sarah Jane Fulks): St. Joseph, MO, Jan. 4, 1914.

WYMORE, PATRICE: Miltonvale, KS, Dec. 17, 1926.

WYNN, MAY (Donna Lee Hickey): NYC, Jan. 8, 1930.

WYNTER, DANA (Dagmar): London, June 8. 1927. Rhodes U.

YORK, MICHAEL: Fulmer, England, Mar. 27, 1942. Oxford.

YORK, SUSANNAH: London, Jan. 9, 1941. RADA.

YOUNG, ALAN (Angus): North Shield, England, Nov. 19, 1919.

YOUNG, BURT: Queens, NY, Apr. 30, 1940.

YOUNG, CHRIS: Chambersburg, PA, Apr. 28, 1971.

YOUNG, LORETTA (Gretchen): Salt Lake City, UT, Jan. 6, 1912. Immaculate Heart College.

YOUNG, ROBERT: Chicago, IL, Feb. 22, 1907.

YOUNG, SEAN: Louisville, KY, Nov. 20, 1959. Interlochen.

ZACHARIAS, ANN: Stockholm, Sweden, Sweden, 1956.

ZADORA, PIA: Hoboken, NJ, 1954.

ZELLWEGER, RENEE: Katy, TX, Apr. 25, 1969.

ZERBE, ANTHONY: Long Beach, CA, May 20, 1939.

ZIMBALIST, EFREM, JR.: NYC, Nov.30, 1918. Yale.

ZUNIGA, DAPHNE: Berkeley, CA, Oct. 28, 1963. UCLA.

OBITUARIES

HY AVERBACK, 76, former actor-turned-director died on Oct. 14, 1997 in Los Angeles following heart surgery. His credits as a director include *Chamber of Horrors, Where Were You When the Lights Went Out?, I Love You Alice B. Toklas, The Great Bank Robbery, Suppose They Gave a War and Nobody Came,* and *Where the Boys Are* (1984). Survived by his wife, two sons, a daughter, a sister, and a grandson.

JOHN BEAL (James Alexander Bliedung), 87, Missouri-born film, theatre and television actor died on April 26, 1997 in Santa Cruz, CA. He came to Hollywood in 1933 to repeat his stage role in *Another Language,* and was thereafter seen in such movies as *Hat Coat and Glove, The Little Minister, Les Miserables* (1935), *Laddie, Break of Hearts, M'Liss, Border Cafe, Double Wedding, Madame X* (1937), *Port of Seven Seas, The Arkansas Traveler, The Cat and the Canary, Ellery Queen and the Perfect Crime, Atlantic Convoy, Edge of Darkness, So Dear to My Heart, Song of Surrender, Chicago Deadline, My Six Convicts, Remains to Be Seen, The Vampire, The Sound and the Fury, Ten Who Dared,* and *The Firm.* He is survived by two daughters and two grandsons.

John Beal   Thelma Carpenter

SALLY BLANE (Elizabeth Jane Young), 87, Colorado-born screen actress died at her home in Los Angeles on Aug. 27, 1997. Debuting as a child in the 1917 film *Sirens of the Sea,* her many other credits include *Casey at the Bat, The Vagabaond Lover, Little Accident, Once a Sinner, Ten Cents a Dance, Night of Terror, I Am a Fugitive from a Chain Gang, Advice to the Lovelorn, One Mile from Heaven, Charlie Chan at Treasure Island* (which was directed by her husband, Norman Foster), *The Story of Alexander Graham Bell* (in which she appeared with sisters Polly and Loretta Young, and her half-sister Gretchen Young) and *A Bullet for Joey.* She is survived by Loretta Young, her son, and her daughter.

THELMA CARPENTER, 77, Brooklyn-born singer-actress was found dead in her Manhattan apartment on May 15, 1997. She was seen in such movies as *Hellzapoppin, The Wiz,* and *The Cotton Club.* No reported survivors.

John Denver   David Doyle

ADRIANA CASELOTTI, 80, Connecticut-born singer who supplied the voice of Snow White in Walt Disney's classic 1937 animated feature *Snow White and the Seven Dwarfs,* died of cancer on Jan. 19, 1997 at her home in Los Angeles.

JOHN DENVER (Henry John Deutschendorf, Jr.), 53, New Mexico-born singer whose hit singles include "Annie's Song," "Rocky Mountain High," and "Thank God I'm a Country Boy" was killed in a plane crash in Monterey Bay, CA, on Oct. 11, 1997. He starred in the 1977 film *Oh God!* and narrated the documentary *Fire and Ice.* Survived by three children.

DAVID DOYLE, 67, character actor best known for co-starring in the hit television series "Charley's Angels," died of a heart attack on Feb. 28, 1997 in Los Angeles. His movie credits include *No Way to Treat a Lady, Paper Lion, Coogan's Bluff, Vigilante Force, Lady Liberty, The Comeback,* and *Capricorn One.* No reported survivors.

CHRIS FARLEY, 33, Wisconsin-born comedian was found dead of a drug overdose in his Chicago apartment on Dec. 18, 1997. A cast member of the series "Saturday Night Live" he appeared in the movies *Wayne's World, Coneheads, Wayne's World 2, Airheads, Billy Madison, Tommy Boy, Black Sheep, Beverly Hills Ninja,* and, released posthumously, *Almost Heroes,* and *Dirty Work.* Survived by his parents, three borthers, and a sister.

GEORGE FENNEMAN, 77, Beijing-born announcer and actor, best known as the affable sidekick of Groucho Marx on the hit game show "You Bet Your Life," died of emphysema on May 29, 1997 at his home in Los Angeles. He was also seen in the movies *The Thing from Another World* and *How to Succeed in Business Without Really Trying.* He is survived by his wife, son, and two daughters.

SAMUEL FULLER, 85, Massachusetts-born cult director-writer of such movies as *The Naked Kiss* and *Shock Corridor,* died of unspecified causes on Oct. 30, 1997 at his home in the Hollywood Hills. He received his first credit in 1949 on the western *I Shot Jesse James,* after which he directed such films as *The Baron of Arizona, The Steel Helmet, Fixed Bayonets, Pickup on South Street, House of Bamboo, Run of the Arrow, Forty Guns, Verboten, The Crimson Kimono, Underworld USA, Merrill's Marauders, The Big Red One,* and *White Dog.* He also appeared as an actor in such movies as *The American Friend, Somebody to Love,* and *The End of Violence.* Survived by his wife and a daughter.

Chris Farley　　　　　　　　Tamara Geva

WILLIAM HICKEY, 69, Brooklyn-born character actor of screen, stage and television, who received an Oscar nomination for playing the decrepit Mafia don in *Prizzi's Honor,* died on June 29, 1997 in Manhattan from complications of emphysema and bronchitis. Among his movie credits are *A Hatful of Rain, The Producers, The Boston Strangler, Little Big Man, A New Leaf, Wise Blood, The Name of the Rose, Bright Lights Big City, Sea of Love, My Blue Heaven, Tales from the Darkside: The Movie, Puppet Master, Forget Paris,* and his last, *Mouse Hunt,* released posthumously. Survivors include his sister.

JUZO ITAMI (Yoshihiro Ikeuchi), 64, Japanese director of the noted film *Tampopo* lept to his death from a rooftop in Tokyo on Dec. 20, 1997. His other credits include *The Funeral* (1984), *A Taxing Woman,* and *A Taxing Woman's Return.* Survived by his wife, actress Nobuko Miyamoto, and his two sons.

TAMARA GEVA, 91, Russian ballet dancer and actress died at her Manhattan home on Dec. 9, 1997. She was seen in such movies as *Their Big Moment, Manhattan Merry-Go-Round,* and *Orchestra Wives.* No immediate survivors.

BRIAN GLOVER, 63, British character actor died from complications from a brain tumor on July 24, 1997 in London. His movie credits include *Kes, Mister Quilp, Jabberwocky, The Great Train Robbery* (1979), *An American Werewolf in London, Britannia Hospital, The Company of Wolves, Kafka, Leon the Pig Farmer,* and *Alien3.* Survived by his wife, two children, and four grandchildren.

GEORGES GUETARY, 82, French singer-actor (born in Egypt to Greek parents), best known to American audiences for singing "I'll Build a Stairway to Paradise" in the 1951 Oscar-winning film *An American in Paris,* died on Sept. 13, 1997 in Mougins, France, of undisclosed causes. He is survived by his wife and two children.

Juzo Itami　　　　　　　　Richard Jaeckel

RICHARD JAECKEL, 70, New York-born character player who went from working in the mailroom at 20th Century-Fox to becoming a character actor in dozens of movies, died on June 14, 1997 of cancer in Woodland Hills, CA. Following his 1943 debut in *Guadalcanal Diary* he was seen in such movies as *Wing and a Prayer, City Across the River, Battleground, Sands of Iwo Jima, The Gunfighter, My Son John, Come Back Little Sheba, The Big Leaguer, The Violent Men, Attack!, 3:10 to Yuma, The Naked and the Dead, Platinum High School, Town Without Pity, Four for Texas, The Dirty Dozen, The Devil's Brigade, The Green Slime, Chisum, Sometimes a Great Notion* (for which he received an Oscar nomination), *Ulzana's Raid, Pat Garrett and Billy and Kid, Chosen Survivors, The Drowning Pool, Grizzly, Twilight's Last Gleaming, Herbie Goes Bananas, ...All the Marbles, Starman,* and *Black Moon Rising.* He is survived by his wife, a sister, and two sons.

Brian Glover　　　　　　　　William Hickey

PAUL JARRICO, 82, Los Angeles-born producer-writer was killed in a car accident on his way home from a ceremony honoring blacklisted writers on Oct. 28, 1997 in California. His credits include *Beauty for the Asking, The Face Behind the Mask, Tom Dick and Harry* (for which he received an Oscar nomination), *Thousands Cheer, Song of Russia, The Search, The White Tower,* and *The Day the Hot Line Got Hot.* He served as producer on *Salt of the Earth,* and wrote, but was not credited due to his blacklisting status, *Five Branded Women* and *Treasure of the Aztecs.* Survived by his wife and his son.

Stubby Kaye   Sheldon Leonard

STUBBY KAYE, 79, Bronx-born screen and stage performer, best remembered for his rendition of "Sit Down, You're Rockin' the Boat" in the original Broadway production and 1955 screen version of *Guys and Dolls,* died of undisclosed causes on Dec. 14, 1997 in Rancho Mirage, CA. His other movies include *Li'l Abner* (repeating his stage role of "Marryin' Sam"), *40 Pounds of Trouble, Cat Ballou* (in which he sang the title song with Nat King Cole), *Sweet Charity, Can Hieronymus Merkin Ever Forget Mercy Humppe and Find True Happiness?,* and *Who Framed Roger Rabbit.* No reported survivors.

BRIAN KEITH, 75, New Jersey-born screen, stage and television actor who went from character parts to stardom in several Disney films and on television, was found dead on June 24, 1997 at his home in Malibu, CA, of a self-inflicted gunshot wound. He had been suffering from cancer. The son of character actor Robert Keith he had made his movie debut at the age

Brian Keith

of three but did not start his film career officially until the 1950s. From that point on his was seen in such motion pictures as *Arrowhead, Alaska Seas, The Violent Men, Five Against the House, Storm Center, Run of the Arrow, Chicago Confidential, Dino, Fort Dobbs, The Young Philadelphians, Ten Who Dared, The Deadly Companions, The Parent Trap, Moon Pilot, Savage Sam, The Pleasure Seekers, A Tiger Walks, Those Calloways, The Hallelujah Trail, The Rare Breed, Nevada Smith, The Russians Are Coming the Russians Are Coming, Reflections in a Golden Eye, With Six You Get Eggroll, Krakatoa: East of Java, Gaily Gaily, Suppose They Gave a War and Nobody Came, Scandalous John, The McKenzie Break, The Yakuza, The Wind and the Lion, Nickelodeon, Hooper, Meteor, Mountain Men, Sharky's Machine, Young Guns,* and *Welcome Home.* Survived by his wife, actress Victoria Young.

Burgess Meredith

DOROTHY KINGSLEY, 87, New York City-born screenwriter, noted for her scripts of several MGM musicals including *Kiss Me Kate* and *Seven Brides for Seven Brothers,* died in Monterey, CA, on Sept. 26, 1997. Her other credits include *The Skipper Surprised His Wife, Bathing Beauty, Easy to Wed, On an Island With You, Look Who's Laughing, A Date With Judy, Neptune's Daughter, Two Weeks With Love, Angels in the Outfield* (1951), *Texas Carnival, It's a Big Country, Small Town Girl* (1953), *Dangerous When Wet, Jupiter's Darling, Don't Go Near the Water, Pal Joey, Green Mansions, Can-Can, Pepe, Valley of the Dolls,* and *Half a Sixpence.* Survived by two sons, two daughters, and nine grandchildren.

BURTON LANE (Burton Levy), 84, New York City-born composer whose scores included *Finian's Rainbow* and *On a Clear Day You Can See Forever,* died at his home in Manhattan on Jan. 5, 1997. His songs were heard in such motion pictures as *Dancing Lady, Kid Millions, Folies Bergere, Reckless* (1935), *College Holiday, Swing High Swing Low, Cafe Society, Las Vegas Nights, Babes on Braodway* (receiving an Oscar nomination for "How About You?"), *Panama Hattie, DuBarry Was a Lady, Presenting Lily Mars, Hollywood Canteen, Royal Wedding* (Oscar nomination for "Too Late Now"), *Give a Girl a Break, Jupiter's Darling,* and *Heidi's Song.* Survived by his wife, a daughter, and three stepdaughters.

Toshiro Mifune   Edward Mulhare

ROSINA LAWRENCE (Rosina Marchisio-McCabe), 84, dancer-actress died on June 23, 1997 in Manhattan. Her film credits include *Ten Dollar Raise, Paramount on Parade, A Connecticut Yankee, Disorderly Conduct, Music is Magic, Reckless* (1935), *The Great Ziegfeld* (as Marilyn Miller), and *Pick a Star.* She retired from films in 1939 following marriage. She is survived by her second husband, writer John McCabe, two daughters, a son, and five grandchildren.

SHELDON LEONARD (Sheldon Leonard Bershad), 89, New York City-born character actor who specialized in tough guy types and later went on to a successful career as a television producer-director, died at his home in Beverly Hills on January 10, 1997. Among his acting credits on film are *Another Thin Man, Buy Me That Town, Rise and Shine, Week-End in Havana, Tortilla Flat, Born to Sing, Lucky Jordan, Tennessee Johnson, Hit the Ice, City Without Men, Taxi Mister, To Have and Have Not, The Falcon in Hollywood, Zombies on Broadway, Captain Kidd, Bowery Bombshell, The Gentleman Bisbehaves, It's a Wonderful Life, Sinbad the*

Don Porter   Denver Pyle

Sailor, The Gangster, Jinx Money, My Dream is Yours, Abbott and Costello Meet the Invisible Man, Come Fill the Cup, Young Man With Ideas, Stop You're Killing Me, Money from Home, Guys and Dolls, Pocketful of Miracles, and *The Brinks' Job.* On television he won two Emmy Awards for directing "The Danny Thomas Show" and one for producing "My World and Welcome to It." He is survived by his wife, a son, a daughter, and four grandchildren.

ROBERT LEWIS, 88, actor,director and founder of the Actors Studio, died of a heart attack on a Manhattan street on Nov. 23, 1997. He acted in such movies as *Dragon Seed, Son of Lassie, Ziegfeld Follies,* and *Monsieur Verdoux,* and was the director of the 1956 remake of *Anything Goes.* On Broadway he directed such works as *Brigadoon, The Teahouse of the August Moon, Witness for the Prosecution,* and *On a Clear Day You Can See Forever.* Survived by his sister.

JEAN LOUIS, 89, Paris-born costume designer died on April 20, 1997 at his home in Palm Springs, CA. His many motion picture credits include *Thousand and One Nights, Gilda, Tomorrow is Forever, The Jolson Story, Dead Reckoning, Down to Earth, The Lady from Shanghai, The Loves of Carmen, Jolson Sings Again, Knock on Any Door, In a Lonely Place, Born Yesterday, The Marrying Kind, Affair in Trinidad, The Big Heat, Miss Sadie Thompson, From Here to Eternity, Salome, Phffft, It Should Happen to You, A Star is Born* (1954), *Picnic, Queen Bee, The Eddy Duchin Story, The Solid Gold Cadillac* (for which he won an Academy Award), *Pal Joey, Bell Book and Candle, Pillow Talk, The Last Angry Man, Suddenly Last Summer, Judgment at Nuremberg, Send Me No Flowers, Ship of Fools, Guess Who's Coming to Dinner, Thoroughly Modern Millie,* and *Waterloo.* Survived by his wife, actress Loretta Young, and his brother.

Marjorie Reynolds   Alexander Salkind

CATHERINE McLEOD, 75, screen and television actress died of pneumonia on May 11, 1997 in Encino, CA. Her film credits include *I've Always Loved You, Courage of Lassie, That's My Man, The Fabulous Texan, So Young So Bad, My Wife's Best Friend,* and *Ride the Wild Surf.* She is survived by her husband, actor Don Keefer, three sons, and a sister.

Robert Mitchum

James Stewart

BURGESS MEREDITH (Oliver Burgess Meredith), 89, versatile Ohio-born screen, stage and television actor whose notable roles included playing George in the 1939 version of *Of Mice and Men* and the fight trainer Mickey in *Rocky* (for which he received an Oscar nomination), died on Sept. 9, 1997 at his home in Malibu, CA. He made his Hollywood debut in 1936 repeating his Broadway role in *Winterset*, and then went on to appear in such films as *Spring Madness, Idiot's Delight, Castle on the Hudson, Second Chorus* (opposite Paulette Goddard who became his third wife), *That Uncertain Feeling, Tom Dick and Harry, The Story of G.I. Joe, Diary of a Chambermaid, Magnificent Doll, On Our Merry Way, Mine Own Executioner, The Man on the Eiffel Tower* (which he also directed), *Joe Butterfly, Advise and Consent, The Cardinal, A Big Hand for the Little Lady, Batman* (as the Penguin, a role he played on the tv series), *Hurry Sundown, Stay Away Joe, Skidoo, There Was a Crooked Man, Such Good Friends, The Day of the Locust* (Oscar nomination), *The Hindenburg, Burnt Offerings, The Sentinel, Magic, Foul Play, The Great Bank Hoax, When Time Ran Out..., True Confessions, Clash of the Titans, Santa Claus, Full Moon in Blue Water, State of Grace, Grumpy Old Men,* and *Grumpier Old Men.* He is survived by his fourth wife, a son, a daughter, and a granddaughter.

TOSHIRO MIFUNE, 77, Japan's leading motion picture actor who became an international star via his work with director Akira Kurosawa in *Rashomon, Yojimbo,* and *Seven Samurai,* among others, died of organ failure on Dec. 24, 1997 at his home in Tokyo. Among his many other films are *Drunken Angel, The Silent Duel, The Lower Depths, Throne of Blood, The Hidden Fortress, Sanjuro, The Legacy of the Five Hundred Thousand* (which he also directed), *Red Beard, Grand Prix, Hell in the Pacific, Red Sun, Paper Tiger, Midway, The Bushido Blade, 1941, Winter Kils, Inchon,* and *The Challenge.*

ROBERT MITCHUM, 79, Connecticut-born screen and television actor, a major star for more than fifty years via his work in such movies as *The Story of G.I. Joe* (for which he earned an Oscar nomination), *Out of the Past, The Night of the Hunter, Heaven Knows Mr. Allison, The Sundowners, Cape Fear* (1962), and *Ryan's Daughter,* died at his home in Santa Barbara, CA, on July 1, 1997. Earlier in the year he had been diagnosed with lung cancer. Among his many other motion pictures are *Border Patrol, The Human Comedy, Bar 20, Thirty Seconds Over Tokyo, Till the End of Time, Undercurrent, Pursued, Crossfire, Rachel and the Stranger, Blood on the Moon, The Red Pony, The Big Steal, Holiday Affair, His Kind of Woman, Macao, The Lusty Men, Second Chance, River of No Return, Track of the Cat, Not as a Stranger, Bandido, Fire Down Below, The Enemy Below, Thunder Road, The Wonderful Country, Home from the Hill, The Grass is Greener, The Last Time I Saw Archie, The Longest Day, Two for the Seesaw, Rampage, What a Way to Go!, Mister Moses, The Way West, El Dorado, Villa Rides!, Five Card Stud, The Wrath of God, The Friends of Eddie Coyle, Farewell My Lovely, Midway, The Last Tycoon, The Big Sleep* (1978), *That Championship Season, Maria's Lovers, Mr. North, Scrooged, Cape Fear* (1991), and *Dead Man.* Survived by his wife of 57 years, two sons, actors James and Christopher Mitchum, a daughter, a brother, and two sisters.

ALVY MOORE, 75, screen and television character actor, perhaps best known for playing Mr. Kimball on the sitcom "Green Acres," died on May 4, 1997 in Palm Desert, CA. His movies include *Susan Slept Here, Five Against the House, Screaming Eagles, The Wackiest Ship in the Army, The Brotherhood of Satan* (which he also produced), *The Witchmaker, Herbie Rides Again,* and *A Boy and His Dog* (also producer). No reported survivors.

EDWARD MULHARE, 74, Irish screen, stage and tv actor, best known in America for following Rex Harrison in the role of Henry Higgins in the Broadway musical *My Fair Lady* and in the television adaptation of *The Ghost and Mrs. Muir,* died of lung cancer on May 24, 1997 at his home in Van Nuys, CA. His movies include *Signpost to Murder, Von Ryan's Express, Our Man Flint, Eye of the Devil, Caprice, Megaforce,* and *Out to Sea.* Survived by two brothers.

DON PORTER, 84, Oklahoma-born character actor, best known for his roles on the tv series "Private Secretary" and "Gidget," died at his home in Beverly Hills on Feb. 11, 1997. He was seen in such films as *Top Sergeant, 711 Ocean Drive, Because You're Mine, The Racket, Our Miss Brooks, Bachelor in Paradise, Gidget Goes to Rome, Youngblood Hawke, The Candidate, Forty Carats,* and *White Line Fever.* Survived by his wife, actress Peggy Converse, a daughter, and a son.

Red Skelton

DENVER PYLE, 77, Colorado-born screen and television actor, who played the sheriff who ambushed *Bonnie and Clyde* in the 1967 film classic, died on Dec. 25, 1997 in Burbank, CA. He had been suffering from lung cancer. Among his other movies are *The Guilt of Janet Ames, The Man from Colorado, Flame of Youth, Rough Riders of Durango, Oklahoma Annie, The Lusty Men, Texas Bad Man, Canyon Ambush, The Boy from Oklahoma, To Hell and Back, Run for Cover, Please Murder Me, I Killed Wild Bill Hickok, The Lonely Man, The Left-Handed Gun, Fort Massacre, The Party Crashers, The Horse Soldiers, The Alamo, Home from the Hill, The Man Who Shot Liberty Valance, Cheyenne Autumn, Shenandoah, Bandolero!, Cahill U.S. Marshal,* and *Escape to Witch Mountain.* On television he became well known for his role on the series "The Dukes of Hazzard." He survived by his wife and two sons.

Jesse White   Fred Zinnemann

MARJORIE REYNOLDS (Marjorie Goodspeed), 79, Idaho-born screen and television actress, best remembered for starring opposite Bing Crosby and Fred Astaire in the classic musical *Holiday Inn* died at her home in Manhattan Beach, CA, on Feb. 1, 1997. Among her other films are *College Humor* (billed as Marjorie Moore), *Overland Express, Streets of New York, Mr. Wong in Chinatown, Robin Hood of the Pecos, Cyclone on Horseback, Dixie, Ministry of Fear, Up in Mabel's Room, Bring on the Girls, Duffy's Tavern, Monsieur Beaucaire, The Time of Their Lives, Bad Men of Tombstone, That Midnight Kiss, The Great Jewel Robbery, His Kind of Woman,* and *Juke Box Rhythm.* On television she starred opposite William Bendix on "The Life of Riley." She is survived by her daughter.

WILLIAM REYNOLDS, 87, film editor who won Academy Awards for his work on *The Sound of Music* and *The Sting,* died of cancer on July 16, 1997 in South Pasadena, CA. He received additional nominations for *Fanny, The Sand Pebbles, Hello Dolly!, The Godfather,* and *The Turning Point.* He also co-produced the 1957 film *Time Limit.* No reported survivors.

ROBERT RIDGELY, 65, New Jersey-born screen and stage character actor died of cancer on Feb. 8, 1997 at his home in Toluca Lake, CA. His movies include *Blazing Saddles, Melvin and Howard, Beverly Hills Cop II, Robin Hood: Men in Tights, The Ref,* and *Boogie Nights.* Survived by his wife and a brother.

ALEXANDER SALKIND, 75, European producer, best known for the 1978 production of *Superman,* died on March 8, 1997 in Neuilly outside of Paris of unspecified causes. His other films include *The Three Musketeers* (1974), *The Four Musketeers* (1975), *Superman II, Superman III, Santa Claus,* and *Christopher Columbus: The Discovery.* He is survived by his son and co-producer Ilya Salkind, his wife and five grandchildren.

RED SKELTON (Richard Skelton), 84, Indiana-born screen and television comedian known for his mix or slapstick and pantomime, died on Sept . 17, 1997 in Rancho Mirage, CA. Following his 1938 debut in *Having Wonderful Time* he was seen in such motion pictures as *The People vs. Dr. Kildare, Lady Be Good, Whistling in the Dark, Panama Hattie, Ship Ahoy, DuBarry Was a Lady, I Dood It, Thousands Cheer, Bathing Beauty, Ziegfeld Follies, The Show-Off, Merton of the Movies, A Southern Yankee, The Fuller Brush Man, Neptune's Daughter, The Yellow Cab Man, Three Little Words, Duchess of Idaho, Watch the Birdie, Excuse My Dust, Lovely to Look At, The Clown, Half a Hero, Around the World in 80 Days,* and *Those Magnificent Men in Their Flying Machines.* His variety series "The Red Skelton Show" ran on CBS for nineteen seasons. Survived by his wife, his daughter, and a grandddaughter.

DAWN STEEL, 51, Hollywood producer and the first woman to head a major movie studio, died on Dec. 20, 1997 in Los Angeles, after suffering from a brain tumor. From 1987 to 1991 she headed Columbia Pictures. Afterwards she served as producer on *Honey I Blew Up the Kid, Cool Runnings, Sister Act 2: Back in the Habit, Fallen,* and *City of Angels.* Survived by her husband, daughter, and brother.

DON STEELE, 61, radio disk jockey , died of lung cancer on Aug. 5, 1997 at his home in Los Angeles. He appeared in such movies as *Rock'n' Roll High School, Death Race 2000, Gremlins, Eating Raoul,* and *Bordello of Blood.* Survived by his wife.

JAMES STEWART, 89, Pennsylvania-born screen, stage and television actor, one of the most popular and beloved of all Hollywood performers, who won the 1940 Academy Award for *The Philadelphia Story* and earned addtional nominations for *Mr. Smith Goes to Washington, It's a Wonderful Life, Harvey,* and *Anatomy of a Murder,* died at his home in Beverly Hills, CA, on July 2, 1997 from a blood clot in his lung. His other movies are *Murder Man* (1935 debut), *Rose Marie* (1936), *Next Time We Love, Wife vs. Secretary, Small Town Girl* (1936), *Speed, The Gorgeous Hussy, Born to Dance, After the Thin Man, Seventh Heaven* (1937), *The Last Gangster, Navy Blue and Gold, Of Human Hearts, Vivacious Lady, The Shopworn Angel* (1938), *You Can't Take It With You, Made for Each Other* (1933), *Ice Follies of 1939, It's a Wonderful World, Destry Rides Again, The Shop Around the Corner, The Mortal Storm, No Time for Comedy, Come Live With Me, Pot o' Gold, Ziegfeld Girl, Magic Town, Call Northside 777, On Our Merry Way, Rope, You Gotta Stay Happy, The Stratton Story, Malaya, Winchester 73, Broken Arrow* (1950), *The Jackpot, No Highway in the Sky, The Greatest Show on Earth, Bend of the River, Carbine Williams, The Naked Spur, Thunder Bay, The Glenn Miller Story, Rear Window, The Far Country, Strategic Air Command, The Man from Laramie, The Man Who Knew Too Much* (1956), *The Spirit of St. Louis, Night Passage, Vertigo, Bell Book and Candle, The FBI Story, The Mountain Road, Two Rode Together, The Man Who Shot Liberty Valance, Mr. Hobbs Takes a Vacation, How the West Was Won, Take Her She's Mine, Cheyenne Autumn, Dear Brigitte, Shenandoah, The Flight of the Phoenix, The Rare Breed, Firecreek, Bandolero!, The Cheynne Social Club, Fools' Parade, The Shootist, The Big Sleep* (1978), *The Magic of Lassie, The Green Horizon/Afurika Monogatari,* and *An American Tail: Fievel Goes West* (voice). His many honors include the Kennedy Center Honors, the American Film Institute Life Achievement Award, the Presidential Medal of Freedom, and a special Academy Award in 1984. He is survived by his stepson and two daughters.

TOMOYUKI TANAKA, 86, Japanese film producer best known for the series of "Godzilla" films starting with *Godzilla King of the Monsters* in 1954 (1956 in America), died in Tokyo on Apr. 2, 1998. Survived by his wife and three sons.

JESSE WHITE, 79, Buffalo-born screen, stage and tv character actor who first came to prominence playing gruff orderly Wilson in the Broadway and film versions of *Harvey,* died on Jan. 9, 1997 in Los Angeles following complications of surgery. Among his other movies are *Death of a Salesman, Bedtime for Bonzo, Francis Goes to the Races, Million Dollar Mermaid, Forever Female, Hell's Half Acre, The Girl Rush, Designing Woman, Country Music Holiday, Marjorie Morningstar, The Rise and Fall of Legs Diamond, On the Double, Sail a Crooked Ship, It's Only Money, It's a Mad Mad Mad Mad World, Pajama Party, A House is Not a Home, Dear Brigitte, The Spirit is Willing, The Ghost in the Invisible Bikini, The Reluctant Astronaut, Bless the Beasts and Children, The Cat from Outer Space,* and *Matinee.* Television viewers knew him best as the Maytag repair from a series of commercials that ran for over twenty years. Survived by his wife, two daughters, a son, five sisters, two brothers, and three grandchildren.

BO WIDERBERG, 66, Swedish director, best known for the 1967 film *Elvira Madigan,* died of an unspecified illness on May 1, 1997 in Angelholm, Sweden. His other credits include *All Things Fair* (which was nominated for an Oscar for foreign-language film), *Adalen '31, Raven's End,* and *Joe Hill.* No reported survivors.

MAX YOUNGSTEIN, 84, Hollywood executive and producer, died at his Los Angeles home on July 8, 1997. He was head of production at United Artists from 1951 to 1962. Later he served as producer on such movies as *Fail Safe, The Money Trap,* and *Welcome to Hard Times.* Survivors include his wife, four daughters, and a son.

FRED ZINNEMANN, 89, Austria-born Hollywood director who won Academy Awards for his work on *From Here to Eternity* and *A Man for All Seasons* (also winning a second Oscar for producing) died on Mar. 14, 1997 at his home in London. He received additional nominations for *The Search, High Noon, The Nun's Story, The Sundowners,* and *Julia.* His other credits include *Kid Glove Killer* (his debut in 1942), *Eyes in the Night, The Seventh Cross, My Brother Talks to Horses, The Men, Teresa, The Member of the Wedding, Oklahoma!, A Hatful of Rain, Behold a Pale Horse, The Day of the Jackal,* and *Five Days One Summer.* Survived by his wife, a son, and four grandchildren.

INDEX

A.D. Vision, 261
Aalam, Schahla, 260
Aaron's Magic Village, 263
Aaron, Caroline, 142, 267
AB Svensk Filmindustri, 262
Abbott, Mark, 175
Abbott, Steve, 12, 219
Abela, Pierre, 259
Abercrombie, Ian, 61, 146
Abernathy, Lewis, 186
Abernathy, Louisa, 78
Abou-Ganim, Tony, 168
Abraham, F. Murray, 99, 214, 267
Abraham, Marc, 84, 106, 122
Abraham, Nancy, 161
Abrahams, Jon, 169
Abrahamson, Peter, 163
Abramowitz, Richard, 161
Abrams, Jeffrey, 63
Abrams, Peter, 164
Abramson, Neil, 160
Abrell, Brad, 77
Abrell, Jorge Luis, 20
Absolo, Roland, 69
Absolute Power, 22,
Ace, Martin, 261
Achilles, Damien, 166
Acimovic, Dejan, 112
Ackerman, Tom, 81
Acosta, David, 132
Acovone, Jay, 112
Adair, Catherine, 119, 184
Adair, Sandra, 19
Adair, Sean, 156
Adair-Rios, Mark, 68
Adam, Ken, 102
Adams, Daniel, 176
Adams, J. Todd, 163
Adams, Joey Lauren, 41, 197
Adams, Joshua G., 184
Adams, Kim, 97
Adams, Mason, 24, 267
Adams, Max D., 98
Adams, Rebecca Rae, 176
Adams, Wendy, 176
Adamson, Barry, 21
Adamstein, Dana, 63
Adcock, Steve, 33
Addicted To Love, 181,
Addy, Mark, 232-233
Adelman, Jason, 33
Ader-Brown, Jamie, 161
Adi, Alexandra, 93
Adkins, Seth, 186
Adkisson, Jim, 166
Adler, Laura, 184
Adler, Matt, 11
Adler, Michael, 37
Adoti, Razaaq, 141
Adrian, Walter, 128
Aesha, 50
Affleck, Ben, 40-41, 104, 138-139, 197, 267
Affleck, Casey, 41, 138-139
Affrime, Mindy, 38
Afrakhan, Behrooz, 181
Afshangol, Arlene, 151
Afterglow, 153
Afterman, Peter, 30
Agee, Tawatha, 71
Agostino, Salvatore, 153
Agredo, Robert, 69
Agromonte, Adrian, 178
Aguilar, Anthony, 184
Aguilar, G.A., 181
Ahern II, Lloyd, 8
Ahern, Liam, 158
Ahern, Tim, 114
Ahlberg, Mac, 83
Ahlf, Al, 122
Ahrens, Lynn, 130
Aibel, Douglas, 105
Aiello, Danny, 29, 156, 267
Aihara, Hiromi, 261
Aikens, David, 104
Aim, Pierre, 259
Air Bud, 87
Air Force Crew, 157
Air Force One, 84
Aitken, Maria, 12, 210
Akerman, Chantal, 265
Akhurst, Lucy, 42
Aki, 179

Akiko, 42
Ako, Yuda, 158
Akrawi, Mike, 90
Akrawi, Romeo, 90
Akwiri, Noella, 167
Alacchi, Marianna, 79
Alaouie, Afifi, 56
Albala, Michael, 181
Albarez, Angela, 49
Alberico, Danette, 131
Albert, Arthur, 11
Albert, Ross, 20
Alberti, Maryse, 241, 264
Albino Aligator, 9
Albinus, Jens, 260
Albright, Dan, 119
Alby, Claire, 262
Alcalá, Felix Enriquez, 182
Alcott, Todd, 169
Alda, Alan, 180, 183, 267
Alda, Rutanya, 184
Aldenhoven, Lisa, 262
Alderman, Jane, 34
Alderton, Kate, 12
Aldredge, Tom, 52
Aldridge, Eddie, 183
Alejan, Sam, 49
Aleksander, Stefan, 137
Alert, Red, 157
Alessandro, Anthony, 53
Alexander, David, 177
Alexander, Elle, 27
Alexander, Jason, 58-59, 267
Alexander, John, 12, 77, 247
Alexander, M.T., 109
Alexander, Matt, 62
Alexander, Newell, 182
Alexander, S.M., 23
Alexander, Sharon L., 148
Alexander, Steve, 167
Alexander, Terry, 181
Alexandra, Danielle, 94
Alexopoulos, Heléne, 157
Alford, Vicky, 160
Alfredson, Hans, 259
Algarin, Miguel, 166
Ali, Kenshaka, 100
Ali, Tatyana M., 114
Alien Resurrection, 133
Alive and Kicking, 125
Alkali, Iowa, 33
Alkoholiks, The 156
All About Eve, 187
All Over Me, 52
Alla, 261
Allain, Stephanie, 66
Allan, Mark, 184
Allan-Headley, Hamish, 163
Allard, Dennis, 260
Allaux, Bérangère, 262
Allbright, Landry, 65
Allegro Films, 167
Allen, Alise, 167
Allen, Debbie, 141, 267
Allen, Georgia, 183
Allen, Hope, 37
Allen, Joan, 74-75, 110-111, 267
Allen, Karen, 62, 163, 267
Allen, Keith, 261
Allen, Kevin, 237, 261
Allen, Krista, 37
Allen, Mary, 261
Allen, Natalie, 181
Allen, Patti, 61
Allen, Randee, 105
Allen, Sage, 182, 184
Allen, Scott, 159
Allen, Tim, 6, 15, 29, 137, 267
Allen, Todd, 145, 184
Alley, Kirstie, 137, 142-143, 267
Allison, Cynthia, 11
Allison, Don, 39, 165
Allman, Sheldon, 81
Allodi, James, 138
Allouache, Merzak, 259
Allred, Mike, 41
Allyson, Dana, 68
Almebäck, Lasse, 259
Alonso, Jain V., 175
Alonso, Tite Curet, 264
Alpert, Jed, 96
Alpert, Richard, 164

Alphasa, Joe, 127
Alphaville, 131
Alsobrook, Allen, 63
Alston, Brian, 181
Alston, Macky, 170
Alt, Carol, 30, 267
Altar Rocks Films Inc., 171
Altay, Derin, 173
Alterian Studios, 163
Alterio, Hector, 259
Altman, Bruce, 93
Altman, Robert, 153
Altman, Stephen, 45
Altro, Melissa, 262
Alumkal, Neil William, 176
Alvarez, Adalberto, 264
Alves, Joe, 154, 182
Amadeus, Adrian, 13
Amalbert, Juan, 100
Amalgamated Dynamics Inc., 128
Amalric, Mathieu, 215, 263
Amatullo, Marianna, 168
Amatullo, Nicolas, 168
Amatullo, Tony, 168
Amber Images, 155
Ambriz, Domingo, 178
Ambrose, Lauren, 102
Ambrose, Tangie, 147
Ambuehl, Cindy, 15
Amend, Kate, 104
Amendolia, Don, 121
American Hero, 151
American History Project, 171
American Playhouse, 116
*American Werewolf in Paris,*An, 254
American Zoetrope, 66, 135
Amiel, Jon, 183
Amin, Mark, 60, 162
Amis, Suzy, 159, 186, 267
Amistad, 141
Amodeo, Luigi, 158
Amorós, Juan, 263
Amos, David, 155
Amstutz, Roland, 263
Amuwa, Edward, 37
Anaconda, 46
Ananthakrishnan, Vyas, 152
Anastasia, 130
Ancona, Amy B., 164
Ancona, Amy, 50
Andabo, Yoruba, 264
Anderson, Azikiwee, 181
Anderson, Carol, 180
Anderson, Cherine, 264
Anderson, Darius, 184
Anderson, Ernie, 28
Anderson, Euva, 260
Anderson, Gillian, 163
Anderson, Jamie, 45
Anderson, Kevin, 106, 122, 267
Anderson, Kort, 132
Anderson, Mark Edward, 161
Anderson, Michael John, 163
Anderson, Nathan, 95
Anderson, Paul Thomas, 28, 121
Anderson, Paul, 91
Anderson, Robin, 258
Anderson, Scott E., 128
Anderson, Scott G., 186
Anderson, Sherry, 169
Anderson, Stanley, 154
Anderson, Stephen M., 161
Anderson, Taylor, 161
Andersson, Jon Kriestien, 144
Andorai, Peter, 266
Andre, Charles, 157, 169
Andreacchio, Mario, 265
Andres, Brandi, 114
Andrews, Jason, 50, 121, 159
Androsky, Carol, 17
Andrus, Mark, 148
Andujar, Elena Camunez, 183
Anezin, Danielle, 262
Angarano, Michael, 137
Angel Baby, 204
Angel Dust, 258
Angel, Jack, 71
Angelica, George, 27
Aniston, Jennifer, 62, 88, 267
Anka, Amanda, 21
Annaud, Jean-Jacques, 117

Annen, Paule, 263
Annenberg, Eve, 177
Anthem, 166
Anthony, Christine, 162
Anthony, David, 260
Anthony, Fran, 53
Anthony, Gerald, 264
Anthony, Marc, 264
Antico, Pete, 45
Antico, Peter, 65
Antin, Steven, 62
Antuofermo, Vito, 176
Anvar, Cas, 153
Anzel, Hy, 142
Anzilotti, Perry, 172, 244
Anzur, Terry, 49, 151
Apeximova, Irina, 42
Apisa, Bob, 173
Apo-Tsang, Karma, 117
Appel, Deena, 56
Appel, Travis, 9
Appiah, Edward, 141
Applecross, 117
Applegate, Christina, 60, 267
Appleton, Tracy, 102
Apps, Greg, 262
Aprea, John, 101
April, Renée, 179
Aptekman, Igor, 29
Aquila, Deborah, 91, 114
Aquilino, Macky, 171
Aragon, Angelica, 264
Araki, Gregg, 60
Arana, Tomas, 182
Aranguiz, Manuel, 105
Aranha, Ray, 86, 142, 178
Arbit, Bernard, 178
Arbogast, Thierry, 96, 216
Archer, Mark, 89
Archibald, Craig, 166
Arenberg, Lee, 163
Arent, Eddi, 264
Argentinian, Jorge Ferrari, 259
Argue, Alan, 99
Argue, David, 204, 265
Arias, Imanol, 259
Arias, Joey, 158
Arias, Yancey, 161
Aris, Jonathan, 131
Aristotle, Augusto, 220
Arizmendi, Vareli ., 174
Arkin, Alan, 45, 124, 267
Arkin, Matthew, 37
Arkoff, Lou, 63, 81
Armas, Grace, 180
Armato, Leonard, 184
Armbruster, Andrew, 62
Armendariz, Pedro, 141
Armeno, Joe, 179
Armitage, Brent, 45
Armitage, George, 45
*Condor*****
Armour, Norman, 165
Armstrong, Alun, 42
Armstrong, Bess, 23, 268
Armstrong, Carrie, 37
Armstrong, Chris, 222
Armstrong, Don, 174
Armstrong, Gillian, 257
Armstrong, Jerome, 49
Armstrong, Su, 138
Armstrong, Valorie, 146, 181
Armstrong, Vic, 253
Armus, Sidney, 53
Arndt, Denis, 10
Arnold Kopelson Production, 180, 183
Arnold, Annette, 158
Arnold, Brian, 107
Arnold, David, 240, 253
Arnold, Madison, 27, 163
Arnold, Susan, 45
Arnold, Tom, 24, 56, 160
Aronson, Alexa, 142
Aronson, Letty, 142
Arost, Lynn, 98, 106
Arquette, Alexis, 175
Arquette, David, 14, 69, 144, 268
Arquette, Lewis, 15-16, 144
Arquette, Patricia, 21, 268

Arquette, Richard, 175
Arquette, Richmond, 13, 69
Arquette, Rosanna, 63, 208, 268
Araras, Maria Celeste, 181
Arredondo, D.K., 144
Arribas, Oscar, 250
Arrick, Larry, 172
Arrighi, Luciana, 257
Arrington, James, 166
Arrow, 155, 218
Arrowood, LeAndra, 182
Arroyave, Karina, 184
Arsovski, Petar, 248
Artenstein, Isaac, 174
Arteta, Miguel, 83
Arther, Cydney, 21
Arthur, Brett, 203
Arthur, Richard, 77
Arthurs, Douglas, 169
Artificial Eye, 231
Artiles, Alexis, 171
Artistic License, 137, 154, 171, 266
Arturo, Michael, 176
Arundel Films, 258
Arvanitis, Yorgos, 203, 245
As Good As It Gets, 148-149
Asada, Nobuo, 261
Ascher, Steven, 154
Ash, 176
Ash, Albert, 125
Ash, Margaret, 43
Ashby, Linden, 159
Ashforth, Justin, 135
Ashong, Derrick N., 141
Ashton, David, 225, 253
Ashton, Joseph, 179
Ashton, Richard, 186, 216
Ashton-Griffiths, Roger, 242
Askew, Ingrid, 69
Askew, Luke, 47
Askin, Peter, 31
Aslan Pictures, 156
Asner, Edward, 104, 268
Asner, Kate, 68
Asp, Anna, 206, 259
Asphalt Films, 167
Assad, Richard, 172
Assas, Madeleine, 262
Assayas, Olivier, 213
Assefi, Christo, 172
Assignment, The 105
Assogba, Luc, 141
Assouline, P., 262
Astin, Sean, 104, 268
Aston, Susan, 94
Astrakhan, Yoram, 173
Astrudillo, Peter, 180
Asymmetrical production, 21
Atara Releasing, 264
Atherton, Claire, 265
Atherton, Sonia, 265
Atherton, William, 97, 183, 268
Atkin, Harvey, 126
Atkins, Peter, 172
Atkinson, Holly, 137
Atkinson, Linda, 183
Atkinson, Rowan, 244, 268
Atlantis Entertainment, 89
Atlas, Natacha, 261
Atlas, William, 145
Attal, Yves, 260
Attanasio, Paul, 27
Attieh, Fida, 24
Atwood, Colleen, 66, 124, 164, 210
Atwood, Dana, 114
Auberjonois, Rene, 180, 268
Aubrey, Juliet, 248
Audiard, Jacques, 236
Audsley, Mick, 220
Auerbach, Esther, 174
Aufray, Frederic, 221
August, Bille, 206, 259
August, Lance, 82
August, Pernilla, 259
Augustine, John, 169
Aukema, Dewald, 32
Aulisi, Joseph G., 30, 53
Aulisio, Curnal, 128
Aumont, Michel, 263, 265
Aumuller, Alycia, 19
Austell, Jan, 21
Austin, Ivy, 263
Austin, Jeff, 182

Austin, Shay, 68
Austin Powers: International Man of Mystery, 56-57
Australian Broadcasting Corporation, 258
Australian Film Finance Corporation, 204, 214, 230, 235, 243, 257
Auteuil, Daniel, 207
Auty, Chris, 25, 208
Avalanche, 173, 176, 241
Avalos, Luis, 29
Avant, Nicole, 151
Avellone, Gregory, 184, 260
Avent, Jon, 126
Aventura Films, 262
Avery, Teodross, 34
Avery, Val, 27
Avila, Christine, 37
Avildsen, Jonathan, 63
Avital, Mili, 100
Aviv, Oren, 174
Aviva, Rachel, 178
Avnet, Jon, 81, 126
Aybar, Andrew, 83
Ayer, Debbon, 35, 181
Ayers, Stephen Michael, 23
Ayers, Tom, 160
Aykroyd, Dan, 45, 267-268
Ayler, Ethel, 129
Aylesworth, Reiko, 159
Aylward, John, 66
Ayres, Mark, 222
Ayres, Rosalind, 186-187
Ayusheyev, Dashinima D., 265
Azadani, Rasoul, 71
Azar, Azita, 172
Azaria, Hank, 45, 130
Azéma, Sabine, 231
Azizi, Anthony, 137, 160
Azmi, Shabana, 235
Azrie, Abed, 261
Azulay, Jom Tob, 258
Azuma, Ryuko, 220
B, Anthony, 264
B, Beth, 154
B*A*P*S, 158
Ba, Inday, 183
Babelsberg Film Produktion, 265
Baca, Jimmy Santiago, 166
Baca, Marika, 180
Baca, Rupert, 21
Baca-Asay, Joaquin, 171
Bacarella, Mike, 8, 72, 109
Bachar, Carmit, 83
Bachar, Ronny, 258
Bacharach, Burt, 56
Bacik, Boris, 169
Bacon, Kevin, 88, 123, 267-268
Badalamenti, Angelo, 21
Badalato, Bill, 133
Badalucco, Michael, 52, 175
Baden, Vanessa, 179
Badger, Jennifer S., 68
Badland, Annette, 210
Baehr, Caroline, 255
Baer, Willi, 153
Bafaloukos, Eugenie, 45
Bafaloukos, Ted, 116
Bagby, Jason, 173
Baggett, Paul, 145
Baggish, Joy, 49
Bähler, Tom, 151
Baifang, Liu, 126
Baigelman, Gayle Fraser, 137
Bailey, Ewan, 131
Bailey, John, 148
Bailey, Scott, 178
Bailey, Tom, 11
Bailey-Gates, Charles, 176
Bailly, Jean-Pierre, 262
Baily, Kirk, 38
Bair, Dina, 8
Bairstow, Scott, 181, 184
Bait and Switch, Inc., 157
Baka, Joe, 123
Baker, Becky Ann, 77, 102
Baker, Bryan, 230
Baker, Carroll, 101, 268
Baker, Danielle, 158
Baker, Diane, 180, 268
Baker, Edwin, 172
Baker, Ian, 12
Baker, Joe Don, 253, 268
Baker, Kathy, 43, 268
Baker, Ray, 106
Baker, Richard, 29, 137
Baker, Rick, 29, 77, 137, 182

Baker, Robert S., 42
Baker, Sharlene, 174
Baker, Simon, 118, 182, 249
Baker, Tab, 97
Baker, Todd, 168
Bakija, Bianca, 170
Bakke, Brenda, 182
Bakula, Scott, 180, 268
Bakunas, Steve, 155
Balaban, Bob, 16, 142, 268
Balagtas, Bernadette, 148
Balahoutis, Alexandra, 65
Balan, Ovidiu, 260
Baldacci, David, 22
Baldini Pictures, 52
Baldwin, Alec, 107, 268
Baldwin, Declan, 260
Baldwin, Doug, 156
Baldwin, Peter, 15
Balgobin, Jennifer, 181
Balibar, Jeanne, 263
Ball, Angeline, 218, 231
Ball, Seamus, 212
Ball, Tulsy, 9
Ball, Vincent, 211
Ballard, J.G., 208
Ballard, Laurence, 13
Ballard, Mai, 168
Ballard, Maurice, 50
Ballerini, Edoardo, 20
Ballhaus, Michael, 84
Ballot, Steve, 30
Ballou, Mark, 102
Balmer, Jean-François, 265
Balsan, Humbert, 250
Baltimore Pictures, 27, 151
Baltz, Kirk, 75, 175
Baluev, Alexander, 112
Ban, Prosperous, 155
Bancroft, Anne, 94, 126, 268
Band Apart, 4
Bandeira Entertainment, 14, 118
Bandis, Helen, 209
Bandit, Alan, 175
Bandwagon, 169
Bang, 176
Bang, Glen, 99
Bangalie, Charlean Isata, 141
Banister, Reggie, 172
Bank, Frank, 98
Banks, Boyd, 208
Banks, Caerthan, 249
Banks, Ernie Lee, 118
Banks, Lenore, 145
Banks, Russell, 249
Banks, Tommy, 155
Banner Entertainment, 47, 123
Baptiste, Nicole, 170
Bara, Carisa, 174
Barak, Ari, 172
Barbachano, Paolo, 265
Barbeau, Francois, 153
Barbee, Carol, 78
Barbella, Victor, 156
Barber, Gary, 181
Barber, Gillian, 165
Barber, Gloria, 156
Barber, Paul, 232-233
Barber, Sandy, 27
Barclay, Bill, 241
Barclay, Caroline, 101
Barclay, Jane, 166
Bardem, Javier, 263-264
Barden, Kerry, 53, 99, 138, 178
Bardon, John, 12
Bareikis, Arija, 105
Barentin, Nadia, 236
Barget, Cristina, 255
Bari, Jenna, 63
Bariha-Simsolo, Khadicha, 239
Baril, Alan, 202
Barker, Adam, 253
Barker, Phillip, 249
Barker, Rick, 11
Barker, Simon, 162
Barkham, David, 154
Barkhordarian, Samson, 121
Barkley, 260
Barkoff, Victoria, 179
Barkus, Arnold, 96
Barlow, John Perry, 166
Barlow, Tom, 136
Barmonde, Peter, 102
Barnaba, Joe, 37
Barndt, Perry, 162
Barnes, Avis-Marie, 172
Barnes, Chris, 210
Barnes, Randee, 65

Barnes, Susan, 43, 68, 82, 132
Barnett, Shawn, 171
Barnett, Craig, 37
Barnett, Ronnie, 180
Barnier, Luc, 213
Barnwell, Javon, 99
Baró, Amparo, 263
Baron, Caroline, 181, 207
Barone, Anita, 69, 178
Barone, Tracy, 179
Barranco, María, 263
Barrass, David, 216
Barret, Alison, 260
Barrett, Alison, 204, 235, 257
Barrett, David, 45
Barrett, Josh, 170
Barrett, Ray, 259, 262
Barrett, Shirley, 235
Barrett, Venetia, 183
Barrie, Barbara, 71, 268
Barrile, Anthony, 166
Barringer, Dan, 84
Barrington, Marcus, 179
Barris, Chuck, 178
Barron, Chris, 30
Barron, Dana, 32
Barron, Doug, 178
Barrow, Johnny, 177
Barrow, Michael, 82, 96
Barry, Bernie, 176
Barry, Georganna, 49
Barry, Jason, 186
Barry, Matt, 65
Barry, Matthew, 96
Barry, Neill, 96, 268
Barry, Nina, 96
Barry, Raymond J., 163, 183
Barry, Raymond, 136
Barry, Simon, 39
Barry, Thom, 84, 184
Barry, Tracey, 31
Barsky, Brett, 33
Bart the Bear, 107
Bart, Roger, 71
Bartek, Steve, 51
Bartels, Lisa, 89
Bartkowiak, Andrzej, 17, 182
Bartle, James, 266
Bartlett, Bonnie, 50
Bartlett, Kevin, 127
Bartlett, Nick, 12
Bartok, Jayce, 19
Bartoli, Adolfo, 162
Barton, Roger, 23
Barton, Shawn, 34
Barton, Suzy, 125
Barton, Will, 257
Barudin, Amanda, 142
Basham, Jerry A., 156
Bashore, Juliet, 177
Basic, Senad, 248
Basil, Harry, 15
Basil, Laura, 15
Basile, Joe, 44, 182
Basinger, Kim, 182, 191, 269
Baskerville, Derek J., 169
Baskin, Elaya, 84-85
Baskin, Elya, 56
Baskins-Leva, Lulu, 173
Basler, Antonie, 213
Bass, Bobby, 45
Beebe, Steve, 126
Bass Jr., Eugene, 61
Bass, Greg, 161
Bass, Nicole, 30
Bass, Seth, 173
Bassett, Angela, 181, 269
Bassett, Linda, 225, 257
Bassett, Richard, 172
Bassett, Steve, 131
Basso, Serge, 254
Bastens, Robert, 133
Bastian, Ali, 125
Basu, Debi, 207
Basulito, Armando, 160
Basulto, David, 118, 155
Bates, Alan, 210, 269
Bates, Edward, 164
Bates, Kathy, 186-187, 269
Bates, Kenny, 65
Bates, Tyler, 164
Bates-Renaud, Kirsten, 176
Bathurst, Robert, 242
Batigne, Marc Andre, 261
Batinkoff, Randall, 112, 148, 183
Batman & Robin, 181
Batson-Smith, Diane, 83
Batt, Bryan, 166

Battaglia, Eve, 176
Batten, Shawn, 171
Battista, Bobbie, 181
Battista, Franco, 105
Battista, John, 163
Bauchau, Patrick, 262, 266
Bauer, Chris, 21, 75, 105
Bauer, Christopher, 132, 182
Bauer, Hans, 46
Bauer, Kristin, 51
Bauer, Richard, 154
Bauerlein, Judy, 142, 158
Baum, Barbara, 206
Baum, Mike, 177
Baumgarten, Craig, 175
Baumgarten-Prophet Entertainment, 175
Baun, Jack, 144
Baur, Marc, 162
Baxley, Bill, 80
Baxter, John, 225
Bayley, Kate, 182
Bayonas, Katrina, 259
Bazac, Miro, 177
BBC Films, 215, 220, 229, 237
Beach, Lisa, 144
Beach, Michael, 108-109, 112
Beach, Stephen, 53
Beach, Steven, 159
Beach, Wayne, 180
Beacham, Stephanie, 68, 269
Beacon Pictures, 84, 106, 122, 220
Beal, Geoffrey, 266
Beale, Melody, 177
Beall, Aaron, 175
Beals, Jennifer, 173, 269
Bean, 244
Bean, Henry, 265
Bean, Reathel, 86
Bean, Sean, 180, 269
Bean, Steve, 146
Bear, Bart the, 107
Beard, John, 247
Bearde, Nicholas, 168
Bearne, Chris, 220, 254
Beasley, Allyce, 69
Beasley, John, 145
Beasley, William S., 119
Beason, Eric L., 160, 175
Beaucaire, J.E., 142
Beaudoin, Sydni, 90
Beaufoy, Simon, 232
Beauman, Nicholas, 257
Beaumarchais The Scoundrel, 265
Beautician And The Beast, The, 18
Beauvois, Xavier, 218
Beck, Karin, 223
Beckel, Graham, 182
Beckendorff, Ghita, 235
Becker, Brooke, 184
Becker, Gerry, 27, 101
Becker, Heinz, 105
Becker, Josh, 178
Becker, Louis, 29, 105
Becker, Max, 183
Becker, Randy, 58-59
Beckett, Diane, 69, 175
Beckett, Ian, 216
Beckett, Lee, 69
Becton, Shelton, 71
Bedi, Bobby, 235
Beebe, Steve, 126
Beecroft, Jeffrey, 101, 164
Beene, Dan, 182
Bega, Leslie, 21
Beghe, Jason, 94
Begine, Ed, 176
Begley Jr., Ed 172, 269
Beijing Youth Film Studio, 260
Beinhart, Larry, 151
Beinö, André, 259
Beiser, Brendan, 98
Beita, Amanda, 250
Beitel, Teri, 104
Beitler, Maureen, 29
Béjart, Maurice, 157
Belanogov, Valentin, 258
Belfrage, Crispian, 245
Bell, Barry, 79
Bell, Dan, 65
Bell, E.E., 84, 175
Bell, Elisa, 179
Bell, Kevin, 34
Bell, Marshall, 100, 128, 162
Bell, Nicholas, 230
Bellamy, Bill, 34, 168
Bellamy, Diana, 84
Bellamy, Ned, 23, 65

Bellando, Tara, 170
Belle, Anne, 157
Belle, Camilla, 61
Bello, Gregg, 94
Bellville, Hercules, 25
Below the Belt, 173
Belshaw, George, 171
Belson, Michael, 151
Belt, Stephanie, 144
Beltrami, Marco, 99, 144
Beltzman, Mark, 68, 83
Belushi, James, 172, 269
Belushi, Jim, 151
Ben-Victor, Paul, 10, 38
Benabiles, M., 44
Benaiche, Wilfred, 236
Benavides, Lisa, 122
Benayoun, George, 260
Benayoun, Georges, 213, 239
Benazzo, Maurizio, 181
Benbry, Carlton, 124
Bender, Lawrence, 138, 147
Bendewald, Andrea, 88
Bendocchi-Alves, André, 264
Benedek, Tom, 11
Benedetti, Caprice, 183
Benedict, Jay, 44
Benedict, Shelly, 144
Benedict, Tannis, 8, 163
Benesh, Mark, 260
Benevides, Rob, 178
Benguigui, Jean, 259, 263
Benítez, César, 263
Benjamin, Paul, 97, 179
Benjamin, Richard, 142, 269
Benjamin, Shant, 155
Bennes, John, 47, 119
Bennet, Douglas, 172
Bennett, Beresford, 69
Bennett, Bill, 243
Bennett, Charles, 97
Bennett, Elise, 163
Bennett, Fran, 98
Bennett, Jennifer, 243
Bennett, John, 21, 81, 216
Bennett, Joseph, 91
Bennett, Kathy D., 160
Bennett, Michael, 13, 129
Bennett, Nigel, 180
Bennett-Jones, Peter, 244
Bennetts, Bruce, 102
Benninghofen, Mark, 95
Benoit, Jean-Louis, 265
Benousilio, Dora, 263
Benousilio, Jacqueline Galia, 263
Benrubi, Abraham, 81, 113
Bens, Paul G., 155
Bensen, Jackie, 180
Benson, Bruce, 182
Benson, Jodi, 136
Benson, Ray, 159
Benson, Wendy, 172
Bent, 245
Bentham, Richard C., 130
Bentley-Griffin, Shay, 179
Benton, Kevin, 38
Benton, Mark, 234
Benton, Nina M., 52
Benullo, David, 157
Benyaer, Michael, 162, 169
Benz, Julie, 43, 148
Benzakein, Simona, 250
Benzali, Daniel, 100, 180
Benzinger, Suzy, 142
Beraldo, Elisabetta, 179
Berberian, Vahe, 95
Berckmans, Nicole D.V., 260
Berdan, Brian, 45, 260
Berdy, Magaly, 259
Berenbaum, Michael, 170
Berendt, John, 183
Beresford, Bruce, 211
Berg, Barry, 78
Berg, Eva Jean, 115
Berg, Peter, 92-93, 269
Berganza, Teresa Jose, 236
Bergen, Bob, 71
Berger, Alan, 180
Berger, Daniel M., 176
Berger, Daniel, 176
Berger, Howard, 90, 172
Berger, Peter E., 10, 126
Berger, Robert, 118, 172
Bergeron, Phillip, 181
Bergin, Joan, 251, 256
Bergman, Anthony, 105
Bergman, Mary Kay, 71
Bergman, Ram, 68

Bergman, Tal, 68
Bergman, Yael, 209
Bergmann, Alan, 8
Beridze, Guiorgui, 213
Beringer, Paul, 18
Beristain, Gabriel, 63
Berk, Ailsa, 12
Berke, Mayne, 51
Berkeley, Laura, 222
Berkeley, Pamela, 163
Berkeley, Xander, 84, 124, 132, 141
Berkey, Brian Fair, 160
Berleand, François, 236, 239
Berliner, Alain, 255
Berliner, Alain, 255
Berlinger, Cain, 175
Berman, Lucas, 181
Bermel, Pat, 264
Bermeo, Cheryl, 68
Bernard, Constance, 100
Bernard, Jason, 37
Bernard, Lionel, 100
Bernardi, Barry, 182
Bernardo, Michael, 181
Bernd Eichinger, 206
Bernheim, Shirl, 52, 157
Bernieri, Laura, 69
Berns, Judy Jean, 38
Bernstein, Armyan, 84, 106, 122
Bernstein, Elmer, 66, 97
Bernstein, Gregory, 63
Bernstein, Howard, 105
Bernstein, Marcos, 264
Bernstein, Sara, 63
Bernstein, Steven, 162, 180
Berodot, Philippe, 236
Berquist, Douglas, 178
Berry, Halle, 158, 269
Berry, Norman, 183
Berry, Tom, 105
Berry, Vincent, 55, 182
Bersaqc, Alberte, 262
Bertenshaw, Michael, 238
Berthelsen, Anders Wodskou, 260
Berthon, Henri, 218
Bertino, Tom, 136
Bertish, Suzanne, 245
Bertolli, John, 11, 44, 172
Bertram, Susan, 162
Bertuccelli, Giorgio, 174
Berube, Michelle, 147
Besio, Olga, 250
Besman, Michael, 117
Besnehard, Dominique, 265
Besse, Jacques, 262
Bessen, Steve, 124
Besset, Jean-Marc, 265
Besso, Claudia, 153
Besson, Luc, 216
Best, Cheridah, 97
Bestrop, Juel, 21
Betancourt, Anne, 21
Betancourt, Jeff, 83
Bettany, Paul, 245
Betti, Laura, 266
Betts, Donnie L., 127
Betts, Dorothy, 166
Betts, Jack, 181
Beucler, Rebecca T., 181
Beuman, Nicholas, 260
Bevan, Tim, 244
Bevans, Loren, 175
Bevel, Reverend James, 80
Beverly Hills Ninja, 11
Bexton, Nathan, 60
Bey, Abdullah, 123
Bey, Richard, 15
Beyer, Brad, 93
Beyer, Troy, 158
Beyond Barbed Wire, 167
Beyond Films, 171, 209
Beyton, Katherine Dow, 219
Bezahler, Alysse, 110
Bhagat, Sheetel, 132
Bhalla, Suresh, 235
Bhansali, Surabhi, 207
Bhasker, 218, 261
Bhatt, Vasudeo, 207
Bhatti, Ahsen, 218
Bianco, Marco, 180
Biase, Michael A., 176
Bibb, Leslie, 30
Bibby, Andrew, 259
Bibby, C.K., 173
Bibot, Laurence, 255
Bice, Patricia, 174
Bick, John, 160
Bickford, Laura, 122

Bidaman, Robert, 23, 180
Biddle, Adrian, 12, 91
Biderman, Ann, 206
Bidhartsang, Sonam, 117
Bidou, Jacques, 259
Biehn, Michael, 161, 269
Biel, Jessica, 67
Bierkens, Theo, 263
Bierko, Craig, 14, 62
Big Bad Prods., 171
Bigelow, Lynn, 65
Bigelow-Kouf, Lynn, 172
Biggers, Dan, 183
Biggerstaff, Sean, 251
Biggine, Edward, 176
Biggs, Casey, 154
Bigham, John, 63
Bigwood, Jim, 176
Bikel, Theodore, 154, 269
Bileschi, Bailee, 38
Bill Todman, Jr., 181
Bill, Jennifer, 49
Billeskov-Jansen, Janus, 259
Billing, Roy, 214
Billings, Earl, 65
Billingsgate Prod., 169
Billingsley, Barbara, 98
Billingsley, Brian Levant, 98
Billows, Angela, 38
Billy, Jean-Marie, 215
Bilotta, Bruno, 44
Biltcliffe, Martin, 222
Bilzerian, Laurence, 45
Bimini, 11
Bina, Tal Ben, 258
Bingwa, 183
Binkow, Bruce, 184
Binoche, Juliette, 265-266, 269
Binx, 81
Binyon, Dory, 157
Biondi, Lidia, 224
Birke, David, 173
Birkett, Jeremiah, 182
Birman, Matt, 180
Birnbaum, Claire, 174
Birnbaum, Michael, 160
Birnbaum, Roger, 10, 18, 45, 63, 94, 115, 174
Birth Of Love, The 263
Bishop, Anthony, 155
Bishop, Dan, 13, 179
Bishop, Kelly, 30, 167
Bishop, Larry, 162
Bishop, Loanne, 114
Bishop, Patrick, 128
Bishop, Paul, 211
Bishton, Jamie, 163
Bisset, Jacqueline, 165, 268-269
Bissonnette, Genevieve, 153
Bjelogrlic, Dragan, 264
Bjelogrlic, Goran, 264
Bjorklund, Jennifer, 49
Björn, 186
Bjornstad, Ketil, 262
Black, Charles, 183
Black, Chris, 169
Black, Edward, 27
Black, Gerry, 49
Black, Jack, 131
Black, Shane, 148
Black, Tim, 183
Blackburn, Richard, 180
Blackkettle, Maggie, 181
Blackmun, Harry A., 141
Blackwell, Chris, 32, 264
Blackwell, Paul, 209
Blades, Lynn, 13
Blades, Ruben, 35, 269-270
Blainey, Sue, 175
Blair, Selma, 102
Blaire, Ronnie Dee, 135
Blaisdell, Nesbit, 102, 181
Blake, Andre, 50
Blake, Blue, 166
Blake, Clement E., 146
Blake, Geffrey, 151
Blake, Geoffrey, 181
Blake, Jerome, 216
Blake, Julia, 259
Blake, Perry Andelin, 98
Blake, Robert, 21, 270
Blake, Susie, 12
Blake, Sydnee, 259
Blake, Teresa, 230
Blakesley, Weston, 114
Blaki, 236
Blalock, Steve, 181
Blanc, Jennifer, 161

Blanc, Manuel, 265
Blancard, Jarred, 33
Blanch, Dennis, 232
Blanchard, Ron, 257
Blanchard, Terence, 62, 80, 129
Blanche, Roland, 265
Blancherie, Laure, 239
Blanchett, Cate, 211, 257
Blanck, Curtis, 11
Blanco, Fred, 161
Bland, Jennifer, 119
Bland, John, 131
Blane, Steve, 28
Blaney, Tim, 77
Blank, Kim, 38, 78
Blanks, Billy, 114
Blaze, 50
Bleckner, Ross, 148
Blick, Hugo, 242
Blicker, Naomi, 126
Blier, Bertrand, 231
Bliss, 165
Bliss, Thomas A., 84, 86, 106, 122
Bloch, Bernard, 236
Bloch, Scotty, 142
Block 2 Pictures, 243
Block, Charles X, 156
Blocker, David, 47
Blocker, Dirk, 183
Blommaert, Susan, 146
Blomquist, Alan C., 90
Blood And Wine, 25
Bloody Child, The 162
Bloom, John, 75
Bloom, S.J., 161
Bloomfield, John, 184
Blossier, Patrick, 183
Blount, Lisa, 86, 270
Blue Sky Studios Inc., 80
Bluford, Dawn, 65
Blum, Len, 30
Blum, Mark, 157, 264, 270
Blumenthal, Hank, 163, 171, 176
Blunden, Christopher, 244
Bluteau, Lothaire, 137, 245
Bluth, Don, 130
Bluthal, John, 216
Bluto, Tony, 222
Bly, Stan, 148
Blythe, Benedick, 117
Blythe, Bernhard, 168
Blythe, Domini, 153
Blythe, Evelyn, 170
BMG Independents, 68, 178
Boal, Peter, 157
Boatman, Michael, 112
Bocabuca Prouccienes, 263
Bock, Carolyn, 230
Bock, Crystal, 137
Bock, Frank, 225
Bode, Ralf, 80
Boden, Kristina, 207
Bodine, Hunter, 128
Bodison, Wolfgang, 118
Bodkin, Greg, 156
Bodnar, Serena, 165
Bodrov, Sergei, 202
Bodry, Pierre, 254
Boebbis, Sabine, 241
Boehm, Bob, 61
Boeke, Valerie, 212
Boeken, Ludi, 11
Boeving, Christian, 181
Boey, Vincent J., 63
Boga, Manize, 207
Bogardus, Stephen, 58-59
Bogart, Peter, 65
Bogdanove, Jon, 184
Bogdanova, Bill, 83, 157, 183
Bogosian, Eric, 19, 142, 270
Bohem, Leslie, 17
Bohne, Bruce, 170
Boisson, Noële, 117
Bolado, Carlos, 264
Bolanca, Dijana, 248
Bolender, Bill, 17
Bolger, John Michael, 30
Bolger, Michael, 30, 178
Bolles, Susan, 105
Bolt, Jeremy, 91
Bolt, Neville, 210
Boltanzer, Lisa C., 11
Bolton, Guy, 130
Bolton, Michael, 15, 38
Bonansinga, Jeanne, 169
Bonaparte, John, 69
Bonaventura, Jindrich, 264
Bond, Maude, 177

Bond, Paula, 49
Bond, Samantha, 253
Bondelli, Roger, 21, 81
Bonds, De'aundre, 177
Bondy, Arpad, 258
Boneyard Film Company, 212
Bonezzi, Bernardo, 263
Bongo, 81
Bonham Carter, Helena, 193, 205, 246-247
Bonilla, Michelle, 63
Bonmatí, Nereida, 263
Bonner, James, 160
Bonnevie, Maria, 259
Bonneville, Hugh, 253
Bonnier, Céline, 105
Bonnot, Francoise, 183
Bontempo, Pietro, 224
Boogie Nights, 121
Booher, Dee, 15
Booker, Rev. Marvin Lewis, 166
Boon, Ed, 177
Boone's Animals for Hollywood, 146
Boone, J.J., 82
Boone, Mark, Junior, 101, 175, 178-179
Boone, Steve, 184
Boorem, Mika, 179
Booth, David, 155
Boothe, Powers, 113, 270
Bootsie, 23
Booty Call, 23
Borack, Carl, 50
Boraine, Nick, 154
Borden, Bill, 98
Borders, Archie, 170
Bordon, Roy, 154
Boretski, Peter, 205
Borg, Annika, 259
Borges, Alexandre, 264
Borghesi, Anna, 230, 235
Borgis, Yannis, 184
Borglund, Mikael, 243
Borgnine, Ernest, 124, 160, 270
Borisy, Troy, 34
Bornedal, Ole, 99
Borrachero, Alicia, 236
Borrego, Jesse, 65, 155
Borriello, Bobby, 30
Bortnik, Aida, 259
Bortz, Jason, 177
Borza, Don, 175
Bosch, Johnny Yong, 158
Bosch, Jordi, 263
Bosco, Philip, 72-73, 126, 142, 270
Boscovic, Boris, 131
Boss, May R., 68
Bossell, Simon, 259
Bossetta, Brian, 182
Bostick, Michael, 37
Boswell, John, 242
Botauzer, Lisa, 97
Botchan, Ronald L., 128
Botcher, Di, 261
Bothur, Günter, 263
Bottin, Rob, 99
Bouabdallah, Ben Salem, 254
Bouakline, Bouziane, 250
Bouchard, Louis, 105
Bouchard, Michel Marc, 241
Bouchareb, Rachid, 261
Bouchitey, Patrick, 265
Boudreau, Pierre, 179
Bouillette, Christian, 263
Bouin, Frederic, 167
Bouix, Bernard, 96
Bouix, Evelyne, 265
Boulanger, Noel, 212
Bould, Sam, 210
Bouquet, Carole, 262
Bourboulon, Frederic, 239
Bourchier, Michael, 265
Bourdieu, Emmanuel, 263
Bourgeois, John, 180
Bourgeois, Nicholas, 105
Bourland, Kevin, 49
Bourne, Billy, 175
Bourne, Kim, 39
Boutefeu, Nathalie, 213
Boutella, Safy, 259, 261
Bowden, Mandy, 230
Bowen, Charles, 154
Bowen, Christopher, 253
Bowen, Deirdre, 208
Bowen, Julie, 254
Bowen, Michael, 98, 147
Bowen, Richard, 164, 168

Bowens, Malick, 44
Bower, Humphry, 204
Bower, Tom, 155, 164
Bowles, Lauren, 81
Bowman, Debbie, 160
Bowser, Kenneth, 162
Box Of Moonlight, 86
Boxer Films, 238
Boxer, Maximilian, 238
Boxer, The 256
Boy of the Year and All Girl Productions, 39
Boy, Gouchy, 105
Boyce, Alan, 60
Boyce, David, 183
Boyce, Frank Cottrell, 248
Boyce, Frank, 225
Boyce, Jim, 177
Boyd, Blake, 174
Boyd, Bob, 107
Boyd, Lindsay, 98
Boyd, Martin David, 127
Boyd, Michael T., 160
Boyd, Russell, 37
Boyer, Katy, 61
Boyer, Marta, 168
Boyfriends, 205
Boyle, Consolata, 212, 220, 231
Boyle, Danny, 240, 261
Boyle, Lara Flynn, 153, 155, 167, 270
Boyle, Lisa, 21, 75
Boyle, Marc, 216
Boyle, Peter, 23, 184, 270
Boyle, Valerie, 23, 80
Boyles, Steve, 181
Boys Life 2, 33
Bozeman, Todd, 38
Bozian, James, 65, 96
Bradbury, Jane, 221
Braddell, Valerie, 180
Braddock, Diane, 80
Bradford, Conor, 256
Bradford, Richard, 97
Bradley, Charlotte, 231
Bradley, Danna, 30
Bradley, John, 125, 179
Bradley, Stewart, 38
Bradshaw, Carl, 264
Bradshaw, Joan, 181
Brady, Lance, 155
Brady, Mark, 61
Braeden, Brad, 121
Braeden, Eric, 186, 270
Braga III, Louis Martin, 98
Bragnier, Cyrille, 263
Brahm, Henry, 224
Braiden, Des, 256
Brailsford, Chris, 232
Brainard, Cam, 75
Bralove, Karen, 154
Brambilla, Marco, 98
Brancato, Chris, 97
Brancato, John, 101
Branch Davidians, 165
Branch, Taylor, 80
Branco, Paulo, 215, 263
Brandhagen, Clinton, 179
Brandise, Thomas, 171
Brando, Conchita, 224
Brandon, Maryann, 106
Brandstein, Matthew G., 95
Brandt, Andreas, 154
Brandt, Victor, 183
Brandt, Walker, 17
Brandt-Burgoyne, Anita, 83
Brandywine, 133
Branklyn, Charles, 101
Branner, Charles, 67
Brannick, Dick, 125
Branson, Ken, 174
Brantley, Betsy, 115, 159, 270
Brashear, George, 109
Brassard, Denise, 175
Brassed Off, 219
Bratt, Benjamin, 155
Bratt, Peter, 155
Brattan, Laura, 253
Braun, Tamara, 199
Braverman, Bart, 44
Braxton, Mary Lynette, 145
Brazeau, André, 101
Brazeau, Jay, 87, 169, 212
Breakdown, 55
Breaugh, Todd Patrick, 173, 181
Brechin, Derek, 55
Brecon, Anna, 125
Breen, Andy, 28

Breen, Charles, 172
Breen, Mark, 174
Breen, Patrick, 77
Breen, Renee, 28
Bregman, Anthony, 110
Bregman, Martin, 82
Bregman, Michael, 82
Bregovic, Goran, 213
Brehat, Jean, 261
Brena, Sean Patrick, 163
Brendan O'Carroll, 220
Brendan O'Hea, 229
Breneman, April, 182
Brener, Shirly, 167
Brenn, Janni, 244
Brennan, Brid, 231
Brennan, Dan, 27
Brennan, Eileen, 33, 270
Brennan, Richard, 260
Brennan, Sean Patrick, 163
Brennan, Norman, 63
Brent, Kimberly, 29
Brereton, Cecelia, 225
Bresin, Marty, 49
Brett, Fannie, 186-187
Brett, Jonathan, 8
Brett, Nick, 44
Bretz, Matthew Allen, 182
Breuse, Bernard, 265
Brevig, Eric, 77
Brewer, Bobby, 183
Brewer, Derek, 60
Brewer, Griffith, 179
Brewer, Juliette, 179
Brewer, Keith, 60
Brewer, Ryan, 13
Brewerton, Kevin, 216
Brewster, Joe, 100
Breznahan, Kevin, 121
Brialy, Jean-Claude, 263, 265, 270
Briaud, Laurence, 263
Brice, Natasha, 216
Brice, Ron, 100, 161, 175
Brick, Richard, 142
Brickle, Justin, 209
Brickman, Gary, 69
Bricmont, Wendy Greene, 180
Bridgeman, Derrick, 138
Bridger, Margot, 168
Bridges, Beau, 174, 270
Bridges, David, 165
Bridges, Mark, 28, 121
Bridges, Penny Bae, 82
Bridie, David, 105
Bridwell, Dennis, 162
Briese, Candice, 147
Briggs, Pat, 52
Briggs-Graves, Anasa, 135
Brigham, Beverly, 154
Bright, Dick, 10
Bright, Richard, 53, 157
Brightbill, Susan, 184
Brightwell, Paul, 186, 222
Brill, Dianne, 176
Brill, Jason, 169, 178
Brilliant Lies, 262
Brimble, Nick, 63
Brimley, John, 162
Brimley, Wilford, 102-103, 270
Brin, David, 184
Brind, Jack, 175
Bringelson, Mark, 56
Brinkley, Bonnie J., 31
Brinkley, Christie, 179, 270
Brinkley, Douglas, 166
Brinkley, Ritch, 55
Brinkman, Leight E., 180
Brion, Jon, 28
Brisbin, David, 182
Briscoe, Brent, 113
Brisebois, Danielle, 148
Brisk, Angelica, 175
Brisse, Joel, 221
Bristow, Patrick, 56, 173
Brisville, Jean-Claude, 265
British Columbia Film, 212
British Screen And Little Bird, 212
Brito, Steve, 176
Britt, Amy IcIntyre, 44
Britton, Chris, 138
Broadbent, Graham, 248
Broadbent, Jim, 206, 260
Broadhurst, Kent, 33, 265
Broadway, Jimmy, 96
Brochu, Don, 49
Brock, Benjamin, 136
Brock, Brett, 145

Brock, Christo, 104
Brock, Jeremy, 229
Brockman, Ungela, 78, 128
Brockmann, Hans, 28
Brocksmith, Roy, 169
Brockton, Jeff, 68, 95
Brockway, Dennis, 160
Broderick, Matthew, 181, 270
Brodsky, Ilya, 96
Brody, Adrien, 164
Brogan-Smith, Paige, 248
Brogger, Ivar, 88
Broken English, 214
Broken Twig Prods., 167
Brolin, Josh, 99
Bromwell, Lisa, 60
Bronson, Lisa Marie, 158
Bronson, Tom, 13, 144
Bronson-Howard, Aude, 27
Brook, Jayne, 124
Brook, Michael, 9
Brooke, Haynes, 181
Brookfield, William, 260
Brooks, Albert, 126, 270
Brooks, Chloe, 148
Brooks, Colin, 216
Brooks, Cooper, 148
Brooks, Geoff, 204
Brooks, James L., 148
Brooks, James, 101
Brooks, Mylin, 128
Brooks, Rodney, 116
Brooks, Ron, 60
Broom, Shea, 119
Broome, Ivory, 68
Broomfield, Nick, 161
Brophy, Antony, 212
Brophy, Brian, 32, 114, 177
Brosnan, Pierce, 6, 17, 252-253, 270
Brosset, Claude, 239
Brother's Kiss, A 50
Brothers In Trouble, 80
Broughton, Bruce, 80, 154
Broughton, Jennifer, 20
Broughton, June, 232
Broughton, Linda, 183
Brous, Nancy, 163
Brown, Andre Rosey, 15
Brown, Andy, 31
Brown, Ben, 37
Brown, Bill, 18, 61, 166
Brown, Bille, 12, 257
Brown, Bryan, 266, 271
Brown, Carolyn Lee, 80
Brown, Charles, 14
Brown, Clancy, 38, 128, 136
Brown, Clare, 172
Brown, David, 42, 114
Brown, Downtown Julie, 159
Brown, Eamon, 256
Brown, Earl, 114
Brown, G. Mac, 102
Brown, Gannon, 184
Brown, Garrett M., 43
Brown, Garrett, 8
Brown, Gavin, 256
Brown, Henry, 264
Brown, J. Anthony, 168
Brown, Jaki, 147
Brown, Jared F., 166
Brown, Jeffrey, 50
Brown, June, 244
Brown, Kevin, 169
Brown, Larry, 170
Brown, Lewis, 168
Brown, Lillie, 80
Brown, Marcus Lyle, 129
Brown, Mark, 37, 168
Brown, Jr., Mayor Willie L., 81
Brown, Megan Leigh, 79
Brown, O. Nicholas, 181
Brown, P.J., 11
Brown, Pat Crawford, 51
Brown, Paul, 126, 168
Brown, Ralph, 141
Brown, Randy, 160
Brown, Rosey, 15, 95
Brown, Samantha, 63
Brown, Stephen, 180, 183
Brown, Steven, 145, 168
Brown, Susan, 123
Brown, Suse, 223
Brown, Velina, 183
Brown, Walter, 155
Brown, Wayne, 179
Brown-Karman, Jaki, 83, 129, 168

Browne, Kale, 62
Browning, Nadine, 181
Browning, Norman, 87
Brownlee, Jerry Mongo, 65
Brownson, Amy, 69
Brownson, Malcolm, 136
Brownstein, Rob, 244
Brubaker, James D., 37
Bruce, David, 94
Bruce, Ed, 182
Bruce, Lynn Robertson, 66
Bruch, Max, 230
Bruckheimer, Bonnie, 39
Bruckheimer, Jerry, 65
Brugeille, Olympe, 221
Brummer, Richard, 172
Brun, Catherine, 260
Brunett, Sean, 256
Bruni-Tedeschi, Valeria, 239
Bruning, Jurgen, 171
Brunner, Bridget, 135
Brunner, Dominique, 265
Bruno, Richard, 97
Brunson, Kitty, 240
Bruskotter, Eric, 128
Brutus, Izudina, 248
Bruynbroek, Frank, 95
Bryan, Clifton Lloyd, 216
Bryant, Daniel, 97
Bryant, Katherine Jane, 159
Bryant, Troy, 156
Bryce, Roberto, 216
Brychta, Edita, 132, 182
Brydern, Benedikt, 156
Brynolfsson, Reine, 259
Bryson, Eric, 180
Brzeski, Bill, 148
Bubble Factory, 20, 39, 80, 137, 160
Buchanan, Jenny, 184
Buchman, Alexander, 254
Buck, Samantha, 102
Buck, Sibyl, 216
Buck, Waltrudis, 142
Buckel, Dave, 123
Buckler, Robert, 218
Buckley, Frank, 49
Buckley, Sean, 125, 216
Buckman, Phil, 254
Buckmaster, Paul, 118
Buckner, Bari, 61
Bucknor, Paul, 232
Budaska, Robert, 174
Budd, Robin, 262
Buddy, 87
Buddy, 66,
Budoff, Gary, 156
Buelterman, Jeff, 104
Buena Vista Pictures, 10, 13, 23, 38, 51, 65, 71, 81-82, 87, 106, 115, 122, 144, 152, 154, 174, 254
Bueno, Rico, 121, 133
Buff, Conrad, 17, 127, 186
Bufford, Takashi, 23
Bugg, Daryl, 69
Buggy, Niall, 180
Bugin, Harry, 157
Bugis Street, 265
Bugos, Rebecca, 171
Buhler, Andreas, 52
Bujold, Genevieve, 118, 271
Bukowski, Bobby, 62, 104, 164
Bukowski, Bubba, 177
Bukowski, Marta, 174
Bulic, Vanja, 264
Bull, Charley, 171
Bulleit, Jim, 27
Bulley, Richard, 260
Bullock, Craig, 180
Bullock, Donna, 84
Bullock, Gregg, 158
Bullock, Sandra, 7, 68, 271
Bulos, Burt, 11
Bumpass, Rodger, 71
Bumstead, Henry, 22, 178, 183
Bumstead, J.P., 183
Bunel, Marie, 265
Bunyan, Maureen, 180
Bunyik Entertainment, 266
Burch, Jackie, 78
Burder, Barbara, 259
Burdoe, Phyllis, 142
Bureau, Matiaz, 218
Burg, Mark, 158, 168
Burge, Emma, 231
Burgess, Don, 181
Burgess, Michael, 173

Burgess, Rick, 144, 182
Buric, Sanja, 248
Burig, Susan, 183
Burke, Alan, 212
Burke, Graham, 211
Burke, Jim, 168
Burke, Michael Reilly, 174
Burke, Robert John, 93
Burke, Robert Karl, 13
Burkes-Nossiter, Emily, 241
Burkett, Brandi, 37
Burkhart, Betty, 161
Burkhart, Kathe, 132
Burkholder, Scott, 65
Burkley, Dennis, 24, 180
Burks, Willis, 96
Burlage, Roger, 160
Burmann, Hans, 224
Burmester, Leo, 127, 183
Burns, Keith Brian, 158
Burns, Pepper, 171
Burns, R.J., 17
Burns, Tim, 254
Burns, Traber, 67
Burr, David, 181
Burrise, Nakia, 158
Burrows, Darren, 141, 271
Burrows, Justin Lee, 163
Burrows, Saffron, 132, 259
Burrows, Victoria, 137, 181
Burson, Greg, 144
Burstyn, Thomas, 32
Burt, Donald Graham, 27
Burton, Billy, 8
Burton, Corey, 71
Burton, Geoff, 262
Burton, Henry, 265
Burton, Kate, 110
Burton, Linda, 145
Burton, Matthew, 265
Burton, Rory, 141
Burton, Tony, 155
Burton, Tyrone, 69
Burum, Stephen H., 180
Burwell, Carter, 88, 116, 131, 181
Burz, Christina, 156
Buscemi, Michael, 175
Buscemi, Steve, 64-65, 271
Busey, Gary, 21, 271
Busey, Jake, 128, 181
Bush, Grand L., 8
Bush, Marlene, 133
Bush, Tommy, 65
Busia, Akosua, 177, 179, 183
Bussi, Franck, 221
Butch Camp, 169
Butcher, Lindsey, 125
Butchers Run Films Production, 145
Butler, Bill, 46
Butler, David, 93, 153
Butler, Gerard, 229, 253
Butler, Gill, 163
Butler, Lucy, 21
Butler, Robert, 8
Butler, William, 69
Butterworth, Paul, 232
Buttle, Stephanie, 265
Buxton, Susannah, 237
Buzzini, Brian, 60
Byars, Floyd, 169
Byers, Frank, 50
Byers, Kate, 234
Bylander, Sheri, 173
Byner, John, 172
Bynum, Nate, 135
Byrd, David, 21
Byrd, Donald, 163
Byrd, James L., 154
Byrd, Toni Lynn, 240
Byrne, Chris, 183
Byrne, Christopher, 186
Byrne, Gabriel, 100, 206, 271
Byrne, Jack, 155
Byrne, Jenna, 183
Byrne, Jenny, 151
Byrne, Larry, 256
Byrne, Michael, 42, 253
Byrne, Peter, 174
Byrne, Seamus, 231
Byrnes, Josephine, 257
Byrnes, Patrick Joseph, 183
C&P production, 161
Caan, Scott, 60
Caballero, Joseph L., 178
Cabasa, Lisa Ann, 132
Cabin Fever Entertainment, 205
Cacho, Daniel Gimenez, 265-266

Cadieux, Jason, 241
Cadiff, Andy, 98
Cadillac Ranch, 159
Caesar, Sid, 179, 271
Cafe Society, 167
Cafferty, Jack, 53
Cage, Nicolas, 6, 64-65, 74-75, 271
Cagle, Kenya, 97
Cahill, Laura, 89
Cahill, Stan, 106
Cahn, Jodi Faith, 63
Cahoon, Kevin, 157
Cain, Christopher, 63
Cain, Sons of, 260
Cain, William, 110
Caine, Michael, 25, 271
Calabro, Jac, 161
Calabro, Kevin, 13
Calamari, Paolo, 181
Calder, David, 125, 210
Caldera, Carolyn, 236
Calderon, Paul, 93
Calderon, Sergio, 77
Calderwood, Andrea, 229
Caldinez, Sonny, 216
Caldwell, Michael, 83
Caldwell, Sandra, 180
Cale, John, 263
Cale, Paula, 178
Calegrai, Maria, 157
Calf, Anthony, 125, 180
Calissano, Paolo, 44
Callaham, Jill, 114
Callahan, E.J., 51, 146
Callaway, Liz, 130
Calley, John, 132
Callie, Dayton, 49
Calon, Jean-Claude, 239
Caloz, Michael, 105
Calzado, Rudy, 264
Camacho, Mark, 153
Camarda, Tom, 157
Camargo, Cristina, 264
Cambridge, Ed, 18
Camen, Joey, 166
Cameron, Allan, 128, 253
Cameron, Dale, 175
Cameron, James, 186
Cameron, Nadia, 253
Caminer, Sylvia, 175
Cammallere, Mike, 53
Camp, Bill, 102
Camp, Casey, 155
Camp, Colleen, 68, 271
Camp, Joanne, 30
Campbell, Alan, 80
Campbell, Amelia, 88
Campbell, Bill, 162, 271
Campbell, Bruce, 160, 178
Campbell, Carolyn, 133
Campbell, Danny, 176
Campbell, Edward, 101, 176
Campbell, J. Kenneth, 8, 67
Campbell, John J., 260
Campbell, John, 21
Campbell, John Lyle, 22
Campbell, John, 65
Campbell, Julia, 51
Campbell, Kathleen, 28
Campbell, Keith, 77
Campbell, Malcolm, 82, 178
Campbell, Mariah, 141
Campbell, Michael, 136, 158, 176
Campbell, Neve, 6, 144, 271
Campbell, Pat, 261
Campbell, Paul, 264
Campbell, Scott Michael, 136
Campbell, Tisha, 60, 271
Camroux, Ken, 165
Camus, Michel, 81
Canady, Christian, 145
Canady, Christopher, 145
Canal+, 215, 218, 220-221, 223, 231, 236, 239, 241, 250, 255, 260, 262, 265
Canellias, Laura, 78
Canijo, Joao, 262
Canini, Tracey, 265
Cannavale, Bobby, 53
Cannom, Greg, 44, 184
Cannon, Bruce, 179
Cannon, Dyan, 23, 44, 78, 271
Cannons, Joe, 138
Canosa, Fabiano, 264
Cantarini, Louis, 181
Canter, Nina, 170
Canto, Marilyne, 221
Canton, Danny, 102
Cantone, Mario, 146

Cantrell, Anthony E., 181
Cantrell, Trick, 160
Capaldi, Peter, 206, 244
Cape, Yves, 255
Capella International, 56, 164
Capella Intl., 164
Capitaine Conan, 239
Capitol Films, 166, 251
Capo, Fran, 96
Capodice, John, 68
Caponera, John, 137
Capote, Truman, 137
Cappachione, Emile, 254
Cappatti, Joe, 137
Cappuccilli, Joanna, 62
Cappucci, Francesca, 11
Capra, Bernt, 11
Capra, Francis, 80
Capra, Frank, 162
Caprari, Toni, 155
Capri, Mark, 186
Capshaw, Jessica, 116
Capshaw, Kate, 116, 271
Capucilli, Billy, 27
Caputo, Jay, 90
Caracciolo, Joe Jr., 183, 241
Caratozzolo, Nino, 162, 169
Caravan Co., 202
Caravan Pictures, 10, 45, 63, 115, 174
Caravella, Bobby, 157
Carballido, Palmy, 236
Carberry, Michelle, 39
Cardellini, Linda, 83
Cardenas, Michael, 11
Cardenas, Steve, 158
Cardinal, Tantoo, 179
Cardona, Cora, 180
Cardone, Thomas, 71
Cardoso, Laura, 264
Cardoza, Benjamin John, 81
Cardoza, Dave, 181
Cardoza, Noah John, 81
Career Girls, 234
Carey, Amie, 19
Carey, Anne, 173
Carey, Clauda, 173
Carey, Helen, 154
Carey, Matthew Thomas, 98
Carey, Peter, 257
Cargi, Garic, 177
Carides, Gia, 230, 262
Carides, Zoe, 262
Carin, Ashley, 35
Carkner, Derek, 80
Carle, Cynthia, 38
Carlin, Amanda, 37
Carlin, Nancy, 168
Carliner, Rob, 145
Carlson, Jonathan, 23
Carlyle, Robert, 232-233, 271
Carman, James, 171
Carmody, Don, 126
Carmona, Christophe, 239
Carneiro, Geraldo, 258
Carnes, Otto, 160
Carnes, Tara, 102
Carney, Karen, 122
Carney, Liam, 256
Carnvial Night, 223
Caron, Danny, 14
Caron, Glenn Gordon, 88
Caron, Jean Luc, 216
Carouso, Tom, 158, 166, 178
Carp, Jean-Philippe, 118
Carpenter, Angel, 160
Carpenter, James, 10
Carpenter, Russell, 95, 186
Carpenter, Willie C., 9, 77
Carr, Bubba, 78
Carr, Cornelius, 256
Carr, Katy, 222
Carr, Patricia, 12
Carradine, Keith, 106, 271
Carrafa, John, 59
Carrasco, Manuela, 213
Carraway, James, 69
Carré, Isabelle, 265
Carreiro, Tony, 37
Carrera, David, 155
Carrere, Tia, 169
Carrey, Jim, 6, 36-37, 271
Carrillo, Erick, 180
Carrillo, Mark, 180
Carrington, Debbie Lee, 77
Carrington, Sarah, 216
Carrodus, Peter, 230
Carroll, Burke, 176

Carroll, Diahann, 129, 271
Carroll, Earl, 18, 62
Carroll, Ginger, 182
Carroll, Gordon, 133
Carroll, Larry, 49
Carroll, Marjorie, 174
Carroll, Ronn, 263
Carroll, Thomas Joseph, 8
Carrow, Lynne, 182
Carson, Lisa Nicole, 34, 129
Carson, T.C., 172
Carter, Allen, 151
Carter, Carmen, 151
Carter, Doyle, 159
Carter, Forrest, 179
Carter, Gary, 159, 164
Carter, Jim, 210, 219
Carter, John, 109, 175
Carter, LaJuan, 27
Carter, Rick, 61, 141
Carter, Ruth E., 141, 179
Carter, Ruth, 158
Carter, Thomas, 10
Carter, Wendy, 104
Carthane, Lynn, 135
Cartlidge, Katrin, 234
Cartwright, Peter, 222
Cartwright, Veronica, 95, 272
Carubia, Saverio, 146
Caruso, David, 175, 272
Caruso, Fred, 123
Carvalho, Walter, 264
Carver, Brent, 241
Carver, Lisa "Suckdog", 166
Carver, Stephen James, 37
Caryn Horwitz Presents, 166
Cascone, Nicholas, 186
Case, Caroline, 114
Casella, Max, 63, 272
Caselnova, Richard, 132
Cash, Jim, 46
Cash, June Carter, 145
Cashen, Irina, 176
Cashman, Dan, 114
Caso, Christopher, 181
Caso, Don, 180
Caso, Maria, 82
Cass, Marc, 186
Cass, Robin, 241
Cassavetes, John, 96
Cassavetes, Nick, 75, 96, 272
Cassel, Ferne, 33
Cassel, Seymour, 79, 272
Cassell, Paul, 88, 157
Cassella, Mark, 93
Cassidy, Althea, 30
Cassidy, Jay, 9
Cassinelli, Martine, 263
Cassini, Frank, 169
Cassini, John, 38, 101
Castaldi, Jean-Pierre, 263
Castanedo, Rafael, 265
Castel, France, 153
Castel, Lou, 213, 263
Castellanos, Vincent, 46
Casterline, Thomas, 169
Castillo, Enrique, 100
Casting, Margiotta, 68
Castle Hill, 122, 156, 159, 222, 231, 262
Castle, Keith Lee, 242
Castle, Maggie, 131
Castle, Robert, 93
Castleway Entertainment, 177
Castro, Canto E., 262
Castro, Eduardo, 32, 207
Castronovo, T.J., 177
Catalano, George, 13
Cathell, Cevin, 129
Catherine, Mistress, 161
Cathey, Reg E., 177
Catlin, Gordon, 112
Caton-Jones, Michael, 131
Cats Don't Dance, 180
Cattaneo, Peter, 232
Caucheteux, Pascal, 263
Caufield, Laura, 102
Caulfield, Maxwell, 183, 272
Cava, Elizabeth, 38
Cavalier, Alain, 266
Cavalier, Charles, 112
Cavallary, Jonathan, 182
Cavalli, Valeria, 44
Cavanagh, Megan, 23, 137
Cavanaugh, Kathy Lyn, 102
Cave, Des, 231

Cavendish, Jonathan, 212
Cavendish, Nicola, 87
Caviezel, Jim, 94
Cayla, 11
Caz, Grand Master, 156
Cazès, Lila, 24
Ceballos, Roy, 163
Cecere, Fulvio, 98
Cecil, Jennifer, 159
Cecil, Sarah, 159
Cedar, Larry, 114
Cedar, Phyllis, 264
Cederna, Giuseppe, 224
Cee, Frank, 80
Ceja, Jose Angel, 161
Celedonio, Maria, 24
Cellario, Maria, 21
Celli, Jack, 176
Centre National De La
    Cinematographie, 218, 236, 262
Ceraso, Chris, 163
Ceredig, Huw, 261
Cerezo, Enrique, 236
Cerf, Muriel, 265
Cerna, J.D., 33
Cerquetti, Anita, 262
Cervantes, Carlos, 49
Chaback, J.J., 18
Chaban, Michael, 181
Chabat, Alain, 265
Chabert, Lacey, 130
Chablis, The Lady, 183
Chacras Filmworks, 155
Chadwick, Aaron, 182
Chadwick, Mark, 181
Chaet, Mark, 37
Chaffin, Céan, 101
Chaffin, Stokely, 119
Chaidez, Jose, 121
Chaix, Jérémy, 250
Chakir, Blaise, 265
Chalfant, Kathleen, 163
Chalsma, Melissa, 171
Chamberlain, Emily, 137
Chamberlain, Nicole, 173
Chamberlain, Suzanne, 230
Chamberlin, Kevin, 102
Chambers, Jennifer, 161
Chambers, Michael, 161
Chamian, Denis, 146
Champetier, Caroline, 218, 260
Champion, Fern, 15, 160, 177
Champion, Rene, 171
Champnella, Eric, 160
Champness, Charlotte, 125
Chan, Da Ming, 11
Chan, Jackie, 203, 230, 272
Chan, Joe GM, 121
Chan, Kam Ray, 23
Chan, Kim, 30, 152, 183, 216
Chan, Michael Paul, 181
Chan, Pauline, 211
Chan, Shirley, 163
Chan, Thang, 168
Chan, Yau Gene, 20, 22
Chan, Yuo, 265
Chance, Carlton, 216
Chancellor, Anna, 125, 183
Chandler, Jared, 112
Chandler, Simon, 183, 210
Chandler, Vincent, 83
Chandu, Lama Champa, 117
Chang, Gary, 44
Chang, Terence, 75
Changmin, Chen, 222
Changui, Grupo, 264
Channel 4, 203, 240
Channel Four Films, 207, 210, 212, 219-220, 225, 231, 234, 245, 248, 251
Channing-Williams, Simon, 234
Chant, Holley, 91
Chantal, Aline, 221
Chantrell, Shirley, 247
Chao, Jian Rui, 126
Chao, Rosalind, 100
Chapa, Damian, 95
Chapin, Doug, 59
Chaplin, Ben, 115
Chapman, Alexander, 241
Chapman, Jan, 235
Chapman, John, 237
Chapman, Mark Lindsay, 186
Chapman, Pamela Tice, 135
Chapman, Stephen, 125
Chappelle, Dave, 65
Chappey, Antoine, 221
Character Shop, The 99

Character, 196
Charbonnet, Pat, 155
Chardiet, Jon, 95
Chardin, Pascal, 221
Charette, Cynthia, 56
Charles De'Ath, 237
Charles, Andre, 157, 169
Charles, Brandon, 230
Charles, Nancy Linehan, 63
Charles, Rebecca, 229
Charles, Scott, 244
Charlton, Lafe, 266
Charlton, Orla, 231
Charmelo, Eric C., 11
Charone, Irwin, 142
Charteris, Leslie, 42
Charters, Rodney, 169
Chartrand, Lauro, 38, 169
Chase, Chevy, 179, 272
Chase, David, 155
Chase, James Hadley, 260
Chase, Johnie, 23
Chase, Maraya, 171
Chase, Vincent, 47
Chasing Amy, 41,
Chasman, Julia, 34
Chasse, Maurice, 184
Chatinover, Marvin, 142
Chatton, Charlotte, 186
Chattot, François, 236
Chau, 11, 32, 220
Chau, Francois, 11, 32
Chavanne, Brian, 130
Chavez, Carmen M., 144
Chavez, Chuy, 83
Chavis, Gabie, 179
Chaykin, Maury, 63, 146, 240, 249, 272
Che, Cindera, 78
Cheadle, Don, 48-49, 121, 179
Cheater, Jason, 225
Chee, Yow Wah, 205
Cheetwood, Derk, 184
Chefin Love, A, 213
Chemchok, 117
Chen, Chang, 243
Chen, Dehong, 220
Chen, Mei-Juin, 126
Chen, Paul, 126
Cheng, Carol, 230
Cheng, Cecil, 216
Cheng, Mayling, 8
Cheng-zhi, Zhang, 260
Chenoweth, Ellen, 10, 104, 131, 151
Cheriguene, Fatiha, 259
Chering, Chris, 222
Cherniawsky, Todd, 167
Cherry, Donna, 118
Cheshatsang, Yama Nugdup, 117
Cheshier, Lydell, 81
Cheshire, Polly, 257
Chesler, Derek, 100
Chesler, Janie, 157
Chesler, Wayne, 157
Chesley, Kevin, 100
Chester, Craig, 166
Chester, SaMi, 181
Chester, Vanessa Lee, 61
Chestnut, Morris, 94
Cheung, Leslie, 222, 243
Cheung, Maggie, 213
Cheung, Peter, 203
Chevrier, Arno, 259
Chi, Chao-Li, 163
Chianese, Dominic, 53, 176
Chiang, Peter, 242
Chiaravalle, Matt, 161
Chieffo, Michael, 182
Child, Bob, 154
Child, Lincoln, 8
Childhood's End, 159
Children Of The Revolution, 214
Childress, Patricia, 148
Childs, Martin, 229
Chiles, Lois, 68, 165, 272
Chimènes, Flavia, 250
Chin, Tsai, 126
Ching, Chan Man, 203
Ching-Chao, Christophe Tseng, 243
Chinich, Michael, 52, 180
Chinlund, Nick, 50, 65, 144
Chinn, Anthony, 216
Chino, Conroy, 181
Chinyamurindi, Michael, 81
Chirinos, Monica, 265
Chisem, James L., 178
Chisholm, Cara, 39

Chisholm, Elizabeth, 145
Chisholm, Jimmy, 229
Chisholm, Kathleen, 175
Chitlaphone, Gilles, 261
Chiu-Wai, Tony Leung, 243
Chmaladze, Teimour, 213
Cho, Henry, 160
Cho, John, 151
Cho, Margaret, 75
Chocolate, 213
Choe, Stella, 83
Choedon, Tenzin, 265
Choedrak, Tenzin, 265
Choi, Peter Y., 178
Chojor, Ven. Ngawang, 117
Cholodenko, Marc, 263
Chong, Alvin, 209, 230
Chong, Michael, 122
Chong, Precious, 182
Chong, Tommy, 160
Choquart, Alain, 239
Chory, James A., 154
Choudhury, Sarita, 207
Chow, Ho, 180
Chow, Raymond, 203, 230
Chowdhry, Ranjit, 207, 235
Christ, Bill, 112
Christ, Chad, 124
Christensen, Erika, 98
Christiaenssens, Serge, 131
Christian, Roger, 162, 169
Christianson, Bob, 160
Christie, Julie, 153, 193, 272
Christie, Sandra Marie, 170
Christmas, Eric, 87, 146
Christofferson, Debra, 146
Christopher, Donald, 171
Christopher, Dyllan, 183
Christopher, Mark, 23, 33, 60
Christopher, Scott, 162
Christopher, Thom, 25
Christopher, Tom, 180
Christy, George, 173
Chronicle Of A Disappearance, 261
Chronopoulos, Gene, 18
Chua, Jeni, 10
Chubb, Caldecot, 129
Chubb, Paul, 260
Chubbco, 129
Chung, Cheung Yiu, 230
Chung, Danny, 243
Chung, David, 211
Church, Eleanor, 210
Church, Thomas Haden, 81, 132
Churchyard, Graham, 210
Churgin, Lisa Zeno, 124
Cianfione, Mario, 194
Ciarfalio, Carl N., 65
Ciby 2000, 21, 100
CiBy Sales Limited, 237
Ciccolella, Jude, 53, 100
Ciesinski, Katherine and Kristine, 262
Cina, Maria, 179
Cinefax Workshop Co. Ltd., 230
Cinema Guild, 176-177
Cinema Parallel, 260
Cinema Village Features, 154, 161
Cinematografica-Istituto Luce-RAI, 203
Cinepix Film Properties, 132
Cinergi, 154
Cineville, 167
Cioffi, Charles, 154
Cioffi, Louis F., 160
Citro, Anthony, 93
Citti, Franco, 266
Citti, Sergio, 266
City Block, 156
City Lights International, 156
City Of Industry, 32
CL Cinema Line Films Corporation
    Production, 46
Clack, Boyd, 261
Claman, June, 137
Clancy, Deirdre, 229
Clanton, Rony, 183
Clapperton, Robert, 216
Clapton, Eric, 220, 272
Clario, Emma de, 209
Clark, Ashley Monique, 37
Clark, Ian D., 241
Clark, Ian, 39
Clark, Jim, 127, 131, 241
Clark, Lynda, 119
Clark, Mark, 184
Clark, Richard, 162
Clark, Sandra, 49

Clark, Tony, 209
Clark-Hall, Steve, 205, 251
Clarke, Bernadette L., 34
Clarke, Caitlin, 173
Clarke, Cheryl, 158
Clarke, Emma, 251
Clarke, Gin, 216
Clarke, Larry, 102
Clarke, Lenny, 15
Clarke, Melinda, 90
Clarke, Stanley, 60, 155, 158
Clatterbuck, Tamara, 32
Claude "Pete" Bryant, 168
Claus, Richard, 254
Clauzel, Nigel, 42
Clavel, Francoise, 213
Clavel, Garance, 221
Clay, Jim, 183
Clayburgh, Jill, 21, 104, 272
Clayton, Curtiss, 38
Clayton, Judy, 63
Cleese, Cynthia, 12
Cleese, John, 12, 81, 242, 272
Clegg, Terence, 131
Clegg, Wade, 13
Cleitman, Rene, 96
Clem, Frank, 135
Clement, Dick, 98
Clemente, Francesco, 138
Clemente, Ralph, 172
Clements, Linda, 51
Clements, Ron, 71
Clemons, Hamp, 109
Clendenin, Bob, 182
Clennon, David, 183
Cleuzo, Sandro, 130
Cleveland, Rob, 23
Cleverdon, Scott, 160
Clifford, Wendy, 44
Clifton, Judy, 238
Cline, Emily, 89
Clinica Estetico production, 32, 67
Clinton, George S., 11, 56, 177
Clinton, George, 83
Cliver, Craig, 162
Clooney, George, 112, 181
Close, Glenn, 84, 102, 211, 272
Cloud Nine Entertainment, 8
Clough, Ina, 125
Clown, Roger, 99
CLP-Dacia Films, 260
Clubb, Jim, 12
Cluff, Caleb, 259
Clyde Is Hungry Films, 96, 113
Clyde, Craig, 162
Clyde, Shthd Right-Turn, 29
Coates, Anne V., 78
Coates, Bill, 23
Coates, Conrad, 126
Coates, Nelson, 9, 114, 180
Coatte, Kirk, 144
Cobalt Films, 176
Cobb, Mel, 259
Cobb, Randall "Tex", 37, 176
Cobb, Sloan, 79
Cobb, Walter, 47
Cobbs, Bill, 87
Cobbs, Willy, 79
Coblenz, Walter, 95
Cobra Film Department, 264
Cobra, Roger, 44
Coburn, Candy, 8
Coburn, James, 160, 272
Coca, Richard, 180
Coccioletti, Philip, 159
Cochran, Dean, 181
Cochrane, Michael, 42
Cochrane, Nicki, 183
Cockburn, Andrew, 112
Cockburn, Arlene, 251
Cockburn, Leslie, 112
Codron, David, 163
Cody, Alan, 68
Cody, Bill, 177
Cody, Jill Mazursky, 63
Cody, Karyn V., 154
Cody, Mike, 135
Coe, Ashley, 159
Coe, George, 176
Coe, Richard, 24
Coffey, David, 205
Coffey, Freeman, 178
Coffey, Scott, 21, 272
Cofimage 7, 236
Coh, Roslyn, 53
Cohen, Adrianna AJ, 90
Cohen, Bruce, 146
Cohen, David Aaron, 35

Cohen, Jaffe, 148
Cohen, Joel, 95
Cohen, Joseph Newton, 105
Cohen, Leonard, 261
Cohen, Lester, 93
Cohen, Neil, 236
Cohen, Norma, 125
Cohen, Scott, 30, 50
Cohen, Steven, 25
Cohn, Peter, 158
Coinman, John J., 184
Colantoni, Enrico, 9
Colares, Ricardo, 262
Colbert, Afonda, 129
Colbert, Catero, 172
Colbert, Gerald, 80
Colbert, Gino, 166
Colbert, Joanna, 98
Colbert, Reginald C., 154
Colby, James, 112
Cold Around The Heart, 175
Cole, Alex, 160
Cole, Gary, 172
Cole, Jude, 162
Cole, Kimberly, 182
Cole, Natalie, 168, 180
Coleman II, James Edward 179
Coleman, Ceal, 99
Coleman, Charlotte, 237
Coleman, Danilo Randjic, 175
Coleman, Jack, 90, 272
Coleman, Jim R., 11
Coleman, Kirby, 168
Coleman, Lisa, 109
Coleman, Patricia, 175
Coleman, Tom, 174
Coles, Lisa, 182
Coles, Stan, 165
Colesberry, Robert F., 35
Colgan, Joe, 256
Colicchio, Victor, 100
Colichman, Paul, 173
Colin, Gregoire, 239
Colin, Margaret, 35, 272
Coll, Ivonne, 20, 236
Coll, Ivonne, 20, 236
Collaso, Joan, 109
Colleary, Michael, 75
Collet, Nancy, 68
Collette, Toni, 260
Colley, Ken, 219
Collie, Mark, 182
Collie, Stephanie, 222
Collier, Marian, 181
Collin, Anthony, 125
Collins Jr., Frank 145
Collins, Andy, 219
Collins, Bill, 131
Collins, Elaine, 229
Collins, Greg, 38, 65
Collins, Jesse, 168
Collins, Junie, 80
Collins, Kennita, 182
Collins, Michael, 231
Collins, Myles, 209
Collins, Pauline, 211, 263-264, 272
Collins, Rickey D'Shon, 163
Collins, Robert, 155
Collis, Terry, 154
Collison, Frank, 66
Collister, Peter Lyons, 18
Collodow, Allen, 53
Colombier, Michel, 15
Colomby, Harry, 55
Colon, Gil, 127
Colon, Liza, 100
Colon, Sally, 44
Colonna, Xavier, 250
Colpaert, Carl-Jan, 167
Colquhoun, Mary, 88, 182
Colston, Robert, 175
Colt, Beth, 83
Colton, Craig A., 33
Colton, Michael, 126
Coltrane, Robbie, 66, 270, 272
Coluca, Teddy, 53
Columbia, 21-23, 35, 44, 46, 66, 77, 84, 98, 119, 124, 162, 169, 216, 242,
Columbus, Pam, 177
Colvey, Peter, 179
Combs, Annie, 21, 155
Combs, Gil, 21
Combs, Sean "Puffy" 157
Comden, Danny, 49
Comeau, Andy, 44
Cometstone Pictures, 254
Comfort, Bob, 156

Comisky, Chuck, 177
Commandments, 52
Communicado Production, 214
Compton, Norm, 75
Con Air, 65
Conaway, Christi, 162
Concorde Films, 203
Conde, Concha Gomez, 236
Condra, Julie, 24
Congdon, Dana, 173
Conley, Jack, 182
Conlon, Oscar, 132
Conn, Diane, 59
Connell, David, 11
Connelly, Jennifer, 43, 272
Connelly, Joe, 98
Conner, David, 176
Connick, Jr., Harry, 98, 272
Connolly, Billy, 228-229, 272
Connolly, Bob, 258
Connolly, Brendan, 186
Conoley, Terence, 12
Conrad, Chris, 177
Conroy, Kelly Anne, 37
Conroy, Neili, 220
Conroy, Ruaidhri, 212, 220
Conroy, Samantha, 35
Conspiracy Theory, 181
Conspirators Of Pleasure, 262
Constable, Gary Griffin, 161
Constantini, Brian, 30
Constellation Films, 135
Contact, 181
Contawe, Ron, 172
Conte, Chris, 93
Conte, Mark, 32
Conte, Paolo, 265
Conteh, Habib, 141
Conteh, Stephen, 141
Conti, Bill, 265
Conti, Carlos, 250
Conti, Walt, 46
Contreras, Ernie, 125
Contreras, Luis, 166
Converse-Roberts, William, 114
Convertino, Michael, 29, 126
Conway, Dan, 106
Conway, Frank, 106, 231
Conway, Sulanya "Sue" 97
Conway, Tim, 68, 273
Cooder, Ry, 100
Coogan, Steve, 242
Cook, Ancel, 55
Cook, Bonnie, 47
Cook, Carl D., 145
Cook, Christopher, 238
Cook, Dane, 66
Cook, Harve, 81
Cook, Jonathan, 158
Cook, Lauri, 160
Cook, Leslie, 78
Cook, Rachael Leigh, 118
Cooke, Gregory, 186
Cooke, John, 256
Cooke, Vince, 159
Coolidge, Jennifer, 63
Coolidge, Martha, 78
Coolio, 181
Coon, Neal Preston, 184
Cooney, Kevin, 65, 127, 183
Cooper, Bobby, 96, 113
Cooper, Chuck, 112
Cooper, Danny, 204
Cooper, Helmar Augustus, 181
Cooper, Jake, 29
Cooper, Jane DeVries, 63
Cooper, Justin, 37
Cooper, Michelle B., 23
Cooper, Nathanael, 138
Cooper, Robert, 141
Cooper, Roy, 170
Cooprider, Coop, 174
Coote, Greg, 211
Cop Land, 93
Copeland, Joan, 29, 112, 273
Copeland, Stewart, 13, 83
Copello, Carlos, 250
Copenhaver, Katherine, 69
Coppin, Gary, 154
Coppola, Chris, 90
Coppola, Francis Ford, 66, 135
Coral, Matilde, 213
Corbally, Sandra, 256
Corbeil, Normand, 105
Corbeil, Yves, 153
Corbett, John, 49, 68
Corbett, Ronnie, 12
Corbin, Barry, 173, 273

Corbin, Kathleen Brown, 83
Corbould, Chris, 253
Corby, Jennifer, 157
Corcoran, Adrienne, 163
Corcos, Flaminio, 250
Cordero, Humberto, 175
Corduner, Allan, 225
Core, Ericson, 184
Corella, John R., 78
Corella, John, 83
Corey, Dave, 63
Corley, Al, 50
Corley, Annie, 86, 182
Cormack, Lynne, 165
Cornelius, Robert, 97
Corner, Clive, 244
Cornwell, Charlotte, 42
Coronado, Jose, 236
Corone, Antoni, 25, 63
Coronel, Xavier, 68
Corosky, Emma, 165
Corr, Eugene, 13
Corradi, Pio, 265
Corrado, Manuel, 93
Corrigan, Blaise, 112
Corrigan, Kevin, 158, 169-170
Corriveau, Andre, 241
Cortes, Antonio Vargas, 183
Cortés, Joaquín, 213
Corwin, Hank, 113
Cosby, Bill, 80, 273
Cosham, Ralph, 154
Cosi, 260
Cosmatos, George P., 154
Cosmos, Jean, 239
Cossacks Of The Kuban River, 223
Cossens, Anne, 255
Cosso, Pierre, 254
Costa, Danny, 181
Costa, James, 99
Costain, Matt, 125
Costales, Larry, 184
Costantini, Isabelle, 254
Costanzo, Julie, 155
Costanzo, Robert, 162
Costas, Celia, 30
Costello, Deirdre, 232
Costigan, C.C., 179
Costner, Anne, 184
Costner, Joe, 184
Costner, Kevin, 184, 273
Costner, Lily, 184
Cotillard, Marion, 263
Cottet, Mia, 51
Cottle, Jason, 151, 183
Cotto, Gelian, 236
Cotto, George Lian, 236
Cotton, Brant, 151
Cotton, Oliver, 222
Cottrell, Kevin, 157
Cottrell, Mickey, 49
Couch In New York, A 265-266
Coughlan, Frank, 256
Coulson, David, 214
Coulson, Peter, 125
Coulter, Bridgid, 179
Coulter, Clare, 80
Coulter, Michael, 125
Court, Gretchen Rennell, 82
Courtney, Dustin, 121
Courtney, Jeni, 67
Courtney, Judy, 67
Courtney, Lydia, 212
Coussein, Sophie, 263
Coutard, Raoul, 263
Couturier, Monique, 250
Couzan, Ras Majah, 109
Covarrubias, Jesus, 161
Covington, Maury, 11
Cowee, Stephen, 101
Cowgill, David, 114
Cowitt, Allison, 17, 98
Cowley, John, 256
Cox, Alex, 166
Cox, Brian, 114, 256, 273
Cox, Courteney, 52, 144, 273
Cox, Darryl, 122
Cox, Joel, 22, 183
Cox, Johanna, 137
Cox, John Henry, 175
Cox, Penney Finkelman, 62
Cox, Ronny, 180, 273
Coyle, Brendan, 253
Coyne, Susan, 165
Cozart, Cylk, 181
Crabbe, Ray, 181
Crabson, Tom, 49
Crabtree, Ane, 264

Cracchiolo, Dan, 181-182
Cracking Up, 169
Craft, Dirk Wallace, 184
Craig, Andrew, 174
Craig, Dana, 178
Craig, Donald, 173
Craig, Janet, 212
Craig, John, 104
Craig, Naomi, 145
Craig, Tony, 39
Crain, Gene, 168
Cramer, Rick, 118
Crane, Baynor Foy, 63
Crane, Simon, 186
Crane, Tony, 172
Cranham, Kenneth, 256
Cranna, Jim, 168
Cranshaw, Patrick, 82
Crash, 208,
Craven, Jayceen, 240
Craven, Matt, 169
Craven, Wes, 144, 172
Cravens, Nellie, 10
Crawford, Alexander, 154
Crawford, Harold G., 179
Crawford, Jared, 182
Crawford, Loren, 170
Crawford, Nikki, 151
Crawford, Rod, 38
Crawford, Thomas, 84
Crawley Creatures, 254
Crawley, Jane, 32
Crean, David, 80
Creevay, Allorah, 127
Creighton, Georgia, 159
Cremades, Michel, 263
Crenshaw, Michelle, 158
Crewson, Wendy, 84-85, 172
Crichton, Michael, 61
Crisafulli, Rachele, 247
Criscuolo, Lou, 79
Critical Care, 126
Crivello, Anthony, 178
Crockett, Tessa, 12
Crockett, Todd, 171
Croft, Bill, 98
Croft, Emma, 206
Croft, Jamie, 265
Croghan, Emma-Kate, 209
Croghan, Kate, 209
Cromwell, David, 88
Cromwell, James, 179, 182, 273
Cronauer, Gail, 180
Crone, Erik, 235
Cronenberg, David, 208
Cronenberg, Denise, 180, 208
Cronin, Jim, 194
Cronin, Juliet, 256
Cronin, Michael, 210
Cronkite, Walter, 80
Cronnelly, David, 186
Crosby, Denise, 147, 273
Crosby, Michael, 182
Crosby, Suzanne, 175
Crosman, Peter, 136
Cross, Alison, 25
Cross, Barbara, 84
Cross, Ben, 8, 273
Cross, Bill, 8
Cross, David, 16, 77
Cross, Jake, 28, 121
Cross, Jason "Jake", 28
Cross, Marcia, 38
Cross, Melissa, 168
Cross, Reverend John, 80
Cross, Roger R., 182
Crossan, Denis, 119
Crossley, Paul, 259
Crouch, Angie, 49
Crouch, Tim, 210
Crouse, Lindsay, 13, 273
Crow, Sheryl, 253
Crowden, Graham, 222
Crowden, Sarah, 183, 242
Crowe, Russell, 182, 260, 273
Crowley, Bob, 215
Crowley, June, 165
Crowson, Hilary, 222
Crudup, Billy, 13, 43, 159
Cruickshank, Marty, 225
Crumbley, Jennifer, 181
Crumpton, J.R., 168
Cruttwell, Greg, 81
Cruz, Anthony Jesse, 160
Cruz, Art, 176
Cruz, Carlos, 224
Cruz, Celia, 264
Cruz, Raymond, 133

Cruz, Wilson, 14, 52
Cruze, Josh, 21, 184
Cryer, Andrew, 125
Cryer, Jon, 173, 273
Cryer, Suzanne, 151
Crystal, Billy, 142-143, 180, 273
Crystal, Jennifer, 180
Csath, Geza, 266
Csokas, Marton, 214
Cuadra, Ulises, 100
Cuba, Joe, 264
Cube, Ice, 46, 155, 281
Cubillas, Fernando, 180
Cubison, Richard, 42, 131, 183
Cudlitz, Michael, 45
Cuel, Francois, 260
Cuervo, Alma, 112
Cuhr, Aaron, 178
Cui, Hans Hanbo, 126
Cuk, Vladimir, 38
Cuker, Elliot, 53, 170
Culkin, Michael, 216
Cullen, Max, 243
Cullen, Sean, 93
Cullison, Cherish, 157
Culp, Robert, 118, 273
Cumler, Tom, 105
Cumming, Alan, 51, 66, 271, 273
Cummings, Howard, 135
Cummings, Jim, 71, 130
Cummings, Richard, 100
Cummins, Gregory Scott, 127, 172
Cummins, Jack, 43
Cummins, Ron, 8, 13, 173
Cumpsty, Michael, 110
Cundari, John, 96
Cundey, Dean, 136
Cundieff, Rusty, 60
Cunliffe, Shay, 63
Cunlin, Tong, 222
Cunningham, Claire, 245
Cunningham, Glenn, 232
Cunningham, James, 10, 135
Cunningham, John, 102, 128, 131
Cunningham, Laura, 123
Cunningham, Lowell, 77
Cunningham, Michael, 154, 261
Cunningham, Officer Ken, 69
Cunningham, Patrick, 175
Cunningham, Sandra, 249
Cuoco, Kaley, 88
Cup a' Joe, 104
Curb Entertainment, 68,167
Curb, Mike, 68
Curnuck, Keelin, 173
Curran, Lynette, 257
Currie, Brian Hayes, 65
Currie, Bryan Hays, 11
Currie, Gordon, 161
Currie, Michael, 94
Currie, Richard, 174
Currie, Sheldon, 205
Currier, Terrence, 131, 137
Curry, Christopher, 128, 178
Curry, Mark, 127
Curry, Tim, 160, 273
Curtis, Austin, 109
Curtis, Bonnie, 61, 141
Curtis, Jamie Lee, 7, 12, 273
Curtis, Richard, 244
Curtis, Sarah, 229
Curtis, Simon, 215
Curtis-Brown, Robert, 244
Cusack, Ann, 45, 183
Cusack, Bill, 45, 65
Cusack, Joan, 45, 102-103, 168, 195, 273
Cusack, John, 45, 65, 130, 183, 271, 273
Cushman, Jessica, 88
Cutanda, Eddie, 69
Cutler, Emily, 157
Cutler, Max, 69
Cutler, Maximilian, 69
Cutler, Miriam, 159
Cutt, Michael J., 114
Cutt, Michael, 49
Cvijanovic, Zoran, 264
Cypress Hill, 157
Cyrille, Dufaut, 44
Czalkin, Juan Jose, 250
Czapla, Sanda, 160
Czerny, Henry, 110
D, Chuck, 157, 166
D, Deezer, 51
D, Donald "Notorious", 176
D, Heavy, 156, 159, 175
D'Adamo, Amadeo , 177

D'Adamo, Heather, 177
D'Addario, Paul, 175
D'Allessandro, Peter, 28
D'Alto, Louis 93
D'Amato, Senator Alfonse 183
d'Amboise, Jacques, 157
D'Angelo, Beverly , 60, 174, 179, 274
d'Angerio, Joe 68
D'Arbanville, Patti, 180
D'Augustine, Joe 178
D'Carol Randle, 177
D'Leon, Oscar, 264
D'Lyn, Shae 179
D'Olive, Gabriella 44
D'Onofrio, Vincent, 33, 77, 156, 166, 266, 275
D, Chuck, 157, 166
D, Deezer, 51
D, Heavy, 156, 159, 175
Da, Brat, 157
da Cunha Telles, Antonio, 258
Da Silva, Viriato José, 262
Dacia Films, 213
D'Acosta, Michelle, 161
Dafoe, Willem, 68, 273
Daggett, Richard, 168
Daher, Jamal, 261
Dahlbäck, Mats, 259
Dahlberg, Ingrid, 259
Dahlquist Jr., Eric, 22
Daiea, 226
Daily, Dan, 25
Dalarsurong, 260
Dalcour, Julian, 129
Daldoul, Hassen, 215
Dale, Laurence, 262
Dalesandro, Anthony, 174
Daley, Jennifer, 104
Daley, Pat, 104
Daley, Robert, 53
Dalferes, Lola, 129
Dalton Films, 257
Dalton, Ninkey, 11
Dalton, Robin, 257
Dalton, Azalea, 38
Dalton, Timothy, 18, 257, 273
Dalton, Wally, 13
Daly, Beth, 69
Daly, Nancy, 115
Daly, Peter-Hugo, 237
Daly, Tyne, 172, 273
Damant, Andrée, 221
Damer, Rod, 133
Damidov, Israel, 258
Damme, Kaatje Van, 255
Damon, Mark, 162, 166
Damon, Matt, 41, 134-135, 138-139, 192, 274
Damon, Una, 124
Dampf, Sarah, 146
Danaher, James, 125
Danan, Stephanie, 69
Dancehall Queen, 264
Dandry, Joseph, 35
Danes, Claire, 113, 134-135, 241, 274
Danese, Connie, 15
Dangar, Henry, 243
Dangerfield, Rodney, 15, 274
Dangerous Ground, 155
Daniel, Chic, 75
Daniel, Elisa, 184
Daniel, Gregory, 121
Daniel, Jesus, 236
Daniel, Lee, 19
Daniel, Sean, 131
Daniels, Alex, 181
Daniels, Glenn, 165
Daniels, Jeff, 63, 274
Daniels, Mark, 223
Danielson, Shell, 158
Dann, Frederick E., 47
Danna, Mychael, 110, 207, 241, 249
Danner, Blythe, 105, 183, 274
Danowsky, Joshua, 50
Dante's Peak, 17
Danvers, Mark, 264
Danylo, Roman, 182
Danza, Tony, 15, 274
Dao, Catherine, 181
Dapar, Jose, 49
Daperis, Daniel, 204
Dapkunaite, Ingeborga, 117
Darbo, Patrika, 68, 183
Dardenne, Jean-Pierre, 215
Dardenne, Luc, 215

DaRe, Eric, 122, 128
Daring, Mason, 13, 175
Darius, Armand, 128
Darko, Juliette, 141
Darling, David, 262
Darling, Jennifer, 71
Darlow, David, 97
Darr, Harriet Goldstein, 258
Darr, Lisa, 173
Das, Nandita, 235
Dash, Stacey, 175
Dashia, 171
Dasti, Sanayeh, 223
Dauda, Raven, 180
Daughtrey, Ben, 170
Daum, Menachem, 165
Davallou, Sara, 101
Davalos, Raul, 15
Davenport, Jack, 12
Davenport, Mark, 63
Davenport, Verda, 135
Davey, Bruce, 125, 180, 184
Davey, Edward, 212
Daviau, Robert, 179
David, Adam, 80
David, Alan, 39, 160, 174, 278
David, Angel, 94
David, Ellen, 153
David, Keith, 14, 71, 155, 175, 274
David, Pierre, 168, 172
Davidian, Peter, 101
Davidovich, Lolita, 24, 29, 274
Davids, Paul, 164
Davidson, Adam, 31
Davidson, Alan, 170
Davidson, Holly, 245
Davidson, Jeffrey L., 118
Davidson, John-Paul, 210
Davidson, Mary, 245
Davidson, Tommy, 23
Davies, Jeremy, 104, 116
Davies, Joseph, 144
Davies, Julie, 261
Davies, Oliver Ford, 229
Davila, Azalea, 38
Davila, John Bryant, 171
Davimos, John, 173
Davis Entertainment, 78, 159
Davis, Andrew Z., 49
Davis, Anna Maria, 21
Davis, Carl, 264
Davis, Cisco, 158
Davis, Colonius, 168
Davis, Dan, 106
Davis, Deanna, 176-177
Davis, Derek, 175
Davis, Don, 65, 163
Davis, Edythe, 63
Davis, Elliot, 157
Davis, Faye, 80
Davis, Garret, 21
Davis, Gene, 8
Davis, Hope, 31, 105, 266
Davis, Jason, 11, 116
Davis, John E., 86
Davis, John, 78, 159
Davis, Judy, 22, 25, 142, 214, 271, 274
Davis, Kate, 168
Davis, Kaye, 178
Davis, Kevin, 158, 169
Davis, Laura, 183
Davis, Margaret R., 183
Davis, Michael Reid, 151
Davis, Milton, Jr., 183
Davis, Noah Eli, 212
Davis, Ossie, 80, 274
Davis, Paul, 164
Davis, Philip, 237
Davis, Reginald, 154
Davis, Sharen, 95
Davis, Shaun, 216
Davis, Stan, 178
Davis, Tina, 168
Davis, Trina, 60
Davison, Jon, 128
Davison, Matthew, 179
Davitt, Karen, 230
Davoli, Ninetto, 266
Dawson, Brendan B., 178
Dawson, Judith, 183
Dawson, Kamala, 68
Day, Larry, 179
Day, Matt, 209, 243
Day-Lewis, Daniel, 256
Daylight productions, 167
Dayne, Taylor, 264
Dayton, Gregory, 250

Dayton, Jonathan, 132, 296
Daytrippers, The, 31
DC Comics, 181, 184
De Arce, Freddie, 236
de Baudry D'Asson, Armand, 236
De Bankole, Isaach, 100
De Fina, Barbara, 152, 170
De Garcia, Eva Cobo, 230
De Hart, Peggy, 171
de Keyser, David, 215
De La Fuente, Azucena, 236
De Laurentiis, Dino, 55
De Laurentiis, Martha, 55
De Laurentiis, Raffaella, 169
Del Frate, Gilles, 236
De Llano, Aymara, 100
De Luca, Michael, 151, 158
de Lucía, Paco, 213
De Marco, Dominick, 154
De Marco, Fabienne, 220
de Marco, Ross, 102
De Martini, Michael, 155
De Niro, Drena, 151
De Niro, Robert, 7, 92-93, 147, 150-151
Deacon, Gwenda, 182
Dead Heart, 266
Dead Men Can't Dance, 161
Deadly Films, 220
Deakins, Mark, 183
Deakins, Roger, 152
Dean, Allison, 68
Dean, Beverlee, 169
Dean, Everette, 34
Dean, Loren, 100, 124, 179, 274
Dean, Robertson, 95
Deane, Fredrick, 163
Dear, Devon, 181
Dear, H. Clay, 182
Dear, Susan, 181
Dear, William, 181
Dearing, Joanne, 178
Dearlove, James, 205
Dearsley, Verity, 42
Dearth, Doug, 45, 65
Deason, Paul, 141
Death In Granada, 236
Deathe, Jennifer, 138
de Azevedo, Lex, 166
Deblinger, David, 166, 170
Debney, John, 8, 37, 119
DeBonis, Marcia, 52, 88, 183
DeBono, Terri, 167
De Bont, Alexander, 68
De Bont, Jan, 68
deBorman, John, 231
DeBroux, Lee, 118
DeCadenet, Amanda, 164
De Capitani, Grace, 263
DeCerchio, Tom, 33
Decker, Anne Cullimore, 240
Decker, Joe, 11
Deckers, Daphne, 253
Deckert, Blue, 182
Decleir, Jan, 196
Deconstructing Harry, 142
DeCook, Irene, 30
De Costa, Sofia Bénard, 262
De Cotiis, Franco, 260
Dedet, Yann, 239, 260, 263
Dee, Kool Moe, 172
Dee, Ruby, 80, 274
Deedrick, Jeffrey, 147
Deegen, Sandrine, 255
Deep Crimson, 265-266
DeepFocus Prod., 159
Deeter, Monica, 137
Def Jam's How To Be A Player, 168
Def Pictures, 13
De Fabel, Erik Cazals, 255
De Falco, Luciana, 224
De Felitta, Raymond, 167
De Fries, Maya, 258
De Gaetano, Alessandro, 169
De Garmo, Diana, 173
Degennaro, Nino, 10
DeGovia, Jackson, 49
DeGregorio, Kayli, 49
DeGregorio, Kelsi, 49
Deguchi, Keiko, 172
Dehart, Wayne, 145
DeHaven, Gloria, 78, 274
de Heer, Rolf, 209
Deimel, Mark, 164
Deisgner, 107
De Jaeger, Tania, 220
de Jerez, La Paquera, 213

Dejesus, Anjeanette, 50
DeJesus, Anthony James, 32
Dekker, Leon, 216
de la Fontaine, Bertrand, 263
De La Fuente, Azucena, 236
De La Fuente, Francisco J., 180
de la Gandara, Beatriz, 171
De La Paz, Danny, 83
De La Pena, E.J., 98
De La Riva, Teresa, 157
de Mora, Robert, 39
De Neck, Didier, 207
De Poncheville, Marie Jaoul, 262
De Rossi, Portia, 144
De Rossi, Ugo, 266
de Salgado, Domini Hofmann, 61
De Salvo, Joe, 164
de Saumserez, Ben, 222
De Segonzac, Sylvie, 265
De Sol, Gabriel, 30
de Thibault, Montalembert, 263
De Victor, Claudio, 162
De Villiers, Gys, 155
Delaney, Hana, 83
Del Coro, Christopher, 41
Del Mundo, Liza, 184
Del Ruth, Thomas, 98
Del Sherman, Barry, 88
Del Sol, Gerald, 174
Del Sol, Gerry, 11
Del Toro, Benicio, 98
Del Toro, Guillermo, 99
Del Valle, Elaine, 27
DeLeon, Idalis, 159
Delfino, Majandra, 11
Delgado, Issac, 264
Delgado, Kim, 83
Del Gastor, Paco, 213
Delhomme, Benoit, 221
Deli, The , 175
Delilah, Mistress, 161
Delinquent, 171
Delk, Denny, 155
Dell'Abate ,Gary, 30
Dell'Agnese, Norma, 205
Dell'Olio, Joseph 171
Dell, Charlie, 37
Del Castillo, Mark, 260
Della Casa, Roberto, 224
Dellarosa, Frankie, 166
DeLoach, Heather, 18
Deloach, Nikki, 47
Delpy, Julie, 254, 272, 274
Delta, The, 168
Delterme, Marine, 221
DeLuca, Michael, 132
DeLuca, Thomas, 78
Delvecchio, Francis, 105
DeMarco, Frank, 175
Demeger, Robert, 237
Demetrakas, Johanna, 181
Deming, Peter, 21, 56, 144
Demme, Jonathan, 32, 67
de Moleron, Arnaud, 239
DeMornay, Rebecca, 166-167, 274
Dempsey, Patrick, 178, 274
Dempsey, Tim, 177
DeMunn, Jeffrey, 8, 174, 274
DeMuth, Manao, 34
Denard, David, 155
Denault, Jim, 157
Denberg, Lori Beth, 83
Dench, Judi, 193, 228-229, 253, 274
Denchev, Kliment, 105
Deniau, Jean-François, 236
Denicourt, Marianne, 263
Denis, Claire, 239
Denk, Alexander, 81
Denman, Trevor, 10, 78
Dennehy, Elizabeth, 101, 124
Dennen, Barry, 186
Dennis, Les, 238
Dennison, Gail, 169
Denniston, Paul, 169
Denny, Damien, 256
Denny, Simon Baker, 118, 182
Denove, Russell, 137, 160
Dente, Joey, 13
Denton, Allegra, 249
Denton, Jamie, 39, 75
Denys, Holly, 148
Denzongpa, Danny, 117
Deodhar, Neil, 157
DePalma, Laura, 216
DePaola, Dan, 94
Depardieu, Gerard, 96, 274

Depp, Johnny, 26-27, 201, 274
Deprez, Therese, 86, 104, 159
Deren, Nancy, 28
Deret, Jean-Claude, 254
Derman, David, 250
Derryberry, Debi, 71
DeRussy III, Myles, 173
Derval, Adrien, 98
Dervaux, Benoit, 215
Derwin, Jordan, 30
Desager, Frederic, 105
DeSalvo, Joe, 52
DeSando, Anthony, 166
DeSantis, Stanley, 21, 121
DeSarro, Candace, 173
Descanville, Tonio, 239
Descas, Alex, 213, 239
DeScenna, Linda, 37, 146
DeSena, Grace, 102
Desert, Alex, 122
Deshon, Donna, 17
Desiato, Ed, 170
Designated Mourner, The 215
Desjardins, Stephan, 181
Desmond, Patrick, 172
Desperate Pictures, 60
Desplat, Alexandre, 236
Desplechin, Arnaud, 263
Desplechin, Fabrice, 263
Desselle, Natalie, 158, 168
Dessler, Bruno, 126
Desyatnikov, Leonid, 202
Detoro, Kathleen, 144
Detour Film production, 19
Deutchman, Ira, 166
de Utrera, Fernanda, 213
Devaney, Gary, 179
Devany, William J., 176
DeVargas, Val, 79
Deveau, Marie-Sylvie, 99
Devenish, Desmond, 171
de Venere, Carmen, 222
Devilla, Debbie, 171
Devil's Advocate, The , 182
Devil's Own, The , 35
de Villenueve, Daisy, 245
de Villeneuve, Jane, 245
de Villeneuve, Poppy, 245
Devin, Miranda, 171
DeVincentis, D.V., 45
DeVincentis, Sarah, 45
Devine, Christine, 118, 151
Devine, Kelly, 83
Devine, Loretta, 97
Devine, Margaret, 158
DeVito, Danny, 71, 124, 134-135, 182, 274
DeVito, Tommy, 63
De Vivaise, Caroline, 236
Devlin, Billy, 65
Devlin, C. Tad, 81
Devlin, Tim, 159
Devon, Helen, 251
Devon, Tony, 123
Devos, Emmanuelle, 263
DeWalt, Robert, 155
Dewey, Alice, 71
Dewey, Rebecca, 179
deZarn, Tim, 184
Dhargyal, Samdup, 117
Dhat, 261
Dhillon, Vinny, 232
Dhondup, Tashi, 152
Dhup, Garima, 207
Di Ciaula, Pia, 238
Di Giacomo, Franco, 266
Di Giaimo, Louis, 94
Dial, Rick, 145
Diallo, Gregory, 255
Diamant, Illana, 44
Diamant, Moshe, 44
Diamant, Sigal, 44
Diamond, Lou, 98
Diamond, Val, 10
DiBenedetto, John, 27, 53
DiCaprio, Leonardo 4, 6, 185-187, 200, 272, 274
DiCicco, Kevin, 87
DiCillo, Tom, 86
Dick, Kirby, 132, 266
Dickens, Kim, 162

Dickerson, Angela, 60
Dickie, Maggie, 230
Dickinson, Elizabeth Anne, 13
Dickson, Deborah, 157
Dickson, Neil, 51
Die Hauskunst & Romb, 241
Diego, Eliseo Alberto, 224
Diehl, John, 38, 100, 118, 182
Diem, Rob, 44
Different For Girls, 237
Diggs, Kip, 176
DiGiaimo, Louis, 27
Digital Media, 171, 264
Dilberti, Luigi, 224
Dill, Bill, 158
Dillane, Frank, 248
Dillane, Stephen, 248
Dillard, Angie, 144
Dillard, Richard, 159, 174
Dilley, Leslie, 112
Dillon, Kevin, 264, 275
Dillon, Matt, 9, 102, 272, 275
Dillon, Paul, 56
Dillon, Teddy-Lee, 179
DiLucca, Jeff, 63
DiMaggio, Lou, 179
DiMauro, Joanne, 102
Dimension Films, 99, 144, 230
Dimitri, Nick, 155
Dimitrijevic, Slobodan, 112
Di Napoli, Ruben Orlando, 250
Dindal, Mark, 180
Dingas, Jack, 175
Dingman, Tony, 135
Dingo, Ernie, 266
Dinkins, Lisa, 173
Dion, Celine, 186
DiPalma, Carlo, 142
DiPaola, Frank, 164
Dippé, Mark A.Z., 90
DiSanti, John, 8
Disappearance Of Garcia Lorca, The 236
Dishy, Bob, 29
Ditty, Scott, 65
Diveny, Mary, 102
Divoff, Andrew, 84, 172
Dixie, Jason, 89
Dixon, Jade Janise, 177
Dixon, Jerry, 112
Dixon, Leslie, 39
Dixon, MacIntyre, 102
Dixon, Matthew, 171
Dixon, Richard, 183
Dixon, Shane, 63, 182
Dixon, Tim, 212
Diz, Jessica, 68
Djabri, Aissa, 221
Djadam, Mostefa, 259
Djodat, Shaghayegh, 223
Djola, Badja, 179
Djordjadze, Nana, 213
Doake, Michelle, 257
Dobbin, Simon, 259
Dobrowolski, Marek, 44
Dobtcheff, Vernon, 180
Docstar, 223
Dodd, Marian, 87
Dodds, K.K., 45, 123, 240
Doe, John, 24, 121, 164
Doel, Frances, 128
Doerk, Chris, 223
Doernberg, Dave, 174
Dog, Sen, 157
Dogg Pound, 157
Dogs: The Rise and Fall of an All-Girl Bookie Joint, 177
Doherty, Christine, 168
Doherty, Josie, 256
Doherty, Kathryn, 168
Doherty, Matthew, 168
Doherty, Shannen, 60, 275
Doillon, Jacques, 218
Dokuchitz, Jonathan, 130
Dolan, Michael, 163, 275
Dolker, Lobsang, 265
Dollar, Aubrey, 137, 173
Dolleris, Helle Charotte, 260
Doman, John, 93
Domingue, Norris, 179
Dominguez, Lara, 236
Dominguez, Wade, 32
Don, Diezzle, 157
Don, Robin Cameron, 251
Donachie, Ron, 12, 186
Donaghy, Michael, 163
Donaghy, Sean, 256
Donaldson, J. Mark, 84

Donaldson, Peter, 249
Donaldson, Roger, 17
Donat, Peter, 101, 126, 275
Donatacci, Camille, 30
Donati, Danilo, 266
Donato, Marc, 249
Donatone, Mario, 224
Dong, Arthur, 159
Dong, Jeffrey, 126
Dongtse, Ama Ashe, 117
Donley, Maureen, 130
Donnelly, Candice, 241
Donnelly, Daragh, 256
Donnelly, Jesse J., 173
Donnelly, Miles, 224
Donner, Lauren Shuler, 49, 182
Donner, Richard, 181-182
Donnie Brasco, 27
Donohoe, Amanda, 37, 132, 275
Donohue, John, 184
Donoso, Carlos, 221
Donovan, Ida, 205
Donovan, Martin, 210
Donovan, Noel, 231
Donovan, Tate, 71, 180, 275
Dons Quixote Production, 178
Donsky, Seth Michael, 178
Doolan, Robbie, 212
Dooley, Paul, 16, 123, 275
Doolin, Richard, 126
Dooling, Richard, 159
Doonan, Mark, 13
Dopazo, Cecilia, 259
Doppelganger Films, 156
Doraine, Allen, 33
Dorcester Youth Collaborative Extreme Close-Up, 69
Dorff, Stephen, 25, 32, 273, 275
Dorfmeister, Tom, 121
Dorin, Ryan, 124
Dority, Traci, 45
Dorjee, Ngawang, 152
Dorleac, Jean Pierre, 98
Dorn, Dody, 132, 266
Dornan, Kevin, 178
Doroudt-Chi, Khalil, 223
Dorrian, John, 175
Dossett, John, 176
Dossey, David, 171
Doty, David, 244
Doudina, Jenia, 258
Doug, Doug E., 23
Dougherty, Darby, 174
Dougherty, Jill, 181
Dougherty, Marion, 179-181, 184
Dougherty, Suzi, 209
Doughten, Chris, 180
Doughty, Richard, 144
Douglas, Amy Lee, 181
Douglas, Freddy, 225
Douglas, Illeana, 68, 88, 275
Douglas, Lionel, 127
Douglas, Michael, 7, 75, 101, 135, 275
Douglas, Monique, 69
Douglas, Norman, 167
Douglas, Sam, 216, 251
Doukoure, Cheik, 259
Doumanian, Jean, 142
Doumanian, John, 142
Dourdan, Gary, 122, 133
Douridas, Chris, 100, 184
Dourif, Brad, 133, 275
Dove Entertainment, 155
Dove, Billy, 158
Dove, Rita, 166
Doven, Andrea, 112
Dow, Bill, 144
Dow, Jo, 183
Dowd, Ann, 50, 52
Dowd, Billy, 94
Dowe, Don, 8
Dowling, Roger, 265
Dowling, Suzanne, 209
Dowling, Timothy, 18
Down, Lesley-Anne, 15
Downe, Pam, 210
Downer, Jeffrey, 172
Downey, Laura, 178
Downey, Leo, 155
Downey, Robert, Jr., 132, 178, 273, 275
Downey, Robert, Sr., 121
Downie, Ian, 39
Dowridge, Denver, 141
Dowse, Denise, 128
Doyle, Carol, 115

Doyle, Chris, 144
Doyle, Christopher, 222, 243
Doyle, Jessica, 213
Doyle, Julian, 242
Doyle, Patrick, 27
Doyle, Richard, 84
Doyle, Roddy, 220
Doyle-Murray, Brian, 16, 148
Dozo, Marie-Helene, 215
Drago, Joe, 53, 132
Dragojevic, Srdjan, 264
Dragon Pictures, 13, 248
Draizin, Doug, 21
Drake, Bebe, 168
Drake, Dolores, 144
Drake, Larry, 244
Drake, Nick, 260
Draper, Ted, 155
Dre, Dr., 157
Dream Quest Images, 65, 81
Dream With The Fishes, 69
DreamWorks Pictures, 112
Dresbach, Terry, 55
Drescher, Fran, 18, 275
Dreyer, Nelle, 132
Dreyfus, James, 205
Dreyfuss, Richard, 53, 275
Driesschen, Mark, 144
Driscoll, Robin, 244
Drissi, Tomy E., 176
Drivala, Jenny, 262
Driver, Minnie, 45, 138-139, 195, 273, 275
Dromkert, Wichert, 220
Droog, Bernhard, 196
Druce, Kim, 158
Drumgold, David, 158
Drummond, Alice, 52, 62, 102, 178
Drummond, Carlos, 266
Drunks, 158
Druyan, Ann, 181
Dryden, Tom, 155
DuArt, 30, 171, 173
Dube, Desmond, 154
Dubinchak, Lucy, 258
Dubinet, Ann, 115
Dublin, Jessica, 157
Dubroux, Daniele, 215
Dubroux, Daniele, 215
Dubrow, Michael, 163
Du Bois, Victor, 180
Dubus, Jack, 250
Duchovny, David, 122, 275
Duclos, Philippe, 236, 263
Ducret, Hélène, 261
Ducsay, Bob, 179
Dudelson, Robert, 169
Dudgeon, Neil, 237
Dudley, Anne, 210, 232
Duell, William, 102
Duff, Julia, 219
Duffin, Shay, 164, 186
Duffy, Brendan "Reno", 68
Duffy, Helen, 55, 167
Duffy, John, 8
Duffy, Karen, 15
Duffy, Thomas F., 61
Duffy, Veronica, 256
Du Fresne, Georges, 255
Dugan, Charles, 11
Dugan, Dennis, 11, 181
Dugarov, Chimit-Dorzhi, 265
Duge, Melissa, 174
Duggan, Kerrie, 256
Duggan, Patrick, 222
Duguay, Christian, 105
Dukakis, Olympia, 88, 259, 275
Duke, Bill, 97, 275
Duke, Deborah, 177
Duke, O.L., 100
Dukes, Eloise, 135
Dumas, Charles, 93, 112
Du Merle, Antoine, 218
Dumont, James, 112
Dumont, Myles, 165
Dun, Dennis, 156, 163
Dunaway, Faye, 9, 158, 173, 275
Duncan, Adrianne, 178
Duncan, Cerall, 34
Duncan, Chip, 199
Duncan, John, 183
Duncan, Lois, 119
Duncan, Peter, 214
Duncan, Virginia, 183
Duncombe Jr., Charles A., 162
Dunford, Christine, 67
Dunham, Pamela, 155
Dunigan, Alverta Perkins, 129

Duning, John, 264
Dunlop, Alan, 222
Dunn, Andrew, 181, 210
Dunn, Barry, 205
Dunn, Beverley, 262
Dunn, John, 52
Dunn, Kathleen, 186
Dunn, Kevin, 38, 88
Dunn, Melissa, 168
Dunn, Wally, 102
Dunn, William, 44
Dunn-Hill, John, 153
Dunne, Catherine, 256
Dunne, Dominick, 181
Dunne, Griffin, 181, 275
Dunne, Martin, 35, 256
Dunne, Pecker, 231
Dunne, Shane, 35
Dunne, Sharon, 256
Dunne, Stuart, 220
Dunst, Kirsten, 130, 151
Dunster, Maurice, 162
Dunster, Wilson, 155
Dunwell, Peter, 216
Dunye, Cheryl, 158
Duong, Phuong, 69
Duplat, Francois, 28
Dupontel, Albert, 236
Dupree, Stephen, 86
Dupri, Jermaine, 157
Du Prez, John, 242
Dupuis, Matthew, 105
Dupuy, Marcelle, 221
Duquenne, Pascal, 207
Duran, Bonnie, 155
Duran, Dan, 180
Duran, Eduardo, 155
Duran, Jim, 212
Duran, Perico, 236
Duran, Richard, 65
Durand, Patrick, 215
Durango, Christian, 79
Durbin, Wade, 38
Durden, Denny, 261
Durden, Paul, 261
Durden, Richard, 210
Durham, Sarah, 161
Duris, Romain, 221
Duritz, Adam, 116
Duronslet, Mara, 122, 128
Dury, Ian, 237
Dusseldorp, Marta, 211
Dust Of Life, 261
Duthie, Michael J., 118
Dutt, Avijit, 207
Dutton, Charles S., 99
Duva, Christopher, 105
Duval, Daniel, 250
Duval, James, 60
DuVall, Howard, 49
Duvall, Robert, 145, 192, 274-275
Duvall, Shelley, 174, 275
Dworkin, Paul Joseph, 63
Dwyer, Finola, 210
Dwyer, Karyn, 165
Dye, Dale A., 128
Dye, Dale, 63
Dyer, Gretchen, 164
Dyer, Julia, 164
Dyer, Stephen, 164
Dykstra, John, 181
Dyktynski, Matthew, 209
Dysinger, Elaine, 60
Dyson, Maisha, 177
Dyson, Michael, 180
Dzambazov, Igor, 248
Dzevad, Pejdah, 248
Dzingeni, Godrey, 155
Dzundza, George, 23, 275
E-40, 157
Eagan, Daisy, 161
Eagle Eye Films Inc., 176
Earl, Elizabeth, 125
Early Morning Films, 176
Early, Austin Howard, 184
Easley, Doug, 86
Eason, Bo, 49
East Side Story, 223
East West Film Partners, 156
East, Guy, 164
East, Martin, 186
Easterbrook, John, 47
Eastin, Steve, 65
Eastman, Rodney, 161
Eastwood, Alison, 22, 183
Eastwood, Clint, 22, 183, 275
Eastwood, Jayne, 39
Eastwood, Kimber, 22

Eastwood, Lora Gomez, 178
Eaton, Ian, 171
Eaton, Lance, 151
Eaton, Rebecca, 229
Eaves, John, 203
Ebden, John, 162
Eberhard, Jude Pauline, 174
Eberlein, Scott, 182
Ebersole, Christine, 62
Ebert, Gerardo, 117
Eberts, Jake, 179, 242
Ebouaney, Eriq, 221
Eccles, Ted, 151
Echegoyen, Helena, 34, 156
Echols, Jennifer, 180
Eckert, John M., 23
Eckhart, Aaron, 89, 197
Eckstein, Paul, 97
Ecoffey, Jean-Philippe, 255
Economou, Bruce, 29, 137
Ecosse Films, 229
Eddy, Jan, 182
Eddy, Steady, 230
Edell, Elaine Hastings, 161
Edelman, Abra, 87, 162
Edelman, Daniel, 171
Edelman, Randy, 46, 63, 98, 137
Edelson, Kenneth, 142
Edelstein, Lisa, 148
Edelstein, Polly, 168
Edgar, Fiona, 214
Edge, The , 107
Edlund, Richard, 84
Edmond, Martell Hill, 109
Edmond, Valerie, 12
Edmonds Entertainment, 109
Edmonds, Brian, 266
Edmonds, Chris, 132
Edmonds, Kenneth "Babyface" 109
Edmonds, Kevon, 109
Edmonds, Melvin, 109
Edmonds, Tracey E., 109
Edson, John, Jr., 49
Edson, Richard, 68, 79, 166
Education Of Little Tree, The , 179
Edward, Wilma, 68
Edward-Stevens, Michael, 230
Edwards, Chris, 132
Edwards, Daryl, 88
Edwards, Edward, 173
Edwards, Eric, 93
Edwards, Jessica, 69
Edwards, Jonathon, 176
Edwards, Paddi, 71
Edwards, Rick, 100
Edwards, Ross, 211
Edwards, Stacy, 89, 197
Edwards, Steve, 49
Efimov, Igor, 180
Efron, Marshall, 167
Efros, Mel, 127
Efthymiou, Stavros Andonis, 209
EFX, 157
Egan, Peter, 244
Egan, Susan, 71
Egerman, Michael, 110
Eggar, Samantha, 71, 275
Egi, Stan, 211
Egleson, Shannon, 138
Ego Film Arts, 249
Egoyan, Atom, 249
Eguren, Raúl, 224
Ehle, Jennifer, 211
Ehrlich, Joy, 22
Eichinger, Bernd, 206
Eidel, Carey, 61
Eidelman, Cliff, 18, 182
Eidsvold, Eindride, 235
Eidsvold, Gard B, 235
Eigeman, Chris, 163
8 Heads in a Duffel Bag, 44
Eighth Day, The 207
Eiht, MC, 157
Einstein, Clifford, 75
Eisenmann, Albert Able, 15
Eisner, David, 138
Eisner, Philip, 91
Ejiofor, Chiwetel, 140-141
Ejogo, Carmen, 10
Ekins, Bud, 179
Ekins, Susan, 179
Eklund, Nils, 259
El Dror, Joseph, 258
El-Kadi, Nameer, 81
Elbaum, Stéfan, 236
Elder, Judyann, 10
Elder, Stacey, 132
Eldridge, Lehla, 222
Elephant Studio, 172

Elfman, Danny, 77, 136, 138, 144
Elfman, Jenna, 45
Elgood, Rick, 264
El Gran Combo, 264
El Rincon, Banda, 60
El Zabar, Kahil, 34
Elias, Buddy, 264
Elise, Gillian, 261
Elizondo, Hector, 8, 275
Elk, Rob, 83, 181
Elkin Entertainment, 154
Elkin, Michelle, 78
Elkins, Hilly, 154
Ellaraino, 182
Ellen, Cliff, 230
Ellerni, Ben, 93
Ellery, Peter, 180
Ellingson, Tyruben, 99
Elliot, Bill, 68
Elliott, Alison, 247
Elliott, Paul, 109
Elliott, Peter, 12, 66
Elliott, William, 10
Ellis, Chris, 65, 151, 244
Ellis, Greg, 186
Ellis, Jimmy, 160
Ellis, Margaret, 23
Ellis, Mike, 219
Ellis, Riley Kathryn, 10
Ellis, Terrance, 173
Ellison, Brian, 260
Ellroy, James, 182
Ellwood, Eddie, 216
Elmaleh, Gad, 259
Elmblad, Jonas, 154
Elmes, Frederick, 110
Elmiger, Suzy, 153, 167
Elohev, Halil, 258
El'Ouzeri, Djellali, 239
Elrod, Lu, 151
Elsen, John, 8
Elston, Tim, 262
Elswit, Robert, 121, 253
Elswitt, Robert, 13
Elvin, William M., 181
Elwes, Cary, 37, 114, 275
Elysian Dreams, 153
Emanuele, Richard, 180
Embesi, Connie, 182
Embry, Ethan, 179, 274-275
Embry, John, 144
Emely, 81
Emeralde Productions, 176
Emerson, Sayuri Higuchi, 172
Emery, Lisa, 102
Emiabata, Tasilimn, 230
Emmanuelli, François, 221
Emmerich, Noah, 93
Emmett, Charles, 37
Emmich, Cliff, 146
Emmons, Wayne, 135
Emory, Tracy O., 93
Emoto, Akira, 226
End Of Summer, 165
End Of Violence, The , 100,
Endelman, Stephen, 32, 160, 170,
  230
Endre, Lena, 259
Engelman, Robert, 132
English, Dean, 212
English, Eve, 99
Englund, Robert, 172, 275
Engstrom, Charles, 67
Engstrom, Lars, 259
Ennis, John, 66
Enos III, John, 60
Enquist, Per Olov, 235
Ensign, Frank, 122
Ensign, Michael, 186-187, 260
Entriken, Matt, 128
Entwisle, Julie, 102
Eon Productions, 253
Epling, Charley J., 182
Epp, Michael, 263, 265
Epper, Tony, 14
Eppolito, Lou, 21
Epps Jr, Jack ., 46
Epps, Omar, 144
Epstein, Alvin, 175
Epstein, Brothers, 258
Epstein, Jonathan, 141
Epstein, Julie, 258, 266
Epstein, Max, 258
Epstein, Willie, 258
Erb, Greg, 174
Erb, Stephanie, 128
Erbe, Kathryn, 69

Eric's Boy, 56
Erickson, C.O., 114
Ericson, Mark, 13
Eriksen, Geir, 164
Ermey, R. Lee, 13, 127, 161, 276
Ernest Perry, Jr., 37
Ernesto, 25, 160, 245, 264
Ernotte, Marc, 236
Ernst, Robert, 155
Ertmanis, Victor, 180
Ervin, Julia, 147
Escalera, Rachel, 132
Escamilla, Joaquin, 78
Escandon, Jose, 260
Escobar, Daniel R., 18
Escoffier, Jean Yves, 98, 138, 174
Eser, Janin, 154
Esformes, Jack, 151
Esmeralda, Merche, 213
Esparza, Moctesuma, 179, 236
Esphagen, Claes, 259
Espindola, Patricia Reyes, 265
Espinoza, Jeremy, 183
Esposito, Giancarlo, 82, 100, 276
Esposito, Jennifer, 50, 166
Essex Features, 205
Essman, Susie, 49
Esten, Charles, 184
Estevez, Ramon, 154, 292
Eszterhas, Joe, 123
Eszterhas, Naomi, 123
Ettema, Dale, 49
Ettinger, Wendy, 122
Eubanks, Shannon, 183
Eureka Pictures, 105
Euro Space, 258
Eustace, Mary Jo, 39
Evangelisti, Noel, 182
Evans, Art, 10
Evans, Bruce A., 29
Evans, Catherine, 37
Evans, David Wayne, 23
Evans, Dick "Skip", 65
Evans, Fred, 12
Evans, Jenny, 261
Evans, John H., 182
Evans, Lee, 146, 198, 216
Evans, Llyr, 261
Evans, Robert, 42
Evans, Stephen, 210, 247
Evans-Jones, Jonathan, 186
Evanson, F., 31
Eve's Bayou, 129
Evein, Agnes, 239
Event Horizon, 91
Everberg, Kirsten, 49
Everett, Tom, 84
Evetts, H.P., 184
Ewan, Nick, 170
Ewell, Dwight, 40-41, 166
Excess Baggage, 98
Eye Of God, 122
Eyre, Peter, 250
Eyres, Jeff, 169
Ezekiel, Jerry, 216
Ezenagu, Derek, 216
Ezralow, Marc, 116
Faber, Christian, 163
Faber, George, 218, 237
Faber, George, 218, 237
Fabre, Jean-Marc, 236
Fabrizio, 155, 186
Fagan, Jo Ann, 166
Fahey, Emma, 205
Fahey, Mary-Anne, 230
Faia, Renee, 172
Fair and Square, 89
Fairbank, Christopher, 216
Faison, Frankie R., 170
Faison, Frankie, 9
Faithfull, Marianne, 260
Falco, Edie, 93, 159
Falcon, Andre, 239
Falconer, Hamish, 180
Falgoux, Denis, 221
Falk, Anders, 186
Fall, 164
Fallon, Siobhan, 21, 77, 176
Fallteen, Brian, 180
Faltisco, Robert, 133
Family Name, 170
Fancovic, Ines, 248
Fancy, Richard, 24, 62
Fangmeier, Stefen, 68
Fanning, Dennis, 96
Fano, Jacqueline, 218

Fanzy, Monguehy, 141
Faragallah, Ramsey, 112
Farah, Jamila, 239
Faranda, Lee, 84
Farbman, Robin, 174
Fardon, Joshua, 49, 83, 182
Farer, Ronnie, 27
Fargeau, Jean-Pol, 239
Farid, Zaid, 63
Farina, Dennis, 39, 276
Farkas, Jo, 72, 83
Farleigh, Lynn, 125
Farley, Chris, 11, 297-298
Farley, John, 11
Farley, Kevin, 11
Farley, Rupert, 229
Farmer & Chase, 155
Farmer, Alvin, 11
Farmer, Bill, 71
Farmer, Blaine, 179
Farmer, Cyrus, 32
Farmer, Gary, 241
Farmer, Jim, 86
Farmer, Ken, 174
Farrar, Robert, 183
Farrell, Christine, 110
Farrell, Suzanne, 167
Farrell, Tom Riis, 52, 183
Farrell, Victoria, 52, 166
Farrelly, Sue, 262
Farruco, 213
Farruquito, 213
Fasanella, Jody, 184
Fassio, Anne, 250
Fast, Adam, 160
Fast, Cheap & Out Of Control, 116
Fathers' Day, 180
Fatt, Lester, 177
Fattori, Laura, 152
Faulcon, Kent, 77, 126
Faust, Leo, 259
Favre, Marianne, 218
Fawcett, Alan, 153
Fawcett, Farrah, 145, 174, 276
Fawcett, John, 171
Fay, Meagen, 180
Faye, Denise, 27, 163
Faysse, Dominique, 213
Fazio, Santo, 53
Featherstone, Angela, 65
Fedotova, Valentina, 202
Feeney, Caroleen, 159
Fei, Xie, 260
Feig, Erik, 119
Feignboim, Tal, 258
Feinstein, Bruce, 253
Feitshans IV, Buzz, 137, 154, 160
Feldberg, Mark, 11
Feldman, Randy, 10
Feldman, Shari, 172
Feldsher, Paul, 247
Feldshuh, Tovah, 263, 276
Feliciano, Cheo, 264
Fellner, Eric, 244
Fellowes, Julian, 253
Fellows, Graham, 237
Fellows, Nicole, 133, 183
Fellows, Russell Lee, 122
Feng, Hsu, 222
Fenn, Suzanne, 260, 264
Fennel, Mitch, 176
Fennell, Chris, 179
Fenner, Lowell, 179
Fenton, Mike, 17, 98
Fenton, Sean, 151
Feore, Colm, 53, 75, 126
Ferguson, Chamblee, 159
Ferguson, Chloe, 209
Ferguson, David, 262
Ferguson, J. Don, 119
Ferguson, John Pyper, 160
Ferguson, Matthew, 241
Ferguson, Meresa, 160
Ferguson, Phoebe, 209
Ferguson, Sharon, 78
Ferland, Guy, 123
Fernandes, David, 236
Fernandes, Joao, 60
Fernandes, Millor, 258, 264
Fernandez, Benjamin, 169
Fernandez, Fil, 171
Fernandez, Giselle, 151
Fernandez, Jonathan, 55
Fernández, Pedro, 224
Ferraro, Chris, 156
Ferraro, Geraldine A., 181

Ferraro, Geraldine, 166
Ferreira, Joel, 262
Ferrell, Conchata, 24, 276
Ferrell, Stephanie, 169
Ferrell, Will, 56
Ferrer, Miguel, 144, 236, 276
Ferrerira, Victor, 101
Ferretti, Daniele, 224
Ferretti, Dante, 152
Ferretti, Robert A., 154, 182
Ferri, Claudia, 105
Ferrier, Noel, 211
Ferrigno, Lou, 71
Ferrin, Ingrid, 181
Ferris, Michael, 101
Ferris, Peter, 209
Ferro, Pablo, 178
Ferrol, Sharon, 121
Ferrucci, Frank, 162
Ferry, April, 136, 154
Fesch, Pierette, 202
Fessenden, Hart, 175
Fessenden, Larry, 175
Fetishes, 161
Feyz, Nick, 172
Fiander, Lewis, 230
Fichtner, William, 9, 127, 181
Fiedler, John, 241
Field, Arabella, 17
Field, Ted, 13
Field, Todd, 155
Fields, Christopher John, 101
Fields, Gigi, 244
Fields, Karyn, 180
Fieldsteel, Robert, 159
Fiennes, Ralph, 257, 275-276
Fierce Creatures, 12
Fierstein, Harvey, 169, 276
Fifth Element, The , 216
Figgis, Mike, 132
Figgis, Susie, 210, 232
Figment Film, 240
Figment Films, 261
Figueroa, Efrain, 83
Filipe, Ruy, 155
Filleau, Jean-Baptiste, 265
Film Australia, 258, 265
Film Board Berlin Brandenburg,
  265
Films Sans Frontieres, 266
Filmstifung North Phine
  Westphalia, 241
FilmWorks, 155, 173, 264
Filpi, Carmen, 15, 146
Finan, Tom, 71
Finch, Pandora, 230
Finch, Roy, 155
Fincher, David, 101
Finck, Bill, 212
Fine Line Features, 52, 59-60, 142,
  164, 170, 174, 208-209, 224,
  249, 251
Fine, Nancy, 164
Fine, Russell Lee, 122
Fine, Russell, 178
Finelli, Lenny, 156
Finerman, Wendy, 125
Finfer, David, 51
Finizza, Mark, 28
Fink, John, 181
Fink, Kellen, 62
Finkel, Fyvush, 263
Finkelman, Alexandria Nicole, 161
Finkelman Cox, Penney, 62
Finlayson, Bruce, 259
Finley, Buck, 170
Finley, Cameron, 98
Finn, Devon, 249
Finn, John, 8
Finn, Mali, 96, 181-182, 186
Finnegan, John, 179
Finney, Albert, 115, 276
Fiondella, Jay, 182
Fiorentino, Linda, 76-77, 170, 276
Fire Down Below, 182
Fire, 235
Firesten, Marcia, 166
Firestone, Roy, 156
Firkins, Christine, 68
First Kiss production, 98
First Look Pictures, 14, 50, 177,
  215, 225, 237, 259
First Run Features, 158, 165, 205,
  218, 235, 258, 266
Firth, Colin, 106, 276
Firth, Peter, 141, 276
Fischer, David Lloyd, 165
Fischer, Marc S., 11

Fischera, Lanie, 175
Fish Productions, 12
Fish, Chad, 67
Fishburne, Laurence, 91, 97, 276
Fisher, Carrie, 56, 276
Fisher, Danny, 156
Fisher, Frances, 38, 181, 186, 276
Fisher, George, 98
Fisher, Jack, 156
Fisher, John, 177
Fisher, Stephanie, 79
Fisher, SW, 37
Fisher, Tom, 81
Fisher, Warna, 99
Fishley, Dave, 216
Fishwick, Daryl, 232
Fitzgerald, Ciaran, 212, 256
Fitzgerald, Glenn, 110
Fitzgerald, Lewis, 266
Fitzgerald, Tara, 219, 276
Fitzgerald, Wilbur T., 23
Fitzhugh, Adam, 13
Fitzpatrick, Colleen, 37
Fitzpatrick, Delanie, 27
Fitzpatrick, Peter, 262
Fitzpatrick, Richard, 138, 180, 262
Fitzpatrick, Tom, 177
Fitzpatrick, Tony, 97
Five Before the Miracle, 164
Flack, Sarah, 159
Flagg, Tom, 110
Flagge, Ron, 129
Flaherty, Lanny, 80
Flaherty, Stephen, 130
Flamenco, 213
Flan de Coco Films, 83
Flanagan, Bob, 132
Flanagan, Markus, 137
Flanagan, Tommy J., 75
Flanagan, Tommy, 42, 101
Flanigan, Sara, 137
Flannery, Bill, 101
Flaska, Carrie, 30
Flatman, Barry, 165
Flaum, Erica, 116
Flaum, Seth, 179
Flav, Flava, 30
Fleck, Jane Allison, 173
Fleder, Gary, 114
Fleet, James, 210
Fleischer, Charles, 13
Fleischer, Henrik, 260
Fleming, Jacqueline, 34
Fleming, Rachael, 240
Fleming, Rachel, 261
Fleming, Robert Barry, 173, 182
Fleming, William, 205
Flemyng, Jason, 210, 225
Flenoury, Roosevelt, 141
Fletcher, Anne, 121, 144
Fletcher, Brendan, 87
Fletcher, Damen, 137
Fletcher, Dexter, 183
Fletcher, Edward, 186
Fletcher, Louise, 63, 276
Fletcher, Russell, 230
Flex, 32, 38
Flint, James "Bruiser", 38
Flipping, 155
Floch, Jérôme, 236
Flockhart, Calista, 123, 158
Flodin, Christer, 259
Floquet, Anton, 167
Flordio, Bianca, 265
Flores, Lysa, 83
Flores, Martha, 180
Flores, Victoria Elena, 180
Flores, Von, 105
Florido, Giovanni, 265
Flotats, Josep María, 263
Flower, Buck, 172
Flowers, Jim, 47
Flowers, Kim, 133
Floyd, Darren, 168
Flubber, 136
Fluharty, Orril, 69
Flury, Myriam, 265
Flynn, Beau, 14, 118
Flynn, Jimmy, 138
Flynn, Kimberly, 169
Flynn, Larry, 122
Flynn, Miriam, 16, 179
Flynn, Neil, 178
Flynn, Steven, 67
Foch, Nina, 62, 276
Fofanah, Abu Bakaar, 141
Fogarassi, Alpar, 266
Fogerty, Adam, 183, 219

Folache, Macarena, 265
Folan, Berts, 256
Foley, Don, 256
Foley, Jeremy, 17
Foley, Joe, 177
Foley, Shannon K., 11
Folgert, Emmett, 69
Folk, Alexander, 21, 122, 172
Folk, Robert, 23, 33, 82
Folkes, Karen, 118
Folland, Alison, 52, 138
Follow Me Home, 155
Folman, Ari, 258
Folsom, Betsy, 51
Fonda, Bridget, 24, 147, 260, 276
Fonda, Nancy, 132, 136
Fonda, Peter, 67, 192, 276
Fong, Alex, 157
Fonlupt, Jean François, 100
Fontaine, Bruce, 230
Fontaine, Stéphane, 263
Fonteyn, Christina, 155
Foo, Sasha, 49, 118
Foolish Mortal Films, 169
Foord, Cameron, 159
For Ever Mozart, 262
For Richer Or Poorer, 137
For Roseanna, 224
Forbes, Elwood, 8
Ford, Dawn, 179
Ford, Harrison, 6, 35, 84-85, 276
Ford, Kay, 180
Ford, Michael James, 256
Ford, Roger, 214
Ford, Steven, 128, 181
Ford, Travis, 38
Ford, Victoria, 159
Forde, Jessica, 44
Fordham, Carly, 93
Fordham, Nicholas, 257
Foreign Land, 264
Foreman, Dave, 166
Forensic Films, 154
Forest, Denis, 161
Forlani, Claire, 164
Forman, Michele, 80
Forrest, Frederic, 100, 276
Forrest, Susan, 238
Forrest, Tom, 181
Forrestal, Terry, 186
Forrester, David, 173
Forristal, Susan, 181
Forster, Robert, 147, 194, 276
Forster, T.J., 83
Forsythe, Frederick, 131
Forte, Christian, 9
Forte, Patricia, 15, 121
Forté, Smith, 160
Fortea, Isabelle, 171
Fortin, Andre, 78
Fortin, Dominique, 253
Fortune, Roger, 34, 50
Forward, Blair, 184
Foster, Blake, 158
Foster, Ellis, 97
Foster, Jodie, 6, 181, 277
Foster, Joe, 68, 80
Foster, John, 96
Foster, Lilibet, 167
Foster, Neil, 80
Foster, Penelope L., 179
Foster, Robert, 182, 276
Foster, Sheri, 113
Foster, Terrence, 60
Foster, Tim, 44
Fothergill, Janey, 225
Foto-Kem, 104, 174, 260
Fotso, Jimmy, 141
Fouassier, Dominique, 44
Foucheux, Rick, 137
Foundation Elf, 262
Foundation Gan pour le Cinema, 262
Fountain, Thom, 77
Fouquet, Marthe, 221
Fourth Floor Productions, Inc., 116
Fowler, Blaque, 47
Fowler, Cate, 183
Fowler, Colby, 45
Fowler, Hal, 162
Fowler, Philip, 125
Fowler, Rachel, 161
Fowler, Scott, 121
Fox 2000 Pictures, 109
Fox Family Films, 130
Fox Lorber, 173, 203, 262, 264, 266

Fox Searchlight, 25, 83, 110, 206, 209, 211, 220, 232, 238, 257
Fox, Bernard, 186-187
Fox, Colin, 165
Fox, Edward ., 131, 277
Fox, James, 180, 277
Fox, Kerry, 248
Fox, Kirk, 184
Fox, Lauren, 102, 241
Fox, Richard, 131, 186
Fox, Rick, 80
Fox, Veronica, 171
Fox, Vivica A., 23, 108-109, 181, 201
Foxx, Jamie, 23
Foy, Nancy, 132, 136
Foye, Eldrid, 179
Fraim, Tracy, 174
Frain, James, 212
Fraisse, Robert, 117, 160
Fraker, William A., 179
France 2 Cinema, 221, 265
France 3 Cinema, 236
France, Marie, 13, 23, 160
Francis, David Paul, 110, 162
Francis, David, 105, 153
Francis, Joe, 27
Francis, Peter, 266
Francis, Romeo, 186
Francis, Sean, 12
Francis-Bruce, Richard, 84
Franco, David, 105
Francois, Guy-Claude, 239
François, Jacques, 231
Frank Capra Prods., 162
Frank Capra's American Dream, 162
Frank Eugene Matthews, Jr., 172
Frank, Dan, 160, 177
Frank, Jason David, 158
Frank, Joe, 63, 101
Frank, Peter, 13
Frankel, Mark, 224
Frankfather, William, 146
Franklin, Bruce, 116
Franklin, Howard, 183
Franklin, Jeff, 169
Franklin, John, 151
Franklin, Lula, 39
Franklin, Richard, 262
Franklyn, Chevelle, 264
Franks, Adam, 125
Franks, Walter, 144
Frantz, Lisa, 175
Franz, Elizabeth, 178
Franzoni, David, 141
Fraser, Angus, 212
Fraser, Billy, 205
Fraser, Brendan, 7, 81, 173, 277
Fraser, David, 173, 180
Fraser, Duncan, 117
Frazer, Tiffany, 265
Frazier, Charles Stan, 180
Frazier, David, 43
Frazier, Deborah, 135
Frazier, Kermit, 53
Frears, Stephen, 220
Free, Scott, 94
Free Willy 3: The Rescue, 182
Freeman, Cheryl, 71
Freeman, David, 263
Freeman, Davis, 254
Freeman, Doug, 155
Freeman, J.E., 69, 133
Freeman, Je, 183
Freeman, Jim, 13
Freeman, Jonathan, 110
Freeman, K. Todd, 45, 100
Freeman, Kathleen, 71, 277
Freeman, Messiri, 84
Freeman, Morgan, 104, 114, 141, 277
Freeman, Paul, 44
Freeway Films, 255
Freihofer, Chris, 122
Frejkova, Hana, 264
Frenais, Ian La, 98
French, Arthur, 100
French, Colby, 45
French, Mark, 203
Fresco, David, 33, 37, 146
Freshwater, Geoffrey, 210
Fresson, Bernard, 231
Freundlich, Bart, 105
Frewer, Matt, 71, 277
Freyd, Bernard, 263
Frias, Carmen, 224

Friberg, Ulf, 259
Friberg, Viktor, 259
Fricker, Brenda, 169, 277
Friday, Gavin, 256
Fridley, Tom, 75, 183
Frieberg, Camelia, 249
Fried, Jonathan, 158
Friedberg, Mark, 110, 207
Friedenberg, Richard, 179
Frieder, Sol, 170
Friedlander, Barry, 262
Friedman, Brent V., 177
Friedman, Derrick, 37
Friedman, Laura, 11
Friedman, Matthew, 30
Friels, Colin, 204, 260, 277
Friend, Judy, 177
Friendly, David T., 78
Frislev, Michael, 178
Frith, Rebecca, 235
Frizzell, John, 17, 133
Froelich, Keith, 170
Froelich, Lily Soh, 101
Frogley, Louise, 68
Fronk, Dean, 162
Froom, Mitchell, 253
Frost, Charles Lynn, 65
Frost, Sadie, 245
Fruitman, Sarah Rosen, 249
Frutkoff, Gary, 43
Fry, Carla, 177
Fry, Stephen, 242, 277
Frye, Mia, 216
Fuchs, Fred, 66, 135
Fuentes, Chris, 33
Fugees, The, 156
Fuhrman, Ben, 127
Fuji Television, 265
Fujimoto, Michael N., 61
Fujimoto, Paul, 61
Fujimoto, Tak, 106
Fujita, Takahiro "Engin", 172
Fujitani, Ayako, 261
Fukaya, Akira, 261
Full Monty, The, 232
Fuller, Amanda, 62
Fuller, Arthus Louis, 32
Fuller, Gabriel, 33
Fuller, Penny, 154, 277
Fuller, Sam, 100, 297
Fulton, Larry, 88
Fung, Wellington, 260
Fung-kwok, Ma, 260
Funk, Greg, 172
Funke, Alex, 128
Furla, George, 174
Furlin, Matthew Daniel Moses, 8
Furlong, Kevin, 151
Furman, Allison, 30
Furman, Rosa, 265
Furness, Deborra-Lee, 204
Furry Feature Films, 265
Fusillo, Mariko H., 172
Futch, Mark, 63
Fyregård, Ann-Margret, 259
G.I. Jane, 94
Gabay, Eli, 107, 165
Gabbeh, 223
Gabel, Shainee, 166
Gabison, David, 263
Gabor, Lauren, 178
Gabriel, Igor, 215
Gabrielle, Francesco, 224
Gaddy, John, 175
Gaden, John, 214
Gadzic, Gordana, 248
Gaeckle, Richard, 104
Gaelic Storm, 186
Gaff, Toby, 89
Gagano, Ambassador Charles, 183
Gage, Kevin, 94
Gage, Melanie A., 121
Gagnon, Steven M., 37
Gail, Max, 156, 277
Gail, Scanlon, 183
Gailey, Lynn, 260
Gaines, Greta, 132
Gaines, Janie, 80
Gaines, Marle, 168
Gainey, M.C., 55, 65
Gaipa, Amy, 186
Gajdecki, John, 163
Gal, Uzi, 181
Galabru, Michel, 231
Galafilm Inc., 241
Galasso, Frankie, 29
Gale, Alison, 51
Galecki, Johnny, 119, 244

Galin, Mitchell, 173
Galitzine, Irène, 250
Gallagher, Joe, 256
Gallagher, John Andrew, 175
Gallagher, Peter, 167, 183, 277
Gallagher, Steve, 171
Gallagher, Susan, 179
Gallanders, James, 180
Gallant, Matthew, 83
Gallienne, Guillaume, 250
Gallini, Matt, 155
Gallo, Vincent, 162, 239
Gallop, Sammy, 39
Gallotte, Jean-Francois, 255
Galloway, Jenny, 12
Galloway, Michael, 179
Galone, Gary, 176
Galssman, Arnold, 162
Galuppo, Flavia, 100
Galvin, Bill, 176
Galyean, Kyle, 66
Gamble, Brian, 79
Gamble, David, 237
Gamble, Mason, 124
Gamboa, Jamielyn, 121
Gambon, Michael, 212, 222, 247, 277
Game, The , 101
Gamera: Guardian of the Universe, 261
Gammell, Robin, 56, 181
Gammon, James, 47, 145
Gandolfini, James, 53, 96
Gang of Four, 171
Gang Related, 172
Gann, Merrilyn, 165
Gannaway, Roberts, 180
Gano, Debra, 131
Gant, Richard, 244
Ganun, John, 60
Ganz, Lowell, 180
Ganzel, Teresa, 83
Garb, Helen Hewitt, 178
Garber, Hope, 151
Garber, Victor, 186-187, 277
Garcia, Andrew, 83
Garcia, Andy, 53, 97, 236, 277
Garcia, Caesar, 83
Garcia, Eddie, 78, 121
Garcia, Ernest, 122
Garcia, John, 236
Garcia, José, 265
Garcia, Luis C, 224
Garcia, Luis, 264
Garcia, Philippe, 221
Garcia, Rick, 49
Garcia, Risa Bramon, 68, 112
Garcia, Stella, 122
Garciadiego, Paz Alicia, 265
Garcillán, Fernando, 263
Garcin, Henri, 207
Gardea, Belinda, 83
Gardiner, Lizzy, 63
Gardiner, P. Holt, 14
Gardner, Cliff, 63
Gardner, Danielle, 167
Gardner, David, 180
Gardner, Kesean, 175
Gardner, Mario, 177
Gardner, Melissa, 151
Gardner, Tony, 163
Gareis, Jennifer, 30
Garfield, Harry, 159
Garity, Troy, 181
Garlacki, Toni, 219
Garland, Chase A., 184
Garlington, Lee, 17
Garner, Alice, 209
Garner, Jennifer, 115, 142, 144
Garner, Pat, 67
Garner, Patrick, 52, 102
Garner, Thomas, 181
Garofalo, Janeane, 24, 51, 92-93, 277
Garoutte, David L., 179
Garr, Roderick, 13
Garr, Teri, 80, 277
Garrel, Philippe, 263
Garréton, Andrés, 238
Garrett, Al, 21
Garrett, Hank, 82
Garrett, James, 186
Garrett, Spencer, 9, 81, 84
Garrick, Babara, 110
Garrick, Barbara, 254
Garrison, Andy, 184
Garti, Steve, 232
Gartin, Christopher, 14

Gartin, Sandy Russell, 180
Gartland, Ann, 175
Garver, James, 177
Garvey, David, 216
Garvey, Ray, 142, 183
Gasc, Christian, 231
Gaskill, Andy, 71
Gasperik, Dave, 176
Gasser, Wolfgang, 264
Gassot, Charles, 265
Gaston, Michael, 93
Gates, Damien, 203
Gatliff, Tony, 260
Gato, Nicolette, 60
Gattaca, 124
Gatton, Joe, 170
Gauchi, Nathalie, 262
Gauchy, Eric, 44
Gauderlier, Patrick, 44
Gauditz, Wolf, 264
Gaultier, Jean-Paul, 216
Gaumont Production, 216
Gauthier, Susan, 130
Gautier, Eric, 213, 263
Gautier, Jean-Yves, 213
Gavanski, Ogden, 163
Gaver, Duffy, 94, 101
Gavin, Madeleine, 96
Gavras, Costa, 183
Gawkowksi, Julie, 30
Gay, Alan James, 177
Gay, John, 24
Gayheart, Rebecca, 82, 144
Gayne, Matthew, 32
Gayner, Kay, 170
Gaynes, George, 151
Gayraud, Pierre Yves, 221
Gazecki, William, 165
Gazelle, Wendy, 161
Gazomiros, Dennis, 110
Gazzara, Ben, 154-155, 264, 277
Geary, Jo Ann, 12
Geary, Patrick, 122
Gédigier, François, 263
Geels, Laurens, 196
Geer, Ellen, 184
Gehringer, Linda, 148
Geier, Chris, 118
Geisnæs, Karsten, 260
Gelarden, James, 123
Gelbart, Arnie, 241
Gelfman-Randazzo, Juliet, 142
Gellar, Sarah Michelle, 119, 144
Geller, Libby, 138
Gellman, Steven, 169
Gelwicks, Riley, 172
Gemini Films, 215
Gendron, Louise, 179
Genelle, Richard, 158
Genest, Claude, 105
Genetti, Dan, 32, 264
Genevie, Michael, 23
Gent, Martin, 125
Gentlemen Don't Eat Poets, 210
George Of The Jungle, 81
George, Tami-Adrian, 51, 128
George, Brian, 56
George, Howard, 44
George, Kent, 8
George, Peter, 179
George, Ralph St., 138
George, Russell, 160
George, Tami-Adrian, 51, 128
George, Terry, 256
Georger, Diana, 24
Georgeson, Tom, 12, 125
Georgijev, Alex, 216
Gephart, Ron, 168
Geraghty, Karen, 151
Geraghty, Mark, 212, 220, 248
Gérard, Pierre, 265
Gérard-Hirne, Claire, 263
Gerdes, George, 141
Gere, Richard, 126, 131, 276-277
Gergely, Szaboles, 266
Gerhard, Kay, 15
German, Parish, 177
Gershin, Scott Martin, 136
Gershon, Gina, 24, 75, 79
Gerson, Betty Lou, 180
Gertz, Paul, 180
Gesbert, Bernard, 261
Gethering, Russell, 100
Gething, Russ, 38
Gettinger, Don, 38
Getty, Balthazar, 21, 277
Ghaffari, M.B., 183
Gheorghiu, Petru, 230

Ghinin, Romano, 224
Ghir, Kulvinder, 218
Ghiringhelli, Paul, 168
Ghoulardi Film Company, 121
Giakoumis, Hasmi, 262
Giamatti, Paul, 27, 30, 72, 142
Gian, Nicole, 167
Giangiulio, Nicholas J., 29
Giannini, Giancarlo, 99, 236, 277
Gianopolous, David, 84
Gibbon, Katie, 125
Gibbs, Amil, 177
Gibbs, David Gene, 61, 131
Gibbs, Keith, 38
Gibbs, Ric, 154
Gibbs, Richard Kendall, 23
Gibney, Rebecca, 230
Gibney, Terrence, 23
Gibs, Matyelok, 257
Gibson, Caroline, 90
Gibson, Charles, 146
Gibson, Donal, 181, 184
Gibson, Ian, 236
Gibson, Kathleen, 160
Gibson, Lynda, 230
Gibson, Margaret, 88
Gibson, Mel, 125, 180-181, 277
Gibson, Moses, 47
Gibson, Paul, 167
Gibson, Reginald, 34
Gibson, Rob, 160
Gibson, Robert, 12
Gibson, Scott, 39
Gibson, Thomas, 163
Giddings, Al, 186
Giddings, Peter F., 81
Gideon, Llewella, 237
Gideon, Raynold, 29
Giem, Gary, 127
Gifaldi, Sam, 98
Gifford, Barry, 21
Gifford, Dan, 181
Giggenbach, Robert, 263
Giggie, Bill, 262
Giguere, Edi, 118
Gika, Hector C., 66
Gilbert, Andrew S., 243
Gilbert, Jo, 162
Gilbert, Lance, 45
Gilbert, Peter, 13
Gilbert, Ron, 155
Gilborn, Stephen, 68
Gilborn, Steven, 30, 133
Gilder, Sean, 222
Giler, David, 133
Giles, David, 211
Giles, Gilbert, 175
Gilkey, Bernard, 77
Gilks, Mark, 203
Gill, Akesh, 165
Gill, Ned, 82
Gill, Patricia A., 168
Gillard, Stuart, 174
Giller, Boris, 202
Gillespie, Craig, 259
Gillespie, Jim, 119
Gillett, Chris, 180
Gilliam, Seth, 128, 175
Gillie, Nick, 183
Gillings, Robert, 157
Gillis, Alec, 128, 133
Gillis, Mary, 180
Gillis, Ruth, 179
Gillott, Nick, 91
Gilmore, Danny, 241
Gilmore, Gail, 262
Gilmore, Susan, 222
Gilmore, William S., 182
Gilpin, Jack, 52, 173
Gilpin, Paul, 155
Gilroy, Jason, 231
Gilroy, Tom, 171
Gilroy, Tony, 182
Gilstrap, Jim, 151
Ginsburg, Isaac, 265
Ginter, Lindsey Lee, 124
Ginther, Mark, 65
Gio, Frank, 176
Giorgio, Tony, 93
Giovaninetti, Arnaud, 260
Girard, Remy, 241
Girardeau, Frank, 52
Girardin, Michael, 135
Girardin, Mike, 155
Girardot, Pascaline, 44
Gish, Annabeth, 184, 278
Gish, Hilary, 12
Gish, Lou, 245

Gitlin, Kieve, 175
Gjonola, Dick, 97
Gladstein, Richard N., 147
Glascoe, Jon, 170
Glaser, Ariel, 258
Glaser, Bedrich, 262
Glasgow, Gil, 174, 180
Glasgow, Tom, 13
Glasko, Michel, 221
Glass Eye Pix, 175
Glass, Ann Gisel, 259
Glass, Philip, 152, 245
Glass, Philip, 152, 245
Glasser, Shelly, 13
Glattes, Wolfgang, 183
Gleason, Joanna, 121, 278
Gleason, Paul, 95, 154, 278
Gleeson, Brendan, 8, 231
Gleich, Shoshanna, 181
Glen, Georgie, 229
Glen, Michael, 170
Glenn, Scott, 22, 278
Glenn, Sean, 178
Glennie-Smith, Nick, 178, 182
Glick, Michael S., 80, 137
Glickman, Jonathan, 45, 174
Glickman, Rana Joy, 38
Glimcher, Marc, 180-181
Glinwood, Terry, 220
Glon, Georges, 231
Glover, Cory, 100
Glover, Danny, 63, 127, 135, 181, 276, 278
Glover, John, 58-59, 181, 183, 278
Glyn-Jones, David, 165
Goatworks Films, 96
Godard, Agnes, 239
Godard, Jean-Luc, 262
Godeau, Eléonore, 236
Godeau, Patrick, 236
Godeau, Philippe, 207
Godrèche, Judith, 265
Godsick, Christopher, 75
Godwin, Christopher, 125
Goe, Jane, 178
Goessens, Fred, 196
Goggins, Walt, 127
Goggins, Walter, 145
Going All The Way, 197
Going, Joanna, 43, 160
Gold, Ari, 171
Gold, Eric L., 118
Gold, Janine, 38
Gold, L. Harvey, 144, 162
Gold, Nina, 224, 261
Gold, Paul, 172
Gold, Sara, 27
Goldberg, Daniel, 30, 52, 180
Goldberg, David, 65
Goldberg, Michael, 174
Goldberg, Whoopi, 102, 278
Goldblatt, Mark, 128
Goldblatt, Stephen, 181
Goldblum, Jeff, 61, 278
Golden Eye Films, 137
Golden Monkey Pictures, 175
Golden, Joey, 157
Golden, Julie, 62
Golden, Noah, 25
Goldenberg, Michael, 181
Goldenthal, Elliot, 181
Goldfarb, Phillip M., 162
Goldfinger, Michael, 77
Goldie, Alison, 244
Goldin, Ricky Paull, 51
Golding, Meta, 114
Golding, Ziggi, 176
Goldman, Adina, 183
Goldman, Clint, 90
Goldman, Gary, 130
Goldman, Michael, 178
Goldman, William, 22
Goldner, Rich, 49
Goldring, Danny, 244
Goldsman, Akiva, 181
Goldsmith, Jerry, 12, 84, 107, 182
Goldsmith, Joel, 50, 169
Goldsmith, Laura, 132
Goldstein, Al, 154
Goldstein, Brett, 27, 94
Goldstein, Irina, 223
Goldstein, Jenette, 186, 278
Goldstein, Jess, 59
Goldstein, Steve, 180
Goldstone, John, 242
Goldthwait, Bobcat, 71
Goldwag, Elliott, 61
Goldwyn, 28, 212, 230, 245, 260,

265
Goldwyn, Tony, 114, 278
Goliath, 121
Golin, Steve, 101, 106
Golov, Brett, 11
Gomez, Andres Vicente, 210
Gomez, Carlos, 21, 112
Gomez, Henry, 80
Gomez, Panchito, 180
Gomez, Tito, 264
Gonçalves, Affonso, 168
Gonzales, Ronald, 180
Gonzales, Sherlyn, 265
Gonzales, Steve, 94
Gonzalez, Clifton Gonzalez, 184
Gonzalez, Elisabeth, 180
Gonzalez, Juan Carlos, 49
Gonzalez, Ruben, 180
Gonzalez, Umberto, 171
Gonzalez, William, 171
Good Fear, 178
Good Luck, 156
Good Machine, 105, 110, 178
Good Will Hunting, 138
Good, Meagan, 129
Good, Melanie, 30
Good, Paula, 160
Goodall, Howard, 244
Goodall, Matthew Michael, 37
Goode, Christopher, 93
Goode, Conrad, 11, 65
Goodhew, Philip, 238
Goodich, Frederic, 172
Goodloe, J. Mills, 181
Goodman, Elisa, 87, 162
Goodman, Hazelle, 142-143
Goodman, Henry, 30, 42
Goodman, Joel, 174
Goodman, Ken, 230
Goodman, Lorraine, 225
Goodman, Miles, 62
Goodman, Sue, 37
Goodrow, Garry, 157
Goodspeed, Margie, 182
Goodwin, Alexander, 86, 99
Goodwin, Karen, 165
Goodwin, Richard, 117
Goody, Bob, 210
Goossen, Gregory, 183
Goossens, Jennie, 12
Gorai, Tom, 104
Gordean, William D., 174
Gordin, Alixe, 35
Gordon, Bill, 83
Gordon, Dan, 105
Gordon, Jay, 101
Gordon, Jonathan, 138
Gordon, Lawrence, 35, 91, 121
Gordon, Lynda, 180
Gordon, Mark, 8, 68, 131
Gordon, Paul Christian, 68
Gordon, Randy, 176
Gordon, Robert, 35, 181
Gordon, Steve E., 166
Gordon, Steven E., 166
Gordon, Yonathan, 105
Gordons, The, 23
Gore II, George 183
Gorecki, Henryk Mikolaji, 231
Gorfil, Gillian, 155
Gorham, Christopher, 240
Gorham, Mel, 93
Goritsas, Demetri, 98
Gorman, Ned, 61
Gorney, Karen Lynn, 161
Gorr, Rita, 262
Gorski, Tamara, 180
Gosnell, Raja, 178
Gossett, Jr., Louis 154, 278
Goth, Sophia, 216
Gottfried, Gilbert, 15, 168
Gottlieb, Andrew, 23
Gottlieb, Heather, 159
Gottlieb, Lisa, 159
Gottlieb, Max, 232
Gottlieb, Nicholas, 170
Gough, Michael, 181
Gould, Dana, 180
Gould, Dominic, 44
Gould, Elliott, 14, 32, 278
Gould, Roger L., 71
Goulem, Alain, 179
Gourmet, Olivier, 215
Gourson, Jeff, 11
Govine, Jasen, 13
Govan, Sam, 67

Gowdy, Barbara, 212
Gowdy, Chuck, 240
Goz, Harry, 263
Grabowsky, Paul, 230
Grac, Nathalie, 44
Grace, Alison, 87
Grace, April, 244
Grace, Wayne, 49
Gracie Films, 148
Gradwell, Josephine, 183
Graef, Vicki, 23
Graf, Allan, 121, 182
Graff, David Allen, 176
Graff, Randy, 160
Graff, Todd, 18, 278
Graff, Zeta, 216
Graham, Aimee, 147
Graham, Bruce, 130
Graham, Chili, 145
Graham, Clarence, 124
Graham, Gary, 184
Graham, Heather, 60, 121, 144, 278
Graham, Jeremy A., 182
Graham, Richard, 186
Graham, Samaria, 82
Graham, Scott, 172
Graham, Stephen X., 52
Graham, Zane, 184
Grahame, Kenneth, 242
Grahame, Olga, 219
Grall, Andre, 213
Gramercy, 13, 52, 104, 160, 168, 207, 244, 261, 266
Grammer, Kelsey, 130
Granat, Cary, 144
Granat, Gary, 99
Granata, Dona, 126
Granath, Björn, 259
Grand, Suzanne, 232
Grandison, Pippa, 259
Granger, Philip, 162
Granger, Phillip, 169
Granillo, Guillermo, 265
Granli, Elisabeth, 182
Grant, Amy, 184
Grant, B. Casey, 98
Grant, Beth, 106, 174
Grant, Edith, 168
Grant, Garrett, 116
Grant, Salim, 210
Grant, Stacy, 98
Grant, Stuart, 127
Granville, Hollis, 183
Grapey, Marc, 31
Grason, Anika, 264
Graubart, David, 8
Gravel, Dinah, 102
Graves, Keiven McNeil, 178
Graves, Nevaina, 177
Graves, Rupert, 222, 237-238, 245, 278
Gravesend, 171
Gray's Anatomy, 157
Gray, Bruce, 112, 128
Gray, Casey, 24
Gray, Chris, 135
Gray, Jeri, 60
Gray, John, 135
Gray, Pam, 177
Gray, Pamela, 52, 157, 177, 182
Gray, Shayne, 168
Gray, Spalding, 157-158, 165, 278
Grayson, Milt, 71
Grazer, Brian, 37, 43
Great Oaks, 136
Greatrex, Richard, 229
Great Parrot, 28
Green, Anthony, 253
Green, Bobby, 145
Green, Bruce, 178
Green, Fanni, 158
Green, Graham, 179
Green, Hilton, 11, 178
Green, Jack N., 22, 68, 183
Green, Jack, 47
Green, Janet-Laine, 165
Green, Merrett, 169
Green, Peter, 209
Green, Seth, 33, 56
Greenaway, Peter, 220
Greenberg, Bob, 157
Greenberg, Paul, 148
Greenberg, Richard, 157
Greenberg, Robbie, 21
Greenbury, Christopher, 5
Greene, Bob, 136
Greene, Everett, 104
Greene, James R., 63

Greene, Justis, 38, 144
Greene, Kim Morgan, 174
Greene, Melanie, 122
Greene, Peter, 176
Greene, Sarah, 183
Greenfield, Hayes, 156
Greenfield, Matthew, 83
Greenleaf, Anthony, 171
Greenly, Theo, 24
Greenpoint Film, 215
Greenquist, Brad, 172
Greenspan, Alan, 27
Greenwood, Bruce, 180, 249
Greenwood, Jane, 137
Greenwood, Laura, 121
Greer, Ben, 182
Greer, Dabbs, 65
Greer, Stuart, 86, 119, 145
Greer, Wililam H., 182
Greetham, Kate, 209
Gregory, Jon, 27
Gregory, Laura, 237
Gregory, Paul, 222
Gregory, Peter, 69, 146
Gregson, Victoria, 183
Greif, George, 15, 160
Greif, Leslie, 15, 160
Greif, Marzia, 15
Grenier, Zach, 27, 158, 167
Grenville, Lewis, 180
Greville-Morris, Caroline, 238
Grevioux, Kevin, 184
Grey, Donna, 215
Grey, Ernie, 230
Grey, Larry, 30
Greyson, John, 241
Griakalova, Nora, 180
Gridlock'd, 13
Grieco, David, 266
Grief, Leslie, 161
Grief, Mike, 37
Griego, Penny, 49
Grier, David Alan, 160, 278
Grier, Erica Nicole, 50
Grier, Pam, 147, 278
Gries, Jon, 77
Grieve, Neal, 156
Grieve, Thomasina, 162
Grifasi, Joe, 96
Griffen, John, 63
Griffin, Aaron, 100
Griffin, Felicia, 174
Griffin, Garett, 155
Griffin, Garrett, 81, 155
Griffin, Gerry, 181
Griffin, Marian Tomas, 35
Griffin, S.A., 179
Griffis, Rhoda, 183
Griffith, Aaron, 33
Griffith, Bill, 173
Griffith, Helen, 261
Griffith, Thomas Ian, 169
Griffith, Tracy, 163
Griffiths, Derek, 12
Griffiths, Heidi, 163
Griffiths, Keith, 262
Griffiths, Michael, 174
Griffiths, Rachel, 72, 214, 260
Griffiths, Sophy, 125
Grigoriani, Guili, 213
Grillo, John, 125
Grillo, Michael, 112
Grills, Erin, 168
Grimalschi, Sergei, 223
Grimes, Martin, 118
Grimshaw, Jim, 131
Grinberg, Anouk, 231, 236
Grind, 159
Grindlay, Annie, 173
Grindlay, Murray, 214
Grinshpun, Olga, 202
Grisham, John, 135
Grives, Steven, 211
Grizzly Mountain, 174
Grobet, Xavier Perez, 174
Groener, Harry, 141
Groh, David, 118, 279
Groh, Michael, 44
Groh, Norma Jean, 77
Grohl, David, 24
Grosby, David, 13
Gross, Andrew, 44
Gross, Jennifer, 151
Gross, Larry, 79
Gross, Molly, 144, 177
Gross, Richard, 28, 183
Grosse Pointe Blank, 45
Grossman, Todd, 181

Grossmann, Goetz, 175
Grote, Vernon, 122
Grote, Veron, 160
Grotesque, The 210
Grove, David Paul, 169
Grove, William, 12
Grover, Gulshan, 162
Groves, Stewart, 156
Grower, John, 254
Gruault, Isabelle, 236
Grubb, Robert, 211
Grubbs, Gary, 63
Grube, Thomas, 174
Grubman, Alan, 183
Grueninger, Joachim, 254
Gruffudd, Ioan, 186
Grundy, Rueben, 183
Grunenwaldt, Luce, 239
Grünmandl, Otto, 264
Grunseld, Ernie, 183
Grusin, Dave, 179
Gryff, Stefan, 42, 180
Guadagni, Nicky, 208
Guardino, Chris, 167
Guay, Paul, 37
Guber, Elizabeth, 181
Gudahl, Kevin, 178
Gudgeon, Shanti, 209
Guérin, Isabelle, 157
Guerin, J.P., 164
Guerra, Castulo, 141
Guerra, Jackie, 180
Guerra, Ruy, 258
Guerra, Saverio, 166
Guerra, Tonino, 203
Guerrero, Michael, 180
Guerrini, Orso Maria, 44
Guess, Alvaleta, 100
Guglielmi, Françoise, 213, 239
Gui, Linda, 163
Guichard II, Vernon, 121
Guichard, Eric, 260
Guidance, Charlie, 168
Guidasci, Magali, 44
Guidera, Anthony, 62, 184
Guidry, Cynthia, 116
Guilfoyle, Paul, 53, 84-85, 141, 167, 182, 265
Guillard, Marie, 216
Guillén-Cuervo, Fernando, 263
Guillot, Donatien, 236
Guilloux-Delaunay, Marcel, 250
Guinan, Francis, 68
Guinan, Patricia, 102
Guinee, Tim, 157
Guinness, Peter, 42
Guinzburg, Kate, 106
Guiranov, Victor, 180
Guish, Michelle, 183, 229, 247
Guitierrez, Joaquin, 264
Guiting, Randy, 161
Guitry, Sacha, 265
Guizar, Luis Fernando, 83
Guizar, Luis, 176
Guleen, Igro, 203
Gulino, John R., 182
Gumbel, Bryant, 181
Gummo, 174
Gunn, Kelsey, 105
Gunn, Peter, 219, 224
Gunnarsson, John, 259
Gunstock, Ashley, 183
Gunter, John, 177
Gunther, Mike, 121
Gunton, Bob, 183
Gurko, Abe, 158
Gurland, Andrew, 154
Gurney, Scott, 8
Gurtu, Trilok, 262
Guru, 157, 164
Gurwitch, Annabelle, 62, 132, 146, 169
Guss, Louis, 53
Gustafsson, Sara Li, 125
Gutierrez, Annette Goliti, 68
Gutierrez, Luis, 236
Guttenberg, Steve, 11, 279
Guttman, Ronald, 220
Guy, 266
Guy, Andrew, 212
Guy, Jasmine, 180, 279
Guyant, Daniel, 261
Guyer, Murphy, 112, 131, 182
Guzaldo, Joe, 97

Guzman, Luis, 121
Guzzardi, Lucia, 224
Gwaltney, Jack, 94
Gwynne, Michael, 30
Gyalpo, Tencho, 152
Gyatso, Geshi Yeshi, 152
Gyatso, H.H. Tenzin, XIV Dalai Lama of Tibet, 265
Gyatso, Lobsang, 152
Gyatso, Ven. Ngawang Tenzin, 117
Gyngell, Kim, 209
Haaland, Kendra, 71
Haas, Barbara, 163
Haas, Lukas, 14, 279
Haas, Tito, 250
Habberstad, Jeff, 127
Haber, Aaron Daniel, 156
Habicht, Brian, 32
Hachette Premiere & Cie, 96
Hack, Ginny, 175
Hackett, John, 25
Hackett, Robyn, 63
Hackford, Taylor, 182
Hackforth-Jones, Penne, 215
Hackman, Gene, 22, 279
Hadary, Jonathan, 30, 80
Haddock, Joseph, 157
Haddrick, Ron, 214
Hadzovic, Ines, 248
Haft, Jeremy, 174
Hagan, Kevin, 157
Hagemann, Martin, 258
Hager, Mark, 69
Hager, Molly, 183
Hagerty, Julie, 113, 279
Hagerty, Michael G., 68
Haggard, Merle, 151
Haggerty, Dan, 174
Haggerty, Dylan, 65, 174, 184
Haggerty, Megan, 175
Hagins, Montrose, 8, 50
Hagopian, Dean, 179
Hahn, Archie, 133
Hahn, Kristin, 166
Hahn, Richard, 156
Hahn, Rob, 102
Hahn, Shirley Honickman, 156
Haidar, Kusum, 207
Haig, Sid, 147
Haigh, Paul, 12
Haigis, Jack, 157, 177
Hailey, Jo Jo, 109
Hailey, K-Ci, 109
Hailey, Leisha, 52
Hairlovsky, Ronald, 258
Haitkin, Jacques, 172
Haje, Richard, 83
Hajian, Chris, 137
Hakuhodo, 226
Halbleib, John, 183
Haldeman, Tim, 17
Hale, Tom, 175
Haley, Brian, 23, 160
Haley, Geoff, 13
Haley, R.M., 29
Hall, Alexander, 166
Hall, Anthony C., 172
Hall, Bug, 71
Hall, Dolly, 14, 52
Hall, Douglas, 145
Hall, George, 229
Hall, Henry Hunter, 13
Hall, Irma P., 66, 82, 108-109, 183, 184
Hall, Jennifer, 180
Hall, Keana, 51
Hall, Michael Keys, 135
Hall, Nadira, 132
Hall, Peter, 171
Hall, Philip Baker, 28, 66, 84, 121
Hall, Robert David, 128
Hall, Vernica, 53
Hall, Vondie Curtis, 13, 129
Hall, William, 180
Hallahan, Charles, 17, 20
Hallam, John, 169
Hallinan, Candace, 238
Hallmark Entertainment, 154, 165, 173
Hallo, Dean, 127
Halsey, Richard, 39
Halsted, Dan, 113
Halsted, Dean, 175
Halston, John, 158
Halton, Michael, 69
Halvorsen, Wendy Lou, 151
Hambling, Gerry, 256

Hambrick, Michael, 180
Hambrick, Mike, 84
Hamer, Jason, 163
Hamilton, Anthony Fife, 181
Hamilton, David, 112, 165, 182, 235, 286
Hamilton, Gary, 112, 243
Hamilton, George, 15, 44, 279
Hamilton, Josh, 118
Hamilton, Linda, 17, 154, 277, 279
Hamilton, Lisa Gay, 147, 158, 176
Hamilton, Richard, 77, 178
Hamilton-Latzen, Ellen, 33
Hamlett, Dilys, 210
Hamlett, Nathan, 216
Hammer, 30, 261
Hammerstein, Simon, 245
Hammil, John, 101
Hammond, Brandon, 108-109
Hammond, Fae, 237
Hammond, Glen, 210
Hammond, Nicholas, 211
Hammond, Vincent, 8
Hamori, Andras, 208, 249
Hamsun, 235
Han, Cassandra, 159
Hanafin, Hope, 244
Hancock, Brian, 261
Hancock, John Lee, 183
Hand, Larry, 258
Handel, Bill, 151
Handerson, Hal, 137
Handmade Films, 238
Handman, David, 172
Handwerker, Lloyd, 175
Handy, James, 172
Hanemann, Danny, 179
Hanes Jr, Arthur ., 80
Haney, Anne, 37, 183
Haney, Kevin, 51
Haney, Sarah, 183
Haney, Tony, 90
Hanft, Jacob James, 178
Hanke, Helmut, 23
Hankin, Larry, 95, 179
Hanks, Jan, 240
Hanley, Chris, 79
Hanley, Dan, 102
Hanley, Roberta, 79
Hann-Byrd, Adam, 110-111
Hannah, John, 222
Hannah, Zip, 265
Hannan, Mary Claire, 11, 147
Hannaway, Patrick, 229
Hanover, Donna, 53
Hansen, Dan, 8
Hansen, Danna, 7
Hansen, Jim, 37
Hanson, Curtis, 182
Hanson, Ed, 155
Hanssens, Daniel, 255
Happy Together, 243
Hara, Hideko, 226-227
Hara, Masato, 265
Haratzis, Denise, 235
Hard Edge, 28
Hard Work, Happy Holiday, 223
Hardeman, Jerome, 112
Harden, Marcia Gay, 31, 136
Hardesty, Kevin, 170
Hardin, Melora, 22
Harding, Jan Leslie, 157
Hardinge, Annie, 224
Hardison, Kadeem, 38
Hardisty, Mark, 100
Hardwicke, Catherine, 19, 183
Hardwicke, Edward, 210
Hardy, Gary, 160
Hardy, James, 181
Hardy, John, 157, 159
Hardy, Simon, 238
Hare, David, 215
Harel, Philippe, 236
Harel, Sharon, 166
Hargett, Hester, 169
Hargraves, Missy, 24
Hark, Tsui, 44
Harley, Jim, 61, 84
Harling, Robert, 168
Harlow, Larry, 264
Harlow, Shalom, 102
Harmati, Laszlo, 207
Harmon, Europe, 93
Harms, John, 181
Harney, Michael, 8
Harnick, Sheldon, 263
Harnisch, Barbara, 223
Haro, Claudia, 63

Harper, Angel, 114
Harper, Ben, 262
Harper, Donn C., 109
Harper, Hill, 184
Harper, Hollie, 161
Harper, Kate, 12
Harper, Tess, 131, 163, 279
Harrah, Verna, 46
Harrelson, Woody, 151, 248, 279
Harrer, Heinrich, 117
Harrington, Laura, 182
Harris, Barbara Eve, 126, 161
Harris, Barbara, 45, 279
Harris, Baxter, 35, 178
Harris, Billie, 80
Harris, Burtt, 158
Harris, Corrie, 83
Harris, Darwin L., 178
Harris, Dorian, 14, 164
Harris, Ed, 22, 277, 279
Harris, Enid, 62, 132
Harris, Estelle, 78
Harris Jr., Glenn Walker, 15
Harris Jr., Glenn, 98
Harris, Heather, 173
Harris, J. Todd, 159
Harris, Jared, 96, 180
Harris, Jez, 254
Harris, Julian ., 33
Harris, Kathryn Jean, 101
Harris, Leon, 181
Harris, Liza, 158, 183
Harris, Mark Jonathan, 104
Harris, Mark R., 173
Harris, Moira, 55
Harris, Neil Patrick, 128
Harris, Olivia, 30
Harris, Paul, 20, 209
Harris, Paul, 20, 209
Harris, Richard A., 186
Harris, Richard, 206, 231, 279
Harris, Ricky, 180
Harris, Samantha, 81
Harris, Talent, 50
Harris, Viola, 142
Harris, Wood, 148
Harrison, Matthew, 170
Harrison, Patrice, 264
Harrison, Philip, 8, 90
Harrison, Robert, 182
Harriss, Robb, 170
Harrow, Lisa, 96
Harry Walters, Jr., 33
Harry, Deborah, 93, 279
Harscheid, David, 137
Harston, Wendelin, 127
Hart, Angela, 238
Hart, Charles, 238
Hart, Chris, 174
Hart, George, 238
Hart, Ian, 210, 212
Hart, James V., 181
Hart, Janice, 15
Hart, Joe, 174
Hart, John, 158, 178
Hart, Joseph Sr., 174
Hart, Mark, 89
Hart, Mickey, 172
Hart, Oona, 34
Hart, Veronica, 121
Harte, Christine, 155
Harth, C. Ernst, 98
Hartigan, Danny, 184
Hartley, Clabe, 177
Hartley, Nina, 121
Hartley, Richard, 106, 122, 215, 220, 260
Hartline, Gene, 55
Hartman, David Lee, 119
Hartman, Jesse, 175
Harvey, Alex, 135, 182
Harvey, Amy, 169
Harvey, Don, 8
Harvey, George "Crackhead Bob" 30
Harvey, Robert, 22
Harvey, Terence, 183
Harzer, Jens, 264
Hasak, Adi, 154
Hasomeris, Nick, 176
Hassig, Alfred, 265
Hastings, Valerie, 161
Hatcher, Teri, 253, 279
Hatfield, Mert, 79
Hathaway, Kellen, 71
Hathaway, Robert, 168
Hatosy, Shawn, 43, 52, 102, 184
Hatten, Keith, 127

Hatton, David, 242
Hattou, Mess, 259
Hatz, Jeff, 66
Haufrecht, Marcia, 31
Hauser, Cole, 52, 138-139
Haut et Court, 255
Haviv, Shira, 245
Hawk's Nest, 264
Hawk, Robert, 41
Hawke, Ethan, 7, 124, 278-279
Hawke, Shaun, 38
Hawkes, John, 62, 122, 184
Hawkins, Andrew, 253
Hawkins, John E., 145
Hawkins, Matthew, 250
Hawkins, Peter, 158
Haworth, Peter James, 165, 180
Hawthorne, Dave, 148
Hawthorne, Nigel, 141, 154, 279
Hawtry, Kay, 126
Hay, Colin, 260
Hayashi, Yuki, 220
Hayat, Delphine, 263
Hayden, Dennis, 172
Hayden-Passero, Elizabeth, 169
Hayek, Salma, 21, 155, 279
Hayes, Adam, 257
Hayes, Chris, 89
Hayes, Hunter, 145
Hayes, James, 256
Hayes, Patrick, 184
Haygood, James, 101
Hayman, David, 131, 256, 261
Haynes, Gibby, 60
Haynes, Jerry, 116
Haynes, Randell, 173
Haynes, René, 179
Haynes, Todd, 178
Haynie, Jim, 112
Hays, Chaz, 157
Hays, Sanja Milkovic, 44
Haysbert, Dennis, 22
Hayter, Charles, 99
Hayward, Henry, 96
Haywood, Chris, 243
HBO, 80
Head Above Water, 164
Head, Murray, 265
Headey, Lena, 210
Healey, Jack, 166
Healey, Mary, 219
Healy, Michael, 234
Healy, Pat, 178
Heap, David, 256
Heard, John, 184, 280
Hearn, George, 35
HeartShare, 156
Heath, Darrel, 158
Hebert, Julie, 38
Hebert, Rich, 181
Heche, Anne, 26-27, 49, 119, 150-
    151, 278, 280
Hecht, Paul, 30
Hecht, Tiffany, 132
Heckendorn, David, 43
Hecker, Gary, 66
Heckler, Andrew, 68
Hedaya, Dan, 102, 133, 240, 280
Heddings-Katulka, Sandy, 144
Hee, Dana, 177
Heeren, Brenton, 203
Heffler, Brad, 156
Hegh, Anita, 211
Heim, Alan, 98
Heimann, Betsy, 127
Heinl, Bernd, 170
Heinlein, Robert A., 128
Heinze, Jacqueline, 181
Heitner, David, 155
Helberg, Sandy, 15
Held, Wolfgang, 157, 161, 177
Helde, Annette, 244
Helfet, Tim, 168
Helfrich, Mark, 95, 118
Helgeland, Brian, 181-182, 184
Helgenberger, Marg, 164, 182
Helies, Phillipe, 239
Helkey, James M., 131
Hell's Kitchen, 52, 256
Heller, Peter, 259
Heller, Richard M., 169
Hellerman, Paul, 147
Helling, Paul, 164
Helm, Levon, 182
Helmuth, Mark, 172
Helmy, Michael, 47, 173
Helpern, David, 98
Helvenston, Scott, 94

Hemblen, David, 23, 249
Hemingway, Mariel, 142-143, 280
Hemming, Lindy, 25, 253
Hemmings, Bruce, 126
Hemmrich, Daryl, 100
Hemsley, Sherman, 60, 280
Henderson, Bill, 97, 182
Henderson, Cathy, 159
Henderson, Don, 125, 242
Henderson, Johnny, 69
Henderson, Judy, 19
Henderson, Lynn A., 8
Henderson, Sean, 69
Henderson, Sparkle, 69
Henderson-Martin, Cathy, 172
Hendrickson, Rusty, 184
Hendrickson, Stephen, 80, 137
Hendrie, Chris, 173
Hendrix, Elaine, 51
Heneghan, Mary K., 47
Henfrey, Janet, 183
Heng, Ivan, 216
Hengsleigh, Jonathan, 65
Henkel, Julia, 89
Henkels, Amy, 34, 95
Henkin, Hilary, 151
Hennessey, Matthew, 169
Hennessy, Jill, 118, 168
Hennigan, Dee, 164
Henninger, Corie, 10
Henriques, Samuel, 171
Henry, David, 210
Henry, Gloria L., 183
Henry, John, 93, 175, 184, 297
Henry, Pitof and Erik, 133
Henry, Sonita, 216
Henschke, Frank, 241
Hensen, John, 15
Henshall, Douglas, 169
Hensleigh, Jonathan, 42
Hensley, Lisa, 211
Henson, Brian, 66
Henson, John, 264
Henzel, Richard, 169
Hepburn, Caroline, 132
Herald Ace, 265
Herald, Valerie, 179
Herbert, Leon, 12
Herbert, Paul, 186
Herc, Kool, 157
Herd, Patricia, 183
Herd, Richard, 183
Heredia, Jose, 173
Herman, Mark, 219
Herman, Paul, 31, 93, 178, 180
Herman, Stanley, 176
Herman, Wandi, 176
Hernandez, Bel, 180
Hernandez, Irene, 21
Hernandez, Isabel, 183
Hernandez, Juan, 183
Hernandez, Vanessa L., 25
Heron, Blake, 50
Heron, Nye, 256
Herr, Michael, 135
Herrer, Gerardo, 224
Herrera, Jade, 184
Herrera, Lazaro, 264
Herrick, Robert, 68
Herried, Matthew, 180
Herrmann, Edward, 126, 280
Hersh, Andrew, 60
Hersh, Kristin, 175
Hershfield, Jonathan Michael, 102
Herter, Miles, 141
Hertford, Brighton, 98
Herwick, Justin, 148
Herzberg, Ilona, 17
Heslov, Grant, 17
Hess, Sandra, 177
Hesseman, Howard, 13, 280
Heston, Charlton, 71, 280
Hettiarachchi, Sunil, 162
Hettinger, Tony, 89
Hevenor, George, 39
Hewitt, Howard, 159
Hewitt, Jennifer Love, 119, 201,
    280
Hewitt, John, 256
Hewitt, Paul, 167
Hewitt, Sean, 205
Heya, Kyoko, 226
Heyerdahl, Christopher, 179
Heyman, David, 31
Heyman, Samantha, 37
Hibbard, Brian, 261
Hice, Freddie, 136

Hickey, Jim, 180
Hickey, John Benjamin, 58-59, 110
Hickey, Marguerite, 175
Hickey, Wickey, 146
Hickey, William, 146, 178, 298
Hickman, Craig, 175
Hickman, Daniel, 145
Hicks, Barbara, 125
Hicks, Catherine, 8, 280
Hicks, Daniel Hawk, 132
Hicks, Danny, 172
Hicks, Joe H., 160
Hicks, Lois, 127
Hicks, Richard, 244
Hidaka, Hisashi, 220
Hien, Roger To Thanh, 220
Hier, Rabbi Marvin, 104
Hieu, Joseph, 157
Higgins, Anthony, 225, 280
Higgins, Douglas, 169
Higgins, J. Paul, 162
Higgins, John Michael, 94, 151
High School Sweethearts, 18
Higuchi, Shinji, 261
Hijacking Hollywood, 167
Hilaire, Elvis Saint, 83
Hilaire, Soledad St., 100
Hild, Jim, 181
Hildebrand, Dan, 122
Hildebrand, David, 115
Hildebrand, Frank, 161
Hill, Bernard, 186, 242, 280
Hill, Dave, 232
Hill, Derek R., 160
Hill, Grant, 186
Hill, Jane, 210
Hill, John, 130, 175
Hill, Melanie, 219
Hill, Phillip, 12
Hill, Raelee, 259
Hill, Rick, 37
Hill, Teresa, 60
Hill, Walter, 133
Hill, William, 112, 183
Hilleary, Irene, 100, 182
Hiller, Randi, 68, 112
Hilliard, Margaret, 240
Hillman, Timothy T., 144
Himber, Robert, 127
Himelhoch, Joel, 169
Himoff, Kathryn, 116
Hinds, Ciaran, 257
Hine, Julia, 224
Hines, Gregory, 156, 280
Hines, Suzanne, 160
Hingle, Pat, 106, 181, 280
Hinkley, Brent, 24, 127
Hinrichs, Dag, 13
Hinrichs, Rodger, 264
Hinton, Mary, 172
Hipp, Paul, 183
Hirabayashi, Keith Cooke, 11, 177
Hirakubo, Masahiro, 240
Hiriart, Hugo, 264
Hirsch, Michael, 262
Hirsch, Tina, 17
Hirsch, Wilbert, 254
Hirshenson, Janet, 44, 61, 84, 162
Hitchcock, Paul, 42
Hitner, Harry, 11
Hivju, Erik, 235
Hixon, Ken, 43
Hjejle, Iben, 260
Home Alone 3, 178
Homegrown Pictures, 157
Homemade Films, 207
Honda, Yutaka, 220
Honess, Peter, 182
Hong, James, 126
Hong, Vien, 32
Honigmann, Heddy, 266
Hood, Adrian, 219
Hoodlum, 97
Hook, Tristan, 179
Hool, Conrad, 160
Hool, Lance, 160
Hoopes, Wendy, 30
Hootkins, William, 79
Hoover, Dave, 116
Hoover, Howard, 180
Hope, Lisa, 238
Hope, Richard, 225
Hope, Ted, 105, 110, 173, 178
Hope, William, 42
Hopgood, Alan, 259
Hopkins, Anthony, 107, 141, 194,
    280
Hopkins, Billy, 53, 99, 138, 178,
    241

Hoehn, Marcel, 265
Hoff, Anette, 235
Hoffer, Irmelin Mai, 112
Hoffman, Bidget, 178
Hoffman, Dominic, 184
Hoffman, Dustin, 7, 150-151, 183,
    192, 280
Hoffman, Elizabeth, 17
Hoffman, Holly, 12
Hoffman, Jane, 102
Hoffman, Jeff, 9
Hoffman, Linda, 75
Hoffman, Philip Seymour, 28, 120-
    121
Hoffman, Rick, 182
Hoffman, Sabine, 159
Hoffmann, Gaby, 49
Hoffmann, Sabine, 52
Hofheimer, Charlie, 180
Hofstra, Jack, 63
Hogan, Andy, 118
Hogan, Chris, 24
Hogan, Cindy, 174
Hogan, David Glenn, 118
Hogan, Lisa, 12
Hogan, Michael, 165
Hogg, B.J., 162
Hoisnard, Danielle, 221
Hoke, Kristin, 86
Holbrook, Hal, 71, 122, 180, 280
Holden, Alexandra, 102, 164
Holden, Amanda, 238
Holden, Beth, 116
Holden, David, 44
Holden, Marjean, 61, 177
Holder, Ginny, 42
Holdridge, Lee, 104, 173
Holender, Adam, 44
Holiday, Anthony, 151
Holland, Agnieszka, 115
Holland, David Vincent, 160
Holland, Erik, 186
Holland, Rodney, 225
Hollander, Barbara, 142
Hollander, David, 8
Hollander, Richard, 75
Holler, Carl William, 180
Holliday, Charlie, 168, 183
Holliman, John, 181
Hollister, Tracy, 13
Holloman, Laurel, 13, 105, 121
Holloway, Kamau, 184
Holly, Lauren, 8, 168
Hollywood Pictures, 13, 45, 63, 94,
    115, 154, 254
Hollywood, Gary, 251
Holm, Ian, 53, 216-217, 240, 249,
    280
Holman, Bruce, 84
Holmes, Bob, 183
Holmes, Boise, 114
Holmes, Katie, 110
Holmes, Lee, 169
Holmes, Preston, 13, 168
Holmey, Erik, 206
Holt, Willy, 231
Holten, Daniel, 262
Holton, Mark, 167
Holtzman, Robert "Ratface", 41
Holzman, Ernest, 34
Holzman, Winnie, 62
Home Alone 3, 178
Homegrown Pictures, 157

Hopkins, Bo, 113
Hopkins, Emery, 145
Hopkins, Harold, 214
Hopkins, Jermaine "Big Hugg" 168
Hopkins, Josh, 94
Hopkins, Kaitlin, 148
Hopkins, Morgan, 261
Hopkins, Smith & Barden, 53, 99,
    137-138, 166, 178, 183
Hopper, 81
Horan, Gerard, 237
Horgan, Jason, 144
Hori, Daishi, 220
Horikoshi, Kenzo, 258
Horn, Andrew, 223
Horn, Andrew, 223
Horn, Debbie, 265
Horna, J.J., 123
Horne, Barbara, 180
Horner, Grenville, 237
Horner, James, 35, 186
Horner, Jill, 102
Hornung, Richard, 260
Horrocks, Simon, 109
Horton, Jeremy, 190
Horton, John, 27
Horton, Matthew, 162
Horton, Peter, 100
Horwitz, Caryn, 166
Hosoya, Yoshifumi, 172
Hot Summer, 3, 223
Hotei, Tomoyasu, 261
Hotel De Love, 259
Hotel Manor Inn, The , 157
Hotz, Jeremy, 68
Houde, Serge, 131
Houghton, Stephen, 225
Houghton, Tom, 182
Hoult, Nicholas, 238
Hounslow, David, 183
Hounsou, Djimon, 140-141, 177
Houri, Alice, 239
House, Garrett, 133
House of Yes, The, 118
Houston, Jacquelyn, 184
Houston, Marques, 83
How I Spent My Summer Vacation,
    177
Howard, Arliss, 14, 61, 141, 280
Howard, Cliff B., 151
Howard, Clint, 56
Howard, David S., 142
Howard, James Newton, 17, 72,
    180, 182, 184
Howard, Jean, 47
Howard, Jeff, 127, 129
Howard, Nancy, 11
Howard, Rance, 47, 95, 172
Howard, Robert E., 169
Howard, Ron, 43, 162, 280
Howard, Sheila, 49
Howard, Terrence Dashon, 14
Howe, Monica, 225
Howell, Chris, 84, 100, 162
Howell, James, 155
Howell, Jessica, 11
Howell, Kathryn, 156
Howell, Keith C., 184
Howell, Michael, 137
Howell, Norman, 182
Howell, Peter, 222
Howells, Michael, 125
Howington, Jana, 137
Howman, Dave, 242
Howson, Stewart, 125
Hoy, Carlos, 101
Hoy, Maysie, 34
Hoyte, David Nathaniel, 11
Hrabowski III, Dr. Freeman, 80
Hrzanova, Barbora, 262
Hseih, Emily, 132
Hsiao, Charles, 69
Hsiao, Michael, 69
Hsin, Jim, 203
Huang, Jack C., 126
Hub, Martin, 186
Huband, David, 39
Hubbard, John and Ros, 91, 244
Hubbard, John, 212
Hubbard, Ros, 91, 244
Hubert, Nathalie, 263
Huberty, Martin, 126
Huckabee, Cooper, 8
Hudd, Lawrence, 121
Hudson, Ernie, 144, 281
Huene, Tadie, 263
Huertas, Luisa, 160
Huestis, Marc, 170

Huff, Mary Neva, 119
Huff, Thomas J., 68
Huff, Tom, 95
Huffman, Phyllis, 8, 22, 30, 183
Huffman-Kerr, Ross, 156
Hugel, Serge, 254
Huggins, Erica, 13
Hughes, Diane, 155
Hughes, John, 136, 178, 216
Hughes, Miko, 11, 90
Hughes, Odette, 225
Hughes, Richard Williams, 180
Hughes, Wendy, 211
Hugo Pool, 178
Hugot, Marceline, 178
Hui, Jin Zheng, 126
Huison, Steve, 232-233
Huke, John, 159
Hules, Endre, 44, 112
Hulin, Steve, 65
Hulsey, Lauren, 115
Humphrey, Justin, 11
Humphrey, Renee, 159
Humphreys, Doug, 155
Humphries, Barry, 265
Humphries, Harry, 94
Humphries, Tessa, 211
Hundhammer, Wolfgang, 263
Hung, Jennifer, 203
Hungry Eye Trijbits, 224
Hunsinger, Tom, 205
Hunt, Abigail, 175
Hunt, Brad, 69, 182
Hunt, Gareth, 12
Hunt, Helen, 148-149, 189, 281
Hunt, Kevin, 68
Hunt, Linda, 8, 281
Hunt, Muriel, 232
Hunter, Amber, 121
Hunter, Bruce, 138
Hunter, Holly, 208, 240, 281
Hunter, J. Michael, 173
Hunter, Kelly, 210
Hunter, Kim, 183, 281
Hunter, Martin, 91
Hunter, Neil, 205
Hunter, Trish, 157
Huntington, Sam, 29
Huntley, Debra L, 212
Huntley, Noah, 91
Huppert, Isabelle, 262, 281
Hurd, Gale Anne, 8, 17, 127
Hurley, Elizabeth, 56-57, 155, 281
Hurst, Melissa, 135
Hurst, Michelle, 178
Hurst, Peter, 66
Hurst, Ryan, 184
Hurt, John, 181, 281
Hurt, Mary Beth, 33, 281
Hurt, William, 265-266, 281
Hurwitz, Tom, 157
Huss, Rachel Zan, 168
Huss, Toby, 177
Hussey, Liam, 205
Huston, Danny, 180
Hutchinson, Doug, 65
Hutchinson, Harry, 61, 84
Hutchinson, Peter, 242
Hutchinson, Tim, 60
Hutchison, Doug, 174, 181
Hutchison, Nicholas, 12
Huth, Hanno, 210
Hutson, Vicky, 160
Hutt, Richard, 162
Hutton, P.B., 61
Hutton, Timothy, 32, 122, 281
Huyard, Éric, 250
Huzzar, Elaine J., 21, 122, 128
Hyams, Peter, 8
Hyatt, Ron, 121
Hyde, Jonathan, 46, 186-187
Hyland, Sarah Jane, 30
Hyler, Erik, 144
Hyman, Mark, 168
Hytner, Steve, 75
I Don't Want To Marry, 223
I Know What You Did Last Summer, 119
I Love You, I Love You Not, 241
I Salonisti, 186
Iacangelo, Peter, 162
Iacovone, Rocco, 100
Ibarra, Mirtha, 224
Ibbetson, Brady, 38
Ibled, Carla, 218
Iborra, Juan Luis, 263
Icarus, 266
Ice Storm, The , 110

Ice-T, 175
Icon Prod., 180, 184
Idle, Eric, 148, 242, 281
Idunafilm, 262
Idziak, Slawomir, 52, 124
Ifans, Rhys, 261
Igarashi, Kazuhiro, 226
Iglesias, Richard, 180
Iglodi, Istvan, 264
Igus, Darrow, 159
Ihara, Tsuyosi, 261
Ikeda, Shoko, 230
Ikeda, Testuya, 226
Ikuta, Yorozu, 258
Ildahl, Eirik, 164
Ilian-Waters, Gillian, 147
Ill Gotten Gains, 177
Illia, Elizabeth, 179
Illusion Entertainment, 113, 175
Ilori, Adekunle, 141
Imada, Brian, 32
Imagine Entertainment, 37, 43
Imai, Darryl A., 61
Imalyre, 262
Iman, 175
Imboden, Elizabeth, 79
Immel, Michael, 18
Impact Pictures, 91
Imperioli, Michael, 175, 178
In & Out, 102
In Pictures, 262, 265
In The Company Of Men, 89
In, Lucy, 144
Indaba, Temba, 154
Independent Pictures, 174
Independent Television Service, 162
Infeld, Geoffrey, 180
Ingalls, Alec, 69
Ingber, Amanda, 8
Ingerman, Ivan, 163
Ingle, John, 181
Inglis, Raul, 212
Ingraham, Bill, 169
Ingram, Brad K., 170
Ingram, Charles, 168
Ingram, Sky, 219
Ingrham, Doran, 160
Initial Groupe, 236
Innocent Sleep, The 222
Inscoe, Joe, 114
Inside, 154
Intelligent, Wise, 157
Interama, 263
Interscope Communicatios, 13
Intl. Film Circuit, 261
Intimate Relations, 238
Inventing The Abbotts, 43
Investimage, 265
Inwood, John, 31
Iotti, Carolina, 250
Iovenko, Chris, 83
Ireland, Simone, 222, 248
Irish, Charlie, 176
Irizawa, Art, 144
Ironside, Michael, 180
Irvin, John, 32
Irvine, Andrea, 256
Irving, Amy, 142, 281
Irwin, Mark, 184
Irwin, Pat, 157
Isaac, Frank K., 32
Isaac, Oneal A., 129
Isaacks, Levie, 161
Isaacs, Jason, 91
Isaacson, Donna, 107, 240
Isacksen, Peter, 160
Isbell, Anthony, 168
Isgar, Jonathan, 230
Isham, Mark, 53, 114, 153, 179
Ishii, Sogo, 258
Ishikawa, Chu, 261
Ishimaru, Aki, 220
Ishimaru, Kazushi, 220
Ishimoto, Dale, 11
Isitt, Kate, 42
Island Digital Media, 171, 264
Island Jamaica Films, 264
Island Pictures, 158, 168
Ismael, Gerard, 95
Isyanov, Ravil, 42, 131
ITC Entertainment Group, 160
Ito, Kazunori, 261
Ito, Steven, 181
Iures, Marcel, 112
Ivanek, Zeljko, 27, 170, 281

Ivania Films, 265
Ivanof, Angel, 203
Ivers, Jeffrey D., 11, 44, 172
Ivey, Judith, 115, 182, 240, 281
Ivey, Lela, 244
Ivleva, Gelena, 180
Ivory Way, 118
Ivy, Joe, 156
Iwata, Min, 261
Izumi, Eiji, 258
J&M Entertainment, 210, 254
J, Ray, 184
Jaaferi, Jaaved, 235
Jablow, Michael, 52
Jace, Michael, 121
Jackal, The , 131
Jackie Brown, 147
Jackie Chan's First Strike, 203
Jacks, James, 131
Jackson ,Reverend Jesse L., Sr., 80
Jackson, Anthony R., 160
Jackson, Josh, 144
Jackson, Kevin, 179, 181
Jackson, Leonard, 181
Jackson, Mel, 109
Jackson, Mick, 49
Jackson, Philip, 219
Jackson, Roger L., 144
Jackson, Ryan, 235
Jackson, Samuel L., 28, 129, 147, 184, 278
Jackson, Shar, 83
Jackson, Sharon, 209
Jackson, Victoria, 68, 281
Jackson, Wes, 166
Jackson, Yvette, 144
Jacob, Robert, 172
Jacobi, Ernst, 235
Jacobs, Peter Anthony, 13
Jacobs, Robert Nelson, 78
Jacobsen, John M., 164
Jacobson, Peter Marc, 18
Jacobson, Peter, 30, 52, 142, 148, 182
Jacobus, Ralph, 170
Jacott, Caros, 45
Jacquemin, Andre, 242
Jade, Tracie, 175
Jaeck, Scott, 115
Jaffa, Rick, 8
Jaffe, Sheila, 31, 170, 176
Jaffe, Susan, 157
Jagger, Karis, 132
Jagger, Mick, 245, 281
Jaher, Diana, 159
Jaimes, Marabina, 184
Jain, Sinia, 207
Jakcson, Brenda B., 145
Jakoby, David, 43
Jakub, Lisa, 18
James, Brion, 216
James, Colton, 61
James, Don, 97
James, Emmett, 186
James, Gary Kent, 49
James, Geraldine, 183
James, Grant, 216
James, Harri, 11
James, Harry, 184
James, Hawthorne, 141
James, Henry, 115, 247
James, Jesse, 148, 297
James, Jim, 38
James, Lynne, 212
James, Peter, 165, 180, 211, 244
James, Richard, 242
James, Robert, 49, 222
James, Simon, 34
James, Steve, 13
Jameson, Jenna, 30
Jane, Sara, 14, 60
Jane, Thomas, 75, 121, 164
Janes, Matt, 176
Jang, Michael, 168
Jang, Tali, 168
Jang, Woody, 168
Jangchub, Ven. Tenzin, 117
Janis, Ryan, 102
Janjic, Davor, 248
Janjua, Kaleem, 216
Jankiewicz, Tom, 45
Jankoska, Brankica, 248
Janney, Allison, 30, 110, 170
Jansen, David A., 97
Jansen, Janus Billeskov, 206
Janssen, Famke, 32
Janssen, Helge, 155
Japy, Camille, 221

Jarboe, Harold, 170
Jarmusch, Jim, 173
Jarmusch, Tom, 100
Jarniou, Solenn, 263
Jarratt, John, 266
Jarre, Kevin, 35, 131
Jarre, Maurice, 61
Jarvis, Martin, 186-187
Jason, Harvey, 61
Jason, Peter, 17
Jason, Warren Robert, 266
Jaulima, Gresham Phet, 155
Javan, Maia, 79
Jay, Ricky, 120-121, 253
Jay-Z, 157
Jaymes, Christopher, 180
Jaytex Prods, 265
Jean, Loretta, 60
Jean-Baptiste, Marianne, 234
Jeffcoat, Jeff, 179
Jefford, Barbara, 42
Jeffrey, Myles, 75
Jeffries, Will, 173
Jehanneuf, Jacqueline, 221
Jelinek, Tobias, 181
Jemison, Eddie, 159
Jemison, Edward, 8
Jenay, Dixie, 155
Jenco, Sal, 27
Jendly, Roger, 263
Jenkel, Brad, 9, 11
Jenkins, Jane, 44, 61, 84, 162
Jenkins, Richard, 22, 122, 265
Jenkins, William Arthur, 174
Jenks, T'Erica, 145
Jenner, Rolf, 259
Jenney, Lucinda, 94, 183
Jennings, Alex, 246-247
Jennings, Bob A., 122
Jennings, Brian M., 99
Jennings, Byron, 110
Jennings, Christie, 237
Jennings, Nolan, 165
Jennings, Roger, 166
Jennings, Will, 186
Jennison, Gordon, 178
Jenny, Lucinda, 164
Jensen, Anne, 51
Jensen, Bradley, 61
Jensen, David, 159
Jensen, Eric, 161
Jensen, Johnny E., 179
Jensen, Lisa, 81
Jensen, Peter Aalbaek, 260
Jeremy, Ron, 15
Jerge, Jim, 164
Jeria, Tonya, 176
Jernigan, Sister Jewell, 145
Jerry Weintraub Productions, 179
Jersey Films, 12, 124
Jerusalem, 259
Jery O'Leary, 256
Jessup, Gayle, 131
Jeter, Leon "Jelly Belly", 160
Jeter, Michael, 87, 146, 281
Jeunet, Jean-Pierre, 133
Jew, The , 258
Jewesbury, Edward, 210
Jezek, Robert, 91
JGM Enterprises, 165
Jharkov, Alexei, 202
Ji-wu, Jim, 260
Jie, Zhou, 222
Jim Henson Pictures, 66
Jim Henson's Creature Shop, 66, 81
Jin, Hong-An, 163
Jing-sheng, Fu, 260
Jinhua, Lu, 220
Jiping, Zhao, 222
JKG Production, 172
Jobin, Daniel, 241
Jody O'Neil, 175
Joe & Joe, 163
Joe, Gordon, 205
Joe, Terilyn, 81
Joel Schumacher Film, 181
Joel, Richard, 184
Joffe, Charles H., 142
Joffe, Mark, 260
Johansen, Allan, 260
Johansen, Dave, 176
Johansen, David, 175, 180, 281
Johansson, Douglas, 259
Johansson, Paul, 96
Johansson, Scarlett, 178

John Cothran, Jr., 90, 114
John, Alexander, 12, 77, 247
John, Priscilla, 12, 117, 219
John, Royston, 261
Johns, 14
Johnsen, René, 260
Johnson, A.J., 158, 168
Johnson, Amanda Mackey, 62, 81, 97, 180-181, 183
Johnson, Amy Jo, 158
Johnson, B. Philly, 121
Johnson, Barry, 27, 71
Johnson, Bayard, 162
Johnson, Beverly, 168
Johnson, Brian, 30
Johnson, Bridget, 148
Johnson, Brooke, 249
Johnson, Bruce Douglas, 159
Johnson, Carl J., 77
Johnson, Caroline Lee, 42
Johnson, Charles, 145
Johnson, Christine Toy, 181
Johnson, Danny, 175
Johnson, Darryle, 184
Johnson, Demetria, 168
Johnson, Eric, 13
Johnson, Ernestine, 175
Johnson, Hassan, 35
Johnson, Haylie, 180
Johnson, Hugh, 94
Johnson, Jack Stubblefield, 170
Johnson, Jeff, 181, 184
Johnson, John S., 171
Johnson, John, 93, 175
Johnson, Julie, 145
Johnson, Junie Lowry, 37, 45
Johnson, Kenneth, 184
Johnson, Kurt, 183
Johnson, L.A., 173
Johnson, Lisa, 163
Johnson, Mark, 27, 112
Johnson, Pat, 177
Johnson, Penny, 22
Johnson, Rebekah, 148
Johnson, Rick, 182
Johnson, Rodney, 81
Johnson, Stacii Jae, 168
Johnson, Wes, 137
Johnston, Adrian, 248
Johnston, Becky, 117
Johnston, Joanna, 181
Johnston, Sue, 219
Johnstone, Iain, 12
Johnstone, Johan, 245
Johston, Ed, 145
Jokanovic, Vladimir, 248
Joksimovic, Dusan, 264
Jokubeit, Joe, 20
Jolie, Angelina, 122, 199
Jonas, Michelle, 132
Jones, Amy, 8
Jones, Angela, 162
Jones, Antonia, 148
Jones, Brett, 83
Jones, Bruce, 232
Jones, Bryan, 15
Jones, Charity, 130
Jones, Cherry, 170
Jones, Christopher, 79, 281
Jones, Corinna Harney, 179
Jones, Damian, 13, 248
Jones, Darryl "Munch" , 13 34
Jones, Dean, 23, 281
Jones, Donald, 180
Jones, Dooney, 168
Jones, Doug, 99, 163
Jones, Gareth, 238
Jones, Gary, 38
Jones, Gene Ellison, 179
Jones, Gillian, 257
Jones, J.P., 122
Jones, James Earl, 156, 172, 278, 281
Jones, Jeffrey, 20, 182, 281
Jones, John Christopher, 102
Jones, John Marshall, 65, 96
Jones, John Randolph, 53
Jones, Jon Paul, 155
Jones, Kenny, 167
Jones, L.Q., 107, 281
Jones, Laura, 106, 257
Jones, Leslie, 180
Jones, Loretha, 158
Jones, Melvin, 122
Jones, Milagros, 69
Jones, Moon, 37, 60
Jones, Nathan, 65, 203, 232
Jones, Neal, 94, 171, 183

Jones, O-Lan, 24
Jones, Paula, 23
Jones, Quincy, 184
Jones, Richard T., 91, 114
Jones, Richard Timothy, 14
Jones, Richard, 37
Jones, Rick, 37, 130
Jones, Robert, 28, 270
Jones, Rupert Penry, 245
Jones, Russell G., 69
Jones, Shawnee Free, 182
Jones, Simon, 35
Jones, Steve, 203
Jones, Steven Anthony, 155
Jones, Tamala, 23
Jones, Terry, 242, 281
Jones, Tommy Lee, 6, 48-49, 76-77,
    281
Jones, Tony, 102
Jones, Trevor, 94, 219, 224
Jones, Tyrone Granderson, 65
Jones-Eveans, Steven, 235
Jongdahl, Henrik, 260
Jonze, Spike, 101
Jordan, Alan, 165
Jordan, Don, 153
Jordan, Jeanne, 154
Jordan, Jeremy, 60
Jordan, Lawrence, 162
Jordan, Petrice, 161
Jordan, Russel and Mary Jane, 154
Jordan, Steven, 83, 154, 181
Jordan, William, 181
Jorden, Kandeyce, 83
Jørgensen, Peter Heidemann, 260
Joseph, Daniel, 102
Joseph, Jeffrey, 8
Joseph, Michael Anthony, 23
Josephson, Erland, 203
Josiah, Andrew L., 141
Josifov, Milko, 264
Joslin, Burr, 173
Joslin, Elizabeth, 173
Jostyn, Jennifer, 175
Journal Film, 266
Jovovich, Milla, 216-217
Joy, Homselle, 60
Joy, Michael, 105
Joyce, William, 66
Joyner, Tom, 39
Juan, Jean-Marie, 239
Juarbe, Israel, 121
Judd, Ashley, 114, 116, 282
Judd Jr., Gen. Fermon,173
Juhasz, Alexandra, 158
Julian Po, 170
Julian, Yolande, 208
Julien, Max, 168
Julius, Nicky, 182
Jung, Nathan, 11
Jungle 2 Jungle, 29
Juraga, Slavko, 112
Jurgensen, Randy, 27
Jury, Chris, 222
Jusko, James A., 87
Justice, Felix, 69
Justus, Mike, 183
Jutras, Richard, 105, 179
Jympson, John, 102
K.G. Productions, 260
Kabillio, Eli, 160-161
Kacandes, Georgia, 135
Kaci, Adam, 44
Kaczmarek, Jan A.P., 115, 165
Kaczmarek, Kristoff, 203
Kadanyov, Alexander, 42
Kadawaki, Amy, 153
Kael, Ron, 155
Kagan, Elaine, 22
Kagy, Tom, 135
Kahan, Stephen, 181
Kahmhadze, Teimour, 213
Kahn, Dave, 98
Kahn, Harvey, 159
Kahn, Karen, 10
Kahn, Michael, 61, 141
Kahn, Sheldon, 180
Kaige, Chen, 222
Kain, Judy, 33
Kain, Khalil, 34
Kairys, Ted, 56
Kalaidjian, Father William, 93
Kalari, Mahmoud, 223
Kalas, Brad, 151
Kaldan, Ngawang, 152
Kaleb, 81
Kaleiwo, M.S., 141
Kalesniko, Michael, 30

Kalfus, Renee Ehrlich, 181
Kalin, Tom, 178
Kalinowski, Waldemar, 132, 260
Kaliski, Michael, 77
Kalli, Mario, 12
Kallista, Jaromir, 262
Kalmbach, Scott, 155
Kalos, Peter, 155
Kam, Ma, 265
Kama Sutra A Tale Of Love, 207
Kambon, Camara, 170
Kamen, Michael, 43, 91, 251
Kamen, Robert Mark, 216
Kameno, Jin, 176
Kamerman, Lawrence S., 31
Kaminski, Albert Hanan, 263
Kaminski, Janusz, 61, 141
Kammermeier, Matthias, 254
Kamrowski, Andrzej, 156
Kanae, Big Nate, 15
Kanafuji, Ai, 220
Kanagawa, Hiro, 98, 165
Kanaoka, Nobu, 261
Kane, Bob, 128
Kane, Brad, 128
Kane, Carol, 63, 178, 282
Kane, Michael, 214
Kane, Tom, 220
Kaneko, Shusuke, 261
Kang, Low Houi, 203, 230
Kanig, Frank, 240
Kanupi, Ike, 155
Kapelos, John, 8
Kaplan, Avram Butch, 96
Kaplan, Brandon, 174
Kaplan, Caroline, 157
Kaplan, Dr. Louise J., 28
Kaplan, Harvey, 178
Kaplan, Larry, 178
Kaplan, Michael, 101
Kappes, David R., 173
Kar-Wai, Wong, 243
Karaindrou, Eleni, 203
Karasick, Paul, 241
Karaszewski, L.A., 23
Kardana Films, 158
Kardos, Ferenc, 266
Kareem, Claudia, 176
Kargbo, Sheriff, 141
Karges, Matthew Murphy, 180
Karim, Patricia, 263
Karlitz, Chris, 245
Karlsen, Elizabeth, 210
Karlstein, Dotti, 78
Karo, Paul, 230
Karp, Robert, 156
Karsch, Andrew, 260
Kartheiser, Vincent, 169
Karuletwa, Jack, 38
Karyo, Tcheky, 181, 264
Kasamatsu, Norimichi, 258
Kasander, Kees, 220
Kasanoff, Lawrence, 177
Kasdan, Lawrence, 148
Kasdorf, Lenore, 128
Kaslow, Keith, 180
Kasper, Pete, 49
Kassovitz, Mathieu, 216, 231, 236
Kasten, Jeremy, 174
Katarina, Anna, 101
Kates, Brian A., 171
Kates, Malek, 259
Kato, Hiroyuki, 226
Katt, Nicky, 14, 19, 181
Katz, David Bar, 20
Katz, Elyse, 14
Katz, Gail, 84, 126
Katz, Jim, 180
Katz, Judah, 208
Katz, Perry, 160
Katz, Robert, 179, 236
Katzenbach, Nicholas, 80
Katzin, Staey, 173
Kaufman, Avy, 33, 110, 126
Kaufman, Jeffrey Howard, 132
Kaufman, Jeffrey, 93
Kaufman, Stephen E., 183
Kaufman, Wendy, 179
Kavadas, Andrew, 169
Kavanagh, Jessica Marie, 35
Kavanagh, Leonard, 125
Kavanaugh, Maria, 148
Kavner, Julie, 142-143, 282
Kawai, Miwako, 220
Kawamura, Naonori, 265
Kay, Barnaby, 183, 257
Kay, Daryll, 183

Kay, Kelly, 144
Kay, Stephen, 164
Kayano, Naoki, 226
Kazan, Vangelis, 203
Kazanskaya, Alla A., 42
Kazmierski, Stephen, 105, 159, 163
Kazui, Kaz, 123
Keanan, Stacy, 60
Keane, Dolores, 231
Keane, John, 231
Keane, Kerrie, 184
Keane, Willem, 155
Keaney, Dermot, 159
Kearns, Sean, 256
Keating, Dominic, 29
Keating, Kevin, 102
Keating, Robert, 97
Keaton, Joshua, 71
Keaton, Michael, 43, 147, 282
Keefer, Don, 37, 300
Keegan-Dolan, Michael, 225
Keel, Keena, 176
Keeley, Cliff, 28
Keeley, Paul, 51
Keeley, Tom, 79
Keen, Lisa Hewlett, 63
Keen, Pat, 12
Keena, Monica, 161, 183
Keenan, Caroline, 82
Keenan, Paddy, 47
Keenen, Mary Jo, 82
Keener, Catherine, 86
Keenleyside, Eric, 13
Keeper, The, 100
Keeslar, Matt, 16, 144, 175
Kehela, Karen, 43
Kehler, Jack, 21, 184
Kehoe, Jack, 101
Kehoe, Pat, 112
Kei, Shu, 222
Keiffer, Dennis, 177, 181
Keir, Andy, 32
Keitel, Harvey, 32, 92-93, 125,
    164-165, 203, 279, 282
Keith, Katernia, 155
Kelamis, Peter, 165
Keller, Annie, 238
Kellerman, Claire, 172
Kellerman, Sally, 172, 282
Kellermann, Susan, 183
Kelley, Donna J., 181
Kelley, Hugh, 163
Kelley, John Patrick, 116
Kelley, Steve, 13
Kellner, Catherine, 163, 179
Kellogg, Robert, 240
Kelly, Brendan, 35, 65
Kelly, Brian, 159
Kelly, Brigid, 209
Kelly, Chance, 35
Kelly, Craig, 186
Kelly, David Patrick, 167
Kelly, Elsie, 238
Kelly, Emma, 183, 209
Kelly, Errol, 162
Kelly, Gabrielle, 173, 264
Kelly, Ian, 50
Kelly, Joseph Patrick, 65
Kelly, Kevin, 182
Kelly, Michael F., 8
Kelly, Mitchell, 35, 83
Kelly, Nicole, 69, 112
Kelly, Norman, 256
Kelly, Peter, 248
Kelly, Renee, 147
Kelly, Sean B., 176
Kelly, Terence, 144
Kelso, Moe, 180
Kemp, Barry, 51
Kemp, Stephanie, 151
Kemp, Tara, 125
Kemp, Tom, 176
Kemp, Vera, 145
Kemper, Steven, 8, 75
Kempf, Robert Louis, 82
Kempster, Victor, 113
Kendall, Greg, 169
Kendall, Tom, 172
Kennedy, Carol, 205
Kennedy, Chris, 204, 260
Kennedy, Christine, 87
Kennedy, Christopher, 180
Kennedy, David, 216
Kennedy, Gavin, 256
Kennedy, George, 180, 282
Kennedy, Jamie, 144, 148
Kennedy, Kathleen, 61, 181, 212
Kennedy, Maria Doyle, 212

Kennedy, Merle, 127
Kennedy, Mike, 182
Kennedy, Mimi, 66
Kennedy, Patrick, 158
Kenney, Bill, 68
Kenny's Kings, 167
Kenny, Francis, 244
Kent, Dana, 247
Kent, Mignon, 265
Kent, Miranda, 102
Kent, Oliver, 229
Kent, Rolfe, 118
Kentis, Chris, 159
Kenyatta, Stogie, 181
Keogh, Jimmy, 231
Keramidas, Harry, 97
Kerby, Bill, 161
Kerdelhue, Jean-Marc, 265
Kerman, Ken, 49
Kern, Kenneth, 151
Kern, Lis, 42
Kerner, Jordan, 81, 126
Kerns, Linda, 186
Kerr, E. Katherine, 183
Kerr, Rowen, 176
Kerray, Brent, 38
Kerrigan, Dermot, 222
Kershaw, Annabel, 212
Kersnowski, Maud, 174
Kerwin, Brian, 105, 282
Kess, Georgina, 29
Kesselman, Wendy, 241
Kessler, Carolyn, 98
Kessler, Paul, 179
Kessler, Stephen, 179
Kesting, Hans, 196
Kestner, Boyd, 94
Kettle, Ross, 122
Key, Steve, 106
Keyes, Joe, 160
Keys To Tulsa, 160
Keymah, T'Keyah Crystal, 147
Keystone Pictures, 87, 162
Kha, 220
Khan, George, 216
Khan, Shaheen, 210
Khan, Sylvia, 93
Khangsar, Tsewang Migyur, 152
Khanjian, Arsinée,213, 249
Kharbanda, Kulbushan, 235
Khomblassen, Melissa, 69
Khondji, Darius, 133
Ki, Kenny, 126
Kiberlain, Sandrine, 236, 260, 265
Kid N' Play, 157
Kidd, Bryan, 166
Kidde, Geoffrey, 175
Kidder, Margot, 175, 282
Kidman, Nicole, 112, 279, 282
Kidnie, James, 23, 99
Kiefel, Russell, 214
Kieferle, Kirsten, 249
Kieffer, Doug, 83
Kiely, Mark, 107
Kier, Udo, 100, 282
Kierny, Tyde, 56
Kieser, Father Ellwood, 141
Kievit, Paul, 78
Kightley, Timothy, 210
Kihlstedt, Rya, 178
Kijak, Stephen, 175
Kikuchi, Junichi, 226
Kikuta, David, 37
Kilbride, Kerry, 49
Kiledjian, Koko, 84
Kilgore, Diedre, 156
Killick, David, 210
Kilmer, Val, 42, 282
Kilner, Kevin, 178
Kilpatrick, Eric, 97
Kilpatrick, Laurie, 148
Kilpatrick, Patrick, 182
Kilroy, Colette, 110
Kim, Daniel Dae, 131, 181
Kim, Jacqueline, 49
Kim, James, 181
Kim, Simon, 181
Kim, Sujin, 261
Kim, Young Joo, 96
Kimball, Frederic, 141
Kimberley, Meggan, 168
Kimilcko, John, 169
Kimura, Hideo, 11, 101
Kimura, Satomi, 220
Kimura, Tatsuya, 220
Kincaid, Brenda, 114
Kind, Richard, 14, 175

Kinder, Sandra, 122
Kindlin, Kevin, 181
Kindred, Oliver, 37
Kiner, Kevin, 20
King Pictures, 83
King, Brian, 12, 180
King, Coretta Scott, 80
King, Don, 183
King, Jeffrey, 23
King, Kevin, 93
King, Larry, 131, 181
King, Lorelei, 42
King, Mark, 230
King, Randall, 135, 155
King, Raymond, 182
King, Rick, 47
King, Robb Wilson, 95
King, Robert, 126
King, Scott, 80, 83
King, Shirley Wesley, 80
King, Zalman, 38
Kingdom, Bob, 131
Kingdom, Robert, 137
Kingelesi, Jules, 256
Kingery, Amanda, 183
Kingery, Dorothy, 183
Kingery, Susan, 183
Kings of Klezmer, 258
Kingsley, Ben, 105, 282
Kingston, Stuart, 163
Kininmonth, Mathew Walker, 203
Kinkade, Chris, 96
Kinlaw, Chuck, 47, 173
Kinnear, Greg, 148-149, 168, 194,
    282
Kinney, Mike, 180
Kinnunen, Jari, 186
Kino, 100, 223, 239, 243, 258
Kinowelt Film Produktion, 218
Kinski, Nastassja, 132, 180, 282
Kinsly, Kelsa, 107
Kipling, Rudyard, 162
Kipper, David A., 148
Kirby, Bruno, 26-27, 280, 282
Kirby, Johanna, 245
Kirby, Michael, 26, 100
Kirk, Justin, 58-59
Kirk, Roger, 262
Kirkland, Sally, 98, 282
Kirkley, Marcia, 157, 177
Kirkpatrick, David, 168
Kirkpatrick, Eric, 176
Kirkpatrick, Kathryn, 80
Kirschenbauer, Karen, 131
Kirschner, David, 180
Kirshner, Mia, 180, 183
Kirtadze, Nino, 213
Kisicki, James, 123
Kiss And Tell, 173
Kiss Me, Guido, 166
Kiss Or Kill, 243
Kiss The Girls, 114
Kiss, Cornelia, 144
Kissed, 212
Kissel, Audrey, 45
Kit, Chen Tsun, 96
Kitson, Ken, 219
Kitt, Eartha, 177, 282
Kiyabo, Randy, 15
Kjellgren, Katherne, 259
Klapisch, Cédric, 221
Klar, Paul, 155
Klass, David, 114
Klaus, Fenja, 183
Klaus, Peter, 115
Klebanoff, Mitch, 11
Klein, David, 41
Klein, Ericka, 160
Klein, Kathleen, 66
Klein, Nicholas, 100
Kleinman, Daniel, 253
Klemp, Matt, 170
Klima, Herbert, 265
Klimenko, Peter, 230
Kline, Kevin, 12, 102-103, 110-111,
    282
Kline, Richard, 11, 15
Kling, Elizabeth, 181
Kling, Heidi, 8
Klingler, Rebecca Jane, 182, 186
Kliot, Jason, 159
Klopper, Nancy, 106, 182
Klugman, Brian, 172
Klvana, Kathryn, 180
Knatchbull, Melissa, 42
Knaus, Darren T., 178
Kniep, Nancy, 71
Knight, Christopher, 60

Knight, Jack, 182
Knight, Ruben, 38
Knight, Shirley, 148-149, 282
Knight, Tuesday, 123
Knight, Wayne, 71, 137
Knittridge, Viggis, 175
Knobelspiess, Roger, 239
Knoeffel, Mark, 105
Knoeral, Bobby, 167
Knoll, R.J., 8
Knopfler, Mark, 151
Knot, Jiri, 264
Knotts, Don, 180
Know-Mawer, Vanessa, 219
Knower, Rosemary, 137
Knowledge Of Healing, The , 265
Knue, Michael N., 90
Ko, David, 33
Koch Company production, 18
Koch, David, 181
Koch, Jr., Howard "Hawk" 18
Koch, Oscar, 158
Koch, Pete, 181
Kocka, Jerry, 174
Kodiak Productions L.L.C., 159
Koechner, David, 151
Koefoed, Christopher, 13
Koehler, Tammy, 101
Koepenick, Brad, 9
Koepp, David, 61
Koff, Barry, 156
Koffler, Pamela, 178
Koford, James D., 166
Kohler, Jon, 23
Kohn, Edgar, 254
Kohout, Pavel, 258
Koizumi, Hiroshi, 261
Kojo, Nikola, 264
Koker, Danny, 68
Kolar, Evzen, 32
Kolman, Allan, 84
Kolsrud, Dan, 182
Kolstein, Harry, 258, 266
Koltai, Lajos, 78
Koman, Jacek, 230
Komarek, Heidi, 132
Komarov, Shelley, 112
Komino, Kumi, 220
Komorowska, Liliana, 105
Konckier, Régine, 265
Konrad Pictures, 144
Konrad, Cathy, 93, 144
Konsgaard, Susanne Birkemose, 260
Konstant, Nicholas, 174
Koon, Rebecca, 23
Kopache, Thomas, 55, 132
Kopelow, Kevin, 83
Kopelson Entertaiment, 182
Kopelson, Anne, 180, 182-183
Kopelson, Arnold, 180, 182-183
Koppekin, Adam M., 183
Koppel, Murit, 171
Koppel, Nurit, 161
Koppelman, Jennifer, 15
Koretzky, Nicolas, 221
Korine, Harmony, 174
Kornis, Anna, 266
Koromzay, Alix, 99
Kosminsky, Oleg, 180
Kosseh, Joseph, 141
Koster, Iren, 178
Kostrin, Valery, 202
Kostroff, Michael, 37
Koteas, Elias, 124, 208, 282
Kotecki, Robert, 118
Kouf, Jim, 65, 172
Koumpaan, Alexander, 44
Kourotchkine, Christophe, 236
Kousnetsova, Larissa, 180
Kouzouyan, Jono, 112
Kovacs, Danny, 155
Kovacs, Lajos, 266
Kove, Martin, 175
Kowalski, Stanley, 216
Koyama, John, 32
Koyama, Seitaro, 220
Koysta, Charles, 97
Kozak, Harley Jane, 174, 282
Kozeluh, John, 173
Kozlowski, Steven, 138
Krabbe, Jeroen, 236, 282
Krajewski, Guido, 223
Kramar, Hubert, 112
Kramer, Bert, 49
Kramer, Clare, 102
Kramer, Josh, 53
Kramer, Oscar, 250

Kramer, Tracy, 95
Krane, Jonathan D., 75, 172, 183
Krasnova, Julia, 180
Krasny, Kevin, 155
Kratzig, Sadie, 114
Kravat, Amanda, 118, 164
Kravetz, Carole, 236
Krawic, Michael, 182
Krayenbuhl, Sabine, 175
Kressel, Lynn, 52
Krevoy, Brad, 9, 11, 29, 44, 116, 172
Kriechbaum, Philipp, 117
Kriel, Helena, 207
Kriesa, Christopher, 155
Krimer, Jorge, 224
Kris Kross, 157
Kriski, Mark, 68
Kristelle, 221
Kristofferson, Kris, 182, 282
Kristopher, Jason, 101
Kroeger, Wolf, 107
Kroetsch, Neil, 105
Kroll, Mark, 156
Kronenfeld, Ivan, 110
Kroopf, Scott, 13
Krost, Barry, 59
Krucker, Fides, 249
Kruger, Brit, 223
Kruglova, Vera, 202
Kruk, Tony, 174
Krull, Suzanne, 44, 146
Krumholtz, David, 110
Krupa, Howard, 170
Krupa, Olek, 170, 178
Krutonog, Boris, 84
Kubheka, Peter, 155
Kublak, Martin, 262
Kuchan, Josip, 164
Kuczynski, Brittney, 39
Kudrow, Lisa, 51, 282
Kufrin, Ben, 177
Kufus, Thomas, 258
Kuhn, Toni, 264
Kujaca, Nikolina, 248
Kukhareshen, Valery, 180
Kuldin, Tamara, 260
Kull The Conqueror, 169
Kumar, Anand, 207
Kumar, Pravesh, 218
Kundun, 152
Kunga, Selden, 152
Kunzler, Kurtis, 14
Kuoch, Koing, 160
Kuras, Ellen, 80
Kurepova, Ludmila, 180
Kurita, Toyomichi, 153
Kuroiwa, Hisami, 245
Kurokawa, Fumio, 261
Kurtag, Gyorgi, 262
Kurtis Blow and Crew, 156
Kurtz, Ada, 39
Kurtz, Marcia J., 53
Kurtz, Michael, 181
Kurtz, Swoosie, 36-37, 282
Kurtzman, Robert, 90, 172
Kurtzman, Wendy, 20
Kurzer, Edie, 266
Kusakari, Tamiyo, 226-227
Kusamura, Reiko, 226-227
Kusatsu, Clyde, 211
Kusenko, Nick, 181
Kushida, Alice, 181
Kushner, Donald, 164
Kux, Bill, 181
Kuznetsov, Alexander, 112
Kuzui Enterprises, 123
Kuzui, Fran, 123
Kvirikadze, Irakli, 213
Kwapis, Ken, 18
Kwok, Philip, 253
Kwok-Wing, Leslie Cheung, 243
Kybartas, Sandra, 23, 241
Kyle & Tyler Wilkerson, 18
Kymlicka, Milan, 205
Kynman, Paul, 169, 245
Kyris, Marco, 65, 75
L.A. Confidential, 182
L'Hirondelle, Tyronne, 38
La Page, Roger, 173
La Region Rhone Alpes, 218
La Promesse, 215
La Rencontre, 266
La Sept ARTE, 258
Labao, Cece Neber, 181
LaBarbara, Joan, 133
Labarthe, Francoise-Renaud, 213
Labaton, Arnold, 165

Laborie, Gustavo, 68
Laboriel, Raymond, 121
LaBorne, Kali, 157
Labowitz, Amy, 59
Labrie, Richard, 156
Labus, Jiri, 262
LaBute, Neil, 89
LaCause, Sebastian, 121, 144
LaChanze, 71
Lachman, Ed, 24
Lachman, Edward, 179
LaCoco, Joe, 179
LaCombe, Andy, 181
Lacopo, Jay, 68
Lacroix, Ghalia, 262
Lacroix, Peter, 182
Ladburty, Hattie, 229
Ladd, Cheryl, 173, 282
Ladd, Jordan, 60
Laduke, Winona, 166
La Ferriere, Natacha, 177
Laffan, Pat, 42, 231
Laffont, Axelle, 265
La Fleur, Art, 167
LaFleur, Art, 178
LaFond, Rick, 63, 172
Lagarto, João, 264
Lagerda, Felipe, 264
Lagerlöf, Selma, 259
Lagle, David, 112
Laguardia, Ernesto, 264
Lah, Saye, 141
Lahouassa, Farid, 221
Lai, Rocky, 203
Laing, James, 11
Laing, Martin, 186
Laing, Richard, 245
Laird, Jere, 49
Lakatos, Alexi, 128
Lake, Don, 16, 174
Lake, Mark, 8
Lake, Michael, 259
Lakeshore Entertainment, 62, 86, 104, 169
Lakey, John, 130
Lalama, Pat, 49
Lally, Brian, 182
Lally, James, 126
Lally, Krista, 178
Lalonde, Robert, 241
Lam, Doris, 203
Lam, Kheim, 220
Lam, Michael, 265
Lam, Siu Lin, 261
Lamarca, Andrew G., 44
Lamb, Amy Jo, 205
Lamb, David B, 205
Lamb, Irene, 242, 250
Lambert, Anne, 265
Lambert, Catherine, 265
Lambert, Kayla, 184
Lambert, Steve, 182
Lambton, Anne, 186
Lamont, Peter, 186
Lamontagne, Cynthia, 56
LaMorte, Robia, 90
Lamotte, Martin, 265
Lampley, Oni F., 100
Lampley, Oni Faida, 29
LaNasa, Katherne, 159
Lancaster, James, 186
Landa, Suzy, 161
Landaas, Robert William, 159
Landau, Jon, 186
Landau, Martin, 104, 158, 283
Landau, Natasha, 163
Landel, Buddy, 86
Landers, Christy, 166
Landey, Clayton, 96
Landis, John, 183, 254
Landis, Laramie, 186
Landra, Sylvie, 216
Landre, Lou, 196
Landsburg, Shana, 184
Lane, Darren, 176
Lane, Diane, 180, 232, 283
Lane, Fredric, 65, 77
Lane, Nathan, 59, 146, 280, 283
Lane, Yuri, 155
Lang, Elaine, 117
Lang, Stephen J., 13
Lang, Stephen, 154, 182, 283
Lange, Andres, 105
Lange, Jessica, 106, 283
Langer, Claus, 264
Langer, Jean, 28
Langford, Lisa Louise, 52
Langlois, Yves, 105

Langmead, John, 203
Langrishe, Barry, 214, 243
Langway, Douglas, 156
Langway, Stephen, 156
Lannom, Les, 20
Lansbury, Angela, 130, 283
Lanthier, Sean, 101
Lantieri, Michael, 61
Lantos, Robert, 208, 249
Lanvin, Gérard, 231
Lanza, Angela, 21
LaPaglia, Anthony, 52, 230, 262, 283
Lapiower, Hélène, 263
Lappin, Arthur, 256
Laquit, Gisele, 221
Larby, Ahmed Ben, 132
Lardner, Lonnie, 49
Laresca, Vincent, 161, 183
Largo Entertainment, 32, 79, 94
Larin, Sergueï, 262
Larkin, Linda, 159
Larkin, Peter, 244
Laroque, Michele, 255
LaRose, Scott, 23, 38
Larralde, Onelia, 224
Larriva, Tito, 96, 118
Larrivaz, Estelle, 221
Larseca, Vincent, 93
Larsen, Barbara, 168
Larsen, Ken, 29
Larsen, Ronnie, 166
Larson, Mark S., 160
Larson, Murphy, 163
LaRue, Chi Chi, 166
LaSardo, Robert, 172
Lasater, Barbara, 159
Lasdun, James, 96
Lasher, Estelle, 164
Laskin, Michael, 78
Lasovich, Bill, 99
Lass, Jeff, 172
Lass, Ruth, 225
Lassez, Sarah, 60
Lasser, Louise, 157, 283
Last Time I Committed Suicide, The , 164
Laswell, Bill, 171
Late Bloomers, 164
Latham, Elester, 84
Lathan, Stan, 13, 168
Lathem, Laurie, 49
Latifah, Queen, 97, 283
Latin Boys Go To Hell, 171
LaTour, Nick, 60
Lattaker, Robyn, 60
Latter, Greg, 155
Lau, Eric, 156
Lau, Jim, 20
Lau, Laura, 159
Lauder, Maureen, 182
Laumeister, Shannah, 179
Laupus, Arthur, 115
Lauren, Andrew, 182
Lauren, Greg, 121, 181
Lauren, Tammy, 172, 183
Laurence, Henry, 179
Laurents, Arthur, 130
Laurie, Darcy, 162
Laurier, Lucie, 105
Laval, Marie-Paule, 263
Lavallée, Jacques, 105
Laventhall, Donald, 35
Lavidis, Achilles, 175
Lavine, Larry, 157
LaVorgna, Adam, 18
Lavrova, Alexandra, 180
Law Brothers production, 163
Law, Christopher, 163
Law, Darren, 177
Law, Dennis, 163
Law, Jeremy, 163
Law, Joseph, 163
Law, Jude, 124, 183, 198, 241, 245, 283
Law, Lindsay, 116
Law, Phyllida, 180, 251
Law, Ronald, 163
Lawford, Christopher, 158, 166
Lawless, Fenton, 84
Lawlor, Sean, 231
Lawrance, William, 125, 242
Lawrence, Andrew J, 244
Lawrence, Mark Christopher, 23, 60
Lawrence, Martin, 82, 283
Lawrence, Scott, 8, 30, 291

Laws, Pamela S., 183
Lawson, Peta, 230
Lawson, Richard, 151
Lawther, Chas, 138
Lawton, Cassandra, 23
Lawyer, Pat, 160
Lay of the Land, The, 172
Layden, Kate, 232
Lazaneo, Steven, 183
Lazar, Max, 122
Lazarev, Evgeny, 42
Lazaro, Eusebio, 236
Lazenberg, Christophe, 161
Lazerine, Loren, 121, 167
Lazich, Stevan, 168
Lazlo-Carr, Linzi, 183
Lazzarini, Rick, 99
Lazzarus, Q, 178
Le Studio Canal+, 231, 236, 239, 260, 265
Le, Hiep Thi, 161, 265
Lea, Dave, 82
Lea, Derek, 186
Leaf, Richard, 216
Leahy, Mark P., 181
Leahy, Senator Patrick, 181
Leake, Damien, 35
Leal, Jack, 155
Leal, Tomas, 160
Lear, Kristina, 53
Leary, Denis, 151, 162, 283
Leary, Franci, 183
Leary, Timothy, 164
Leaud, Jean-Pierre, 213, 215, 263, 283
Leave It To Beaver, 98
Lebenzon, Chris, 65
Le Besco, Maïwenn, 216
Lebeshev, Pavel, 202
Le Bihan, Samuel, 239
Lebrón, Juan, 213
Calm, Renée Le, 221
Lecesne, James, 33
Lechterman, Bob, 175
Leckner, Brian, 182
Le Clezio, J.M.G., 260
Le Compte, Rick, 69
Le Coq, Bernard, 231, 239
Lecube, Graciela, 93
Leder, Mimi, 112
LeDon, Horacio, 44
Ledoux, Patrice, 216
Lee, Allan, 165
Lee, Ang, 110
Lee, Anthony, 37
Lee, Bill, 175
Lee, Candy Jack, 155
Lee, Carmen, 41
Lee, Casey, 118
Lee, Clarence, 171
Lee, Henry, 121
Lee, Howard, 250
Lee, Jason, 40-41
Lee, Jennifer, 60
Lee, Leo, 32, 181
Lee, Luann, 49
Lee, Madeline, 39
Lee, Moonyeenn, 154
Lee, Mushond, 181
Lee, Nikki, 122
Lee, Phillipa, 230
Lee, RonReaco, 176-177
Lee, Sacha, 245
Lee, Sheryl, 79, 165
Lee, Spike, 80, 283
Lee, Tony, 159
Lee, Wing, 159
LeFevre, Adam, 29-30, 102, 265
Lefevre, Dennis, 181
Lefko, Carol, 172
Legacy, 50, 68, 159, 162, 166, 174, 262
Legato, Robert, 186
LeGault, Lance, 177
Legrand, Michel, 263
LeGros, James, 105, 283
Leguizamo, John, 20, 50, 90, 280, 283
Lehembre, Philippe, 236
Lehman, Kristin, 165
Le Henry, Alain, 236
Lei, Ren, 262
Leibman, Ron, 53, 283
Leigh, Jennifer Jason, 106, 115, 283
Leigh, Lexi, 121
Leigh, Mike, 234
Leisenring, John, 154

Leisure Time Features, 178, 215
Leisure, David, 60
Leitch, Donovan, 132
Leker, Larry, 130
Lekshe, Lama Jampa, 117
Leland, Brad, 159
Lemkin, Jonathan, 182
Lemmon, Chris, 172, 283
Lemmon, Jack, 78, 283
Lemmons, Kasi, 13, 62, 129
Lemon Sky, 86
Lemon, Ben, 37
Lemore, George, 184
Lemus, Luis, 160
Lenard, Melvyn, 98
Lence, Robert, 180
Lenk, Thomas, 121
Lennon, Gary, 158
Lennox, Kai, 121, 128
Leno, Jay, 15, 102, 151, 181, 183, 283
Lenthall, David, 79
Lenzer, Don, 104, 157
Leo Films, 163
Leo Tolstoy's Anna Karenina, 180
Leon, 159
Leonard, Elmore, 24, 147
Leonard, Lawrence, 154
Leonard, Robert Sean, 241, 280, 283
Leonetti, John R., 177
Leonetti, Matthew F., 177
Leong, William, 32
Leopard, Mary, 161
Leopard, Michael, 37
Leos, Cindy, 83
Lerer, Shifra, 142
Lerner, Fred, 32
Lerner, Michael, 18, 137, 283
Leroy, Liane, 221
Les Comperes, 180
Les Films Alain Sarde, 218, 231, 239
Les Films Balengicaga, 265
Les Films Du Fleuve, 215
Les Films Du Rivage, 213
Leshcinkov, N, 203
Leskin, Boris, 77
Lesley Clare O'Neill, 218
Lesley, Bradley J., 66
Leslie, Brooke, 75
Leslie, Georgette, 69
Lesser, Anton, 125
Lesser, Elana, 180
Lesser, Robert, 8
Lester, Dan, 8, 90
Lester, David, 84
Lester, Derrell Keith, 177
Lester, Mary, 135
Lester, Ron, 83
Letham, Ronnie, 42
Leto, Jared, 13, 127
Leto, Shannon, 13
Letterman, David, 30
Letts, Dennis, 160, 182
Letts, Don, 283
Leubner, Marilyn, 17
Leung, Ken, 126
Leung, Kwok-Wing, 80
Leung, See Wah, 220
Leung, See Yan, 220
Leupp, Clinton, 176
Leustig, Elisabeth, 42, 164, 260
Leva, Gary, 173
Leva, Shelly, 173
Levani, 84-85
Levant, Brian, 98
Levantal, François, 236, 239
Levels, Calvin, 44, 155, 283
Leventon, Annabel, 225
LeVert, Benjamin, 34
Levi, Michelle, 225
Levi, Nino, 248
Levi, Rick, 30
Levin, Gail, 254
Levin, Harvey, 49
Levin, Lloyd, 35, 91, 121
Levin, Matt, 128
Levin, Robert, 154
Levine, David, 175
Levine, Floyd, 83
Levine, Jeff, 75
Levine, Jerry, 151, 283
Levine, Judi, 230
Levine, Ted, 127, 136, 183
Levinsohn, Gary, 8, 131
Levinson, Barry, 27, 151
Levinson, Michelle, 151

Levitas, Andrew, 102
Levitt, Heidi, 100
Levitt, John, 242
Lévy, Krishna, 263
Levy, Lisa, 173
Levy, Marty, 49, 95
Levy, Robert F., 164
Levy, Shuki, 158
Lewin, Alexandra, 230
Lewin, Ben, 230
Lewis, Carol, 55, 172
Lewis, Don W., 163
Lewis, Ellen, 152
Lewis, Geoffrey, 183, 283
Lewis, Jazmsin, 168
Lewis, Keith, 155
Lewis, Mark, 38
Lewis, Richard, 158, 178
Lewis, Ross, 251
Lewis, Selina, 170
Lewis, Stephen Brimson, 245
Lewis, Thyme, 60
Lewis, Todd, 184
Lewis, Vicki, 146
Leyh, Blake, 132
Leys, Polly, 232
Leyser, Jamie, 237
Lhamo, Tsering, 152
Lhermitte, Thierry, 29, 254
L'Heureux, Gerard, 65
Lhomme, Pierre, 231
Li'l Caesar, 157
Li, Gong, 222
Li, Lian-Yi, 163
Li, Yang, 126, 214
Lianqun, Lin, 222
Liapis, Peter, 172
Liar Liar, 37
Libby, Brian, 84
Libby, Linda, 86
Licensed To Kill, 159
Lichtenstein, Gregory, 183
Lichtenstein, Mitchell, 171
Liddell, Eric, 13
Liddell, Mickey, 47, 123
Lieberman, Arthur M., 169
Lieberman, Hal, 131
Lieberman, Iris, 97
Liebling, Terri, 63
Liesche, Jochen, 13
Life Apart: Hasidism in America, A, 165
Ligardes, Patrick, 236
Ligeti, Barbara, 178
Liggett, Agnieszka, 42
Liggins, Maleah, 69
Light, Kevin, 60
Light, Michael, 158
Lightfoot, Sally, 259
Lightstorm Entertainment, 186
Like A Bride, 264
Lilies, 241
Lill, Denis, 12
Lima, Omar, 183
Limas, Jim Adhi, 220
Limperis, Constantine, 156
Lin, Ge, 222
Lin, Kevin, 222
Lin, Lily L., 126
Lin, Robert, 126, 152
Linares, Aida, 113
Linares, Carmen, 213
Linari, Peter, 77, 80
Lind, Josefina, 264
Lind, Traci, 100
Lindberg, Lorri, 173
Linde, David, 173
Lindeman, Doug, 166
Lindemulder, Janine, 30
Linden, Hal, 78, 283
Lindenlaub, Karl Walter, 126, 131
Linder, Dixie, 245
Linder, Stu, 151
Lindgren, Astrid, 262
Lindinger, Natacha, 44
Lindley, Audra, 8
Lindo, Allan, 38
Lindo, Delroy, 166, 183, 240
Lindsay, Brad, 262
Lindsay, Delia, 229
Lindsay, Robert, 12, 283
Lindsay-Hogg, Michael, 266
Lindsey, Joseph, 145
Lindsey, Kent, 94
Lindsley, Blake, 128
Lindstedt, David, 107
Lindstrom, Kara, 175

Lindstrom, Lisa, 126
Lineback, Richard, 131
Ling, Bai, 126
Ling, Barbara, 181
Ling, Van, 186
Linhart, Ken, 184
Link, Andre, 264
Link, John F., 184
Linke, Shannon L., 183
Linklater, Richard, 19
Linkovoin, Dolgor B., 265
Linn, Rex, 55, 184
Linney, Laura, 22, 284
Linson, Art, 107
Lintz, Gertrude Davies, 66
Linz, Alex D., 178
Liotta, Ray, 8, 93, 284
Lip, Tony, 27
Lipper, David, 17
Lipper, Ken, 205
Lipsky, Jeff, 159
Lipsky, Mark, 10
Lipson, Biran, 222
Lipson, Mark, 104, 116
Lipton, Geoff, 230
Lipton, Peggy, 184
Lisbon Story, 262
Lisi, Joe, 159
Lisi, Richard, 93
Liska, Stephen, 182
Lister, Tommy "Tiny", Jr., 147, 216
Litefoot, 169, 177
Littenberg, Susan, 157
Little Bear Films, 239
Little, Carole, 46
Little, Dwight, 180
Little, Martha, 164
Little, Nicollette, 96
Little, Pauline, 179
Little, Russ, 162
Little, Tawny, 95
Liu, Lucy Alexis, 13, 32
Liu, Symantha, 203
LIVE Entertainment, 126, 161, 166-167, 172, 210, 259
Lively, Ernie, 182
Livingston, Victor, 177
Livingstone, Andrew, 232
Livingstone, Paul, 214
Livingstone, Steve, 203
Lizzi, John, 33
Llanaj, Gert, 203
Llewellyn, Wes, 177
Llewellyn-Jones, Tony, 260
Llewelyn, Desmond, 252-253
Llewelyn, Doug, 95
Llosa, Luis, 46
Lloyd, Barnett Milton, 30
Lloyd, Caleb, 125
Lloyd, Caroline, 209
Lloyd, Christopher, 130, 159, 284
Lloyd, Emily, 248, 284
Lloyd, Eric, 142-143, 181
Lloyd, John Bedford, 173
Lloyd, Peter, 254
Lloyd, Samuel, 136
Lloyd, Walt, 30
Lo, Chi Muoi, 8
Lo, Ming, 126
Lo, Mrs, 220
Lobotsky, Igor N., 84
Lobst, Annie, 171
Locane, Amy, 13, 104, 165
Locatell, Carol, 31
Loch, Philip, 79
Locke, Michael, 168
Locke, Peter, 164
Locke, Tembi, 184
Lockhart, Doris, 80
Lockhart, Dugald Bruce, 225
Locklear, Heather, 95
Locksley, 264
Locusts, The , 116
Lodoe, Tenzin, 152
LoDuca, Joseph, 178
Loewenthal, Dan, 159
Loftin, Lennie, 182
Logan, Bellina, 88
Logan, H. Forrest, 69
Logan, Harlem, 69
Loggia, Robert, 21, 206, 284
LoGiudice, Gaetano, 27
Logo Entertainment, 154
Logue, Donal, 10
Lohmann, Dietrich, 112, 265
Lollia, Dominique, 231
Lomax, David, 112
Lombard, Karina, 169

Lombard, Michael, 183
Lombardi, Louis, 180
Lombardo, Tita, 264-265
Lombardo, Tony, 63
Lombardozzi, Domenick, 166
Lomena, June, 168
Lomino, Daniel, 66
Lon, Juliet, 147
London, Bill, 157
London, Frank, 50, 163
London, Lisa, 160
London, Melody, 154
London, Michael, 264, 285
London, Sharon K., 129
London, Sharon, 145
London, Stacie B., 177
Lone, David, 212
Long Way Home, The , 104
Long, Kathy, 51
Long, Nia, 34, 108-109, 201
Longo, Alexandra, 39
Longoria, Valerio, Sr., 180
Longworth, David, 98
Lonow, Mark, 162
Lonsdale, David, 232
Loperz "Cachao", Israel, 264
Lopes, José Manuel, 258
Lopez, Carmen, 25
Lopez, Daniel Steven, 179
Lopez, Diego, 100
Lopez, Irene Olga, 44
Lopez, Jennifer, 25, 46, 113, 179, 198, 284
Lopéz, José, 213
Lopez, Pascal, 44
Lopez, Peter, 179
Lopez, Rigoberto, 264
Lopez, Sal, 100, 180
Lopez, Seidy, 180
Loquasto, Santo, 142
Lordan, John, 104
Lords of the Underground, 157
Lords, Traci, 60, 162
Loren, Eric, 42
Lorenc, Michal, 25
Lorences, Maria Fernanda, 250
Lorente, Isabel, 245
Lorenzo, Oscar Dante, 250
Lorez, Juliane, 262
Loriaux, Fabienne, 207
Loring, Scotch Ellis, 38, 184
Lorre, Alex, 133
Lorusso, Theodore P., 169
Lory, Shan, 41
Lost Highway, 21
Lost World: Jurassic Park, The, 61
Lott, Barbara, 220
Lou, Jackson, 203
Loubert, Patrick, 262
Loudon, Dorothy, 183
Loughlin, Terry, 131
Louis-Dreyfus, Julia, 142, 180, 284
Louiso, Todd, 44
Loup, Jean, 178
Lourwood, Heath, 156
Loustau, Olivier, 239
Louthan, Guy J., 160
Louvart, Hélène, 250
Love Always, 174
Love And Other Catastrophes, 209
Love Jones, 34
Love Serenade, 235
Love! Valour! Compassion!, 58
Love's Debris, 262
Love, Candice, 161
Love, Capt. Greg, 69
Love, David, 118
Love, Faizon, 95, 159
Love, Mother, 49
Love, Ted, 97
Love, Victor, 172
Loveheart, C.C., 157
Lovejoy, Ray, 43
Lovelace, Laura, 147
Lovell, Lexy, 171
Lovemaster, The , 174
Low, Eddie J., 49
Low, Victor, 196
Low, William, 261
Lowe, Jo-Jo, 102
Lowe, Kevin, 95
Lowe, Leslie, 12
Lowe, Marjorie, 39
Lowe, Rob, 181, 284
Lowe, Robert, 259
Lowell, Carey, 12
Lowen, Travis, 128
Lowery, Gary, 86

Loyd, Zelma, 145
Lubatti, Henry, 13
Luca, Claudio, 205
Lucas, Nick, 210
Lucca, Papo, 264
Lucci, Gino, 183
Lucente, Cameron, 50
Lucey, D., 49
Luchak, Joan, 39
Luchich, Aaron Thomas, 101
Luchini, Fabrice, 265
Luchs, Jay, 181
Lucich, Aaron, 183
Luck, Bree, 183
Ludescher, Kurt, 230
Ludwig, James Paul, 176
Ludwig, Tony, 146
Lugo, Pinky, 69
Lui, Lucy, 176
Luisi, Caesar, 11
Luisi, Edwin, 258
Lukanic, Steve, 137
Lukashov, Konstantin, 180
Lukhang, Gyatso, 152
Lumbrezer, Stacy, 128
Lumet, Sidney, 53, 126
Lumpkin, Furley, 151
Lunch, Lydia, 154
Lund, Nicole, 174
Lunden, Joan, 182
Lundmark, Erik, 167
Lundy, Jessica, 174
Lung Ta, 262
Lungtok, Jampa, 152
Lungtok, Kalsang Dhundop, 117
Lunn, Bill, 135
Lunney, Dan, 41
Luntz, The, 157
Luong, Ham Cham, 220
Lupi, Daniel, 28, 121, 144
Lupien, Julie, 175
Lupien, Tabitha, 39
Lurie, Evan, 178
Lurie, John, 98
Lussier, Patrick, 99, 144
Lustig, Aaron, 8
Lustig, Branko, 112
Lustig, Dana, 68
Luthren, Jonathan Taylor, 79
Lutter, Ellen, 86, 93
Lutz, Jon, 13
Lutz, Karl, 265
Lux, Frank "The Gator" 176
Luzier, Aimee, 30
Lycan, Jeff, 170
Lychnikoff, Pavel D., 84
Lydon, Christine .D M., 147
Lydon, Gary, 212
Lykes, Theron Touché, 109
Lynch, Aubrey, 163
Lynch, Colin Patrick, 162
Lynch, David, 21
Lynch, Edward, 176
Lynch, John Carroll, 49, 75, 106, 161
Lynch, John, 5, 204, 212
Lynch, Kelly, 144, 175, 284
Lynch, Martin, 256
Lynch, Roy J., 69
Lynchnikoff, Pavel D., 122
Lyndenberg, Joshua, 154
Lynds, Bob, 138
Lynn, Edward, 63
Lynn, Jonathan, 63
Lynn, Patsy, 182
Lynn, Peggy, 182
Lynn, Sherry, 71
Lynn, Theresa, 30
Lynwood, Alex, 101
Lynwood, Michael, 101
Lyon, Gail, 124
Lyons, J., 177
Lyons, James, 166, 171
Lyons, John, 28, 121
Lyons, Rob, 138
Lyons, Susan, 265
M6 Films, 236, 265
Ma Vie En Rose, 255
Ma, Yo-Yo, 117
Ma, Christina, 114
Ma, Eddie, 230
Ma, Jingle, 144, 203
Ma, Margaret, 99
Ma, Raymond, 32
Ma, Tzi, 17, 126
Maa, Lei, 155
Maas, Henry, 260
Mabandla, Nkululeko, 155

Mabowe, David T., 49
Maby, Elisabeth, 263
Mac, Bernie, 23, 158, 168
MacAdam, Elise, 178
Macary, Hubert Saint, 215
Macat, Julio, 178
Macaulay, Marc, 25, 179, 181
Macaulay, Scott, 174
Maccarone, Michael, 30
MacConkey, Holly, 174
MacCrae, Taylor, 86
MacDonald, Andrew, 240, 261
MacDonald, Bill, 23
MacDonald, Brenda, 144
MacDonald, Don, 212
MacDonald, James G., 49
MacDonald, James, 8
MacDonald, Lance, 121, 144
MacDonald, Laurie, 77, 112
MacDonald, Murdoch, 205
MacDonald, Sharman, 251
MacDonald, Shaun, 144
MacDonald, William J., 42
MacDougall, Alec, 205
MacDowell, Andie, 100, 284
Mace, Doug, 156
Mace, Thad, 79
Macedo, Augusto, 264
MacEoin, Aoife, 231
Macfadyen, Angus, 163
MacGregor-Scott, Peter, 181
Machado, Justina, 96
Machado, Maria, 254
Machinova, Jelena, 258
Machuel, Laurent, 215
MacIsaac, David, 84
Mack, Craig, 157
Mack, Steve, 145
MacKay, Donald Sage, 166
Mackay, John A., 171
MacKay, Michael Reid, 66, 181
Mackie, Kathleen, 257
MacKinnon, Gillies, 231
Mackintosh, Steven, 210, 237
Macklin, Albert, 178
MacLachlan, Kyle, 132, 284
MacLaine, Shirley, 168, 284
MacLaughlin, Steve, 49
Maclean, Peter, 205
MacLellan, Don, 8
MacLeod, Alan, 205
MacLeod, Bruce, 205
MacLeod, Wendy, 118
MacMillan, Doug, 169
MacMillan, Kenneth, 43
MacMillan, Patty Raya, 17
MacNeill, Peter, 208
MacNicol, Peter, 244, 284
Macon, Brian, 118, 141
MacPherson, Elle, 107, 181, 284
MacPherson, Walt, 27, 131, 154
MacQueen, Melanie, 146
MacRae, Michael, 169
MacTavish, Elspeth, 257
MacVittie, Bruce, 112
Macy, William H., 84-85, 120-121, 151
Mad City, 183
Maddalena Films, 144
Maddalena, Marianne, 144
Madden, John, 229
Madden, Molly, 88
Madigan, Alix, 96
Madigan, Amy, 38, 284
Madragoa Films, 262
Madrid, Larry M., 23
Madsen, Michael, 26-27, 166-167, 281, 284
Madsen, Virginia, 135, 284
Maduemezia, Theresa, 232
Maes, Michèle, 207
Maetlind, Jenna, 21
Maffei, Joe, 212
Maffia, Roma, 114
Mafuya, Mabel, 155
Magaloni, Honorato, 160
Magee, Ken, 8, 63
Mager, Madeline, 137
Magicon, 254
Maginnis, Molly, 148
Maglayev, Nikita B., 265
Magnuson, Ann, 178, 284
Magnuson, Tom, 17
Magrath, Cassandra, 259
Maguire, Amanda, 212
Maguire, George, 69, 101, 155
Maguire, Oliver, 212, 256
Maguire, Tobey, 110-111, 142, 199,

284
Maguire, Tom, 256
Mahaffey, Valerie, 29
Maher, Ben, 245
Maher, Joseph, 102
Maher, Kerry, 47
Mahmoudi, Khalil, 223
Mahmud-Bey, Shiek, 53, 100
Mahon, John, 182
Mahon, Lizzy, 102
Mahon, Philippe, 236
Mahoney, Brian, 63
Mahoney, Pat, 127
Mahtani, Lili, 137
Maibaumn, Paul, 173
Maille, Claudette, 264
Maillet, Geraldine, 250
Mainprize, James, 23
Mainz, Steven, 49
Maisler, Francine, 50, 117, 124, 148
Maistre, Philip Le, 131
Majestic Films, 164
Major, Mary, 114
Majowski, Rachel, 138
Mak, Shirley, 203
Makaj, Steve, 169
Makem, Tommy, 176
Makenzie, Sam, 263
Makhmalbaf, Mohsen, 223
Maki, Taro, 258
Makinen, Karl, 181
Makinen, Margaret, 132
Makkar, Joseph Merzak, 94
Makkena, Wendy, 87
Mako, 117, 284
Makovsky, Judianna, 182
Maksimovic, Dragan, 264
Malahide, Patrick, 18, 62
Malavarca, Eddie, 178
Malberti, Suset Pérez, 224
Malcolm , 205
Maldonado, Aixa, 132
Maldonado, Norma, 171
Malet, Arthur, 130
Maley, Michael, 155
Maley, Shamus, 155
Malhotra, Pavan, 218
Malibu Comic, 77
Malik, Art, 23
Malina, Judith, 175
Malkin, Barry, 135
Malkovich, John, 65, 284
Mallinson, Matthew, 156
Malloy, Matt, 89, 148
Malloy, Tom, 102, 171
Malm, Mona, 259
Malofilm Communications, 205
Malone, Jena, 181
Malone, Mike, 159
Maloney, Denis, 166
Maloney, Jacqueline, 102
Maloney, Kevin, 182
Maloney, Peter, 30, 115
Malota, Kristina, 96
Malpaso production, 22
Maly, Xavier, 259
Malzahn, Richard, 169
Mamet, David, 107, 151
Mami, Cheb, 260
Man Who Knew Too Little, The , 183
Man, Beenie, 264
Man, Choy-Ling, 12
Man, Gary, 147, 170
Mancina, Mark, 65, 68
Mancini, Ray "Boom Boom", 176
Mancuso Jr., Frank 97
Mandalay Entertainment, 27, 44, 117, 119
Mandel, Babaloo, 180
Mandela, 32
Mandeville Films, 38, 81
Mandic, Milorad, 264
Mandt, Ann, 167
Mandt, Neil, 167
Manfredini, Harry, 172
Manfro, Marc, 183
Manga, 261
Mangano, Anthony, 44
Mangini, Mark, 159
Mangold, James, 93
Manheim, Camryn, 51
Mani, Maya, 182
Mani, P.D., 78
Manion, Karen, 170
Mankuma, Blu, 39, 165
Manley, Jennifer, 151

Manley, Lee Ann, 183
Mann, Byron, 126
Mann, Leslie, 81
Mann, Marijke, 211
Mann, Rosie, 166
Mann, Sharon, 186
Mannen, Tracey, 162
Manning, Ann, 184
Mannix, Ernie, 175
Manoel, Viktor, 38
Manon, Christian, 257
Manor Films, 157
Mansaray, Peter, 141
Mansfield, David, 145, 265
Mansfield, Mark, 133
Manson, Alan, 167, 183
Manson, Jono, 184
Manson, Marilyn, 21
Manson, Ted, 47, 183
Mantegna, Joe, 9, 162, 284
Mantello, Joe, 59
Manton, Marcus, 162
Manuel, Lole y, 213
Manuel, Michael, 49
Manz, Linda, 101, 174, 284
Manzoni, Franck, 221
Mao, Snakey, 172
Maples, David, 137
Maples, Marla, 137
Maquignon, Charles, 254
Maranville, George, 170
Marassi, Horacio, 250
Marber, Samuel J., 179
Marceau, Sophie, 180
Marchal, Robin, 229
Marchand, Guy, 263
Marchand, Mitchell, 100, 118
Marchant, Tony, 237
Marchetti, Will, 10
Marcoen, Alain, 215
Marcus, Bea, 38
Marcus, Dominic, 23
Marcus, Trula, 132, 135
Marder, Henry, 182
Marder, Jordan, 182
Mardis, Bobby, 60
Marean, Simone, 102
Marechal, Joan, 155
Marek, Miles, 110
Maressa, Mauro, 71
Margaret's Museum, 205
Margiela, Martin, 220
Margin Films, 265
Margiotta, Karen, 60, 105
Margiotta, Mary, 60, 105
Margolin, Stuart, 172
Margolis, Mark, 22
Margolyes, Miriam, 104, 237
Margulies, Juliana, 47, 211
Mari, Gina, 182
Maria O'Brien, 156
Maria, Constance, 179
Marie, Heather, 56
Marie, Madeleine, 221
Marie, Tara, 125
Marie, Theresa, 164
Marin, Mindy, 46, 75, 184
Marinelli, Anthony, 162, 169
Marinker, Peter, 91, 205
Marinkovic, Dragan, 248
Marino, Ken, 124
Marino, Mandana, 186
Mark, Laurence, 51, 148
Mark, Tony, 118
Markaris, Peros, 203
Markell, Andrew, 32
Markie, Biz, 176
Markinson, Brian, 49
Markland, Ted, 127
Markovic, Petar, 264
Markovitz, Barry, 145
Markovitz, Russ, 172
Marks, Beau, 46
Marks, Leo, 177
Marks, Richard, 62, 148
Marks, Ross, 173
Markwood, Jonathan, 257
Marling, Stefan, 245
Marquez, Michael, 42
Marquez, Willie, 236
Marquis, Andre, 177
Marr, Tony, 38
Mars, Kenneth, 260, 284
Marsalis, Branford, 129
Marsan, Eddie, 183
Marsden, Joel B., 177
Marsden, Sarah, 125

Marsh, Ali, 30, 88
Marsh, Stephen, 81
Marshall, Alan, 128
Marshall, Anna Calder, 180
Marshall, Dale C., 67
Marshall, E.G., 22, 284
Marshall, Garry, 173
Marshall, Gary Dewitt, 102
Marshall, Kathleen, 173
Marshall, Mark, 182
Marshall, Morris, 80
Marshall, Nathaniel, 128
Marshall, Paula, 39
Marshall, Phil, 63
Marshall, Ryan, 67
Marshall, Sara Constance, 115
Marsico, Tony, 96
Martells, Cynthia, 124
Martens, Rica, 86
Marti, Christian, 265
Martin, Adrian, 209
Martin, Andrea, 130, 151, 284
Martin, Ben, 184
Martin, Dan, 82
Martin, Duane, 144
Martin, George, 158, 284
Martin, Helen, 114
Martin, James, 156
Martin, Jean Luc, 181
Martin, Jonathan Komack, 60
Martin, K. Douglas, 166
Martin, Keith, 216
Martin, Lionel C., 168
Martin, Michael, 89, 271
Martin, Pamela, 118, 169, 284
Martin, Peter, 219
Martin, Rudolph, 164
Martin, Sandy, 38
Martin, Sasha, 30, 163
Martin, Simon, 214
Martin, Ursula, 87
Martindale, Margo, 122, 126
Martinet, Charles, 101
Martinez, Carmen, 180
Martinez, Cliff, 157, 159
Martinez, Crystal, 240
Martinez, Jessica, 250
Martinez, Leonardo, 180
Martinez, Melba, 53
Martinez, Olivier, 231
Martinez, Richard, 31
Martini, Maximilian, 181
Martini, Stephanie, 176
Martiniz, Charles, 44
Martirez, Jean, 49
Martling, Jackie, 30
Martschewski, Vessela, 213
Martt, Mike, 177
Marvin, Richard, 161
Masada, Jamie, 174
Masekela, Hugh, 32
Mashimo, Fritz, 8
Maskell, Tina, 12
Masko, Walter, 180
Maslansky, Judd, 163
Mason, Anna, 245
Mason, Laurence, 100
Mason, Steve, 39, 66
Massalas, Valorie, 173
Massaquoi, Sylvestre, 141
Massaro, Orazio, 250
Massee, Michael, 21, 101, 122, 141
Massey, Anna, 210
Massey, Drew, 77
Masson, Anne, 235
Masson, Laetitia, 260
Massone, Nicoletta, 205
Masten, Gordon, 179
Masterminds, 169
Masterpiece Theatre, 229
Masterson, Danny, 75
Masterson, Fay, 141
Masterson, Mary Stuart, 184, 284
Masterson, Owen, 101
Masterson, Sean, 151
Mastrantone, Lucia, 265
Mastro, Michael, 29
Mastroianni, Chiara, 60, 215, 263
Mastropierro, Teresa, 157
Masui, Shoji, 226
Masur, Richard, 182, 284
Matacunas, Ann, 138
Matarazzo, Heather, 182
Matchinga, Caryn, 183
Mathe, Tibor, 266
Matheisen, Mark, 173
Mather, Jessebel, 87
Mather, Kati, 87

Mathers, James, 182
Mathers, Jerry, 98
Matheson, Margaret, 129
Mathews, Eddie, 32
Mathews, Gisella, 224
Mathews, Thom, 112
Mathias, Anna, 11
Mathias, Sean, 245
Mathias, Sean, 245
Mathieson, John, 261
Mathison, Melissa, 152
Mathonnet, Guillaume, 250
Matlin, Olga, 171
Matlock, Norman, 53
Matloff, Jeff, 168
Matschoss, Ulrich, 126
Matsuda, Masaru, 220
Matsuo, Hiroshi, 258
Matsuo, Kentaro, 220
Matsuo, Michiko, 220
Matte World Digital, 80
Matthau, Walter, 78, 284
Matthews, Al, 216, 253
Matthews, Dakin, 136, 244
Matthews, Lester, 96
Matthews, Liesel, 84-85
Matthews, Sally Ann, 219
Matthews, Tom, 183
Mattila, Steve, 184
Mattison, Michael, 182
Mattson, John, 182
Matwijkow, David, 156
Mau, Leonore, 264
Maugran, Morgane, 250
Maura Fay & Associates, 259
Maurer, Shawn, 169
Maurette, Marcelle, 130
Mauri, Paco, 160
Maurin, Maurice, 260
Mauro, Jim, 53
Mauro, Rich, 176
Mauro, Richard, 156
Maus, Rodger E., 20
Mavimbela, Isaac, 155
Mavrakis, Eve, 222
Mavric, Elizabeth, 214
Mavros, Claudine, 250
Max, Arthur, 94
Maxcy, Jennifer, 69
Maximov, German, 180
Maxwell, David, 175
Maxwell, Max, 79
Maxwell, Raquel Caballes, 177
Maxwell, Roberta, 164, 184
Maxwell, Wayne, 178
May, Jack, 160
May, Joseph, 125
May, Mathilda, 131
May, Mona, 51
Maya, Mario, 213
Mayanja, Issac, 141
Mayer, Chip, 37
Mayers, Michael, 167
Mayesh, Joe, 83
Mayfield, Les, 136
Maylam, Genevieve, 216
Maynard, Elizabeth, 173
Mayne, Colleen, 147
Mayo, Alfredo F., 259
Mayo, Josiah A, 241
Mayron, Maya, 258
Mays, Benjamin, 182
Mayweather, Joshua Gibran, 60
Mazar, Debi, 15, 60, 96, 175
Mazin, Craig, 174
Mazur, Monet, 56
Mazur, Stephen, 37
Mazursky, Paul, 24, 284
Mazzello, Joseph, 61, 284
Mazzocco, Kerri, 204
Mazzola, Michael, 178
Mazzola, Nick, 179
Mazzotti, Anna, 224
Mbanzi, Ernest, 155
MC, Young, 157
McAleese, Peter, 261
McAlpine, Andrew, 136
McAlpine, Donald M., 107
McArdle, Tom, 83, 100, 178
McArthur, Alex, 114, 181
McAskill, Trish, 204
McAtee, Jeff, 13
McAuley, Nichole, 114
McAuliff, Steve, 181
McAvoy, Edward T., 65
McBee, Deron, 177
McBlain, David, 256
McBride, Chi, 97

McCabe, Anne, 31
McCabe, Stephen, 163, 170
McCaffrey, James, 176
McCaffrey, Valerie, 95, 118, 158
McCallany, Holt, 112
McCallum, Jon, 174
McCamus, Tom, 249
McCardie, Brian, 68
McCarthy, Andrew, 264, 284
McCarthy, Bruce, 166
McCarthy, Dennis, 160
McCarthy, Eoin, 253
McCarthy, Francis X., 8
McCarthy, Julianna, 128
McCarthy, Thomas, 182
McCartney, Justin, 69
McCartney, Paul, 180, 284
McCarty, Bruce, 161
McCary, Michael, 97
McCauley, Colleen, 138
McCauley, James Michael, 27
McCauley, James, 131
McClain, Saundra, 38
McClanahan, Rue, 78-79, 128, 284
McClarin, Curtis, 30, 100, 161
McClary, J. Michael, 163
McClean, Brennan, 156
McCleery, Michael, 182
McCleister, Tom, 20
McClelland, Derbhla, 256
McClory, Belinda, 259
McCloskey, Kristin, 127
McClung, Patrick, 17
McClurg, Edie, 136, 284
McComb, Theresa, 256
McConaughey, Matthew, 140-141, 181
McConnachie, Brian, 142
McConnel, Bridget, 229
McCord, Rocky, 97
McCormack, J. Patrick, 38, 61, 151, 183
McCormack, Mary, 30
McCormick, Patrick, 27
McCormick, Randall, 68
McCourt, Malachy, 8, 35
McCoy, Matt, 182
McCoy, Ron, 151
McCoy, Scott, 65
McCracken, Cameron, 241
McCracken, Dafidd, 173
McCrary, Vladimir, 216
McCulloch, Malcolm, 243
McCullough, Lonnie, 114
McCurley, David, 75
McCurry, Michael, 157
McCusker, Frank, 212
McCutchen III, Bill, 176
McDaniel, Charles, 22, 182
McDaniel, James, 162
McDeed, Samantha, 260
McDermott, Carolyn, 169
McDermott, Dylan, 62, 281, 285
McDermottro, Maria, 256
McDermottroe, Maria, 231
McDevitt, Trenton, 47
McDonald, Christopher, 98, 136, 168
McDonald, Daniel, 110
McDonald, Dominic, 209
McDonald, Mac, 12, 216
McDonald, Roy, 180
McDonnell, Leverne, 257
McDonnell, Michael, 21
McDonnell, Tim, 256
McDormand, Frances, 211, 285
McDougall, Martin, 216
McDowall, Roddy, 23, 162, 285
McDowell, Malcolm, 144, 178, 285
McElhaney, Billy, 251
McElhenny, Rob, 35
McElhinney, Danny, 212
McElhinney, Ian, 256
McElhone, Natascha, 35
McElroy, Alan, 90
McEnery, Donald, 71
McEntee, Brian, 180
McEveety, Stephen, 180, 184
McEwan, Hamish, 126
McFadden, Davenia, 30, 72
McFarland, Rebecca, 144
McFarlane, Todd, 90
McGahan, Alannah, 125
McGann, Luke, 219
McGann, Paul, 125
McGann, Whitney Alexandra, 175
McGarry, Joan, 256

McGarry, Victoria, 105
McGarty, Michael, 164
McGarvey, Seamus, 251
McGary, Amy, 137
McGaughey, Nicholas, 261
McGaw, Patrick, 69
McGee, Bobby, 60
McGee, Carl A., 83
McGee, Jack, 29, 55, 80
McGill, Bruce, 179
McGill, Desi, 185
McGinley, John C., 14, 82, 162, 285
McGinley, Sean, 231
McGinn, Chris, 52
McGlocklin, Michelle, 160
McGlynn, Jim, 47
McGovern, Brian, 13
McGovern, Danielle, 35
McGovern, Don Charles, 65
McGovern, Elizabeth, 247, 285
McGovern, George, 166
McGowan, Mickie, 71
McGowan, Rose, 60, 104
McGowan, Tom, 148, 175, 244
McGrady, Michael, 49
McGrail, Jeff, 184
McGrath, Douglas, 31
McGrath, John, 210, 255
McGrath, Mark, 180
McGrath, Martin, 214
McGrath, Michael, 205
McGrath, Patrick, 210
McGraw, Melinda, 9
McGregor, Brian, 51
McGregor, Ewan, 219-220, 240, 285
McGregor, Robbie, 214
McGruther, Michael, 102
McGuckin, Aislin, 231
McGuigan, Barry, 256
McGuinness, Janine, 256
McGuire, Betty, 172
McGuire, Kim, 155
McGuire, Scott Hunter, 101
McGuirk, Sean, 141
McHale's Navy, 160
McHenry, David, 205
McHugh, Bill, 167
McIlvaine, Julia, 179
McInerney, Bernie, 112
McInerney, Elizabeth, 147
McInnerny, Tim, 125
McIntosh, Bill, 162
McIntosh, Shannon, 156
McIntyre, Gerry, 163
McIvor, Ben, 214
McKay, Craig, 93
McKean, Michael, 16, 23, 82, 285
McKechnie, Elizabeth, 238
McKechnie, Sarah-Jane, 238
McKee, Monty, 182
McKellar, Don, 175
McKellen, Ian, 245, 285
McKenna, Alan, 254
McKenna, Chris I., 102
McKenna, Joseph, 184
McKenzie, Jacqueline, 204
McKenzie, Rita, 15
McKenzie, Stacey, 216
McKeown, Dave, 153
McKerrell, Simon, 229
McKillop, Jack, 35
McKinley, Tom, 20
McKinney, Chris, 175
McKinney, Kee, 177
McKinney, Roslyn, 13
McKinney, Tony, 160
McKinnon, Jake, 172
McKinstry, Carolyn M., 80
McKnight, David, 60
McLachlan, Duncan, 162
McLachlan, Rod, 163, 181
McLain, David, 95
McLaren, Conrad, 181
McLarty, Ron, 184
McLaughlin, John, 262
McLean, Kinsey, 23
McLean, Lenny, 216
McLean, Rod, 224
McLellan, Zoe, 43
McLeod, Eric, 56, 151
McLeod, Mary, 181
McLindon, James, 153
McLoughlin, Timothy, 172
McLoughlin, Tom, 125
McLouglin, Tom, 125

McMahon, Frank, 174
McMahon, Patricia, 254
McManus, Don R., 84
McManus, Michelle, 180
McMillan, Dawn, 11
McMillan, Fernie E., 145
McMillan, Mary, 119
McMillon, Doris E., 180
McMullan, Jim, 56, 181
McMullan, Tim, 216
McMullen, Cliff, 180
McMullen, Gail, 116
McMurray, Rocky, 155
McMurry, Gregory L., 8
McNab, Eric, 212
McNabb, Barry, 163
McNabb, Murray, 214
McNair, Chris, 80
McNair, Harold, 80
McNair, Maxine, 80
McNally, Loretto, 115
McNally, Terrence, 59
McNamara, Jennifer, 178
McNamara, Madeline, 214
McNamara, Pat, 31, 52, 164
McNamara, William, 175, 264, 285
McNeely, Joel, 179, 181
McNeese, Patrick, 170
McNeice, Ian, 18, 240
McNeil, Timothy, 128, 181
McNickle, Jim Taylor, 102
McPheely, Alan, 156
McQuaide, James, 62
McQuarn, Michael, 109
McQueen-Mason, Edward, 265
McRae, Clay, 163
McRobbie, Peter, 88, 142
MCRS, 264
McSorley, Gerard, 212, 256
McSorley, Martin, 65
McSweeney, Tom, 264
McTavish, Graham, 242
McTavish, Patrick Lawrence, 37
McVerry, Maureen, 156
McVey, Carrie, 28
McWatt, Chris, 49
McWilliam, Jill, 235
McWilliams, Debbie, 253
MDP Worldwide, 162
Meachem, Stewart, 245
Mead, Brad, 172
Mead, Tara, 144
Meade, Donald J., 35
Meader, Martin, 211
Meadows, Arlene, 39
Meaney, Colm, 65, 220
Meaney, Nick, 186
Means, Angela, 60
Means, Randy, 160
Meara, Anne, 31, 285
Meaux, Jimmie J., 145
Mecchi, Irene, 71
Mechera, Katernia, 250
Mechoso, Julio Oscar, 62, 127, 179, 183
Meckler, Nancy, 225
Medeiros, Michael, 158
Media Asia Distribution, 230
Media Asia Films, 260
Mediaworks, 126
Medina, Teresa, 38
Medjuck, Joe, 30, 52, 180
Medlen, John, 177
Medoff, Mark, 173
Medrano, Frank, 180
Medrano, Joseph, 166
Medusa Pictures, 52
Medvesek, Rene, 112
Meedin, Riz, 216
Meegan, Anna, 256
Meet Wally Sparks, 15
Mega Communications, Inc., 174
Meheux, Phil, 42
Mehr, Elizabeth, 160
Mehta, Deepa, 235
Mei, Wei, 183
Mei, Wu, 220
Meisle, Kathryn, 179
Meiss, Greg, 144
Meissel, Petr, 262
Meistrich, Larry, 158
Meistrich, Shireen, 158
Mejia, Paul, 157
Mekhralieva, Susanna, 202
Mel, Melly, 157
Melendez, John "Stuttering" 15, 30
Melery, Veronique, 255
Melhus, Marianne, 125

Mell, Randle, 184
Mellin, Maggie, 151
Mello, Tamara, 18
Mellon, Brett, 182
Mellor, Cherith, 229
Mellott, Greg, 203
Melniker, Benjamin, 181
Melo, Luis, 264
Melocchi, Vince, 56
Melton, Pat, 155
Meltzer, Ileane, 118
Melville, Neil, 262
Melvoin, Wendy, 109
Memme, Tanya, 29
Men In Black, 77
Mende, Lisa, 82
Mendel, Juel, 21
Mendel, Sharon, 179
Mendelsohn, Aaron, 87
Mendelsohn, Ben, 260
Mendelsohn, Michael, 86, 104
Mendez, Frank, 180
Mendez, Ray, 116
Mendicino, Gerry, 39
Mendillo, Stephen, 94
Mendonça, George, 116
Mendonga, Frank, 179
Menell, Jo, 32
Menese, José, 213
Meneses, Alexandra, 180
Meng, Jessey, 126
Menges, Chris, 256
Menglet, Alex, 214
Menke, Sally, 147
Menken, Alan, 71
Menkes, Nina, 162
Menkes, Tinka, 162
Menkesfilm, 162
Menshikov, Oleg, 202
Mention III, Richard A., 154
Menton, Kevin, 231
Menza, Gina, 151
Menzies, Alex, 229
Menzies, Robert, 257
Meoli, Christian, 33
Mercado, Esther "Tita", 184
Mercado, Hector, 78
Mercé, José, 213
Mercedes, Yvette, 53
Mercer, Alex, 160
Mercer, Sam, 8
Merchant, Alpheus, 77
Merchant, Veronica, 265
Mercier, Matt, 138
Meredith, Gary, 238
Meredith, Kim, 155
Merediz, Olga, 158
Merims, Adam, 175
Merkin, Michelle, 132
Merkitch, Arnold, 174
Merlin, Claudine, 231
Merlin, Joanna, 163
Merlin, Serge, 215
Merola, Pat, 258
Merrifield, Douglas C., 182
Merrill, Jayson, 182
Merrill, Shondra, 116
Merry, Nicole, 216
Mertinz, Johanna, 264
Mery, Amin, 180
Meskell, Katie, 156
Meskimen, Jim, 82
Messam, Dane, 216
Messica, Vicky, 262
Messick, Kevin J., 162
Messina, Rick, 29, 137
Messing, Debra, 160
Messmer, Emily, 181
Mestres, Ricardo, 136, 178
Metcalf, Laurie, 113, 144, 285
Metcalf, Mark, 167
Metcalf, Toby, 122
Metcalfe, Robert, 144
Metchik, Aaron Michael, 71
Method Man, 93, 184
Methven, Eleanor, 256
Metro, 10
Metrocolour London, 232
Metzger, Gary, 169
Metzler, Jim, 159, 182, 285
Mewes, Jason, 40-41
Meyer, Daniel, 116
Meyer, David, 245
Meyer, Dina, 128
Meyer, Hans, 44
Meyer, Kevin, 168
Meyer-Wiel, Christoph, 262

Meyers, Henry, 123, 182
Meyers, Janet, 43
Meyers, Lawrence Steven, 178
Meyers, Rusty, 179
Meylan, Gerard, 239
Meza, Rebecca Lee, 180
Mézières, Myriam, 263
MGM, 11, 24, 71, 97, 100, 116, 126, 163, 172, 187, 2-3, 230, 245, 253, 265
Mhall, Marcella, 160
Miall, Tristram, 214
Miano, Clipper, 206
Miano, Robert, 27
Michael "Kevin" Harry, 183
Michael, Christopher, 21, 127, 183
Michael, Simon, 263
Michael, Terence, 164
Michaels, David, 183
Michaels, Gordon, 61, 84
Michaels, Mya, 35
Michaels, Ryan "Rhino", 180
Michaels, Suzanne, 84
Michaels, Tommy, 263
Michalakopoulos, Yorgos, 203
Michalski, Jeff, 83
Michele, Michael, 38
Michell, Scott, 222
Michelman, Ken, 179
Michiel, Joy, 168
Michos, Anastas, 179
Mickelson, Pam Dixon, 13, 127, 181
Mickelson, Robert, 47
Middleton, Gregory, 212
Middleton, Joseph, 47, 69, 182
Midkiff, Jr., J. Williams., 154
Midler, Bette, 39, 282, 285
Midnight In The Garden Of Good And Evil, 183
Midnight Revue, 223
Midwood, Ramsay, 156
Mighton, John, 138
Mighty Reel, 175
Miglin, Duk, 84
Migliore, Jim, 179
Mika, Dennis, 256
Mikado Film, 218
Mikelson, Jennifer, 181
Mikesch, Elfi, 262
Mikkelsen, Monika, 100
Milano, Alyssa, 178, 285
Milchan, Arnon, 180, 182-183
Miles, Ben, 247
Miles, Charlie Creed, 216-217
Miles, Lynda, 220
Miles, Vincent Dee, 61
Milhoan, Michael, 118
Milian, Tomas, 21, 141
Millen, Lorna R., 182
Millenotti, Maurizio, 180
Miller, Cory M., 181
Miller, Courtney, 83
Miller, Dennis, 180
Miller, Emmett, 151
Miller, George, 11, 173
Miller, Greg, 131
Miller, Howard S., 37
Miller, Jane Jean, 123
Miller, Jennifer, 264
Miller, Jim, 77
Miller, Joel, 161
Miller, Jonny Lee, 153
Miller, Joshua Wade, 102
Miller, Kelly, 81
Miller, Larry, 16, 137
Miller, Laurie A., 69
Miller, Lawrence, 63
Miller, Marcus, 38
Miller, Mark Jeffrey, 79, 179
Miller, Matt, 123
Miller, Max, 163
Miller, Michael R., 46, 144, 160, 164
Miller, Michael Ray, 84
Miller, Owen, 166
Miller, Paul, 20
Miller, Penelope Ann, 8, 285
Miller, Randall, 38
Miller, Reginald W., 173
Miller, Richard Dale, 179
Miller, Richard Hoyt, 8
Miller, Richard, 93
Miller, Rick, 11
Miller, Robert Sean, 53
Miller, Selwyn Emerson, 121
Miller, Stephen E., 87, 182

Miller, Thomas G., 159
Miller, Tim, 176
Miller, Tracey Lynne, 142
Miller, Vera, 179
Milligan, Brian, 256
Milliken, Angie, 266
Milliken, Sue, 211
Millington, James, 180
Mills, Adam, 163
Mills, Charles, 177
Mills, Christopher, 177
Mills, Hayley, 23, 285
Mills, John, 210, 244, 285
Mills, Keith, 63
Mills, Sir John, 244
Mills, Thomas, 172, 244
Mills, Todd Easton, 164
Milne, Paula, 210
Milsome, Doug, 55
Milton, Russell, 124
Mimic, 99,
Minami, Kaho, 258
Mindel, Allan, 170
Mindy Affrime Productions, 38
Ming-Lam, Wong, 243
Ministre de la Culture de la
    Francophonie, 262
Minjares, Joe, 82, 160
Minnow Pictures, 122
Minter, Kelly Jo, 161
Minter, Paul, 250
Mintz, Daniel, 230
Minucci, Frank, 50, 175
Miou-Miou, 207, 285
Mira Vista Films, 176
Mirabai Production, 207
Mirage Releasing, 162
Miramax, 9, 41, 69, 87, 93, 96, 99,
    118, 138, 144, 147, 156, 181,
    190, 214, 219, 222, 226, 229-
    230, 235, 247-248, 260, 263
Miranda, Alex, 61
Miranda, Dianna, 114
Miranda, Marcus A., 175
Mirano, Virgil, 67
Miras, Fernan, 259
Miravista Films, 178
Mirindo, Djunawong Stanley, 266
Mirkin, David, 51
Mirkovich, Steve, 65, 119
Mirman, Brad, 162
Mirojnick, Ellen, 75, 128
Mirowitz, Sheldon, 154
Mirren, Helen, 126, 285
Mirza-Khani, Mustafa, 223
Misauer, Mark, 245
Misawa, Goh, 78
Mishalska, Maya, 264
Missel, Renee, 266
Mitas, George, 156
Mitchell, Aleta, 183
Mitchell, Antonio, 179
Mitchell, Arthur, 157
Mitchell, Chris, 181
Mitchell, Cleveland, 132
Mitchell, Colin, 182
Mitchell, Donna, 84, 110
Mitchell, E. Roger, 177
Mitchell, Gene, 155
Mitchell, Heather, 214
Mitchell, Iain, 12
Mitchell, James, 212, 249, 285
Mitchell, Jim, 171
Mitchell, Katharine, 8
Mitchell, Kel, 83
Mitchell, Lou, 259
Mitchell, Lynn, 155
Mitchell, Radha, 209
Mitchell, Robyn M., 83, 129, 147
Mitchell, Rod, 222
Mitchell, Rodney, 133
Mitchell, Ruby ., 171
Mitchell, Veronica, 155
Mitevska, Labina, 248
Mitges, Christine, 173
Mitler, Lilli, 169
Mitler, Matt, 169
Mitsuishi, Ken, 220
Miura, Atsushi, 220
Mix-a-Lot, Sir, 15
Mixon, Bernard, 109
Mixon, Jamal, 168
Mixon, Jerod, 168
Mixon, L. Christian, 145
Miyashima, Joey, 65
Miyeni, Eric "Waku",155
Miyori, Kim, 10

Mizerski, Barrie, 20
Mizota, Diane, 78, 121
MK2, 223, 265
Mobley, Clarence, 141
Mocanu, Florentine, 101
Mockus, Tony, Jr., 178
Modl, Martha, 262
Moeller, Ralf, 181
Moffat, Donald, 168, 286
Moffett, D.W., 260, 286
Mofokeng, Jerry, 154
Mogwaza, Simo, 155
Moharami, Hossein, 223
Moharami, Roghieh, 223
Mohr, Jay, 88, 286
Moiselle, Nuala, 285
Mokoena, Fana, 155
Mol, Gretchen, 27, 164, 175
Molen, Gerald R., 61
Molen, Jerry, 141
Molenaar, Reynier, 171
Molina, Alfred, 121, 180, 183, 286
Molina, Antonio, 32
Molina, Dan, 180
Molina, Ralph, 173
Molinaro, Edouard, 265
Mollet, Clotilde, 236
Mollo, John, 91
Molloy, Kevin, 216
Molloy, Mike, 65
Molom: A Legend Of Mongolia,
    262
Moloney, Janel, 62
Moloney, Sean, 101
Momtchilova, Natalia, 78
Mon Frere Motion Pictures, 155
Mon Homme, 231
Monas, Stephen, 162
Monastesse, Genevieve, 125
Mondesir, Merwin, 126
Mondo, 260
Mones, Paul, 44
Money Talks, 95
Money, Eddie, 173
Mongolian Tale, A 260
Mongrel Movies, 175
Monk, Debra, 102, 182
Monk, Isabell, 179
Monk, Roger, 216
Monks, Michael, 84
Monroe, Jarlon, 101
Monroe, Steve, 56
Montanez, Andy, 264
Montano, Glice, 25
Montano, Hector, 25
Monte, Tino, 180
Monteith, Felice, 177
Montejano, Peter P., 180
Montel, Germane, 33
Montemayor, Renee, 216
Montero, Tony, 44
Montesino, Alex, 68
Montgomery, Chuck, 157, 169
Montgomery, Joseph, 178
Montgomery, Karen, 62
Montgomery, Rick, 60, 63, 174
Montgomery, Sam, 55
Montgomery, Toni, 9
Monti, Alicia, 250
Montiel, Cecilia, 166
Montilla, Carlos, 68
Montillier, Georges, 263
Monton, Vince, 230
Moody Blues, The, 164
Moody, Hans, 93
Moody, James, 183
Moody, Jim, 53
Moody, Rick, 110
Moon, Amy, 162
Moon, Cadillac, 183
Moon, Philip, 122
Moon, Warren, 163
Mooney, Debra, 130
Mooneyhan, Charles, 159
Moonstone Entertaiment, 153
Moor, Bill, 183, 286
Moore, Andrea, 257
Moore, Ann, 56
Moore, Benny, 118
Moore, Bob, 94
Moore, Chris, 138
Moore, Christopher Michael, 183
Moore, Dan, 79
Moore, Demi, 7, 56, 94, 142, 286
Moore, Frank, 180
Moore, Jarion, 155
Moore, Julianne, 61, 105, 120-121,
    195, 282, 286

Moore, Katie, 137
Moore, Kevin, 12
Moore, Lisa Bronwyn, 179
Moore, Maggie, 122
Moore, Mary Tyler, 160, 286
Moore, Mary, 180,
Moore, Muriel, 183
Moore, Phil, 179
Moore, Rebecca, 175
Moore, Roger, 42, 286
Moore, Rudy Ray, 159
Moore, Stephen, 219
Moore, Tracey Marable, 50
Moore, Wiley, 23
Moorer, Margo, 23
Moorhouse, Jocelyn, 106
Moos, Richard, 69
Moraitis, John, 23
Morajele, Sechaba, 155
Morales, Esai, 236, 286
Morales, Mio, 163
Morales, Santos, 8, 260
Moran, Dan, 142
Moran, Jackie, 47
Moran, Janet, 212
Moran, Michael P., 163
Moran, Michael, 177
Moran, Mike, 163
Moran, Toni, 260
Morapedi, Roslyn, 155
Moreau, Jacqueline, 239
Moreau, Jeanne, 241, 286
Moreau, Jennie, 163
Moreau, Marguerite, 151
Morel, François, 265
Morell, Jason, 229
Moreno, Belita, 45
Moreno, Lucy, 160
Moreno, Patricia, 69
Morente, Enrique, 213
Moreu, Kristin, 163
Moreu, Raphael, 163
Morf, Martin, 105
Morgan Creek Prod., 181
Morgan, Andre, 144
Morgan, Debbi, 129, 198
Morgan, Derrick, 151
Morgan, Diana, 186
Morgan, Edwin T., 151
Morgan, Gary, 63
Morgan, Lara, 125
Morgan, Scott Wesley, 154
Morgenstern, Danny, 179
Morgenstern, Maïa, 203, 266
Morgenstern, Stephanie, 249
Mori, Mineko, 160
Moriah Films, 104
Moriarty, Cathy, 50, 69, 93, 178,
    286
Moriarty, Michael, 50, 286
Moricz, Barna, 138
Morison, Akiko, 169
Morita, Noriyuki "Pat", 167, 286
Moritz, Neal H., 49, 119
Moriyama, Syuichiro, 226
Morley, Natasha, 212
Morley, Vanessa, 169
Morlidge, Roger, 183
Mornell, Sara, 173
Mornin, Daniel, 212
Moro, Fernando, 130
Moroney, Molly, 180
Morong, Donna, 144
Morozova, Kathy, 177
Morrell, Geoff, 257
Morricone, Ennio, 113, 266
Morris, Al, 256
Morris, Alex Allen, 160
Morris, Andrea, 205
Morris, Brian, 256
Morris, Chris, 167
Morris, Errol, 116
Morris, Haviland, 178
Morris, Howard, 121, 286
Morris, Kathryn, 148
Morris, Nic, 169
Morris, Phil, 151
Morris, Steve, 203
Morrison, Campbell, 222
Morrison, Julie, 136
Morrison, Shelley, 21
Morrison, Temuera, 68
Morrissette, Billy, 179
Morrissey, John, 23
Morrow, Carrie, 168
Morrow, Katherine, 135
Morrow, Kevin, 97
Morrow, Mari, 168

Morse, Christo, 182
Morse, David, 181, 286
Morse, Natalie, 263-264
Morse, Richardson, 181
Morse, Susan E., 142
Morshower, Glenn, 84
Mortal Kombat: Annihilation, 177
Mortensen, Viggo, 9, 94, 283, 286
Mortimer, Emily, 42
Mortison, Hayley, 179
Morton, Jessica, 138
Morton, Joe, 20, 283, 286
Morton, Philip, 182
Morton, Rebecca, 153
Mortorff, Lawrence, 164
Moschin, Gastone, 266
Moses, Albert, 162
Moses, Burke, 157
Moshe Diamant, 44
Mosher, Bob, 98
Mosier, Kristin, 41
Mosier, Scott, 41, 138
Mosley, Jeff, 10
Mosley, Ken, 8
Moss, Elizabeth, 106
Mossier, Michael, 170
Mosso, Joe, 53
Most Wanted, 118
Mostow, Jonathan, 55, 101
Moszkowicz, Martin, 206
Motion Picture Corporation of
    America, 9, 11
Motoki, Masahiro, 226
Mottet, Alain, 263
Mottola, Greg, 31
Motubatse, Maimela, 155
Mouis, Marie-Christine , 157
Moulévrier, Gérard, 231
Mount, Thom, 53
Mouse Hunt, 146, 198
Mouse, The , 176
Mouth To Mouth (Boca A Boca),
    263
Moving Pictures, 56, 94
Movius, Kate, 83
Moya, Felipe, 221
Moyer, Betty, 184
Moyer, Dan, 157
Moyes, Zach, 179
M'Punga, Denis, 215
Msize, Eddy, 155
Mr. Magoo, 144
Mrs. Brown, 229
Msize, Eddy, 155
Mudgal, Shubha, 207
Mudie, Jessie Winter, 212
Mueller, Robert, 162
Mueller-Stahl, Armin, 101, 112,
    283, 286
Muellerleile, Marianne, 18, 37, 168
Mugford, Ian, 205
Muhoberac, Jamie, 161
Mui, Eddie, 33
Muir, Linda, 241
Muldoon, Patrick, 128
Mulhare, Edward, 78, 300, 303
Mulholland, Mark, 256
Mulinar, Liz, 230
Mullan, Peter, 125
Mullarkey, Neil, 56
Muller, Michael, 260
Müller, Paul, 224
Müller, Robby, 250
Mullins, Julie Dawn, 182
Mulroney, Dermot, 72-73, 86, 283,
    286
Mulroney, Kieran, 155
Mulrooney, Kelsey, 96
Mulryan, Pat, 256
Mulvehill, Charles B., 126
Mulvey, Louis, 264
Mumford, Dean, 79
Munasinha, Madonna, 259
München, 264
Mundy, Robert, 260
Munge, Julio, 163
Munoz, Emilio, 236
Muñoz, Isidro, 213
Munoz, Jose, 171
Munro, Ronn, 93
Munz, Manuel, 221
Munzi, Maximo, 156
Murder And Murder, 163
Murder At 1600, 180
Muren, Dennis, 61
Muresan, Crina, 239
Murney, Christopher, 167
Muro, Marissa Anna, 115

Murofush, Wataru, 220
Murphy, Annette, 83
Murphy, Bill, 259
Murphy, Doreen, 27
Murphy, Douglas, 251
Murphy, Eddie, 10, 286
Murphy, Fred, 10
Murphy, Geoff, 17
Murphy, Hugh, 20
Murphy, Maeve, 210
Murphy, Michael, 10, 30, 286
Murphy, Mike, 33
Murphy, Vinny, 256
Murray, Abigail, 114, 137
Murray, Bill, 183, 286
Murray, Christopher, 17
Murray, Doug, 39
Murray, Forrest, 100
Murray, Keith, 157
Murray, Mick, 174
Murray, Tom, 24, 151
Murray-Leach, Roger, 12
Murtaugh, James, 30
Murtaugh, Jim, 53
Murton, Iain, 262
Musacchia, Carmelo, 27
Musacchia, Rocco, 27, 183
Musker, John, 71
Musky, Jane, 35
Muslim, Bilal, 168
Mussenden, Isis, 9, 17
Mussenden, Roger, 179
Musser, Larry, 107
Must Be The Music, 33
Mustillo, Lou, 112
Mustillo, Louis, 14
Mutrux, Gail, 27
Mutual Film Company, 131
Mwakutuya, Paul, 141
My Mother's Courage, 263-264
*My Sex Life ... Or How I Got Into
    An Argument*, 263
Mybrand, Jan, 259
Myer, Mark, 180
Myers, Chris, 49
Myers, Dee Dee, 181
Myers, Douglas, 23
Myers, Lou, 49
Myers, Mike, 56-57, 286
Myers, Ruth, 106, 182
Myerscough, Damian, 183
Myhre, John, 180
Myles, Meg, 171
Mylod, Patrick, 102
Mylrea, David, 144
Myrin, Arden, 102, 142
Myron, Ben, 98, 123, 132, 144
Myth Of Fingerprints, The , 105
Nacco, John, 176
Nadoolman, Deborah, 183
Naebig, Kurt, 8
Nagasawa, Toshiya, 172
Nagashima, Hiroyuki, 258
Nagata, Yoshihiko, 220
Nagle, Kevin, 35
Naidu, Ajay, 19
Naipo, Al, 49
Nair, Mira, 207
Nair, Urvashi, 207
Najimy, Kathy, 180
Nakamura, Saemi, 181
Nakanishi, Masayuki, 172
Nakashima, Frank, 138
Nakashita, Genee, 168
Nakayama, Shinobu, 261
Nally, Kiersten, 183
Nance, Jack, 21
Nance, Richard, 145
Nancy Tenenbaum Films, 31
Naor, Yigal, 258
Napier, Charles, 56, 184
Napier, Hugo, 253
Napier, Jessica, 235
Napier, Marshall, 214, 230
Napoleon, 265
Napolitano, Dennis, 37
Napor Kids, 174
Nappo, Tony, 180
Naranhua, 260
Narita, Darling, 176
Narita, Jude, 176
Narration, 135, 170
Narvy, Jason, 158
Nascarella, Arthur, 50, 92, 93, 159
Nash, Diane, 80
Nash, Gresby, 245
Nasso, Frank, 63
Nasso, Julius R., 182

Natasha, Mistress, 161
Nathanson, Jeff, 68
Nathanson, Michael, 180, 182-183
Nathanson, Rick, 44
Nathenson, Zoe, 132
National Center for
    Cinematography, 260
National Center for Jewish Film,
    263
National Center Of
    Cinematography, 215
Naudon, Jean-Francois, 215
Nava, Gregory, 179
Navaro, Guillermo, 147
Navarro, Demetrius, 184
Navarro, Guillermo, 90
Navarro, Jorge, 183
Navazio, Miki, 52
Naveira, Gustavo, 250
Nayar, Deepak, 21, 100
Nayar, Nisha K, 237
Naylor, Jacqueline, 219
Naylor, Phyllis Reynolds, 50
Nayor, Nancy, 39
Nayyar, Harsh, 77, 112, 183
NDF International Ltd., 207
Ndlovu, Ernest, 155
Neal, Barbara, 110
Neal, Billie, 13, 129
Neal, Elise, 95, 144, 168, 179
Neale, David, 144
Neapel Film, 258, 266
Neate, Anthony, 209
Nebout, Claire, 218, 265
Nechunayev, Alexander P., 265
Necoechea, Miguel, 265
Nee, Phil, 49
Neely, William, 119
Negron, Rick, 163
Nehls, Roger, 181
Nehme, Tania, 209
Neiderman, Andrew, 182
Neidich, Melissa, 167
Neidlinger, John, 75
Neighbors, Amelia, 182
Neil, Ed, 158
Neil-Fisher, Debra, 56
Neill, Sam, 91, 214, 286
Neilson, Phil, 94
Neilson, Sandy, 251
Neilson, Torquil, 209
Nelligan, Kate, 205, 286
Nelson, Christopher, 181
Nelson, Connie, 164
Nelson, Craig T., 151, 182, 286
Nelson, Danny, 183
Nelson, Dave, 38
Nelson, Fiona, 232
Nelson, Fred, 97
Nelson, Ian, 127
Nelson, Jessica, 170
Nelson, John Allen, 155
Nelson, John, 46
Nelson, Judd, 184, 286
Nelson, Karlotta, 60
Nelson, Michael, 122
Nelson, Novella, 100, 183
Nelson, Peter, 44
Nelson, Tim Blake, 27, 122
Nelson, Willie, 63, 151, 166, 286
Nelvana, 262
Nemec, Joseph III, 42, 68
Nemeth, Stephen, 159
Nemeth, Vincent, 263
Nemmers, Joe, 164
Nemoy, Carole Curb, 68
Nenette And Boni, 239
Neo Motion Pictures, 177
Nepita, Sean M., 186
Nero, Franco, 222, 286
Nesbitt, James, 248
Nessler, Brad, 38
Nest Entertainment, 166
Nester, J., 183
Nesvold, Roy, 147
Netterville, Ned, 181
Nettles, Joyce, 210, 251
Neubauer, Donnie, 180
Neuenschwander, Brody, 220
Neufeld, Mace, 42
Neuhaus, Ingo, 17, 182
Neuhoff, Ted, 163
Neumann, Birthe, 260
Neumeier, Ed, 128
Neuwirth, Bob, 177
Never Met Picasso, 175
Neville, Cyril, 155
Neville, John, 216

Nevin, Robyn, 230
Nevins, Sheila, 161
New Crime Production, 45
New Deal Productions, 179
New Line Cinema, 5, 34, 56, 63,
    90, 95, 118, 121, 132, 151, 155,
    158, 177, 203
New Millennia Films, 155
New South Wales Film and
    Television Office, 257
New Year's Punch, 223
New Yorker, 213, 215, 223, 260,
    262, 265-266
New Zealand Film Commission,
    214
New Zealand On Air, 214
Newall, Patrick, 161
Newberry, Paul, 130
Newborn, Gayle S., 33
Newcomb, Bodie, 182
Newell, Douglas, 169
Newell, Mike, 27
Newell-Easton, Jennifer, 155
Newhall, Deborah, 176
Newhart, Bob, 102-103, 286
Newitt, Elizabeth, 157
Newland, Michael, 176
Newland, Robin, 175
Newman, Andrew Hill, 21
Newman, Ari, 69
Newman, David, 78, 130
Newman, Johnny, 154
Newman, Kim, 168
Newman, Phyllis, 18
Newman, Randy, 180
Newman, Sam, 257
Newman, Steve, 263
Newman, Thomas, 126, 183, 257
Newman, Vernon, 135
Newman, William, 24
Newmark, Charles, 102
Newmyer, Bobby, 181
Newmyer, Robert, 168
Newton, John, 163
Newton, Thandie, 13
Newton, Wayne, 179
Next Step, The , 163
Nga, Jehad, 171
Ngaujah, Mike, 177
Ngokhang, Chewang Tsering, 152
N'Gom, Abddoulaye, 81
Nguyen, Eric, 261
Nguyen, Ha, 10, 181
Nhan, Nguyen Duc, 220
Nicastro, Michelle, 166
Niccol, Andrew, 124
Nicholas, Gregor, 214
Nicholls, Patrick, 216
Nicholls, Phoebe, 125
Nichols, Chet, 83
Nichols, David, 66, 117
Nichols, Marisol, 144, 179
Nichols, Mike, 215
Nichols, Reno, 179
Nichols, Sue C., 71
Nichols, Taylor, 163
Nicholson, Jack, 6, 25, 148-149,
    188, 287
Nicholson, Mariska M., 260
Nicholson, Michael, 25, 248
Nicholson, Scott, 35
Nick And Jane, 176
Nickel, Nancy, 97
Nickelodeon, 83
Nickles, Michael, 44
Nicksay, David, 136
Niclass, Ivan, 262
Nicolaides, Steve, 66
Nicole, Jamillah, 177
Nicolella, John, 169
Nicolic, Mile, 203
Nicolson, Clair, 229
Nicosia, Mojoee, 95
Nicotero, Frank, 172
Nicotero, Greg, 172
Nicotero, Gregory, 90
Niehaus, Lennie, 22, 183
Niehus, Vicki, 265
Nielsen, Anne, 100
Nielsen, Connie, 182
Nielsen, Leslie, 144, 285, 287
Nielson, Caroline, 126
Nielson, Vincent, 124
Nienhuis, Terry, 79
Nieto, José, 224
Nieves, Benny, 183
Night Falls On Manhattan, 53
Nightingale, John, 39

Nighy, Bill, 125, 225
Nikodym, Martin, 112
Nikolaev, Valery, 42, 113
Nikos, Constantine, 156
Niles, Maja, 80
Nilsson, Stefan, 259
Nimoy, Leonard, 165, 287
Nippon Herald Films, 265
Nishida, Akihiro, 220
Nishida, Yuki, 172
Nishio, Masami, 220
Nissan, Rosa, 264
Nissen, Brian, 166
Nissen, Frank, 262
Nissile, Bernard, 213
Nittoli, Alfred, 63
Nittoli, Andrea, 106
Nivola, Alessandro, 43, 74-75
Nixon, Stuart, 84
Nkosi, Thokozani, 155
Nkwanyana, Peter, 155
No Cheating Darling, 223
No Ordinary Love, 160-161
Noa, Jorge, 18
Noakes, Carol, 125
Noble, Bob, 63
Noble, James 176, 287
Noel, Maria, 250
Noiret, Philippe, 263, 287
Nolan, Barry, 15
Nolan, Mick, 256
Nolens, Marc, 266
Nolot, Jacques, 239
Nolte, Nick, 113, 153, 285, 287
Nomadic Pictures, 178
Nomura, Eugene, 172
Nonna, Grishajeva, 203
Noon Pictures, 263
Nørby, Ghita, 235
Nordberg, Thomas J., 113
Norkat Company, 262
Norman, David, 49, 125
Normant, Anne-Katerine, 263
Norment, Elizabeth, 51
Norona, David, 178
Norr, Chris, 174, 176
Norris, Dean, 124, 128
Norris, Fred, 30, 157
Norris, Lance, 176
Norris, Patricia, 21, 100
Norris, Sabrina, 235
Norris, Terry, 230
North Rhine Westfalia Filmfund,
    266
North, Alan, 167
Northam, Jeremy, 99, 141, 287
Northern Arts Entertainment, 157-
    159, 167, 172, 178, 258, 265-
    266
Northern Lights Entertainment, 52,
    180
Northup, Harry E., 180
Norton, Juanita, 265
Norton, Kristin, 20
Norton, Rosanna, 182
Norwood, Lakia, 175
Noseworthy, Jack, 55, 91
Nossiter, Jonathan, 96
Noth, Christopher, 175
Nothing Personal, 212
Nothing To Lose, 82
Noto, Vic, 53
Notorious B.I.G., The, 156
Nott, Juliann, 263
Nou, Yuki, 220
Novak, Robert D., 181
Novak, Tom, 184
Novat, Pierre, 241
Noveck, Fima, 160
Novello, Don, 24, 287
Novembre, Tom, 254
Novoa, Luis Alberto Garcia, 224
Novoselic, Krist, 166
Novotny, Michael, 32
Novy, Pavel, 262
Nowaki, Nick, 172
Nowra, Louis, 260
Noy, Menashe, 258
Noyce, Phillip, 42
Noyce, Richard, 95, 118
NTV, 226
Nubla, Malou, 10
Nucci, Danny, 39, 186
Nugdup, Lama Thupten, 117
Nugent, Cameron, 259
Nugent, Daniel, 182

Nugent, Ted, 30
Nugiel, Nellie, 52
Nunez, Miguel A., Jr., 137
Nunez, Rafael, 50
Nunez, Victor, 67, 69
Nunn, Barbara, 80
Nunn, Bill, 114, 183
Nunn, Queen, 80
Nunzio's Second Cousin, 33
Nusevic, Emira, 248
Nussbaum, Mike, 77
Nuttall, Jeff, 265
Nuttgens, Giles, 235
Nuyen, France, 168, 287
Nuzollo, Gerry, 69
Nuzzo, Chip, 133
Nyberg, Rick, 165
Nyemba, Nandi, 154
Nyma, Geshe Lobsang, 117
Nyman, Michael, 124
Nyqvist, Michael, 259
Nyström, Anders, 259
Nyswaner, Ron, 83
O Amor Natural, 266
O'Bannon, Dan, 133
O'Boyle, William B., 163
O'Brien, Colm, 212
O'Brien, Elizabeth ,12
O'Brien, Eugene, 231
O'Brien, Kelly, 161
O'Brien Livingstone, Wendy, 212
O'Brien, Patrick T., 114
O'Brien, Peter, 259
O'Brien, Skip 37
O'Bryan, Sean 78, 173
O'Callaghan, Daniel, 135
O'Callaghan, John, 175
O'Connor, Frances. 209, 243
O'Connell, Jack, 29
O'Connell, Jerry, 144, 287
O'Conner ,Gladys, 126
O'Connor, Dennis, 165
O'Connor, Donald, 78, 287
O'Connor, Kevin J., 141
O'Connor, Pat, 43
O'Connor, Matthew, 165, 169
O'Connor, T. Michael 169
O'Dell, Nancy, 144
O'Donahue, Dan, 182
O'Donnell, Catherine, 229
O'Donnell, Chris, 181, 287
O'Donnell, David, 84
O'Donnell, Ernie, 41
O'Donnell, Jerry, 174
O'Donnell, Patrick, 138
O'Donnell, Rosie, 173, 287
O'Donohue, John F., 148, 184
O'Donoghue, Peter , 256
O'Donovan, Noel 256
O'Driscoll, Angela, 231
O'Flanagan, Roisin 231
O'Grady, Gail, 39
O'Grady, Sean, 176
O'Hagan, John, 173
O'Hagan, Michael, 68, 183
O'Halloran, Brian, 41
O'Hara, Catherine, 16, 262, 287
O'Hara, David, 35
O'Hara, Jack, 162
O'Hara, Jenny, 172
O'Hara, Robin, 174, 265
O'Hare, Gareth, 212
O'Henry, 126
O'Herlihy, Cornelia Hayes, 162
O'Kane, Sean 42, 183
O'Keeffe, Douglas, 180
O'Keefe, Terry, 205
O'Kelly, Donal 220
O'Leary, Celine, 209
O'Leary, William, 183
O'Malley , Jason, 96
O'Malley, Jim, 13
O'Neal, Demetrice, 97
O'Neal, Mattie, 164
O'Neal, Shaquille 83, 184
O'Neal, Ty, 184
O'Neil, Pat, 13, 45
O'Neil, Tommy, 256
O'Neil, Tricia, 186,287
O'Neill, Chris, 21
O'Neill, Ed, 13, 287
O'Neill, Steve, 162
O'Neill, Terry, 169, 183
O'Quinn, Jamil Akim, 63
O'Quinn ,Terry, 154, 287
O'Reilly, Ciaran, 35
O'Reilly, Robert, 156
O'Ross, Ed, 97

O'Rourke, Kevin, 8
O'Steen, Sam 53
O'Sullivan, Donald, 183
O'Sullivan ,Kevin, 93
O'Sullivan, Thaddeus, 212
O'Toole, Max, 79
O'Toole,Matt, 24
O'Toole, Peter, 125, 287
Oakes, Chad, 178
Oates, Robert, 216
Oberg, Catherine, 69
Oblowitz, Michael, 79
Oblowitz, Orson, 79
Obst, Lynda, 181
Ocean, Ivory, 21
October Films, 21, 38, 145, 170,
    173, 243
Oda, Takashi, 261
Odede, Samson, 141
Odell, Deborah, 80
Odessa, Devon, 60
Oditz, Carol, 110
Odoardi, Franco, 224
Odom, George, 170
Odum, Ralph, 95
Oedekerk, Steve, 82
Offerman, Nick, 104
Office Killer, 178
Ogata, Ken, 220
Ogata, Yuji, 226
Ogawa, Yuri, 173
Ogg, Ernest R., 86
Ogier, Bulle, 213
Oglesby, Randy, 37, 82
Ognon Pictures, 250
Ogrodnik, Mo, 161
Ogura, Toshie, 183
Oh, Sandra, 244
Oh, Soon-Tek, 11
Ohanneson, Jill, 146, 168
Ohlsson, Fredrik, 259
Ohnishi, Chizuru, 220
Ohno, Shigeru, 226
Ohnuki, Taeko, 226
Ohtani, Koh, 261
Oida, Yoshi, 220
Ojeda, Rene, 93
Okada, Daryn, 180
Okada, Shunji, 172
Okamura, Seiji, 181
Okonedo, Sophie, 131
Okpala, Chike, 141
Okumoto, Yuji, 101, 181
Olcott, Nick, 154
Oldman, Gary, 84, 200, 216-217,
    287
Olejnik, Craig, 205
Oleschak, Edward, 172
Olin, Lena, 53, 287
Oliver, Chris, 258
Oliver, Dave, 118
Oliver, James Louis, 182
Oliver, Mark, 144
Olmos, Edward James, 179, 236,
    287
Olney, Warren, 49
Olsen, Agga, 206
Olsen, Dana, 81
Olsen, Nancy, 136
Olson, Heather Lauren, 98
Olson, Jeff, 65
Olstead, Renee, 159
Olyphant, Timothy, 144, 240
Oman, Chad, 65
Omewenne, 175
Omundson, Timothy, 128
Onafesso, Tony, 141
Onafesso, Willie, 141
One Eight Seven, 184
One Mind Productions Feature, 164
One Night Stand, 132
One Story Pictures, 44
Ongg, Judy, 220
Onodera, Akira, 261
Onorati, Peter, 174
Ontiveros, Lupe, 148, 180
Opel, Nancy, 110
Opelika Pictures, 170
Operation Condor, 230
Opinato, Mario, 44
Oplev, Niels Arden, 260
Oppewall, Jeannine, 182
Orange, Gerald, 176
Orange, Mac, 35
Orange, Rhasaan, 176
Oranntia, Joe, 130
Orchid, Bruce, 49
Ordaz, Terry Elena, 180

Ordesky, Mark, 224
Orekhio, Samuel, 141
Orel, Vesna, 248
Orent, Kerry, 93
Oreskes, Daniel, 183
Orieux, Ron, 23
Orion, 32, 44, 67, 79, 116, 172, 202
Oristrell, Joaquín, 263
Orland, John, 160
Orlandi, Daniel, 174
Orlando, Silvio, 266
Orloff, Stephen, 156
Orly Films, 263
Ormeny, Tom, 173
Ormieres, Jean-Luc, 265
Ormond, Julia, 206
Ornstein, Fred, 173
Oropeza, Luis, 155
Orozco, Regina, 265-266
Orr, Lorenzo, 38
Orr, Mack, 160
Orrison, George, 22
Orsatti, Noon, 96
Orser, Leland, 98, 133
Orth, Zak, 102
Orth-Pallavinci, Terri, 168
Ortiz, Elia, 180
Ortiz, John, 141
Osborn, Michael K., 127
Osborne, Angelique, 123
Osborne, Barrie M., 75
Osborne, Jewdyer, 100
Osborne, Rachel, 115
Osbourne, Ozzy, 30
Oscar And Lucinda, 257
Oseciuc, Gabriel Marian, 105
Osian, Matte, 182
Osmond, Ken, 98
Osorio, Yelba, 20
Ossa, Irwin, 171
Ossman, Michael, 182
Ostalowska, Dominika, 266
Osterwald, Bibi, 148
Ostiguy, Richard, 105
Ostrow, Randy, 115
Oswald D'Andrea, 239
Oteri, Cheri, 31
Other Voices, Other Rooms, 137
Otlkan, James, 162
Ottavio, John, 112
Ottens, Rita, 258,
Otterson, William, 169
Ottey, Oral Norrie, 261
Otto, Barry, 243, 257, 260
Otto, Brian, 163
Otto, Chris, 260
Otto, Götz, 252-253
Otto, Miranda, 235
Ouedraogo, Assita, 215
Ouedraogo, Rasmané 215
Oumi, Darryl, 61
Ourdach, Mohamed, 259
Ousdal, Sverre Anker, 235
Ousley, Benea, 179
Out of the Blue, 171
Out Of The Present, 258
Out To Sea, 78
Outerbridge, Peter, 212
Outlaw Productions, 168, 181
Outsider Enterprises, 170
Outtrabady, Leon, 261
Ove, Indra, 216
Overby, Rhonda, 94
Overmyer, Robert, 114
Overton, David, 94
Owe, Baard, 260
Owen, Alison, 224, 245
Owen, Clive, 245
Owen, Sion Tudor, 261
Owen, Tony, 141
Owens, Albert, 84
Owens, Alexandre, 186
Owens, Gordy, 8
Owers, Kevin, 186
Oz, Frank, 102, 287
Ozier, Michael, 38
P'Tit Louis, 221
P, Fernando Colomo .C., 171
P, Master, 157
P.T. Anderson Pictures, 28, 121
Pace, Chip, 130
Pace, John, 169
Pacheco, Johnny, 264
Pacific Data Images, 80
Pacific Motion Pictures, 165, 169
Pacific Western, 8, 17, 127
Pacino, Al, 26-27, 182, 285, 287
Pack, Roger Lloyd, 210

Packer, 38, 245
Packer, Billy, 38
Padamsee, Pearl, 207
Padden, Bernard, 242
Paddock, Charlie, 65
Padgett, Anna, 83
Padilla, Marcos, 180
Padraic O'Neill, 256
Padura, Leonardo, 264
Pagano, Rick, 80, 133
Page, Jessica, 159
Page, Oliver, 186
Pagès, Jéhan, 261
Paglia, Camille, 158
Paichang, Tenzin Yeshi, 152
Paige, Kimberly, 62
Paik, Greg Joung, 161
Paisley, Ray, 180
Pakula, Alan J., 35
Paladini, Mark, 15, 160, 177
Paladino, Dennis, 53
Paley, Andy, 47
Palin, Michael, 12, 242, 287
Pallascio, Aubert, 241
Pallavicino, Giovanni, 224
Pallister, Joe, 159
Palmer, Geoffrey, 229, 253
Palmer, Gretchen, 172
Palmer, Hugh, 157
Palmer, Jim, 181
Palmer, Joseph, 184
Palmer, Richard, 50
Palmero, Rafael, 213
Palmier, Marina, 160
Palmieri, Eddie, 264
Palmisano, Kerry, 182
Palmisano, Victory Grace, 182
Palter, Lew, 186
Paltrow, Gwyneth, 28, 286
Palud, Herve, 29
Pamlico Pictures, 169
Pan-Européenne, 207
Panatieri, Jerry, 104
Pandora Film, 266
Pandora Films, 207
Pankin, Stuart, 265, 287
Pankow, Bill, 44
Pankow, Joanne, 47
Panorama Entertainment, 176
Panoramic Pictures, 178
Pansullo, Ed, 166
Pantaeva, Irina, 177
Panzarella, Patrick, 161
Paolino, T.J., 161
Paoloni, 44
Papadimitriou, Mania, 203
Papajohn, Michael, 90
Papamichael, Phedon, 116, 146
Papazian, Robert A., 20
Paperback Romance, 230
Papick, Barry, 30
Paplia, Giuseppe, 224
Pappé, Stuart, 81, 144
Pappas, James, 156
Papsidera, John, 56
Paquin, Anna, 141, 288
Parada, Dan, 38, 60, 63, 174
Paradise Films, 265
Paradise, Richard, 132
Parady, Ron, 176
Paragon Entertainment, 238
Paramor, Aron, 216
Paramount, 8, 18, 30, 42, 53, 55,
   62, 75, 83, 91, 102, 114-115,
   125, 127, 135, 166, 168, 179,
   186
Parati, Tim, 162
Pardo, Etela, 42
Parducci, Michael, 171
Parducci, Paul, 83, 127
Paredes, Marisa, 265
Parelle, Monic, 215
Parent, Mary, 63
Parent, Michele, 250
Parfitt, David, 247
Parikh, Devika, 168
Parilo, Markus, 180, 208
Parish, Diane, 225
Parisi, Cliff, 42, 183
Park, Kris, 241
Parke, Andy, 174
Parke, Eva, 175
Parker, Adam, 83
Parker, Ann, 174
Parker, Brad, 49
Parker, Corey, 144, 288
Parker, David, 259

Parker, F. William, 21, 28
Parker, Laurie, 260
Parker, Leni, 105, 179
Parker, Michael, 212
Parker, Molly, 165, 212
Parker, Nathaniel, 11, 288
Parker, Nicole Ari, 120-121
Parker, Nicole, 98, 100
Parker, Paula Jai, 60
Parker, Sarah Jessica, 62, 165, 288
Parker, Timothy Britton, 171
Parkes, Walter F., 77
Parkes, Walter, 112, 141
Parkinson, Eric, 174
Parks, Andrew, 27
Parks, Charles, 68
Parks, Michael, 170, 288
Parks, Stan, 127
Parlavecchio, Steve, 169
Parmele, Don, 180
Parmet, Phil, 155, 174
Parnes, Fred, 154
Parnes, Uzi, 191
Parnet, Veronique, 265
Parra, Alejandro, 81
Parrondo, Gil, 236
Parry, William, 102
Parshin, Sergei, 180
Parsons, Estelle, 23, 288
Parsons, Jennifer J., 177
Parsons, Nicholas, 266
Parsons, Willy, 82
Part, Arvo, 235
Partridge, Ross, 61
Pasco, Richard, 229
Pasdar, Adrian, 50
Paseka, Lawton, 170
Paseornek, Michael, 264
Pasolini, Uberto, 232
Pasqualone, Rick, 51
Pasquin, John, 29
Pass, Cyndi, 172
Passero, Jeffery, 169
Passewe, Steve, 141
Passport Cinemas, 175
Past, Melodie, 182
Pasternak, Beth, 249
Pastko, Earl, 169, 249
Pastore, Garry, 93
Pastore, Vincent, 52-53
Pastorelli, Robert, 80
Pasztor, Beatrix Aruna, 96, 98, 113,
   138
Patel, Bhasker, 261
Patel, Harish, 207
Patel, Raju, 162
Patel, Sharad, 162
Paterson, Fiona, 209
Paterson, Spencer, 96
Patino, Alejandro, 160
Patlock, Tomer, 258
Paton, Julia, 23
Patric, Jason, 68, 288
Patrick, John, 116, 144
Patrick, Robert, 93, 179
Patrick, Vincent, 35
Patsas, Yorgos, 203
Patten, Michael, 13
Patteri, Robert, 174
Patterson, Gene, 86
Patterson, James, 114
Patterson, Janet, 257
Patterson, Paulette, 144
Patton, Frank, 78
Patton, Lynda, 69
Patton, Tyler, 68
Patton, Will, 43, 79, 184, 288
Patton-Spruill, Robert, 69
Pau, Peter, 44, 163
Paul, Adam, 177
Paul, Adrian, 161
Paul, D.J., 96
Paul, Jarrad, 37
Paul, Jeff, 171
Paul, Megan, 75
Paul, Victoria, 55, 63
Paul-Davidson, John, 210
Pauldine, Michael, 132
Paulin, Viveca, 95
Paulk, Marcus, 82, 132
Paulovic, Lubomir, 112
Paulson, Dan, 154
Paulson, William, 35
Paumier, Christian, 263
Paur, Frank, 166
Pavel, Philip, 144
Pavlich, John Charles, 13
Paxton, Bill, 47, 186, 288

Paxton, Collin Wilcox, 183
Paxton, John, 47
Paxton, Sara, 37
Pay, Chris, 69
Paymer, David, 38, 104, 141, 172,
   286, 288
Payne, Eric, 13
Payne, Freda, 60
Payne-Gabriel, Laura, 56
Payton, Christian, 97
Pazienza, Vinny, 176
Peace, Moses J., 168
Peaces, 69
Peacock, Trevor, 224
Pearce, Guy, 182, 288
Pearlman, Stephen, 30, 52
Pearlstein, Julia, 244
Pearson, James A., 175
Pearson, Tania L., 11
Pecanins, Marisa, 265
Pecanins, Tere, 264
Peceva, Viktorija, 248
Peck, Bob, 125, 206
Peck, Brian, 83
Peck, James, 222
Peck, Jonathan Earl, 35
Peck, Rodney, 135
Pecora, Robert, 160
Pedersen, Aaron, 266
Pedersoli, Giuseppe, 209
Pedley, Anthony, 12
Peduto, Ralph, 10
Peel, Darren, 181
Peet, Amanda, 159
Pegues, Helen, 80
Peister, Gail, 122
Pejakovic, Nikola, 264
Peldon, Ashley, 180
Pellegrino, Frank, 93
Pellegrino, Vince, 216
Pelletier, Michele-Barbara, 153
Pelletier, Michelle, 183
Pelletier, Polly, 105
Pelligan, Francois, 155
Pellington, Mark, 104
Pelzman, Richard, 137
Pema, Jetsun, 117
Pemrick, Don, 162
Pena, Ailinda Camile, 100
Peña, Candela, 263
Pena, Cantilo, 250
Pena, Jose "Esau", 180
Peña, Michael, 83
Penche, Gonzalo, 236
Pendergrass, Torry, 38
Pendleton, Austin, 63, 141, 288
Pendleton, Richard, 162
Penman, Simon, 125
Penn, Arthur, 154
Penn, Michael, 28, 83, 101, 121
Penn, Richard, 49
Penn, Robin Wright, 96
Penn, Sean, 96, 101, 113, 178, 286,
   288
Penn, Zak, 83
Pennell, Jon, 81
Penner, Jonathan, 68
Pentz, Robert, 174
Pepito, Alaina P., 160
Peploe, Clare, 260
Pepper, Jason, 176
Peraza, Mike, 130
Percival, Lyn, 230
Percival, Michael, 12
Perczel, Zita, 224
Pereira, Gilvan, 258
Pereira, Manuel Gómez, 263
Pereira, Rui Luis, 258
Pereira, Vanessa, 248
Perell, Tim, 105
Perella, Marco, 160
Perepeczko, Agnieszka, 230
Pereyra, Rene, 260
Pérez, Carla, 158
Perez, Charles, 49
Perez, Danilo, 178
Perez, Eddie, 65, 178
Perez, Gary, 161, 170
Perez, George, 180
Perez, Jesse, 122
Perez, Josie, 216
Perez, Miguel, 44, 259
Perez, Rosie, 50, 288
Perez, Salvador, 109
Perez, Tony, 20, 173
Perilch, Max, 162
Perine, Kelly, 63

Périphéria, 262
Perkins, Garwood, 156
Perkins, Kari, 159
Perkins, Ron, 49
Perlich, Max, 174
Perlich, Miles, 3
Perlman, Bonnie, 156
Perlman, Ron, 133, 288
Permenter, David, 84
Permut, David, 75
Perri, Linda, 142
Perri, Paul, 161
Perri, Valerie, 81
Perrier-Royer, Dominique, 263
Perrineau, Harold, 25, 107
Perrineau Jr., Harold, 25
Perrochaud, Christian, 230
Perron, Michel, 179
Perry, Chancz, 144
Perry, Douglas, 145
Perry, Ernest, 34, 37
Perry, J.J., 177
Perry, John Bennett, 21, 81
Perry, Kate, 256
Perry, Luke, 216, 288
Perry, Matthew, 21
Perry, Nickolas, 33
Perry, Pamela, 165
Perry, Penny, 8, 44
Perry, Steve, 68
Persistence of Vision Films, 174
Persky, Lisa Jane, 38
Persson, Jörgen, 206, 259
Persuasions, The, 154
Pertier, Michelle, 163
Pertronzio, Nina, 144
Pertwee, Sean, 91
Perugorria, Jorge, 224
Pesce, Frank, 27
Peschcke-Koedt, Nina, 69
Pesci, Joe, 44, 63, 288
Peskov, Alexander, 112
Pest, The , 20
Peterman, Don, 77
Peters Entertainment, 179
Peters, Bernadette, 130, 288
Peters, Jon, 179
Peters, Paul, 44
Peters, Robert, 47, 84, 114, 122,
   127, 162
Petersen, John, 100
Petersen, Sally, 161
Petersen, Wolfgang, 84, 126
Peterson, Clark, 172
Peterson, Janie, 181
Peterson, Johnny, 258
Peterson, Kristine, 177
Peterson, Lisa, 164
Peterson, Robyn, 25
Pethig, Hazel, 12
Petit, Aurélia, 221
Petit, Jean-Claude, 265
Petit, Philippe, 260
Petricini-Buxton, Barbara, 180
Petrick, Paris, 41
Petrone, Bettina, 259
Petrov, Jouri, 203
Petrovic, Dragan, 264
Petruccelli, Kirk M., 46
Petrucci, Darren, 205
Petruna, Peter, 169
Pettengill, Theresa, 180
Pettersson, Dan, 186
Pettijohn, Benjamin, 11
Petty, Lawrence, 109
Petty, Tom, 184
Pevner, Stephen, 89
Peyser, Michael, 68
Peysson, Julie, 250
Peyton, Harley, 160
Pezyos, George, 96
Pfah, Kembra, 154
Pfarrer, Chuck, 131
Pfeffer, Andrew, 166
Pfeifer, N. Dylan, 178
Pfeifer, Paul, 157
Pfeiffer, Carolyn, 264
Pfeiffer, Chuck, 53
Pfeiffer, Michelle, 7, 106, 288
Pflug, Jo Ann, 47, 183
Phaedra Cinema, 13, 156-157, 160-
   161, 163, 169, 171-172, 174,
   177
Pham, Hoang N., 168
Pharcyde, 154
Phelan, David, 225, 245
Phelan, Walter, 172
Phelps, Nigel, 133

Phifer, Mekhi, 108-109
Phifer, Sylvester, 109
Phifer, Zack, 51
Phillippe, Ryan, 60, 119, 286, 288
Phillips, Arianne, 104
Phillips, Arlene, 242
Phillips, Don, 101
Phillips, Erica Edell, 84
Phillips, Ethan, 137
Phillips, Grace, 98, 162
Phillips, Jacqueline, 183
Phillips, John, 105
Phillips, Johnny, 186
Phillips, Karentiio, 179
Phillips, Leslie, 131
Phillips, Lloyd, 107
Phillips, Michael, 99
Phillips, Rod, 78
Phillips, Tamara, 53
Phillips, Todd, 154
Phillips-Palo, Linda, 135
Phoenix Pictures, 113
Phoenix, Joaquin, 43, 113, 288
Phuntsok, Sonam, 152
Picard, Don, 29
Piccoli, Michel, 265
Picerni, Charles, 44
Pickens, James, Jr., 13, 174
Pickens, Jimmy, 116
Picker, Si, 142
Pickering, Denise, 71
Pickering, Donald, 183
Pickering, Steve, 97
Picture Perfect, 88
Pieh, Samuel, 141
Piel, Jean Louis, 220
Pierce, Charleston, 10
Pierce, Fred, 146
Pierce, Justin, 50
Pierce, Sarah, 11
Pierce-Roberts, Tony, 29
Pierpoint, Eric, 37, 184
Pierreux, Jacqueline, 215
Pierrot, Frédéric, 262
Pierson, Geoff, 98
Pierson, John, 41
Pierson, Joseph, 170
Pieter van Huystee Film, 266
Piggott, Richie, 266
Pigott, Johanna, 214
Pike, Nicholas, 123
Pilato, Josef, 172
Pilcher, Lydia Dean, 207
Pilhofer, Herb, 163
Pilkington, Lorraine, 256
Pillars, Jeffrey, 79
Pillow Book, The 220
Pillsbury, Sam, 182
Pillsbury, Suzanne, 154
Pilon, Daniel, 105
Pinard, Bruce, 169
Pinckes, Craig A., 68
Pine, Larry, 96, 110, 181
Pine, Ted, 164
Piñeyro, Marcelo, 259
Ping, Zong, 126
Pingarron, Gabriel, 260
Pinheiro, Felipe, 258
Pink, Steve, 45
Pinkett, Jada, 144, 292
Pinkney, Rose Catherine, 168
Pinney, Clay, 49
Pinney, Patrick, 71
Pinnock, Emil, 38
Pinon, Dominique, 133
Pinsent, Gordon, 109
Pinter, Herbert, 211
Pinto, Fernando Alves, 264
Pippi Longstocking, 262
Pirner, David, 41
Piro, Salvatore Paul, 53
Pisoni, Edward, 21
Pistor, Julia, 83
Pite, Crystal, 132
Pitoniak, Anne, 106
Pitt, Brad, 6, 35, 117, 287-288
Pitt, Malcolm, 232
Pitts, Oscar, Jr., 154
Pitts-Wiley, Richard, 176
Piven, Jeremy, 45, 114, 288
Piyasena, EA, 162
Pizano, Beatriz, 23
Place, Graham, 77
Place, Mary Kay, 122, 134-135, 288
Plainview Pictures, 159
Plakson, Suzie, 151
Plan B, 173

Plana, Tony, 184
Planer, Nigel, 242
Planet Pictures, 211
Plant, Briony, 125
Plasson, Suzanne, 221
Platnick, Jonathan, 165
Platt, Howard, 179
Platt, Lucas, 166
Plateau, Antoine, 263
Platz, Tom, 44
Playing God, 122
Playten, Alice, 163, 288
Plimpton, George, 184
Plimpton, Martha, 122, 287-288
Plistina, Milan, 248
Plotch, Joel, 89
Plowman, Anna-Louise, 125
Plumb, Eve, 60, 288
Plumer, Andrew, 243
Plummer, Amanda, 71, 80, 158, 288
Plummer, Glenn, 68, 132
Plummer, Mark, 9
Plummer, Sean, 77
Plumpis, John, 62
Plunkett, Maryann, 21
Podalydès, Denis, 263
Podesta, Patti, 60
Podgurski, Jeff, 181
Poe, Richard, 112
Pogue, Charles Edward, 169
Poindexter, Jeris, 65
Pointer, Chandra, 156
Poirier, Gregory, 179
Poitier, Pamela, 131
Poitier, Sidney, 131, 289
Pokorny, Diana, 106
Polaire, Michael, 136
Polar Entrainment, 241
Polar, 183, 241
Polcsa, Juliet, 170
Polcyn, Beverly, 78
Polden, Donald, 135
Poledouris, Basil, 55, 127, 128
Polhemus, Pamela, 105
Poling, Chan, 170
Polit, Mario, 35
Polizos, Vic, 184
Poll, Jon, 18
Pollack, Bernie, 35
Pollack, Christophe, 262
Pollack, Jeff, 23
Pollak, Kevin, 162, 289
Pollard, Korey Scott, 184
Pollard, Sam, 80
Pollard, Yvonne, 182
Polley, Sarah, 199, 249
Pollock, Patsy, 42
Pollock, Steven, 151
Poloni, Dario, 224
Polstein, Claire Rudnick, 56, 151
Polstein, Jay, 129
PolyGram Filmed Entertainment, 13, 104, 168, 207, 244, 261, 266
Ponder, Nezester, 83
Ponette, 218
Pons, Sebastien, 239
Ponti, Antonio, 156
Pony Canyon Inc., 207
Pony Canyon, 207, 265
Ponzo, Rosemary, 178
Poole, Alyson, 169
Poole, Mary Alvena, 205
Poole, Michelle, 34
Poon, Alice, 208
Poor, Bray, 88
Pope, Angela, 210
Pope, Bill, 13
Pope, Carole, 262
Pope, Conrad, 169
Pope, Dick, 212, 234
Pope, Francis, 12
Pope, Martin, 225
Popkova, Oxana, 42
Popovska, Joana, 248
Popper, John, 30
Popperwell, Paul, 125
Poppick, Eric, 146, 159, 184
Popson, Hedy, 167
Por, Mike, 69
Porcaro, Steve, 10
Porizkova, Paulina, 38, 68
Porrett, Susan, 42
Porter, Adina, 112
Porter, Aldric, 148
Porter, Andrew, 47
Porter, Billy, 135, 178
Porter, Shiree, 184

Porter, Steven M., 82
Porter, Susie, 211
Porter, Vern, 127
Portier Sr., Harold, 145
Portland, 260
Portman, Rachel, 181
Portnow, Richard, 30, 183
Porto, Lidia, 174
Posey, Parker, 16, 19, 31, 118, 158, 287, 289
Post, Andrea, 43
Post, Tim, 105
Poster, Meryl, 93
Poster, Randall, 240
Poster, Steve, 33
Poster, Steven, 174
Postlethwaite, Pete, 61, 141, 219, 289
Postman, The ,184
Poteat, Brian, 183
Potkins, Michael, 87
Potte, Monica, 65
Potter, Barr, 32, 79
Potter, Bob, 50
Potter, Leigh-Anne, 160
Potter, Richard, 99, 144
Potter, Sally, 250
Potter, Tim, 12
Potter, Will, 20
Potts, Michael, 112, 181
Pouille, Hubert, 207
Poul, Alan, 62
Poulos, George, 13
Pounder, CCH, 75
Poupaud, Melvil, 174
Powell, Brian, 45
Powell, Esteban, 164
Powell, John, 75
Powell, Linda, 178
Powell, Melissa, 159
Powell, Nik, 210
Powell, Rickey, 80
Powell, Robert, 181, 289
Powell, Sandy, 247
Powell, Tony, 97
Power, Ashley, 172
Power, Pamela, 183
Powers, Alexandra, 78
Powers, Eddie, 21
Powers, Jonathan, 169
Powsey, Clive, 262
Poyser, Mark, 38
Pozenko, Yegor, 42
Pozer, John, 212
Pradal, Yann, 236
Prael, William, 264
Prasad, Udayan, 218
Pratt Films, 259
Pratt, Kyle, 183
Pratt, Lauren, 65
Pratt, Susan, 30
Prefontaine, 13
Prefontaine, Steve, 13
Preising, Donna, 23
Preisner, Zbigniew, 125
Preller, Ross, 154-155
Presar, Barbara, 31
Prescott, Nicole, 175
Presle, Micheline, 213, 215, 289
Presnell, Harve, 75, 170, 289
Press, Fiona, 214, 265
Pressman Lipper, 251
Pressman, David, 49
Pressman, Edward R, 251
Pressman, Lawrence, 63
Prestia, Shirley, 98, 151
Preston, Carrie, 72, 137
Preston, David, 15, 176
Preston, Douglas, 8
Preston, Grania, 38
Preston, Kelly, 82, 181, 289
Preston, William, 157, 289
Pretty Village, Pretty Flame, 264
Prettyman, Jeff, 63
Prevost, Nathan Frederic, 121
Price, Frank, 11
Price, Gary, 95
Price, Kenneth, 12
Price, Louis, 97
Price, Molly, 166
Price, Officer Mike, 69
Price, Vernon Oliver, 97
Prichard, Jennifer, 169
Prichard, Robert, 169
Priestley, Paul, 216
Priestley, Tom, Jr., 79

Prigunov, Lev, 42
Primes, Robert, 95
Primi, Keith, 159
Primus, Barry, 155, 289
Prince, Daisy, 142
Prince, Faith, 88
Prince, Richard H., 63, 174
Prinze Jr., Freddie, 118-119, 199, 201
Prisco, Tom, 176
Prisoner Of The Mountains, 202
Private Parts, 30
Procacci, Domenico, 209
Processen Mod Hamsun, 235
Prochnow, Jurgen, 84-85, 289
Procirep, 236, 265
Procopio, Fortunato, 50
Proctor, Phil, 71
Proft, Pat, 144
Proletariat Pictures, 177
Prominent Features, 219
Propaganda Films, 101, 106
Prophecy Pictures Inc., 176
Prophets of Da City, 155
Prosky, Andy, 77
Prosky, John, 182
Prosky, Robert, 183, 289
Proval, David, 8, 155, 289
Provine, Dorothy, 23, 289
Pruitt-Hamm, Robyn, 184
Prulhiere, Timi, 69
Pryce, Jonathan, 252-253, 288-289
Pryor, Andy, 245
Pryor, J.F., 167
Pryor, Nicholas, 180
Pryor, Richard, 21, 289
Przygodda, Peter, 100, 262
Puccio, Nicholas A., 154
Puente, Carlos, 166
Puente, Tito, 264
Puett, Dallis, 169
Puett, Tommy, 127
Pugh, Robert, 237
Pugh, Willard, 84
Pulbrook, David, 262
Pulford, Don, 68, 182
Pullman, Bill, 21, 100, 288-289
Punch Productions, 183
Puny But Loud Prods., 173
Puopolo, L.A., 163
Pupello, Angela, 159
Puri, Om, 218
Purwin, Alan, 51, 61
Pustelnik, Claudio, 259
Putnam, Andree, 220
Puttnam, Michael, 144
Putzulu, Bruno, 236
Py, Olivier, 221
Pyle, Missi, 148
Pyper-Ferguson, John, 137

Q Productions Inc., 179
Qiagui, Huang, 222
Qiang, Gao, 126
Quaid, Dennis, 127, 172, 289
Quaid, Randy, 179, 289
Quaki, Fabien, 262
Quan, Stuart, 32
Quast, Philip, 265
Quettier, Nelly, 250
Quevedo-Stoll, Teresa, 49
Quiet Room, The 209
Quigley, May, 88
Quigley, Peter, 176
Quincy & Carson Welch, 165
Quincy Jones-David Salzman Entertainment, 184
Quinlan, Kathleen, 11, 54-55, 91, 289
Quinn, Aidan, 52, 105, 289
Quinn, Declan, 132, 207
Quinn, Declan, 132, 207
Quinn, Kave, 240
Quinn, Linda, 231
Quinn, Tom, 154
Quinones, Leo, 49
Quint, Jonathan, 119, 121
Quintanilla, Abraham, 179
Quirk, Brian, 157
Quivers, Robin, 30

Rabaeus, Johan, 259
Rabaud, Pascal, 100
Rabe, Pamela, 211, 260
Rabin, Trevor, 65
Rabinowitz, Elliot, 173
Rabinowitz, Jay, 173
Rabinowitz, Leonard, 46
Rabson, Jan, 71

Rachins, Alan, 15, 98
Rack, B.J., 99
Racki, Branko, 180
Racz, Marra, 38
Racz, Yvonne, 163
Rada Films, 100
Radclyffe, Sarah, 245
Rader, Jack, 156
Radiant Production, 84
Radley, Ken, 214
Radtke, Peter, 264
Radzull, Lydia, 159
Rae, Charlotte, 60
Rae, Douglas, 229
Rae, George Anthony, 121
Rae, James, 179
Rae, Karen, 154
Rafelson, Bob, 25
Rafferty, Bill, 183
Raffo, John, 8
Ragazzi, Rossella, 263
Ragland, Gary, 122
Ragsdale, Georgia, 175
Ragusa, Angelo, 44
Raho, Umberto, 44
Raimi, Ted, 172
Rainbow, D.D., 168
Rainer, Yvonne, 163
Raines, Howell, 80
Rainmaker, The , 135
Rainone, Thomas C., 172
Rajabali, Anjum, 207
Rajinovska, Natali, 248
Rajski, Peggy, 33
Ralston, Ken, 181
Ramanee, Sakuntala, 225
Rambis, Kurt, 174
Rambo, 78, 221
Rambo, Bubba Dean, 78
Ramessar, Ron, 133
Ramez, Jill, 236
Ramirez, Juan A., 97
Ramirez, Paola, 221
Ramirez, Twiggy, 21
Ramis, Harold, 148, 289
Ramminger, Michelle, 184
Ramos, Juan Antonio, 236
Ramos, Richard Russell, 30
Ramos, Sixto, 35, 100
Rampa, Tenzin, 152
Rampage Entertainment, 264
Rampling, Charlotte, 246-247, 289
Ramsay, John, 229
Ramsay, Remak, 181
Ramsay, Robin, 260
Ramsay, Todd, 172
Ramsey, Anna, 125
Ramsey, Carol, 29
Ramsey, David, 65
Ramsey, George, 23
Ramsey, Kennard, 160
Ramsey, Kevin, 53
Ramsey, Stephen, 94
Rand, Ronald, 102
Randall, Gary, 174
Randall, George, 65
Randle, Theresa, 90
Randolph, John, 53, 157
Randolph, Shari, 60
Random, Ida, 184
Ranga, Dana, 223
Rank Film Distributors, 44
Ranken, Liz, 225
Rankin, Steve, 77, 182
Ranquet, Joan, 163
Ransen, Mort, 205
Ransohoff, Martin, 8
Rao, Arundhati, 207
Rao, Bhanumathi, 207
Raoul, Dale, 78
Raoul, Nathalie, 250
Rapaport, Michael, 10, 50, 92-93, 170
Raphael, Sally Jessy, 15
Rappaport, Alex, 156
Rappazzo, Carmela, 18
Rappoport, Ksenia, 180
Rasche, David, 39, 289
Raschke, Claudia, 166
Rashleigh, Andy, 210
Ras Kass and Crew, 157
Rasool J'Han, 119
Ratchet Productions LLC, 171
Ratchet, 171
Ratcliffe, Ken, 222
Rathaus, Jeffrey, 166
Ratier, Ellea, 236

328

Ratliff, Pat, 145
Ratner, Brett, 95
Rats In The Ranks, 258
Ratzenberger, John, 23, 132
Ratzin, Lisa E., 121
Raudaschl, Tom, 117
Rauf, Kurt, 178
Raulerson, Steve, 179
Raunsbjerg, Preben, 260
Raveling, George, 38
Raven, 180
Raven, Elsa, 186
Raven, Mistress, 161
Ravera, Gina, 109, 114
Rawlings, Terry, 42
Rawlins, Adrian, 237
Rawlins, David, 20, 144
Ray Murphy, Jr., 10
Ray, Billy, 49, 135
Ray, Connie, 68
Ray, Johanna, 21, 122, 128
Ray, Robyn, 174
Ray, Warren, 170
Ray, Wendy, 13
Ray, William Earl, 159
Ray-Gavras, Michèle, 260
Raybourn, Philip, 180
Raymond, Bill, 132
Raymond, Deborah, 172
Raymont, Daniel, 133
Raynor, Michael, 50
Razzano, Tom, 161
Rea, Brad, 182
Rea, F.T., 154
Rea, Joe, 212
Rea, Joseph, 256
Rea, Karen, 11
Rea, Stephen, 231, 289
Read, Bobbie, 65
Read-Wilson, Jane, 125
Reagon, Toshi, 158
Reamer, Keith, 171
Reaves, Harvey, 23
Reback, Katherine, 21
Rebecca O'Brien, 231, 244
Rebhorn, James, 101
Rebolledo, Juan, 160
Recasens, Alina, 49
Recorded Picture Company, 25, 260
Rector, Cynthia, 169
Rector, Jerry, 118
Rector, Mark, 89
Red Corner, 126
Red Mullet, 132
Red Sky Films, 155
Redback, Katherine, 21
Redden, Leslie, 121
Reddy, Brian, 17
Redeemable Features, 166
Redfield, Dennis, 8
Redford, Dan, 144
Redford, Elisabeth, 172
Redford, Robert, 166, 289
Redgrave, Vanessa, 206, 289
Redman, Crispin, 222
Redmond, Elaina, 167
Redstall, Victoria, 82
Redwave Films, 232
Reece, Gabrielle, 124
Reece, Georgia, 12
Reed, Aaron, 163
Reed, Ben, 75
Reed, Christopher, 38
Reed, Pamela, 244, 289
Reed, Rondi, 29
Reed-Humes, Robi, 13, 34, 109
Reedus, Norman, 99
Rees, Roger, 157, 289
Reese, Larry, 181
Reese, Star, 163
Reeves, Clinton Lee, 174
Reeves, Keanu, 164, 182, 289
Reeves, Lucia, 160
Reeves, Phil, 173
Reeves, Saskia, 237
Reeves, Steve, 71, 289
Reevis, Steve, 155
Reffie, Peter, 163
Regency Enterprises, 180, 182-183
Regent Entertainment, 173
Regidor, Carlos, 213
Reichardt, Kelly, 175
Reichel, Stephane, 208
Reichle, Franz, 265
Reichle, Luke, 80
Reid, Audrey, 264
Reid, Sheila, 251
Reidy, Gabrielle, 35

Reidy, Joseph, 142
Reidy, Kevin, 177
Reilly, Brian M., 29
Reilly, Brian, 29
Reilly, John C., 28, 120-121
Reilly, Luke, 30
Reimbold, Bill, 216
Reimer, Chris, 38
Reimer, Nadine, 155
Reiner, Carl, 39, 289
Reiner, Clark, 82
Reinke, Randall, 168
Reisberg, Barney, 237
Reisz, Barney, 237
Reitano, Robert, 88
Reitman, Caroline, 180
Reitman, Ivan, 30, 52, 180
Reitman, Jason, 180
Reitz, Ric, 179
Reitz, Tymme, 160
Rekha, 207
Rekhi, Kushal, 235
Relic, The , 8
Remar, James, 177, 290
Remsen, Bert, 178, 182, 290
Remy, Tony, 234
Ren, Esmond, 203
Renaissance Films, 247
Renard, Frederick, 44
Renaud, David, 155
Renaud, Francis, 221
Renaud, Line, 263
Rendino, Sal, 49
Rendon, Kevin, 158
Renegade Films, 218
Renfro, Brad, 123, 290
Renfro, Bryan, 180
Renier, Jérémie, 215
Renna, Melinda, 114
Rennard, Deborah, 173
Rennie, Callum Keith, 169
Rennie, Callum, 98
Rennie, David, 178
Reno, Jean, 224, 290
Renoly, 65
Renshaw, Alan, 155
Renshaw, Blair, 155
Renuault, Dalia, 259
Repanis, Dimitri, 155
Reperage and Vanguard Films, 117
Represa, Guillermo, 263
Reshovsky, Marc, 33, 118
Resnick, Floyd, 142
Resnick, Gina, 38
Restivo, Justin, 98
Reubens, Paul, 66
Reuther, Steven, 75, 135
Revell, Graeme, 42
Revilla, Gil, 175
Revuelta, Leon, 236
Rey, Antonia, 166, 290
Rey, Jose, 146
Rey, José, 181
Rey, Reynaldo, 60
Reyburn, Leigh, 127
Reyes, Alejandro, 160
Reyes, Christopher, 175
Reyes, David, 184
Reymond, Dominique, 250
Reynolds, Billy Ray, 135
Reynolds, Brian J., 172
Reynolds, Burt, 15, 120-121, 194, 244, 289-290
Reynolds, Debbie, 68, 102-103, 290
Reynolds, Hilary, 225
Reynolds, Jacob, 174
Reynolds, Kelly, 167
Reynolds, Kevin, 184
Reynolds, Larry, 168
Reynolds, Michael J., 39
Reynolds, Patrick, 35
Reynolds, Tom, 75
Reynolds, Wayne, 205
Rhames, Ving, 64-65, 155, 179
Rhind-Tutt, Julian, 42, 253
Rhine, Gary, 155
Rhoads, Terry, 37, 183
Rhodes, Shari, 182
Rhodri, Steffan, 261
Rhue, Geoffrey, 69
Rhyme And Reason, 156
Rhymes, Busta, 156
Rhys Meyers, Jonathan, 123
Rhys-Davies, John, 180, 290
Rhythm & Hues, Inc., 68
Ribeiro, Pedro, 258

Ribisi, Giovanni, 19, 21, 184, 290
Ricard, Eduardo, 44
Ricci, Christina, 23, 110-111, 289-290
Rice, Brett, 179
Rice, Georg D., 32
Rich Animation Studios, 166
Rich, Allan, 78, 141
Rich, Catherine, 239
Rich, Claude, 239
Rich, Katie, 49
Rich, Richard, 166
Rich, Tony, 97
Richard Speight, Jr., 68
Richard, Nathalie, 213
Richard, Pierre, 213
Richards, Ariana, 61
Richards, Denise, 60, 128
Richards, J. August, 83
Richards, Jeff, 63, 212
Richards, Jerome, 157
Richards, Michael, 63, 290
Richards, Walter, 49
Richardson, Alex, 222
Richardson, Charles L., 180
Richardson, Elizabeth, 205
Richardson, Henry, 158
Richardson, Ian, 158
Richardson, Jackie, 126
Richardson, James, 86
Richardson, Joely, 91, 210, 290
Richardson, LaTanya, 170
Richardson, Miranda, 145, 215, 290
Richardson, Nancy, 145
Richardson, Nolan, 38
Richardson, Patricia, 67
Richardson, Robert, 113, 116, 151
Richardson, Stina, 216
Richardson, Sy, 166
Riche, Alan, 146
Richerson, Mackie, 182
Richings, Julian, 99
Richman, Lucas, 173
Richman, Robert, 258
Richmond, Anthony B., 122
Richmond, Tom, 14, 173
Richter, Jason James, 182
Richter, Jason, 56
Ricketson, Greg, 214
Rickman, Alan, 251, 290
Ricupero, Michael, 180
Rider, Robert, 38
Ridgely, Robert, 28, 121, 182, 304
Ridgeway, Lindsay, 180
Ridgewell, Colin, 237
Ridgle, Elston, 180
Ridgway, Josh, 160
Riding The Rails, 171
Ridings, Richard, 12, 242
Ridley, John, 113, 175
Ridley, Merle-Anne, 262
Riehle, Richard, 184
Riemens, Peter, 254
Riera, Jose M., 264
Rifkin, Adam, 146
Rifkin, Ron, 182, 290
Rigby, Terence, 253
Rigby, Tim, 32
Riley, Claire, 98, 144
Riley, Jack, 121
Riley, Leslie, 173
Riley, Michael, 141
Riley, Paul, 262
Riley, Stu "Large" 52
Ringberg, Kirk, 148
Ringwald, Molly, 178, 290
Ringwood, Bob, 133
Rinpoche, Lobsang Gendun, 117
Rinpoche, Sharpa Tulku, 117
Rinpoche, Tenzin Gyaltsen, 117
Rinpoche, Zongra Tulku, 117
Rinzler, Liza, 262
Riofilme, 264
Riojas, Juan, 181
Rios, Guillermo, 160
Rios, Mark Adair, 21
Ripe, 161
Ripley, David, 180
Ripley, Fay, 224
Ripoux Contre Ripoux (My New Partner At The Races), 263
Rippy, Leon, 183
Ripstein, Arturo, 265
Rispoli, Michael, 49
Riss, Wendy, 166
Ristovski, Laza, 264
Ritchie, Lillian, 80
Ritchie, Michael, 80

Ritchie, Miriam, 80
Ritson, Blake, 237
Ritter, John, 60, 290
Ritter, Sonia, 257
Riva, Marie, 221
Rivera, Alfredo, 69
Rivera, Emillio, 65
Rivera, Geraldo, 15, 156, 181
Rivers, Brad, 168
Rivers, Joan, 265, 290
Rivers, Lucy, 238
Rivers, Victor, 141
Rivett, Julian, 222
Riviere, Julien, 255
Rivkin, Stephen, 98
RMM FilmWorks, 264
Roach, Jay, 56
Roach, Pat, 169
Roache, Linus, 246-247
Roache, Paul, 37
Road Movies Filmproduktion, 262
Roan, Jean-Yves, 239
Robards, Jason, 106, 290
Robbie Thibaut, Jr., 11
Robbins Entertainment, 69
Robbins, Amy, 162
Robbins, Brian, 83
Robbins, Kristina, 69
Robbins, Matthew, 99
Robbins, Mitchell B., 69
Robbins, Pastor Truman, 28
Robbins, Tim, 82, 290
Robbins, Tom, 166
Roberson, David, 65
Roberts, Adrian, 135
Roberts, Amy, 219
Roberts, Arthur, 177
Roberts, Bruce, 181
Roberts, Diana, 29
Roberts, Eric, 118, 290
Roberts, Evan, 30
Roberts, Ian, 154
Roberts, Jeremy, 178
Roberts, Jordan, 169
Roberts, Julia, 6, 72-73, 181, 290
Roberts, Ken, 162
Roberts, Kim, 126
Roberts, Leonard, 34, 97
Roberts, Mario, 65, 84
Roberts, Michael D., 118
Roberts, Randall R., 182
Roberts, Selwyn, 125
Roberts, Steve, 157
Robertson, Alpha, 80
Robertson, Andy, 156
Robertson, George R., 180
Robertson, Jessie, 116
Robertson, Kathleen, 60
Robertson, Kimmy, 68
Robertson, Scott, 102
Robertson, Wamo Reed, 80
Robicheaux, Jay, 145
Robillard, Kim, 55
Robin, Diane, 8
Robins, Laila, 38
Robinson, Andrea C., 173
Robinson, Claudia, 177
Robinson, David, 27, 183
Robinson, Elisabeth, 183
Robinson, Elizabeth, 164
Robinson, J Peter, 203
Robinson, James G., 181
Robinson, Jane, 78, 88
Robinson, Joan, 162
Robinson, Judith, 183
Robinson, Karen, 23
Robinson, Larry, 174
Robinson, Marc, 90
Robinson, Michael, 68
Robinson, Philip David, 183
Robitaille, Lucie, 105, 153
Robles, Walt, 155
Robotham, John, 65
Rocamora, Isabel, 125
Rocca, Peter Anthony, 146
Rocha, Elisabete Cunha, 262
Rocha, Father Michael, 75
Rocha, Vera Cunha, 262
Roche, Billy, 231
Roche, Eamonn, 15
Roche, Sabastian, 112
Rochelle, Lauren, 160
Rochetin, Fanny, 250
Rochon, Lela, 172
Rock, Chris, 11, 290
Rocket Pictures, 174
Rocket, Charles, 180
Rocketman, 174

Rockett, Eliot, 170
Rocksavage, David, 137
Rockwell, Sam, 86, 158
Roddy, Andrew, 212
Rodero, José López, 213
Rodger, Struan, 222
Rodgers, Aggie Guerard, 43, 135
Rodgers, Bill, 127
Rodgers, Bob, 219
Rodgers, David, 44
Rodgers, Mic, 49
Rodman, Dennis, 44, 159
Rodman, Roberta, 176
Rodov, Florina, 178
Rodriguez, Eva, 45
Rodriguez, Evangelina, 38
Rodriguez, Freddy, 20
Rodriguez, Gary, 8
Rodriguez, Jacinto, 75
Rodriguez, Jason, 162
Rodriguez, Joe Xavier, 44
Rodriguez, Juanita, 69
Rodriguez, Paul, 260
Rodriguez, Tresha, 114
Rodriguez, Valente, 49
Roe, Channon, 121
Roe, Jack A., 69
Roebuck, Dan, 95
Roeck, Peter, 212
Roelfs, Jan, 124, 210
Roessingh, Karel, 89
Roger, Alexandre, 250
Rogers, Herb, 175
Rogers, Jean, 112
Rogers, Kivi, 51
Rogers, Mimi, 56, 290
Rogers, Reg, 62
Rogers, Rick, 49
Rogerson, Gus, 102
Roget, Vincent, 262
Rohatyn, Michael, 168
Rohner, Clayton, 8
Roisman, Harper, 14, 146
Rojas, Eduardo Lopez, 160
Rojo, Eduardo, 250
Roleder, Garry R., 151
Roles, Natalie, 225
Rolf, Tom, 35
Rolle, Esther, 179, 290
Rollins, Henry, 21
Rollins, Howard, 158
Rollins, Jack, 142
Rom, Adam, 166
Roma, Niki, 102
Roman, Frank, 44
Romano, Andy, 260
Romano, Larry, 27
Romero, Irene, 155
Romig, Emily-Jane, 262
Romney, Clive, 175
Romvary, Jozsef, 266
Romy And Michele's High School Reunion, 51
Rona, Andrew, 99, 144
Ronan, Paul, 35, 256
Ronan, Paul, 35, 256
Ronson, Rena, 38
Roodt, Darrell James, 155
Rooker, Michael, 15, 160, 179, 290
Rooker, Tom, 22, 183
Rooney, Jonah, 33, 184
Roos, Camilla Overbye, 186
Rosa, Gilberto Santa, 264
Rosales, Gilbert, 65
Rosales, Thomsa, 61
Rosales, Tommy, 65
Rosario, Bert, 78
Rosario, Jose Ramon, 181
Roscher, Gudrun, 241
Rose, Adam, 142
Rose, Alison, 148
Rose, Andrew, 173
Rose, Andy, 160
Rose, Bernard, 180
Rose, Bonnie, 53
Rose, Christie, 164
Rose, Gabrielle, 249
Rose, Jasmine, 180
Rose, Rochelle, 186-187
Rose, Sheree, 132
Rose, Vanya, 153
Roseanna's Grave, 224
Roseanne, 15, 290
Roseen, Irene, 182
Rosefunk Pictures Ltd. production, 50
Roselius, John, 21, 65, 122
Rosemore, Terrence, 145

Rosen, Arthur, 169
Rosen, Charles, 30
Rosen, Edward J., 182
Rosen, Marty, 84
Rosen, Robert L., 144
Rosen, Steve, 167
Rosenbaum, Michael, 183
Rosenberg, Brett, 259
Rosenberg, Craig, 259
Rosenberg, Ilan, 158
Rosenberg, Philip, 53, 126
Rosenberg, Scott, 65
Rosenberg, Tom, 62, 86, 104
Rosenblatt, Bart, 50
Rosenblatt, Elliot, 15, 160
Rosenblatt, Jana, 171
Rosenblatt, Marcell, 110
Rosenbloom, Cantor Aviva, 20
Rosenbloom, Dale, 50
Rosenbloom, David, 112
Rosenfeld, Seth Zvi, 50
Rosengren, Clive, 43
Rosenstein, Edward, 258
Rosenstein, Howard, 179
Rosenstock, Harvey, 114, 136
Rosenthal, Jane, 151
Rosewood, 179
Roshovich, Gordana, 157
Rosier, Bill, 122
Rosner, Louise, 164
Rosow, Gene, 11
Ross, Caroline, 68, 128
Ross, Gary, 63
Ross, Gene, 21
Ross, Justin, 173, 290
Ross, Kenneth, 131
Ross, Liza, 253
Ross, Marcia, 51, 144
Ross, Mark, 171
Ross, Matt, 75, 157
Ross, Michael, 146
Ross, Ricco, 12, 172
Ross, Toni, 171
Ross, Tracey, 175
Ross, William, 168
Ross, Willie, 125
Ross-Norris, Vicki, 154
Rossal, Kerry, 100
Rossberg, Susana, 207
Rossetter, Kathryn, 68
Rossi, Claudia, 177
Rossi, George, 224
Rossi, Leo, 68
Rossi, Tony Ray, 27, 166
Rossovich, Rick, 162, 290
Rossow, Jim, 167
Roswell, Maggie, 127
Rotenberg, Michael, 11
Roth, Ann, 102
Roth, Donna Arkoff, 45
Roth, Eric, 184
Roth, Shira, 50
Roth, Tim, 13, 97, 290
Rothberg, Jeff, 80
Rothery, Teryl, 163, 169
Rothman, John, 88, 159, 183
Rothpan, Mitchell David, 105
Rothschild, Richard Luke, 51
Rothwell, Caroline, 220
Rough Magic, 260
Roughley, Lill, 219
Roumel, Katie, 166
Round, Jason, 183
Roundtree, Richard, 81, 184, 290
Rourke, Mickey, 44, 135, 290
Rouroua, Vakhtang, 213
Rouse, Christopher, 161
Roussel, Hélène, 207
Roussel, Yann, 261
Rousselot, Renee, 29, 145
Rowan, Barbara, 47
Rowan, Kelly, 184
Rowat, Bill, 153
Rowat, William, 179
Rowe, David, 133
Rowe, Hansford, 17
Rowe, Jill, 31
Rowe, Michael J., 28
Rowe, Tonia, 13
Rowell, Victoria, 129
Rowland, Bruce, 11
Rowlands, Gena, 96, 290
Roxburgh, Richard, 214, 257
Roy, Rita, 205
Royer, Luckie, 218
Rozenbaum, Marek, 258
Rozycki, Christopher, 42
RTBF, 215, 255

RTBF-Television Belge, 265
Ruark, Ann, 33
Rubacky, Louise, 122
Ruben, Patricia, 163
Rubeo, Bruno, 182
Rubin, David, 9, 72, 77, 126
Rubin, Jackie, 45
Rubin, Joel, 258
Rubin, Joshua, 62
Rubinstein, Richard P., 173
Ruby, Cliff, 180
Rucker, Bo, 175, 183, 290
Rudavsky, Oren, 165
Rudd, Paul, 116, 290
Rudd, Phil, 30
Rudin, Lou, 183
Rudin, Scott, 102
Rudin, Stuart, 30
Rudkin, Holly, 137
Rudnick, Paul, 102
Rudolf, Gene, 160
Rudolph, Alan, 153
Rudolph, Maya, 124, 148
Rudyard Kipling's The Second
    Jungle Book: Mowgli & Baloo,
    162
Ruehl, Mercedes, 224, 290
Rufli, Peter, 35
Ruge, George Marshall, 124
Ruginis, Vyto, 106, 182
Rugolo, Pete, 79
Ruivivar, Anthony, 128
Ruiz, Anna, 261
Ruiz, Eli, 32
Ruiz, Mike, 171
Rumph, Ashley, 37
Rundell, Steve, 251
Runnette, Sean, 93
Rupert, Michael, 105, 291
Ruscart, Marc, 213
Ruscio, Michael, 47
Ruscoe, Alan, 216
Rush, Deborah, 102
Rush, Geoffrey, 214, 257, 291
Rushton, Darrell Scott, 156
Rushton, Kevin, 138
Ruskin, Judy L., 37
Ruskin, Susan, 46
Rusli, Fay, 159
Russell, Andrew, 259
Russell, Anne, 102
Russell, Carlton Lee, 56
Russell, Chad, 183
Russell, Clive, 205, 257
Russell, Grant, 44
Russell, Kimberly, 101
Russell, Kurt, 54-55, 291
Russell, Robin, 162, 169
Russell, Shirley, 125
Russell, Theresa, 210, 291
Russi, Celeste, 18
Russian State Film Commission,
    202
Russo, James, 26-27, 184, 290-291
Russo, Kathleen, 157
Russo, Rene, 66
Russof, Ted, 44
Rusu, Monique, 144
Ruth, Glenn, 86
Ruth, Patrick, 69
Rutherford, Christopher, 160
Rutkowski, Eddie, 175
Rutowski, Richard, 113, 175
Rutter, Kate, 232
Ruzicka, Sara, 115
Ryack, Rita, 151, 180
Ryan, Dick, 176
Ryan, Ellery, 204, 260
Ryan, Ger, 220
Ryan, Jennifer, 175
Ryan, Jim, 88
Ryan, Joy Ann, 101
Ryan, Lata, 45
Ryan, Leroy, 209
Ryan, Marisa, 174, 177
Ryan, Mitchell, 35, 37, 45
Ryan, Paul, 45, 86, 137
Ryan, Roz, 71
Ryan, Terry, 211, 214
Ryan, Thomas, 8
Ryan, Ursula, 175
Ryder, Winona, 133, 291
Rymer, Michael, 204
Rysher Entertainment, 8, 11, 28, 30,
    42, 114, 158, 260
Rza, The, 157

Saachiko, 11
Saal, Philippe, 215
Saarbrücken, 264
Sabag, Uri, 258
Sabatino, Joe, 181
Sabbatini, Enrico, 117
Sabella, Ernie, 102, 146
Sabo, Timothy E., 169
Sabourin, Marcel, 241
Sachdev, Achla, 207
Sachs, Ira, 168
Sachs, Robin, 61
Sachs, Sharon, 178
Sackheim, Ken J., 105
Sackman, Jeff, 264
Sacks, Howard, 245
Sacrey, Rachel Layne, 115
Sadler, Laura, 238
Sadler, Sonya, 238
Sadler, William, 174
Sadness Of Sex, The, 260
Sadovnikov, Father Vadim, 180
Sadoyan, Isabelle, 207
Safavi, Julian, 156
Safir, Shari-Lyn, 171
Safire, Beverly, 172
Safran, Peter, 174
Sagal, McNally, 63
Sagalevitch, Dr. Anatoly M., 186
Sagan, Carl, 181
Saget, Bob, 15
Sagoes, Ken, 179
Sagona, Katie, 27
Saharov, Barry, 258
Sahay, Vic, 138
Sahraoui, Youcef, 261
Saiet, Eric, 184
Saifei, He, 222
Saito, James, 178, 183
Sajnani, Arjun, 207
Sakai, Richard, 148
Sakelaris, Anastasia Nicole, 56
Sakharov, Alik, 59
Saklofsky, Danielle, 38, 98
Saks, Gene, 142
Salas, Andre, 171
Salas, Fabian, 250
Salas, Iris Prado, 171
Salata, Greg, 35
Salazar, Rita, 62
Saldaña, Salvador, 21
Salek, Pavel, 175
Salem, Peter, 225
Sales, Robin, 229, 234
Saliba, Troy, 130
Salijevic, Berina, 248
Salimbeni, Michele, 266
Salinas, Juanita, 176
Salinger, Emmanuel, 263
Salkey, Jason, 125, 216
Salles, Walter, 264
Sallows, Ken, 209
Salmon, Colin, 253
Salmond, Jodi, 174
Salt-N-Pepa, 156
Salter, Jim, 214
Saltouros, Jim, 97
Saltzman, Mark, 265
Salut Cousin!, 259
Salvail, Eve, 216
Salvin, Pedro, 23, 39
Salzman, David, 184
Samaan, Gerard, 264
Sampedro, Frank "Poncho", 173
Samples, Brandon, 168
Samples, Carol, 168
Samples, Craig, 168
Samples, Ellen, 168
Samples, Jennifer, 168
Samples, Karen, 168
Samples, Katie, 168
Samples, Keith, 8, 28, 30, 127, 168
Samples, Kent, 168
Samples, Sheridan, 168
Sampson, Caleb, 116
Sampson, Donre, 162
Sams, Jeffrey D., 108-109

Samsa Film, 215
Samson, Cedric Gradus, 32
Samten, Lobsang, 152
Samuel Goldwyn Company, 265
Samuels, Jeremiah, 34
Samuels, Ken, 44
Samuelson, Jerome, 170
Sanchez, Adrian, 171
Sanchez, Alfred Brel, 230
Sanchez, Joanna, 181, 184
Sanchez, Mario Ernesto, 25
Sanchez, Marisol Padilla, 100, 182
Sanchez, Monique, 169
Sánchez-Gijón, Aitana, 263
Sanchini, Rae, 186
Sandberg, Francine, 221
Sandeen, Darrell, 182
Sandell, William, 84
Sanderford, Austin, 128
Sanders, Elizabeth, 181
Sanders, Jay O., 114, 137, 291
Sanders, Jeff, 44, 182
Sanders, L.V., 118
Sanders, Lowell, 29
Sanders, Mark, 264
Sanders, Rick, 55
Sanders, Ronald, 208
Sanders, Thomas, 180
Sandow, Nick, 132, 159
Sandrich, Cathy, 62, 81, 97, 180-
    181, 183
Sands, Julian, 132, 165, 291
Sands, Mark, 205
Sandy, J. Craig, 180
Sanford, Isabel, 60
Sanford, Kate, 122
Sanford, Sherry, 135
Sanko, Anton, 161, 174
Sanlúcar, Manolo, 213
Sanna, Jeff, 83
Santa Barbara Studios, 254
Santana, Cesar, 21
Santiago, Chad, 182
Santiago, Saundra, 176
Santiago, Socorro, 53, 183
Santiago-Hudson, Ruben, 182
Santini, Raphaelle, 255
Santo, Anton, 168
Santoni, Reni, 30
Santos, Joe, 184
Saperstein, Henry G., 144
Saperstein, Richard, 132
Sapiel, John, 141
Sarabia, Ric, 44
Saraf, Peter, 32, 67
Sarde, Alain, 218, 231, 239, 262
Sarde, Philippe, 218
Sarin, Vic, 205
Sarlatte, Bob, 136
Sarles, Matthew, 141
Sarmiento, Christian Keller, 250
Sarony, Paul, 229, 248
Sarosiak, Ronn, 208
Sarossy, Paul, 88, 249
Sarr, Ndiouga, 105
Sarvan, Haris, 248
Sasse, Heribert, 263
Sasso, William, 38
Sassoon, Elan, 167
Saucedo, Michael, 33
Saucido, Paul, 176
Saunders, David, 105, 169
Saunders, Julie, 12
Saunders, Ron, 265
Saunders, Tony, 155
Saunier, Nicole, 263
Saura, Carlos, 213
Saura, Marina, 236
Sauvageau, Jean-François, 153
Savage, John, 176, 291
Savides, Harris, 101
Savin, Eric, 221, 239
Savin, Jody, 38
Savitch, Alison, 177
Savitt, Jill, 123
Saw, Lady, 264
Sawa, Devon, 181
Sawade, Coralie, 265
Sawalha, Julia, 242
Sawi, Lansana, 141
Sawyer, David, 61
Saxon, Edward, 32, 67
Saxon, Rolf, 253
Saxton, Richard L.D., 49
Saxton, Richard, 151
Sayahi, Abbas, 223
Sayeed, Malik Hassan, 175
Sayles, John, 13

Sayour, Chris, 181
Saypol, Ben, 123
Scala, 210
Scalia, Pietro, 94, 138
Scallon, Lia, 211
Scalora, Joseph, 63
Scanlan, Carol, 256
Scantlebury, Glen, 65
Scarborough, Victoria, 210
Scarfe, Gerald, 71
Scarpa, Renato, 224
Scarry, Rick, 151
Schadt, Rachel, 101
Schaefer, Art, 95
Schaefer, Josh, 14
Schaefer, Louis, 127
Schaeffer, Eric, 164
Schaeffer, Jerry, 39
Schaffer, Lauren A., 173
Schakatt, Beth, 167
Schamus, James, 105, 110, 173,
    178
Schanley, Tom, 182
Schanz, Heidi, 114, 162
Scharf, William, 80
Schatzmann, Pierre-Alain, 263
Schaub, Mary-Cristina, 240
Schaufele, David, 177
Scheafer, Josh, 33
Scheider, Cynthia, 137
Scheider, Roy, 105, 135, 291
Scheine, Raynor, 63, 291
Schell, Maximilian, 123, 291
Schell, Ruth, 165
Schellenberg, August, 182
Schepisi, Fred, 12
Scherbina, Sergei, 180
Schiavelli, Vincent, 18, 253
Schicker, Maria, 254
Schiff, Charlie, 159
Schiff, Laura, 50
Schiff, Richard, 24, 49, 61, 260
Schiff, Robin, 51
Schiffer, Michael, 112
Schifrin, Lalo, 95
Schilling, Laurent, 239
Schilling, Vincent, 79
Schiltz, Delphine, 218
Schirg, Ralf, 170
Schizopolis, 159
Schlather, Sage, 159
Schlattman, Craig, 177
Schlesinger, John, 173
Schliessler, Tobias, 182
Schlueter, Stephen, 156
Schmeer, Karen, 116
Schmidt, Andrea, 223
Schmidt, Arthur, 181
Schmidt, Trudeliese, 262
Schmidtke, Ned, 8, 72
Schmock, Jonathan, 32
Schneid, Herve, 133, 250
Schneider, Anne, 262
Schneider, Aaron, 114, 205
Schneider, Dan, 83
Schneider, David, 42
Schneider, Jochen, 254
Schneider, Marliese, 17
Schneider, Rich, 180
Schneider, Rick, 180
Schöbel, Frank, 223
Schoemaker, Craig, 174
Schoene, Reiner, 177
Schoenke, Victoria, 163
Schofield, David, 180
Schofield, John D., 148
Scholes, Robin, 214
Schombing, Jason, 169, 264
Schoonmaker, Thelma, 152
Schorr, Daniel, 101
Schorr, Michael, 79
Schotte, Anne, 215
Schouten, Chris, 130
Schouweiler, John, 173
Schrader, Paul, 24
Schreiber, Avery, 172
Schreiber, Catherine, 49, 53
Schreiber, Ginny, 83
Schreiber, Liev, 31, 144, 291
Schreiner, Charmain, 50
Schrier, Paul, 158
Schröder, Karin, 223
Schrody, Eric, 176
Schroeder, Adam, 102
Schroeder, Rasila, 144
Schroeter, Werner, 262

Schuch, Robert, 160
Schull, Rebecca, 23
Schulman, Sarah, 158
Schulman, Tom, 44
Schultz, Jacqueline, 61
Schultz, Jay, 130
Schultz, John, 169
Schultz, Scott, 47
Schultz-Keil, Wieland, 262
Schulze, Paul, 159
Schumacher, Joel, 181
Schuster, Tom, 179
Schuurman, Betty, 196
Schwabl, Herbert, 265
Schwartz, Alan, 157
Schwartz, Cary, 157
Schwartz, Judy B., 172
Schwartz, Paul, 171
Schwartz, Scott L., 15, 182
Schwartz, Steven, 126
Schwartzman, John, 181-182
Schwarz, Bill, 164
Schwarzenegger, Arnold, 181, 291
Schweber, Emily, 123
Schwenker, Kenneth, 166
Schwieterman, Jan, 83
Schwietert, Stefan, 258
Schwimmer, Rusty, 13, 141
Schyfter, Guita, 264
Sciorra, Annabella, 93, 162, 222, 290-291
Sciutto, Nellie, 155, 173
Scoggin, Nick, 10, 168, 183
Scooper, 81
Scope, Clairmont, 184
Scorgie, Rachel, 261
Scorpio, 157
Scorsese, Martin, 152, 170, 260
Scotland, Simon, 238
Scott Free, 94
Scott, Campbell, 31, 291
Scott, Darin, 60
Scott, Deborah L., 186
Scott, Dougray, 261
Scott, Esther, 78, 184
Scott, Hunter, 101, 166
Scott, Jack William, 157
Scott, John, 132, 162
Scott, Joseph John, 132
Scott, Kathryn Leigh, 184
Scott, Keith, 81
Scott, Kimberly, 181
Scott, Ridley, 94
Scott, Ronald Joshua, 8
Scott, Tom Everett, 254
Scott, Walter, 75
Scott, Wendy, 110
Scott, William Lee, 124
Scott-Masson, William, 253
Scotta, Carole, 255
Scotti, Nick, 166
Scoy, Hillary Van, 159
Scream 2, 144
Screwed: Al Goldstein's Kingdom Of Porn, 154
Scriba, Mik, 13, 181
Scrimm, Angus, 172
Scripnik, Rusean, 203
Seagal, Steven, 182, 291
Seager, Chris, 225
Seagoat Films, 158
Seahorse Films, 157
Sealey, Mark, 66
Seamon, Ed, 33
Seamon, Edward, 183
Sears, B.J., 158
Sears, Eric, 38
Seaton, Mark, 216
Seaward, Tracy, 212
Sebastian, John, 184
Sebastian, Lobo, 161, 184
Secic, Haris, 248
Seda, Jon, 179
Sedaris, Amy, 52
Sedgwick, Kyra, 126, 290-291
Seeger, Mindy, 180
Seezer, Maurice, 256
Segal, Susan, 183
Seganti, Paolo, 182
Segedin, Richard, 176
Seguin, François, 59, 153
Sehring, Jonathan, 157
Seidman, Bob, 165
Seifert, Heath, 83
Seifert, Pastor D., 183
Seiler, Sonny, 183
Seitz, John, 25, 53, 94
Seitzman, Michael, 155

Sekhon, Sanjot Kaur, 209
Seldahl, Viveka, 259
Selden, Eli, 129
Seldes, Marian, 178
Selena, 179-180
Self Made Hero, A, 236
Sellar, Joanne, 121
Selleck, Tom, 102-103, 291
Seller, The , 133
Sellers, Dylan, 78
Sellers, Latrice, 168
Sellers, Lynda Marie, 168
Selway, Mary, 125
Selzer, Tony, 83
Semel, Stephen, 184
Semenov, Ed, 112
Semler, Dean, 63
Senator Films, 210
Sender, Julie Bergman, 63, 94, 115
Senger, Frank, 169
Senia, Jean-Marie, 215
Seowoo Film Col. Ltd., 243
Sequeira, Vasco, 262
Serafini, Georgio, 247
Serano, Greg, 184
Serbedzija, Lucija, 42
Serbedzija, Rade, 42, 214
Serefin, Bruce, 69
Serkis, Andy, 234
Sermon, Erick, 157
Serpico, Terry, 27, 93, 112
Serra, Eduardo, 247, 258
Serra, Eric, 216
Serrault, Michel, 265, 291
Serre, Leopoldine, 218
Serreau, Karen Muller, 255
Server, Josh, 83
Seth, Aradhana, 235
Setrakian, Mark, 77
Seus, Doug, 107
Seven Years In Tibet, 117
Seventh Art, 104, 259
Sevi, Mark, 161
Sevigny, Chloe, 174
Sewell, Jacob, 174
Sewell, Jan, 242
Sexton, Will, 67
Seymour, Carolyn, 177
Seymour, Jeff, 68
Seymour, Patrick, 165
Seymour, Ralph, 8
Sfat, Dina, 258
Shaalan, Hashem, 94
Shabtai, Sabi H., 105
Shack, Andrew, 156
Shackelford, David, 18, 83
Shadow Conspiracy, 154
Shadow Distribution, 260
Shadyac, Tom, 37
Shaff, Edmund L., 15
Shaffer, Paul, 71
Shahbazian, Ara, 155
Shai, Patrick, 154
Shaiman, Marc, 81, 102
Shakey Pictures, 173
Shakey, Bernard, 173
Shaklin, Aleks, 84
Shakur, Tupac, 13, 157, 172
Shale, Kerry, 12, 248
Shalhoub, Tony, 76-77, 124, 240, 292
Shall We Dance?, 226
Shamas, Roger, 183
Shamberg, Michael, 12, 124
Shanahan, Niall, 256
Shand, Jan, 251
Shaner, Michael, 47
Shankman, Adam, 144, 240
Shanks, Don, 162
Shanks, Priscilla, 244
Shannon, Polly, 165
Shannon-Smith, Jane, 91, 114
Shanta, James, 13
Shapiro, Eden J., 83
Shapiro, Esther, 83
Shapiro, Mel, 172
Sharian, John, 216
Sharma, Barbara, 65
Sharp, Colleen, 59
Sharp, Duane, 169
Sharp, Eric, 37
Sharp, Howard, 171
Sharp, Lesley, 232
Sharpe, Beverly, 182
Sharpe, James, 176
Sharrar, Jack, 168
Sharry, Isaac, 259
Shatner, Marcy Lafferty, 68

Shattuck, Kim, 180
Shaun, Dominic, 253
Shaver, Billy Joe, 145
Shaw, Bernard, 61, 181, 214
Shaw, Bob, 71
Shaw, Denise, 170
Shaw, Fiona, 180
Shaw, Joe, 169
Shaw, Jonathan, 66
Shaw, Michael, 135, 158
Shaw, Zanne, 141
Shawhan, April, 172
Shawn, Wallace, 126, 179, 215, 292
Shawzin, Gregg, 75
Shay, Peggy, 35
She's So Lovely, 96
Sheaks, Christine, 28, 38, 105, 121
Shearer, Jack, 151
Shearer, Johnetta, 155
Shearer, Licia, 168
Shearer, Paul, 183
Shearmur, Ed, 247
Shebby, Brianna, 146
Shebby, Danielle, 146
Sheehan, Gladys, 231
Sheehan, Julia, 116
Sheehan, Kathi, 184
Sheehan, Mike, 53
Sheehy, Joan, 256
Sheen, Charlie, 95, 154, 291-292
Sheen, Martin, 90, 162, 292
Sheen, Ruth, 237
Sheffer, Craig, 164-165, 291-292
Sheffield, Jeremy, 180
Sheffield, Peggy, 179
Sheinberg, Bill, 20, 80, 160
Sheinberg, Jon, 20, 80, 137, 160
Sheinberg, Sid, 20, 80, 160
Shelley, Adrienne, 159
Shelley, Carole, 29, 71
Shelly, Adrienne, 157
Shelton, Don, 180
Shelton, Marc P., 8
Shelton, Marley, 163
Shelton, Thomas, 154
Shen, Brian, 32
Shend, 237
Shepard, Maxine, 109
Shepard, Robert, 159
Shepherd, Elizabeth, 165
Shepherd, Peter, 162
Shepherd, Suzanne, 172
Sheppard, Anna, 115
Sheppard, Christopher, 250
Sheppard, Richard Borg, 180
Sher, Antony, 225, 229, 242, 292
Sher, Stacey, 124
Sher, Travis, 33
Sheridan, Jamey, 110-111, 292
Sheridan, Jamie, 161
Sheridan, Jim, 256
Sheridan, John, 256
Sheridan, Kirsten, 256
Sheridan, Liz, 68
Sheridan, Nicollette, 11
Sheridan, Paul, 256
Sheridan, Peter, 256
Sheridan, Tess, 256
Sherman, Amanda, 43
Sherman, Arnold, 167
Sherman, Cindy, 178
Sherman, Geraldine, 245
Sherman, Martin, 225, 245
Sherman, Patrick, 118
Sherman, Steven, 86
Sherman-Godfrey, Jay, 171
Shermis, Boyd, 75
Sherohman, Tom, 144
Sherpa, Major Angphurba, 117
Sherpa, Pemba Norbu, 117
Sherwood, Brad, 23
Sherwood, Ian, 102
Shestack, Jon, 84
Shestack, Marciarose, 84
Shevloff, Michael, 169
Shevtsov, George, 235
Shi, Nansun, 44
Shi, Zhang, 222
Shieh, Wella, 203
Shield, Jim, 178
Shields, Malcolm, 237
Shiffman, Scott, 99
Shiloh, 50
Shimizu, Keenan, 27
Shimizu, Misa, 226
Shimono, Sab, 211
Shinohara, Hiroko, 243
Shipman, Claire, 181

Shipton, Susan, 249
Shire, Talia, 96, 292
Shishido, Fuminori, 261
Shivas, Mark, 215, 220
Shively, Debby, 21
Shoaf, Rory J., 13
Shoaib, Samia, 19
Shoemaker, Craig, 144, 174
Shohan, Naomi, 122
Sholohov, Peter, 180
Shonka, J. Scott, 61, 84
Shooting Gallery, 158
Shooting Porn, 166
Shopmaker, Susan, 171
Shor, Dan, 84
Shore, Howard, 93, 101, 208
Short, Chris, 182
Short, Martin, 29, 80, 292
Short, Sylvia, 183
Shou, Robin, 11, 177
Showtime Cable Network, 173
Showtime, 154, 158, 165, 173
Shragge, Lawrence, 238
Shriver, Tim, 141
Shropshire, Terilyn A., 129
Shroyer, Sonny, 135, 181
Shteinman, Jonathan, 204
Shue, Andrew, 135
Shue, Elisabeth, 42, 142-143, 292
Shuger, Dale, 38
Shull, Jennifer, 168
Shull, Richard B., 30, 167, 292
Shulman, Marcia, 86, 100
Shusett, Ronald, 133
Shute, Mike, 180
Shuttlesworth, Reverend Fred, 80
Siatidis, Georges, 236
Sible, Todd, 49
Sibley, Sherry, 162
Sichel, Alex, 52
Sichel, Sylvia, 52
Sick: The Life & Death Of Bob Flanagan, Supermasochist, 132
Sideropoulos, John, 69
Sidique, Abu, 141
Sidney, Deana, 96
Siebert, Steven, 13
Siegel, David, 115
Siegfried and Roy, 179
Siegler, Ben, 68
Siegler, Marc, 101
Siemaszko, Casey, 165, 265, 292
Siemaszko, Nina, 14, 104
Siff, Greg, 102
Sifuentes, Everett, 180
Sifuentes, Kevin, 184
Sigall, Eve, 83
Sigel, Newton Thomas, 25
Sighvatsson, Sigurjon, 62, 86, 104, 106
Sigloch, Matt, 21
Siguenza, Herbert, 83
Sikharulidze, Djemal, 202
Silberg, Tusse, 42
Silijee, Susan, 156
Silijee, Nicolas, 156
Silk, Greg, 102
Sillas, Karen, 38
Silliman, Maureen, 159
Sills, Douglas, 166
Silva, Geno, 61, 141
Silva, Leslie, 21
Silvas, Daniel Rey, 122
Silver Pictures, 180-181, 183
Silver, Amanda, 8
Silver, Amy Beth, 14, 52
Silver, Harvey, 184
Silver, Jeffrey, 168, 184
Silver, Joel, 180-181
Silver, Ruth, 14
Silver, Scott, 14, 118
Silver, Seth, 30
Silver-Smith, Donia, 161
Silverleaf, Peter, 12
Silverman, Cara, 24
Silverman, David Michael, 10
Silverstein, James, 33
Silverstone, Alicia, 98, 181
Silvestri, Alan, 21, 49, 146, 181
Simanton, Jon, 158
Simard, Jenifer Lee, 171
Simchowitz, Stefan, 14, 118
Simkin, Margery, 102
Simmonds, William C., 156
Simmons, Bobby, 170
Simmons, Derrick, 23
Simmons, J.K., 131
Simmons, Jim, 163
Simmons, Jon, 66, 181

Simmons, Matty, 179
Simmons, Russell, 13, 168
Simms, Michael David, 162, 169
Simms, Tasha, 182
Simon Wiesenthal Center, 104
Simon, Charles, 183
Simon, Joel, 184
Simon, Len, 130
Simonds, David Hamilton, 112, 182
Simonds, David, 157
Simonds, Lincoln, 182
Simonds, Robert, 23, 98
Simonson, Louise, 184
Simpkins, Kelli, 41
Simple Wish, A, 80
Simpson, Charlene, 173
Simpson, Geoffrey, 257
Sims, Annabel, 265
Sin, Ammie, 23
Sinbad, 83, 292, 300
Sinclair, Caroline, 175
Sinclair, Lauren, 75
Sincoff, Paul Allan, 79
Sine, Jeff, 157
Siner, Guy, 21, 122
Singer, Garrison, 90
Singer, Isaac Bashevis, 263
Singer, Joseph M., 17
Singer, Kelly, 35
Singer, Leon, 78, 141, 180
Singer, Stephen, 52
Singh, Prabeen, 207
Singh, Roy Garcia, 216
Singleton, John, 179
Singleton, Ralph S., 180
Sinise, Gary, 9, 292
Sinkovics, Geza, 132
Sinnar, Don, 181
Sinor, Paul, 161
Sirico, Tony, 93, 142, 175
Sirola, Joe, 96
Siskin, Alex, 169
Sisti, Michelan, 66
Sisto, Meadow, 164
Sisto, Rocco, 27
Sit, Ailen, 203
Sivak, Drazen, 248
Sivan, Divan, 258
Sivan, Ori, 258
Six, Eva Gayle, 184
Sixth Man, The , 38
Sizemore, Tom, 8
Sjödin, Jan, 259
Sjöholm, Torsten, 259
Skaggs, Jimmie F., 162, 173
Skalski, Mary Jane, 105
Skarsgård, Stellan, 138-139,141, 292
Skee, Mickey, 166
Skelley, Jack, 123
Skelton, Jerry H., 145
Skerritt, Tom, 181, 292
Skies, Roni, 163
Skinner, Carole, 265
Skinner, Claire, 206
Skipper, Pat, 20
Sklar, Kate C., 98
Sklar, Paul, 84, 181
Sklaroff, Jon, 157
Skloff, Michael, 174
Skorstad, Ben, 61
Skye, 121
Skye, Ione, 132, 292
Skyler, Robb, 51
Skyline Entertainment, 167
Skyvision Partners, 260
Slade, John, 182
Slam Pictures, 52
Slan, Jon, 238
Slanger, Alexander D., 121
Slansky, Paul, 88
Slater, Christian, 170, 292
Slater, Helen, 104, 292
Slaughter, Ginger, 182
Slaughter, Richard, 162
Slaves To The Underground, 177
Slaza, Carrie, 241
Sleepy Heads, 172
Slevin, Kenneth Valentine, 130
Slezak, Victor, 35
Slifkin, Michael, 174
Sloan, Carolyn, 265
Sloan, Jerry, 122
Sloss, John, 19, 67
Slotnick, Sara Jane, 14, 60, 175
Smallwood, Tucker, 118, 181
Smart, Amy, 128, 164
Smerczac, Ron, 155

Smiar, Brian, 141
Smile Like Yours A, 168
Smiley, Jane, 106
Smiley, Tava, 132
Smiljanic, Bozidar, 112, 230
Smilla's Sense Of Snow, 206
Smith, Aaron, 60
Smith, Adam, 42
Smith, Afton, 81
Smith, Alexander, 9
Smith, Allison, 127
Smith, Amber, 30, 168, 182
Smith, Amelinda, 51
Smith, Arturo, 60, 266
Smith, Britta, 231, 256
Smith, Charles Martin, 68, 87, 292
Smith, Charlie, 175
Smith, Clive, 262
Smith, Dana, 75
Smith, Danny, 181
Smith, Darryl, 98
Smith, Derek, 29
Smith, Douglas Hans, 136
Smith, Ebbe Roe, 183
Smith, Ed "Booger", 167
Smith, Eddie "Bo", Jr., 97, 131
Smith, Frank, 23
Smith, Horace E., 86
Smith, Howard, 17
Smith, Iain, 117, 216
Smith, Irby, 13, 181
Smith, Ivan, 153
Smith, J., 186
Smith, Jamie Renée, 17
Smith, Jerry, 260
Smith, John, 132, 177
Smith, Kevin, 40-41, 138, 292
Smith, Kieran, 222
Smith, Kurtwood, 13, 292
Smith, Maggie, 115, 292
Smith, Mark Haskell, 122
Smith, Max, 219
Smith, Mel, 244
Smith, Michael Raye, 121
Smith, Mike, 121, 183
Smith, Morgan Méchelle, 108-109
Smith, Nicholas Crawford, 209
Smith, Parrish, 157
Smith, Patricia, 183
Smith, Peter, 170
Smith, Rita, 98
Smith, Robin, 155
Smith, Roger Guenveur, 129
Smith, Ronald G., 182
Smith, Roy Forge, 174
Smith, Rusty, 18
Smith, Sara, 56
Smith, Sarah Christine, 144
Smith, Scott, 41, 138, 146
Smith, Seth, 178
Smith, Shawnee, 38, 161
Smith, Shepard, 49
Smith, Silan, 127
Smith, Sly, 179
Smith, Suzanne, 53, 99, 138, 178
Smith, Symba, 182
Smith, Tammy L., 17
Smith, Verdell, 176
Smith, Virgil, 100
Smith, Virginia, 41
Smith, Will, 6, 76-77, 292
Smith, Yeardley, 148-149
Smith-Cameron, J., 102
Smitherman Esq, Carole C. 80
Smitrovich, Bill, 84
Smock, Ashley, 65
Smolanoff, Bruce, 166
Smollett, Jake, 129
Smollett, Jurnee, 129
Smrz, Brian, 75
Smyj, Brian, 154
Snaider, Meredith, 175
Snape, William, 232-233
Snee, Richard, 175
Sneed, Chonique, 83
Snider, Dee, 30
Snik, Jeannette, 196
Snipes, Wesley, 132, 180, 292
Snooks, Susie, 262
Snyder, David L., 179
Snyder, Suzanne, 21
Sobchak, Victor, 131
Sobiesky, LeeLee, 29
Sobol, Ken, 262
Soderbergh, Steven, 31, 157, 159
Söderling, Asa, 235
Soeberg, Camilla, 146
Soeterboek, Corrie, 243

Softley, Iain, 247
Sogetel, 263
Sogne, Herve, 254
Soham, Bodi, 86
Soisson, Joel, 177
Sokoloski, Magdalena, 249
Sokolow, Alec, 95
Solan, Sean, 169
Solann, Evelyn, 110
Solari, John, 21
Solarz, Ken, 32
Solberg, Shayn, 87
Soles, Linden, 181
Solinger, Michael, 245
Sollberg, David, 172
Sollinger, Daniel, 156
Solofilm, 264
Solokow, Peter, 258
Solomon, Charles, 159
Solomon, Ebony Monique, 184
Solomon, Ed, 77
Solomon, Oliver, 93
Solomon, Rick, 181
Solondz, Todd, 148
Soltani, Bahman, 96
Solum, Mark, 161
Somers, Robert L., 127
Somerville, Frank, 10
Somford Entertainment, 165
Sommers, Michael Rae, 146
Sommerville, Trish, 101
Son, Joe, 56
Song, Brenda, 98
Sonnenfeld, Barry, 77
Sontheim, Claudia, 263
Sony Pictures Classics, 16, 19, 69,
    89, 105, 116, 152-153, 213,
    250, 255
Sony Pictures Imageworks Inc., 128
Sooster, Evert, 112
Soravilla, James, 96
Sorbo, Kevin, 169
Sorel, Edmond, 156
Soren, Tabitha, 181
Sorensen, Kristian, 84
Sorkin, Arleen, 88
Sorlet, Gregoire, 263
Sorrento, Lamar, 168
Sortino, Sal, 21
Sorvino, Mira, 51, 99, 292
Sorvino, Paul, 95, 118, 292
Sostillio, Troy, 156
Soto, Talisa, 177, 292
Soualem, Zinedine, 221
Soucy, Jin Hi, 183
Soul Food, 109,
Soul In The Hole, 167
Soule, Chris, 94
Sousa, Ana-Teresa, 264
South Side Amusement Co., 181
Southon, Mike, 87
Sova, Peter, 27
Sow, Elhadju Malik, 141
Sowers, Scott, 52, 161
Spacey, Kevin, 9, 182-183, 292
Spade, David, 44, 292
Spader, James, 126, 160, 208, 292
Spain, Douglas, 83
Spala, Miroslav, 262
Spalding, Mark, 253
Sparber, Herschel, 157
Sparks, Carrie Cain, 98, 144
Sparx, 255
Spats Films, 177
Spawn, 90
Spear, Susie, 17, 161
Spearhead, 157
Spears, Aries, 20
Speck, David, 137
Speech, 155-156
Speed 2: Cruise Control, 68
Speer, Hugo, 232-233
Spell, Melissa, 83, 121
Spelling Films, 53, 55, 102, 118,
    224
Spelling, Tori, 118, 144
Spence, Gerry, 63
Spence, Jerry, 183
Spence, Richard, 237
Spencer, Bobbi, 172
Spencer, Bradley Jordan, 13
Spencer, Chris, 38
Spencer, Danielle, 148
Spencer, James, 78
Spencer, John, 9, 93, 167, 175
Spencer, Octavia L., 38
Sperdakos, George, 180, 183
Sperling, Andrea, 60

Spero, Richard, 156
Speth, Benjamin P., 168
Spice 1, 157
Spicer, Bryan, 137, 160
Spiegel, Howard, 142
Spiegel, Karen, 22
Spielberg, Steven, 61, 77, 141
Spier, Carol, 99, 208
Spiers, Bob, 23
Spiller, Michael, 118
Spinder, Christopher, 49
Spinella, Stephen, 58-59, 131
Spiner, Brent, 78
Spinola, Michael, 166
Spinotti, Dante, 182
Spinuzza, Doug, 9
Spirer, Peter, 156
Spirggs, Elizabeth, 211
Spisak, Neil, 75
Spivey, Anastasia, 181
Spivey, Carlos, 141
Spohnholtz, Drenda, 137
Spore, Richard, 88
Sposit, Laurie, 144
Spottiswoode, Roger, 253
Spread The Word: The Persuasions,
    154
Spriggs, Sondra, 8
Springer, Jerry, 15
Springer, Trishia, 127
Spruill, James, 69
Sprung, 60
Spybey, Dina, 19, 170
Squeeze, 69
Squibb, June, 102
Squyres, Tim, 110
Stabile, Salvatore, 171
Stabler, Alexandra, 11
Stabler, Nicolas, 11
Stabler, Steve, 9, 11, 44, 116, 172
Stacey, Eddie, 177
Stackelberg, Catharina, 262
Stadlen, Lewis J., 102, 263, 293
Stadvec, Michael, 15
Stag, 264
Stagg, Bima, 154
Stahl, Andy, 182
Stahl, Nick, 122, 293
Stahlbrand, Sandi, 180
Stallone, Sylvester, 92-93, 293
Stamatelatos, Miranda, 83
Stamos, John, 30
Stamp, Terence, 165, 293
Standefer, Robin, 52, 181
Stander, Ron "The Butcher" 176
Standing, John, 183
Stanley, Don, 182
Stanley, Larue, 23
Stanley, Margo, 234
Stanley, Mike, 86
Stansfield, Claire, 184
Stanton, Harry Dean, 96, 182, 293
Stanton, Robert, 115, 126
Stanwyck, Barbara, 187
Stanzler, Wendey, 176
Staples, Pops, 151
Stapleton, Maureen, 181, 293
Stapleton, Oliver, 215, 220
Star Line Productions, 263
Star Maps, 83
Stark, David, 245
Stark, Jonathan, 179
Starke, John H., 53
Starkey, Steve, 61
Starks, Joyce Jolivet, 145
Starr, Beau, 97
Starr, Mike, 25, 97, 155, 175
Starrs, Adrienne, 175
Starship Troopers, 128
Starski, Allan, 115
Staub, Tom, 159
Stavrou, Sarah, 122
Steadman, Lynda, 234
Stearns, Craig, 62
Stebner, Greg, 35
Steckelberg, Mandy, 30
Stedelin, Claudia, 127, 181
Steeg, Ted, 104
Steel, 184,
Steele, Brian, 8
Steele, Danny, 144
Steele, Jim, 167
Steele, Philmore, 155
Steele, Theo, 229
Steen, Alisa, 83
Steen, Amanda, 259
Steen, Ira, 155
Steen, Jessica, 63

Stefanek, Sophia, 69
Stefano, Kathleen, 156
Stefanson, Leslie, 136, 148
Steggert, Bobby, 137
Stegman, Richard, 163
Steiger, Rod, 50, 162, 293
Stein, Ben, 168
Stein, Jacob, 37
Stein, Mike, 121
Stein, Mitchell, 69
Stein, Saul, 159
Steinberg, David, 180
Steinberg, Rachel, 101
Steinberg, Robert, 174
Steiner, Riley, 71
Steinkamp, William, 114
Stella, Stefani, 221
Stellby, Eva, 259
Stencil, Michael Scott, 121
Stepanov, Yuri, 131
Stepashkin, Vadim, 42
Stephan, Rafi, 33
Stephanopoulos, George, 166
Stephen O'Rourke, 211
Stephen-Daly, Christine, 209
Stephens, Betty Wills, 86
Stephens, Duane, 240
Stephens, Heather, 17, 21
Stephens, Perry, 174
Stephenson, Robert J., 101
Stephenson, Robert, 65
Stepp, Laura, 90
Sterki, Fritz, 265
Sterling, Jim, 181
Sterling, Mindy, 56
Stern, Alison, 30
Stern, Donna, 50
Stern, Howard, 30
Stern, Jay, 34, 95, 158
Stern, Jenna, 88
Stern, Merrill, 178
Stern, Selma, 82
Stern, Tom, 254
Stetson, Mark, 216
Steve Stabler, 9, 44, 116, 172
Steve Tisch Company, 181
Stevens, Joe, 159, 180
Stevens, Maggie, 230
Stevens, Nigel, 47
Stevens, Robert, 183
Stevens, Ronnie, 219
Stevenson, J.P., 60
Stevenson, Charles C., Jr., 77
Stevenson, Michael A., 29, 136
Stewart Pictures, 165
Stewart, Aaron, 69
Stewart, Alana, 15
Stewart, Allyn, 165
Stewart, Annie, 132
Stewart, Barbara, 80
Stewart, Bill, 125
Stewart, Clayon, 256
Stewart, Eve, 234
Stewart, Ewan, 186
Stewart, French, 160
Stewart, Jane Ann, 156
Stewart, Jean-Pierre, 44
Stewart, Kate McGregor, 102
Stewart, Lesley, 232
Stewart, Marlene, 42
Stewart, Melissa, 138
Stewart, Missy, 38, 98
Stewart, Nils Allen, 15
Stewart, Olivia, 219
Stewart, Pamela, 170
Stewart, Patrick, 169, 181, 293
Stewart, Paul, 105, 157
Stewart, Sara, 229
Stewart, Terrance, 135
Stewart, Will Foster, 122
Stickney, Timothy, 93
Stiefel, Arnold, 183
Stiers, David Ogden, 15, 29, 293
Stifel, David, 240
Stigwood, Robert C., 137
Stikney, Timothy D., 179
Stiles, Julia, 35
Still, Mary Elizabeth, 148
Stiller, Amy, 31
Stiller, Jerry, 175, 264, 293
Stillman, R. Sparkle, 18
Stilwell, Dick, 182
Sting, 210, 293, 304
Stinton, Colin, 253
Stipe, Michael, 166
Stiti, Mosefa, 259
Stitt, Kevin, 55, 181
Stockwell, Dean, 84-85, 135, 160,

293
Stockwell, John, 264, 293
Stockwell, Tracey, 132
Stoeber, Orville, 127, 146
Stoff, Erwin, 88, 182
Stoffers, Rogier, 196
Stojanovich, Christina, 145
Stojanovich, Nicholas, 145
Stokey, Michael, 128
Stole, Mink, 21, 177
Stoltz, Eric, 46, 154, 160, 293
Stone, Ahimsa, 155
Stone, Alan, 259
Stone, Andrea, 169
Stone, Barry, 69
Stone, Danton, 160
Stone, Doug, 166
Stone, James, 11
Stone, Jessica, 110
Stone, Joshua, 172
Stone, Mandy, 245
Stone, Nancy Rae, 122, 163
Stone, Oliver, 113, 171
Stone, Randy, 33
Stone, Rip, 166
Stone, Sean, 113
Stone, William, 245
Stone-Myrie, Pauline, 264
Stoneham, John, 208
Stonehouse, Marilyn, 208
Stoneman, Rod, 231
Stopkewich, Lynne, 212
Storaro, Vittorio, 213
Storer, Stephen, 184
Storey, Gerry, 256
Storey, Howard, 38
Stormare, Peter, 61, 122
Storry, Malcolm, 183
Stott, Ken, 256
Stouffer, Mark, 181
Stovall, Joyce, 27
Stover, Garreth, 168
Stover, Hunter and Scout, 137
Stover, Susan A., 175
Strand, 33, 154, 164, 168, 171, 176,
    178-179, 236, 239
Strang, Deborah, 114
Strange, Adario, 157
Strange, Alluring, 168
Strange, Michael, 87, 162
Stratas, Fabian, 250
Strathairn, David, 182, 293
Stratton, Anna, 241
Strauss, Alexandra, 263
Strauss, Bruce "The Mouse", 176
Strauss, Guy, 176
Strauss, Jane, 157
Strauss, Johann, 235
Strauss, Peter, 160, 293
Street, Victoria, 176
Streitfeld, Susan, 38
Strick, Wesley, 42
Strickland, Amzie, 50
Stripe, 11
Stripling, Randy, 160
Stritch, Elaine, 78, 293
Strittmatter, Cyd, 61, 184
Strobele, Alexander, 112
Strober, Carol, 83, 173
Stroh, Ernst, 153
Stroller, Louis A., 82
Strom, Yale, 165
Strong, Brenda, 128
Stroud, Catherine, 160
Stroud, Don, 181, 293
Strozier, Henry, 154, 181
Strummer, Joe, 45
Struycken, Carel, 77
Stuart, Gloria, 186-187, 195
Stuart, Jason, 179
Stuart, Jeb, 187, 182
Stuart, Katie, 169
Stuart, Lexie, 127
Stuart, Marty, 182
Stuart, Mimi, 102
Stuart, Thomas, 61
Studebaker, Gay, 176
Studio Babelsberg, 213
Studio Images, 231, 236, 239
Studios Adam Et Eve, 213
Study, Lomax, 78
Stuhler, Anne, 162
Sturla, Luis, 250
Sturridge, Charles, 125
Sturridge, Matilda, 125
Sturridge, Thomas, 125
Stutes, Ronnie, 145
Styler, Trudie, 210

Suave, 157
Subkoff, Tara, 52, 148
Suburbia, 19
Sucharetza, Marla, 102, 137, 178
Suchet, David, 96
Sudzin, Jeffrey, 55
Sugland, Helen, 97
Suk-ping, William Chang, 222, 243
Sukowa, Barbara, 178
Suleiman, Elia, 261
Suleiman, Fuad, 261
Suleiman, Nazira, 261
Sullivan, Grace, 124
Sullivan, Lea, 56
Sullivan, Peter, 131
Sullivan, Sarah, 32
Sultan, Malek, 239
Sulu, Eric, 155
Sumanapala, Raja, 162
Sumatra, Aristide, 81
Sumida, Yukio, 167
Summers, Leanne, 238
Sumner, Anita, 210
Sunara, Igor, 100
Sunday Sun, 222
Sunday, 96
Sundstrom, Carl, 21, 82
Sunwood Entertainment, 167
Suo, Masayuki, 226
Suo, Yoshikazu, 226
Suozzo, Mark, 176
Suplee, Ethan, 41
Suran, Renee, 30
Suriano, Phillip, 44
Surillo, Laura Elena, 181
Surma, Ron, 37, 45
Surratt, Harold, 154, 183
Suschitzky, Peter, 208
Susi, Carol Ann, 68
Sussman, Matthew, 88, 112
Sutcliffe, Philip, 256
Sutherland, Catherine, 158
Sutherland, Donald, 13, 105, 154, 293-294
Sutherland, Kiefer, 162, 293
Suttles, M. Darnell, 49
Sutton, Carol, 129
Sutton, Michael, 43, 168
Sutton, Nick, 174
Sutton, Randy, 21
Sutton, T. Michael, 168
Sutton, Ted, 94
Suvari, Mena A., 114
Suvari, Mena, 60
Suzanne Farrell: Elusive Muse, 157
Suzman, Peter, 154
Svankmajer, Eva, 262
Svankmajer, Jan, 262
Svenson, Bo, 68, 293
Svezia, Joe, 172
Swaby, Donn, 94
Swain, Dominique, 74-75
Swain, Joanna, 232
Swan, Bob, 104
Swan Princess: Escape from Castle Mountain, The, 166
Swaney, Roxy, 179
Swanson, Arnita, 220
Swanson, Gaard, 13
Swanson, Grant, 33
Swanson, Kristy, 44
Swanson, Rochelle, 15
Swanson, Ryan Lee, 144
Swanson, Ted, 165
Swardstrom, Brian, 47, 123
Swarts, Cheryl, 208
Swartwout, Tom, 126
Swedlin, Rosalie, 126
Swee, Helen, 168
Sweeney, D.B., 90, 293
Sweeney, Julia, 15, 179
Sweeney, Mary, 21
Sweet Hereafter, The, 249
Sweetland Films, 142
Swenson, Erin, 160
Swenson, Jeep, 181
Swerdlow, Ezra, 93, 151
Swift, Francie, 164, 173
Swimar, Barry, 158
Swindall, Jerry, 123
Swinton, Tilda, 38
Switchback, 127
Sylbert, Paul, 179, 181
Sylbert, Richard, 25, 72, 126
Sylvester, Colin Bradley, 97
Sylvester, Harold, 38
Syme, Jennifer, 21
Symmonds, Bob "Guitar Whitey",

171
Syson, Lucinda, 216, 218
Szasz, Janos, 266
Szkolnic, M., 44
Szumlas, Peter, 177
T&C Film AG, 265
T, Suga, 157
Tabakin, Ralph, 151
Tabari, Ula, 261
Tabio, Juan Carlos, 224
Tabori, George, 263
Tabori, Katrina, 154
Tackett, Lonnie Duran, 182
Tadic, Ljuba, 203
Tadross, Michael, 182
Taft, Robert, 65
Tager, Aron, 180
Taglang, Tom, 177
Taglialatela, Justina, 39
Taguchi, Hiromasa, 226-227
Taguchi, Tomoroh, 261
Tahir, Faran, 88
Tai, 81
Tai, Wong Ngok, 230
Tait, Anne, 205
Takahama, Kan, 261
Takama, Kenji, 261
Takano, Mak, 181
Takenaka, Naoto, 226
Taketani, Maskai, 220
Takeuchi, Nobuo, 261
Takizawa, Ryoko, 258
Takmatsu, Shiho, 220
Taktarov, Oleg, 84
Talavera, Miriam, 264
Talbot, Billy, 173
Talidi, Said, 216
Talmadge, Victor, 101
Talvano, Robert, 138
Tamada, Paige, 183
Tamasy, Paul, 87
Tamayo, Rafael, 180
Tambellini, Flávio R., 264
Tambini, Catherine, 157
Tames, David, 175
Tamia, 68
Tamma, Nanni, 266
Tan, Philip, 32, 81
Tanaka, Eiichi, 220
Tanaka, Miho, 220
Tanaka, Tom, 181
Tanaru, I, 215
Tang, Edward, 230
Tang, Hon Ping, 216
Tang, Jacky, 265
Tango Feroz, 259
Tango Lesson, The 250
Tanguay, Bernard, 153
Tanklow, Jerry, 241
Tankson, Larry C., 109, 178
Tann, Tyrone, 128
Tannebaum, Ted, 62, 104
Tanner, Antwon, 184
Tanvir, Moneeka Misra, 207
Tapestry Films, 164
Taplin, Jonathan, 260
Taplitz, Daniel, 52
Tapping, Amanda, 23
Tar, 175
Tara, 259-260
Tarantina, Brian, 27
Tarantino, Quentin, 147, 293
Taranto, Glenn, 44
Tarbes, Jean-Jacques, 263
Tardif, Graham, 209
Tare, Nello, 173
Tarkanian, Jerry, 38
Tarlov, Mark, 183, 241
Tartaglia, Gregory, 230
Tarver, Andrew "J.R.", 179
Tasco, Maryn, 60
Tasco, Rai, 60
Tate, Jack, 163
Tate, Larenz, 34, 184, 293
Tate, Mark, 51, 125
Tatsuno, Koji, 220
Tattersall, David, 65, 242
Taub, Myer, 245
Taube, Sven-Bertil, 259
Tavera, Michael, 144, 174
Tavernier, Bertrand, 239
Tavernier, Elisabeth, 239
Tax, Yan, 207
Taxi Lisboa, 264
Taylor, Annie, 158
Taylor, Camille, 33

Taylor, Charles Gould, 156
Taylor, Colin, 257
Taylor, Cooper, 184
Taylor, Dayton, 175
Taylor, Don, 219, 293
Taylor, Duffy, 45
Taylor, Finn, 69
Taylor, Frank, 137
Taylor, Holland, 81
Taylor, Jack Stewart, 22
Taylor, Jackie, 97
Taylor, Jill, 232
Taylor, Joan, 21
Taylor, Judy, 180, 182
Taylor, Juliet, 142
Taylor, Lili, 170, 293-294
Taylor, Mark L., 15
Taylor, Nokie, 160
Taylor, Regina, 100
Taylor, Rocky, 186
Taylor, Sandra, 172, 181-182
Taylor, T.A., 164
Taylor, Tate, 51
Taylor-Vince, Pruitt, 100, 175
Taylor-Williams, Laurie, 158
Tchkhikvadze, Ramaz, 213
Teal, Danny, 10
Teang, Srey, 160
Tecosky, Eric, 156
Teddy Lane, Jr., 173
Tedeschi, Daniel, 117
Tedeschi, Tony, 121
Tedeschi, Valéria Bruni, 231
Tehranian, Yalda, 126
Teitler, Williem, 88
Tele Munchen, 203
Telek, April, 169
Téléma, 265
Telford, Todd, 209
Tellefsen, Christopher, 174
Telling Lies In America, 123
Temperilli, Tres Trash, 60
Templin, Bayard, 259
Temptress Moon, 222
Tenenbaum, Nancy, 31
Tengger, 260
Tennant, Andy, 21
Tennant, Nicholas, 257
Tenney, Anne, 266
Tenney, Jon, 21, 173
Tenuta, Judy, 169
Tenzin, Jamyang, 152
Tenzin, Tulku Jamyang Kunga, 152
Teo, 122, 128
Ter Steege, Joanna, 211
Ter Steege, Johanna, 263
Terisi, Jason, 169
Terkel, Studs, 166
Termo, Leonard, 21, 63
Terrell, Florence, 80
Terreri, Bert, 68
Terry, John, 173
Terry, Marty, 173
Terry, Ruby Francis, 145
Tertipis, Emmanuelle, 250
Teschner, Peter, 30
Testa, Joe, 97
Testaverde, Damon, 157
Tester, Hans, 132
Tethong, Gyurme, 152
Tetlow, Christopher, 219
Tetsuo II: Body Hammer, 261
Tewes, Lauren, 60, 294
Tezuka, Hideaki, 261
TF1 Films, 207, 239, 263
Thakar, Vimesh, 88
Thal, Jeffrey, 177
Thaler, Todd, 93, 170
Tharp, Kenneth, 225
That Darn Cat, 23
That Old Feeling, 39
Thatcher, Ken, II, 8
Thedford, Marcello, 49
Theirse, Darryl, 8
Theismann, Joe, 156
Theodore, Marie-Francoise, 34
Theriault, Alexandra, 62
Theron, Charlize, 63, 182, 294
Theroux, Justin, 51
Thewlis, David, 117, 294
Thiam, Lamine, 141
Thigpen, Angela, 177
Thigpen, Kevin, 50, 96, 175
This World, Then The Fireworks, 79
Thivel, Caroline, 259
Thivisol, Victoire, 261
Thomas Rosales, Jr., 182
Thomas, Alex, 159

Thomas, Betty, 30
Thomas, Bill, 181
Thomas, Bradley, 116
Thomas, Brent, 182
Thomas, Carmen, 75
Thomas, Clarence, 179
Thomas, Daniela, 264
Thomas, Dave, 262
Thomas, Dorien, 261
Thomas, Gee, 155
Thomas, Henry, 167, 294
Thomas, Isa, 163
Thomas, Jaqui, 12
Thomas, Jeremy, 25, 208
Thomas, Jess, 182
Thomas, John, 121, 170
Thomas, Jonathan Taylor, 181
Thomas, Ken, 49
Thomas, Kendal, 163
Thomas, Larry, 56
Thomas, Leonard L., 184
Thomas, Leonard, 129
Thomas, Mark, 261
Thomas, Naim, 236
Thomas, Pat, 146
Thomas, Ransford, 141
Thomas, Ray, 164, 258
Thomas, Rhonda Nunn, 80
Thomas, Robin, 83
Thomas, Robin, 123
Thomas, Scott, 231, 251, 291
Thomas, Sean Patrick, 88, 181
Thomas, Sherry Lapham, 167
Thomas, Valerie, 67
Thomas, Vaneese, 71
Thomas, Vanita, 168
Thomas, Victoria, 65, 141
Thomas, William, 261
Thomas, Wynn, 151
Thomason, Mark, 181, 184
Thomassin, Florence, 265
Thommessen, Vendela K., 181
Thomsen, Anna, 167
Thompson, Bess S., 183
Thompson, Brian, 177
Thompson, Caroline, 66
Thompson, Chris, 224
Thompson, Donald, 264
Thompson, Emma, 251, 294
Thompson, Hunter S., 166
Thompson, Ian, 256
Thompson, Jack, 98, 183, 294
Thompson, Jeffrey, 154
Thompson, Jeremy, 49
Thompson, Jim, 79
Thompson, John, 38
Thompson, Kenan, 83
Thompson, Kevin, 170, 178
Thompson, Krist, 100
Thompson, Reece P. III, 186
Thompson, Richard, 177
Thompson, Samuel, 182
Thompson, Sarah, 180
Thompson, Scott, 167
Thompson, Vernon P., 118
Thomsen, Cecilie, 253
Thomsen, Ulrich, 260
Thomson, Anna, 137, 158
Thomson, John, 183
Thomson, Mark, 84
Thomson, Sabine, 80
Thonden, Phinsto, 152
Thorin, Donald E., 82
Thorlakson, Wendy, 45
Thorley, Ken, 77, 127
Thorn, Richard, 168
Thorne, Callie, 8
Thorne, Jared, 49
Thorne, Taylor, 49
Thorne, Tracy, 132
Thorne-Smith, Courtney, 174
Thornhill, Lisa, 15
Thornton, Billy Bob, 113, 145, 166, 294
Thornton, David, 96, 178
Thorsen, Sven Ole, 169
Thorton, Fonzi, 71
Thousand Acres, A, 106
Thrane, Edith, 260
3 Arts Production, 88
3 Ring Circus Films, 69
Threshold Entertainment, 177
Thurman, Uma, 124, 181, 294-295
Thurston, Robert, 212
Tian, Xie, 222
Tibbins, Hayley, 125
Tichenor, Dylan, 121

Ticotin, Rachel, 8, 64-65, 294
Tidy, Frank, 97
Tiedt, Fred, 256
Tien, Annie Mei-Ling, 113
Tiernan, Andrew, 122
Tierney, John, 144
Tierney, Malcolm, 42
Tierney, Maura, 37
Tig Productions, 164-165, 184
Tigar, Ken, 159
Tigar, Kenneth, 106, 182
Tiger Aspect Films, 244
Tigrett, Darline, 180
Tikaram, Ramon, 207
'Til There Was You, 62
Tilden, Leif, 66, 81
Tillen, Jodie, 178
Tiller, Stephen, 42
Tillman, George, Jr., 109
Tillman, Kimberly A., 21
Tilly, Grant, 262
Tilly, Jennifer, 36-37, 294
Timbes, Graham, 145
Timeless, 174
Timer, 148
Times, Temsie, 155
Timmermann, Bonnie, 180
Timmons, James, 212
Timms, Neusa, 265
Timoney, Bill, 181
Timothy Leary's Dead, 164
Tinajero, Cynthia, 155
Tindersticks, 239
Tingey, James, 257
Tintori, John, 33
Tiny Tim, 30
Tippe, Annie Maginnis, 148
Tippet Studio, The, 128
Tippett, Phil, 128
Tirelli, Jaime, 80
Tisch, Steve, 181, 184
Tischhauser, Peter, 32
Tisdall, Richard, 205
Titanic, 186-187
Tittle, Jim, 170
Tittle, La Donna, 8
Tittot, Robert, 49
To Have (Or Not), 260
To, Chan Wai, 203
Tobias, John, 177
Tobie, Ellen, 159
Tobin, Jason J., 11
Tobolowsky, Stephen, 33, 144, 294
Todd McFarlane Entertainment, 90
Todd, Antonio, 154
Todd, Jennifer, 56
Todd, Lina, 52, 158
Todd, Norman, 177
Todd, Suzanne, 56, 94
Todd, Tony, 172
Todoroff, Tom, 8
Tohill, Mickey, 256
Toilers And The Wayfarers, The, 170
Tokui, Yu, 226-227
Tokuma, Yasuyoshi, 226, 261
Toler, Ray, 106
Toles-Bey, John, 97
Tolins, Jonathan, 173
Toll, John, 135
Tolle, Hillary, 23
Tollin, Mike, 83
Tolson, Dickon, 225
Tolstoy, Leo, 180
Tomandandy, 104, 260
Tomasello, Duchess, 11
Tomasetti, Pamela, 176
Tomé, Marina, 221
Tomei, Concetta, 78
Tomei, Marisa, 50, 248, 294
Tomita, Tamlyn, 24
Tomlinson, Ryan, 15
Tomorrow Never Dies, 253
Tompkinson, Stephen, 219
Tong, Elliot, 203
Tong, Kaity, 53
Tong, Stanley, 144, 203
Toniolo, Camilla, 86
Tonninger, Wolfgang, 117
Too-Short, 157
Tookie, 81
Toole, David, 250
Toon, John, 214
Tootoosis, Gordon, 107
Topalian, Garen, 69
Topic, Velibor, 42

Topjar, Tenzin, 152
Topping, Lesley, 163
Torchiaro, Antonio, 264
Torell, Johanna, 132
Torelli, Francesco, 266
Torin, Tony, 41
Tormey, John, 29, 52, 166
Torn, Angelica, 176
Torn, Rip, 63, 71, 76-77, 176, 294
Torn, Tony, 177
Toro, Hernan, 178
Toronjo, Paco, 213
Torrel, Johanna, 132
Torrens, Pip, 253
Torrent, Jordi, 100
Torrero, Ulysses, 50
Torres, Albert, 78
Torres, Angelina Calderon, 21
Torres, Fernanda, 264
Torres, Jose Fernandes, 183
Torres, Olivier, 213
Torres, Pep, 146
Torreton, Philippe, 239
Torry, Guy, 184
Torry, Joe, 60
Toscano, Shelly, 156
Tosin, Omo Lara, 141
Toth, Melissa, 175
Touch, 24
Touchstone, 10, 38, 51, 65, 82, 106,
   122, 128, 152
Toussaint, Allen, 129
Touza Films, 215
Towers, Constance, 8
Towers, Jim Torres, 25
Towers, Lisa, 165
Towles, Tom, 13, 155, 163
Towns, Terri, 93
Townsend, Chris, 218
Townsend, Clayton, 113
Townsend, Robert, 115, 158
Townsend, Stuart, 231
Townsend, Tammy, 20
Townshend, Marisa, 171
Towry, James B., 145
Toy, Christine, 29-30, 181
Toyokawa, Etsushi, 258
Tozawa, Junichi, 261
Trac, Michael, 32
Tracey, Ian, 182
Tractor Drivers, 223
Tracy, Christopher, 179
Trainor, Saxon, 181
Traissac, Astrid, 218
Trammell, Sam, 157, 159
Tramontane, Nick, 203
Trank, Richard, 104
Trans Atlantic Entertainment, 38
Traveller, 47
Traver, Mark, 169
Travis, Greg, 21, 128
Travis, Neil, 107
Travis, Randy, 135, 182
Travis, Stacey, 122
Travolta, John, 6, 74-75, 96, 183,
   294
Trayer, H.D., 80
Traylor, Susan, 96, 180
Trejo, Danny, 46, 64-65
Trevis, Sarah, 125
Trevor, 33
Tribe Called Quest, A, 156
Tribeca, 151
Trickompany, 262
Tricky, 216
Trigg, Derek, 222
Triggelis, Takis, 181
Trigger, Sara, 156
Trijbits, Paul, 224
Trimark Pictures, 15, 60, 86, 129,
   161-162, 207, 212
Trinkwater, Yvonne, 163
Trinley, Tenzin, 152
Trintignant, Jean-Louis, 236, 294
Trintignant, Marie, 218
Tripet, David, 172
Tripp, John, 21
Tripplehorn, Jeanne, 62, 178-179
Triptych Media, 241
TriStar, 11, 20, 27, 72, 105, 113,
   117, 128, 148, 162-163, 188-
   189
Tritt, Travis, 182
Triumph, 105, 162, 165, 236
Troell, Jan, 235
Troell, Jan, 235
Trojan Eddie, 231

Trombetta, Leo, 38, 104
Tronick, Michael, 49
Tronto, Marilise, 174
Troob, Danny, 33
Troobnick, Eugene, 142
Tropicana, Carmelita, 171
Trotinier, Glen, 29
Trott, Natalie, 132
Trotta, Ed, 37
Troub, Shaun, 78
Troublesome Creek: A Midwestern,
   154
Troyano, Ela, 171
Troyer, Verne, 77, 172
Truby, Tim, 13
Trudel, Billy, 151
True, Rachel, 60
Truitt, Mark Rafael, 186
Truman, Tim, 156, 173
Trumper, John, 205
Trunk, Peter, 49
Truong, Jean-Marc, 221
Truong, The Cuong, 265
Trustman, Kathy, 116
Trutner, Kirk, 17
Tsamardos, Noda, 262
Tsamchoe, Lhakpa, 117
Tsarong, Tenzin Thuthob, 152
Tsarong, Tsewang Jigme, 152
Tseded, 262
Tseng, Derrick, 41
Tsering, Choeden, 117
Tsering, Dorjee, 117
Tsitsopoulos, Yannis, 203
Tsondu, Lama Champa, 117
Tsui, Siuming, 163
Tsukamoto, Shinya, 261
Tsultrim, Geshe Yeshi, 117
Tsuruyama, Kinya, 220
Tsyrengarmayeva, Viktoria, 265
Tubbs, Vicky, 160
Tubert, Miriam, 236
Tucci, Christine, 30
Tucci, Stanley, 31, 142, 240, 294
Tucci, Tony, 171
Tuchman, Eric, 130
Tucker, Chris, 95, 147, 216
Tucker, Cody, 159
Tucker, Dexter, 95
Tucker, Joe, 234
Tucker, Michael, 62, 294
Tucker, Norris, 95
Tucker, Paul, 95, 125
Tudisco, Joseph, 174
Tudor-Pole, Edward, 169, 237
Tuerpé, Paul, 181
Tufano, Brian, 240
Tugend, Jennie Lew, 182
Tuiasosopo, Peter Navy, 173, 177,
   181
Tuinstra, Brad, 13
Tuke, Sioban, 230
Tukker, Martin, 220
Tukur, Ulrich, 263
Tulchin, Harris, 176
Tulliver, Barbara, 24
Tung, Barbie, 203
Tung, Bill, 203
Tunie, Tamara, 112, 129, 182
Tunney, Jim, 176
Tunney, Robin, 170
Tuohy, Liam, 186
Turbiville, Tom, 23
Turbo: A Power Rangers Movie,
   158
Turbulence, 8
Turbulence, Verna, 175
Turbulent Arts, 175, 241
Turcott, Sheldon, 180
Tureltaub, Paul, 224
Turk, Brian, 61
Turley, David, 163
Turnbull, Mark, 257
Turner Feature Animation, 180
Turner, April, 137
Turner, Chris, 87
Turner, Christopher, 38
Turner, Dennis, 90
Turner, Frank C., 87, 144
Turner, Guinevere, 41, 158, 166,
   171
Turner, Hilary Shepard, 158
Turner, Janine, 98, 294
Turner, Jimme, 160
Turner, Kathleen, 80, 294
Turner, Keena, 101
Turner, Leonard O., 173

Turner, Pilar, 157
Turner, Richard, 154
Turner, Stephanie, 259
Turning, The, 163
Turorskaya, Maya, 223
Turteltaub, Jon, 174
Turturice, Robert, 8, 181
Turturro, John, 86, 294
Turturro, Nicholas, 98, 154
Tusar, Majda, 248
Tutin, Alexander, 42
Tutin, Dorothy, 225, 294
Tuttleby, Robert, 259
Tweedley, Sean, 174
20th Century Fox, 43, 49, 68, 78,
   88, 107, 109, 130, 133, 158,
   175, 178, 186-187, 240
Twigden, Michelle, 259
Twilight Of The Golds, The, 173
Twin Town, 261
Twins Japan Inc., 258
Twisted, 178
Twohy, David, 94
Twomey, Anne, 88, 294
Tyabji, Khalik, 207
Tygner, Rob, 66
Tyler, Liv, 43, 113, 294
Tyler, Steven, 179
Tylor, Evan, 264
Tyng, Christopher, 159
Tyrell, Tyrone, 216
Tyrone, Kirstie, 38
Tyson, Cicely, 97, 294
Tyukodi, Anton, 180
Tzachor, Jonathan, 158
Tzarfati, Asher, 44
Tzudiker, Bob, 130
U Turn, 113
Ubach, Alanna, 14
Udenio, Fabiana, 56
Udoma, Charles, 141
UGC Images, 260
Ujica, Andrei, 258
Ulbrich, Brigitte, 223
Ulee's Gold, 67
Ullian, Seth, 102
Ulrich, Skeet, 9, 24, 148, 294
Ulsamer, Sibylle, 169
Ulysses' Gaze, 203
Underwood, Blair, 124, 294
Underwood, Jay, 153
Underworld, 162
*Unforgotten: Twenty-Five Years
   After Willowbrook*, 156
Unger, Deborah Kara, 101, 160,
   208
Unger, Kimberly, 169
Unger, Michael, 9
Universal, 12, 17, 37, 39, 61, 80,
   98, 131, 137, 160, 169, 254,
   256
Unlimited Effects, 230
UPA Productions of America, 144
Upson, Leslie, 146
Upstate Films, 260
Upton, Brad, 13
Urena, Julian Scott, 20
Uribe, Diana, 147
Urich, Justin, 33
Urich, Tom, 180
Urich, Vern, 186
Urioste, Frank J., 181
Urla, Joseph, 68
Urquidez, Benny, 45
Urquidi, Sergio, 49
Urquieta, Xavier, 132
Urushido, Seiji, 226
Urwin, Michael, 205
Uslan, Michael K., 181
Ustichenko, Alexander, 203
Utazawa, Toraemon, 261
Utopia Pictures, 50
Uys, Michael, 171
Uzzaman, Badi, 218
Vacation On The Black Sea, 223
Vacher, Laurent, 231
Vachon, Christine, 166, 178
Vadim, David, 84, 94
Vail, Justina, 114
Vajna, Andrew G., 154
Val, Pierre, 239
Valadié, Dominique, 231
Valdes, Chucho, 264
Valdes, David, 8
Valdes, J.R., 171
Valdez, Angel, 21
Valencia, Rita, 132
Valencia, Vance, 181

Valentin, Dave, 264
Valentino, Venessia, 147
Valentino, Venssia, 13
Valle, Jamie, 174
Van Bergen, Lewis, 8
Van Betten, Melanie, 118
van Boem, Het Paleis, 196
Van Damme, Jean-Claude, 44, 294
Van Dang, Nhan, 168
Van Den Bergen, Francois, 220
van den Dop, Tamar, 196
Vanden Ende, Walther, 207
Van Der Beek, James, 241
vander Stappen, Chris, 255
Van de Sande, Theo, 49
van Diem, Mike, 196
Van Dien, Casper, 128
Van Dormael, Jaco, 207
Van Dormael, Pierre, 207
van Dorp, Wilbert, 220
Van Gerena, Densi, 172
Van Gorkum, Harry, 181
Van Hales, Sean, 237
Van Horn, Kelly, 98
Van Huffel, Filip, 245
van Huet, Fedja, 196
van Huystee, Pieter, 266
van Iderstine, Nancy, 177
Van Lindt, Robert, 174
Van Nickerk, Louis, 154
Van Nuygen, Wayne, 177
Van Peebles, Mario, 264, 295
Van Putten, Chekesha, 56
Van Rossum, Bob, 177
Van Sant, Gus, 138
Van Schuylenburch, Ellen, 225
Van Sharner, Robin, 159
Van Slyke, Joe, 97
Van Sprang, Alan, 169
van Straalen, Dien, 220
Van Tassel, Sabrina, 132
Van Tieghem, David, 122
Van, Alex, 23
Van, The, 220
Van Voorhis, George, 176
Van Wormer, Steve, 167
Van Wyck, Jim, 181-182
Vance, Ladd, 176
Vance, Marilyn, 94
Vander, Musetta, 177
Vandestien, Michel, 236
Vann, David J., 80
Vann, Marc, 97
Vanterpool, Curtis, 101
Vardy, Adam, 156
Varelli, Alfred, 224
Varenstov, Leonty, 180
Vargas, Jacob, 51, 179
Vargas, Jorge, 98
Vargo, Mark, 8
Varma, Indira, 207
Varney, Jim, 170, 295
Vartan, Michael, 105
Vasquez, Alberto, 151
Vasquez, Ana Cristina, 260
Vass, Phaedon, 260
Vassallo, Marie Stuart, 183
Vassallo, Nicole M., 43
Vassie, Lana, 182
Vassort, Cecile, 239
Vaughan, Hannah, 183
Vaughan, James, 229
Vaughn, Alice, 148
Vaughn, Matthew, 222
Vaughn, Michael, 69
Vaughn, Vince, 61, 116, 295
Vazquez, Diego, 160
Veadov, Alex, 84, 181
Veber, Francis, 180
Vecchio, Pat, 27
Vega Film, 262
Vega, Omar, 250
Veitch, Michael, 262
Vela, Ricky, 180
Velasco, Howard, 181
Velasco, Marta, 25
Velez, Eddie, 118
Velez, Martha, 83, 184
Velez-Mitchell, Jane, 49
Venditto, Stephanie, 31
Venezia, Danny, 176
Veneziano, Sandy, 39
Vengos, Thanassis, 203
Venora, Diane, 131, 295
Ventimiglia, John, 93, 170
Ventimiglia, Milo, 33

Ventresca, Vincent, 51
Ventura, Jesse, 181
Ventura, Joe, 170
Venture, Richard, 126
Verbinski, Gore, 146
Verbois, James, 162
Vercel, Roger, 239
Verduzco, Noah, 155
Verea, John, 180
Verhoeven, Michael, 263
Verhoeven, Paul, 128
Verhoeven, Simon, 263
Verhoeven, Yves, 236
Verica, Tom, 180
Verillon, Aurelie, 218
Vernaccio, Dorian, 172
Vernieu, Mary, 14, 23-24, 79, 113,
   118-119
Vernotico, Ryan, 33
Veron, Pablo, 250
Veronika, Eva, 29
Verreaux, Ed, 181
Vertigo Productions, 221
Vesbit, Erc, 175
Veselov, Nikolai, 42
Vessey, Tricia, 114, 244
Veysset, Sandrine, 250
Viard, Karen, 215
Vicente, Al, 83
Vicente, Joana, 159
Vicino, Cyndi, 172
Vickerman, Michael, 163
Vickey, Karen, 257
Victor, Renee, 145
Vidal, Gore, 124, 154
Vidal, Lisa, 164
Videofilmes, 264
Vidler, Steven, 265
Vidovic, Petar, 8
Viederman, Laura, 131
Viegas, Mário, 258
Vieha, Mark, 151
Vieluf, Vince, 254
Vierny, Sacha, 220
Vietch, Michael, 230
View Askew, 41
Vigil, Rhiannon, 128
Vigoda, Abe, 83, 162
Vilar, Tracy, 13
Vilhelmova, Tatjana, 264
Village Roadshow Pictures, 211,
   214, 259
Village Roadshow-ASQA Film
   Partnership, 126
Villalobos, Reynaldo, 51, 123
Villamil, Mercedes, 37
Villani, Michael Louis, 49
Villani, Michael, 151
Villatuya, Marie, 10
Villemaire, James, 30
Villepique, Greg, 33
Villiers, Nick, 25
Villis, Ray, 222
Vince, Anne, 87
Vince, Barrie, 218
Vince, Robert, 87, 162
Vince, William, 87, 162
Vincent, Amy, 129
Vincent, Brian, 175
Vincent, Craig, 166
Vincent, Frank, 53, 93, 159, 175
Vincent, Helene, 255
Vincent, Joe, 10
Vincent, Lawrence, 157
Vindevogel, Thomas, 236
Vinovich, Steve, 166
Virkler, Dennis, 35, 181
Viscidi, Marcus, 86
Visiting Desire, 154
Visnjic, Goran, 112, 248
Vitale, Anthony, 166
Vitale, Mario, 118
Vitale, Ruth, 59, 224, 251
Vitale, Tony, 166
Vitarelli, Joseph, 52, 96
Vithana, Kim, 12
Vives, Camilo, 224
Vizents, Eric, 177
Vlahou, Agni, 203
Vlaskalic, Diana, 162
Voe, Sandra, 251
Voetmann, Hans Henrik, 260
Vogel, Jürgen, 206
Vogler, Rudiger, 262
Vogt, K.T., 182
Vogt, Mary E., 77
Vohra, Rahul, 207
Voight, Clint, 170

Voight, Jon, 46, 113, 118, 134-135, 179, 295
Volanaki, Dora, 203
Volcano, 49
Volga Volga, 223
Volkle, Peter, 263
Volokh, Ilia, 84, 113, 173
von Bargen, Daniel, 94, 141, 184
Von Detten, Erik, 71, 98
Von Dohlen, Lenny, 178, 295
von Flotow, Michelle, 182
von Klaussen, Ronald, 53
von Meyer, Jeffrey, 177
Von Oelffen, Petra, 96
von Sydow, Max, 235, 259, 295
von Sydow, Stina, 259
Von Watts, Hamilton, 83
Voorhies, Lark, 168
Vosloo, Arnold, 11
Voss, Philip, 225
Vrana, Vlasta, 105
Vuillermoz, Michel, 263
Vujcic, Aleksandra, 214
Waco: The Rules Of Engagement, 165
Wada, Emi, 220
Waddell, Amber and Alison, 186
Waddell, Amy Monique, 23
Waddell, Justine, 180
Waddington, Steve, 55
Wade, Alan, 170
Wade, Kay, 56
Wade, Kaye, 118
Wade, Melinda, 157
Wadkins, Rick, 184
Wadman, Glenn, 205
Wag The Dog, 151
Wagner, Christian, 75
Wagner, Dawn, 160
Wagner, Karyn, 129, 172
Wagner, Len, 180
Wagner, Micah, 166
Wagner, Natasha Gregson, 21, 295
Wagner, Richard, 235
Wagner, Robert, 56-57, 295
Wagner, Roy H., 20
Wah, Ridley Tsui Po, 177
Wahlberg, Mark, 47, 120-121
Wahrman, Hua, 126
Wahrman, Wayne, 168, 179
Wainwright, Rupert, 260
Waislitz, Alex, 259
Waislitz, Heloise, 259
Waitaire, Gnarnay Yarrahe, 266
Waite, Ric, 162
Waite, Trevor, 248
Waites, Thomas G., 118
Wakamatsu, Takeshi, 258
Wakefield, Dan, 104
Wakeford, Kent, 68
Walch, Hynden, 157
Walcutt, John, 186
Waldau, Nikolaj, 245
Waldburger, Ruth, 262
Walden, Leigh, 168
Waldron, Pat, 144
Walerstein, Marcela, 236
Walken, Christopher, 24, 98, 146, 295
Walken, Georgianne, 31, 170, 176
Walker, Alexandra, 15
Walker, Amanda, 12
Walker, Bruce, 13
Walker, Charles, 37
Walker, Fuschia, 163
Walker, Jennifer Jarman, 262
Walker, Kerry, 260
Walker, Mandy, 235
Walker, Matthew, 182, 238
Walker, Polly, 224
Walker, Randy, 109
Walker, Rebecca, 166
Walker, Seth, 179
Walker, Shirley, 8
Walker, Stephen, 237
Walker, Steve "Biscuit" 179
Walker, Stuart, 210
Walker, Valarie, 158
Walker, Wyatt Tee, 80
Walker-McBay, Anne, 19
Walkrop, Jesse, 145
Wall, David, 163
Wall, Father John, 256
Wall, Julian, 183
Wall-Asse, Marilyn, 67
Wallace, Andrew, 75
Wallace, Ed, 264
Wallace, George, 15, 80

Wallace, Hugh P., 13
Wallace, Jack, 120-121, 175
Wallace, Julie T, 216
Wallace, Leighanne, 181
Waller, Anthony, 254
Waller, John, 254
Wallis, Peter, 219
Walls, Allen, 78
Wallstein, Hans-Joachim, 223
Walrod, Ransom, 61
Walsh, Bill, 23, 136
Walsh, Brian, 186
Walsh, E. Bennett, 50
Walsh, J.T., 54-55, 295
Walsh, Jesse Joe, 44
Walsh, Joan Brosnan, 256
Walsh, Laurence, 75
Walsh, M. Emmet, 9, 72, 295
Walsh, Martin, 224
Walsh, Raymond, 260
Walsh, Robert, 141
Walsh, Wendy, 98
Walshe, Dermot, 262
Walt Disney Pictures, 23, 29, 71, 81, 87, 135-136, 144, 174
Walter, Alphonse V., 122
Walter, Jimmy, 176
Walter, Tracey, 122, 181, 295
Walters, Bruce, 254
Walters, Happy, 156
Walters, Hugh, 222
Walters, Ingrid, 141
Walters, Julie, 238, 295
Walters, Melora, 28, 121
Walters, Patrice, 182
Walters, Susan, 62
Walthall, Romy, 75
Walton, Jim, 50
Waltz, James J., 115
Waltz, Wendy, 123
Wan, Ai, 32
Wanda Films, 265
Wandell, Joe, 184
Wands, Alan J, 231, 251
Waney, Rick, 220
Wang, Ben, 152
Wang, Charles, 261
Wang, Danny, 251
Wang, Ding Yi, 126
Wang, Tien Sing, 220
Wang, Vincent, 253
Wang, Yao, 126
Wang, Yvonne, 126
Wangchuck, Karma, 152
Wangchuk, Jamyang Jamtsho, 117
Wangchuk, Sonam, 117
Wangda, Jurme, 152
Wangdue, Tsering, 117
Wansey, Skye, 260
Warakagoda, Wijeratne, 162
Warbeck, Stephen, 218, 229, 237
Ward, Dave "Squatch", 162
Ward, Jay, 81
Ward, Jeffrey L., 229
Ward, Lauren, 102
Ward, Sandy, 127
Ward, Vincent, 132
Ward, Zack, 181
Warden, Rick, 237
Wargert, Stina, 259
Waringo, Claude, 215
Warmflash, Stuart, 156
Warnat, Amber, 212
Warnat, Kimberly, 163
Warner, David, 95, 144, 186, 295
Warner, Edrie, 151
Warner, Julie, 68
Warner, Mark, 182
Warner, Rick, 79, 114
Warren, Darryl, 90
Warren, Diane, 168
Warren, Lesley Ann, 104, 295
Warren, Madeline, 183
Warren, Mervyn, 184
Warren-Green, Nigel, 229, 231
Warrington, Chaz, 86
Warriors Of Virtue, 163
Warry, Jillian, 49
Warshofsky, David, 75, 94
Warwick, James, 141
Warwick, Michael, 182
Wasco, David, 24, 96, 147
Washington Square, 115
Washington, Beverly, 175
Washington, Dan, 138
Washington, Dennis, 181
Washington, Isaiah, 34
Washington, Joe, 144

Washington, Karreem, 182
Washington, Manner "Mooky", 184
Washington, Tsemach, 41
Washington, Yvonne, 171
Washko, Frank, Jr., 179
Wasserman, Jerry, 144
Watanabe, Eriko, 226
Watanabe, Gedde, 23, 176
Water Street Pictures, 159
Waterford, Lon, 175
Waterman, Steve, 169
Watermelon Woman, The , 158
Waters, Aiden, 225
Waters, Gillian Iliana, 168
Waters, Hilary, 222
Waters, Jack, 256
Waters, John, 166
Waters, Julia, 151
Waters, Mark, 118
Waters, Maxine, 151
Waters, Oren, 151
Waterston, Sam, 154, 295
Watkin, David, 53, 126
Watkins, Dennis, 214
Watkins, Jason, 253
Watkins, Royale, 68, 170
Watros, Cynthia, 159
Watson, Alberta, 249
Watson, David, 230
Watson, Emily, 256, 296
Watson, Joe, 167, 256
Watson, John, Sr., 34, 97, 109
Watson, Sr., John M. 34, 109
Watson, Muse, 119, 179
Watson, Tom, 251
Watson, William, 118, 160
Watson, Woody, 122
Watt, Tracy, 262
Watts, Charlie, 245
Watts, Fiona, 232
Watts, Helen, 266
Watts, James D, 249
Watts, Peggy, 179
Watts, Rolanda, 15
Watts, Tonya, 18
Wavelength, 163
Waxman, Al, 105, 126
Waxman, Rebecca, 41, 166
Way, Wendy, 265
Wayans, Craig, 38
Wayans, Keenen Ivory, 118, 296
Wayans, Marlon, 38
Waye, Anthony, 253
Wayne, Archer, 230
Wayne, Hilary, 162
WCG Entertainment, 75
We Free Kings (I Magi Randagi), 266
Weatherly, Michael, 15
Weathers, Dee Dee, 121
Weaver, Daniel, 56
Weaver, Jacki, 260
Weaver, Lee, 180, 183
Weaver, Sigourney, 110-111, 133, 295-296
Weaver, Tyrone Lee, 183
Webb, Bunty, 80
Webb, Charlie, 104
Webb, Chloe, 96
Webb, David, 249
Webb, Gordon, 180
Webber, Brian, 245
Webber, Charlie, 167
Webber, John, 44
Webber, Tim, 125
Weber, Al, 66
Weber, Billy, 180
Weber, Dewey, 67
Weber, Jacques, 265
Weber, Jake, 141
Weber, Thomas, 15
Webster, 13, 104, 169, 284
Webster, C. Brett, 169
Webster, Dave, 104
Webster, Paul, 13
Wechsler, Nick, 34, 129
Wechsler, Ron, 118
Wedding Bell Blues, 68
Wegner, Lisa, 105
Weidman, Wendy, 28
Weil, Dan, 216
Weiland, Paul, 224
Weincke, Jan, 154
Weiner, Mark, 178
Weinstein, Amy, 184
Weinstein, Bob, 87, 93, 96, 99, 138, 144, 147, 181, 241, 247
Weinstein, Harvey, 87, 93, 96, 138,

144, 147, 181, 241, 247
Weintraub, Carl, 84
Weintraub, Helene, 175
Weintraub, Jerry, 179
Weis, Bob, 230
Weisenberg, David, 146, 173
Weisgal, Jonathan, 59, 251
Weisgel, Jonathan, 224
Weisman, Sam, 81
Weiss, Barry, 180
Weiss, Gordon Joseph, 30, 100
Weiss, Julie, 24, 107
Weiss, Larry, 167
Weisz, Rachel, 104, 245
Welch, Bo, 77
Welch, Daniel, 176
Welch, Sandy, 44
Welch, Wally, 122, 159
Welcome To Sarajevo, 248
Welfling, Juliette, 236
Welker, Frank, 66, 90, 180
Wellburn, Tim, 211
Weller, Peter, 165, 296
Wells, Audrey, 81
Wells, Claudette, 180
Wells, Frank T., 141
Wells, Jane, 49
Wells, John, 112
Wells, Lee, 132, 181
Wells, Llewellyn, 24, 109
Wells, Tico, 8
Welsh, Harry, 251
Welsh, Ken, 22
Welsh, Kenneth, 205
Welsh, Margaret, 171
Wen, Ming-Na, 132
Wendel, Tammy, 135
Wender, Angela, 159
Wenders, Wim, 100, 262
Wendt, David, 260
Wendt, George, 174, 296
Wenger, Brahm, 87
Wenham, David, 260
Wentworth, Peter, 137
Wentworth, Scott, 110
Werb, Mike, 75
Werby, Doug, 155
Werdin, Egon, 254
Werntz, Gary, 112
Werntz, Hannah, 112
Werthmann, Colleen, 159
Wesley, Paul, 256
Wessler, Charles B., 116
Wesson, Howard, 163
West, Kit, 169
West, Pamela, 174
West, Red, 135
West, Simon, 65
Westcott, Lisa, 229
Westenberg, Rob, 110
Westhead, David, 229
Westlake, Nigel, 214
Westmore, Mark, 50
Weston, Douglas, 21
Weston, Jennifer, 144
Weston, Paul, 169
Westover, Richard, 174
Wetlinska, Anna, 262
Wexler, Gerald, 205
Wexler, Joshua, 177
WFE, 255
Whalen, Sean, 77
Whaley, Frank, 166-167, 296
Whaley, Robert, 167, 171
Whalley, Joanne, 183
Whalley, Tat, 183
Whalley, Tristan, 164
Wheaton, Wil, 136, 296
Whedon, Joss, 133
Wheeler, Andrew, 169
Wheeler, Gary, 94
Wheeler, Harold, 59
Wheeler, Joan, 170
Wheeler, Julianna, 66
Wheeler, Rick, 61
Wheeler-Nicholson, Dana, 176
When The Cat's Away, 221
Whitaker, Kenn, 118
Whitaker, Yolanda, 60
Whitcomb, Ian, 181
White, Barry, 231
White, Bridget, 159
White, Cary, 179
White, Cathy, 212
White, Christopher, 170
White, Damon, 122
White, Freeman, 132
White, Gregory, 182

White, Gwendolyn, 80
White, Henry, 156
White, James D, 237
White, Kenneth, 63
White, Lillias, 71
White, Michael Jai, 32, 90
White, Michael, 83, 131
White, Michole Briana, 49
White, Noni, 130
White, Patrick, 123
White, Peter, 174
White, Reverend Reggie, 80
White, Robert, 65
White, Sam, 205
White, Steve, 145, 182
White, Timothy, 204, 214, 257, 260
White, Tracey, 60
White, Warren, 155
White, Welker, 41
White, Wynn, 28
Whitehead, Paxton, 174
Whitehead, Robert, 155
Whitehouse, Helen, 245
Whitehurst, James, 67
Whitfield, Lynn, 63, 129
Whitfield, Peter, 242
Whitford, Brad, 169
Whitford, Bradley, 126
Whitford, Peter, 257
Whitham, Fred, 183
Whiting, Joshua, 167
Whitmore, James, 8, 296
Whitrow, Benjamin, 42, 125
Whittal, Ted, 105
Whittemore, Gloria, 33
Whittemore, Libby, 23
Whittle, Brenton, 265
Whitton, Frank, 265
Whitworth, Johnny, 135
Whodini, 157
Why Not Productions, 60
Whyte, Stephanie, 175
Wiatt, Kevin, 168
Wickham, Jeffry, 210
Wickham, Saskia, 180
Wickwire, Caroline, 122
Widmer, David, 166
Wieczorkowski, Donna, 173
Wieger, David Michael, 181
Wiener, Danielle, 47, 62
Wierson, Tere, 38
Wiest, Dianne, 158, 296
Wiggins, Jim, 125
Wiggins, Tyrone, 177
Wightman, Robert, 86
Wigman, Denis, 220
Wilbur, David, 68
Wilchie, Carrie, 160
Wilcox, Elizabeth, 87
Wilcox, Steve, 172
Wild America, 181
Wild, John, 265
Wild, Patrick, 181
Wilde, Adam, 166
Wilden, Gert, Jr., 264
Wilder, Alan, 114
Wilding, Gavin, 264
Wiles, Michael Shamus, 21, 181, 184
Wilhelmova, Gabriela, 262
Wilhoite, Kathleen, 107
Wilkerson, Laurnea, 97
Wilkey, Jim, 162
Wilkin, Catherine, 262
Wilkins, Joseph, 159
Wilkins, Mac, 13
Wilkinson, Gary, 203
Wilkinson, Tom, 206, 232-233, 257
Wilkof, Lee, 30, 131, 263
Wilkop, Michael, 265
Will It Snow For Christmas?, 250
Willems, Brian, 65
Willett, John, 144
Willett, John, 165
William Long, Jr., 13
William, Ellis E., 147
Williams, Barbara, 43
Williams, Bernie, 25
Williams, Biddug, 261
Williams, Brian J., 181
Williams, Cindy, 15, 296
Williams, Clarence, III, 60, 97, 296
Williams, Clark D., 53
Williams, Cliff, 30
Williams, Ellis E., 44
Williams, Eric, 183
Williams, Finty, 229
Williams, Fred, 174, 216

Williams, Gareth, 49, 122, 175
Williams, Gary Anthony, 183
Williams, Ginger R., 102
Williams, Gregalan, 264
Williams, Harland, 151, 174
Williams, Harry Gregson, 206
Williams, Heathcoat, 250
Williams, Jamie, 162-163
Williams, Jim Cody, 63
Williams, JoBeth, 29, 296
Williams, John H., 117
Williams, John, 47, 61, 141, 179
Williams, Junior, 180
Williams, Justin, 17
Williams, Kate, 105
Williams, Keith, 180, 216
Williams, Kenyon, 61
Williams, Ken, 71, 89, 105
Williams, Leigh, 69
Williams, Leo, 216
Williams, Lia, 237
Williams, Lynn Red, 177
Williams, Michelle, 106
Williams, Mykal Wayne, 77
Williams, Nadean S., 80
Williams, Natashia, 168
Williams, Olivia, 184
Williams, Omar Hibbert, 216
Williams, Patrick, 39, 170
Williams, Philip, 138
Williams, Robin, 6, 136, 138-139,
   142-143, 180, 190, 296
Williams, Ronnie, 261
Williams, Sherly Acosta, 141
Williams, Sherman, 116
Williams, Steve "Spaz", 90
Williams, Tim, 159, 176
Williams, Treat, 35, 296
Williams, Vanessa L., 97, 108-109,
   201, 296
Williams, Veron T., 184
Williams, Victor J., 93
Williams, Vikki, 97
Williams, Warren "Slim", 153
Williamson, Jake, 166
Williamson, Kate, 24, 164
Williamson, Kevin, 119, 144
Williamson, Mykelti, 64-65, 162
Williamson, Nicol, 90, 242, 296
Willigham, Kevin, 123
Willis, Bruce, 131, 216, 296
Willis, Gordon, 35
Willis, Michael, 77
Willis, Rachel, 216
Willis, Ronnie, 78
Willis, Ronny, 60
Willyung, John, 41
Wilmot, David, 35
Wilmot, Mike, 39
Wilmsen, Herbert Hans, 147
Wilsey, Pamela, 181
Wilson, Andrea Paige, 78
Wilson, Andy, 122
Wilson, Brad, 83
Wilson, Brian Anthony, 184
Wilson, Bridgette, 119
Wilson, Cate, 158
Wilson, Colin, 61, 141
Wilson, David, 156, 164
Wilson, Debra, 13, 159, 169
Wilson, Hamish, 212
Wilson, Jane Edith, 163
Wilson, Jim, 164, 184
Wilson, Luke, 123, 144
Wilson, Mak, 66
Wilson, Mara, 80
Wilson, Michael G, 253
Wilson, Owen, 46
Wilson, Peta, 260
Wilson, Phaedra, 13
Wilson, Rainn, 163
Wilson, Reno, 32
Wilson, Richard, 183
Wilson, Scott, 50, 94, 296
Wilson, Stewart Harvey, 216
Wilson, Suzanne Lemieux, 130
Wilson, Tom, 23
Wilson, Victor, 51
Wilson, Warren, 151
Wilton, Garth, 186
Wiltsey, Larry "Bait", 160
Winant, Bruce, 62
Winant, Scott, 62
Winborne, Hughes, 158
Wincott, Michael, 10, 133, 296

Wind In The Willows, The 242
Windon, Stephen, 184, 259
Winestine, Zack, 163
Winfree, Rachel, 50, 63, 83
Wings Of The Dove, The , 247
Winikoff, Cami, 129
Winkler, Mel, 240
Winn, Fay, 145
Winner, The , 166
Winning, David, 158
Winslet, Kate, 4,185-187, 193, 200,
   296
Winston, Hattie, 147
Winston, Matt, 112
Winston, Stan, 8, 61
Winter Guest, The , 251
Winterbottom, Michael, 248
Winters, Dean, 181
Winters, Kristoffer Ryan, 181
Winters, Scott Williams, 138
Winton, Marvin, 184
Winzenried, Eric, 121
Wisden, Robert, 98
Wisdom, Robert, 49, 75
Wise, Bill, 159
Wise, Naomi, 263
Wise, Nina, 38
Wise, Peter, 93
Wise, Steve, 63
Wiseman, Debbie, 38
Wishart, Paul, 230
Wishmaster, 172
Wisnievitz, David, 179
Wisnik, Jose Miguel, 264
Wissner, Gary, 119, 184
Witcher, Guy, 125
Witcher, Theodore, 34
Witer, Oleh, 209
Witherspoon, John, 60
Without Air, 160
Witkins, Doug, 160
Witten, Brian, 90, 177
Witter, Karen, 174
Witz, Barry, 178
Wizan, Joe, 114
Wodoslawsky, Stefan, 105
Woinski, Marcos, 250
Wolande, Gene, 182
Wolf, Catherine, 30
Wolf, Daniel, 142
Wolf, Eugene, 86
Wolf, Jeffrey, 170
Wolfe, Nancy, 184
Wolff, Joanna, 102
Wolff, Natasha, 241
Wolff, Patrick, 128
Wolheim, Donald A., 99
Wolk, Andy, 173
Wollter, Sven, 259
Wolos-Fonteno, David, 53
Wolper, David L., 182
Wolsky, Albert, 126, 131
Womersley, David, 180
Wonderland, 173
Wong, B.D., 117, 296
Wong, John, 152
Wong, Oliver, 203, 230
Wong, Victor, 117
Woo, John, 75
Woo, Terry, 203
Wood Entertainment, 93
Wood, Carol Winstead, 13
Wood, Charles, 177
Wood, Craig, 146
Wood, David, 12
Wood, Dennis, 172
Wood, Elijah, 110, 296
Wood, Jody, 121, 182
Wood, Oliver, 75, 127
Wood, Tom, 67
Wood, Victoria, 242
Woodall, Andrew, 183
Woodard, Alfre, 155, 296
Woodbury, Heather, 175
Woodbury, Judy, 182
Woodeson, Nicholas, 183
Woodruff, Tom, Jr., 128, 133
Woodhouse, Andrew, 170
Woodman, Jori, 165
Woods, Cary, 93, 174
Woods, Maurkice, 151
Woods, Melete, 145
Woods, Michael, 155, 181

Woods, Richard, 102
Woods, Rowan, 214
Woods, Scott, 216
Woodside, Bruce, 166
Woodson, Charles Richard, 167
Woodward, Joanne, 2-3, 296
Woodward, Lawrence, 260
Woof, Emily, 232
Woolf, Alan, 84-85, 135
Wooll, Nigel, 94
Woolley, Stephen, 210
Woolvett, Jaimz, 179
Wordes, Smith, 51
Worgan, Simon, 250
Working Title, 207, 244
Workman, Jimmy, 148
Worth, Stan, 81
Worthen, Jock, 9
Worthington, Sheldon, 65
Worthington, Wendy, 83
Worthy, Lisa, 182
Worthy, Rick, 184
Woulard, Keith, 84
Wow, Johnny, 69
Wray, Dean, 98, 162
Wrenn, Clyde, 18
Wrenn, Tommy, 80
Wright, Barclay, 91
Wright, Carl, 109
Wright, Io Tillett, 170
Wright, J. Madison, 50
Wright, Jeffrey, 126
Wright, Jocelyn F., 179
Wright, Karl T., 49
Wright, Marcia, 109
Wright, Michael, 95, 179
Wright, Peter, 125
Wright, Philip, 247
Wright, Richard S., 62
Wright, Sam E., 100
Wright, Stewart, 12
Wright, Teresa, 135, 296
Wright, Tom, 13
Wright, Tori, 50
Wrigley, Bernard, 219
Wu, Chen Chun, 203
Wu, David, 163, 222
Wu, Mike, 126
Wu, Ping, 118
Wu, Vivian, 220
Wu-Tang Clan, 156
Wuhl, Robert, 83, 296
Wuhrer, Kari, 46
Wurtzel, Stuart, 29
Wyatt, Chris, 220
Wyatt, Sue, 210
Wycoff, Eric, 183
Wyle, Noah, 105
Wyman Production, 79
Wyman, Brad, 79
Wyman, Nick, 30
Wyner, George, 182, 184
Wynn, Andrea, 49
Wynne, Christopher, 68
Wysocki, David ., 163
Wysocki, David, 163
X Pictures, 237
Xalabarder, Ferran, 130
Xaleese, 28
Xiangting, Ge, 222
Xiao-Hua, Gao, 126
Xiaonan, Pei, 222
Xingu Films, 210
Xiong, Xin Xin, 44
Xiu-qin, Zhao, 260
Xris, 69
Xynidis, Michael A., 11
Xzibit, 157
Yagemann, Scott, 184
Yager, George, 182
Yagher, Kevin, 75
Yakusho, Koji, 226-227
Yamamoto, Robie, 132
Yamamoto, Ulala, 225
Yamamoto, Yoshinori, 183
Yamauchi, Takayuki, 49
Yanay, Eli, 230
Yancey, Happy, 164
Yancey, John, 135
Yancey, William, 34
Yancy, Minnie Bates, 170
Yang, Bing, 126
Yang, Catherine T., 84
Yang, Gu Xiao, 126
Yanne, Jean, 265

Yansick, Eddie, 32
Yao, Li Jia, 126
Yap, Andrew, 211
Yap, Olivia, 23
Yardley, Stephen, 222
Yarnold, Pauly, 13
Yassine, Ali, 216
Yasuda, Kelvin, 180
Yates, Janty, 183, 248
Yatsko, Alexander, 112
Yau, Chi Wai, 203
Yaura, Yukki, 220
Ye-Cheng, Chan, 243
Yeager, Bigg, 166
Yeager, Caroline, 165
Yearby, Roy, 127
Yearby, Roy, 127
Yedidia, Mario, 163
Yee, Nancy, 114
Yellen, Linda, 165
Yellen, Mark, 50
Yemang, Zhou, 222
Yenque, Jose, 164
Yeoh, Michelle, 252-253
Yeomans, Charles, 230
Yeskel, Ronnie, 23-24, 244
Yiasoumi, George, 250
Yin, Lei, 126
Ying, Qu, 163
Ying, Wang, 222
Yinh, Jesus, 132
Yiu, Lo Ka, 230
Yo Soy, Del Son A La Salsa, 264
Yoba, Malik, 93
Yoda, Malik, 109
Yon, Fan, 265
Yondejunai, 262
Yong-ling, Du, 260
York, Kathleen, 161
York, Michael, 56, 104, 295-296
Yorktown Productions, 137
Yorn, Julie Silverman, 129
Yoshida, Hideko, 220
Yoshikawa, Yuko, 172
Yoshioka, Yoshino, 220
Yoshizaki, Michiyo, 207
Yost, Graham, 68
You, Pitzly, 50
Young, Aden, 211, 259-260
Young, Angus, 30
Young, Burt, 96, 170, 175-176, 296
Young, Chris, 183, 296
Young, Christopher, 164, 180
Young, Dave, 38
Young, Dey, 154
Young, Harrison, 101
Young, Jeffrey Michael, 101
Young, Keone, 122
Young, Lance, 165
Young, Leigh Taylor, 165
Young, Lenny, 179
Young, Malcolm, 30
Young, Neil, 173
Young, Nina, 253
Young, Norris, 184
Young, Paul, 100, 205, 262
Young, Reverened Andrew, 80
Young, Ric, 23, 117
Young, Robert, 12, 296
Young, Russell, 66
Young, Seldon O., 166
Young, William, 141, 151, 168
Youngdung, Gawa, 152
Youngs, Susan, 176
Yourgrau, Barry, 260
Youri, Franklin, 177
Youth, Sonic, 19
YTC Pictures, 211
Yu, Li Chi, 126
Yu, Ronny, 163
Yuan, Roger, 126
Yuen, Joyce, 209
Yui, 216
Yuk, Henry, 152
Yukun, Lu, 126
Yulin, Harris, 180, 244
Yuman, Bernie, 179
Yuricich, Richard, 91
Yusef, Mohammed, 162
Yzerman, Kristie, 144
Z, Danny, 178
Zabel, Bruce, 177
Zabriskie, Grace, 161
Zacher, Rolf, 266

Zachery, 81
Zagnit, Stuart, 265
Zaharova, Tatiana, 180
Zahn, Steve, 19
Zahonero, Coraly, 221
Zahrn, Will, 182
Zajonc, Bobby, 154
Zajonc, Robert "Bobby Z", 61
Zamora, Del, 75, 166
Zamsky, Meredith, 86
Zanchi, Michela, 132
Zane, Billy, 79, 164, 186-187
Zane, Debra, 77, 115, 151
Zanitsch, Noel A., 172
Zanoline, Carrie, 81
Zanone, Christian, 251
Zapata, Carmen, 236
Zappa, Moon, 174
Zaricor, Debbie, 13
Zavaglia, Richard, 27
Zaver, George, 49
Zavradinos, Giannis, 203
Zayas, David, 156
Zayed, Hisham, 105
Zaza, Paul J., 264
Zazou Productions, 172
Zea, Kristi, 148
ZéBranco, 262
Zed, 77, 245
Zegers, Kevin, 87
Zeigler, Jesse, 172
Zeigler, Zack, 136
Zeitgeist, 163, 166, 213, 235, 250,
   262-263
Zem, Roschdy, 260
Zemanova, Marie, 262
Zemeckis, Alex, 181
Zemeckis, Robert, 181
Zentropa, 260
Zerbe, Anthony, 24, 296
Zero Film, 258, 266
Zeta Entertainment, 50
Zeus And Roxanne, 11
Zeust, Dianne, 260
Zevalia, Sebastian, 117
Zhan, Grace, 126
Zhang, Daxing, 126
Zhao, Jing, 214
Zhong, Wei De, 126
Ziakas, Yorgos, 203
Zidi, Claude, 263
Zieff, Rick, 38
Zielinski, Jerzy, 23, 115
Ziembicki, Bob, 121, 144, 165
Zien, Chip, 263
Ziker, Dick, 68
Zilberschatz-Banai, Orly, 258
Zima, Madeline, 62
Zima, Vanessa, 67
Zima, Yvonne, 62
Ziman, Richard, 30
Zimmer, Christopher, 205
Zimmer, Hans, 112, 148, 206
Zimmerman, Don, 37
Zimmerman, Jeff, 174
Zimmerman, Matt, 205
Zimny, Thom, 164, 171
Zinsser, Sarah, 30
Zippel, David, 71
Ziskie, Daniel, 131
Ziskin, Laura, 148
Zivojinovic, Velimir-Bata, 264
ZM Prods., 162
Zobeida, 250
Zola, Brian David, 178
Zolli, Robert, 156
Zolotin, Adam, 98
Zook, Tamara, 180
Zophres, Mary, 122
Zorich, Louis, 52
Zorn, John, 171
Zotoff, Andre, 180
Zoubtov, Helena, 258
Zoumas, Michael, 99
Zovkic, Lydia, 42
Zuckerbrod, Gary M., 11
Zuckerbrod, Gary, 23
Zuckerman, Anita, 183
Zuckerman, Dori, 172
Zumbrum, Harley, 65
Zuniga, Jose, 65
Zupcevic, Miralem, 248
Zurinaga, Marcos, 236
Zurlo, John, 44